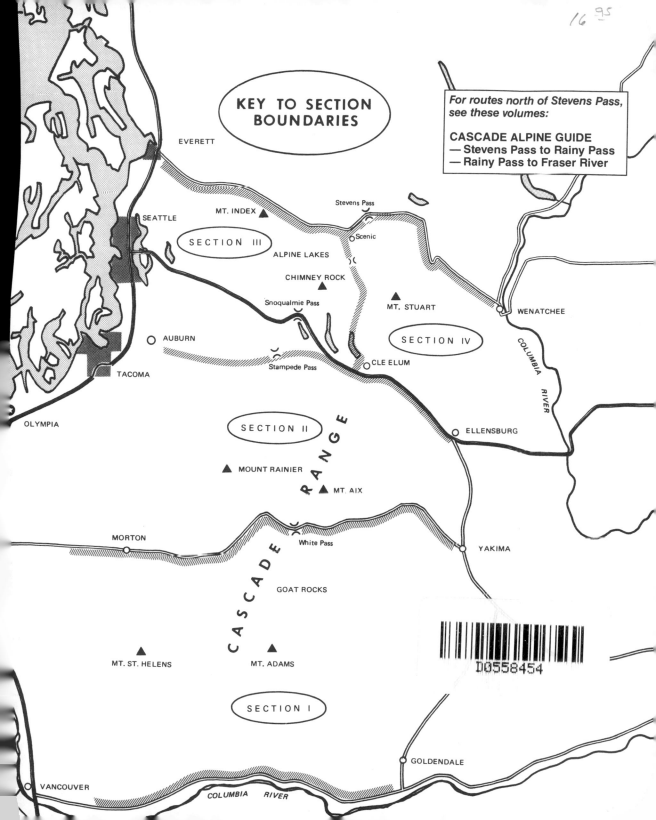

16 95

KEY TO SECTION BOUNDARIES

For routes north of Stevens Pass, see these volumes:

CASCADE ALPINE GUIDE
— Stevens Pass to Rainy Pass
— Rainy Pass to Fraser River

EVERETT

MT. INDEX ▲

Stevens Pass

SECTION III

Scenic

SEATTLE

ALPINE LAKES

CHIMNEY ROCK ▲

MT. STUART ▲

Snoqualmie Pass

WENATCHEE

SECTION IV

AUBURN ○

C
O
L
U
M
B
I
A

CLE ELUM ○

Stampede Pass

R
I
V
E
R

TACOMA

OLYMPIA

SECTION II

ELLENSBURG ○

R
A
N
G
E

▲ MOUNT RAINIER

▲ MT. AIX

C
A
S
C
A
D
E

MORTON ○

White Pass

YAKIMA ○

GOAT ROCKS

D0558454

▲ MT. ST. HELENS

▲ MT. ADAMS

SECTION I

GOLDENDALE ○

○ VANCOUVER

COLUMBIA RIVER

CASCADE ALPINE GUIDE

CLIMBING AND HIGH ROUTES
Vol. 1: Columbia River to Stevens Pass

by FRED BECKEY

Second Edition

THE MOUNTAINEERS Seattle

THE MOUNTAINEERS

Organized 1906

To explore and study the mountains, forests and watercourses
    of the Northwest;
To gather into permanent form the history and traditions of
    this region;
To preserve by the encouragement of protective legislation
    or otherwise the natural beauty of Northwest America;
To make explorations into these regions in fulfillment of the
    above purposes;
To encourage a spirit of good fellowship among all lovers of
    outdoor life.

First edition 1973, revised 1979. Second edition 1987
Printed in the United States of America

Published by The Mountaineers
306 Second Avenue West
Seattle, Washington 98119

Published simultaneously in Canada by
Douglas & McIntyre, Ltd.
1615 Venables Street
Vancouver, British Columbia V6L 2H1

Photo overlays by Richard Pargeter and Nick Gregoric
Maps by Richard Pargeter and Helen Sherman
Topos by Richard Pargeter and Nick Gregoric
Sketches by Dee Molenaar and Nick Gregoric
Frontispiece: Mount Adams from northeast. (Austin Post,
U.S. Geological Survey)

Library of Congress Cataloging in Publication Data

Beckey, Fred W., 1921 —
    Cascade alpine guide.

    Includes index.
    1. Mountaineering — Cascade Range — Guide-books.
2. Cascade Range — Description and travel — Guide-books.
3. Washington (State) — Description and travel —
1981-   — Guide-books. I. Title.
GV199.42.C37B4 1986   917.95   86-23899
ISBN 0-89886-127-6 (soft)

0 9 8 7

5 4 3 2 1

Contents

Preface

It is hoped this guide will materially contribute to the multiple rewards of enjoyment and knowledge of the Cascade Range in Washington. As an alpine guide, it is directed not only to those who wish to climb its peaks, but to forest and alpine pedestrians ... those who would hike its high trails, fish, and explore the valleys and uplands in the rich and varied range called the Cascades, one of America's great mountain ranges.

My initial guidebook, *Climber's Guide to the Cascade and Olympic Mountains,* published by the American Alpine Club in 1949, was the first comprehensive study of the alpine approaches and mountaineering routes of these mountains. It provided a summit inventory of the extremely complex Cascades, and was immensely influential in developing detailed knowledge for a variety of users. In 1961 this book was rewritten by a committee of the American Alpine Club, bringing its content up to date. It has been out of print since 1967, leaving a vast information gap. Therefore it is hoped this guide will serve as the needed pictorial and written exposition on the range.

Recent increase of human use in the Cascades is manifold, pointing to a need for new and additional information, detail which cannot be adequately covered in one volume. As I pointed out in the earlier guide, "climbing has reached a state of acceptance and maturity in the Pacific Northwest that gives it a new recognition and popularity, reflecting the history of the sport in the Alps." This same popularity is exemplified by a great influx of mountain hikers who will find some coverage specifically to their benefit.

It is assumed the user will obtain topographic maps to complement his specific needs. Much additional interpretation has been provided in the form of specific area maps, sketches, climbing "topos," and photography. The user should be aware of deceptions in the use of oblique aerials. The scale of mountain terrain is never fully perceived in them. The angle and proximity of view may distort correct height, distance, and slope gradient. The farther from center, the greater the image distortion in scaling distance and estimating direction.

Particular gratitude for the use of excellent photographs is due Austin Post of the U.S. Geological Survey, Wallace C. Guy of the U.S. Forest Service, Ed Cooper, Ira Spring and William A. Long.

This volume includes the Cascade Range from the Columbia River to a demarcation along the Skykomish River, Stevens Pass, and the Wenatchee River.

For convenience, this volume is divided into four sections generally following principal drainage patterns.

Each section is prefaced by an introductory overview and a listing of ranger stations and maps pertaining to the area covered. References to specific roads, trails, and cross-country routes related to the alpine areas are signaled in the text by a diamond ◆. These approaches are described in alphabetical order in the "Approaches" section (marked by shaded page margins), located near the end of this volume, following the route descriptions.

Space does not permit a listing of peripheral roads and trails, or of those confined to the foothills or built for timber harvesting. Fishermen will find valuable advice on trail and cross-country routes to high-country lakes, but space does not allow a description of all lakes and their approaches.

The guide's primary purpose is to help the user enjoy the Cascade Range, its peaks and high places; keeping a person on a precise route used by others is secondary. An attempt has been made to characterize a mountain, and a known route, presenting an overview, with enough detail and flavor to assure success, rather than a total concentration on how to climb the objective. In general, an equitable rather than selective coverage of peaks and routes is intended.

Names used fall in several categories: (1) names with the official approval of the Board on Geographic Names and shown on U.S.G.S. maps; (2) other accepted names, some shown on U.S. Forest Service maps, some not; (3) provisional names in common usage by mountain visitors or applied by explorers and other specialists, many of which will likely become official by precedent. In the case of modified names, duplicates, or pseudonyms, these will be noted. When no name has been given official approval for a feature, for purposes of ready identification, the adopted name, derived from written references or applied by the most authoritative usage, is used; otherwise locations are defined by elevation shown on the most recent topographic map. The author has been anxious to see attractive names applied to major features and to alleviate the growing confusion of identification by elevation or description, for such a procedure is constantly subject to revision.

LITTLE TAHOMA from northeast
ED COOPER

It should be pointed out that some peak names and certain elevations in the Cascades differ on various map *editions* as well as on different maps. The vast U.S. Geological Survey project of remapping the range from aerial photography and producing the results on 7½-minute topographic sheets is incomplete. Various editions of maps mass-produced by technical processes are subject to error in feature portrayal, lettering placement, and interpretation. This guide will show locations, names and elevations to the highest standard of accuracy, and if a discrepancy in recent maps is known, it will be pointed out in the text. Elevations, when not shown on maps as a triangulated altitude, are shown as the height of the highest contour of the associated topographic map, often with a plus-mark added. The abbreviation "est." denotes estimated elevation.

Descriptive terms used are those common in hiking and mountaineering, and in the case of multiple meaning, an attempt is made to conform to popular usage. The glossary will be helpful to climbers, for it includes some technical terms. Directions such as "turn left" or "left" are used in the sense of direction of movement and assumes the hiker or climber is facing the slope. The various routes on a mountain are listed in a clockwise direction, beginning with the most popular route as known.

When trail and cross-country mileages are given or estimated, travel time is rarely shown in the guide because of the many individual variables, including routing and surface conditions. In the case of some alpine cross-country routes, as well as for many climbs, a time estimate is made for the *average party,* competent to follow the given route or climb, under normal conditions. Rock climbing times assume competence as practiced by a group likely to attempt the particular ascent. The more popular a route becomes, the more accurate this estimate should be. In the case of certain rarely done ascents, the time of the first climbing party may be given for appraisal. Few specific time studies have yet been made on routes in the Cascades; eventually more accurate estimates will be available through accumulated reports.

Among the thousands of facts incorporated in the guide, there will inevitably be a certain percentage open to personal interpretation; there is, after all, no substitute for experience and judgment. Usually only the more important points of routes are given in detail, and these will vary by need, complexity, and the availability of reliable data. The best information that could be obtained from written journals, publica-tions, photographs, and volunteer sources has been conveyed in these pages; efforts here have been hindered by insufficient recording by both participants and editors. Since route priority is a fair subject of increasing interest to technical climbers, it deserves accurate publication.

It is hoped this guide will inspire hikers, climbers, and editors to record routes more carefully; its publication will provoke some corrections, and it is sincerely hoped new information, missing history, as well as errors discovered, will be sent to The Mountaineers.

In Britain there is an unusually high standard of accuracy in guidebooks, for it is usually feasible for an author to either climb a route or get a consensus view. In the Cascades, a *wilderness range* not yet fully explored, the standards of Britain (or even the Alps) are impossible to attain at this time.

A high degree of responsibility rests with the individual climber to interpret the information at his disposal in a rational way. It must be remembered that two parties following a specific route invariably describe it differently (as do witnesses to accidents and natural events).

Within the context of this guide, it has seemed superfluous to include all bibliographical references to an area or route; they are given only when they contain significant route information or are of unusual historical value.

A list of regional outdoor clubs and their publications is given here:

ALPINE CLUB OF CANADA; 1200 Hornby St., Vancouver, B.C. V6Z 2E2 — *Avalanche Echoes* and *Canadian Alpine Journal*

BOEING EMPLOYEES ALPINE SOCIETY; P.O. Box 3707, Seattle, WA 98124 — *Alpine Echo*

B.C. MOUNTAINEERING CLUB; P.O. Box 2674, Vancouver, B.C. V6B 3W8 — *B.C. Mountaineering Club* newsletter and *B.C. Mountaineer*

THE CASCADIANS; P.O. Box 2201, Yakima, WA 98907 — *The Cascadian*

INTER-MOUNTAIN ALPINE CLUB; P.O. Box 505, Richland, WA 99352 — *The Yodeler*

ISSAQUAH ALPS TRAILS CLUB; P.O. Box 351, Issaquah, WA 98027 — *The Issaquah Alpineer*

THE MAZAMAS; 909 N.W. 19th St., Portland, OR 97232 — *The Mazama*

MT. BAKER HIKING CLUB; P.O. Box 73, Bellingham, WA 98223 — *The Rambler*

MT. ST. HELENS CLUB; P.O. Box 843, Longview, WA 98632 — *Loo-Wit Kla-Ta-Wa*

THE MOUNTAINEERS; 300 Third Ave. West, Seattle, WA 98119, (Branches in Everett, Tacoma, Olympia) — *The Mountaineer Bulletin, The Mountaineer*

MOUNTAIN RESCUE COUNCIL; P.O. Box 67, Seattle, WA 98111

THE PTARMIGANS, P.O. Box 1821, Vancouver, WA 98663

SIERRA CLUB - CASCADE CHAPTER; 1516 Melrose Ave., Seattle, WA 98122 — *Cascade Crest*

SKAGIT VALLEY ALPINE CLUB; P.O. Box 513, Mt. Vernon, WA 98273

TACOMA MOUNTAIN RESCUE UNIT; P.O. Box 696, Tacoma, WA 98401 — *The Rescue Rucksack*

SPOKANE MOUNTAINEERS; P.O. Box 1013, Spokane, WA 99210 — *The Kinnikinnick*

WASHINGTON ALPINE CLUB; P.O. Box 352, Seattle, WA 98111

U.S. Forest Service and National Park headquarters are:

U.S. Forest Service - Pacific Northwest
 Regional Headquarters
P.O. Box 3623 (319 S.W. Pine St.)
Portland, OR 97208
(503) 221-2877

Gifford Pinchot National Forest
500 W. 12th St., Vancouver, WA 98660
(206) 696-7500

Mount Baker - Snoqualmie National Forest
1022 - 1st Ave., Seattle, WA 98174
(206) 442-5400

Forest Service - National Park Service
 Information Center
1018 - 1st Ave., Seattle, WA 98174
(206) 442-0170

Wenatchee National Forest
301 Yakima Ave., Wenatchee, WA 98801
(509) 662-4335

Okanogan National Forest
219 - 2nd Ave. South, Okanogan, WA 98840
(509) 442-2704

Mount Rainier National Park
Ashford, WA 98397
(206) 589-2211
Recorded information: (206) 589-2343

North Cascades National Park
Ross Lake and Lake Chelan
 National Recreation areas
Sedro Wooley, WA 98284
(206) 856-5700

BACKCOUNTRY INFORMATION
Marblemount, WA 98267
(206) 873-4590

NCAA weather radio KBB-60 provides the Cascade area latest forecasts. A VHF broadcast, Pacific Northwest Weather Reporter, is given on KHB-60; this includes avalanche forecasts and pass reports from December 1 to April 15.

Snow recreation and current avalanche forecasts: The Forest Service has advisory numbers —
 (206) 526-6677 (Cascade Range);
 (503) 221-2400 (Southern Washington).

The vast amount of gratitude for assistance on this project, as well as the debt to those who wrote portions of the 1961 American Alpine Club Guide is beyond a simple flow of words. The innumerable persons who have contributed information and provided review are appreciated silent assistants. Much of this publication's validity is due to their documentation of routes and interpretation of personal experiences. Various persons in the U.S. Forest Service and the National Park Service have been most helpful in obtaining aerial photographs and reviewing route information.

I am especially grateful for the critical review and route information provided by Alex Bertulis, Norman Bishop, Dwight R. Crandell, Dan Davis, Pete Doorish, Keith Gehr, Donald J. Goodman, Mike Hiler, William A. Long, Lex Maxwell, Dee Molenaar, Jim Nelson, Garry Olson, John Pollock, Austin Post, Gene Prater, Roy Ratliff, Will F. Thompson, Joseph Vance, James Wickwire, and Jim Yoder. Further gratitude is due to Joseph Vance and Paul E. Hammond for their review of the geologic material.

An appreciative note is given to Peggy Ferber, Tom Miller, and John Pollock, who accepted the liaison between the author and the Literary Fund Committee at the inception of this guidebook in the early 1970s. The revision has been a comprehensive project with the editing and production supervised by Stephen Whitney, Ann Cleeland, and Donna DeShazo.

FRED BECKEY

Introduction

BACKGROUND ON THE CASCADE RANGE

Various early explorers had their selections for a name of the range of "Western Mountains"[1] and "mountains covered with snow" that Lewis and Clark wrote about in general terms in 1805 and 1806. In the year 1792 Captain George Vancouver, who had sailed from England on an expedition to acquire more complete knowledge of the "north-west coast of America" and negotiate the Nootka dispute for George III, beheld at a distance the "eastern snow range."[2] This was merely a description, not a specific place name. Historians believe that probably the first attempt at a name for the range was by the Spaniard Manuel Quimper, who in 1790 mapped it as "Sierras Nevadas de S. Antonio."[3]

The botanist David Douglas, who visited the margins of the range, found he had a need for a name for those mountains. He refers to them as the "Cascade Mountains" in his journal between 1826 and 1827, but he does not claim to have originated the name, which perhaps came from where the Columbia River formed a *cascade* in breaking through the range.[4] John Lambert, a topographer with the Pacific Railroad Survey in 1853, perhaps sensed the origin of the name when he wrote, "Going down the Columbia, the reason of the Cascade mountains being so named becomes apparent from the steep sides of that tremendous chasm through which the gathered waters seek the ocean . . . numerous and beautiful little falls which pour from every crevice, at every height, and frequently from the very mountain top."[5] In 1841 the Wilkes Expedition charted the mountains as the *Cascade Range*.[6] That name — or Cascade Mountains —, the wording used on early Washington territorial, military, and survey maps — prevailed with the wide distribution of maps.

The only serious threat to this usage came from Hall J. Kelley, an early enthusiast on the Oregon question, who sought to change the names of the great volcanos from Shasta to St. Helens by naming them after former presidents of the United States and to label the range the "Presidents' Range." T.J. Farnham, in 1843, in modifying Kelley's plan, tried to change Mount Baker to "Tyler" and Mount Rainier to "Harrison." The scheme failed due to lack of map circulation and confusion of interchanging names.[7]

In the earliest use the name Cascade Range included only those mountains that could be seen from the cascades of the Columbia, but the terminology soon spread far north and south. On the Wilkes map the "Cascade Range" is emphasized well in both directions from the river. In the Sixth Report, 1933, of the U.S. Geographic Board, the Cascades were defined as "limited on the south by the gap south of Lassen Peak and extending northward into British Columbia." As Francis P. Farquhar has pointed out, this is obviously a definition of convenience.[8] Marked so distinctly on the south by the Columbia, the Cascade Range in Washington has become the best known portion of this long mountain chain because of its high, easily visible ice-clad volcanos, its many rugged rock peaks, and its vast scattering of glaciers. In Washington, the Cascade Range is clearly bordered by the Puget Sound lowland on the west and the Columbia and Okanogan rivers on the east.

General usage has not fixed precise northern limits to the Cascade Range, but the Fraser River clearly supplies the required boundary between the Cascade and Coast ranges, if the principle of limiting units by master valleys is applied. Canadian usage 100 years ago showed the name "Cascade Range" extending to the Bella Coola River.[9] Professor I.C. Russell considered the Coast Mountains of Canada to be a direct northward extension of the Cascades.[10] National Geographic Society maps mark the Cascades extending to the confluence of the Thompson and Fraser rivers. This definition where the Fraser bears north has been confirmed by Canadian accord, with the *Cascade Mountains* marking a narrow belt west of the transition to the high Thompson Plateau.[11]

H. Bauerman,[12] geologist to the British Boundary Commission, and Smith/Calkins[13] recognized the need to subdivide the system in Northern Washington and Canada, and near the turn of the century applied three divisions, separated by the north-south valleys of the Skagit and the Pasayten-Similkameen. The subranges were the Okanogan Range (from the Okanogan River to the Pasayten River), the Hozameen Range, and the Skagit Range (west of the Skagit-Sumallo trench). This and other proposals for subrange and special-area nomenclature have not been universally accepted; most specific areas are referred to by the names of the major peaks, principal passes, and subranges, rather than the names of the principal rivers.

A summer snowstorm dusts the north face of SUMMIT CHIEF MOUNTAIN
PHILIP LEATHERMAN

Originally, Indian names were applied to the major peaks, but these were seldom retained by the white explorers as were those for rivers, lakes, and features bordering salt water. While the name of the range is broadly descriptive, the pattern of peak and place-names is predominantly personal and secondarily descriptive. Until the coming of the Pacific Railroad Survey in 1853 few features and high peaks had been named or mapped; unfortunately much of their charting of Indian names was not perpetuated as was the intent. Maps prepared by the U.S. Army Corps of Topographical Engineers tended to give permanence to place names, but in later years the U.S. Geological Survey in field mapping often chose local names different from those on Army maps.

Some names that evolved from early mountain travels are purely descriptive (Three Fingers); many are honorary (Stuart); others are commemorative of an incident (Overcoat); some are of Indian derivation (Kaleetan).[14] The term "North Cascades" has had varying boundary interpretations since early application; perhaps the most fitting is to apply it to the region north of Stevens Pass, though much usage applies it north of Snoqualmie Pass.

As a point of historical interest, the Cascade Range was only distantly known to early navigators and most overland explorers, and had been deeply probed only by a few surveyors, geologists, trappers, and numerous prospectors when it became the center of gold rush frenzies.

Indian trails, used in sporadic trading between the coast and interior, crossed some Cascade passes. One of these routes was used by Alexander Ross in his vague exploration through the range in 1814. Although the Pacific Railroad Survey (1853) under Capt. George B. McClellan did not nearly achieve Gov. Isaac I. Stevens' directive to "thoroughly explore this range from the Columbia River to the Forty-ninth Parallel," it yielded much knowledge.[15] Though the exploration's geologist George Gibbs believed that a large basin was enclosed between the ranges bordering the Okanogan River and Puget Sound, he and Lt. Johnson K. Duncan made the first sound regional interpretation of Cascade Range systems, to describe these with a degree of accuracy on the resultant maps.[16] Topographic engineers of the Northwest Boundary Survey, gained a detailed knowledge of a broad transect of the range near the 49th parallel beginning in the late 1850s. The first gold rush in the Cascades developed at Ruby Creek in 1878. Others followed, the most notable being another there in 1880, and the booms at Monte Cristo and near Twin Lakes (Mount Baker district). By 1910 the mining heyday had largely ended.

Records of early Cascade climbs are unfortunately very incomplete, with much of the source material missing. Few early pioneers, most of whom were economically concerned with the mountains, considered their climbing achievements of an importance to record. One cannot expect much else when even educated men in the early days of the West, such as John Muir, once wrote "I have never left my name on any mountain, rock, or tree in any wilderness I have explored." Translated into problems of the historian, the maintenance of accuracy on early climbs is an impossible task. Some non-technical summits are given no "first party" priority because of the great likelihood that the earliest known climbers had been preceded by a pioneer.

The Cascade Range has a great allure for the trail and alpine hiker, the wilderness explorer, and the serious climber. A distinctive thing about the Cascades is its consistently exciting alpine terrain on a scale suited to individual ventures in a setting which is true wilderness in the most rigorous ecological sense. The unusual related factor is the range's proximity to a large population, and that it does not extend into physiologically stressful altitudes (except for Mount Rainier), or require camps uncomfortably far above timberline (same exception). Outside of Alaska, no area of the United States can match the Cascades for alpine mountaineering, though the Tetons, which are famed for their excellent rock and more limited snow climbing, are comparable on a smaller scope. The Cascades have not been climbed as intensively as the Tetons, except in the case of the volcanos, but they have been climbed more thoroughly than the Sierra Nevada or the Wind River Range. While the Cascades offer an unlimited opportunity for wilderness adventure and a great variety of mountaineering problems, the golden age of discovery is over.

Inevitably pioneering interest has shifted from the highest peaks to the new and harder routes, following the pattern of climbing progress in other ranges. New routes have been pioneered that have provided rapid advance in climbing ambition, competence, and courage, requiring the utmost in technical skill. The use of direct aid, which was a rarity prior to 1948, has become a necessity on some of the harder rock routes.

Numerous climbs and variations of existing routes have now been made on less significant yet imposing walls or ridges, since the initial efforts in technical climbing chose the most obvious features leading to summits.

To gain a broader understanding of the climbing history, topography and geology of the range, it is suggested one read selections from the brief list of supplementary material.

The scope of the range is such that there is room for many varieties of experience, and to understand the history and deeper values of these mountains it is well to read of the style and experience of earlier times. In this guide occasional use is made of older appelations to preserve the spirit of a historic episode. Past climbing journals report many of the meaningful ascents in the first person, and are effective supplements for a broader viewpoint.

A guidebook cannot dictate where to go, where safety limits are strained, nor is it a substitute for climbing or wilderness skill. One should remember that all climbs are not for everyone. Those inexperienced or incapable of certain standards should wait until they are ready or forfeit the experience. This ethic should apply, as it not only enhances safer climbing, but sometimes protects the rock from needless bolting and perhaps pitoning. It is recommended that those who newly venture into rough terrain learn their technique on easy ground, seek adequate companionship and proper instruction, and gain knowledge from such volumes as *Mountaineering — Freedom of the Hills, Learning to Rock Climb, Climbing Ice, Basic Rockcraft, Advanced Rockcraft,* and ski touring guides or textbooks. It is hoped that every reader of this guide heeds the principles of mountain-travel safety; otherwise these pages are an invitation to disaster. Further it is hoped the reader will share John Muir's thought: "Climb the mountains and get their good tidings. Nature's peace will flow into you as sunshine flows into trees. The winds will blow their own freshness into you and the storms their energy, while cares will drop off like autumn leaves."

GEOGRAPHIC ASPECTS

"The life of a glacier is one eternal grind"

The striking characteristic of the Cascades in Washington State is the vivid contrasts and diversity of ecological zones. The peaks are often majestically al-pine, with compact groupings, immense local relief, dazzling snowfields, and crevassed glaciers. Their contrasts can be sublime, with a range of subtle and strong earth colors emanating from the great variety of vegetation, the dark forest shadow, and the formerly ice-protected alp slopes. The intriguing Cascade landforms have been produced by the interaction of Pacific moisture and winds, ice, and complex geologic forces. Towering above the average crest line of the range are five large stratovolcanos of Quaternary age, stationed like sentinels at regular intervals. The Cascades are quite unlike any other American range: from Lassen to Baker, the volcanos stand above a very characteristic setting of old-rock crests of strikingly regular altitude. The Chilean Andes may be analogous, but such landscapes are otherwise unique.

Washington's Cascades have the most glaciers, densest and most magnificent forests, and least disturbed wilderness in our contiguous western states. They are the southern limit of a typical Northwest Coast alpine topography which extends to Prince William Sound in Alaska (the North Cascades have much more affinity with the southern British Columbia Coast Mountains than with the Oregon Cascades). In spite of the contrasts cited, certain consistent characteristics and many individual peak similarities create a strong impression of regional unity.

The hydrologic divide of the Cascade Range is erratic and often obscure; it rarely follows one ridge for any large distance. Precipitation therefore drains into a complex stream network. The western slope is drained by 19 important rivers, most of them flowing into the Puget Sound Basin. East of the main watershed all drainage is directed to the Columbia, which turns west to bisect the range. The Columbia and Fraser rivers are both antecedent to the Cascade uplift.

The principal west-draining valleys have been more deeply eroded than those east of the main divide. The valley floors are usually above 3000 ft except at their heads, and many equally deep tributary gorges incise the range almost to their origin on high divides. Valley floors east of the drainage divide lie at relatively higher elevations. Cascade valleys are deeply filled with drift material. Most rivers are fast-flowing; few of them flow tortuously through the pre-glacial depressions, as is often the case in the Rocky Mountains and Interior Ranges of Canada. Water and its effects are visible everywhere in the Cascades: one striking feature is the frequency and beauty of waterfalls in lateral glens.

Plateau Height and Relief: Plateau height is low but relief is high throughout the Cascades. Comparative studies have shown that the 4000- to 7000-ft local relief is quite extensive in the old-rock areas of the Cascades (55 to 108 miles over an east-to-west span between the 48th and 49th parallels) and involves a broader region than is found elsewhere in mid-latitude North America outside nearby British Columbia. Equal relief does exist in a few other places in the western United States, but the area involved is much less. Mount Shuksan, in fact, has been singled out as one of three non-volcanic peaks in the nation whose rise exceeds 3000 ft above timberline on adjacent south slopes. A spectacular example of height differences is Bonanza Peak, whose summit stands over 8400 ft above the surface of Lake Chelan.

Summit Levels: The skyline formed by the higher non-volcanic summits of the North-Central Cascades is so consistent that it was once considered a uniformly uplifted plain which had become dissected by valleys. That concept, originated elsewhere, was applied beyond original expectations to the high Cascades by geologists Bailey Willis and Israel Russell just before the turn of the century. Russell was quite correct in writing that the Cascades are "one of the best illustrations of a deeply dissected mountain mass that the United States affords,"[17] since very little plateau underlies that mass relative to that which supports ranges of greater absolute height such as the Sierra Nevada and the mid-latitude Rockies. Henry Gannett, a prominent geographer early in this century, supported the "peneplain" hypothesis. He said of the Cascades, "the altitude of its crest line averages about 7500 feet, nowhere rising much above or going much below this elevation." However, it is now doubted that the seemingly level (accordant) crest of the range is a remnant of an ancient continuous surface.

Instead, an explanation by Canadian geologist George M. Dawson in 1896 has been revived. Dawson noted the prevalent accordance of ridge crests and minor summits at timberline in both the Coast Mountains and the Cascade Range. He also observed that the Coast Mountains weather and waste away more vigorously above timberline, where they are less protected by the stabilizing root-mat of the subalpine forest.

More recently, it has been proposed that although timberlines were at various heights during the Ice Ages, the crest-leveling action described by Dawson has always been powerful, and that summits in the treeless alpine are bound to waste — to approach the accordance with tree-covered neighbors. Two and possibly three distinct summit accordances have developed: one at the level of present timberlines and one 2000 ft above, with a less well-defined level roughly halfway between. The intermediate accordance is particularly well seen between Glacier Peak and Snoqualmie Pass.

Each level is believed to record a timberline which existed during a different period of persistent interglacial Pleistocene climate as warm or warmer than that of the present. During the warmest such period, only the highest non-volcanic summits in the Cascades were affected by alpine erosion. The more continuous parts of the level ridges which then developed have since mostly been dissected by couloir (avalanche) erosion to form individual peaks.

On the other hand, meadow-crowned accordant crests at the present timberline level often run for miles with only minor peaks and gaps. A broad zone of such level crests, roughly 20 mi. broad, flanks the high range between Mount Rainier and Mount Baker.

The erosional tendency of frost action and glacial quarrying at and above timberline has formed extensive alp slopes (inclined meadow benchlands) at and near timberline. These include floors of many small Ice Age cirques. Many such timberline benches have moderate slopes, which contrast with steeper lower canyon walls. High alpine gradients and steep subalpine canyon walls allow rock and soil to be transported freely downslope by avalanche, stream transport, and solifluction, whereas detritus accumulates as a substantial mantle on the alp slopes. Such meadow slopes likely developed very slowly, and they have been moderated by frost-caused creep and nivation pockets.

Throughout the higher ranges of the western United States, alp slopes coincide with timberlines except where timberline lies on Tertiary desert pediments, as it often does in the Rocky Mountains. The prevailing height of the alpine zone above timberline is about the same in each major alpine region in our western states. Will F. Thompson observes that accordance 2000 ft above timberline is represented in the western North Cascades by near-7000-ft peaks above 5000-ft timberlines (Three Fingers, Columbia, Twin Sisters) and in the eastern Cascades by 9000-ft peaks above 7000-ft timberlines (Stuart, Maude, Silver Star), as well as by large numbers of 8000-ft peaks above 6000-ft timberlines in mid-range. The alpine relief cited is based on regional, not local,

MOUNT DANIEL, MOUNT HINMAN, and valley of the East Fork Foss River
ED COOPER

south-slope timberline. The eastward rise of timber-line, and thus of both the high and timberline accordances, is due to warmer mid-summer temperatures and less snow accumulation. The Cascade Range also exhibits a gradual southward rise in timberline, which eventually reaches 9000 ft in southern Oregon. The alp slope level rises accordingly, both eastward and southward.

Climate and Vegetation: Cascade Range climate is mid-latitude, west-coast marine, with most air masses having a Pacific source. Temperatures are seldom below 10° F or above 80° F (afternoon summer temperatures are usually about 60°). Both low and high extremes occur with a high pressure system centered east or north of the Cascades, causing the flow of continental air from the interior westward across the range.

The climate of Washington State is strongly influenced by alternating, semipermanent high- and low-pressure cells over the North Pacific. These control flow of air across the western continental margin. Counterclockwise circulation around the low-pressure system reaches its maximum intensity in midwinter and produces a southwesterly flow of moist maritime air, resulting in a distinct rainy season, usually from October to April. During summer, the low-pressure cell weakens, while a high-pressure system intensifies and spreads over much of the North Pacific. Clockwise circulation around this system usually brings a north-westerly flow of relatively cool, dry air over Washington during the summer months. The Cascades form a major topographic barrier to air flow and divide the state into two contrasting climatic regions — a belt of strongly maritime conditions west of the range and one of increasingly continental climate to the east.

Annual precipitation ranges over 150 inches on the wettest slopes, with July and August accounting for less than 5 percent of the average total. The following are the average seasonal clear or partly-cloudy days: 4 to 7 in winter, 10 to 15 in spring and fall, and 20 in summer. The Cascade Range in Washington State is not only notable for rainfall, but for extensive winter snow cover, which is often heavy as low as 2000 ft. The maximum snowfall is not always at the highest altitudes because it is controlled by the mean freezing level (the greatest snowfall occurs at or near the freezing level).

Because of the moderating effects of Pacific air and a high percentage of cloudiness, the January and July mean temperatures at timberline differ by only 25° F (the corresponding difference in Colorado averages nearly 40° F). Permafrost level is probably near 8000 ft (or higher), much higher relative to timberline than in most North American ranges. Locally, the margins of permafrost are affected by their directional exposure and by their position in the range.

Under the strongly maritime conditions of the western side of the range, timber is dense and, except where logged, is essentially continuous below timberline. However, avalanches, together with persistent snowdrifts that extend through much of the growing season, hinder timber growth on some slopes, and thus have a pronounced local effect on timberline and timber density. Dwarfed timber and open, brush-filled areas are common on both flanks of the range. East of the highest Cascade crests, a drier climate results in open timber stands with less undergrowth and soil occurring on steep slopes. Meadows and extensive taluses are more evident. At the lee margins of the range, the forest zone ends and is replaced by a semi-arid climate and vegetation (Okanogan averages 12 inches annual precipitation).

The picturesque high-level conifers of the Cascades highlight a heavy forest mantle that makes the complex geology difficult to decipher. The complete stratification of life zones may occur in just a few miles when there is vast local relief. The belts of mountain vegetation are basically determined by altitude, soil, moisture, and exposure. The scale of size decreases from the immense and prolific firs and cedars of the low "rain forest" to the montane (Canadian) zone, where trees grow with increasing economy and elegance. Here and in the ascetic subalpine (Hudsonian) zone exists the threat of destruction by wind, snow-drifts, and dehydration. In testimony to the tenacity of life, delicate perennial plants, a distinct species related to lowland types, have only about three months to grow.

In the more naked landscape of the alpine zone the few plants, for literally a moment of exuberance, have to adapt to unusually cruel conditions; plants and scrub evergreens tend to survive and preserve heat by hugging the ground, often in seclusion behind rock outcrops. Here lichens create seedbeds for the more advanced flower-bearing plants. The greatest survival ability is shown by "pink snow," (*proctococcus nivalis*), which owes its characteristic tint to invisible algae that secrete a reddish gelatinous protective covering.

Geology: Although the evolution of the Cascades has taken several tens of million years, the modern range came into existence only near the end of the

Tertiary Period, perhaps six m. y. ago or less. The range in southern and central Washington is a broad uplift of gently folded sedimentary and volcanic rocks, upwarped at an angle to the northwest-trending bedrock structures.

By the end of an earlier Cretaceous time, mountain-building movements intensified, and a general uplift began forcing the sea out of what is now eastern Washington. By the beginning of Pliocene time, the seashore had been pushed to near its present location. Cascade uplift was sufficiently slow that the Columbia River was not deterred in its flow, but trenched the weak volcanic rock barrier as it rose. Lesser streams adjusted to the configuration of the new range.

The chain of Cascade volcanos is a topographic consequence of the ongoing collision between the westward-pushing North American crustal plate and the tiny offshore Gorda plate (which drifts northeastward about one inch annually). New sea floor is added to the western margin of the oceanic Gorda plate along the San Juan rift as it moves on a collision course toward the Oregon-Washington coast, where it is subducted beneath the Cascade volcanos.

The main volcanic axis lies above where the oceanic plate descends into the deep, hot mantle. Complex physical and chemical reactions occur in the deep part of the subduction zone and cause the rocks to liquefy. Molted magma arrives at the surface through weak zones (conduits) in the continental crust to periodically erupt at volcanos.

The high composite volcanos — Mount Adams, Mount St. Helens, and Mount Rainier — are young features built in Pleistocene time atop a range which already possessed its present relief and elevation. These large Quaternary (within the past one million years) volcanos rise above a deeply dissected platform of older lavas and volcanic clastic rocks. They overlie the deeply eroded, warped, and faulted Tertiary volcanic strata and diverse pre-Tertiary rocks.

It is convenient to divide the Washington Cascades into two geological provinces: the *Southern Cascades* and the *North Cascades*. In the latter the Tertiary rocks have been stripped away by erosion, or are preserved only as remnants, exposing deformed and metamorphosed, structurally complex pre-Tertiary rocks. The boundary between these two provinces lies near the latitude of Stevens Pass.

The Cascades south of Stevens Pass exhibit a younger geologic environment than that to the north, and are composed predominantly of Tertiary volcanic rocks and subordinate sedimentary rocks that are also invaded by Tertiary and pre-Tertiary igneous rocks. West of the Straight Creek fault (extending from north of Skykomish through Lake Kachess) the oldest rocks are scattered, relatively unmetamorphosed Mesozoic and Paleozoic melanges.

The oldest rocks of the Snoqualmie Pass to Skykomish River area are generally the thick Swauk Formation sediments of arkose sandstone, shale, and conglomerate of Eocene age. These tilted and deformed rocks extend in a belt west of the fault from near the Skykomish River to Little Kachess Lake. Striking examples of the formation are Bears Breast and Summit Chief mountains. Following the deformation and erosion of the Swauk, a variety of volcanics and sandstones of the Naches Formation were also deposited west of the fault, nearer the Cascade crest. This extensive formation is composed of some 5000 ft of interbedded, folded volcanics and sedimentary rocks: examples of a narrow band of the Naches Formation are Lemah Mountain, Overcoat Peak, Chimney Rock, and Three Queens. The formation extends southward to approximately Naches Pass, where it grades with the Ohanapecosh and other formations.

The andesite Denny Peak-Tooth Rock unit crops out northwest of Snoqualmie Pass. The Guye Formation, a sedimentary member of the Naches Formation, is exposed in an area north of the pass. The Mount Garfield volcanics, between the Middle Fork Snoqualmie and Taylor rivers, are massive breccias, tuffs, and ash flows with little stratification. Other complex Tertiary volcanic rocks include an extensive and widespread grouping in the area of Mount Daniel, and in the watershed of the Tolt River through Mount Persis.

Batholiths invaded the southern and central Cascades at roughly the same time as the volcanic events. The Snoqualmie and Grotto batholiths cooled at about 25 m. y. ago, and the Mount Index about 34 m. y. ago. The younger Tatoosh pluton, underlying Mount Rainier, is dated between 17 and 14 m. y. ago. The White River pluton, northeast of Mount Rainier, and the Bumping Lake batholith, to the west of Mount Aix, are of similar age.

Heat from emplacement of the Snoqualmie batholith metamorphosed and indurated such rock units as the Naches, Denny, and Garfield. This batholith, estimated to occupy an area exceeding 270 mi^2, is one of the larger intrusions exposed in the Cascades. It is resistant and is carved into high peaks and ridges such as Granite and Snoqualmie moun-

COLLIDING PLATES CAUSE VOLCANIC ACTIVITY

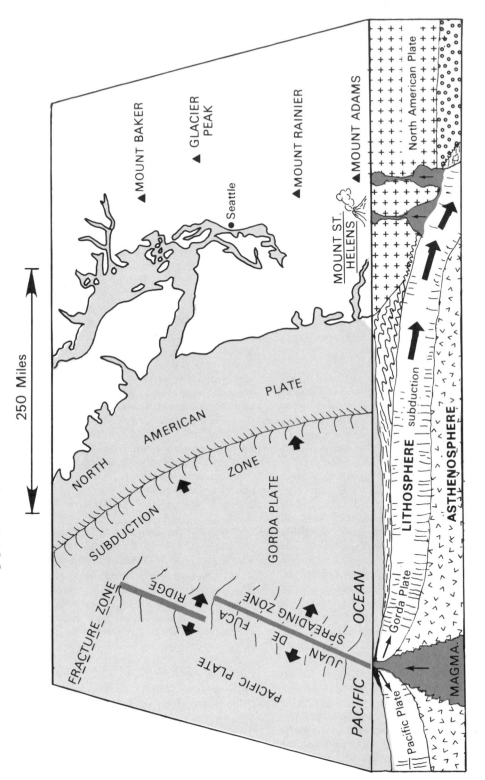

The Gorda plate is slowly thrusting under the North American plate and into the earth's hot mantle. This process results in the formation of magma and causes zones of weakness in the North American plate through which magma rises to feed the Cascade volcanoes. The lithosphere is cool enough to be rigid and strong; it includes the entire crust and also the top of the mantle. The hot asthenosphere beneath is plastic, allowing the lithospheric plates to slide over it easily.

tains, and is the bedrock for many of the west-side Alpine Lakes.

East of the Straight Creek fault, the strongly folded and widespread Swauk Formation (dated at about 50 m. y. in age) unconformably covers pre-Tertiary peridotite and schist. South of Mount Stuart, the Swauk Formation is overlain by Teanaway Basalt.

The principal high-grade metamorphic rock units are the Chiwaukum Schist (exposed east of the fault) and the late Jurassic Ingalls Complex, which was thrust over the schist. Both the Ingalls and Chiwaukum rocks were intruded by the Mount Stuart batholith, much of it dated at about 93 m. y. of age.

A thick sequence of volcanic rocks underlies the area south of Naches Pass and the White River, and the Quaternary volcanos of the southern Cascade Range. The oldest unit, the Ohanapecosh Formation of mostly Oligocene age, consists principally of colorful breccia, sedimentary rocks, and basalt and andesite flows. These rocks are overlain by widespread ash-flow tuffs, designated as the Stevens Ridge Formation, and by andesite lava flows of the Fifes Peak Formation. Rocks of the Tatoosh pluton sharply crosscut these bedded formations.

Flood-lava flows of the Yakima Basalt locally separate the Ohanapecosh-Stevens Ridge-Fifes Peak group from the High Cascade volcanic rocks at White Pass, Goat Rocks, and Mount Adams.

Glaciers: The present Cascade topography of jagged ridges and deep gorges is the product of stream erosion modified and sharpened in the last several million years by Pleistocene glaciation. Repeated glacier oscillations in cirques and over the floors of outlet valleys produced the glacial basins and deep U-shaped valleys. Turbid glacial streams and ancient moraines are examples of the immense erosive power of glacial ice.

Aside from those mantling the volcanos, Cascade Range glaciers are not only very numerous, but are located with surprising consistency on alp slopes. They filled valleys during the Ice Ages, but do so no longer. The ice-covered area in the Cascades is triple that of all the remainder of the contiguous United States. The state of Washington is particularly well endowed in this respect; it is estimated that 77 percent of the glacier area in the United States south of Alaska occurs in Washington (Meier, 1961). Mount Rainier National Park alone holds 34 square miles of ice. The U.S. Geological Survey has completed an atlas listing 756 glaciers 0.1 square km (.04 sq mi) or larger in area

north of Snoqualmie Pass, covering a total of 103 square miles.[18]

Glaciers in the maritime western Cascades are nourished chiefly by direct accumulation brought in by warm Pacific air masses, and augmented by avalanches. Prevailing westerly winds drift some snow onto eastern faces. Such drift is more important in the eastern than in the western Cascades because snow is drier and less abundant there. In climatically continental ranges cirques are located precisely where accumulation of drift snow is greatest; but the situation in the Cascades is quite different: drift is significant, but does not play a major role.

Late summer glacier firn limits range from 6000 to 8000 ft in elevation, varying with slope exposure and position in the range. Below 8000 ft glaciers generally tend to melt back from rock margins as the summer progresses. Moats due to melt-back from rock contact with snow or ice tend to become increasingly broad as altitude decreases. Where bedrock is below freezing, bergschrunds occur which are not due to melting but to withdrawal of deep ice downslope from the shallow ice frozen to the mountain face.

Cascade glaciers are especially numerous on shady north and northeast-facing slopes. These glaciers are of diverse forms: while there are a few small valley glaciers and several small icefields, patch, slope, and cirque glaciers are the most common. The self-descriptive "hanging" glaciers (either cirque or slope) are the most spectacular. Cascade glaciers and snowfields have vast and complex hydrologic significance: they act as reservoirs that release meltwater in summer, which comes at a time to build up depleted groundwater storage.

Glaciers located so that most of their surface is lower than the summer snowline, are wasting most rapidly, yet each glacier responds independently to climate. Conditions are most favorable to expansion when most of the glacier's area is above the accumulation zone. Some glaciers located in deeply glaciated canyons on Cascade volcanos are in a self-defeating situation for expansion, for they are severely restricted by their own structural boundaries.

Relatively mild winters, high permafrost level, and heavy snowcover are the primary reasons for the lack of rock glaciers west of the crest of the North Cascades. However, there are many in the lee of Mount Rainier (D.R. Crandell mapped nearly 20 there) and in the easternmost Cascades. Rock glaciers are more prevalent in other U.S. alpine ranges.

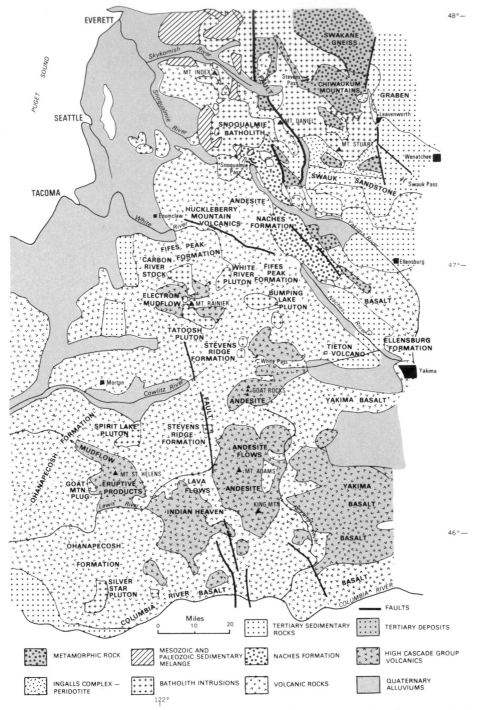

48°—

EVERETT

PUGET SOUND

SEATTLE

TACOMA

Skykomish River

Snoqualmie River

SWAKANE GNEISS

CHIWAUKUM MOUNTAINS

GRABEN

Leavenworth

MT. INDEX

Stevens Pass

MT. DANIEL

SNOQUALMIE BATHOLITH

MT. STUART

Wenatchee

Snoqualmie Pass

SWAUK SANDSTONE

Swauk Pass

ANDESITE

HUCKLEBERRY MOUNTAIN VOLCANICS

Enumclaw

White River

NACHES FORMATION

FIFES PEAK FORMATION

CARBON RIVER STOCK

WHITE RIVER PLUTON

FIFES PEAK FORMATION

Yakima River

Ellensburg

47°—

ELECTRON MUDFLOW

MT. RAINIER

BUMPING LAKE PLUTON

BASALT

TATOOSH PLUTON

STEVENS RIDGE FORMATION

White Pass

TIETON VOLCANO

ELLENSBURG FORMATION

Yakima

Morton

Cowlitz River

GOAT ROCKS

ANDESITE

YAKIMA BASALT

SPIRIT LAKE PLUTON

STEVENS RIDGE FORMATION

OHANAPECOSH FORMATION

MUDFLOW

ANDESITE FLOWS

MT. ADAMS

GOAT MTN. PLUG

ERUPTIVE PRODUCTS

MT. ST. HELENS

LAVA FLOWS

ANDESITE

KING MTN.

YAKIMA BASALT

FAULT

Lewis River

INDIAN HEAVEN

46°—

OHANAPECOSH FORMATION

BASALT

SILVER STAR PLUTON

COLUMBIA RIVER BASALT

COLUMBIA RIVER

Miles
0   10   20

━━━ FAULTS

⋰⋰ TERTIARY SEDIMENTARY ROCKS

∴∴ TERTIARY DEPOSITS

▨ METAMORPHIC ROCK

▨ MESOZOIC AND PALEOZOIC SEDIMENTARY MELANGE

∴∴ NACHES FORMATION

˅˅ HIGH CASCADE GROUP VOLCANICS

∴∴ INGALLS COMPLEX — PERIDOTITE

+++ BATHOLITH INTRUSIONS

˅˅ VOLCANIC ROCKS

▨ QUATERNARY ALLUVIUMS

122°

GEOLOGIC MAP of the CENTRAL AND SOUTHERN CASCADE RANGE, WASHINGTON

From: Geologic Map of Washington, U.S. Geological Survey (A.E. Weissenborn - 1969), and Southern Cascade Range (Paul E. Hammond - 1980)

Glacial Sequence: During early glacial episodes of the Pleistocene Epoch much of the Cascade Range was mantled with icefields, and long alpine glaciers extended to or beyond the western front of the range. These valley glaciers merged with a massive lobe of the Cordilleran Ice Sheet which originated in Canada and spread into northern Washington to form the Puget Lobe. In the southern lowland it terminated against the Cascade and Olympic foothills, while north of the Skagit River it engulfed valleys and passes. Ice sheet movement has left a complex record of till and outwash along the western mountain front and in mountain river valleys.

Major stream valleys record the multiple advances and retreats of alpine glaciers. Great glaciers whose flow force and weight extensively modified the river-carved master valleys were broad and long: the Chelan Glacier 90 mi.; the Skagit over 100 mi. When glaciers invaded river valleys, they concentrated their erosion on spurs and cirques, often truncating them — the effect being to straighten valleys. Because excavation of the major ice streams was faster and channel depth lower than that of tributaries (though they met at about the same surface levels), many "hanging valleys" remained when these valley glaciers melted.

About 15,000 years ago, the Puget Lobe spread onto foothills and high onto northern peaks, damming lakes in valleys that had just previously been occupied by alpine glaciers. Cascade mountain glaciers receded and no longer joined ice lobes to the east and west. However, the Puget Sound trough and Strait of Georgia were still occupied and deeply scoured by ice lobes which later withdrew to expose present lowlands and waterways.

After the last glaciation some 8000 to 10,000 years ago, a warmer climate than the present lasted about 4000 years, and led to melting and disappearance of most Cascade mountain glaciers.

The climate then became more rigorous, to result in rebirth of small modern glaciers in the more protected cirques and valleys (Neoglaciation), characterized by at least three main intervals of glacier growth. In the Cascades such redevelopment has been mostly on alp slopes. In the Pacific Northwest, maximum advances have occurred at widely different times for individual glaciers. The diversity in the pattern of fluctuations was such that some advanced 5000 years ago, while most reached a maximum 2500 to 3000 years ago, or during the 19th century. Many moraines formed during the mid-19th century advances are well preserved. Receding ice has extensively uncovered polished bedrock. Most Cascade glaciers lie below the altitude zone of maximum snowfall and suffer accordingly in terms of nourishment. At present there is about 385 km² of ice in the Washington Cascades, about half being on the volcanos.

Beginning about 1950 a moderating climatic trend generated advances on many glaciers. During the past decade, general equilibrium has persisted. Neoglacial chronology in the Cascade Range has been established largely by relative dating of moraines, using associated layers of volcanic ash found deposited over wide areas. One of the older layers originated about 6700 years ago in a catastrophic eruption of Mount Mazama (Crater Lake, Oregon); significant ash layers came from St. Helens volcano and from an eruption of Glacier Peak.

The present wide variety of Cascade Range topography is largely due to oft-repeated glaciation, revived by each deterioration of regional climate. At alpine levels, the enlargement and headward erosion of cirques was the principal effect of the various ice ages. During each major advance, the larger cirques at the head of each great gorge were deepened, broadened, and eroded headward. Many lesser cirques, produced partially by inter-glacial frost action above timberline, are found primarily on alp slopes. The topography of the Cascade timberline zone seems quite completely explained by that sequence. Cascade Range meadow uplands are pitted with hundreds of such small glacial cirques, many containing lakes in ice-gouged basins; others still contain glacial ice and perennial snow in nivation pockets.

CAMPING AND TRAILS

"People who sleep in tents lead sheltered lives"

Campgrounds in national parks and forests are open to the public on a first-arrival basis. While many national forest camps are open to the public without charge, under the Land and Water Conservation Fund Act passed by Congress in 1965, certain designated developed sites require a camping fee.

Entrance to these sites is gained by (1) purchase of an annual Golden Eagle Passport, available at National Park entrances, good for one car including all occupants (currently $10), or (2) purchase of a daily permit. Permits are on sale at forest headquarters and ranger stations. Daily permit and user-fees may be purchased at charge sites (self-paying; exact change needed).

Campfire permits are not needed in national forests, but are required in national parks except at designated

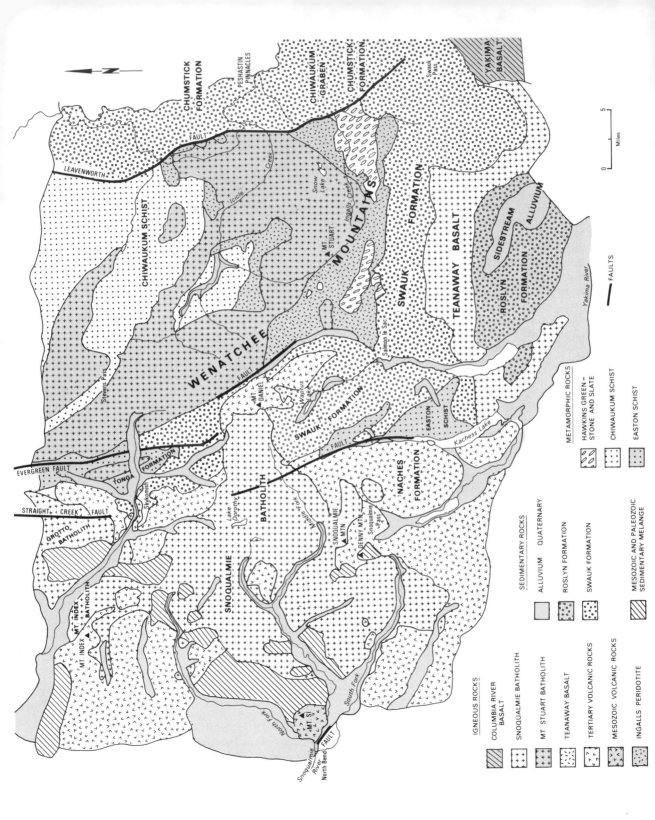

campgrounds. During periods of extreme fire hazard, be prepared for forest closures or special restrictions.

State Parks: There is an overnight camping charge. (Generally parks are closed to entrance or exit during late night hours.)

The Pacific National Scenic Crest Trail follows the approximate watershed of the Cascade Range some 450 mi. from the Columbia River to the Canadian Boundary. Nearly all of the trail is on public lands, but there are minor private crossings and various road and highway interruptions. While there are no stores at highway crossings to replenish provisions, it is possible to leave vehicles at parking lots and sometimes make caches.

The Forest Service began the construction of this trail in 1935. Since then, there have been several relocations with new grade standards, the most recent major one being the portion between Snoqualmie Pass and Deception Pass covered in this volume. The Crest Trail and its branches are not designed for motorized equipment and such vehicles are prohibited on the entire trail.

Prior to July one should expect the higher trail sections to be snow-covered and the meadows wet. In the southern Cascades of Washington, late summer conditions may be very dry and water sources infrequent.

Environmental Impacts:

Trail use: Hikers should not take shortcuts. The resulting new scars from boots pounding downhill leave gullies, which erode the soil and quickly become deeper.

Pets impair the enjoyment of others. Do not take pets on trails or into the mountain environment.

Newcomers often need guidance in maintaining the wilderness aspect of trails, camps, and lakeside settings. You can help by good example and direct instructions. There is a constant danger that those who litter the highways and cities will enter our mountain areas and expand their abuse.

Carry out all trash, including plastics, cans, peels, and wrappers. Encourage others to do so.

Camping: It is best to camp and build fires at previously used sites, both from the standpoint of safety and to minimize ground surface damage. Gravel bar or forested sites are preferable to meadows. In fragile meadow regions the use of liquid fuel or butane stoves conserves wood supply and eliminates ground damage. *The campfire has long been part of the charisma of the outdoor experience, but it is no longer in vogue.* The Cascade Range ecosystem is one which is balanced for a low level of disturbance. The pressure of human needs at vulnerable timberline areas can cause vast damage.

Do not make unsightly marks about a campsite. Avoid using an axe except in forest camps where saw logs are available for burning. Do not hack trees with axe or knife, and do not cut green boughs for sleeping beds.

Do not dig trenches for tents. Try to avoid camping on passes or ridge lines; select benches at a lower level. Do not build rock windbreaks at campsites. Avoid camping within 100 ft of any lake.

Camping may not be allowed at certain overused locations, and near certain lakes. Check maps and signposts for such restrictions.

Human wastes: Bury human wastes and tissues, if possible about 8 inches deep; dig a small hole to begin the toilet and later cover with soil. Otherwise the stool on surfaces will stink, draw flies, and remain. Always make the toilet at least 100 ft from any stream, lake, or water source, and away from trails and campsites.

Avoid burying excrement in snow. The decay is retarded by freezing temperatures, and melting snow exposes the remains at a later time. Pack out anything not completely biodegradable. The use of sealed plastic bags is becoming encouraged for solid excrement disposal, especially on the higher snow and glacier-covered mountains, such as Mount Rainier.

Water: Most Cascade water sources are free of contamination and may safely be used for drinking without treatment. Water taken from areas of suspicious quality should be treated with iodine or boiled. There is an increasing danger from *Giardia* and other water-borne diseases.

Never pollute streams, lakes, or meadowland ponds. Do not drop food remains or wash dishes in our water resources.

A vast quantity of rock flour is carried in turbid glacial streams. The silt suspended in glacial water will settle out if allowed to stand undisturbed.

Horses are generally permitted on the Pacific National Scenic Crest Trail. Watch for posted restrictions and group size limitations. Horse travel is permitted on many other trails; for specific restrictions, trail and bridge re-routing, consult the District Ranger. Horse packing and grazing continue to damage alpine meadow soils, which can be lost rapidly; riders should take great care to avoid eroding trails and to keep stock at specified areas. Packing should flatly be forbidden in many places.

Motorized equipment, including mountain bikes, of any sort is prohibited in wilderness areas, as well as on many trails; trail signs and maps indicate those trails closed to motorized usage. Motorized equipment and bicycles are prohibited on the Crest Trail. Motorbikes have caused considerable trail and highland surface damage, and should be forbidden in all alpine areas and predominantly pedestrian trails.

Provisions are not for sale at forest stations or campgrounds. A few resorts, forest lookouts, and forest stations are equipped with telephones, available to the public only in an emergency.

MOUNTAIN AND WILDERNESS TRAVEL

"The musquitoes charged in from all directions on our heads, necks, ears, faces and hands, from whence it was imposible to dislodge them, until a fresh supply of saw-dust, thrown over the dying embers, put them once more to flight."
CHAMBERS EDINBURGH JOURNAL

Frequently the major defenses of a mountain in the Cascades lie far below timberline. It must be remembered that approaches may suddenly be changed by stream washouts, destroyed bridges, timber blow-downs, and area closures due to fire hazard. Some private roads in mountain areas have locked gates to prevent equipment theft. Logging roads can wash out readily if not maintained; grades are often abandoned after timber harvesting is completed. It is wise to carry an axe and saw in the car when driving seldom-used roads to avoid being trapped by windfall. Many trails are of a transient nature, and their identity covered quickly by brush growth, or windfall. Some formerly excellent trails and even wagon roads have entirely vanished.

A burned-over or logged "second growth" area is especially difficult to cross due to the deadfall and thick new brush. In the Cascades the combined effects of brush and gorges may make untracked valleys unpleasant; young streams cut typically narrow canyons; where creeks have cut through glacial till, a steep cut may be deceptively difficult. Larger streams may have boulder beds and gravel bars suitable for travel in late summer and fall. Only a few of the broader valleys are plagued by beaver ponds, which should be carefully avoided. Often one can follow animal trails near stream banks or along a valley wall. Old trails and game paths generally follow the easiest route through a wilderness, so one should watch for blazes and other signs. If traveling through average Cascade brush,

allow *at least* two hours for one mi. on the flat, and more if on a gradient. Very dense, untracked west-side valleys may require a much greater time allowance.

Willow, red alder, and vine maple often grow very densely in low valleys and along streams, and they compete to thicken bottomlands. Plants ranging from the harmless sword fern to the unpleasant devil's club may be found in moist areas. On slopes the mountain alder may fill avalanche tracks through timber zones; usually these areas are hard to traverse and a swath tends to fan out on the valley floor. Make a detour if necessary to stay in the heaviest timber. While travel east of the main divide is generally easier, do not assume there cannot be dense thickets; these may occur along streams, gulches, and where the forest is smashed down by snowslides.

Accordance of ridges at timberline often provides ridge routes which link up with continuing alp-slope traverses at the same level on larger peaks. Timberline is lower when rock, talus, and snow force it down; slopes usually grow timber and vegetation higher on the south than on the shadow slopes. Where alp slopes head under cliffs, rockfall debris and soil creep tend to leave bedrock thinly covered at this point, often allowing brushless travel here; likewise, early in summer snow accumulation at such points may allow good traversing. When advancing upvalley it is sometimes feasible to follow a pattern of travel along the tops of talus sections and alluvial cones to keep above lower brush areas. In general, try to travel on scree, snow and grass rather than through brush; large detours or added elevation gains and losses are often worth taking to avoid brush and dwarf timber.

When ascending a spur or ridge that is later to be descended, take note of branching ridges; keen memory or the taking of notes may be valuable. When descending it is much easier to lose the crest and become involved in sub-ridges and steep side-canyons. The Cascades, especially to the northern limits, often have multiple cirques. The upper cirque may still support a glacier while steep cliffs of the lower cirque are defended by alder, cedar shrub, and waterfalls. Many valley bottom routes are more feasible in spring or early summer than later, if snow covers brush, provided high water does not otherwise impede movement. Gulches and couloirs running up brushy mountain slopes may provide fast early-season routes if snow-filled; however, always stay alert here for dangerous avalanche conditions and for *thin snow* above stream-melt. The meltwater percolation of snowfields and glaciers drains away almost entirely through stream hollows or in sub-glacial drainage channels.

In general, the validity of an alpine route described in the guide may depend on snow conditions, season, crevasse conditions, weather, high water, and other variables. Warm daytime temperatures in late spring and early summer often render snow conditions very poor for progress. To achieve firmer and safer snow it may be wise to wait for a cooler air mass; or climb extremely early or at night. But, avoid making night-time descents. *A number of serious accidents have occurred solely because those policies were not followed!* Snow surfaces that provide firm early-season footing will become icier and may require crampons in late season. One should anticipate that most slopes above 5000 ft in altitude will be snow-covered from November until July.

On difficult stream crossings use of a long pole or the ice axe on the down-side is helpful for depth probing, especially in opaque glacial water. At stream fords, try to wade at the widest point; where the river is swiftest and broadest, it is also shallowest. Avoid wearing a safety rope above a snag; one should approach log jams and sweepers from the downstream side. Should you fall off a low log, fall downside if possible; beware of sagging logs that touch fast water, as the tendency here is to be thrown to the dangerous upstream side. Because of their stretch factor, nylon ropes are poor for handlines and tyrolean traverses.

When traveling off-trail it is wise to carry a topographic map, altimeter, and compass — and be certain you know how to use these aids. One problem that may arise (not always anticipated) is rapid incursion of fogs; this may obliterate progress viewing, or it may render a return to the trailhead quite difficult. When in a fog above timberline beware of the danger of traversing across a spur or ridge, then traveling in the wrong direction (reliability of "slope direction" is thereby lost).

If it is deemed absolutely necessary to mark a route for the return, bright colored crepe paper is acceptable, since it will vanish with time. Never use bright plastic ribbons to mark routes. *They destroy the Wilderness Experience.*

Good behavior in marking routes preserves the wilderness quality for others. Never paint rocks to mark routes. Such an act defaces natural features, and is subject to a fine.

Should you become lost, first stop to collect your thoughts. By retracing the route to a known position, the chances of locating or understanding the route are

increased. Should this fail, and night is approaching, gather a good supply of wood (if available) for a fire. Remember, ground searchers and aircraft can find you most easily in open areas where colors and a smoky fire capture attention.

If outside assistance is needed two should be sent out. An injury or hypothermia victim should be looked after by others — never left alone. The route should be marked or otherwise identified so rescuers can be quickly led or directed to the scene. Liaison should stand by to direct assistance back, or to give first-person instructions.

IN CASE OF ACCIDENT OR FOR MOUNTAIN EMERGENCIES:

In *National Park,* notify nearest park ranger.

In *National Forest,* notify county sheriff or forest ranger.

In *British Columbia,* contact the nearest R.C.M.P.

If someone becomes lost or overdue, notify the nearest forest or national park ranger, or the county sheriff.

Before leaving for a climb or hike in the Cascades, always leave your plans, estimated return time, and car license number with a responsible person.

For distress or emergency, three signals or signs is the standard for alert.

To minimize the danger of thefts from parked cars on mountain roads, take only the needed valuables, and lock the remainder in the trunk. In case of theft, notify the county sheriff.

CASCADE WEATHER

"The weather man is always correct — sooner or later."

The strongest winds are from the south or southwest and usually occur as the more intense winter-season storms move inland. The frequent alternation in winter of warm southerly air currents with the colder northern winds is a fixed climatic characteristic of the Puget Sound region. But the prevailing wind in fall and winter is from the southwest, gradually shifting to northwest in late spring and summer.

The upper-level "low," a pool of high cold air that generates much cloudiness in the Cascades and considerable rain, is a common occurrence; entire systems of these "lows" may move slowly. Fronts may be broken up by irregularities of the mountains, especially those of the turbulent zones in a cold front, with squalls going off in various directions, hitting certain peaks and missing others. The existing currents of an unstable air mass are exaggerated by the mountains, and the lifting of air as it passes over mountains both lengthens and intensifies any storm system. Typically, the cooling on the windward side may cause condensation of vapor into clouds. On the lee slope the warming effect from air compressing quickly dispels clouds, and it may be clear there when it is raining only a few miles west. The western slopes are transverse to prevailing winds, and even after the passing of a weather system, clouds tend to linger in comparison to the lee slopes; the higher percentage of cloud-cover reduces the mean flux of thermal radiation.

Chinook winds, a transitory climatic phenomena, and a version of the föehn wind of the Alps, develop on the eastern slope of the Cascade Range. As air crosses the mountain crest line and descends, it brings a warming effect instituted by compression heating. Warming at the dry adiabatic rate is greater than the cooling of the wet adiabatic rate during ascent on the windward slope.

The chinook wind may arrive with violence and continue for several days, and in spring it can bring a rapid snow thaw. The chinook develops typically with a ridge of high pressure on the windward slope and a low-pressure trough on the leeward, creating a steep pressure gradient across the range.

Stable air masses that move in, bringing fair weather, often bring onto the coast fog that pushes well up into mountain valleys. Such fog or clouds may hang very low and rise to 4000 ft or higher, with clear weather above. Sometimes these low mists clear in the afternoon, while morning may have a deep gloom and drizzle.

July and August normally have the most stable and driest weather, with June and September following. There is generally a stable winter weather period, sometimes with firm snow conditions. Some years record excellent autumns, but it must be remembered that heavy snowfalls can occur above timberline at any time during that season — although they rarely arrive before late October. Light snowfall often occurs at the beginning of September, rendering northern and eastern mountain faces quite iced and wintry thereafter.

Mountaineers should be alert to the signs of weather instability and the dangers caused by rapid lack of visibility where continuation or retreat is slow or difficult. Cloudcaps on the high volcanos can form rapidly. Watch for the appearance of thickening cirrus and lenticular clouds. Spring and fall storms can be especially savage, with driving winds accompanied by sleet that stings the face and makes visibility zero. In general, it is wise to make a hasty retreat under such conditions, as such storms may last several days without respite. *A number of tragedies have occurred because a party underestimated the severity of such storms, and "dug in" or kept climbing with inadequate equipment.*

SPECIAL DANGERS

"Look well to each step . . . and remember the risk."
EDWARD WHYMPER

It is assumed that those using this guide are aware of and accept the normal hazards associated with hiking and climbing, but it should be remembered that the Cascades are a complex wilderness range, with attendant hazards. Everyone who hikes or climbs must assume all attendant risks for his own safety. Some of the principal dangers are outlined.

Cornices and avalanches: Special dangers in the Cascades at all altitudes because of strong prevailing winds and steep lee slopes; may be dangerous at any time from early winter to early summer. Beware of heavy early season snowfalls where cornices may break suddenly from ridges and glacier-moat edges due to poor adhesion. In spring and early summer both rainy weather conditions and warm daytime temperatures can trigger dangerous wet-snow avalanches; especially treacherous are narrow couloirs and canyons, as well as thin snow patches or fingers atop rock slabs or streams. Freezing altitudes can be predicted from forecasts or the weather bureau. Dangerous wet snow avalanches can occur in spring when significant amounts of melting take place at the snow surface. Large wet, loose snow slides are more likely to occur during warm cloudy weather and during wind and rain, when melting proceeds both day and night, with large quantities of liquid water penetrating deeply into the snowcover. Steeply pitched hanging glaciers, common in the North Cascades, present unusual hazards as large avalanches may occur unpredictably.

Loose rock: Rain is the greatest cause of rockfall from faces; intermittent freezing and thawing is the greatest cause of rockfall on the volcanos, and a dangerous cause on any wall. The timing of an ascent can be important in relation to avoiding a period when sun warms frozen areas. The danger in gullies can in part be ascertained by looking for scars on adjacent rock walls and for strewn rock pitting snow in and below the gully.

Avoid following below another party on a rock wall; needless to state, there are great dangers in having any

SUMMIT CHIEF MOUNTAIN and Overcoat Glacier from Chimney Rock
PHILIP LEATHERMAN

but a small party on a rock or alpine route where stonefall could hit the members below.

High water: Flash floods are rare in the Cascades, but a hard crossing may readily become impassable in periods of rain or hot weather. The usual period of high water is May and June; many creek and river barriers ordinarily moderate may be quite impassable or dangerous; even overflow stream channels can be dangerous. The amount of water in and velocity of the current of glacier-fed streams can vary over a short period of time.

Snakes, insects: There are occasional rattlers on lower slopes east of the main Cascade crest. Ticks are common in the drier forests in spring and early summer, but do not carry Rocky Mountain spotted fever. One may meet wasps, but no poisonous insects.

Animals: Bears and goats are prone to raid unattended camps, even above timberline; food should be hung out of reach. Rodents are likely to cause damage to food, clothing and boots, if not properly hung out of reach.

Windfalls: These are an uncommon danger in the Cascades, but one should be alert to the danger of falling snags and certainly so during high winds.

Lightning: Not common in the Cascades, but if it is seen nearby, the best advice is to leave ridges and summits by the fastest route.

WINTER TRAVEL AND CLIMBING

"Nature, to be commanded, must be obeyed."

FRANCIS BACON

Winter travel and climbing are becoming increasingly popular in the Cascades in spite of their rigors and the pattern of frequent and heavy snowfalls from strong Pacific onshore air flows. In winter, most of the peaks involve long and serious snow approaches; foul weather is the rule and one should not count on clearing periods to last long. But when they do occur, the rewards of touring and alpinism can be great. Occasional winters have extended periods quite favorable for difficult undertakings. In winter the peaks are invested with a beauty unknown in other seasons. There are many unpredictable hazards, many new potential adventures. Climbs that involve intricate crevasse fields, loose pumice, or tedious talus may well be more ideal and enjoyable in winter than summer. This applies to the high volcanos in the range — from California northward — which offer potentially excellent winter climbing and touring opportunities.

The mountain traveler should have a broad awareness of the significance of snow conditions, position of slopes and terrain, and the temperature as related to dangers. Only a brief review of some of these causes and factors is possible here.

Winter storm temperatures are usually relatively warm at timberline elevations; when it is clear very cold snaps may occur from continental air, especially east of the main divide. Above timberline, one should be prepared for quite strong wind; sleet that is wind-driven can make visibility, and therefore travel, impossible. Avalanches are a danger after heavy snowfalls at any elevation and during periods of rising temperature at low to medium elevations. One should beware of being caught by dangerous conditions on the return trip across a slope which may have been quite safe during an earlier crossing. Since an instability is transient, it may be wise to delay a trip, wait for an evening freeze, or more settled snow. Rainfall may occasionally occur in winter above the timberline level. Rainfall acts as a medium of heat exchange at the snow surface, as the liquid water will always be at the temperature equal to or higher than that of ice.

However, the air is a greater medium of heat exchange; to the degree that the air is warmer than the snow surface, heat is transferred to the snow. The higher the wind velocity, the greater is the amount of heat transferred. The chinook wind that quickly brings warm air can shortly cause avalanches. The condensation of water vapor on snow can be a large source of heat, and this increases with wind velocity. Warm wind and condensation have more effect toward a heavy snow melt than mere rain, for the latter itself rarely delivers much heat to the snow surface.

A winter climber must understand cornices, the underlying snow conditions, and the attendant dangers. A high rate of snowfall alone may quickly render a slope dangerous, for the stabilizing effects of settlement will not have had time to act. Generally, a new light snowfall will run off steep slopes and cliffs almost as soon as it falls, creating a stabilizing effect. This may take longer east of the main Cascade Crest, where winter temperatures tend to be lower, and snow drier.

Hard wind slabs may exist when wind action has occurred on high, exposed areas with low temperature. Even a windward slope may remain unpredictable for a long time period. Wind alone is one of the prime agents in slab formation; when high winds accompany a heavy snowfall, slab avalanches may form without respect to exposure, and any slope may become unstable. Soft slabs can form readily during Cascade snowstorms.

Wind crust is caused by mechanical wind action; once the surface snow layers are disturbed, age-hardening is initiated and these layers become harder than the undisturbed ones beneath. Warming compounded by the wind's heat followed by cooling when the wind dies provokes additional hardening. A winter sun crust may hold a slope together well. This crust is formed when water melted at the snow surface by solar radiation is refrozen at night and bonds snow crystals into a cohesive layer. In late winter one may get solid corn snow conditions, good for footing during clear weather, from nightly freezing and morning thawing.

Surface drifting may hide a space between a mature cornice and solid snow. Great care is indicated in early season (fall) accumulations when ridge and snowfield edges are hard and new snow is yet unconsolidated. Generally south and west exposures above timberline or along ridge crests allow surest travel. Staying in forested slopes on spur ridges, and on ridge crests, is often a way to minimize the potential of the avalanche. Glaciers are generally safer and easier than in summer, once a significant snow pack has accumulated; this does not mean a rope should not be used, as dangerous hidden crevasses may still exist.

Rime covering rock may be very solid, especially if the temperature remains low. These deposits, derived from the freezing of water droplets, are built up toward the wind direction. Careful study of *past and present* temperatures, snowfall, and weather patterns is sensible procedure when planning and conducting winter trips, not only to avoid danger but to locate the most suitable places to travel. Winter conditions in the Cascades can readily approximate severe summer conditions in northern Canada or Alaska; an inexperienced party should seek counsel or join a stronger group rather than experiment with hazards they may not recognize.

Generally, skis or snowshoes will be found so desirable as to be necessary to reach timberline; but slopes exposed to the prevailing winds will often allow foot or crampon travel higher, providing there has not been a heavy recent snowfall. Even then, exposed windy ridges and slopes may remain solid for footing. Wind-blown slopes can produce sheet ice so hard crampons may be needed on level surfaces. *In winter, never move above timberline without having crampons available.*

Known winter climbs are recorded in this guide. Few records have been kept, so this information is necessarily incomplete.

For the purpose of record, alpine climbs in the range are termed winter climbs December through March, though "winter" conditions certainly may exist outside of this time span. The above time limits seem generous and in accordance with usage at comparable latitudes.

CLIMBING CLASSIFICATIONS

A need for a rating system had long been recognized by American rock climbers, for simple words such as "easy," "moderate," and "difficult" are subject to a variety of interpretations. The intent of a scale of arbitrary divisions is to permit experienced climbers to compare difficulties with a set of standards, a frame of reference derived from experience. Ratings are only an approximation, and no system is without its imperfection. One such is that the same criterion of significance is hard to apply everywhere.

The accepted system of ratings in the United States is a modification of the Sierra Club system, developed at Tahquitz Rock and introduced in 1937. This system uses a class rating from 1 to 5, following the Welzenbach system begun in Germany in the 1920s, adding decimals for class 5 (free climbing). One of its limitations is the fact that the system's validity is based on the equipment needed.

In this guide, to preserve historical continuity and the most popular usage, the old classes 1 to 4 have been left unchanged, and class 5 expanded in decimal fashion, 5.0 to 5.11 or higher. Following popular usage, the former class 6 decimals are replaced by A (aid) ratings, 1 to 5.

Several aspects of the decimal system should be mentioned here:

(1) A classification compares the difficulty of the hardest move on a pitch, or climb, but this does not mean the entire pitch, or climb, will reach the maximum difficulty as so expressed.

(2) Care must be taken not to confuse class (Arabic numerals) with overall grade (always Roman numerals), which evaluates the overall difficulties of a climb from I to VI.

(3) Estimates of difficulty generally average the opinions of many climbers in an attempt at uniformity with other areas of the United States. Such grad-

ing, of course, may only roughly reflect climbs and peaks still under exploration and not sufficiently climbed to average varying opinion. Many ratings in the Cascades will need revision for this reason.

(4) Climbs are rated according to a standard for the average climber, who might do *that* climb. One cannot always assume that everyone will climb each 5.6 pitch equally well, as different challenges are likely to arise, and varying abilities will reflect the challenge of a variety of problems (chimneys vs. friction).

(5) Climbs or pitches rated as class 3 (rope not needed) and class 4 (roping suggested) may have individual areas that are as difficult or exposed as some class 5. The exposure of a climb may have a bearing on the rating. It should be noted that on alpine climbs experienced climbers sometimes climb some 5th class pitches unroped to speed the pace and call them "class 3." A moderate rating should not be interpreted to fortify a concept of simplicity.

Class 1 may range from hiking scrambles to a rocky gradient; generally the hands will not be needed more than very occasionally. An example would be Snoqualmie Mountain.

Class 2 will involve some scrambling and likely use of the hands; all but the most inexperienced or clumsy climber will not want the use of a rope. Examples would be Guye Peak and Mount Persis.

Class 3 initiates elementary climbing, scrambling with frequent use of hands. There may be moderate exposure; for the average climber a rope will not be desired, but one should be available. Some strength and technique may be needed on specific moves. Examples would be Mount Thompson, East Ridge and Little Tahoma.

Class 4 involves intermediate climbing where most climbers will want a rope because of exposure and sometimes use pitons at belay points. Some class 4 climbs would be certain minimum class 5 if it were not for the security of ledges or the availability of trees, shrubs, chockstones, or rock horns to protect the rope leader. Examples would be the Grand Teton (Owen-Spalding route, Tetons) and The Tooth, North Ridge.

In class 5, the average climber will wish to use some protection (chocks, Friends, pitons, runners). There can be no aid to qualify as "class 5," and this includes devices or techniques such as shoulder stands, and holding onto a carabiner, piton, or sling. There are various stages within the protected free climbing

zone. The easiest climbs are at the bottom of the scale (5.0), with the order of difficulty increasing to 5.11 or higher.

TABLE I

Comparative examples for class 5 ratings are:

5.0	Orchard Rock, Tunnel Route
5.1	The Tooth, South Face — first pitch
5.2	Forbidden Peak, West Ridge
5.3	Castle Rock, Sabre Route — first pitch
5.4	Castle Rock, Midway Route — second pitch
5.5	Liberty Bell, Beckey Route
5.6	Castle Rock, Midway Route — first pitch
5.7	Snow Creek Wall, White Slabs Route
5.8	Midnight Rock, Orbit Route
5.9	Snow Creek Wall, Outer Space Route
5.10	Midnight Rock, Easter Overhang

Arabic numbers are used to rate aid climbing. It should be remembered that the numbers represent maximums on a pitch or route, and that there are likely easier areas of aid within the coverage. Ratings tend to be flexible in aid, partly due to changing conditions of cracks. The solid placement and easy movement of A1 becomes tricky or awkward in A2. Generally, difficult placements and specialized items will be needed for the difficult aid of A3. Sophisticated equipment, ingenuity and nerve will certainly be needed for A4 and A5.

TABLE II

A table of comparative difficulty is given here:

A1	Index Town Wall, City Park — first pitch
A2	Index Town Wall, Narrow Arrow Overhang
A3	Liberty Crack — third pitch
A4	Liberty Bell, Independence Route

The overall grade of a route is indicated by Roman numerals from I to VI. This grade evaluation consists of factors involving a sense of commitment on the climb, the objective dangers and overall physical strain. Specific factors weighed are:

length of climb
ascent time
number of hard pitches

average pitch difficulty
difficulty of hardest pitch
escape factors — commitment
routefinding problems
stonefall, icefall
weather problems

Thus, the overall grade defines difficulty only by means of example standard climbs (see Table III) which represent comparison with other well-known areas as rendered by informed, competent climbers. Because so many diverse factors enter into the rating appraisal, one cannot always assume that two grade IIIs, for example, can be climbed equally well, or within the same time limits. One may expect, however, that all grade IIIs will present noticeably more problems than grade IIs, even though conceivably some pitches or moves on the latter could be harder.

Classification for rock climbs, both in the decimal system and the overall grading, assumes optimum conditions. The basis of comparison shifts as externals change.

Since climbs which are principally snow and ice vary enormously by year, time, and season, the overall grade is less reliable, and generally meaningless if compared to a rock climb. A general description of the climb, time estimates, slope inclination, and its length provide factors that a climber should evaluate along with the given estimate of overall grade. Pitch ratings by class are not given on snow/ice climbs unless there is a need to evaluate a rock section of the ascent, because technical difficulties of snow and ice climbs depend on current conditions.

In the six categories using Roman numerals it is now felt that the grades I, II, and III are too inflexible, since there are certain climbs with a great range of difficulty within these grades. In general, the technical portions of a grade I can be done in several hours, grade II in a half day, grade III in most of a day. A grade I, II, or III rock climb may have any number of variations of difficulty, but there need not necessarily be a minimum pitch difficulty rating; however a grade IV's hardest pitch is usually never less than 5.7, and the climb can be expected to cover one long hard day of technical climbing (generally longer, with bivouac on the first ascent).

A grade V can be expected to be more difficult and take longer than a IV, although some can be done in one day; at least 1½ days is average. The hardest pitch is rarely less than 5.8. A grade VI is usually a climb of two or more days and generally includes considerable very difficult free climbing and/or aiding.

TABLE III

Examples of overall grade ratings:

Grade I	Yosemite:	Monday Morning Slab, Right Side
	Cascades:	Chair Peak
		Mt. Adams, South Spur
Grade II	Tetons:	Grand Teton, Exum Route
	Yosemite:	Lower Cathedral Spire, Regular Route
	Cascades:	Mt. Stuart, West Ridge
		Mt. Adams, Adams Glacier
Grade III	Tetons:	Grand Teton, East Ridge
	Yosemite:	Nutcracker Route
	Cascades:	Mt. Rainier, Sunset Ridge
		Mt. Stuart, North Ridge
Grade IV	Tetons:	Grand Teton, North Ridge
	Yosemite:	Yosemite Point Buttress
	Cascades:	Mt. Rainier, Ptarmigan Ridge
		Mt. Stuart, Complete North Ridge
Grade V	Colorado:	Longs Peak, The Diamond
	Yosemite:	Washington Column, South Face
	Cascades:	Liberty Bell, Liberty Crack
Grade VI	Yosemite:	Half Dome, Northwest Face

ROCK DESTRUCTION

The increased popularity of climbing is contributing to deterioration of rock. Responsible climbers recognize that mountains are finite and hardware usage needs to be restrained. A few guidelines:

Stay off technical climbs you do not intend to complete.

Observe the clean climbing ethic — use jam nuts (chocks) and runners when possible. Pitons will still be a factor on aid routes and unknowns where clean routes are not established.

Don't overdrive pitons. This merely flakes the nearby rock and reduces holding power.

Don't bolt as a substitute for climbing. Don't pound established bolts, for it weakens them. And —

indiscriminate bolt chopping is as bad as over-placement.

Don't use paint to mark routes.

Remember, the climbing adventure is not enhanced by merely getting up, but by keeping the climb a challenge. The dividends should be in the motions of the art, concentration, judgment, and technique. Don't use aid on free climbs — leave alone that which you cannot do in good style, for it may diminish the aesthetics for others. With the raising of qualitative standards the rewards are not lost.

TECHNICAL GLOSSARY

This glossary is not intended to cover the complete range of mountaineering terminology, but to review specific definitions and some lesser known terms used in this guide.

Aid climbing: Involves the use of any artificial means of ascent, not relying totally on hands and feet. (This includes any tension from such aids as knotted slings, a lassoo, or a shoulder stand.)

Angle pitons: Commonly range from ½ inch to 1 inch in width (at widest point) as measured from backbone to blade edges. A *regular angle* piton is meant to be a standard ¾ inch size.

Arete, nose, pillar, and *buttress:* Often refer to the same type of corner formation on a mountain. Generally an *arete* is a major edge, not necessarily steep in profile. A *nose* is almost always quite steep. A *pillar* is usually rounded and sharply defined, and is generally steep. A *buttress* is a major formation on a peak, generally implied to be broader than an *arete.*

Bergschrund (schrund): A large crevasse formed by tension where flowing ice of a glacier fractures away from a nearly stagnant ice slope or headwall above.

Blue ice: See *glacier ice.*

Bolt: An anchor placed into a drilled hole to protect or climb a portion of a route that cannot be done by pitons. Necessary bolts and their hangers should not be removed, but their placement should be discouraged.

Bulge: A small steepening of the angle of a face.

Buttress: See *arete.*

Ceiling: See *overhang.*

Chimney: See *couloir.*

Chock: An aluminum device to place in a crack.

Chute: A depression steeper than a gully. See also *couloir.*

Cirque: A deep, steep-walled amphitheater-like recess in a mountain; caused by glacial erosion.

Col: A steep high pass, smaller than a saddle; a saddle is a more rounded ridge depression.

Couloir: A deep chute. Likely to have some snow or ice. Terms for depressions are used in this order of decreasing size: *canyon, gully, couloir, chute, chimney, crack.*

Crack: See *couloir.* The smallest is an *incipient crack* that may take only the thinnest of chocks or pitons (knife blades). When larger, they are referred to as finger or hand cracks. See also *jam crack.*

Dihedral: An *inside corner, open book* or *corner;* a depression generally 90 degrees or more on its facings, as a junction of two rock planes. An angular slab lying against a flat wall may form a left-facing or right-facing *open book.*

Face: A steep mountainside, generally over 30 degrees if mixed snow, ice, and rock; and over 45 degrees if rock.

Firn: A consolidated granular transition of snow not yet changed to glacier ice. The word *firn* refers only to the substance of the material itself. It has survived at least one season of ablation. Its density may require cramponing in climbing situations.

Flaring chimney: A chimney in which the sides are not parallel, but are converging rock planes; generally more difficult than a similar parallel-walled chimney.

Free climbing: Means that no direct support from chock, piton, stirrup, loop, rope, or carabiner is used; any such piece of equipment may be used for safety only. Free climbing may be roped or unroped.

Glacier ice: Clear and relatively unaerated dense glacier ice characterizes the basal parts of glaciers. Usually termed *blue ice* when found of this density on alpine walls. Below the névé line the main material of the glacier is bubbly glacier ice.

Glacier snowline: The term used to describe the transient outer limit of the retained winter snowcover on a glacier. Its elevation gradually rises until the end of the annual ablation season, by which time the old snow has become firn and the glacier snowline becomes the seasonal snowline.

Groove: A very shallow inside corner, often smooth, generally flared.

Gully: A depression grooving a mountainside. See also *couloir.*

Headwall: Where the slope or face of a mountain, cirque, or glacier steepens dramatically in angle; it is often concave in shape.

Icefall: A steep reach of glacier with a chaotic crevassed surface and rapid flow rate.

Inside corner: See *dihedral.*

Jam crack: A crack varying from hand size to room for a leg; it is usually climbed by hand jamming foot wedging techniques.

Knife blade: An exceptionally thin small chromalloy piton.

Lava: Igneous rocks formed from molten magma erupting on the surface.

Lead: See *pitch.*

Ledge or *ramp:* Generally extends some distance; a *ramp* is an ascending ledge.

Moat: The space between snow/ice and a rock wall. It can be expected to widen as the summer progresses.

Move: The act of going from one set of holds to another (usually a few feet).

Nailing: A colloquial term for aid climbing with pitons.

Névé: A French word translated "consolidated, granular snow in the state of transition to glacier ice." Névé refers to the area covered by perennial snow or firn, lying entirely within a glacier's accumulation zone. The line (actually névé-line zone) which equates to the lower elevation limit of the retained winter snowpack. At the end of the annual melt season it separates the névé area from the bare ice area of a glacier. In the accumulation area above, annual snowfall exceeds annual melting.

Nose: See *arete,* and *outside corner.*

Notch: Generally a narrow col or sharp break in a ridge.

Nunatak: Hill or mountain surrounded by ice (derived from the Eskimo).

Off width: A crack too wide for fist jams, but too narrow for stemming.

Open book: See *dihedral.*

Outside corner: A minor edge on a rock face, usually briefer and of less stature than a nose or rib.

Overhang: A section of wall above the angle of 90 degrees. Termed *ceiling* or *roof* when nearly 180 degrees.

Pendulum: A swinging traverse made from a fixed point.

Pillar: See *arete.*

Pitch: A section of the climb between belays; length can vary from a short distance to the full length of the rope; most pitches vary from 80 to 150 ft. Sometimes called a *lead.*

Piton cracks: See *crack.*

Platform: A level rock area, short in length.

Ramp: See *ledge.*

Regional snowline: The altitude at which annual accumulation balances ablation on the ground surface. The summer snow line on non-glacial surfaces is often much higher and generally more irregular than that on slope and valley glaciers.

Rib: See *outside corner.*

Runner: A knotted sling, usually 1-inch nylon webbing, used to loop over rock projections or to lessen rope-drag at carabiner points.

Rurp: A type of knife blade, of shorter and stouter blade; since it can generally only penetrate about ¼ inch, it is exclusively used for aid.

Serac: A block tower or pinnacle of ice or firn formed by the intersection of crevasses, or found standing in ice cascades.

Slope: A mountainside gentler than a face.

Spire, tower, needle: In general, a spire is smaller than a peak or mountain (exceptions: The Bugaboos, Twin Spires), but larger than a *tower.* A *needle* is generally a single thin block.

Squeeze chimney: A chimney of such width that one can barely get the body inside.

Tension traverse: Leaning against a taut rope and utilizing tension plus whatever holds exist to move laterally.

Tie-off loop: Nylon webbing usually of ½-inch size and tied in 6-inch diameter, generally used to reduce carabiner drag or to reduce torque to protruding pitons.

Tower: See *spire.*

MAPS

Topographic Maps

These can be ordered from:

Distribution Section,
U.S. Geological Survey,
Denver Federal Center, Bldg. 41
Denver, Colorado 80225

The Geological Survey is printing a series of topographic maps, quadrangles covering 7½ minutes of latitude and longitude published at the scale of 1:24,000 (1 inch = 2000 ft). Quadrangles covering 15 minutes of latitude and longitude are published at a scale of 1:62,500 (1 inch = approx. 1 mile).

Some areas are covered or partially covered by two or more maps published at different scales but with the same title. Wherever this occurs a map order should also include the map scale designation.

Another USGS map, *North Cascades,* covering the span Snoqualmie Pass to the Canadian Boundary, is available at the 1:250,000 scale.

Some libraries have maps for reference and most retail stores selling climbing equipment stock those covering the Cascades. It should be noted that some errors, primarily trail locations and feature names, may exist on topographic maps. When known, these will be pointed out. Some current road extensions and logging roads may not be shown.

Forest recreation maps, brochures and directories can be obtained by writing to forest headquarters or by visiting ranger stations during business hours. There is a charge for maps. Other useful publications by the Forest Service include the Pacific Crest National Scenic Trail map. Addresses for the Forest Service headquarters and the ranger stations are given with each of the four sections in this volume.

The forest maps concerned within the scope of this book are: Mount Baker-Snoqualmie National Forest, Gifford Pinchot National Forest, and Wenatchee National Forest.

It should be noted that these maps are quite general

and cannot show all current road changes, in particular those related to logging operations. Map revisions are made, usually about every two years.

Other county and private maps at times may show recent changes in roads, particularly those related to hunting and fishing areas. The Weyerhaeuser Company has public road maps concerning their lands in the North Fork Snoqualmie, Green, and White River drainage areas.

SELECTED REFERENCES

The following references provide valuable background material for the portion of the Cascade Range covered in this volume. Other references of localized value, concerning a specific trail, area, or mountain, will be noted at that point in the text.

The references listed include meaningful books and the periodic journals that often contain coverage of the Cascade Range.

Ayres, H. B. "The Washington Forest Reserve," 19th Annual Report (Part V) U.S.G.S. (1897-98).

Beckey, Fred. *Challenge of the North Cascades.* Seattle: The Mountaineers, 1969.

————. *Mountains of North America.* San Francisco: The Sierra Club, 1982.

Easterbrook, Don J. and Rahm, David A. *Landforms of Washington.* Western Washington State University, Bellingham, 1970.

Emmons, Samuel F. "The Volcanoes of the Pacific Coast of the United States." *Jour. Amer. Geog. Soc. of N.Y.,* 10 (1879), pp. 45-65.

Evans, Brock. *The Alpine Lakes.* Seattle, The Mountaineers, 1971.

Farquhar, Francis P. "Naming America's Mountains — The Cascades," *American Alpine Journal.* 1960, pp. 49-65.

LaChapelle, E. R. *The ABC of Avalanche Safety.* Seattle, The Mountaineers, 1985.

Manning, Harvey. *Washington Wilderness: The Unfinished Work.* Seattle, The Mountaineers, 1984.

McKee, Bates. *Cascadia — The Geologic Evolution of the Pacific Northwest.* New York, McGraw-Hill Book Company, 1972.

Peters, Ed (editor). *Mountaineering — The Freedom of the Hills.* Seattle, The Mountaineers, 4th ed., 1982.

Prater, Gene. *Snow Trails: Ski and Snowshoe Hikes in the Cascades.* Seattle, The Mountaineers, 1975.

Plummer, Fred G. "Mount Rainier Forest Reserve, Washington." *21st Annual Report, U.S. Geol. Survey*

1899-1900. Part V (Washington, 1900), pp. 87-143.

Spring, Ira and Manning, Harvey. *100 Hikes in the Alpine Lakes*. Seattle, The Mountaineers, 1985.

———— . *100 Hikes in the South Cascades and Olympics*. Seattle, The Mountaineers, 1985.

Sterling, E. M., and Spring, Bob and Ira. *Trips and Trails, 2*. Seattle, The Mountaineers, 1983.

*   *   *   *

Periodicals

The *American Alpine Journal;* The American Alpine Club, New York, NY.

The *Mazama;* The Mazamas, Portland, OR.

The *Mountaineer;* The Mountaineers, Seattle, WA.

Sierra; The Sierra Club, San Francisco, CA.

The Signpost; Lynnwood, WA.

Summit; Big Bear Lake, CA.

ABBREVIATIONS

hwy	highway
BIA	Bureau of Indian Affairs
R.C.M.P.	Royal Canadian Mounted Police
Crest Trail	Pacific Crest National Scenic Trail
ATP	at time of publication
ft	feet (altitude)
m	meters (altitude)
est.	estimated altitude
km	kilometer (glacier length)
km²	square kilometer (glacier area)
mi.	miles
m. y. (B. P.)	million years (before present) (geology)
F	fahrenheit (degrees)
A.A.J.	*American Alpine Journal*
C.A.J.	*Canadian Alpine Journal*
B.C.M.	*British Columbia Mountaineer*
A.N.A.M.	*Accidents in North American Mountaineering*

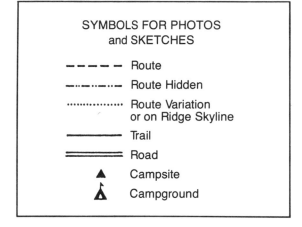

HIDDEN ROUTES:
Route symbols on photos should be carefully studied to differentiate hidden portions (—··—··—··—) of visible routes (— — —)

"This mountain is now a burning volcano. It commenced about a year ago . . . . ashes fell at the Dalles to the depth of one half an inch."
    PETER H. BURNETT, December 28, 1844

SECTION I

Southern Cascades

COLUMBIA RIVER TO WHITE PASS

GEOGRAPHY

White Pass on the Cascade Crest, an important all-season highway route, and the flanking Cowlitz and Tieton river valleys, bound the northern fringe of this section. The other important river drainages in this section are the Cispus on the north, the Klickitat on the east, the White Salmon and Wind on the south, and the Lewis and Toutle on the west.

From the Cascade Crest near Goat Rocks (6000 to 8000 ft in altitude), the eastern flank of the range descends rather gradually to the Naches River at about the 1500-ft level. Ice sheets once were extensive along the crest, and valley glaciers extended down various drainages; the important Tieton valley has deposits of two late Pleistocene glacial episodes. Present ice on the two volcanos and on Goat Rocks is described separately; here glaciers descend well below the regional snowline. Annual precipitation averages about 140 inches at Mount St. Helens and under 100 inches at Mount Adams and Goat Rocks.

Plant life on many of the higher meadows is very fragile, and near Mount St. Helens many species had been growing only a few hundred years before the 1980 eruption. In the high zones alpine (Lyalls) larch appear, mountain hemlock, subalpine fir, and whitebark pine form the thin vanguard of the forest. Along the main crest and to the east open forests of western white pine, ponderosa and lodgepole pine are predominant, while Engelmann spruce and western larch make their appearance. On the west slope Douglas fir (*Pseudotsuga menziesii*), noble fir (*Abies procera*), silver fir (*Abies amabilis*), western hemlock (*Tsuga heterophylla*) and western red cedar (*Thuja plicata*) are the prevalent trees. Most volcanic rubble and scree slopes near and above timberline have become fairly stable and support vegetation. East of the Cascade Crest open forests and scree permit generally feasible cross-country travel. Unfortunately much of the region west of the Cascade Crest is a green-brown logger-blighted checkerboard. Fires have denuded much of this region. The large Cispus fire of 1902, south of Randle, burned much of three counties; the vast Lewis River fire of 1872 may have been started by Indians. Many of the uplands, especially near Mount Adams and Twin Buttes, are heavy producers of berries.

Mammals of the mountain area include black bear, raccoon, blacktail deer, hoary marmot, long-tailed weasel, coyote, bobcat, pine marten, beaver, cougar, mink, snowshoe hare, pika, Douglas' squirrel, and Townsend's chipmunk. Birds frequently seen include blue grouse, spruce grouse, white-tailed ptarmigan, gray jay, and Clark's nutcracker.

HISTORY

The Klickitats, a mountain tribe who inhabited the valleys between Mounts St. Helens and Adams, have traditionally picked huckleberries in the meadow areas. Their mythology, long colored by the two volcanos, consisted of vague and incoherent tales, in much of which Ta-la-pus (the prairie wolf) figures as a supernatural power. The Klickitat Trail across Cispus Pass, long used by the Indians, was one of the first cross-Cascade trails.

The Pacific Railroad Survey of July 1853 with 66 men and 173 animals under Capt. George B. McClellan, made its first crossing of the Cascade Range south of Mount St. Helens and Mount Adams, and correctly identified the volcanos from a height near the Cath-la-poot'l (Lewis River); "Five large snow mountains were in sight ... Rainier, St. Helens, Adams, Hood and Jefferson." (Report of Capt. George B. McClellan to Gov. Isaac I. Stevens; House Exec. Doc. 129, 33rd Congress, 1st session, p. 189.)

Various railroad explorers placed feature names on reports and maps, some of which are no longer used. One map tracing survey travels depicted the Goat Rocks as the "Simcoe Range" and the North Fork Tieton River as "Big Tieton." The name Whites Pass is shown closely south of Cowlitz Pass, not at the present White Pass.

We are indebted to the exploration's geologist, George Gibbs, and topographer Lt. Johnson K. Duncan for the first accurate descriptions of the southern Cascades. These include comments on the craters' positions on the volcanos, lava fields, basalt forma-

Western red cedar in lowland valley
ED COOPER

tions, and the character of the topography and forest zones. But comparing the relative height of the volcanos proved difficult. Gibbs, among others, believed Mount Hood was the highest in the range. "Those familiar with all of them assign the supremacy to Mount Hood. Its probable elevation is 14,999 ft."[19]

GEOLOGY

The Cascade Range between the Columbia River and White Pass consists largely of a thick sequence of Tertiary volcanic rocks. These volcanic strata underlie Mount Adams and Mount St. Helens. Andesitic and basaltic lava, tuff, and breccia are the predominant rock types. An example of important lava flows in this region are those at Council Bluff (about 26 m. y. in age), located northwest of Mount Adams.

The diverse volcanic strata can be separated into a Western Cascade Group and the younger High Cascade Group. The Ohanapecosh Formation is the oldest unit of these Tertiary volcanic rocks. It is particularly visible in the western half of the Mount St. Helens region. The more recent Stevens Ridge Formation, also a unit of the Western Cascade Group, is exposed between Mount Adams and Mount St. Helens, and also near the Columbia River. The extensive Columbia River basalts, which are interstratified with the Western Cascade Group, are of late Tertiary age. Steamboat Mountain, near Mount Adams, is a remnant of thick Columbia River basalt flows. Flows of the Yakima Basalt (related to the Columbia River Basalt Group) underlie Mount Adams and are visible along the valleys of the Klickitat, Tieton, and Yakima rivers, and the Columbia Gorge. Basaltic lava flows have formed extensive fields, notably at the Indian Heaven region southwest of Mount Adams and southeast of Mount St. Helens and the King Mountain fissure system south of Mount Adams, which are noted for underground basalt galleries, some of which were partly filled with ice in the days of early settlers.

The basalt and basaltic andesite of the High Cascade Group (5 m. y. to the present), which unconformably overlies the Western Cascade Group, erupted from shield volcanos, stratovolcanos, and cinder cones, mainly in the region southeast of Mount Rainier National Park. The recent eruptive deposits of Mount St. Helens are of various ages up to 35,000 years. Goat Mountain is a prominent volcanic plug to the southwest of Mount St. Helens.

Local basalt flows and cinder cones of Quaternary age are present in the White Pass area and are widespread farther south. Potato Hill, Red Butte, Goat Butte, and Little Mount Adams are examples of such cinder cones. The Muddy Fork flow, northeast of Mount Adams, is a large Quaternary andesite lava flow.

Recent volcanism has played the dominant role in shaping the landscape of the southern Cascades of Washington. The composite volcanos Mount Adams and Mount St. Helens dominate the topography. These young volcanic centers contrast with Goat Rocks, which are older, deeply eroded volcanos. The recent Tieton Andesite, a Quaternary flow which originated in the Goat Rocks area, underlies Pinegrass Ridge and extends far down the Tieton River canyon.

The principal granitic plutons (Tertiary in age) in this section are at Silver Star Mountain and at Spirit Lake, located southwest and north, respectively, from Mount St. Helens.

LAND MANAGEMENT

Headquarters:

Gifford Pinchot National Forest
500 West 12th St.
Vancouver, WA 98660
(206) 696-7500 and (503) 285-9823

Mount St. Helens National Volcanic Monument
Amboy, WA 98601 (State Hwy No. 503)
(206) 247-5473

Ranger Stations:

Randle: Randle, WA 98377
(206) 497-7565

Packwood: Packwood, WA 98361
(206) 494-5515

Mount Adams: Trout Lake, WA 98650
(509) 395-2501

Wind River: Carson, WA 98610
(509) 427-5645

Naches: Naches, WA 98937 (510 Hwy No. 12)
(509) 653-2205

Visitor Centers:

Pine Creek Information Station
Lewis River Road No. 90 — 18 mi. E of Cougar

Iron Creek Information Station
Road No. 25 — 10 mi. S of Randle

Yale Information Station
Road No. 90 — 2 mi. W of Cougar

Mount St. Helens National Volcanic Monument

Visitor Center is located 5 mi. from I-5 (exit 49), E of Castle Rock. Will be open daily. Phone (206) 274-4038

Motorized travel off roads and trails is permitted in the Gifford Pinchot National Forest, except for Mount St. Helens Restricted Entry Area, Goat Rocks Wilderness, Mount Adams Wilderness, Wind River Experimental Forest land and research natural areas. See the Gifford Pinchot National Forest Travel Plan for details, updates, and map showing closures and restrictions.

All Forest trails are open to vehicles less than 40 inches wide except where restrictions and closures are necessary to minimize resource damage and to avoid user conflicts. Over snow vehicles are permitted to travel over Forest lands, provided snow depth is sufficient to prevent damage to vegetation, except for restricted areas — including those shown on the Travel Plan. The National Volcanic Monument policy is to restrict all ORV's (except snowmobiles) outside the Restricted Entry Area.

In the Forest, areas of closure will be signed on-site at major entry points. Restricted trails will be posted at trailheads. The Pacific Crest National Scenic Trail and its access trails are closed to off-road vehicles.

Many local roads are closed between Forest project uses because of erosion potential. Many of these roads were designed only for dry roadbed use during timber harvesting and will be open only during the dry season for summer recreation use. Some other roads will receive minimum maintenance and will be allowed to close naturally. All roads are subject to winter snow closure.

The Goat Rocks Wilderness Area was established by the U.S. Forest Service in 1940 to protect the meadowlands and forests surrounding the area of high peaks south of White Pass. The Mount Adams Wilderness Area, overgrazed by sheep since before the turn of the century, was designated in 1942.

Roads and trails east of Mount Adams are administered by the Bureau of Indian Affairs. Hikers need permits when in BIA lands; obtain from BIA, Box 632, Toppenish, WA 98948. In the summer season, permits are available from a crew or office at Bird Lake.

Campgrounds

There are camps located on mountain access roads; these are marked on the Gifford Pinchot and Mount Baker-Snoqualmie National Forest maps. Facilities and fee information available on maps, at ranger stations, and in campground directories.

MAPS

Topographic (U.S. Geological Survey)

Burnt Peak (1965)	1:24,000
East Canyon Ridge (1970)	1:24,000
French Butte (1965)	1:24,000
Glaciate Butte (1970)	1:24,000
Lone Butte (1965)	1:24,000
Green Mountain (1970)	1:24,000
Meeks Table (1971)	1:24,000
McCoy Peak (1965)	1:24,000
Old Scab Mountain (1971)	1:24,000
Mt. Adams East (1971)	1:24,000
Mt. Adams West (1971)	1:24,000
Sleeping Beauty Mountain (1970)	1:24,000
Spencer Butte (1965)	1:24,000
Tieton Basin (1967)	1:24,000
Tower Rock (1965)	1:24,000
Rimrock Lake (1971)	1:24,000
Timberwolf Mountain (1971)	1:24,000
Walupt Lake (1970)	1:24,000
Mt. St. Helens (1958)	1:62,500
Spirit Lake (1957)	1:62,500

Topographic (provisional editions)

Mount St. Helens (1983)	1:24,000
Spirit Lake East (1984)	1:24,000
Spirit Lake West (1984)	1:24,000
Goat Mountain (1983)	1:24,000
Elk Rock (1983)	1:24,000
Smith Creek Butte (1983)	1:24,000

U.S. Forest Service

Gifford Pinchot National Forest Map
Mt. Adams Wilderness Area (topographic)
Goat Rocks Wilderness Area (topographic)

MOUNT ST. HELENS   8363 ft/2549 m

Klickitat tribal legends long spoke of symmetrical Mount St. Helens as *Loo-wit-lat-Kla,* a fair maiden who was transformed into a mountain.[20] The Salish culture along the Cowlitz River had a different legend; to one tribe the name meant "one from whom smoke comes." The white man's name for the mountain came from Captain George Vancouver. While sailing on Puget Sound on April 10, 1792 he wrote in his log: "the clearness of the atmosphere enabled us to see the high round snowy mountain, noticed when in the southern parts of the Admiralty inlet, to the southward of mount Rainier . . . . This I have distinguished by the name of Mount St. Helens, in honor of his

MOUNT ST. HELENS in winter — Shoestring Glacier descending from breach
JIM HUGHES, U.S. FOREST SERVICE

Brittanic Majesty's ambassador at the court of Madrid."[21] When Lewis and Clark descended the Columbia River in 1805 they anticipated this mountain, at first confusing it with then-unknown Mount Adams, some 34 mi. eastward. But on November 4 they identified the peak correctly, which Lewis described as "emensely high and covered with snow, riseing in a kind of cone."[22] The explorers suspected it of being the highest peak in America, an illusion that is quite forgiveable, for the lofty volcanic cone dominated the vista from the Columbia — only 37 mi. distant. Even Hall J. Kelley, the humorless Bostonian who believed himself chosen by God to lead a migration to Oregon, was sufficiently impressed to describe St. Helens as the "most remarkable of all the mountains in Western America" and declared that its peak reached a "stupendous height."[23]

Frémont's diary entries indicate he confused St. Helens, Adams, and Rainier. On his return trip (November 26, 1843) at a position E and yet slightly N of Mount Hood, he wrote, "We had a grand view of St. Helens and Rainier, the latter appeared of a conical form, and very lofty, leading the eye far up into the sky."[24] What he then called "St. Helens" was likely Mount Adams, for his October 29 entry clearly indicates he saw the latter, but referred to it as St. Helens. His conception of Rainier would then be St. Helens.

Progress reports by Thomas J. Dryer in the weekly *Oregonian* in 1853 detail the account of the first ascent party, "Messrs. Wilson, Smith, Drew, and myself" who followed a military trail from Vancouver with horses to the S side of the mountain. On the fifth day (August 20) "Mr. Wilson had a chase after a deer, but could not get a shot at him. Mount St. Helens looms up majestically .... It looks more formidable and difficult of ascent than when seen at a longer distance." Eventually the party left the trail and ascended N, leaving the horses at a grass patch, then taking three day's rations for the summit. They succeeded on August 27 "by constant and persevering effort" and from the top could plainly see the Pacific Ocean. The ascent records the first climb of a major snow peak near the coast, and Dryer exulted, "The whole Coast and Cascade range of mountains could be plainly traced with the naked eye. The snow covered peaks of Mounts Hood, Rainier and two others seemed close by."

Several years after this date a number of gold discoveries were made in the upper branches of the Lewis River. A group of prospectors, balked in a search for gold, turned their energies to the climb. Indian guides would not go above timberline on the W side, but five of the party (Jesse Failing, Lyman Merrill, Amos E. Russell, Squire J. Bozarth, and James H. Neyce) reached the top on September 28, 1860 to describe Spirit Lake "looking like a splendid jewel in an enamelled setting, as it reflected the beautiful green deep shadows of the surrounding forests." Believing theirs was the first climb, they placed a flag staff and banner; they made no mention of the pyramid of loose stones Dryer said was built on the summit. One of them left a vivid account of the exploit, first published in the Vancouver *Chronicle* by L. F. V. Coon in 1861, and later preserved in a historical collection. Under the misleading title *Gold Hunting in the Cascade Mountains,* it tells of the route from Vancouver which eventually followed the Simcoe trail across upper Lewis River, where they met an Indian, John Staps, who offered to guide them to the mountain. Indians reported the Failing party had priority, and that the only persons who ever attempted St. Helens were a party of Hudson Bay men, 20 years earlier, who became discouraged in the lowlands. It must be remembered though, Indians were transient; also the prospectors may not have yet homesteaded at the time of Dryer's expedition.

The next known ascent was in 1874; other ascents followed and in 1883 the first woman made the summit. Colonel Frederick Plummer claimed the first climb of the N side in August, 1893: Some skepticism has been expressed because the party did not sign an existing register and because of the stated progress schedule. The route was definitely climbed in 1895 by two Toledo men, who reported an uneventful, satisfactory ascent. The first climb by an organized group, in 1889 by the Oregon Alpine Club, included two Indians. In 1908 a Mazama group climbed the mountain by the "Lizard" and "Boot," with some aspects of a burlesque, though this adventure should be weighed in the light of the times. The descent after nightfall required 7 hours, and on the steepest ice, 25 people clutched a single rope!

Mountaineers have found the eastern and northern slopes of Mount St. Helens to provide a variety of dangers. Writing in 1894, Plummer described the surface of the glacier as a sheet of ice. "The speed of the rocks as they passed us was terrific. They whirled at such a rate that they seemed spherical . . . making a metallic sound as they clipped the ice . . ." Various climbing parties have met serious accidents or tragedy by falls on ice, into crevasses, or from avalanches.

Because the mountain has so few distinctive features, little other climbing history has been left, but by 1910 the Dog's Head route had been done and the S side had been termed "a kindergarten" by Charles E. Forsyth. In August 1908 seven members from a Mazama camp, led by Forsyth, saved the life of a woodsman, one of three Swedish loggers who had crossed the mountain and were descending the S slope when a rock struck the unfortunate adventurer, breaking his leg. After his companions found the Mazamas at Spirit Lake, the combined party hiked around to the S, where the injured man was carried from timberline, almost over the summit, and then down the N side. Forsyth deserved the naming of a glacier in his honor.

The symmetry of Mount St. Helens was indicative of youth: the present cone was not yet built when Pleistocene glaciers carved canyons and cirques into Mount Adams. The mountain had been born of volcanic violence and it had alpine meadows and a uniquely low timberline (4000 to 4400 ft) because of the recency of eruptions and a porous, thick pumice cover. Much of the visible cone probably formed in the last 1000 years, partly concealing the remnants of an older volcano that geologists date back 37,000 years.

Drainage patterns are not concentric to Mount St. Helens, for both the Toutle and Green rivers originate in high terrain to the NE. But as the volcano grew, stream erosion produced a radial system of small canyons. Those of the Toutle became deep trenches cut into soft pumice.

In general, eruptions of Cascade volcanos tend to be much more explosive than those of Hawaiian volcanos, a pattern related to the chemical composition of the magma that feeds the volcanos and the amount of gas contained in the magma.

The building of modern Mount St. Helens of successive basalt and andesite eruptions on a platform of sandstone sediments began at an estimated 400 B.C. Since that time the volcano has had many eruptions in the form of lava flow, pyroclastic flow, and airborne tephra. This youngest and lowest of Washington State's five volcanos is of a composite type, built through a single vent so rapidly that erosion had a minimal effect in hindering its symmetry. The lavas smoothed the earlier topography and created lakes. In some cases the lavas created rough terrain: the S slope of the volcano is mantled by a series of blocky andesite flows.

Significant mudflows occurred intermittently in the past. Evidence shows that one mudflow inundated the Lewis River valley for 40 mi. — perhaps 2500 to 3000 years ago. Other large mudflows streamed down the Toutle and Kalama river valleys. Spirit Lake, which long mirrored the volcano's elegance, is the result of a volcanic mudflow which became a dam. Another molten flow threw a dike across a stream to create Lake Merrill, then veered S to overwhelm forests with basalt sheets. The lava beds nearby reflect violence; there are many caves and galleries, a place where forests struggled to gain a foothold.

The mountain's position well W of the Cascade crest line and only 84 mi. from the Pacific resulted in the establishment of small, vigorous glaciers; the Forsyth on the NE was the largest. The St. Helens glaciers occupied shallow beds except for the remarkable cleft of the Shoestring.

The current cycle of volcanic activity is part of a pattern extending over 4500 years. During a violent eruption 1400 years B.C., ash drifted as far as Alberta, and about 1900 B.C. a great eruption is estimated to have been four times as large as the 1980 eruption that made Mount St. Helens a household word. The eruptive phase between 1831 and 1857 frequently awed settlers and travelers, who reported ashes, columns of smoke, and evening firelight. James D. Dana of the Wilkes Expedition in 1841 was the first of many geologists to mention the mountain's activity.

The missionaries were not the first to write of the eruptions, but they popularized them. On November 22, 1842 Reverend Josiah L. Parrish noted that white steam "rose many degrees into the heavens," and that ash fell eastward to The Dalles (a specimen was given to Frémont the next year). An unknown author wrote that St. Helens still burned February 16, 1844: "Dense masses of smoke rose up in massive columns" (Report of Lt. Thomas W. Symons to Secretary of War, 1882).

Despite all its mystic and ice-clad splendor, the volcano was a time bomb. During climax explosions about 450 years ago, a dacite mass grew atop the volcano from lava of a centered vent, and outbursts blasted a large gap in the SE crater wall, a breach for the escape of Shoestring Glacier. Small earthquakes in March, 1980 attracted scientific interest. Then, on

March 27, observers saw the volcano erupt for the first time in 123 years. There was public clamor when a dense column of volcanic ash rose through the clouds, eventually to a height of some 6000 ft above the volcano.

There were conspicuous changes on the mountain. A new crater had formed in part of the old ice-filled summit crater and the summit area was bisected by a long fracture. Eruptions continued at varying intensity, followed by tremors, through April and into early May. A prominent bulge on the N flank of the volcano became larger as this slope continued to break and distort. This rapid deformation gave spectacular indications of magmatic intrusion into the volcano.

The climactic eruption on May 18 began at 8:32 AM. It probably was triggered by an earthquake of magnitude 5, which caused failure of the bulging N flank, resulting in an immense rockslide-avalanche. Rock blasted out of the fringes of the magma blister as if the cap had moved.

Within 15 seconds of the earthquake the mountain's slumping N slope collapsed: a tremendous explosion hurled steam, superheated groundwater and rock debris from the huge reservoir of volatile, hot magma northward laterally through the new breach. At least half a cubic mi. of pulverized rock and glacial ice surged into Spirit Lake and the pristine North Fork of the Toutle River valley. The collapse sent ice from five glaciers into hot ash and the released meltwater steamrollered a boiling torrent into the valley. The boiling slurry (lahar) that raced down the two forks of the Toutle killed motorists, destroyed highway bridges, and swept away homes, logging equipment, and camps. Catastrophic mudflows and floods were generated from rapid melting of snow and ice derived from the immense landslide which slid into the Spirit Lake basin and down the North Fork Toutle River valley. Volcanic mudflows (lahars) — dense mixtures of ash and rocks mixed with water — flowed down all slopes.

On the mountain a pyroclastic flow composed of rock fragments and volcanic gases as hot as 800° C sped downslope at perhaps 200 mi. per hour, overtaking the avalanche debris. The lateral blast accelerated to an estimated 670 mi. per hour as it swept across the forested land to affect an area of some 230 sq mi., blowing down trees up to 19 mi. from the mountain. At the same time, an ash plume rose more than 80,000 ft, injecting over one cubic mi. of volcanic debris into the atmosphere and profoundly affecting a vast area. Finely pulverized rock of the upper plume drifted eastward, settling in troublesome amounts as far as

Aerial view of catastrophic eruption of MOUNT ST. HELENS, May 18, 1980
U.S. GEOLOGICAL SURVEY

MOUNT ST. HELENS, May 18, 1980 — view looking southeast, showing detail of sharply defined windward edge of plume
U.S. GEOLOGICAL SURVEY

Montana. The ash pillar formed a cloud that gave towns such as Yakima the darkness of midnight. Over 5000 highway travelers were stranded at one time in eastern Washington; some ash drifts were up to three feet thick and in places settled to the amount of 100 tons per acre.

The cataclysmic eruption blasted out a semicircular crater over 2 mi. long, 1½ mi. wide, and 2100 ft deep. The highest remaining point on the mountain was 8363 ft in altitude, a portion of the S rim. The nine-hour eruption and intermittent eruptions during the following three days removed about 0.7 cubic mi.

of new magmatic material and old upper and northern portions of the mountain, including an estimated 170 million cubic yards of glacial snow and ice.

Searchers rescued some 200 persons from the ravaged area; 61 were left dead in the ash and choking debris. An estimated two million animals, fish, and birds perished, 26 lakes were destroyed, and an estimated 156 sq mi. of timber were shredded. Total dollar loss was over $1.5 billion.

After the eruption Spirit Lake was clogged with a mass of fallen trees, logs, mud, and ash. Blocked by the mudflow, the lake level rose from 3198 to 3408 ft.

Various eruptions that have taken place in the horseshoe-shaped crater since the events of May 18, 1980 have built a lava dome 800 ft high and 2200 ft in diameter, rising to a present (1985) altitude of over 6360 ft.

Nature has shown remarkable resiliency in the form of plant and animal recovery within the devastated area. The hot debris that swept life from the mountain was rich in organic residuals and is helping the process of vegetative recolonization. A variety of chance conditions present at the time of the eruption permitted many species to survive.

Surviving organisms have played the major role in the recovery process. The complicated pattern of plant recovery has been affected by the diversity of existing communities, the presence or absence of snow cover at the time of eruption, slope orientation, and the depth of ash deposits. Dormant, unexposed plants, ground-dwelling animals, and fish in ice-glazed lakes survived the eruption, being less susceptible than their exposed counterparts. At higher elevations, snow protected small evergreens, understory species, and plants from the hot volcanic debris. Huckleberry shrubs were able to emerge from ash layers relatively successfully. Slopes facing southward and those unprotected by snow received the full force of the blast and were often swept clean of plant life and soil.

Surviving plants sprouted from beneath ash deposits less than 10 inches deep within one year after the eruption, and those growing on steep hillsides were assisted by erosion that uncovered an otherwise impenetrable deposit. Plant recovery has been slowest in river valleys affected by the debris avalanche and mudflows. Weedy plants such as fireweed, thistle, and pearly everlasting have been quick to recover in clearcuts and meadows, and because their seeds are easily transported by wind, they have been important colonizers of barren surfaces. The first seeds to reforest the devastated area produced alder, whose leaf litter enriched the soil with nitrogen. The short-lived alder will give way to western hemlock, which in turn may be replaced by lodgepole pine and Pacific silver fir. A stable coniferous forest should mature in 100 to 200 years.

The removal of vegetation and deposition of large amounts of volcanic debris by the blast has greatly increased erosion in the Toutle and other stream valleys. The rivers draining Mount St. Helens continue to be among the highest sediment-carrying ones in the world. The Toutle River in 1984 delivered nearly 100 times its pre-eruption yield of sediment to the Cowlitz River. It is estimated that more than 70 percent of this sediment comes directly from the avalanche deposit that buries the North Fork Toutle River to an average depth of 150 ft for 15 mi.; this deposit will continue to be an active source of sediment for many years. A tunnel has recently been constructed through the debris blocking Spirit Lake to prevent a collapse of its dam and subsequent valley flooding.

MOUNT ST. HELENS NATIONAL VOLCANIC MONUMENT

Congress established the 110,000-acre Monument in 1982.

ADMINISTRATION: Mount St. Helens National Volcanic Monument Headquarters is located on State Hwy No. 503 between Amboy and Cougar. Address: Amboy, WA 98601. Phone: (206) 247-5473.

Three special information stations near the volcano are manned by specialists during the summer season. These stations are:

Yale Information Station (2 mi. W of Cougar on Lewis River Road ◆).

Pine Creek Information Station (18 mi. E of Cougar on Lewis River Road ◆).

Iron Creek Information Station (10 mi. S of Randle on Randle-Lewis River Road ◆); one can reach Randle via U.S. Hwy No. 12 in 49 mi. from exit 68 on I-5.

Pine Creek and Iron Creek information stations are open daily through the summer.

ACCESS: Toutle River Mudflow. Drive from Castle Rock on I-5 (exit 49) via State Hwy No. 504 to its end (28 mi. at present). The volcano's crater opening and the massive mudflows are visible from here. A paved road is planned to continue to Coldwater Lake (7 mi. from the volcano's crater). Various facilities, including a restaurant and a cross-country ski center, are planned. A shuttle bus road and service may be available to reach a viewpoint on Johnston Ridge, SE of the lake. As time passes, other proposals and changes will be made. Check for notices and regulation changes.

Windy Ridge: This is a fine viewpoint of devastated Spirit Lake, forest land, and the volcano's crater at the edge of the current restricted zone. Reach via Spirit Lake-Iron Creek Road No. 99; distance is 12½ mi. from the Randle-Lewis River Road ◆.

Strawberry Mountain: Located 10 mi. NE of the volcano on Road No. 2516; this vantage offers a view of the volcano. Reach via Randle-Lewis River Road ◆ to the S of Iron Creek Information Station, then drive 7 mi.

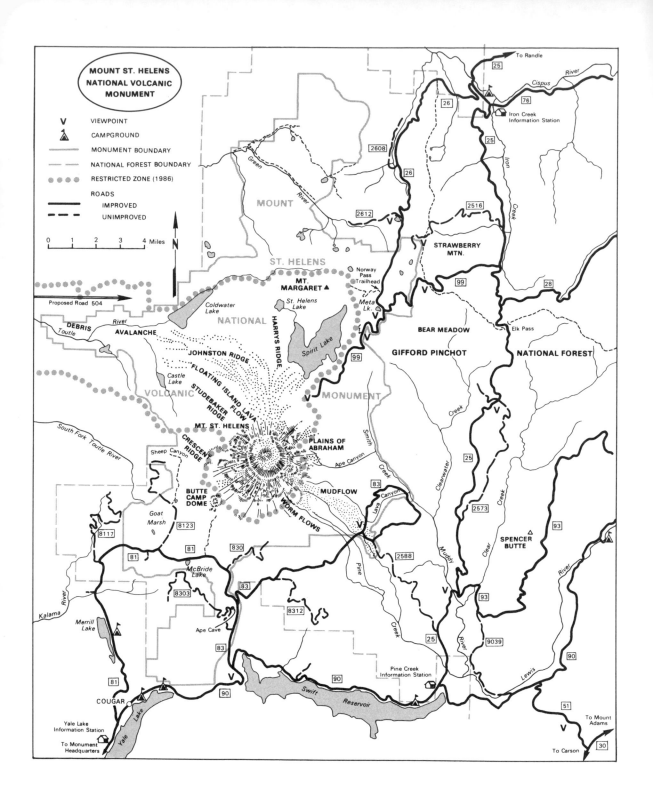

Lahar Viewpoint: Near the site of the Muddy River and Pine Creek mudflows, SE of the volcano. Drive E of Cougar on Road No. 90 for 5½ mi., then take Road No. 83 for 11 mi.

Access Restrictions: Washington State and the U.S. Forest Service have created a Hazard Zone in a limited area surrounding the mountain. Currently, entry to this zone is by permit only and is strictly enforced for the protection of the public. Detailed Hazard Zone maps are displayed at information centers, ranger stations and other public facilities in the area. Information concerning permits and road conditions can be obtained at Monument Headquarters and information centers.

The North Fork of the Toutle River can be extremely dangerous due to deep mud and quicksand on the bed and bank instability. Flash flooding is possible in the Toutle River Valley due to rapid snowmelt caused by an eruption or thermal activity, or the failure of a water-impounding debris dam (such as the one holding Spirit Lake). Siren warning systems at lakes and in the valley have been installed to signal flash flooding. Posted evacuation routes should be followed during emergencies.

Near the junction of state routes 504 and 505 the Department of Transportation has installed a Highway Advisory Radio system; within a mi. radius of this intersection, tune to 1610 megahertz on your AM radio for current status reports or emergency information.

Health Precautions: All water obtained in the vicinity of the volcano should be considered unsafe for drinking. If water must be used, strain debris and boil for two minutes. Minor ashfall from eruptions is a minimal hazard and can be dealt with by breathing through a handkerchief or particle mask.

Place Names: Recently approved (1983) names on and near Mount St. Helens include:

The Breach: The gap in the new crater wall.

Butte Camp Dome: A lava dome on the SW flank, near Butte Camp.

Castle Lake: The 1½ mi. lake formed by the impoundment of the South Fork of Castle Creek, about 4.5 mi. NW of the volcano's summit.

Coldwater Lake: Dammed by a slide from the 1980 eruption.

Coldwater Peak: A small flat-topped summit at 5727 ft that was an old lookout site.

Crescent (West) Ridge: On the W flank of Mount St. Helens one mi. W of the crater.

Harrys Ridge: The 1½ mi. ridge along the W arm of Spirit Lake; the name honors Harry R. Truman, owner of the St. Helens Lodge, killed by the 1980 eruption.

Johnston Ridge: The prominent ridge W of Spirit Lake that commemorates David Johnston, a U.S.G.S. volcanologist who manned an observation post here.

Lava Dome: The actively growing lava dome in the crater of Mount St. Helens; the dome will probably be a permanent feature.

Monitor (South) Ridge: The main spur on the south slope of the volcano.

Muddy River Gorge: The deeply incised canyon of the Muddy River E of the volcano, 2.2 mi. SE of Ape Canyon. The gorge is also known as Lava Canyon.

1980 Crater: The large new crater formed from the explosion.

Pumice Plain: The area extending from the base of the N slope of the volcano to Spirit Lake (about 5 sq mi.).

Sasquatch Steps: The area on the north flank of the volcano where pyroclastic flows cascaded out of the breach over a cliff series, forming canyons with step-like floors.

Studebaker Ridge: The prominent ridge, about 2 mi. in length, alongside Studebaker Creek, on the NW flank of the volcano.

Worm Flows: Lava flows that are uniquely long and narrow, about 500 years in age, on the SE flank of the volcano, 2 mi. SE of the crater rim.

TRAILS: These trails are local to Mount St. Helens and its surroundings. Some trails are old, some new, and some rerouted. This listing is not included in the Trails section at the back of the book.

Norway Pass No. 1 (part of Boundary Trail): This new trail begins on Road No. 26, about 1 mi. N of the junction of Roads No. 99 and 26. Distance to the pass is 2.2 mi. The trail is being continued across Mount Margaret to the summit of Coldwater Peak. There are numerous vistas of Spirit Lake and nearby devastated areas.

Boundary Trail No. 1: This well-established trail, with a length of 35 mi., begins as the Norway Pass Trail. The Boundary Trail descends to Bear Meadow on Road No. 99 and Elk Pass on Road No. 25; the trail offers excellent views of the volcano and the surrounding region. The high point is about 5600 ft.

Windy Ridge: Follow the roadway and trail S from the end of Road No. 99 to just E of Windy Pass. The

MOUNT ST. HELENS from Pumice Plain, showing 1980 crater
JIM HUGHES, U.S. FOREST SERVICE

trail continues to the Plains of Abraham, Pumice Butte, and Ape Canyon, reaching Road No. 83 at Lava Canyon. See also Ape Canyon Trail.

Loowit (Round the Mountain) Trail No. 216: This trail is currently under construction. There is a western connection at Sheep Canyon Viewpoint; the trail traverses SE from Sheep Canyon above Butte Camp Dome, crosses Swift Creek flow, passes June Lake, and is planned to join the Ape Canyon Trail near Pumice Butte. The latter trail can be followed N to Windy Ridge.

Ptarmigan (Monitor Ridge) Trail No. 216A: This new trail is a connection with Loowit Trail on the S flank of the volcano. Begin near the end of Road No. 830, a branch of Road No. 81 to the E of Redrock Pass. A climber's camp is reached in about 2 mi. on this road (trailhead here). This trail, which bears NW, is expected to become the most popular climbing route because of its nearness to the summit and relatively high start (about 3680 ft).

Butte Camp Trail No. 238A: This long-used trail begins as No. 238 from Road No. 81 at Redrock Pass (about 3 mi. from the No. 83/81 junction). The trail crosses ancient lava flows (about 2000 years old) and provides a good access to the ascent of Mount St. Helens. Distance to Butte Camp (about 3950 ft) is 2 mi. A left fork at a trail junction here extends to a meadow and the camp; there is a spring about 200 yards W of the camp — higher locations may have no water. The flat area above Butte Camp is closed to camping due to the intensive research occurring in the area.

The right fork continues about 0.7 mi. to timberline and intersects with Loowit Trail.

Goat Marsh Trail No. 237: This trail to a unique ecological area (including a Noble fir stand) begins on Road No. 8123 just N of Road No. 81.

Goat Mountain Trail No. 217: This trail in the NE portion of the Monument begins at 0.1 mi. past Ryan Lake interpretive site (Road No. 2612). The 9 mi. trail leads to the 5600-ft summit of Goat Mountain. There are good views and, in late summer, berries.

Independence Pass Trail: Begin off Road No. 99. Hike about 3 mi. to Norway Pass. The trail provides excellent views of the Spirit Lake basin and Mount St. Helens. The trail also provides access to Tephra Pinnacle, a 100-ft pinnacle which can be climbed on its S face (class 5.4).

Ape Canyon/Plains of Abraham Trail (No. 234 and 216): Begin on Road No. 83 at E side of the Muddy River/Pine Creek lahar. Follow the trail N on the ridge above the lahar for 5 mi. to Ape Canyon and the edge of the May 18, 1980 devastated area. From Ape Canyon continue N, passing Pumice Butte and Dry Falls before crossing the Plains of Abraham (3 mi. to Road No. 99). Follow the road 2 mi. NE to the gate and Windy Ridge Viewpoint. All hikers should carry water.

Sheep Canyon Viewpoint (to W of Mount St. Helens): Take roads No. 83, 81, and 8123, or follow No. 81 from beyond Yale Information Station for 12 mi. The Loowit (Round the Mountain) Trail can be accessed by a ½ mi. connector trail from the viewpoint.

MOUNTAINEERING: The formerly ice-clad volcano is no longer a technical ascent, and old routes —such as the Dog's Head, Forsyth Glacier, and Lizard —no longer exist in the same form. Mount St. Helens is currently closed to mountaineering, but probably will be opened in 1987. A climbing-permit system will be instituted. Obtain permits at Monument Headquarters, or phone in advance. The S, SW, and W flanks of the volcano will likely be the most popular routes when climbing closures are lifted. It is expected that the crater (N flank) routes will be closed. An ice axe is advisable for the ascent in most conditions. If conditions are icy, crampons and a rope are advisable.

The southern slopes are the most gradual and fea-tureless. Early-season ascents are largely easy snow climbs, and any remaining ice remnants can be avoid-ed in late season by keeping to pumice or snow. Water and snow for camping may be limited above timberline after June on any southern or western route; until August the lower slopes may be afflicted with mosquitoes.

The Monitor Ridge route is expected to become the most popular (see Ptarmigan Trail). From the Swift Creek flow the route ascends almost due N to the rim between Dryer and Swift glaciers (just E of the highest summit point). The distance from the junction of Loowit Trail to the crater rim is about 2 mi.

A traditional route on the SW flank is the one via Butte Camp, then keeping W of the Dryer Glacier. The terrain is mostly a long, gradual snowfield (or pumice in late season) to the crater rim. See Butte Camp Trail.

The western route is Crescent Ridge, using the

MOUNT ST. HELENS from northeast (September 9, 1980)
U.S. GEOLOGICAL SURVEY

Shoestring Glacier · Dogs Head · Studebaker Cleaver · 1980 crater · Windy Pass · former Timberline parking area · Plains of Abraham

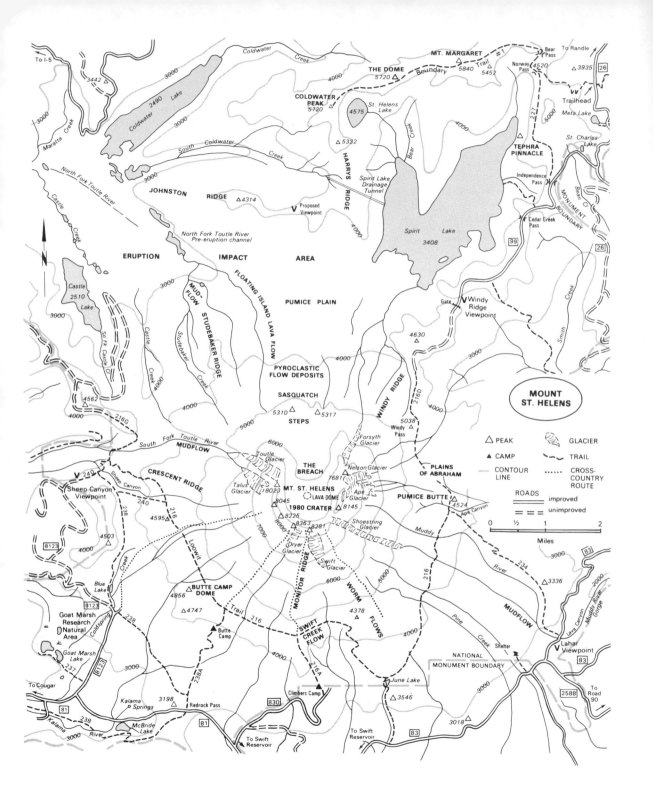

Sheep Canyon approach, with a 3 mi. distance to the crater rim at its SW corner. This is a very straightforward route, beginning from an altitude of about 3600 ft. Approach from roads No. 81 and 8123.

The formerly used Moonbase Route is not difficult, but because of rough lava is optimum when the upper mountain is snow-covered. From Road No. 83, park and hike on an abandoned road to a hilltop junction. Keep right and hike to timberline (about 3400 ft). Continue through the timber fringe to a narrow boulder gully and a trough to a campsite at 5000 ft (Moonbase, 4 hours hiking). This location is on the SE flank of the volcano (to the SW of the terminus of Shoestring Glacier).

The ascent route initially stays left of the SE ridge, then higher connects with it by pumice fingers. The route is safe from falling rock, and has no crevasses. Follow the crater rim westward to the summit.

Interesting references include:

American Forests. October 1980, pp. 26-31, 67-68.

Audubon. July 1980, pp. 24-41.

Mazama. July 1903, pp. 123-137; 1913, pp. 44-46; 1925, pp. 73-78; 1926, pp. 83-92; 1938, pp. 49-54; 1941, pp. 56-60; 1967, pp. 10-12.

Mountaineer. 1910, pp. 56-62; 1915, pp. 10-12; 1917, pp. 9-34; 1922, pp. 24-27; 1932, pp. 9-17; 1937, pp. 42-43; 1980, pp. 9-11.

National Geographic Magazine. "Mount St. Helens, Mountain with a Death Wish." January 1981, pp. 2-65.

Off Belay. June 1980, pp. 19-28.

Science, 80. September–October 1980, pp. 49-52.

Summit. January 1959, pp. 12-13; April 1976, pp. 20-24; April-May 1980, pp. 1-5.

Volcano: The Eruption of Mount St. Helens. Longview Publishing Company, Longview, Washington, and Madrona Press, Seattle, 1980.

Decker, Robert and Decker, Barbara. "The Eruptions of Mount St. Helens." *Scientific American.* March 1981, pp. 68-80.

Elliott, Lt. Charles P. "Mount Saint Helens." *Nat. Geog. Mag.* vol. 8 (1897), pp. 226-230.

Foxworthy, Bruce L. and Hill, Mary. "Volcanic Eruptions of 1980 at Mount St. Helens: The first 100 days." *U.S. Geol. Survey Prof. Paper 1249* (1982).

Holmes, Kenneth L. "Mount St. Helens' Recent Eruptions." *Oregon Hist. Quart.,* vol. 56 (1955), pp. 197-225.

Jillison, Willard L. "Physiographic Effects of the Volcanism of Mount St. Helens." *Geog. Review,* vol. 11 (1921), pp. 398-405.

Lipman, Peter W. and Mullineaux, Donal R. "The 1980 Eruptions of Mount Saint Helens, Washington." *U.S. Geol. Survey Prof. Paper 1250* (1981).

Loo-Wit-Lat-Kla; *pseud.* "Gold Hunting in the Cascade Mountains." Vancouver, W. T., 1861 (New Haven, Yale Univ. Library, 1957).

Miller, Maynard M. "Mount St. Helens Eruption." *American Alpine Journal,* 1981, pp. 99-114.

(del) Moral, Roger. "Life Returns to Mount St. Helens." *Natural Hist.,* vol. 90 (May 1981), pp. 36-46.

Mullineaux, D. R. and Crandell, D. R. "Late Recent Age of Mount St. Helens Volcano, Washington." *Geol. Survey Prof. Paper 400-B* (Washington, 1960).

_____ . "Recent Lahars from Mount St. Helens, Washington." *Geol. Soc. Amer. Bull. 73* (1962), pp. 855-870.

Parrish, J. L. "Eruption of Mount St. Helens." *Steel Points,* vol. 1 (Oct. 1906), pp. 25-26.

Shane, Scott. *Discovering Mount St. Helens: A Guide to the National Volcanic Monument.* University of Washington Press, Seattle, 1985.

MOUNT MARGARET
5840 ft+/1789 m+

The Spirit Lake Road no longer provides access because of the 1980 eruption. The best route to Mount Margaret is via the Norway Pass Trail, starting from Road No. 26 (see Mount St. Helens access). It is planned to continue the trail to Coldwater Peak. Both summits and the trail provide grand panoramas of the volcano and the eruption's devastation.

Mount Whittier (5883 ft) is a summit 0.9 mi. to the N of Mount Margaret. It can be reached cross-country.

PINTO ROCK   5123 ft/1562 m

This locally prominent rock formation is located immediately E of Pole Patch Road (see Randle-Lewis River Road ◆), 14 mi. S of Randle. The rock is a silicified tuff-breccia, apparently the vestige of a large volcanic crater. Its texture is rough, with abundant knobs and projections; it is of varying surface quality — often solid but sometimes loose. The climbs range from 150 to 400 ft, and in difficulty from class 5.0 upward. Allow about 1½ hours per route. There are few cracks for protection, but knobs often provide runner fixing opportunities.

The E summit of Pinto Rock is the highest; there is a deep gap between the two summits. The descent is

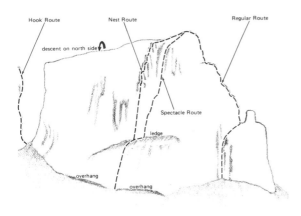

PINTO ROCK from south

PINTO ROCK from east
U.S. FOREST SERVICE

best done by a rappel to a ramp on the N side. Reach the area via Randle-Lewis River Road ◆.

REGULAR ROUTE: This is the easiest of the climbing routes; first climbers unknown. Class 5.0-5.2.

Start in a gully near the E end of the S face and traverse right to a gully on the SE side to the top; 3-4 leads.

SPECTACLE ROUTE: This route offers three interesting leads (class 5.5). First ascent by David Wagner and Richard Crow, June 1967.

The route climbs from the middle of the S face, starting at left edge of lowest part of rock to a ledge, then angles right 30 ft and up a vertical groove just below the top.

NEST ROUTE: This route takes one just right of the great overhang which cuts across the left side of the S face (class 5.6). First ascent by David Wagner and Robert Sprenger, October 1968.

Starts as in Spectacle Route. From the ledge angle left 10 ft and climb the groove in buttress to summit (three leads).

HOOK ROUTE: This route leads to the lower summit; two leads (class 5.6). First ascent by David Wagner and Tom Goman, July 1968.

Climb the first continuous erosion furrow N of the gap to the summit of the W peak.

TOWER ROCK   3335 ft/1017 m

Tower Rock is a prominent crag located about 1 mi. S of the Cispus River and S of Tower Rock Forest Camp (about 7 mi. SE of Randle). Reach the Rock via Randle-Trout Lake Road ◆. There are climbing opportunities on the relatively solid basalt. The easiest approach is from the N, following a logging road, then hiking from the valley to the W side of the Rock. The S ridge is taken to the summit.

The NW face was climbed by Jim Nieland and Francisco Valenzuela on June 20, 1982. The route begins on the left side of the face, left of a large cleft: class 4 to a sloping ledge at the end of a long ramp. Then climb up and right for three pitches (some poor rock; class 5.6-5.7 and minor aid). Then climb about 60 ft, then right for 30 ft, then down into a triangular spot. Climb to gain a large ledge, then to the right. On better rock, move right on a ledge, then climb through a twisted chimney to a small ledge; climb along the minor ridge to a belay (class 5.6). Climb the ridge, then right and face climb to a piton belay (class 5.6 and poor protection). Traverse the open book left of the roof and face climb on moss clumps and small holds to the summit tree (class 5.7-5.8—poor protection). Grade III; class 5.8 and aid.

SUNRISE PEAK   5892 ft/1796 m
and JUMBO PEAK   5801 ft/1768 m

Sunrise and Jumbo peaks are prominent volcanic summits located 13 mi. NW of Mount Adams. Both peaks are best approached by the Randle-Trout Lake Road ◆ and its branch No. 2324 (24 mi. from Randle). Follow the branch road to the Sunrise Peak trailhead (about 5½ mi.). The craggy peak is seen clearly from here. The summit via Trail No. 262 is about 2½ mi. distant; there is a minor bit of scrambling on the NW flank near the summit.

To reach Jumbo Peak, take Trail No. 261 southward at the fork. This trail reaches the summit from the N flank.

BADGER PEAK   5664 ft/1726 m
and KIRK ROCK   5597 ft/1706 m

Badger Peak and Kirk Rock can be reached by Boundary Trail No. 1 from about 3½ mi. along Road No. 2551, which branches from Iron Creek Road ◆ (at est. 26 mi. from Randle).

Trail to Badger Peak Lookout is about 1½ mi. The trail continues E along the high country past Kirk Rock, Shark Rock, Hat Rock, and Table Mountain to meet Road No. 2834 (a short branch of Randle-Trout Lake Road ◆ W of Council Lake junction).

Note: Roads from a northern access along Yellowjacket, McCoy, and East Canyon creeks intersect the main trail. A review of the maps will show these and other approaches, and connecting trails.

The solid outcrops at Kirk Rock and the other formations offer rock-climbing opportunities.

SLEEPING BEAUTY MOUNTAIN
4907 ft/1496 m

The mountain is a prominent basalt outcrop that provides panoramic views of the Mount Adams region. A short trail (1½ mi.) leads to the former lookout site. The southern exposures are steep and offer climbing potential.

From Trout Lake, distance to the summit trailhead is approximately 13 mi. Take Roads No. 88 (Trout Lake Creek), 8810, and 040. Reference: *Trips and Trails, 2.*

MOUNT ADAMS   12,276 ft/3742 m

The majestic hulk of Adams dominates the Cascade landscape N of the Columbia River so much that it became idolized as Pah-to, son of the Great Spirit, or Klickitat, to the Indians, and linked in a legend concerning a fraternal battle with Wy-east (Mount Hood) in the courtship of Loo-wit (Mount St. Helens). Lewis and Clark did not visualize Adams as a mythical warrior, but as "a high humped mountain" (Thwaites, vol. 4, p. 238), a terse description in Captain William Clark's journal dated April 2, 1806 near the Willamette River's mouth — the earliest mention of the mountain. However, when the two explorers first saw it (October 19, 1805 from near the Columbia and John Day rivers) they mistook it for St. Helens, having anticipated this feature from Vancouver's narrative. Clark wrote, "I discovered a high mountain of emance hight covered with Snow" (Thwaites, vol. 3, p. 135). Later that intrepid explorer of the North West Company, David Thompson, saw both Adams and Hood (July 12, 1811), describing each as a "snow mount."[25]

Adams and St. Helens were frequently confused in early observations. Lt. Robert E. Johnson, while in the Yakima Valley in 1841, mistook their identities, as did John C. Frémont in 1843 from the Umatilla uplands.[26] The confusion of geographic position and the names of the two mountains was compounded by Oregon enthusiast Hall J. Kelley's invention, the "Presidents' Range" and his scheme of naming the principal volcanic peaks for early American presidents. Another settler, Thomas J. Farnham, attempted to rearrange Kelley's plan, and when in 1843 he saw Mount Adams to the N of the Cascades of the Columbia, he applied its present name. George Gibbs, writing in 1873, noted the resemblance of the volcanos and recalled they had long been "confounded with each other."[27]

The confusion was not resolved until 1853 when the Pacific Railroad Expedition charted the mountain as Mount Adams. That both its location and height were subject to considerable variance is shown by early maps. Both the 1856 and 1870 maps of Public Surveys in Washington Territory continued to show the Klickitat River on the W side of Mount Adams. The 1866 map of the U.S. Northwest Boundary Survey only listed Adams at 9570 ft in height, while giving Mount St. Helens 9750 ft. These errors apparently developed because Lt. Johnson K. Duncan, topographer for McClellan, and George Gibbs determined that the height of Adams was about equal to that of St. Helens. The vastness and shapeless form of Adams likely had something to do with underestimation of its height in early times, while the steep pointed form of Mount Hood long exaggerated its altitude.

David Douglas, the Scottish botanist who came to the Columbia River area in 1825, was rumored to have climbed the mountain twice. George Gibbs (who accompanied Capt. McClellan) hoped to ascend both volcanos, but survey priority and weather conditions frustrated this idea. The accepted first ascent was made in late summer, 1854. The party probably consisted of A. G. Aiken, Edward J. Allen, and Andrew Burge, who belonged to a military road work party on the Naches Pass route; it was while they were camped a few miles NE of the mountain that they apparently climbed by the North Ridge. The record of this climb was given by George H. Himes in *Steel Points,* July 1907. Himes, a pioneer who knew the men, learned of the ascent through conversation with Aiken.[28]

An early attempt on the mountain by a missionary and three Indian lads was published in 1854 in *Mission Life in Oregon* (author unnamed); they took horses to the snowline on the S side and climbed onward some distance. Their Indian guide said that they were the first men to try the mountain. Himes has also provided the information that in the summer of 1863 or 1864 Henry C. Coe, Mr. Phelps, Julia A. Johnson, and Sarah Fisher reached the summit, leaving from White Salmon. The earliest names on Adams from the *Mazama* are for 1864, and probably were among the first climbers from the south: Rev. Thomas Condon, Charles C. Coe, H. Clayton, Henry C. Coe, William B. Stillwell, and "Johnson" — an Indian.[29] An interesting comment in the *Oregonian* records an ascent on August 6, 1867, when Samuel L. Brooks and six others reached the summit in 7 hours. The notation mentions that on the return "Brooks descended on a tin plate in 1½ hours." The news of these early ascents was retained locally, for as Edmund T. Coleman (who made the first ascent of Mount Baker) commented on Mount Adams in the *Whatcom Reveille* (August 3, 1883): "Little or nothing is known respecting this mountain. I believe it has never been ascended."

Though sheepmen in early times ranged herds on the grasslands at the base of the E side,[30] it was not until 1890 that Claude E. Rusk made a circuit of the mountain; he was likely the first person to visit the Rusk Glacier, named for him by Professor Harry F. Reid of Johns Hopkins University. Not until 1901 when Rusk accompanied Reid, the most eminent glaciologist of his time, on a circuit of the mountain, could the volcano be considered fully explored. During that time the names Adams, Rusk, Lava, and Lyman Glaciers were bestowed (Professor W. D. Lyman of Whitman College, one of the early investigators of the mountain, is commemorated by the Lyman Glacier). Rusk provided early feature names such as Ridge of Wonders, Victory Ridge (for the World War I victory), Wilson Glacier (for the President), and Devil's Gardens for the large breccia outcrops below the Wilson Glacier. On their 1895 outing the Mazamas changed "Hellroaring Glacier" to Mazama Glacier.

In 1919 Rusk made several unsuccessful attempts to scale various eastside routes: he went high on the Wilson Glacier, Lava Ridge, and Victory Ridge. Certainly he was the first to explore the glaciers and cliffs in this extremely rugged area. In 1921 he led his famed climb via The Castle, an anachronism in view of its magnitude; its top now bears Rusk's ashes in a memorial cairn.

A lookout cabin was built on the summit in 1921 and manned for several years. In 1929 a sulphur claim

was staked on the summit and a trail soon built; test holes were dug through the ice to deposits. At the height of activity in 1931, some 168 pack trains reached the summit (climbers still use traces of the pack trail and for years could expect hot coffee with the miners). The Glacier Mining Company had active workings until 1937.

"The cliffs and ice cascades appall even the expert alpinist," wrote John H. Williams in 1912, when describing the E and W faces of Mount Adams. Rusk was the first to dare the difficult routes, but the lack of followers after his notable 1921 climb is surprising. Even the moderately difficult Adams Glacier was not ascended until 1945. Adams was climbed on skis by Hans-Otto Giese, Hans Grage, Otto Strizek, Walter Mosauer, and Sandy Lyons on July 16, 1932, and a winter ascent was made by J. Daniel and W. Liebentritt on January 1, 1937. Adams has become popular with the peak bagger, the many ascents usually taking the easier S and N routes. Mass ascents were popular for many years until phased out because they conflicted with the area's wilderness designation. Group caution and consciousness shine through as the predominant climbing attitude. Note: Wilderness permits are needed April 15 through November 15 for overnight hikes and climbs. Timberline firewood is scarce; use stoves for alpine camps.

While the approaches are long in winter, some winter ascents have been made, with good conditions for climbing generally encountered on the upper, windward slopes. Spring ascents are a problem because of closed roads, but conditions should often be good; early summer is therefore the most appropriate time to make ascents, certainly on routes with stonefall and major crevasse problems, which may be very dangerous if not impossible after about mid-July. The optimum time for any of the more serious routes is when there is ample consolidated snow under well-frozen conditions. Routes exposed to rockfall should not be attempted during periods when freezing level is unusually high. Ascents should be timed to arrive at dangerous areas at the safest time (before sun's rays strike). Rain can cause rockfall and snow and scree slides as readily as sun's heat. Rock climbing on Adams is unpredictable due to alternating strata of varying densities. Most routes on Adams demand more physical effort than technical skill; those in good training may make relatively easy work of them where speed is an essential factor in safety.

Mount Adams conveys the impression of massiveness, and when one climbs it, this impression is prov-

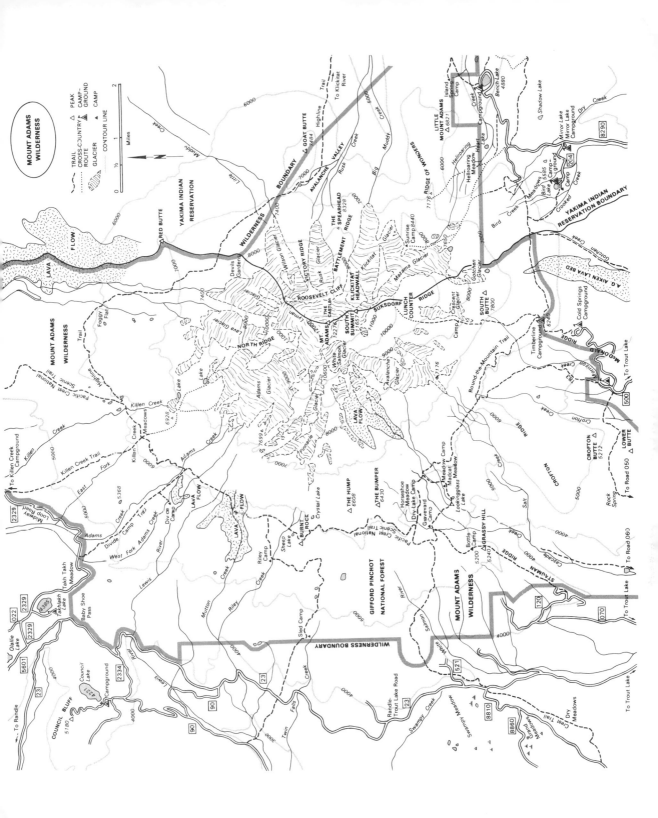

ed correct. It is a vast mountain in all respects. It has a complex array of walls and ridges, which recently have been the object of considerable exploration.

The elongated cone of Mount Adams stands 5000 to 7500 ft above the surrounding peaks of the Cascade Range. The volcano compares closely with Mount Rainier in total volume of extruded material: it is estimated that Mount Adams' volcanics cover approximately 270 mi.[2] Slopes of the main cone average between 25 and 30 degrees, and lava flows that surround the mountain extend out from a broad, gently sloping apron 3 to 6 mi. in width.

The Yakima Basalt of Miocene-Pliocene age underlies much of the Mount Adams area. Early eruptions from the volcano followed widespread olivine basalt volcanism that probably continued to the mid-Pleistocene. Quaternary rocks of the area include andesite lavas from Mount Adams, as well as widespread basalt flows from peripheral vents.

Mount Adams presumably had its last mass-building eruptions well back in the Pleistocene, perhaps a half million or more years ago. The rugged volcano is old enough to be heavily sculptured by the last major glaciation, except on the S slope, the site of repeated eruptions that took place late in its history. A hundred modern vents have added to the interest and topographic variety of Adams' scarred slopes.

Adams was formed and elongated from multiple venting, then shaped by differential erosion. The hard andesite lava is shattered into fragments and interlayered with crumbling softer volcanic ash and pumice. The broad summit area appears to be the result of eruptions from several vents; shifting vents have caused cones to overlap, and the summit cone itself may have been built in post-Glacial time.

The latest eruptions include one of the largest Cascade lava flows, covering some 10.4 mi.[2] This, the Muddy Fork lava flow of blocky andesite, was extruded from a vent near Red Butte. The Big Muddy Creek flow, SE of Mount Adams is a thick intracanyon flow that occupies the Klickitat River valley. A 4½-mi.-long blocky lava flow, extruded near South Butte, is the most recent lava eruption — possibly less than 2000 years old.

Most of the craters on and near the mountain are partly filled and concealed. Lava dikes — resistant longitudinal spurs — have resisted erosion and the undercutting of ice. But without the production of new lava, the volcano is undergoing a continual, slow destruction. A radiating pattern of ridges separated by entrenched valleys has developed, much like near Mount Rainier, but with far less incision.

There have been devastating heat-originated mudflows on the volcano, notably in May 1921 when a slide over 1 mi. in length swept from the SW face and uprooted a forest at its base. Some 5000 years ago a large mudflow from the W flank mantled the White Salmon River valley near Trout Lake.

Mount Adams is covered by ten principal glaciers, ranging 1 to 2 mi. in length. They discharge meltwater to the Cispus, Lewis, White Salmon, and Klickitat river systems. With the exception of the Rusk and Klickitat glaciers, these bodies of ice occupy shallow troughs on the flanks of the cone. The summit ice dome is the feeding ground of the Klickitat, Wilson, Lyman, Adams, and White Salmon glaciers. The others collect snow from direct accumulation or avalanches from cirque headwalls. The greatest cliffs and ice cascades are on the eastern faces, whose cumulative effect is to produce one of the wildest precipices in the Cascades. The glaciers on the E side descend lowest where the Rusk and Klickitat have cut deep amphitheaters, leaving a hanging icecap below the snows of the summit dome. The great cirques were cut where the volcano was most easily eroded and where the strongest glacial action existed. In the Ice Ages, the larger glaciers were periodically shrunk by volcanic activity, as well as climatic fluctuations.

The Klickitat Glacier is a grand spectacle of hanging ice, descending about 6000 ft in its canyon. Lyman (1903) exalted: "the rocks of black and red and saffron are seamed with glistening colors of ice, which, descending from the dizzy pinnacle of the summit, join in the gashed and hummocked surface of the great ice river." The Rusk Glacier breaks off the summit icecap between The Castle and upper Victory Ridge, then below its headwall the main body descends to about 7000 ft.

Most of the mountain's glaciers are not deeply embedded, but lie on its surface, spreading out fan-like and banked by moraines. A good example is the Mazama, which has built up a large lateral moraine at its S flank. A northern lobe of the glacier spills from a saddle to the Klickitat. Prominent Neoglacial moraines flank the Klickitat, Rusk, Wilson, and Adams glaciers.

The White Salmon Glacier begins on the West Peak, at a common source with the Avalanche Glacier, and flows down the southwestern slope to divide into two branches: one ends in a wall and the other turns to the S, flowing along the SW slope, where it has deposited large terminal moraines near the 7500-ft level.

Certainly one of the finest glaciers, and perhaps its

most distinctive, is the 3-mi.-long Adams, which flows down to 7000 ft on the NW flank. Born on the summit, it pours a series of spectacular icefalls through a steep corridor, then spreads into a large fan-shaped sheet having several fronts. Photos from the turn of the century show its ice cascade much larger.

The Lava Glacier on the E side of the North Ridge begins N of the summit dome and fans down to about 7000 ft. The Lyman descends from a vast, drooping summit icecap on the NE side of the summit dome, then breaks chaotically into nearly twin sections, split by a narrow cleaver at its mid-section. Lower, it merges again to continue to about the 7800-ft level. It has not yet scoured the slopes beyond minor indentations.

The Wilson Glacier begins from the summit icecap, just S of the Lyman. Its main body descends in a jumbled, continuous corridor as an icefall. Lower, it broadens and slopes down to about 7500 ft. The icecap mass S of the corridor perches above a great lava cliff (Roosevelt Cliff); beneath it a lower portion of the Wilson merges with the direct flow from the corridor.

Interesting references include: *Mazama,* 1896, pp. 68-103; 1903, pp. 164-175; 1905, pp. 195-200; 1921, pp. 44-46; 1924, pp. 7-30; 1935, pp. 7-16; 1941, pp. 39-42; *Mountaineer,* 1910, pp. 44-45; 1911, pp. 5-10 and 15-25; 1917, pp. 14-41; 1922, pp. 14-20; 1965, pp. 8-14; Claude E. Rusk, *Tales of a Western Mountaineer,* Seattle, 1978; John H. Williams, *The Guardians of the Columbia,* Tacoma, 1912, pp. 89-104; *Summit:* March 1961, pp. 10-15; March 1970, pp. 20-24; *100 Hikes in the South Cascades and Olympics. Trips and Trails, 2; Off Belay:* June 1972, pp. 11-20; Philip H. Overmeyer, "George B. McClellan and the Pacific Northwest," *Pacific Northwest Quarterly, 32.*

SOUTH SPUR: This is the popular non-technical route, following the way of the 1863 or 1864 party. From Cold Springs (see Mount Adams Timberline ♦ — Roads Section) hike an old roadway which enters a basin and emerges as a trail on the left skyline ridge (1½ mi.). Ascend past South Butte (7600 ft +) and across the cauldron of broken basalt known as Devil's Half Acre, up a giant's stairway overlooking the W branch of the Mazama Glacier. The main spur is now known as Suksdorf Ridge, for pioneer German botanist Wilhelm N. Suksdorf, who began his local visits and studies in 1877.

Continue to the "Lunch Counter," a broad shoulder at the 9000-ft level: in winter or spring skis or snowshoes are usually worn to here. When the route steepens at about 9700 ft ascend due N up snow or talus to the 11,657-ft South Summit. Cross the intervening divide to the true (middle) summit, the last pull being on pumice or snow. The route is largely a hike, but one should be prepared for icy snow conditions; crampons are advised in late season. Grade I. Time: 5-7 hours.

Variation: From end of road trace, continue up the wooded ridge; then bypass "South Butte," a minor red cone at 7790 ft, then work up gullies and broken basalt to "Lunch Counter."

SOUTHWEST CHUTE: This is a shallow gully between the South Spur and the Avalanche Glacier; once the chute was a finger of the Avalanche. There are no special difficulties; best to climb in early season. The first ascent was done by Tom Hargis, Jr., Charles Lyon, and Sean Maxwell in June 1965.

From Timberline (same approach as South Spur) bear northwesterly for about 2 mi. to a prominent moraine which marks the terminus of the Avalanche Glacier (since trail descends at first, it is more direct to go cross-country). The route ascends the slope, then the gully to its end, W of the false summit. Note that the route ascends the center of three gullies. Numerous variations are possible if one desires to angle toward the South Spur or to the Avalanche Glacier. Grade I. References: *A.A.J.,* 1966, p. 26; *Mountaineer,* 1966, p. 203.

A gully called Avalanche Glacier Headwall, was climbed by James Bjorgen and Dale Schmidt on July 10, 1976.

AVALANCHE - WHITE SALMON GLACIER: This is a gently-sloping glacier route on the SW slopes, with the attraction of solitude over the South Spur route. But when the White Salmon breaks up, some ice work may be required. Watch for rockfall on upper portions. First ascent by Gene Angus and Roger Moreau, September 1957.

Bear NW from Timberline Camp for about 2 mi. cross-country to the terminus of Avalanche Glacier. The route crosses the lower Avalanche to a cleaver between it and the White Salmon. Climb the cleaver, then work out onto the White Salmon (crevasse detours may be necessary) before climbing the chute between the W summit and the rock wall flanking the glacier's right side. From the saddle at the head of the chute, bear E onto the summit icecap. Grade I. Time: 6-8 hours. References: *Mountaineer,* 1961, pp. 97-98; *A.A.J.,* 1961, p. 366; *Cascadian,* 1960, p. 8.

WEST RIDGE: This is the ridge between the White Salmon and the Pinnacle Glacier. It meets the NW ridge at the W summit. The first climb was done by Ralph Uber, Lex Maxwell, Wallace Juneau, and Gary Faulkes in July 1963. There was an early unsubstantiated report that a Julius Wang of the Forest Service climbed one of the W ridges alone, and if so, this would appear to have been the route used.

The shortest and best approach is via the Crest Trail ♦ from the S; hike to Horseshoe Meadows, then up. One could also reach the Crest Trail via Riley Camp Trail, then continue in same direction toward Pinnacle Glacier. The ridge lies just S of the glacier and the route runs directly up the ridge. Careful but obvious routefinding is needed to bypass some gendarmes and to avoid possible falling rock. No real technical difficulties. Meet Northwest Ridge just below the

Ridge of Wonders

Mazama Glacier Saddle

Devil's Half Acre

South Butte

Lunch Counter

South Summit

South Spur

Summit

Southwest Chute

West Peak

Timberline

trail

Cold Springs

WHITE SALMON GLACIER

AVALANCHE GLACIER

Morrison Creek

Town of Trout Lake

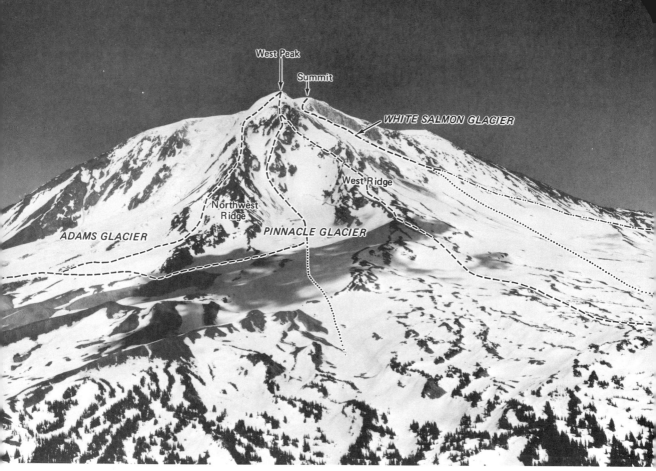

MOUNT ADAMS from west
WALLACE C. GUY, U.S. FOREST SERVICE

West Peak and continue as per directions. Grade I. Time: 6-8 hours from a camp at the foot of the ridge. Reference: *A.A.J.,* 1964, p. 169.

A descent of the White Salmon Glacier, using the cleaver between it and the Avalanche Glacier to avoid the icefall of the White Salmon, is an easy return route if using a southern approach to base camp.

PINNACLE GLACIER HEADWALL: This 2000-ft headwall is located between the West and Northwest ridges. First ascent by Gary Faulkes and Phil Lizee in June 1965.

Approach as for West Ridge route (or from Adams Glacier, crossing its lower spread and traversing around the lower part of the Northwest Ridge). Ascend the lower glacier basin and work left toward rock outcrops in midface. The climb ends just W of the W summit. Best time is early season; to avoid rockfall danger. Grade II. Time: 4½ hours on headwall. References: *A.A.J.,* 1966, pp. 127-128; *Mountaineer,* 1966, p. 204.

NORTHWEST RIDGE: This is the prominent ridge between the Adams and Pinnacle glaciers. It meets with the

West Ridge at the W summit. The ridge is in a magnificent position and by virtue of its own outcroppings, most of the ridge should be safe. The first ascent was made in 1924 by Fred S. Stadter, John Scott, and Lindsley Ross, who spent the night in the summit cabin after bad experience with loose rock. "Another great fragment loosened . . . it dashed down over our very heads," they wrote.

Approach as for the Adams Glacier route; cross the Adams Glacier to its junction with the lower toe of the ridge. Climb up the ridge, keeping generally right of the crest to 10,000 ft, where some rock upthrusts are avoided by working left on a steep slope. The last pinnacle on the ridge is at about 10,500 ft. Continue gently upridge to an ice mound forming the W summit. Cross to the saddle, then follow the icecap E to the summit along the gentle 15-degree slope. Grade II. References: *Mazama,* 1924, pp. 32-39; *Summit,* September 1969, pp. 10-13.

Approach Variation: Reach the Crest Trail ◆ via Divide Camp Trail. Then follow the Crest Trail S a short distance, then turn off SE. Timberline is just below 6000 ft (camp-

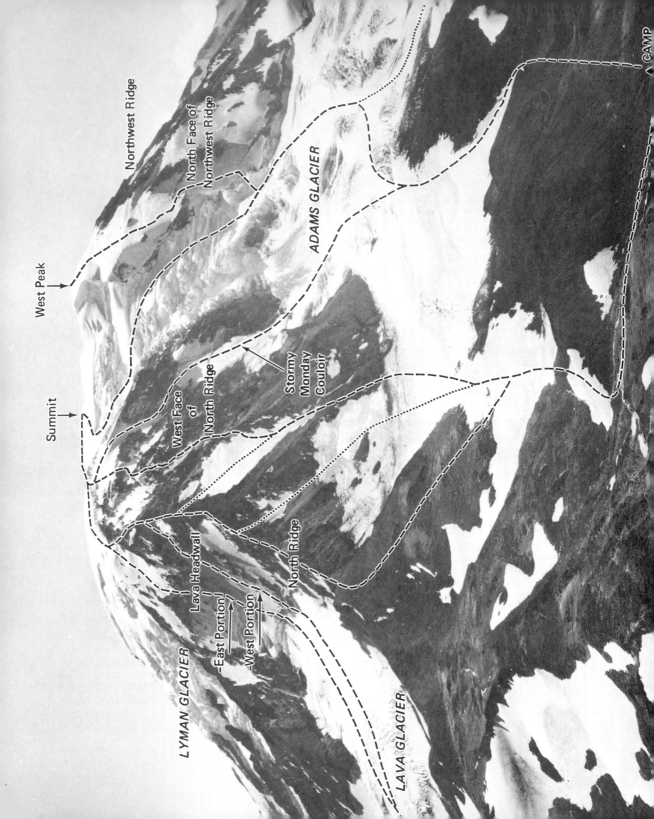

Northwest Ridge

North Face of
Northwest Ridge

ADAMS GLACIER

West Peak

Summit

West Face
of
North Ridge

Stormy Monday
Couloir

Lava Headwall

East Portion

West Portion

North Ridge

LYMAN GLACIER

LAVA GLACIER

CAMP

ing). Cross moraines and reach small steep snowfield just S of Adams Glacier. Below about 10,000 ft numerous variations on the ridge or its flanks can be made.

NORTH FACE OF NORTHWEST RIDGE: This face of about 2000 ft is a sustained 40-45 degrees. Take several ice screws. Best done as early-season climb. First ascent by Al Givler, Dick LeBlond, and Doug McGowan in July 1967.

Approach as for Northwest Ridge or Adams Glacier. Climb lower Adams Glacier route up and right, then cross above large rotten cliff bands (water ice encountered at traverse) to long ice slope flanking the glacier. Follow this slope to near the top of the W summit. Grade II. Reference: *Mountaineer,* 1968, p. 205.

ADAMS GLACIER: This interesting glacier route has become a popular one, especially in early summer, when it is usually in best condition. The ascent involves moderately steep crevassed slopes where the glacier tumbles between rock walls from the summit icecap to 8500 ft. The glacier is profuse with crevasses, which vary with the season and year. First ascent by Fred Beckey, Dave Lind, and Robert Mulhall in July 1945.

See Killen Creek Trail ◆ for route to normal high camp area. Bear SE on moraine or snow toward the lower edge of the Adams Glacier at about 7000 ft. The initial gradient for 1½ mi. to below the icefall is gentle. Either keep left or right of a breakup area, depending on conditions. Most parties first bear to the right, then veer to the left. Ascend the icefall to the summit dome, which is then traversed S to the true summit. Grade II. Time: 4-6 hours for the glacier. References: *A.A.J.,* 1946, p. 44; *Summit,* December 1982, p. 23; *Cascadian,* 1960, pp. 6-7.

STORMY MONDAY COULOIR: First ascent by Craig Reininger and Eric Simonson July 7, 1975. Ascend snow finger to rock band at top. Traverse left two leads (class 4) to the sickle-shaped 50-degree ice gully, then climb to the top of the W face. This route should only be done with firm snow and ice conditions. Reference: *A.A.J.,* 1976, p. 441.

WEST FACE OF NORTH RIDGE: This 4000-ft face lies between the North Ridge and Adams Glacier. First ascent by Dee Molenaar, Forrest Johnson, Robert Ostro, and Robert Startzell in September 1960.

Approach as for Adams Glacier route. The route ascends moderately steep ice and lava ridges above the lower Adams Glacier to reach the snow dome area just left of the upper Adams Glacier icefall; the pattern of ascent is diagonally right, beginning at the base of the depression which is used in the variation to the North Ridge. Grade II. Time: 5½ hours on face. References: *A.A.J.,* 1961, pp. 36-37; *Mountaineer,* 1961, p. 98.

NORTH RIDGE: This long ridge, which trends N-S between the Adams and Lava glaciers, is a relatively easy all-season route, ranking second in popularity on the volcano. At about the 9000-ft level, erosion has made the first portion of the upper ridge quite narrow and exposed. Route finding can be a problem: avoid getting onto the exposed E face of gendarmes.

Hike the Killen Creek Trail ◆ to Mountaineer Camp, then continue to the base of a prominent ridge seen on the right. Keep left here, climbing a large snowfield to a saddle. Follow the rockbed and snow fingers on the right side of the ridge, skirting the lower edge of the Adams Glacier. A broad gradient leads directly to the North Ridge. Ascend near the crest, which is at most a 40-degree stairway of shattered basalt, occasionally skirting outcrops. In late season, there may be some loose rock and occasionally steep portions. From the lower part of the icecap, there is nearly a mile of easy gradient, due S, to a final short ascent on the summit dome. Grade II. Time: 6-8 hours from camp.

Variation: Lower West Flank: Keep W of the ridge's base to a major depression with scree on the right. Ascend depression, usually snow-filled and moderately steep near the top, to the North Ridge; some easy gully scrambling may be encountered below the ridge.

LAVA GLACIER HEADWALL, EAST PORTION: This headwall forms a triangle between the North Ridge and the Lava Ridge (on E). It is best done early season to avoid icy conditions and rockfall. First ascent by Ed Cooper and Mike Swayne in July 1960.

One can reach the Lava Glacier at 8500 ft by traversing around the lower portion of the North Ridge (use any of North Ridge approaches); there are camp spots below the Lava Glacier at timberline; one can camp near the North Ridge crossing, using stoves. One could also approach from Highline Trail, then ascend cross-country to Lava Glacier moraine. The route climbs over two schrunds, then 45-degree névé up the center of the headwall; from there one follows glacier slopes more gentle and the last portion of the North Ridge route to the top. Grade II. Initial party took 5½ hours from timberline camp. References: *A.A.J.,* 1961, pp. 366-367; 1976, p. 442; *Mountaineer,* 1961, p. 92; 1975, p. 102.

LAVA GLACIER HEADWALL, WEST PORTION: By Alex Bertulis and Half Zantop, September 1965.

Approach as for E portion route. Cross the bergschrund to the westerly ice slope on the headwall; the next 1000 ft averages 40 degrees (ice screws may be needed for protection). Use a depression between rock outcrops to exit to the upper North Ridge. Grade II. Time: 12 hours road to summit. Reference: *A.A.J.,* 1966, pp. 126-127.

LAVA RIDGE: This is the cleaver between the Lava Headwall and Lyman Glacier, some 2500 ft high, that eventually merges with the summit icecap. In August 1919 C. E. Rusk and J. Howard Green climbed this cleaver onto the ice slope above its upper end and only turned back because of late season hard ice. Difficulties were generally only moderate. First ascent by Ed Cooper and John Holland, September 1961.

Approach as for Lava Headwall. Either reach the ridge at its lowest point or ascend snow on its right to enter ridge some distance up. Continue up the crest until it merges into a rounded snow/ice slope, then continue upward to the N part of the snow dome. Keep N of outcrops and large

MOUNT ADAMS from northwest
AUSTIN POST, U.S. GEOLOGICAL SURVEY

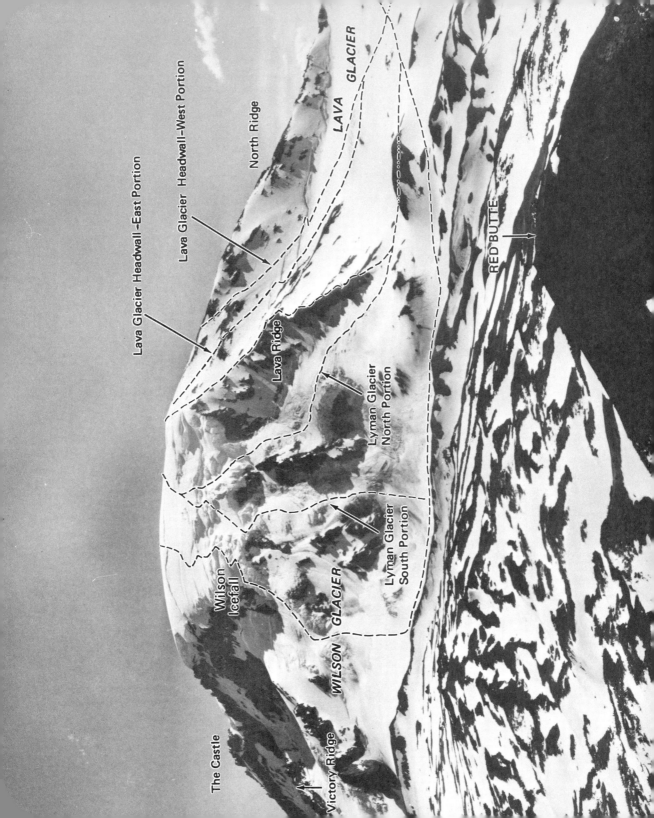

Lava Glacier Headwall–East Portion

Lava Glacier Headwall–West Portion

North Ridge

LAVA GLACIER

RED BUTTE

Lava Ridge

Lyman Glacier North Portion

Lyman Glacier South Portion

WILSON GLACIER

Wilson Icefall

The Castle

Victory Ridge

crevasses of the Lyman. Grade II. References: C. E. Rusk, *Tales of a Western Mountaineer; A.A.J.,* 1962, pp. 205-206; *Mountaineer,* 1962, p. 99.

LYMAN GLACIER, NORTH PORTION: The steep and quite crevassed Lyman Glacier has a narrow outcrop which separates it into halves. The N portion was the original route. First ascent by Cornelius Molenaar and Robert W. Craig in September 1948 on a marathon from the road, to arrive on the summit in 14 hours of travel.

The approach can be made from low on the North Ridge (see North Ridge approaches) and by contouring the Lava Glacier, or from Red Butte via Highline Trail, to névé on the lower glacier. The route ascends the central corridor of the W portion of the glacier; start between two ice snouts on the lower slopes, close to Lava Ridge. Then diagonal up and left to get above the curving ice cliff that runs to the narrow cleaver between the N and S glacier portions. One point between two ice bulges (near 11,000 ft) may reach 45 degrees in angle; large crevasses above may cause detour problems. Grade II. Reference: *Mountaineer,* 1948, p. 53.

LYMAN GLACIER, SOUTH PORTION: The lower half of the route is steep (40-degree) unbroken névé or ice; the upper half is a series of crevasses and serac walls. First ascent by Tom Hargis, Jr., and Chris Cunningham in August 1966.

The route works left of the cleaver that divides the Lyman Glacier, and is best done by keeping to the center of the S half while passing this cleaver. A large bergschrund at 9500 ft deterred earlier efforts and could prevent completion of the climb; on the initial ascent it was crossed on the extreme E side by 20 ft of direct-aid (ice screws). On the next ascent, a snow bridge allowed a schrund crossing to a 30-ft vertical wall; here ice screws were used. Grade III. Time: 8 hours from below Lava Glacier.

WILSON ICEFALL: The Wilson Glacier plunges steeply from the NE edge of the summit icecap, breaking away from the Lyman, with the N icefall section being fringed by two parallel rock walls near 10,500 ft. This is the area of greatest angle and most crevasses; at about 11,000 ft the glacier widens and crevasses are easier to detour. First ascent by Fred Beckey and Herb Staley in July 1961.

Best approach is from the N (see Lyman Glacier approaches); climb to the crest of an 8000-ft moraine to enter the Wilson Glacier. (Keep S of the cleaver separating it from the Lyman.) Choose an ascent line on the lower section of the glacier that minimizes time spent beneath ice cliff; work slightly left between two ice breakups, then climb directly to the narrow steep neck of plunging ice cliffs and seracs. Careful route planning is essential. Steep cramponing may be necessary; bring ice screws. Grade III. References: *A.A.J.,* 1962, pp. 204-205; *Mountaineer,* 1962, pp. 91-92.

WILSON GLACIER HEADWALL: This portion of the E face heads the S portion of the Wilson Glacier and consists of ice and some lava outcroppings, with summit ice cliffs hanging above; one should expect ice and rock showers, unless conditions are perfect; however, the route does not ascend beneath hanging ice. Claude E. Rusk and J. Howard Green explored the ice of this glacier, and the headwall

(which they called "Roosevelt Cliff") between it and Victory Ridge in August 1919. With some cutting they reached approximately 10,000 ft before turning back. They were the first to explore this rugged area and continue N to the Lyman Glacier on their climbing venture. First ascent by Ed Cooper and Mike Swayne, July 1961. First winter ascent by Keith Edwards and Dwain Hess, February 1973.

The approach can be made from the lower glacier slopes of the Wilson Icefall route. Ascend to the wall; pass the schrund to the left and traverse its steep upper slope back right until the chosen gully is reached. Enter the third ice-filled gully to the right. On the intial ascent there were class 4 rock pitches coated with ice; at the top of the gully reach steep névé and approach ice cliffs. There is a wide passage through them to the left, leading to the summit slopes. Take ice screws. Grade III. References: C. E. Rusk, *Tales of a Western Mountaineer; Summit,* December 1961; *Mountaineer,* 1962, pp. 98-99; *A.A.J.,* 1962, p. 205; *A.N.A.M.,* 1974.

VICTORY RIDGE: This ridge separates the headwalls of the Rusk and South Wilson glaciers, centering the steepest lava walls and ice cliffs on the eastern precipices of the mountain.

During his exhaustive explorations of "the great E side," Claude E. Rusk called it the "mighty red ridge sandwiched between it (Wilson) and the Rusk Glacier." Rusk and J. Howard Green went to the top of the second step on the ridge — over 9000 ft — where they found the sharp crest too shattered to continue. Here Rusk made a bivouac and carefully studied his proposed E-side route via The Castle, which he could carefully scan from this high vantage.

Victory Ridge is one of the most unusual routes of its standard, a route of character. The feeling of insecurity experienced gives the climb a serious air. There is likely danger from stonefall after early July, when ice cementing pumice scree in couloirs and faces starts to disappear. Approach as per other N or E side routes (see Lyman Glacier Route), or from Avalanche Valley.

First ascent July 7, 1962 by Fred Beckey and Don (Claunch) Gordon.

Because the lower portions of the ridge form a sharp spine that finally cuts off into a steep notch, the climbing route follows a segment of the South Wilson Glacier (N of the lower ridge), climbing into the upper body of the glacier by a chute between badly crevassed sections and becomes a headwall route rather than a ridge climb. After turning a major schrund on the left the initial ascent party encountered two steep ice leads; then a snow arete on the ridge, followed by a 2-hour traversing climb to the right, into the center of three ice couloirs that sweep upward. This area required stepcutting. Finally three leads to the left, traversing under an ice cliff (both ice and rock pitons used for protection here) led to a corner, where the ice slope around the cliff led toward the summit area. Grade IV. References: *Mountaineer,* 1963, pp. 88-89; *A.A.J.,* 1961, pp. 469-470; C. E. Rusk, *Tales of a Western Mountaineer;* Fred Beckey, *Challenge of the North Cascades,* pp. 218-221.

MOUNT ADAMS from northeast
WALLACE C. GUY, U.S. FOREST SERVICE

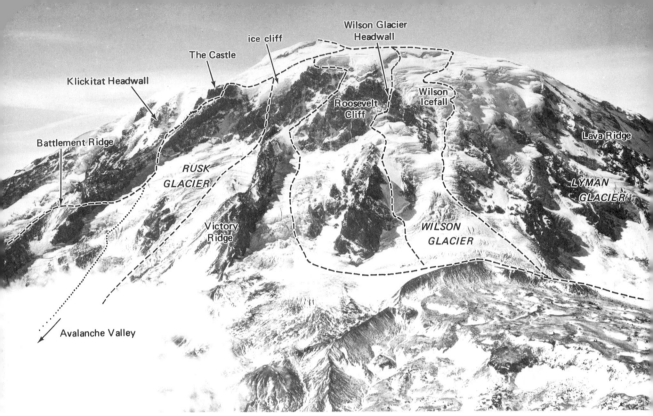

Labels on image: Klickitat Headwall, The Castle, ice cliff, Wilson Glacier Headwall, Battlement Ridge, Roosevelt Cliff, Wilson Icefall, Lava Ridge, RUSK GLACIER, LYMAN GLACIER, Victory Ridge, WILSON GLACIER, Avalanche Valley

MOUNT ADAMS from east
AUSTIN POST, UNIVERSITY OF WASHINGTON

RUSK GLACIER ICE CLIFF: This route climbs the head-wall of Rusk Glacier, an undertaking probably done with minimum risk in winter or early spring. First ascent by Richard Morse and Chet Sutterlin in February 1978. From the upper-right portion of the glacier climb a 40-degree gully of snow/ice until it is feasible to traverse left one pitch on rock to the base of the ice cliff. Climb five pitches of steep ice, then a 30-ft overhang to reach the cliff's top. Grade IV; bring ice screws and tools. Time: 21 hours round trip from Mazama Saddle. Reference: *A.A.J.*, 1979, pp. 182-183.

RUSK GLACIER, THE CASTLE ROUTE: The Castle, between the icefall of the upper Klickitat Glacier and the headwall of the Rusk Glacier, is a prominent feature of the great E face of Adams. It is undoubtedly a resistant remnant of an earlier, greater, bulk. The complexity of the face and attendant routefinding problems render any ascent route delicate. Rusk's climb, during an outing of the Cascadians in the early 1920s, was an outstanding achievement in courage. Many knowledgeable persons, including Prof. Lyman, had long regarded the ascent impossible. The party wore hob-nailed boots; two had Swiss ice axes, the others alpenstocks. The first ascent was made by Claude E. Rusk, W. E. Richardson, Clarence Starcher, Clarence Truitt, Robert E. Williams, Rolland Whitemore, and Edgar Coursen in August 1921. Four Cascadians repeated the route in 1924 and the third ascent was made by a party of three Yakima Boy

Scouts in 1933.

Approach via Mazama Glacier Saddle ◆. Descend N to the lower Mazama, then cross the Klickitat to the base of Battlement Ridge (between the Klickitat and Rusk). This rocky spine actually spurs from timberline to 11,440 ft+, culminating in The Castle. One can ascend the S edge of the Rusk Glacier to bypass some of the gendarmes on Battlement Ridge. From the end of the schrund, ascend the N slope of the ridge, then along the crest (loose and narrow). At the base of The Castle cross a sharp saddle between a minor spire and higher cliffs; then reach a narrow snow chute (on slope of a minor ridge to N) which connects to a snowfield high on the E face of The Castle. Cross almost level to the NE corner; then climb a gully-chimney on breccia (one of three broad chimneys) for about 200 ft (class 3) to the crest of The Castle; final portion also reported as steep, narrow ice chutes. Descend 75 ft on the W side to the summit icecap. Bear NW through a large crevasse field, then climb to the top. Grade II or III. Time: 10-12 hours to The Castle. References: *Mazama*, 1921, pp. 46-47; C. E. Rusk, *Tales of a Western Mountaineer*, pp. 231-265.

Approach Variation: This was the route of the original party. From Avalanche Valley (see Highline Trail and Mazama Glacier Saddle ◆) ascend the S edge of Rusk Glacier directly to the schrund and upper Battlement Ridge.

Variation: South Side of Battlement Ridge: By James

THE CASTLE and RUSK GLACIER

RUSK GLACIER

The Castle

KLICKITAT GLACIER

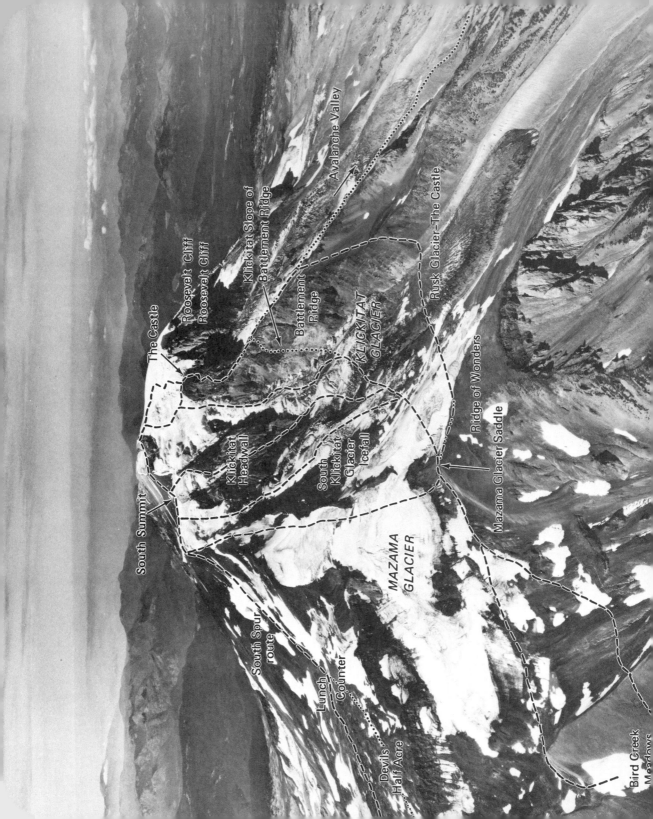

MOUNT ADAMS from southeast
AUSTIN POST, UNIVERSITY OF WASHINGTON

Mount and Everett Darr on August 18, 1934. This variation begins from the icefalls at the N edge of the Klickitat Glacier and ascends the obvious major snow gully 1000 ft to the narrow, rotten crest of Battlement Ridge. This is a direct way to reach the ridge, but the gully is moderately steep and may be subject to rockfall. (Original party angled from glacier rightward to cross the gully, then bore left again beneath the ridge crest.)

Traverse loose gendarmes along the ridge to the snow gully on the slope of The Castle. The 1934 party varied from the original finish by climbing a chimney on the SE face of The Castle; this led to a ledge over the Klickitat, then the route took a chimney a short distance right, then to the top. Time: 9 hours to top of The Castle, then 2½ hours to the summit. References: *Mazama,* 1934, pp. 29-32; *Cascadian,* 1962, pp. 38-39.

KLICKITAT GLACIER: This glacier flows directly from the icecap SE of the summit, and descends on the S side of Battlement Ridge to form the lowest ice on the mountain. The route is in a magnificent position. The climb is best

made in cool temperatures, early season. Ice screws should be taken. First ascent in June 1938 by Joe Leuthold, Russ McJury, and Wendall V. Stout.

Approach via Mazama Glacier Saddle ♦. Cross to the N side of the saddle, then traverse glacier slopes to the far N side of the Klickitat. Ascend the center of the narrow and steep upper section (watch for rockfall and avoid avalanche chutes on either side). At the top of the steep section, keep on the right side under The Castle to avoid ice cliffs; work up to the E end of the summit slopes. Variations of the route may be required due to crevasses. Grade III. Time: 7-10 hours from the saddle.

KLICKITAT HEADWALL: The steep and extensive headwall between the main and South Icefall of the Klickitat Glacier; it should be done only in proper, early season conditions. First ascent by David Beckstead and Fred Beckey on July 1, 1971.

Approach as for South Klickitat Glacier Icefall, then contour the main body of the Klickitat Glacier to just N of the lowest rock toe of the headwall. Cross the bergschrund on its right, then ascend the ice slope, keeping immediately left of a gigantic pinnacle that has a cave on its face. Ascend steep slopes directly upward; the initial party culminated the route via a minor sub-spur to the right of a final ice cliff closely beneath the false summit. Grade III. Reference: *A.A.J.,* 1972, p. 113 and pl. 61.

SOUTH KLICKITAT GLACIER ICEFALL: This narrow ice cascade pours from the false summit to the S edge of the Klickitat Glacier's main body. The relatively gentle slopes of the Mazama Glacier are across the spur to the S. First ascent by Dave Mahre, Lex Maxwell, and Ralph Uber in July 1962 (called "Mazama Glacier Icefall").

Approach as for Mazama Glacier Saddle ◆ . Cross N to the foot of the icefalls. Moderate glacier slopes lead to a steep 1500-ft icefall with cliffs breaking off to the right; some cutting may be necessary. Little variation is possible due to the narrow character of the route here. A transition zone (possible crevasse problems) is followed by a headwall, the last 500 ft of which are quite steep. Grade II or III. References: *A.A.J.,* 1963, pp. 470-471; *Mountaineer,* 1963, pp. 87-88; *Cascadian,* 1962, pp. 36-37.

MAZAMA GLACIER: This is a pleasant route, circuitous but more scenic and less populated than the South Spur.

Approach as for Mazama Glacier Saddle ◆ . Just before reaching the saddle ascend the gradient of the Mazama Glacier to the upper section. Either climb up a narrowing snow tongue to the South Summit (watch for cornices and drop-off to the right) or work left on pumice to join the South Spur route. Grade I. Time: 5 hours from high camp.

GOAT ROCKS

The picturesque Goat Rocks, an alpine mountain group N of Mount Adams, are the eroded remains of Pliocene composite cones from which the recent Tieton Andesite originated. Goat Rocks are a complex of possibly as many as four overlapping volcanos. Thick accumulations of fragmental material indicate a history of very explosive episodes. The Goat Rocks are a jumble of ragged spires resulting from violent volcanic action, followed by periods of rapid cooling. An escarpment bounds the main complex on the W, while the eastern flank is quite dissected and largely modified by glaciation. The Conrad and Meade glaciers, which flank Mount Curtis Gilbert, the highest summit, and the Tieton, Ives, and McCall glaciers (all on the E flank of the massif) give distinctive contrast to the dark craggy summits.

The meadows of the area sparkle with streams and flowers, including lupine, rock penstemon, saxifrage, aster, arnica, paintbrush, phlox, avalanche lily, marigold, and heather (volcanic soils include rich deposits of calcium, potash, and phosphorus). Mountain hemlock, white-bark pine, and subalpine fir form

attractive groves. Elk herds use the area as a summit habitat, and mountain goats are commonly seen. The highest summit was known simply as "Goat Rocks" until mid-century, and was first visited by Fred G. Plummer and A. H. Sylvester; little else is known about climbing history prior to the 1934 Mazama summer outing. In 1940 the 82,680-acre region was designated as the Goat Rocks Wilderness Area. Useful narrative is found in *Mazama,* 1934, pp. 7-21; 1956, pp. 18-23; 1961, pp. 44-46; 1972, pp. 43-47; *Mountaineer,* 1922, pp. 10-14; 1954, pp. 14-15; *Summit,* April 1960, pp. 4-5; *Cascadian,* 1961, pp. 17-20; 1962, pp. 9-10 (winter route).

Goat Rocks are generally approached via Snowgrass Trail ◆ , the Crest Trail ◆ , Packwood Lake Trail ◆ , North Fork Tieton River Trail ◆ , South Fork Tieton River Trail ◆ , or Bear Creek Mountain.

IVES PEAK   7840 ft + /2390 m +

Ives, one of the most prominent summits of the Goat Rocks area, is located between Snowgrass Flat and the North Fork Tieton River about ½ mi. SE of Old Snowy; the Ives Glacier is located on its eastern flank. References: *Mazama,* 1934, p. 16; 1956, pp. 18-21; *Mountaineer,* 1954, pp. 14-15.

ROUTES: The peak can be reached without difficulty from McCall Basin (see Old Snowy) by climbing southward on the McCall and Ives glaciers or from Snowgrass Flat on the Crest Trail ◆ . Ascend gentle alpine slopes eastward. Avoid the craggy NW ridge by an ascent of the sandy final summit slabs on the SE (easy scrambling).

OLD SNOWY   7930 ft/2417 m

This gentle peak, largely of basalt, anchors the northern end of the rugged portion of the principal Goat Rocks crest. McCall Glacier covers most of the N and E slopes. References as for Ives Peak, and *Mazama,* 1934, p. 18.

SOUTH ROUTE: From Snowgrass Flat on the Crest Trail ◆ ascend to the Ives-Old Snowy connecting ridge. Follow easy crest, with occasional traverse on W, to the summit. Time: 2 hours.

NORTH ROUTE: From Snowgrass Flat follow the Crest Trail ◆ some 2 mi. to just NW of the summit (or approach via trail from Elk Pass on N). A talus hike of several hundred ft leads quickly to the top.

EAST ROUTE: Hike to Glacier Basin (see Crest Trail ◆ or North Fork Tieton River Trail ◆). Then ascend SW to the McCall Glacier. Follow it (mostly moderate snowfields) to the summit.

TIETON PEAK   7768 ft/2368 m

This is basically a long ridge, with the high point at

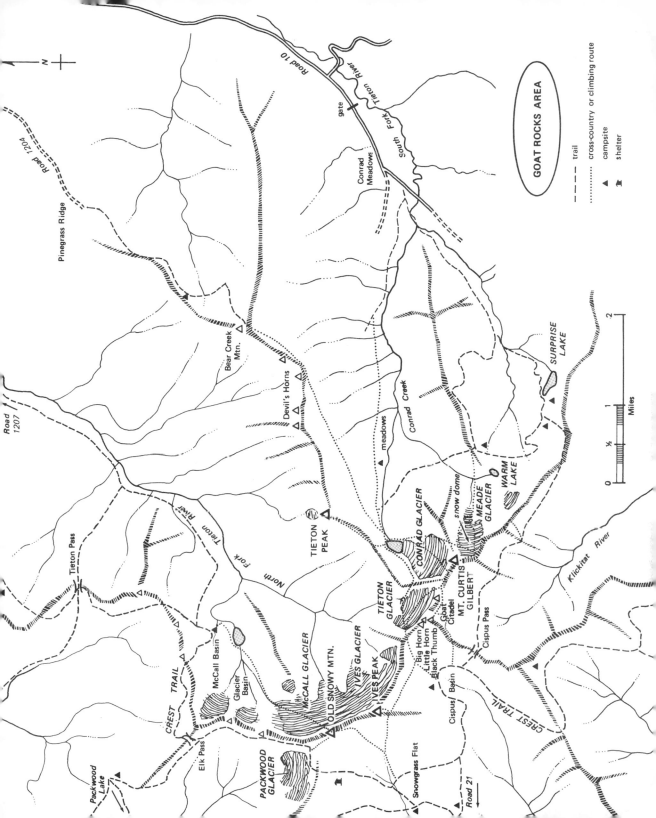

GOAT ROCKS AREA

trail
cross-country or climbing route
campsite
shelter

N

Road 10

South Fork Tieton River

gate

Conrad Meadows

Road 1204 / Pinegrass Ridge

Road 1207

Bear Creek Mtn.

Devil's Horns

Conrad Creek

SURPRISE LAKE

meadows

TIETON PEAK

CONRAD GLACIER

snow dome

WARM LAKE

MEADE GLACIER

North Fork Tieton River

Tieton Pass

Tieton River

TIETON GLACIER

MT. CURTIS GILBERT

Klickitat River

Cispus Pass

McCall Basin

McCALL GLACIER

Glacier Basin

OLD SNOWY MTN.

IVES GLACIER

IVES PEAK

Big Horn
Little Horn
Black Thumb

Goat Citadel

Cispus Basin

CREST TRAIL

Elk Pass

Packwood Lake

PACKWOOD GLACIER

Snowgrass Flat

Road 21

CREST TRAIL

Miles
0 ½ 1 2

the NW end. It is located on the North Fork-South Fork Tieton divide, at 1½ mi. NE of Mount Curtis Gilbert. References: *Mazama, 1934,* pp. 20-21; *Mountaineer,* 1954, pp. 14-15.

SOUTHWEST RIDGE: From Snowgrass Flat (see Crest Trail ◆ or Snowgrass Trail ◆) climb over Ives Peak's shoulder (about 7100 ft) and on to the Ives-Goat Rocks ridge. Drop onto the Tieton Glacier and traverse to a bare ridge leading out NE to Tieton Peak. Follow the ridge crest to the summit; some crumbly rock.

Approach Variation: From the South Fork Tieton River Trail ◆ at 1.3 mi. take Tieton Peaks Trail No. 1131 W for about 2½ mi. to a wet meadow area. Continue on paths and meadows another 3 mi. to Conrad Glacier. From its foot, ascend to long, bare ridge leading out to the peak. Do not traverse the side of the ridge, but follow its top. An approach and climb from the N or W is certainly possible, but less attractive.

MOUNT CURTIS GILBERT

8184 ft/2496 m

This, the highest point in the Goat Rocks, has also been known as "Gilbert Peak" and "Goat Rocks." It has a gentle W ridge and a short steep face falling off to the E. The highest portion of the summit is the northwestern-most point. The Conrad Glacier, ending in a small lake, lies at its northern foot. The peak has three distinct approaches: Snowgrass Flat, Cispus Pass, and Conrad Meadows.

Photographs indicate that Fred G. Plummer made the peak's ascent in 1899; he labelled a vista "Cispus Range from Goat Mountain" (Plummer, 1900). Plummer studied forests and natural features between Mount Rainier and Mount Adams. References: *Mazama,* 1934, pp. 18-20; *Mountaineer,* 1922, pp. 10-14; 1954, pp. 14-15.

GOAT ROCKS — northeast flank
U.S. GEOLOGICAL SURVEY

GOAT ROCKS — southeast flank
MARTIN JOHNSON

From Snowgrass Flat

TIETON GLACIER

Big Horn

Little Horn

Goat Citadel

CONRAD GLACIER

MT. CURTIS GILBERT

MEADE GLACIER

WEST ROUTE: From Snowgrass Flat (see Crest Trail ◆ and Snowgrass Trail ◆) hike S to Cispus Basin (1 hour) at the foot of the rock escarpment. Diagonal up and right to the ridge extended SW from the rocky mass crowned by Big Horn. Cross to the S side, descend below cliffs, and follow the slope to a broad rotten gully. Climb it for several hundred ft, then veer right between the lower cliff line and upper cliffs, crossing a series of small ridges and gullies. Pass the 8000 ft + rock formation termed "Goat Citadel" on the S. Descend a short snow slope and loose rock at the final summit ridge (at head of Conrad Glacier). Hike the broad sandy ridge to a pinnacle; skirt it on the S, then scramble 75 ft to the summit.

Variation: Southwest Side: An old trail from Cispus Pass running E on S-facing Klickitat slope to the E crosses the ridge to the Surprise Lake drainage at 6600 ft. From here hike NW about 2½ mi. (or take a short-cut en route but if so, keep right [S] of some western cliffs when approaching the ridge). Higher up, keep alongside the ridge by the Meade Glacier until level with the top of the ice. Then keep just left of the crest, as cliffs exist on the right above the ice, and the ridge itself is rocky. Meet the main route on the upper SW slope.

NORTH ROUTE: The approach can be made via one of several routes from Conrad Meadows (South Fork Tieton River Trail ◆) or from Bear Creek Mountain ◆. Another approach is the Tieton Peaks Trail (see Tieton Peak, Approach Variation). The old trail which extends from Goat Rocks Trail around the basin to the NW and N to enter the creek branch leading to the base of the Conrad Glacier (5 hours from Surprise Lake) offers another approach. Many camp spots en route, including the high basin under the Conrad.

The final climb is made directly up the glacier, then through a break in the lower cliff band via a snow finger. Bear up and right on snow continuing to a sandy col W of the highest point; then follow the crest E to the summit. Scrambling at top.

Note: the cliff band could be climbed either left or right of the snow finger, but moats and exposed rock could be a problem in late summer.

Variation: Tieton Glacier: One could ascend the broad, easy glacier chute at the head of the Tieton Glacier to the large sandy saddle on the ridge crest between Goat Citadel and Curtis Gilbert (possible icy slopes and crevasses in late season). The approach to the Tieton Glacier is rather pointless unless one is already in the drainage or if planning a traverse from Ives Peak. A possible approach is from Snowgrass Flat (see Tieton Peak, Southwest Ridge).

MEADE GLACIER: From Surprise Lake (South Fork Tieton River Trail ◆) take the trail to the high-point on its loop at ridge (5950 ft). The route is now nearly due W, across open country. Proceed up about 200 ft nearly over a knoll; then dip into a vale, bearing SW toward Warm Lake (may be snow in early season). Proceed toward a point slightly S of the mountain, gaining height to between two large mounds,

onto the foot of the Meade (6350 ft). Make a long traverse up left side of glacier; bear 240 degrees magnetic until glacier is crossed at 7500-ft level (some open crevasses). From small rock outcrop route continues up steep snowfields in a WNW direction to the rocky area SW of the summit. Boulder scrambling, scree, and a snowfield lead to the summit ridge. Time: 4½ hours.

Variation (1): From the base of the Meade, keep to the right of the glacier and small clifflike rock outcroppings (keep right of snowdome on glacier); this alternative offers good descent glissading.

Variation (2): From North Side Route on Conrad Glacier, ascend its E side to the saddle E of the summit, then make a southward crossing of the Meade to the S side of the mountain.

BIG HORN   7960 ft + /2426 m +

This is the largest of the "horn" rock formations leading W from Mount Curtis Gilbert. It has a precipitous face above Tieton Glacier on the N. As seen from Cispus Basin, the cliffs of the "horns" are impressive. Ascents can be combined with that of Curtis Gilbert by a high traverse under the summit of "Goat Citadel."

Approach as for Mount Curtis Gilbert — West Side. Ascend the broad gully cited to a small rocky basin (on S side of Little Horn and E of Big Horn) below the summits. Ascend a gully and chimney system on the S face (many ledges, class 3). The final summit pitch is a difficult 10-ft vertical crack. Class 4.

LITTLE HORN   est. 7750 ft/2362 m

Little Horn is located E of Big Horn, on the main crest. Approach as for Big Horn; from the small rocky basin, then to notch on the ridge E of Little Horn which overlooks Tieton Glacier. Traverse base of pinnacle on S across snowfield, taking a slot upward to the W notch. Ascend by traversing ledges easterly across the S face to a chimney leading directly to the summit. There is 200 ft of rock climbing, extending to class 4.

BLACK THUMB   est. 7750 ft/2362 m

The prominent black spire located just S of Big Horn on the S side of the main crest. Approach as for Big Horn. From the small basin ascend W to a notch separating Black Thumb from Big Horn. Scramble, then climb a 60-ft crack (fairly difficult, 3-8 inches wide) leads to a belay platform ridge just N of the summit. Class 4 (used two chocks for safety).

HAWKEYE POINT   7431 ft/2316 m

From Snowgrass Flat or the Crest Trail ◆ take Lily

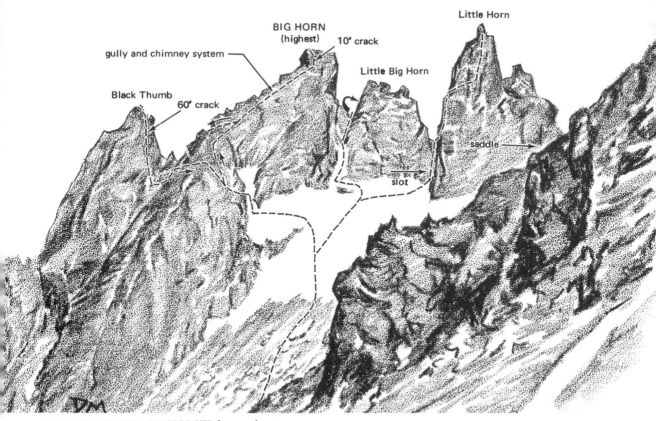

BIG HORN GROUP, GOAT ROCKS from southeast

Basin Trail for 2½ mi. N to 6400 ft + Goat Lake. Scramble grassy slopes W to the summit, or follow the trail W to a summit path ascending from the SW. This is a fine viewpoint to study the region and spot goats.

The approach can also be made by following Goat Ridge Trail No. 95 directly from Berry Patch for 4½ mi. to its junction with Lily Basin Trail at about 6800 ft, then taking the summit path.

JOHNSON PEAK   7487 ft/2282 m

While not as high as the Goat Rocks crest, Johnson Peak, located 3 mi. NW of Old Snowy, is prominent because of the lower flanking drainage valleys. The eastern flank of the peak falls steeply into Lake Creek. Goats often frequent the area.

ROUTES: From Snowgrass Flat (Crest Trail ◆ or Snowgrass Trail ◆) take Lily Basin Trail No. 86 about 5.3 mi. to S side of the peak closely above Heart Lake (est. 6200 ft). Ascend due N; no difficulties.

The ascent would be easy, also, from the NW; one could leave the trail beyond Packwood Lake (see Packwood Lake Trail ◆). Ascend uphill, and bear to the W side near the summit.

THE TALON   est. 4000 ft/1219 m

The Talon is a 90-ft rock sliver on the canyon wall directly opposite U.S. Hwy No. 12 ◆ at about 5 mi. E of White Pass (on N slope of Round Mountain). It is structured of basalt with a weathered base. First ascent by Dave Mahre, Fred Dunham, and Jim Wickwire, September 1961.

ROUTE: Approach via Clear Lake (Tieton Road ◆), then W for about 2½ mi. The Talon is the tallest of several spires grouped about 900 ft above the road. Ascend a large talus slope to its base, then work up along its E side to the S hillside notch. Start here, climb 15 ft to a rotten ledge; traverse right on it to a more solid one 10 ft higher, which leads to a belay spot on the SE corner (some loose rock on this lower portion). Climb 15 ft to twin horizontal cracks bearing right across a face to a small pine on a ledge. From the tree climb 15 ft on a diagonal traversing crack to the N rib, then

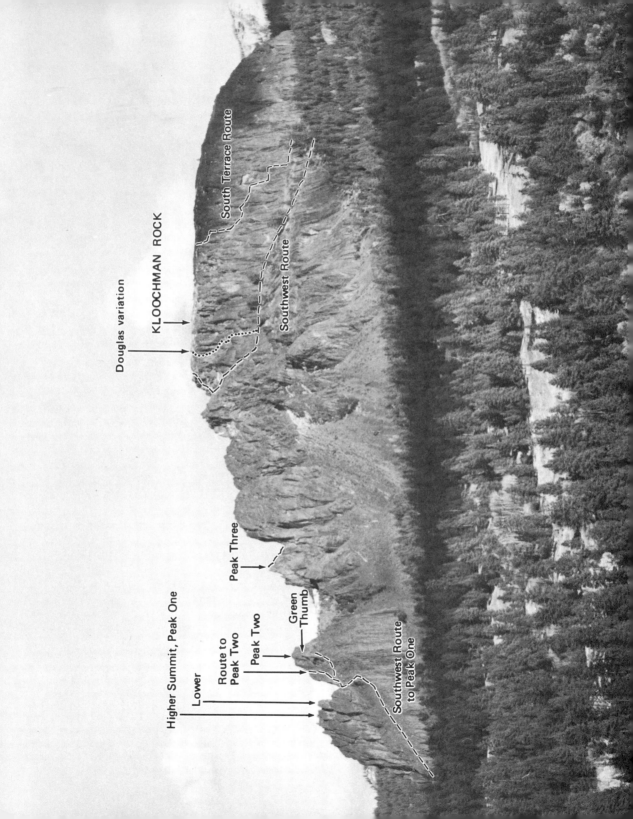

Higher Summit, Peak One

Lower

Route to Peak Two

Peak Two

Green Thumb

Peak Three

Southwest Route to Peak One

Douglas variation

KLOOCHMAN ROCK

South Terrace Route

Southwest Route

up slabs (unprotected) to the summit. Bolts in place for rappel at S summit corner. Class 5.7. References: *Mountaineer,* 1962, pp. 102-103; *Cascadian,* 1951, p. 56; 1964, p. 55; 1967, p. 62; *A.A.J.,* 1962, p. 208.

Variation (East Face, first pitch): By Don and King McPherson, September 1964. Begin at indentation in middle of wall (loose rock) and then traverse upward toward the N side, to a sloping ledge, then work toward middle of E side. Later move almost horizontally toward the S side to where rock overhangs. Place piton under overhang and here one can stretch to touch the small ledge above (hard move, solid). When on ledge continue up to end, and up a large vertical crack which continues to SE corner belay spot. Class 5.

KLOOCHMAN ROCK   4532 ft/1381 m

Kloochman is a NW—SE-trending oval-shaped rock mass lying 2 mi. E of the E end of Rimrock Lake. The highest elevation is in the center of the main mass, which is nearly level for ½ mi. The NW end of the Rock consists of three distinct, rugged lower peaks numbered One, Two, and Three (from the NW). The entire formation extends some ¾ mi. Rock is of volcanic origin, very friable and often treacherous. The name Kloochman comes from the Chinook jargon, meaning "wife." The Indian legends depict Kloochman Rock as a woman turned to stone by Coyote (the medicine man). The Yakima chief known as Meow-wah became Goose Egg Mountain.

The best approach to the formation is take Lost Lake Road No. 1402 off Tieton Road ♦, leaving Hwy No. 12 just W of White Pass Work Center. After passing Lost Lake watch for an unmarked woodcutter road (right) which approaches the SE end of Kloochman Rock. Park and walk around the N end of the rock, keeping in close to end on the sloping ramp that bears to the summit.

From near the SE end of the rock there is a well-traveled game trail that leads along the S face. References: *Mountaineer,* 1952, p. 82; A. J. Splawn, *Ka-Mi-Akin: The Last Hero of the Yakimas,* pp. 428-430; William O. Douglas, *Of Men and Mountains,* pp. 314-329.

SOUTHWEST ROUTE: Follow a rising timbered ramp starting near the SW end of the Rock, for ½ mi. northwesterly to a scree gully; it leads to the high saddle W of the summit; easy ascent from here. Class 3.

Variation: First climbed about 1915 by William O. Douglas and Douglas Corpron; the climb is described with the overstatement of an impressionable youth in *Of Men and Mountains.* Leave the timbered ramp at the last tree group before the scree gully and join the above route between the saddle and summit.

SOUTH TERRACE ROUTE: First ascent by Lex Maxwell, Louis Ulrich, and Rolla Goold in 1961.

Begin about 200 ft SE of the Southwest Route, then scramble upwards westerly from terrace to terrace. A steep 100-ft chimney leads to open face on left. Traverse slabs to a second terrace, then traverse W past a chimney system and gully bearing to the summit. Class 4. Reference: *Mountaineer,* 1962, p 105.

RUMBLE GULLY: First ascent by Lex Maxwell, Joe Gleason, and Louis Ulrich, 1933.

This narrow gully begins just below and N of Deception Chimney's route start. It leads to the high saddle below the main summit to join the Southwest Route. Class 3.

DECEPTION CHIMNEY: First ascent by Lex Maxwell, Joe Gleason, and Louis Ulrich, 1933.

Start from scree slopes N of Staircase Route. Large open gully leads steeply to a face from which three chimneys seem to reach the summit. Take center chimney 40 ft to a chockstone; above, take lesser chimney to right and traverse long exposed ledge right to notch in a small arete from where steep insecure slabs lead to the summit. Class 4.

STAIRCASE ROUTE: First ascent by Dick Oswin in 1929.

From large high scree slope at midpoint of the NE side of the Rock, a short chimney leads to easier rock bearing right to the summit. Class 3.

PEAK ONE   3800 ft+/1158 m+

This northwestern summit has two small pinnacles of almost equal height, not readily seen from below. Each may be approached by separate climbing routes. Reference: *A.N.A.M.,* 1978, pp. 36-37.

NORTHWEST FACE: First ascent by Jim Kurtz and Tom Pinkerton, 1950; the summit was reached again in 1951 by Pete Schoening and Jim Henry, who did not know of the earlier climb.

The route is plainly visible from the road. Ascend scree slopes and steep slabs leading to deep vertical chimney in the "near" face. Several pitches of vigorous stemming lead off a left-traverse up steep slabs. Then a 50-ft crack gives access to a broad N shoulder. Scramble over easy rock to the 25-ft summit pinnacle. Class 4.

Variation: Northeast Gully: Start from scree on E side of the peak, and ascend the deep gully between Peaks One and Two. Take first chimney to right. Several leads to the N shoulder, where join main route below summit pinnacle. Class 4.

SOUTHWEST ROUTE: Approach as in Northwest Face route, except ascend scree slopes southeasterly to post pile rocks (above scree to first tree). Diagonally ascend this rock staircase SW to a deep notch between Peaks One and Two. Route goes N up steep, open chimney (poor rock) about 50 ft, then traverses E about 80 ft on broad ledges to vertical chimney; then 40 ft to the notch between the twin pinnacles. Ascend higher pinnacle by ledge traversing up and N to a 10-ft crack; from upper end the top can be seen and climbed. Class 4.

KLOOCHMAN ROCK — southwest flank
LEX MAXWELL

KLOOCHMAN ROCK — *east flank*
LEX MAXWELL

To climb the lesser pinnacle, climb as above, except take the steep chimney from the notch left to lesser pinnacle. Class 4.

PEAK TWO   3920 ft+/1195 m+
First ascent by Wesley Grande and Dick Widrig, 1951.

From the deep notch between Peaks One and Two (see Peak One, Southwest Route), climb the S side of the ridge, cross gully on left, cross over arete to descend 30 ft on N side slabs to chimney; it leads 60 ft to N shoulder of peak for a short scramble to summit. Class 4.

Green Thumb is a prominent tower, decorated with green lichen, seen high on the S face of Peak Two. Approach as for Peak Two; from the deep notch traverse to climb it on the S side. Class 3.

PEAK THREE   4040 ft+/1231 m+
This peak has three fingerlike spires at its crest, sometimes referred to as "Kloochman Fingers." First ascent of highest (S) finger by Dwight Baker, Fred Beckey, Richard Berge, Jim Henry, and Pete Schoening on

July 29, 1951. The route ascends via the moderately difficult couloir on the E side to near the Kloochman Rock notch. The subsequent E slope and ridge is easy to the summit tower, then use caution. Class 4 — friable rock.

GOOSE EGG MOUNTAIN
4566 ft/1392 m

Located about ¾ mi. to the NW of Kloochman Rock, composed of two prominent basalt rock masses, a denuded intrusive plug of andesite. It has an interesting accumulation of moraine till plastered against the W flank. The W peak is higher; the E peak is 4470 ft. The N area is a timbered ridge, which provides a hike-up.

SOUTHEAST FACE: First ascent by Lex Maxwell and Bob Kershaw, about 1955.

The climb begins within 200 yards of Tieton Road ◆, at the top of an area above a rock-crushing site at the foot of the wall. Start in a broken area of the wall and continue upface in a series of steps and chimneys. Class 4.

SECTION II

Southern Cascades

WHITE PASS TO STAMPEDE PASS

GEOGRAPHY

This portion of the southern Cascades of Washington is so dominated by the massive hulk of Mount Rainier that the coverage in this section largely concerns the volcano. Many lesser peaks and subranges lie within Mount Rainier's shadow, such as the Tatoosh Range, the Mother Mountains, and the Cowlitz Chimneys, but the only peak of significant altitude is sharp-pointed Little Tahoma on the east flank, a remnant of an earlier form of Mount Rainier.

The Cascade Crest, lying east of Mount Rainier, has a few outstanding summits, Mount Aix and Bismarck Peak being the highest of these, but it generally lacks rugged alpine topography. The geology south of Snoqualmie and Stampede passes does not sustain the type of peaks and alpine landscape we associate with the North Cascades. Elevations north of Chinook Pass soon decline toward Naches and Stampede passes, and most of the region here is below timber-line, the Crest assuming largely a logged "foothill" character.

Much of the Crest is heavily forested or glaciated upland underlain by andesite. The broad, relatively flat area on the Crest between White Pass and Twin Sister Lakes contained a small ice sheet. Its former presence is indicated by extensive polished bedrock, numerous small rock-rimmed lakes, and hundreds of ponds and swamps.

The range south of Stampede Pass consists largely of middle Tertiary volcanic rocks. Andesitic and basaltic lava, tuff, and breccia with less voluminous rhyolitic volcanic rocks are the predominant types. These rocks experienced several episodes of mild deformation prior to the outpouring of the Miocene Yakima Basalt which overlaps them unconformably on the east flank of the range.

At least 80 percent of the areas above 5000 ft and below the timberline may be classed as mountain meadows, watered by streams and lakes. The meadows, often called parks, have their greatest floral development near the 5500-ft level. This is also the area of lush herbaceous communities, with the heather-huckleberry community located at a slightly lower altitude. A massive invasion of the meadow areas by tree species has taken place in the last half-century in this region, as well as elsewhere in the range.

The alpine landscape in this portion of the Cascades has a truly unique character. High lakes are plentiful, especially between White and Chinook passes, adding charm to the meadowlands, and Bumping Lake (Tanum to the Indians) adds variety to the scenery. Bumping, Clear Creek, and Tieton (Rimrock) reservoirs are used for water storage, with retaining dams built by the U.S. Bureau of Reclamation.

On the east side of the main crest there are mountain spurs with open stands of ponderosa pine 50 to 75 mi. in length, extending from the foothills to divide the desert valleys. Landforms vary from the steep, rocky canyons of the Rattlesnake to the relatively thick tree-covered slopes of the Little Naches drainage. The principal east-side river drainages are the Yakima, Naches, and Tieton; on the west slope they are the Cowlitz, Nisqually, Puyallup, Carbon, White, and Green.

The rugged region surrounding Mount Rainier is well-dissected by deep stream valleys radiating from the central peak. The streams have often cut canyons into the coniferous forest zone. Such fast-flowing rivers as the White, Carbon, and North Mowich have cut through andesite flows and deeply into underlying rocks.

In the valleys near Mount Rainier and elsewhere west of the divide, there are thick evergreen forests. Typically, dense stands of Douglas fir (*Pseudotsuga menziesii*), western hemlock (*Tsuga heterophylla*), and western red cedar (*Thuja plicata*) predominate below 4000 ft. Between 3000 and 5000 ft western hemlock (*Tsuga heterophylla*), Pacific silver fir (*Abies amabilis*), noble fir (*Abies procera*), western white pine (*Pinus monticola*), and Engelmann spruce (*Picea engelmanii*) are the predominant trees. Tree groups are picturesque aspects of the subalpine parklands. Here mountain hemlock (*Tsuga mertensiana*), subalpine fir (*Abies lasiocarpa*), and Alaska cedar (*Chamaecyparis nuthana*) are common, typically occurring on slight ridges; whitebark pine *(Pinus albicaulis)* grows to 7000 ft east of the main divide, and stunted trees may grow to 7700 ft in favorable locations. In this high region the white-tailed ptarmigan makes its habitat. Mountain goats frequent some high ridges; they are often seen near Panhandle Gap. Elk, which man has successfully reintroduced into the Cascades, are overgrazing parts of Mount Rainier National Park.

GEOLOGY

The southern Cascades in Washington are underlain by a thick and diverse volcanic strata which can be separated into a Western Cascade Group, ranging from 5000 to 8500 m in thickness (50 to 5 m. y. in age), and an unconformably overlying High Cascade Group, up to 1 km thick. These volcanic rocks are locally intensely fractured and faulted.

The rocks of the Western Cascade Group crop out in two structural blocks, separated by the west-northwest trending White River fault. The sequence of volcanic rocks that crop out south of the fault are equivalent and continuous with rocks around Mount Rainier. The eruption of this sequence appears to have begun about 35 m. y. ago and ended about 20 m. y. ago (Frizzell, 1984). The distribution of lava flows indicates that most eruptive centers were located along the western flank of the range.

Tertiary rocks of the Western Cascade Group are divided into the Ohanapecosh Formation and the overlying Fifes Peak Formation and Stevens Ridge rocks. The oldest unit, the Ohanapecosh, consists mostly of colorful well-bedded andesite tuff and breccia, and volcanic sedimentary rock, alternating with massive tuff-breccia and subordinate volcanic flows; the formation is 900 to 5000 m in thickness. Rocks of this formation can be seen in the Chinook Pass area and near Panhandle Gap, above the Cowlitz River valley, and west of Mount St. Helens. From a hiking vantage one can see the lava flows of this formation dipping gently westward above the Sarvant Glaciers. The prominent planar surface of Banshee Peak near Panhandle Gap was formed by the erosion of the Ohanapecosh clastic rocks lying above the thick sequence of lava flows.

North of the White River fault the volcanic rocks of Huckleberry Mountain appear to correlate with the Ohanapecosh Formation south of the fault (Frizzell, 1984).

· The Stevens Ridge Formation, deposited in canyons

cut into the Ohanapecosh Formation, is composed of widely distributed pyroclastic flows and interbedded tuff and breccia. The Stevens Ridge rocks are exposed along the crest of the range north and east of Mount Rainier and also along the Tatoosh Range.

The Fifes Peak Formation generally overlies the Stevens Ridge rocks, but is in part contemporaneous with them. The Fifes Peak rocks consist of andesite and basalt flows, breccias, and pyroclastic rocks. The lava flows of the Fifes Peak Formation form cliffs of Fifes Peak and are also located north of Mount Rainier, at Sluiskin Peak, and on Unicorn Peak. Here the nearly flat strata of flows and alternating volcanic sedimentary rocks lie in the broad trough of the Unicorn Peak syncline. At Naches Pass the White River fault separates the Ohanapecosh Formation on the north from the Fifes Peak Formation on the south.

Overlying the Fifes Peak Formation along the lower Little Naches River is the Yakima Basalt, a member of the Columbia River Basalt Group. This flood basalt is also conspicuous along the Naches, Yakima, and Tieton River valleys.

The east slope of the southern Cascades in Washington is mantled by the Yakima Basalt and locally by the overlying volcaniclastics of the Ellensburg Formation. The generally smooth rise of the eastern flank of the range reflects the gentle dip of these units away from the crest of the Cascade arch.

The Yakima Basalt consists of up to 100 flows, many covering an extensive area, and each ranging in thickness from approximately 50 to several hundred ft.

The interbedded sedimentary and volcanic rocks of the Naches Formation (Oligocene age) extend widely east of the Cascade divide, and are prominent in the watershed of Little Naches River, where the formation is up to 2400 m thick. To the north of this drainage, the volcanic rocks become increasingly interstratified with sedimentary rocks.

The Ellensburg Formation (Miocene age) consists of sedimentary rocks extensively interbedded with Yakima basalts. It is largely composed of huge fans of pyroclastic debris and coarse mudflows; much of the debris was brought in by the ancestral Yakima River. The formation is generally poorly exposed because of extensive landsliding and vegetation, but can be seen in and southwest of the Kittitas Valley.

The Manastash Block consists of strongly deformed volcanics and sandstones of lower Tertiary Age, and some older rocks in the fault zone. The rocks are tightly folded and faulted along structures that help define the intersection of the Straight Creek fault with

MOUNT RAINIER from northwest and Spray Park
ED COOPER

the major northwest-trending Cle Elum lineament. Along Taneum Creek the Manastash Formation is overlain by volcanic rocks called the Taneum Andesite (once known as the Keechelus Formation).

The Easton Schist (pre-Tertiary and the oldest rock in the region) is a low-grade metamorphic suite probably derived from marine basalts and sediments. In this section the suite is located south of Cle Elum.

During Miocene time, there were extensive outpourings of andesites of the Fifes Peak Formation in this section. Several plugs, probably the source of andesite flows, cluster in the headwaters of Little Naches River and the upper Green River: these plugs are exposed in Pyramid Peak, Kelly Butte, and Rooster Comb. Clear West Peak, a plug dome, stands west of the White River. A large radial dike system occurs at Tieton volcano, northeast of Rimrock Lake.

The High Cascade Group, consisting predominantly of basalts and andesites which have erupted from cinder cones and shield volcanos, is located largely south of this section. Rocks of this group are extensive between White Pass and Bumping Lake.

The principal Quaternary unit in this section is the andesite of Mount Rainier. Many surficial deposits, largely mudflows of volcanic derivation, glacial drift, and landslides occurred in the region. The Electron Mudflow, which descended the Puyallup River about 600 years before present, and the Osceola Mudflow (dated 5700 years B. P.), and the even older Greenwater lahar occurred in the White River valley, all left extensive deposits.

Rocks of the Ohanapecosh, Stevens Ridge, and Fifes Peak formations were intruded by the Tatoosh pluton, Carbon River stock, White River pluton, and Bumping Lake pluton between 14 and 17 m. y. ago. The intrusions may be the high-level expression of a continuous Miocene batholith below the surface (Frizzell, 1984).

The intrusive rocks of the Mount Rainier area underwent a complex history of magmatic rise, and as a result are extremely varied and altered in texture and mineral composition. Intrusive rocks include granodiorites, quartz monzonites, and various diorites. During Miocene time the Tatoosh pluton was emplaced in the volcanic rocks at shallow depths over a broad area. The Tatoosh is a roughly oval mass extending beneath Mount Rainier from the Tatoosh Range to Vernal Park. North of the Tatoosh Range the granitic rocks are covered by lavas of Mount Rainier, but reappear along the northern base of the mountain and in outcrops along the east and west flanks of the volcano. The contact of the mass curves across the Tatoosh Range and cuts discordantly through the gently folded and faulted Ohanapecosh and Stevens Ridge rocks. The Tatoosh pluton is bordered by complex swarms of sills and dikes, which are similar in composition to the core rocks but even more varied in texture.

Magma of the Tatoosh pluton broke the surface at some places to cause large-scale volcanic activity: visible manifestations are plugs and welded tuffs. The Palisades Plug is such a remnant; locally here the pluton breached the surface with explosive violence.

Uplift of the range since Pliocene time along a north-south axis was superimposed on an ancient diverging fold-fault pattern, consisting of a northwest structural trend characteristic of the Cordillera. There has possibly been as much as 1.5 km of uplift since middle Miocene time. This uplift continued to about 5 m. y. ago, and appears to have ceased or diminished by 1 m. y. ago.

Strata of the Western Cascade Group are gently to moderately folded, whereas strata of the High Cascade Group are generally flat-lying or gently inclined away from volcanic centers. Deformation by regional folding developed in the Ohanapecosh Formation before deposition of the Stevens Ridge-Fifes Peaks Formations between middle Oligocene and early Miocene time. Renewed folding along the same northwest-trending axes then deformed the Stevens and Fifes Peak rocks.

A structural block of pre-Tertiary metavolcanic rocks between White Pass and Rimrock Lake (Russell Ridge) and the block between the Naches and Yakima rivers (Manastash Ridge) were uplifted in Miocene and Pliocene time.

References: Paul E. Hammond, "Reconnaissance geologic map and cross sections of southern Washington Cascade Range." Portland State University, 1980; Virgil A. Frizzell, Jr., et al., "Preliminary Geologic Map of the Snoqualmie Pass 1:100,000 Quadrangle, Washington. U.S. Geol. Survey Open-File Map QF 84-693 (1984).

HISTORY

For centuries before the arrival of fur traders and settlers, a route across Naches Pass was known to the Indians from both the Columbia Plateau and Puget Sound. This and other Cascade trail routes served as access to neighboring native groups for purposes of trade, as well as hunting, fishing, and berry picking.

As Hudson's Bay Company posts increased in size

early in the 19th century, fur traders traveled between them and ventured into Cascade valleys. Both a fur trader and missionary are purported to have explored Naches Pass in 1839, and about this time Owhi, leader of an Indian band from the Yakima Valley, drove cattle eastward from Fort Nisqually through the pass. It became common practice for the Indians east of the Cascades to drive horses through Naches Pass, returning along the same route with cattle.

In 1841 Lt. Charles Wilkes of the U.S. Navy voyaged into Puget Sound with a squadron of vessels, and while making his headquarters at Nisqually House, sent Lt. Robert E. Johnson in command of a party to cross the Cascade Range. Between May 19 and July 15, Johnson headed the party (with Indians and horses) to round the northern flank of Mount Rainier and to cross Naches Pass. Since Johnson employed two trapper guides, it can be inferred that Company men had previously crossed the pass. Some of the group ascended a peak near the junction of the White and Greenwater rivers that Johnson called "Le Tete." Johnson's was the first crossing of the range by an exploring expedition.

Several years after the United States acquired the Cascade region by the Oregon Treaty of 1846, there was an unsuccessful effort by settlers to establish a wagon road through Naches Pass. Congress recognized the importance of this route for the purpose of attracting immigration and as a military contingency. Accordingly, early in 1853, $20,000 was appropriated for the construction of a military road through Naches Pass. The Secretary of War selected Captain George B. McClellan to survey and locate the road, then arrange for its construction. McClellan was not enthusiastic about his mission after reaching the pass on August 25, but sent Lt. Henry C. Hodges across with packhorses, packers, and soldiers to obtain supplies at Fort Steilacoom. In *Reports of the Pacific Railroad Survey* McClellan commented on a belt of jagged rock cones above the snow line and described Mount Rainier as "Exceedingly massive" (Reports, p. 192; see note 52). McClellan's maps placed Mount Rainier about 15 minutes longitude east of its correct location (near that of Naches Pass), a location that was shown on the Pacific Railroad maps of Oregon. The journal of contemporary geologist and ethnologist George Gibbs mentions his surprise at discovering the mountain well west of the pass during his crossing.

When by July 1853 neither the road nor funds had materialized, settlers and businessmen in Olympia dispatched two work parties. Edward J. Allen led a road building party up the Puyallup, White, and Greenwater rivers to a point east of the summit. Meanwhile in September a wagon train party consisting of Oregon Trail immigrants led by James Longmire, reached the pass after crossing the Naches River 68 times during an exhausting struggle. Descending, the footsore pioneers had to lower each wagon with ropes. Horses, oxen, and cattle were led down a narrow, twisting defile to the Greenwater River.[31]

In the following year, 1854, Lt. Richard Arnold was given the responsibility of building the military road. He explored Allen's route and undertook minor improvements, but was not impressed with its practicability; Arnold recommended a route farther north because surveys and sentiments favored Snoqualmie Pass.[32] That year was the last recorded immigrant use of the Naches Pass road.

The movement of pioneers through Naches Pass was curtailed by the Indian hostilities of 1855-56. However, military and volunteer troops made use of the pass on several occasions. In 1856 Col. B. F. Shaw's volunteers marched (175 mounted soldiers and 107 pack animals) through the pass on an expedition to the interior. After the defeat, Chief Leschi of the Puyallup Indians retreated through the pass under hardship conditions. With the conclusion of the hostilities, enterprising cattlemen established herds in the Klickitat, Yakima, and Kittitas valleys. Naches Pass became a regular route for cattle drives to the communities along Puget Sound. The stockmen maintained and improved the road, using it for cattle and sheep into the 1880s.

Other areas were studied for road surveys, including a route over Cowlitz (Carlton) Pass in 1861-62. In summer of 1867 Northern Pacific Railroad surveyors under J. S. Hurd and W. H. Carlton were dispatched by General James Tilton to explore Cowlitz and Snoqualmie passes, and the area between.

The party followed the Nisqually River, crossed the divide to the Cowlitz River at Bear Prairie, then followed the Cowlitz and Summit Creek to Cowlitz Pass. The survey continued down the Bumping branch of the Naches and along the valley to the Yakima River. A letter by R. M. Walker indicates that the party cut their way through the "nearly impenetrable forests of the mountains, have climbed the loftiest peaks of the range for observations, have run a spirit level and compass line of about 70 miles . . ." The letter stated "The Sno-qual-a-mie has been found to be impracticable without a heavy tunnel" (Northern Pacific

Railroad records, Minnesota Historical Society). Field parties studied passes as far north as the Wenatchee River, and in 1873 the Northern Pacific directors made a decision to end the railroad on Commencement Bay.[33]

Surveys continued, and in March 1878 a party led by D. D. Clarke, with James Longmire as guide, followed the earlier route across Cowlitz Pass, finding seven feet of snow there. Indian trails often provided access routes in valleys, but did not always cross the lowest passes. In railroad correspondence, Engineer-in-Chief Edwin F. Johnson noted these trails often crossed summits 800 to 1200 ft higher to avoid timber and obstructions.

In the season of 1880, surveyors traversed the range from Mount Adams to beyond Naches Pass to study grades and winter snow depth; J. R. Maxwell's surveys indicated that Green River Pass would be less costly than Naches or Snoqualmie, and was chosen for the line. It became known as "Stampede" because during construction a "work faster" order conflicted with the men's idea of pace, so they "stampeded out" of the area. A train finally crossed the pass via switchbacks in July 1887, and less than a year later a tunnel was completed.

Eventually the popularization of the Columbia River as a steamboat route, and railroad construction through other Cascade passes, resulted in the decline of Naches Pass as a transportation route. The old wagon road fell into disrepair until early in the 20th century, when the region became part of the national forest system. Jeep usage of the Naches Trail was initiated after World War II. Such use and logging of adjacent lands resulted in a growing deterioration of the original road tread until the 1970s, when various groups undertook to rehabilitate the historic trail. Between the last ford of the Little Naches River and Government Meadow, just west of the pass, some of the tread and remnant features of the pioneer trail exist today in a semblance of the original environment.

LAND MANAGEMENT

Park Ranger Stations:

>Mount Rainier National Park
>Nisqually Entrance, Longmire, Paradise, Ohanapecosh, White River (May to November), Carbon River (May to November), Sunrise (July to October), Mowich Lake (July 4 to Labor Day)

Park Visitor Centers:

>Longmire, Paradise, Sunrise, Ohanapecosh

Park Headquarters:

>Ashford, WA 98304
>(206) 569-2211
>(same number for ranger stations)

National Forest Ranger Stations:

>Gifford Pinchot National Forest
>Packwood, WA 98361
>(206) 494-5515

>Mt. Baker-Snoqualmie National Forest
>Enumclaw, WA 98022
>(206) 825-2571

>Wenatchee National Forest
>Naches, WA 98937
>(509) 653-2205
>Cle Elum, WA 98922
>(509) 674-4411

Campgrounds

There are campgrounds along all Mount Rainier National Park road entries. Entrance stations, Ranger Stations, and Visitor Centers provide all locations and other information. Campgrounds are located on access roads throughout Gifford Pinchot, Wenatchee, and Mount Baker-Snoqualmie National Forests. These are noted on Forest Service maps and are signed along roadways.

MAPS

Topographic (U.S. Geological Survey)

Chinook Pass (1971)	1:24,000
Golden Lakes (1971)	1:24,000
Mt. Rainier East (1971)	1:24,000
Mt. Rainier West (1971)	1:24,000
Mowich Lake (1971)	1:24,000
Mt. Wow (1971)	1:24,000
Old Scab Mountain (1971)	1:24,000
Rimrock Lake (1967)	1:24,000
Sunrise (1971)	1:24,000
Tieton Basin (1967)	1:24,000
Timberwolf Mountain (1971)	1:24,000
White River Park (1971)	1:24,000
Mt. Rainier National Park (1971)	1:50,000
Bumping Lake (1962)	1:62,500
Cle Elum (1958)	1:62,500
Easton (1961)	1:62,500
Enumclaw (1956)	1:62,500
Greenwater (1956)	1:62,500
Lester (1962)	1:62,500

Packwood (1962)   1:62,500
Randle (1962)   1:62,500
White Pass (1962)   1:62,500

U.S. Forest Service

Gifford Pinchot National Forest Map
Wenatchee National Forest Map
Mt. Baker-Snoqualmie National Forest Map

MOUNT RAINIER
14,410 ft/4392 m

After Captain George Vancouver sailed through the Strait of Juan de Fuca in the sloop *Discovery,* he saw Mount Rainier from his yawl when near Marrowstone Point May 7, 1792 and named "the round snowy mountain" after his friend Rear Admiral Peter Rainier. In 1801 Vancouver published the name Rainier in his journal in London, initiating a controversy that lasted over a century. Though Peter Rainier had a long and honorable career at sea, and later was elected to Parliament, the greatest mountain in the Pacific Northwest is named for one who took an active part in the war against the American colonies.[34] Later a movement arose to restore the Indian name for the mountain — *Tahoma* — which was a generic term applied to all snow peaks. The Puyallup Indians called the volcano "Tah-ko-bah"; the Nisqually Indians called it "Tah-ho-mah"; and the Duwamish Indians used "Ta-ko-bet," all meaning "snow mountain."[35] Tolmie, Winthrop, and Stevens all reported similar names, which probably came from the Chinook jargon term for "white."

The rivalry between Seattle and Tacoma made the mountain's name a subject of bitter strife, the Northern Pacific printing it as *Tacoma* on all maps and in publications. In 1890 the U.S. Board of Geographic Names decided that *Rainier* must stand on all government maps and publications.

The matter came to a climax in 1924 when a joint resolution was passed by the U.S. Senate and introduced into the House of Representatives (but opposed by the Board of Geographic Names) to change Mount Rainier to "Mount Tacoma." One of the strongest proponents of the name "Tacoma" was Theodore Winthrop, who crossed Naches Pass in 1853; in his eloquent book *The Canoe and the Saddle,* he wrote "of all the peaks from California to Frazer's River, this one before me was the royalest."

Dr. William F. Tolmie, a medical officer in the service of Hudson's Bay Company at Nisqually House, the first settlement by white men on Puget Sound, made a botanizing trip to the mountain in September 1833, and was the first white man known to have come close to the great mountain. With Indian companions and three horses he traveled via the "Poyallip" River. From a viewpoint which appears to have been on the Hessong Rock-Mount Pleasant Ridge, Tolmie later wrote that Mount Rainier bore "SS.E and was separated from it only by a narrow glen."[36]

Other pioneers who did notable exploration around the base of Mount Rainier include the first settler James Longmire, naturalist J. B. Flett, and geologist Bailey Willis.

The sketchy early climbing history of Mount Rainier includes a newspaper account of an ascent on the S or SW flank in August 1852 by Sidney S. Ford, Robert S. Bailey, John Edgar, and Benjamin F. Shaw while scouting the Nisqually Valley for a trans-Cascade wagon road, a project that had become an obsession with settlers on Puget Sound.[37] An ascent via the Winthrop Glacier by two men engaged in a survey 1858-1860 was related years later by their Indian guide Saluskin. In the absence of further verification the cautious historian should maintain skepticism here.[38]

The epic attempt on Mount Rainier in 1857 by Lt. August V. Kautz (an officer of the U.S. Regular Army stationed at Fort Steilacoom) most likely reached to a level above 13,000 ft. The Kautz party, which included Dr. Robert O. Craig and soldiers Nicholas Dogue and William Carroll, was directed in their arduous one-week approach by the Indian guide Wapowety. On July 15 the party ascended a glacier (the Nisqually) which Kautz described "with immense furrows" and camped near timberline on its edge. Here Kautz estimated the party would not need more than three hours to reach the summit the next day. On the climb they took homemade alpenstocks, a 50-ft rope, a hatchet, dried beef and biscuit. Climbing via the glacier later named for him, Kautz's party exhausted themselves late in the day, high on the mountain. Kautz continued to where the mountain "spread out comparatively flat;" he later reported that St. Helens, Adams, and Hood stood above the clouds "looking like pyramidal icebergs above an ocean."[39]

The historic first ascent of Mount Rainier was made on August 17, 1870 by Hazard Stevens and Philemon B. Van Trump, after being guided from Olympia to the mountain by James Longmire and to timberline by the Indian Sluiskin. Edmund Coleman, who had led the first climb of Mount Baker, was to have climbed with them, but fell behind and failed to share in the famous ascent. After a reconnaissance to Cowlitz Cleaver, Stevens and Van Trump set out from timberline and climbed via the Gibraltar ledges to the summit ice dome. Stevens, who preferred to call the mountain "Takhoma," wrote of Gibraltar: "loose stones and debris which were continually falling from above."[40] They climbed the SW peak (which they christened "Peak Success"), then crossed over to the rim of the W crater after 11 hours of climbing from camp. Steam issuing from the rocks led to the discovery of a cavern under the ice. Piling large chunks of ice at its front as a windbreak, they spent the night inside. Mist delayed them in the morning before a clearing period allowed them to reach the summit and then descend.

Exactly two months later, on October 17, the noted geologists Samuel F. Emmons and Allen D. Wilson repeated the climb in an effort to survey the mountain's height. The fourth ascent of the Gibraltar Route, in 1888, is of interest because the party included John Muir and Major Edward S. Ingraham, who named Gibraltar Rock, among a number of Mount Rainier's features.[41] The site where they protected themselves by digging into the pumice and building up stones for a windbreak, once called "Cloud Camp," is now known as Camp Muir. The famed naturalist wrote "The night was like a night in Minnesota in December." The first stone shelter was built there in 1916 (now there are two stone huts and two frame buildings).

The early stories of attempts and climbs provide further evidence of the volcano's stimulating influence. In 1890 Fay Fuller became the first woman to reach the summit, and by 1900 over thirty parties had climbed Rainier. Some of the early parties were summer outing groups from the Mazamas, The Mountaineers, and the Sierra Club. In 1906 a Sierra Club outing placed 62 members on the summit. The climbers used a stout alpenstock ending in a sharp iron point. It was felt that the short steep descent along Gibraltar was the most dangerous situation on the mountain. Here the leader tied a long rope around his waist and at the end were two anchormen. Each climber held the rope in his left hand and the alpenstock in his right hand. The anchors prevented a too-rapid descent.

They were a disciplined group: a committee inspected each climber's shoes and steel calks. Each person was given a number, with the request that he stay in place even while resting. The fact that there were no accidents was attributed to such enforcement.[42] It seems that their prudence was justified, for shortly after the outing, a mountain guide broke his leg when falling during a crevasse crossing.

Skis have made their mark on the mountain: the first ski ascent was made by Sigurd Hall on July 1, 1939, but a complete ski descent was not made until July 18, 1948, this by Charles Welsh, Clifford Schmidtke, Kermit Bengtson, and David Roberts. The first winter ascent was made via the Gibraltar Route on February 13, 1922 by Jean and Jacques Landry, Jacques Bergues, and Charles Perryman.

Other of the early mountaineers were geologists and surveyors. The first exploration around the mountain, which included various glacier crossings, was made by Emmons and Wilson in 1870, when they spent a month in the area.[43]

Israel C. Russell, one of America's notable geologists, thoroughly explored and mapped the mountain. In July 1896 he made a N-S traverse of Rainier with a party of five, spending a night in the summit crater. Russell and Bailey Willis studied the Carbon Glacier for one week that summer. Russell observed that early Cascade visitors may not have recognized the volcano was mantled by glaciers, not merely snow-covered.

The first calculation of Mount Rainier's height was made by Lt. Wilkes in 1841 from a base line on Nisqually Prairie. The altitude 12,330 ft, was revised to 14,532 ft by S. S. Gannett of the U.S. Geological Survey in 1895. In 1897 Professor Edgar McClure carried a barometer to the summit, then tragically fell on the descent at a rock that now bears his name.

F. E. Matthes began his topographic survey of the Park in 1910, one which resulted in the first accurate map. In August 1913 C. H. Birdseye led a U.S. Geological Survey party that ascertained the position and altitude of Columbia Crest — after which they survived a severe blizzard in the shelter of the steam caves. Other early explorers of the Park area included copper miners who were active at Camp Starbo in Glacier Basin from 1895 to 1915. They operated a small water-power sawmill and built a wagon road to their camp.

Mount Rainier rises in a commanding fashion about 8000 ft above the surrounding ridges and lesser peaks, and even at this level it has a circumference of over twenty miles. The mountain's great mass is visually enhanced by the fact it stands 11 mi. W of the Cascade Crest — only some 43 mi. from Tacoma. Its highest point, Columbia Crest (14,410 ft), is a mound of snow where the two craters overlap. The truncated summit area has two other significant peaks: Point Success (14,158 ft) and Liberty Cap (14,112 ft).

The size and complexity of Mount Rainier is difficult to comprehend without personal experience on the mountain, and even then its bulk is often grossly underestimated. The early geologist Bailey Willis in 1883, wrote fittingly, "It is the symbol of an awful power clad in beauty." The mountain has been likened to an arctic palace floating on a sea of green trees. A closer view shows that the mountain is textured with a multitude of cliffs, ridges, canyons, cascading glaciers, lakes, meadows, and the incomparable flower fields that color its lower slopes.

Mount Rainier is geologically young: about 700,000 years ago lava began to flow over a rugged surface carved mainly in rocks of Tatoosh pluton and the Stevens Ridge volcanic-sedimentary formation. Repeated extrusions and ejections of lava, ash, and pumice caused the volcano to grow over a great NW-trending downfold into which Tatoosh granites had intruded during Miocene time. The mountain may have reached its present size by about 75,000 years ago (Crandell, *The Geologic Story of Mount Rainier*).

The Cascade Range upon which the volcano stands is far older, being composed of a complex of sedimentary and igneous rocks 20 to 60 m. y. old. About 14 m. y. ago masses of molten rock pushed up into the lower part of other volcanic rocks and solidified to form granodiorite. This rock is exposed at the base of the Tatoosh Range and in some of the lowest valleys.

Various early periods of volcanism produced repeated lava flows out of low volcanos. The ancestral pyroclastic cone of Mount Rainier began with violent eruptions and often produced mud and lava flows that streamed many miles. Most of the earliest eruptions were thick intracanyon lava flows of gray andesite that were poured out on a mountainous landscape carved mainly in the rocks of the Tatoosh pluton. This lava flowed down old valley floors, solidified, and later resisted river and ice erosion so much that it now forms ridgetops such as Klapatche Ridge, Old Desolate, Burroughs Mountain, and Rampart Ridge. The bulk of Ptarmigan Ridge is an immense flow at least 1200 ft thick.

Subsequent eruptions from a central vent alternated between thin successive lava flows and explosions of rock debris to build the great cone. Breccias were formed by violent steam explosions where the thin lava streams became mixed with mud and meltwater as they glided downslope. Alternating layers of solid and fragmented lava interbedded with layers of ash and pumice are magnificently exposed on Willis Wall, South Tahoma Headwall, and Gibraltar Rock. The thin lava flows on the upper walls and cleavers, partly oxidized by escaping gases, are visible in various shades of red, pink, gray, and brown. The blocks in interstratified mudflow breccias formed by the explosive shattering of lava flows often have rough surfaces and are reddened by oxidation. An interesting example of how magma solidifies into rocks whose appearance varies according to the manner of cooling is Gibraltar, the volcano's most notable landmark. Gibraltar is composed largely of S-dipping interlayered lava, breccia, pumice, and tuff-breccia. The lower portion is a thick mass of andesite breccia (shattered lava blocks).

Evidence that Rainier was once higher and of greater bulk is shown by steeply dipping lava flows in Sunset Amphitheatre and South Tahoma Headwall that slant upward — probably toward a vent that lay 500-1000 ft above the present summit. The shape of Mount Rainier's summit area, with Liberty Cap and Point Success on the summit rim as remnants on the side of a higher and more symmetrical cone, adds to the evidence of a former higher summit.

Mount Rainier is a striking example of the complex interplay of eruption and erosion typical of all Cascade Range volcanos. Mudflows caused by violent explosions 6600 to 5700 years ago vastly diminished Rainier's bulk, changed its appearance, and caused great devastation in flanking valleys. Explosions and inward collapse truncated the summit and produced a vast 1½ mi. crater. Weakening by hot gases and solutions over time turned the rock into muddy debris. Cataclysmic explosions and great landslides of hydrothermally altered rock from the old summit created the broad depression between Gibraltar Rock and Russell Cliff. The western half of the great bowl-filled summit caldera was then broken down by explosions and slides. This left a gap for ice to erode the weakened rock that formed Sunset Amphitheatre. This gap is now the site of the Tahoma Glacier.

At various times, melting of snow and ice by volcanic heat triggered some of the mudflows that originated from the crater area and swept into various valleys near the volcano. One vast sliding mass of water-saturated rock probably descended the Emmons and Winthrop glaciers to produce the Osceola Mudflow, which swept down both forks of the White River some 5800 years ago to fan out beyond the present site of Enumclaw. It also has been suggested that this mudflow was formed by collapse of a thick fill of water-saturated sediments in the upper valley.[44] The hydraulic pressure of impounded meltwater has caused devastating slurry floods of turbulent, debris-filled water. Every valley that heads on Rainier contains fills composed of mudflows, stream deposits, and outwash debris. Heat shifts causing subglacial melting are the probable cause of the destructive Tahoma Creek outburst flood of August 31, 1967. Thermal activity was the apparent cause of a massive breakup of the Emmons Glacier from 13,000 to 10,000 ft in 1969.

The most recent explosions have been estimated at 10,000, 6000, 5000, and 2300 years ago. The last major eruptive period (between 3000 and 2500 years ago) saw the eruption of pumice and lava flows, and the formation of many lahars (mudflows).[45] The old hollow, shattered summit caldera was filled by building the present summit cone. During this period, the eastern crater, which marks Columbia Crest, was formed. In summer the crater rims are snow-free except for the summit mound. Inside its rim edges, heat and steam have melted out caverns and passages. These firn caves have long been vital refuges for mountaineers caught in storms. The older western crater is now imperfectly preserved, but the eastern, about 1300 ft in diameter, is almost perfectly circular.

Despite its eruptions since the end of the last major glaciation, the production of new lava and pumice has not kept pace with the piecemeal destruction of the volcano by repeated mudflows, landslides, and glacial erosion. Owing to its northern latitude and high snowfall, Mount Rainier is almost completely covered by glaciers, which flow radially from the summit area. The total glacier area is calculated at 34 mi.[2], the most on any single mountain in the conterminous United States.

Six important ice streams emanate from the summit icecap: the Winthrop, Emmons, Ingraham, Nisqually, Kautz, and Tahoma glaciers. The prominent cirque-born glaciers — the Carbon, Cowlitz, Wilson, South Tahoma, Edmunds, North and South Mowich — begin in the zone of the greatest ice sculpturing, between 12,000 and 10,000 ft. These glaciers are growing headward in this zone of incised cirques and steep gradients. In 1896 the pioneer geologist, I. C. Russell correctly observed, "Carbon Glacier, by enlarging its amphitheatre, is slowly destroying the conditions on which its existence depends."

The many cleavers left as ice erosion remnants owe their comparative resistance to vertical dike material which crosscuts the layered lava and breccia. Erosion differentials on harder and softer materials contribute to protrusion of cleavers and depth of cirques.

Separating Mount Rainier's principal glaciers are secondary, or "inter" glaciers, bodies of ice nourished wholly by snowfall on the middle to lower slopes. An example is the oft-visited Paradise Glacier — actually a combination of two stagnant bodies of ice — on the spreading slope between Paradise River and Stevens Creek. The Van Trump Glacier, lying on an extensive wedge, the Pyramid, Russell, and Inter (on the slope of Steamboat Prow) are typical of such glaciers. More unusual is the broad Fryingpan (named for its unusual shape) on the hollow E slope of Little Tahoma. The Ohanapecosh Glacier, which lies on a shelf just S, is also peculiarly broad in flow direction. Inactive rock glaciers were formed during the late part of the most recent major glaciation. Most rock glacier deposits occupy E- or N-facing cirques within an altitude range of 6600 to 5500 ft (Crandell, *Surficial Geology*).

Glaciers formed very early in the history of Mount Rainier, perhaps even before the volcano as we know it today began to develop. Since the mountain reached its present size, there have been at least five major glaciations. At various times ice completely buried the lower flanks of the volcano and pushed nearly to the Puget Sound lowland. The most recent glaciation (Fraser) occurred 25,000 to 10,000 years ago. Alpine glaciers then heading on Mount Rainier gouged valleys deeply between broad ridges, and radiated away 15 to 40 mi. downvalley (Crandell, *The Geologic Story of Mount Rainier*). A small expansion of glaciers began about 3500 years ago (Neoglaciation), reaching a maximum about 1850, and then gradually receded.

Mount Rainier's glaciers have repeatedly scoured the valleys and left well-formed moraines and gravel deposits to mark past positions. The many long marginal moraines outflanking glacier snouts, and the large areas of terminal debris, are vital proof of general glacial recession (interrupted by temporary equilibriums and minor advances). Various end and lateral moraines from eight glaciers indicate a consistent recession pattern since 1830-50 around the mountain. The location of old ice margins may be established by differences in the size and age of adjacent forests. (The trimline is a term used to designate the boundary between differing ages of plants or trees marking the position from which a valley glacier has recently receded.)

During Neoglaciation, the oldest postglacial advance occurred between 3500 and 2000 years ago (the Winthrop reached its maximum extent during this period); cirques at altitudes of 6000 ft and higher were reoccupied by glaciers. Various glaciers attained maximums at times ranging from the middle of the 14th to the middle of the 19th centuries, as shown by inconsistent patterns.

The Emmons, Mount Rainier's largest glacier, has behaved variably in the past 420 years. At certain times it was broader and formed lateral moraines farther downvalley. Nine moraines have been dated between 1596 and 1901. After a half century of progressive stagnation, the Emmons began an advancing front in 1953, and in the late 1960s, ice above the White River outlet thickened. The present terminus is just over 5000 ft in altitude — some 300 ft higher than the Winthrop, having receded about 1 mi. upvalley since 1900.

The outermost Neoglacial moraine of the Carbon (the lowest glacier in the contiguous United States, with an ice front near 3500 ft) was built near A.D. 1217. About A.D. 1760 the Carbon began to recede from the Wonderland Trail area, but between 1860 and 1906 the glacier advanced some 250 ft over bedrock and ground. The advancing terminus is today close to its maximum advance in the last 10,000 years.

The Tahoma Glacier, which cascades down the W flank of Mount Rainier, was more than 1 mi. farther downvalley in the 1830s, and until about 1910 a southern fork joined the South Tahoma at about 5000 ft, below Glacier Island. The South Tahoma reached a maximum in about 1540, and has retreated to terminate in a gray ice tongue. The nearby Puyallup Glacier, which now terminates at about 5400 ft, curves around a prominent bedrock knob and into a narrow canyon. In the early 19th century, it plunged over cliffs and flowed nearly to the end of the present West Side Road.

The Nisqually, the largest body of ice on the mountain's S side — about 4 mi. in length — is easy to view because of the proximity of its 4714 ft elevation terminus to the road. The glacier's upper half has a mean slope of 30 degrees and is badly crevassed; the lower half is about 14 degrees in angle and is here a fast-moving valley glacier. The Nisqually is nourished by an average annual snowfall of over 45 ft, and by April there is usually 15 or more feet of snow on the glacier. The Nisqually has responded dramatically to climate variations. About 1836 the glacier extended 600 ft below the road bridge and filled the valley wall to wall. The former terminus receded nearly ¼ mi. between 1909 and 1943. Ice sources on the Nisqually appear to be diminishing above 7000 ft since observation of

"kinematic waves" began in 1931. But the glacier thickened in 1946, to begin an advance that continued until recent years at a diminishing rate.

Steep thin glaciers such as the Nisqually sometimes discharge a vigorous ice flow after a thickening build-up, then return to a negative regime for a new accumulation. Glacier flow is predominantly by basal sliding and has a pronounced seasonal variation; the variations do not correlate directly with the meltwater discharge from the terminus. In general, spring-summer velocities in the ablation area are greater than in the fall-winter. The rate of sliding appears to be determined primarily by the amount of water in temporary storage in the glacier. Data supports the idea that glaciers store water in the fall, winter, and spring, then release it in summer. Stored water sometimes is released suddenly: large water storage is suggested by the South Tacoma jökulhlaup (glacial outburst flood) of August 31, 1967.

In general, glacial outburst floods may occur on active temperate glaciers. Other notable floods on Mount Rainier were in October 1955, when the Nisqually River highway bridge was destroyed, and the destructive Kautz Creek flood of October 1947. Bouldery flood plains built up from debris deposited by water, glaciers, and mudflows outflank the terminus portions of the Nisqually, Emmons, and Winthrop glaciers.

Being directly in line with Pacific storms and well on the W side of the Cascade Crest, Mount Rainier's annual precipitation is very high: the long-term annual at Longmire averages 82 inches; the measured norm at Paradise is 110 inches. Winter snow depth often totals 25 ft and in some years deep drifts remain until July. During the past decades, the mean glacier névé line has ranged between 6300 and 6900 ft. On most glaciers this seasonal line is reached in early September.

The snow and ice that accumulates on the slopes of Mount Rainier is important to the runoff characteristics of several important rivers draining to Puget Sound. The principal contribution of the glaciers to the total runoff is their timely release of water during the warm, dry summer months. Snowmelt is the principal source of runoff until the snowpack is largely depleted in July-August, after which there is a delayed contribution through glacier runoff and a groundwater system.

The famed *nieve penitente,* which also may be found on other Cascade volcanos, seems to develop chiefly on the E and S slopes in the low and medium latitudes. Its origin, however, involves complex ablation theories. The pinnacles (snow penitents) lean to the S to correspond to the angle of the midday sun. The highly developed suncups, sometimes 2 or 3 ft deep, can provide laborious travel for the climber; usually they exist only in late summer and at elevations over 11,000 ft. Below 10,000 ft they tend to be less pronounced and are seldom a real impediment to movement.

References of special interest include:

Chase, Evelyn Hyman. *Mountain Climber: George B. Bayley, 1840-1894.* Palo Alto, 1981, pp. 15-30, 135-154.

Crandell, D. R. "The Geologic Story of Mount Rainier." *Geol. Survey Bull. 1292* (1969).

Crandell, D. R. "Surficial Geology of Mount Rainier National Park, Washington." *Geol. Survey Bull. 1288* (1970).

Crandell, D. R. and Mullineaux, D. R. "Volcanic Hazards at Mount Rainier, Washington." *Geol. Survey Bull. 1238* (1967).

Fiske, R. S., Hopson, C. A., and Waters, A. C. "Geology of Mount Rainier National Park, Washington." *Geol. Survey Prof. Paper 444* (1963).

Haines, Aubrey L. *Mountain Fever.* Portland, 1962.

Kirk, Ruth. *Exploring Mount Rainier.* Seattle, 1968.

Kiver, Eugene P. and Mumma, Martin D. "Summit Firn Caves, Mount Rainier, Washington." *Science 23* (July 1971).

Matthes, F. E. "Mount Rainier and Its Glaciers." *U.S. Dept. Interior,* 1914.

Meany, Edmond. *Mt. Rainier: A Record of Explorations.* Seattle, 1914.

Molenaar, Dee. *The Challenge of Rainier.* Seattle, 1979.

Plummer, Fred G. "Mount Rainier Forest Reserve, Washington." *21st Annual Report, U.S. Geol. Survey, 1899-1900;* pt. 5. Washington, 1900, pp. 81-143.

Russell, I. C. "Glaciers of Mount Rainier." *18th Annual Report, U.S. Geol. Survey, 1896-1897;* pt. 2. Washington, 1898, pp. 349-409.

Sigafoos, Robert S. and Hendricks, E. L. "Recent Activity of Glaciers of Mount Rainier, Washington." *U.S. Geol. Survey Prof. Paper 387-B.* Washington, 1972. pp. B1-B24.

Willis, Bailey. "Canyons and Glaciers — a Journey to the Ice Fields of Mount Rainier." *The Northwest,* vol. 1 (1883).

Winthrop, Theodore. *The Canoe and the Saddle.* Tacoma, 1913.

American Alpine Journal: 1957, pp. 1-28.

Mazama: 1900, pp. 1-39 and 93-117; 1905, pp. 201-215; 1914, pp. 5-25; 1919, pp. 301-326; 1927, pp. 7-39; 1941, pp. 7-8 (ski).

Mountaineer: 1909, pp. 4-59; 1912, pp. 14-65; 1915, pp. 9-74; 1919, pp. 9-64; 1920, pp. 44-49; 1924, pp. 25-45; 1930, pp. 9-25; 1939, pp. 30-31 (ski); 1944, pp. 5-15; 1956, pp. 46-54.

Summit: January-February 1963, pp. 30-35; April 1965, pp. 18-25; November 1965, pp. 12-15; April 1966, pp. 4-7; September 1968, pp. 20-23; May 1969, pp. 22-26.

Backpacking: The hiking season in the Park normally extends from early July until early October, although lower-level trails may be open both earlier and later. Some trails may not be free of snow until mid-July, especially on N-facing slopes or in other sheltered locations. Beware of hollow snow bridges when crossing streams (both on and off trail).

The Park has two hiker's centers: At Longmire (7 AM to 7 PM) and at the White River Entrance (8 AM to 6:30 PM; 9 PM Fri. and Sat.). These hiker's centers list trail conditions and available campsites and issue backcountry permits. The centers are staffed by rangers to assist in trip planning.

The average afternoon summer temperature at Longmire is in the mid-70s F, and the night temperature in the upper-40s F. At Paradise (2640 ft higher) the afternoon temperature is usually in the mid-60s F, and at night in the lower-40s F. Frost and below freezing temperatures will occasionally occur at 5000 ft and above even during the warmest summer months.

The most settled weather is between mid-May and mid-September. Snow usually begins to accumulate on the ground at timberline levels in late October, and reaches a depth of 15 to 20 ft by March. At the Longmire level (2761 ft) expect a 4 to 6 ft depth in midwinter. Snow usually leaves the Longmire area by May and Paradise by the first of July.

Backpacking Regulations: All hikers who plan overnight trips into Park backcountry (including trail hikers) are required to have a *backcountry permit* during the summer months (currently June 15 to September 30). Permits are available at visitor centers, hiker's centers, and ranger stations and are issued on a first-come, first-served basis. Advance reservations for permits and campsite allocations are not accepted.

Campsite allocations are made on a first-come, first-served basis on the first day of your trip. There are three types of camping in the Park: (1) Trailside camps; (2) Cross-country camping; (3) Alpine camping.

Camping along trails is permitted only at designated sites (see list of trailside camps). Wood fires are permitted at some camps (within fire rings). Stoves must be used at all other sites. Most camps have toilet facilities, marked sites for camping, and a nearby water source.

The Park has been divided into zones with camping limits. These zones are below 5000 ft (the lower forest zone) and between 5000 ft and 7000 ft. Both zones are limited to five people (or immediate family) per group; some camps have space for groups of twelve.

Off-trail camping is permitted only out of sight and sound of trails, and no less than 100 ft from streams and lakes. In the lower forest cross-country zone, fires are permitted if they are built in metal fire pans. No limit for the number of parties has been set for this zone. Fires are prohibited in all subalpine zones. Limits have been set on the number of parties that may camp in this zone. In either type of cross-country zone, party size is limited to five people or one immediate family.

The alpine zone includes all camping above 7000 ft and all snow and glacier camping. Certain areas may be closed to camping (check with ranger stations). There is a party size limit of twelve for all alpine zones. No limits have been set on the number of parties per night except Muir Snowfield, Camp Muir, Ingraham Flats, Camp Schurman, Camp Curtis, and Ruth Mountain. Fires are not permitted in any alpine zone. Hikers venturing onto glaciers must first register with Park rangers.

Winter backcountry camping is permitted in all areas once a 3-ft snowpack has formed.

Dogs and cats are not permitted away from roads.

Trailside Camps: W = wood fires permitted; S = stove only, no wood fires.

Camp	Indiv. Sites	Group Sites	Elev. Feet
Berkeley Park (S)	4	—	5600
Camp Curtis (S)	23	—	8200
Camp Muir (S)	110*	—	10000
Camp Schurman (S)	35*	—	9510
Carbon River (S)	3	—	3100
Cataract Valley (S)	7	1	4700
Clover Lake (S)	2	—	5732
Deer Creek (W)	3	—	3125
Devil's Dream (S)	7	1	5000
Dick Creek (S)	2	—	4320
Dick's Lake (S)	1	—	5680
Eagle's Roost (S)	5	—	4700
Fire Creek (W)	4	1	4600
Forest Lake (W)	1	—	5600
Glacier Basin (S)	4	1	5960
Golden Lakes (S)	5	1	5000
Granite Creek (S)	2	—	5732
Indian Bar (S)	3	1	5100
Klapatche Park (S)	4	—	5400
Lake Eleanor (W)	3	1	5000
Lake George (S)	5	1	4320
Lake James (S)	6	1	4400
Lower Crystal Lake (S)	2	—	5510
Maple Creek (S)	4	1	2800
Mowich River (W)	8	1	2600
Mystic Lake (S)	7	1	5620
Nickel Creek (S)	4	1	3350
No. Puyallup River (W)	3	1	3600
Ollalie Creek (W)	3	1	3800
Owyhigh Lakes (W)	4	1	5200
Paradise River (S)	3	1	3950
Pyramid Creek (S)	2	—	3760
Shriner Peak (S)	3	—	5800
Snow Lake (S)	2	—	4600
So. Puyallup River (S)	4	1	4000
Summerland (S)	5	1	5900
Sunrise (S)	10	2	6300
Three Lakes (W)	2	1	4650
Upper Crystal Lake (S)	2	—	5800
Upper Palisades Lake (S)	2	—	5840
Yellowstone Cliffs (S)	2	—	5100

*Space in the two high camps at Camp Muir and Camp Schurman is allotted by the number of people rather than the number of parties.

Protect the fragile meadows and plant resources by walking on established paths when possible. The cutting of trail switchbacks leads to the formation of erosion gullies. When hiking in areas without trails, walk on snow and rocks where possible. On fragile meadow terrain, parties should spread out, rather than hiking in single file.

Camp at designated sites or on snow. Do not build rock windbreaks and do not clear tent sites on the rocky areas. Small clearings disturb the alpine soil and the ability of fragile plants to survive. It is recommended to hang food between two trees (if possible) to prevent loss to animals. The Park Service recommends boiling or other treatment for Giardiasis and other water-borne diseases. *Giardia* may be present in all natural waters.

Human wastes should be buried 8 inches deep and

at least 100 ft away from streams and lakes. It is recommended that solid wastes and tissues be brought back by plastic disposal bags (available at ranger stations) rather than be deposited on snowfields and glaciers. There is a continual danger that such wastes may enter the water supply.

Climbing: Because of its altitude, majesty, and proximity to civilization, Mount Rainier receives a disproportionate share of public attention. Ascended mostly by participants in club outings during the first half of the century, the mountain has lately been sought by numerous small independent and guided parties. In the twenty-year period 1962 to 1982, the number of individuals attempting Mount Rainier rose from about 1000 to 8000.

Statistics show a marked increase of successful individual ascents from 141 in 1950 to 4016 in 1985, with a success ratio varying from 42 to 75 percent. The figure of 7368 persons making a summit attempt in 1985 reflects an increase from the previous year.

The Disappointment Cleaver route continues to be the one most popular. Figures for the year 1984 (nonwinter) show that the most attempted routes in the Park were: Disappointment Cleaver, 737 parties (with 1379 persons successful); Emmons Glacier, 246 parties; Ingraham Glacier Headwall (Direct), 76 parties; Liberty Ridge, 71 parties; Fuhrer's Finger, 54 parties; Kautz Glacier, 54 parties; Gibraltar Ledge, 38 parties; Little Tahoma, 18 parties; Tahoma Glacier, 18 parties; Success Cleaver, 13 parties. The 1985 season showed a 54 percent success percentage.

The route from Camp Muir up the Ingraham Glacier and Disappointment Cleaver is often overcrowded. Some of its advantages are: it is well marked; there are usually others available to provide emergency help; and one does not need to carry a tent if there is space available in the shelter at Camp Muir. But crowding poses problems on this route: the shelter is generally full; the smell from the toilets convinces many parties to continue climbing and to camp at Ingraham Flats (about 1000 ft higher). Since this means that a tent must be carried, other routes of the same standard can be considered. Three such routes are the Fuhrer Finger, the Kautz Glacier, and the Emmons-Winthrop Glacier.

In 1984 there were no climbing fatalities in the Park, but 1983 had five — typical in their variety. In May a climber skied off a cornice below Anvil Rock (in a whiteout). A climber who had untied from his rope fell through a snow bridge 100 ft into a crevasse. In June a person climbing on wet rock was killed after falling 200 ft. In September, two climbers were killed after they slipped near the top of Disappointment Cleaver; they had no ice axes and were wearing Army rubber boots with crampons.

A reduction in rescue activity for 1984 may be attributed to good conditions throughout the summer, with better than average weather. These factors are counterbalanced by what appears to be a growing lack of concern for safety. The number of persons traveling on glaciers unroped seems to be increasing, along with an attitude that party members are not responsible for each other's well being. There were incidents of people wearing tennis shoes and not carrying ice axes on glaciers.

Human waste problems at upper elevations on Mount Rainier are becoming serious because of the numbers of mountaineers and the fact that decomposition is slow; human waste contaminates the snow, and eventually the water supply. Privacy toilet screens have been placed at Ingraham Flats (11,000 ft) and Emmons Flats (9700 ft) just above Camp Schurman, to concentrate fecal matter in one area so it can be flown off the mountain. In addition to two pit toilets at Camp Muir, a solar assisted decomposing toilet has been emplaced; at other locations, choose latrines away from campsites and routes.

Due to hazardous terrain and possible severe weather, it is recommended that non-guided climbers have good basic mountaineering knowledge and skills, and have adequate snow and ice experience for the contemplated route. Personal equipment should include: climbing boots, gaitors, full-frame crampons, ice axe, three prusik slings or two jumars, carabiners, sun glasses, sun cream, headlamp, adequate food, sleeping bag, and warm clothing. Party equipment should include topographic map, compass, shelter, first aid kit, stove, fuel, and climbing rope of minimum 9-mm. thickness. Parties should be prepared for crevasse rescue and be familiar with its techniques.

Most climbing on Mount Rainier, as on other Cascade volcanos, demands more physical effort and determination than technical ability. Good judgment is important. Physiological, weather, and glacier-travel factors become important. One should remember that temperatures decrease and winds increase with altitude: when it is a mild 68° F at the Puget Sound level, it will probably be 50° F at timberline, 35° F at high camp, and about 20° F on the summit — possibly with a chilling, strong wind. The formation of a cloudcap (a localized lenticular cloud caused by a rising high wind over the summit) can create hazardous visibility problems. Resulting snowfall may be accompanied by a strong wind that may be difficult to face. Cloudcaps can form very rapidly and envelop the upper mountain regions to make any progress (even descent) difficult. The appearance of air-wave lenticular clouds is a signal of a possible mountain cloudcap and should not be ignored.

Obtain a current weather forecast.

In general, the best period for ascents on the northern and western faces of Mount Rainier is between early May and mid-July; in August and later one may encounter blue alpine ice and rockfall from cleavers and cliff bands. The optimum time for any of the more serious routes is when there is ample, consolidated snow, as during early season, and in well-frozen conditions (so loose rock is frozen in place). *Certain routes should not be attempted during periods of high freezing level.*

Personal risk on mountain facades such as Willis Wall can only be partially calculated. As in the Alps, some climbers have come to accept unstable ice cliffs as an occupational hazard, relying on cold conditions and some luck. The long routes on Mount Rainier make more demands on the speed and general competence of a party. In late summer, some routes become a wall of gray ice above a yawning bergschrund, streaked with rock debris.

Sometimes a rational time to climb is in the fall, when faces may come back into condition from alpine ice after a snowfall and a minimum freeze and thaw cycle. A spell of clearing should provide good conditions if the surface snow is frozen.

The danger of storm and fresh snow persists through mid-June. It is important to monitor weather forecasts. Heavy snow at high altitude can trap a party during any month and make them vulnerable to avalanches and whiteout storm conditions. Parties camped high on Liberty Ridge have been marooned (May 1979).

Climbing Regulations: Backcountry permits are required for all climbers who camp or bivouac overnight on Mount Rainier, Little Tahoma, and other peaks in the Park from June 1 through September 30. Climbers must register year-round for Mount Rainier and Little Tahoma. Limits have been established at Camp Muir (110 persons per night), Camp Schurman (35 per night), Muir Snowfield (36 per night), and Inghram Flats (36 per night). Climbing party size is limited to 12.

No advance reservations can be made for camping at camps Muir and Schurman (permits are issued on a first-come, first-served basis).

For information concerning current mountain or snow conditions and high-risk areas, contact the Paradise or White River ranger stations. It should be noted that Panorama Point has a high avalanche danger in winter and early spring. The safest route is via the treeline on the SW ridge, ascending from Alta Vista.

Other regulations include:

1. Mandatory registration for climbing and hiking on glaciers or above high camps. Minimum of two in party. All climbers must register with a park ranger at the beginning and end of each trip (some locations are self registry).

2. Persons under 18 must have written permission from parent or guardian.

3. Solo climbers must have superintendent's permission (allow two weeks for request reply).

Leading or participating in a commercial, guided climb of Mount Rainier other than with an approved climbing concessionaire is illegal. A special permit is required to engage in any business in the Park.

Approximate times for climbing check-in are as follows:

Summer (June-September): Paradise — 7 AM to Midnight (Fri.-Sat.); to 9 PM weekdays. Other locations — 8 AM to 5 PM.

Winter (October-May): 8 AM to 5 PM.

INGRAHAM GLACIER — DISAPPOINTMENT CLEAVER ROUTE: The Ingraham Glacier is a long, narrow ice stream on Rainier's SE slope, joining the Cowlitz Glacier just below Cathedral Rocks at 6800 ft. On the S it is bounded by Gibraltar Rock and Cathedral Rocks and on the N by Little Tahoma and Disappointment Cleaver (the prominent cleaver separates the Ingraham from the Emmons). The upper Ingraham may be a chaos or very smooth, often changing from year to year. By July it is usually suncupped above 11,000 ft. Between 7000 and 9000 ft the glacier makes its steepest gradient, forming an icefall.

The Ingraham flows from the summit dome, while the Cowlitz, its southerly branch, heads in a cirque immediately beneath Gibraltar Rock. Together the glaciers measure 4.6 mi. in length. Early geologist F. E. Matthes stated "at the point of confluence of the two branches there begins a long medial moraine that stretches like a black tape the whole length of the lower course." The lower ice stream ends at about altitude 5500 ft, in a steep-walled canyon and is bordered by long morainal ridges. The arcuate dirt bands (ogives) of the lower Cowlitz are a noteworthy feature.

In September 1885 or 1886 Allison L. Brown and a party of six or seven Yakima Indians climbed the glacier to an

COLUMBIA CREST

LIBERTY CAP

Curtis Ridge

POINT SUCCESS

Disappointment Cleaver

EMMONS GLACIER

INGRAHAM GLACIER

Cathedral Gap

KAUTZ GLACIER

Nisqually Cleaver

Nisqually Icecliff

NISQUALLY GLACIER

Gibraltar Rock

Cadaver Gap

Cathedral Rocks

COWLITZ GLACIER

Nisqually Icefall

Cowlitz Cleaver

Camp Muir

unknown height; it is uncertain just who made the first completed ascent. Since the late 1950s this has been the most frequently used route on Rainier.

From Paradise ◆ take the Skyline Trail ◆ and continuing snowfield route to Camp Muir, a site selected by John Muir in 1883 and named for him by Major Ingraham (4-7 hours). Here is a public shelter open on a space-available basis. Rock windbreaks on the ridge offer more sites. Climbers commonly often set up tents on the snow. Note that no camping reservations can be made in advance; the space allocation is made first-come, first-served.

A Park ranger with radio is stationed at Camp Muir during the summer season. In winter the shelters may be closed by snow, but can usually be dug into. There is an emergency radio in the stone public shelter in winter.

Use the toilet facilities — not the snow or pumice ridge!

From Camp Muir gain access to the Ingraham Glacier by a near-level traverse of the upper Cowlitz Glacier and ascend the slope through the central of three gaps (Cathedral Gap — 10,500 ft) in Cathedral Rocks Ridge. At this gap climb a snow or long scree slope to the ridge crest, then onto the Ingraham. Traverse across the glacier (Ingraham Flats — about 11,000 ft) to the lower S base of Disappointment Cleaver. Parties usually leave the glacier at 200-300 ft above the cleaver's nose to begin the ascent (see photo). A ledge system of loose rock provides access to the cleaver crest snowfield; continue to its top (12,300 ft). Note: late season rockfall danger on cleaver from persons above (do not linger at any time; rocks kicked off by one party may hit others below). Continue directly toward the E crater rim, crevasses allowing.

The E crater is a circular rock-rimmed volcanic depression filled with snow and marked by steam fumaroles. Columbia Crest, the true summit, is located on the western rim. The summit register is at a three-rock outcrop on the inside of — and about 300 linear ft from — the crater's NNE rim. The western crater is SW of Columbia Crest.

Avoid bottlenecks at critical spots on the route by allowing space between parties. A party stopped and blocking the route may cause others to wait in a dangerous position. If stopping to rest, stand off the route so others may pass.

Note: Although the Disappointment Cleaver Route is the most popular one on the mountain, and generally the most feasible, there are icefall and crevasse dangers. On June 21, 1981 a massive icefall on the glacier caused one of North America's worst mountaineering tragedies. A large ice mass above Ingraham Flats broke off early in the morning and swept eleven persons into a crevasse.

Grade I or II. Time: 5-8 hours from Camp Muir. References: *Mountaineer*, 1920, pp. 49-50; *A.A.J.*, 1957, pp. 14-15; *A.N.A.M.*, 1979, pp. 35-36; 1982, pp. 55-56; 1984, pp. 57-58; 1985, pp. 68-69.

Variation: Cadaver Gap: From Camp Muir ascend the Cowlitz diagonally to a moderately steep snow chute on the Cathedral Rocks Ridge; this leads directly to Cadaver Gap (est. 11,300 ft), between the ridge and Gibraltar Rock.

Cross through to the Ingraham, then either climb the headwall (the direct route), staying close to Gibraltar, or cross to Disappointment Cleaver. Note: This route is most free of crevasses and safest in early season, but is quite exposed to rockfall from the Gibraltar face. A fatal slab avalanche occurred on the route, below Cadaver Gap, in March 1979.

Variation: The Ingraham Headwall, which can be reached either by Cathedral Gap or Cadaver Gap, is usually feasible only in early summer.

Variation: When the upper Ingraham is heavily crevassed and it is difficult to gain access to Disappointment Cleaver (particularly in late season), one may cross the glacier near the 10,600-ft level and then climb the left side of the Emmons Glacier (N of the Cleaver).

GIBRALTAR LEDGE ROUTE: Gibraltar Rock, with the characteristics of a frowning battlement, is a celebrated feature on Rainier and one of its most massive rock outcroppings. At its peak (12,660 ft) it divides the Nisqually and Ingraham glaciers. It has steep faces on the Nisqually, Cowlitz, and Ingraham flanks. Its lower E corner merges with Cathedral Rocks ridge.

Both the first and second ascents of Mount Rainier were made by the Gibraltar Ledge Route. Some of the early parties camped at "Camp of the Stars," about 1000 ft above Camp Muir, and the highest comfortable site. In 1936 a section of the traditional Gibraltar Ledge fell away, closing the route until 1948, when a lower ledge bypass was negotiated. Despite rockfall danger, Gibraltar Ledge is still a frequently used route, but one recommended only in early season. One should schedule the climb early enough to allow descent of the ledges before sun loosens icicles and rocks (hard hats advised).

From Camp Muir (see Skyline Trail ◆) climb diagonally to the head of Cowlitz Glacier at 11,500 ft. Pass the Beehive (a projecting ridge), then cross Cowlitz Cleaver at a high notch (old Camp Misery) to reach the Gibraltar Ledge. Follow snow or steep scree on the W face of Gibraltar. One can scramble down to a lower ledge at the site of an eye bolt (some parties rappel here, leaving a rope for the return); in early season one may be able to step onto the lower ledge's snow cover. Follow the ledge beneath a cliff to a narrow point, then continue across and up narrow gullies to regain the original ledge. Proceed to the ice chute on the left. Ascend this (the most difficult portion) nearly to the upper end of Gibraltar Rock, then to the saddle at the top. Ascend glacier slopes directly to the E crater rim, allowing for crevasses. Grade I or II. Time: 4-8 hours from Camp Muir. References: *Mazama*, 1905; *Sierra Club Bull.*, vol. 6 (1906), pp. 1-6; *Mountaineer*, 1954, pp. 67-68; 1956, pp. 38-45; *A.A.J.*, 1957, pp. 4-13; *Atlantic Monthly* 38 (November 1876), pp. 511-533.

Variation: Nisqually-Gibraltar Chute: By Paul Gilbreath, Stan de Bruler, and a man named "Hewitt" in July 1946. From Camp Muir traverse around the W base of Cowlitz Cleaver to the Nisqually Glacier, then to the base of Gibraltar. Climb directly up the steep snow/ice chute be-

MOUNT RAINIER from east
BOB AND IRA SPRING

Disappointment Cleaver

Gibraltar Rock

Gibraltar Route

INGRAHAM GLACIER

Drop-off

Gibraltar Ledge

Nisqually-Gibraltar Chute

NISQUALLY ICE CLIFF

Nisqually Cleaver

tween the Nisqually Ice Cliff and Gibraltar to join the principal route at the level of the main ledge. The route is safest in early season. There are definite rockfall/icefall hazards. References: *Mountaineer*, 1970, pp. 108-109 (winter); *A.A.J.*, 1957, pp. 25-26; *A.N.A.M.*, 1982, pp. 49-52.

NISQUALLY ICE CLIFF: This 200-ft ice cliff terminates the eastern lobe of the upper Nisqually; the cliff narrows to a point at its lower W extremity, where it is climbed from the amphitheatre beneath. First ascent by Barry Bishop and Luther Jerstad on August 13, 1962. First winter ascent by Jerry Hasfjord and Eric Simonson on March 3-4, 1975.

Approach as for Nisqually-Gibraltar Chute. Plan the route to avoid objective danger. The steepest section is the chute leading to the lowest (left) point of the ice cliff. Grade II. Reference: *National Geographic Magazine*, May 1963.

Variation: Nisqually Cleaver: By Fred Dunham and James Wickwire, June 19, 1967. The route ascends the upper portion of the cleaver, whose total rise is from 10,600 to 13,000 ft. Just above the chute's narrowest point (this bypasses rotten vertical rock step at its base), traverse left on snow and over small rock bands to the cleaver's crest. Bypass several small ice cliffs on the Nisqually Icefall flank, then ascend to the cleavers' termination. Time: 7 hours from Camp Muir. Reference: *A.A.J.*, 1968, p. 130.

NISQUALLY ICEFALL: The Nisqually Glacier, largest and most vigorous on Rainier's S flank, extends from the crater rim some 3.8 mi. into a deep canyon W of Paradise Park, ending at about 4700 ft. The Nisqually and its tributary, the Wilson, are a single glacier system covering an area of 2.2 mi.[2]

At the 13,000-ft level the Nisqually is split by the rock buttress of Nisqually Cleaver; the eastern lobe descends W of Gibraltar Rock to form an ice cliff at about 12,000 ft. Its lower portion heads in a large cirque below the level of Gibraltar (at about 11,400 ft), fed by avalanches from the ice cliff. The Nisqually Icefall originates from the western lobe of the glacier. It forms a narrow ever-changing cascade between Wapowety Cleaver on the W and Nisqually Cleaver on the E, the steepest section being between 10,500 ft and 12,500 ft. Due to crevasse openings it is generally wise to do this climb during low temperatures in spring or early summer. The hazards of seracs in the icefall require acceptance of certain risks. (In 1968 a party had a close escape from falling ice.) First ascent by Dee Molenaar and Robert W. Craig, July 15, 1948.

From Camp Muir (see Skyline Trail ◆) make a traverse W beneath Cowlitz Cleaver and cross the crevassed cirque of the Nisqually Glacier to the base of the icefall. It is then climbed as dictated by crevasse and serac patterns. Large crevasses above the main icefall may be a problem; once above 12,500 ft the slope eases to the crater rim. Grade II or III. Time: 6-10 hours from Camp Muir to crater. References: *Mountaineer*, 1948, pp. 18-19, 23; 1960, pp. 78-79; *A.A.J.*, 1949, pp. 138-143; 1957, pp. 26-27.

FUHRER FINGER: Fuhrer Finger is a narrow couloir named for Hans Fuhrer, the guide who led its first ascent. This 35- to 40-degree slope leads from the head of the Wilson Glacier at 10,000 ft to gentler upper slopes at 11,500 ft on the W edge of the upper Nisqually Glacier. The Finger is separated from the Nisqually by a sharp rock cleaver. The Wilson Glacier was named for topographer Allen D. Wilson, who made the second ascent of Rainier.

This route is the shortest to Rainier's summit. The route is seldom crowded; there is no large, flat campsite area, but good campsites exist at the edge of the Wilson Glacier. The climb should be done before mid-July to avoid large crevasses on the Nisqually Glacier. Occasional parties make the entire ascent from Paradise in one day. Beware of rockfall and avalanche danger in the Finger. First ascent by Hans Fuhrer, Heinie Fuhrer, Joseph Hazard, Peyton Farrer, and Thomas Hermans on July 2, 1920. First winter ascent by Mike Bialos and party, March 1969.

Descend Nisqually Moraine Trail ◆ to the Nisqually Glacier; cross the Nisqually at the 6200-ft contour line to a snow (or rock) gully (Wilson Gully) at the opposite side. Climb this to the W edge of the Wilson Glacier, and ascend left (W) edge of glacier to about 9000 ft, then cross glacier diagonally upward and right toward base of the rock cleaver separating the Wilson and Nisqually glaciers. High camp can be made at about 9500 ft on the cleaver; alternate camp is at same level on rocks at W edge of Wilson Glacier (6 hours).

It is best to begin the climb of the Finger very early; ascend directly upward to its junction with the upper Nisqually Glacier. Ascend the upper W edge of the Nisqually to the top of Wapowety Cleaver at 13,000 ft. From here the summit is reached by working around the crevasses of the upper Nisqually. Grade I or II. Time: 5-7 hours from high camp. Note: The Finger can be icy, making the ascent considerably more difficult. Rockfall can occur, especially on warm days (wear helmets). Glissading descents of the Finger are tempting, but are risky. References: *Mountaineer*, 1970, p. 109; *Cascadian*, 1961, pp. 49-51; 1963, pp. 46-50; *A.A.J.*, 1957, p. 19; *A.N.A.M.*, 1979.

WILSON GLACIER HEADWALL: This is the steep cirque wall of the Wilson Glacier (W of Fuhrer Finger) beneath the apex of converging ridges that end atop Wapowety Cleaver. It offers a fast, direct summit route in early season when surface material is frozen. Watch for icefall danger from Kautz Ice Cliff down the narrow chutes at the lower portion of the headwall. First ascent by Dee Molenaar and Pete Schoening, July 21, 1957.

Use Fuhrer Finger route to high camp at 9500 ft on rocks at W edge of Wilson Glacier. Ascend to the head of the Wilson and cross the bergschrund on the right. Traverse upward-left into the first (central) snow couloir, keeping next to the left side to avoid possible rockfall. Climb over a 15-25-ft rock restriction in the couloir (may be filled in early season), then ascend the broad central ice slope to rock bands at 12,200 ft. Continue to 13,000 ft atop Wapowety Cleaver. Follow upper Kautz route from here to crater rim, on upper

NISQUALLY ICE CLIFF and GIBRALTAR ROCK
JIM STUART

Routes
1. Kautz Glacier
2. Wilson Headwall
3. Fuhrer Finger
4. Nisqually Icefall
5. Nisqually Cleaver
6. Nisqually Ice Cliff
7. Nisqually-Gibraltar Chute
8. Gibraltar Ledge
9. Cadaver Gap
10. Ingraham Glacier-Disappointment Cleaver
11. Little Tahoma

MOUNT RAINIER from southeast
BOB AND IRA SPRING

W side of Nisqually Glacier. Grade II or III. References: *A.A.J.,* 1958, p. 79; *Mountaineer,* 1958, p. 96.

Variation: By Dan Davis, Tom Stewart, and Bruce Loughlin on August 6, 1967. From the bergschrund traverse left *past* the first couloir and ascend snow slopes on the *left* side of the prominent rock island in the center of the headwall to a notch at the top of the island. Then continue up the snow until it is possible to traverse right to the slopes above the main cliff band. Then join the original route at the central snow/ice slope. Note: Both upper, smaller rock bands are passed on the right; original party made bivouac at 10,000 ft on a rock shoulder to the right of the headwall gully.

KAUTZ GLACIER: The Kautz Glacier was named for Lt. A. V. Kautz, who first climbed it and made his heroic summit attempt on July 15, 1857. It is located immediately W of Wapowety Cleaver and descends in a gradually narrow-

ing canyon to below timberline. F. E. Matthes pointed out that the Kautz is a "peculiar ice stream for its exceeding slenderness." From 11,000 to 11,500 ft the Kautz has its steepest gradient and forms an ice chute about 300 ft wide to the W of the famous Kautz Ice Cliff, much of which overhangs the Wilson Glacier. To the W of the ice chute is another curving ring of ice cliffs. Entry to the chute is made on the right, from Wapowety Cleaver.

Kautz's near-ascent route was completed to the crater rim (using a direct ascent over the ice cliff) July 28, 1920 by Hans and Heinie Fuhrer, guides, Roger W. Toll, and Harry M. Myers. In 1924 Joseph Hazard led an exploratory climb of the route to assess Kautz's accomplishment. Camp Hazard, at about 11,400 ft and the usual camp for climbers using this route, is named for him. In the 1940s the Kautz route was used by guided parties because of the closure of the Gibraltar Route. Climbs of the route prior to 1947 were

generally reported as an easy ascent of the ice cliff through a maze of terraces and pinnacles. The changing character of the ice cliff area (between 11,300 and 12,000 ft) is such that it has formed a vertical barrier in some years, forcing an ascent by the ice chute to the W. While the Kautz Glacier Route is relatively long, it is scenic and avoids the crowds that frequent the Disappointment Cleaver Route.

Follow Fuhrer Finger Route to the W edge of Wilson Glacier, then continue upward to 9500 ft. Leave Wilson Glacier and ascend "The Turtle" (turtle-shaped snowfield beginning about 9800 ft) and upper slope of Wapowety Cleaver to Camp Hazard, about 200 ft below the Kautz Ice Cliff (there also are small sleeping spots lower on the cleaver). Allow 8-10 hours to here.

It is advisable to make a very early morning start, when ice is well frozen. Drop down from top of rock ridge and skirt W below the prominent lower point of the ice cliff. Ascend the Kautz Chute to upper end where it merges into a pinnacled area of the ice cliff. Under icy conditions climb into pinnacles and terraces on the right (sometimes a short stretch of steep cramponing), then ascend these to upper smooth portion of the glacier. Ascend either to top of glacier opposite Point Success and cross the saddle to the crater rim, or climb smooth slopes to top of Wapowety Cleaver on the right (13,000 ft) then ascend upper left Nisqually Glacier to the crater. Grade II. Time: 5-7 hours from high camp. Reference: *Mountaineer*, 1924, pp. 57-59.

Note: In some years a rappel can be made directly over the ice cliff, a time-saver on the descent.

Approach Variation: From Van Trump Park ◆ ascend N to gentle slopes of Wapowety Cleaver; follow these to Camp Hazard.

Variation: In some years it is possible to climb terraces in the 100-200-ft ice cliff directly above high camp. Maintain extreme caution against falling ice at all times, particularly when skirting below the cliff.

KAUTZ GLACIER HEADWALL: This headwall contains the glacier finger and the rock-and-snow face W of the upper part of the Kautz Glacier. It is bound on the W by Kautz Cleaver and on the E by the upper portion of the Kautz Glacier. First ascent by Patrik Callis, Dan Davis, and Don (Claunch) Gordon on July 8, 1963.

From high camp at 9800 ft on Wapowety Cleaver (reach by using approach from Van Trump Park; see Kautz Glacier Approach Variation, or use Kautz Glacier approach) descend to the Kautz Glacier and then ascend the glacier to its head left of the ice cliffs between the lower and upper Kautz. Ascend steep snow and over and around rock bands as conditions allow, until feasible to ascend through a gully, followed by snow slopes to Point Success. Grade II or III. References: *A.A.J.*, 1964, pp. 170-171; *Mountaineer*, 1964, pp. 131-132.

KAUTZ CLEAVER: This is the rock ridge separating the Kautz and Success glaciers; at 12,000 ft it merges with upper Success Cleaver. The route has not become popular, probably because of the long approach. A photo taken by C. E. Rusk

indicates that he and F. H. Kiser were high on this route in July 1905. First ascent by George Senner and Charles E. Robinson on September 1, 1957.

From Van Trump Park ◆ continue up the meadows to rock ridges on the E side of Kautz Glacier. At 8000 ft drop onto the glacier and cross diagonally upward to the base of the cleaver at about 9000 ft. It may be necessary to cross a crevassed area above a prominent icefall. Ascend on left side of true cleaver via the long snow finger between the two ribs of the cleaver (parties have followed the cleaver crest, but this is slower). Reach a small saddle on the ridge below a red gendarme (at est. 10,200 ft; good high camp). Circle right-ward around the gendarme and then left across the cleaver. It is simplest to ascend snow along its left but the widening character of the cleaver allows ascent between various minor ribs and gullies. Continue to where the outcroppings broaden into upper Success Cleaver at about 12,000 ft (at these the Success Cleaver and Kautz Cleaver routes merge). Continue to Point Success, keeping generally on the E side of the upper rock slopes. Grade II. Time: 10-12 hours from high camp to crater rim. Reference: *A.A.J.*, 1958, pp. 80-81.

Alternate Approach: Approach as for Success Glacier Couloir; from Success Glacier bear eastward onto the cleaver.

Variation: Success Glacier Couloir ("Success Finger"): This route uses a snow finger above the head of Success Glacier. The Success, which is a tributary of the Kautz Glacier, heads in a cirque against the flanks of Point Success. First ascent by George Senner and Dick Wahlstrom on July 17, 1960.

From lower Success Cleaver at 7500 ft (see Success Cleaver Route) bear E and cross the small Pyramid Glacier to 9000 ft (possible campsite on cleaver between Pyramid and Success glaciers). Then ascend the Success Glacier to its head; a major schrund may have to be crossed at 10,600 ft. Here a broad snow finger tapers to rock outcroppings at the 12,000-ft level (this is the eastern of three main fingers rising above the glacier). References: *A.A.J.*, 1961, p. 336; *Mountaineer*, 1961, p. 97.

SUCCESS CLEAVER: Success Cleaver, the great SW rock spur to Point Success, begins at 6500 ft at the saddle north of Pyramid Peak. In late summer it usually is an all-rock route to the 14,000-ft level (with a number of unpleasant traverses on loose scree). Most of the route is protected from stonefall by its own projection. It is not a difficult route, but it has a moderately long approach and is a long climb. Most parties carry bivouac or sleeping gear, and make a traverse of Rainier to descend by another route.

In the summer of 1905 F. H. Kizer and three others from a Mazama outing had started out for the ascent of the cleaver, when Ernest Dudley and John Glascock, members of the Sierra Club outing camped at Paradise, made the entire ascent from Paradise by traversing intervening glaciers. They reached the summit of Point Success the evening of July 24, continued to the crater for the night, then de-scended to Camp Muir after being without food or sleep for

MOUNT RAINIER from southwest
JIM STUART

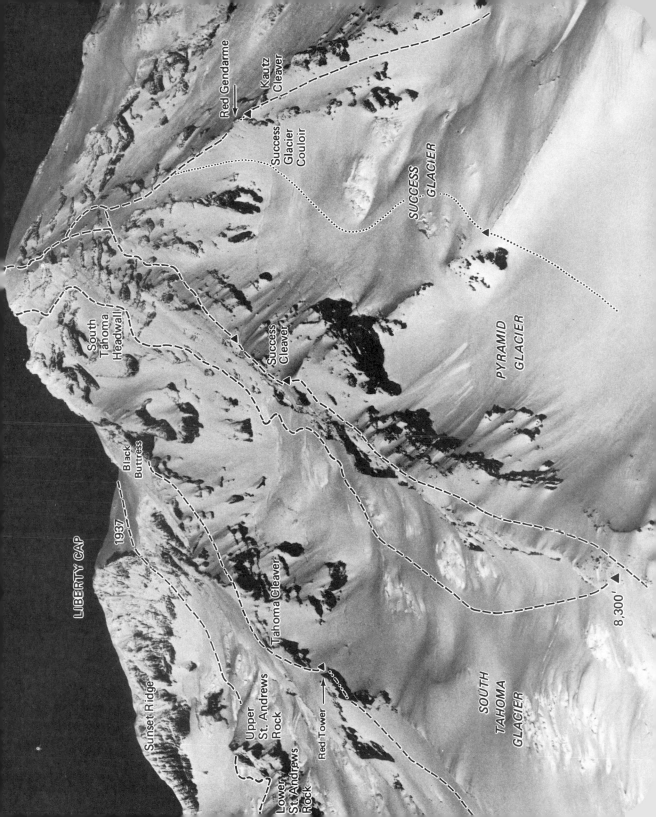

LIBERTY CAP

Red Gendarme

Kautz Cleaver

Success Glacier Couloir

SUCCESS GLACIER

South Tahoma Headwall

Success Cleaver

PYRAMID GLACIER

Black Buttress

1937

Tahoma Cleaver

8,300'

Upper St. Andrews Rock

Sunset Ridge

Red Tower

Lower St. Andrews Rock

SOUTH TAHOMA GLACIER

35 hours. Perhaps some competitive motivation was involved in this feat.

The second ascent was not made until 1912, when guide Joseph Stampfler, Phil Barrett, and Frank Kandle followed the route. Little credence can be given to a single newspaper account of a supposed ascent to Point Success in 1884 by P. B. Van Trump and George Bayley; in 1887 an attempt to about 13,000 ft was made on this SW flank of the mountain by a party including Claude E. Rusk; they reportedly were halted by an ice cliff. First winter ascent by Jerry Hasfjord, Dan Lepeska, and Paul Neilson, 1977.

From Mirror Lake at Indian Henrys Hunting Ground (see Tahoma Creek Trail ♦) ascend meadows and traverse snowfields around the N base of Pyramid Peak at about 5600 ft, to the broad rock crest of Success Cleaver. Some early parties camped as low as 6500 ft at the base of Pyramid Peak, but it is preferable to use good locations at about 8300 ft or just above the 9500-ft level. Just below the latter site the ridge forms the first of two steps; keep right when passing these; at top of second step is a rock buttress with a sandy top (ample room and protective boulders here).

Above 10,000 ft one must pass several crumbly pinnacles on the ridge before the cleaver steepens to force the route to the E. Here (near 11,000 ft) angle below cliffs across a succession of chutes near their tops into a large snow couloir which broadens at its top (this is the first of the three parallel couloirs leading up from the head of Success Glacier). Ascend and then bear right for the shoulder skyline at 12,000 ft at the confluence with Kautz Cleaver. Continue upward on a traverse over rock and snow slopes, keeping on the E side of the cleaver, to Point Success (or stay below it by bearing right on snow). Cross the intervening saddle to the crater rim. Grade II. Time: 7 hours from high camp to Point Success. References: *Sunset,* vol. 16 (1905), p. 44; *Mountaineer,* 1918, pp. 49-50; 1920, p. 47; 1949, pp. 55-56; *Mazama,* 1965; *A.A.J.,* 1957, pp. 17-18; *A.N.A.M.,* 1978, pp. 29-30.

SOUTH TAHOMA HEADWALL: The South Tahoma Glacier is a classic example of a cirque-born glacier, nourished both by avalanches and by direct snowfall. The glacier lies between the Success and Tahoma cleavers; the formidable recessed headwall rises above a schrund system at 10,300 ft and steepens to Point Success. Due to rockfall from many exposed bands, the climb should be done in early season and under cold temperatures. In December 1946, a Marine Corps aircraft crashed on the South Tahoma Glacier. First ascent by Steve Marts and Fred Beckey on July 12, 1963.

From a camp on Success Cleaver at about 8300 ft (see Success Cleaver Route), traverse N to the glacier; it may be necessary to make a short descent. The best route to avoid crevasses is generally near the center or N side of the glacier. Cross the bergschrund and ascend directly upface, keeping right of a curving couloir that slants down from the upper left portion of the face. A left-slanting ice ramp works below a small ice cliff to a corner nearly atop Point Success; here easy slopes are taken to its top. Grade III or IV. Time: 7 hours on the face. Reference: *A.A.J.,* 1964, p. 70.

Note: an alternate approach is that for Tahoma Cleaver.

TAHOMA CLEAVER: This prominent cleaver on the SW side of Mount Rainier separates the Tahoma and South Tahoma glaciers. The route is long and demanding; it begins at 9000 ft and extends to the NW corner of Point Success. Due to rockfall hazard, the climb is recommended for early season. Because a section of rock on the buttress at 12,000 ft appears to have broken away, climbers may be forced to the variation described. The first ascent was made by Klindt Vielbig, Anthony Hovey, Don Keller, Paul Bellamy, and Herb Steiner on June 7, 1959.

Take the Tahoma Creek Trail ♦ to its juncture with the Wonderland Trail; then follow this N toward Emerald Ridge about a mi. and cross below the terminus of Tahoma Glacier on morainal and outwash debris. Head into the major broad gully splitting Glacier Island (long snow slope in early season); this takes one to the broad northern edge of South Tahoma Glacier.

Follow it, keeping right of several rock islands and buttresses to about 8500 ft at the beginning of the Tahoma Cleaver. Ascend the flat cleaver crest until forced onto the large oval shelf on the left of the crest at about 9200 ft. Proceed upslope to a small snow col at 10,000 ft (just above the base of a red rock tower). This is the last good campsite on the Cleaver. Time: 8-10 hours from road.

Proceed upward on moderate snow slopes toward the sharp giant ridge gendarme (11,700 ft). Pass 200 ft below it on the right and traverse diagonally across long steep S-facing snow slopes toward the huge black rock buttress which blocks the crest. Gain the knife-edge snow ridge about 100 yards before the buttress and then follow to its base (12,000 ft). About 40 ft around the N side of the buttress a 25-ft vertical solid rock pitch (original ascent) led to the steep rounded slope of about 500 ft bearing to the buttress crest left of the massive square-topped tower. From the snow saddle bear NE on a steeply inclined snow ramp to its end at 13,700 ft, where it drops steeply to the Tahoma Glacier. Take steep ledges around the corner to the right for 300 ft where broken ice is crossed to the summit icecap; climb NE to the crater rim. Grade IV. Time: 11 hours from camp. References: *A.A.J.,* 1960, p. 114; *Mountaineer,* 1960, p. 76.

Variation: By Dan Davis, Gene Prater, Tom Stewart, and Steve Marts on June 16, 1968. At the buttress base this party found a vertical step of more than 150 ft on both flanks. This party made a traversing ascent up steep snow/ice slopes below the high vertical rock band for about ½ mi. Where the ice joins cliffs, they climbed two rock pitches (exposed class 4) which are long, steep, and loose, to surmount the band and meet the original route. Reference: *A.A.J.,* 1969, pp. 383-384.

Approach Variation: Use Emerald Ridge Trail (see South Puyallup River Trail ♦). Continue to the Tahoma Glacier moraine and proceed NE to the lower S edge of the glacier.

TAHOMA CLEAVER (pre-1959)
BRADFORD WASHBURN

11,700'
Gendarme

Black Buttress

Rock Step

Tahoma
Cleaver

1959

1968

TAHOMA GLACIER

At about 7000 ft bear toward the N edge of the South Tahoma Glacier.

TAHOMA GLACIER: The Tahoma Glacier tumbles vigorously from the depression W of the summit cone through a narrow gap and descends some 4½ mi., to below timberline. The terminus has two lobes, one draining southward to Tahoma Creek, and the larger northern lobe draining westward into the South Puyallup River at 5200 ft. In the 19th century the Tahoma and South Tahoma glaciers flowed in wide detours around the castellated rock mass known as Glacier Island, then united below.

The Tahoma is steepest between 11,500 and 13,000 ft, where the angle varies from 30 to 40 degrees; it is over a mi. wide at places, with a surface alternating between smooth areas and icefalls. Matthes described it as "diversified by countless icefalls and cataracts." In early summer the Tahoma provides one of Rainier's most direct routes, but by August it can be badly broken.

The first ascent was by Philemon B. Van Trump, Alfred Drewry, Dr. Warren Riley, and Riley's deerhound on August 11, 1891. The route was again used by Riley and George Jones when they participated in the first climb of Liberty Cap (then called "North Peak") on July 31, 1892 (with Frank Taggert and Frank Lowe, coming from the crater rim). The early climbs began from the South Tahoma Glacier, then diagonally climbed the Tahoma (see Approach Variations); the presently popular entry to the Tahoma from Puyallup Cleaver was pioneered by Hans Fuhrer and Alfred Roovers in 1934.

From Klapatche Park ◆ take the trail E to St. Andrews Park, then ascend snowfields and ridges to the crest of Puyallup Cleaver just below Tokaloo Rock. Turn it on the S and continue up the crest to a notch at 8000 ft. Follow the Puyallup Glacier around the N side of the monster rock buttress (9063 ft) on the cleaver, then return to the cleaver at 9200 ft. Here is a good camp spot; allow 5-7 hours from road.

To reach the Tahoma first ascend the Puyallup just left of the cleaver to a large snowfield (near 10,000 ft) that drops S through a break. Diagonally descend several hundred ft onto the Tahoma, then choose the best line of ascent to the summit icecap and crater rim; generally it is best to ascend the steep section near center or right-center. Grade II. Time: 6-9 hours from high camp. References: Haines, *Mountain Fever*, pp. 123-129; *A.A.J.*, 1957, pp. 15-17; 1959, p. 301; *Mountaineer*, 1920, p. 46; *Mazama*, 1914, pp. 26-27; *Sierra Club Bull.*, May 1894, pp. 109-132; *Overland Monthly* 8 (September 1886), pp. 266-278; Evelyn Hyman Chase, *Mountain Climber: George B. Bayley 1840-1894*, pp. 135-154.

Approach Variations: Hike in from the Emerald Ridge Trail (see South Puyallup River Trail ◆) via the Tahoma Glacier moraine and proceed NE to the lower S edge of the glacier; then ascend to join the main route at about 10,000 ft. This variation requires longer distances on snow and ice. Another approach is to use that for Tahoma Cleaver, to northern edge of South Tahoma Glacier, then work through

the cleaver dividing the glaciers at a break (8200 ft) to the Tahoma. When nearing the lower cliffs of Tahoma Cleaver, it may be necessary to work well out on the glacier. Reference: *Mountaineer*, 1920, p. 46.

Variation: In late summer the Tahoma below 11,000 ft may be badly crevassed. In this event, climb over lower St. Andrews Rock (easy but loose) and continue on the edge of the South Mowich Glacier around the N side of upper St. Andrews; if crevasses bar the way, climb over its crest.

Variation: South Mowich Icefall and Tahoma Glacier Sickle: By Leroy Ritchie, Larry Heggerness, Allan Van Buskirk, Edward Drues, Bob Walton, Monte and Mark Haun on June 8, 1958.

Starting from the Puyallup Cleaver at 8000 ft work across the Puyallup Glacier to above Colonnade Ridge. The route then climbs the South Mowich Glacier Icefall (steepest from 9500 to 10,800 ft) to the upper end of upper St. Andrews Rock (11,200 ft); the icefall is recommended only in early season because of the vigorous flow from the accumulation zone, and resulting chaos. From here work S and then climb the steep sickle-shaped trough at the extreme N edge of the upper Tahoma Glacier (watch for debris from small ice cliffs on right). The "Sickle" is generally a good route until late summer. Time: 11 hours from 8000-ft camp on Puyallup Cleaver. Reference: *A.A.J.*, 1959, p. 301.

Tahoma Descent Route: May also be used by those ascending other routes, such as Sunset Ridge or Mowich Face. One should (1) descend the steep part of the Tahoma, or the Tahoma Glacier "Sickle" (a safe, fast descent route that avoids the crevasse problems of the Tahoma); (2) rise N to the col above St. Andrews Rock; (3) swing around N side of upper St. Andrews Rock, then descend over lower St. Andrews to the head of upper Puyallup Glacier; one could return to timberline via the Puyallup Glacier, or return to a particular base. Note: In late season or in years when South Mowich is unusually active, crevasses may force a descent over crumbly upper St. Andrews Rock.

SUNSET AMPHITHEATER — TAHOMA GLACIER ICECAP: Sunset Amphitheater, the unique high W-facing cirque at the head of the South Mowich Glacier, is a great ice-accumulation reservoir nearly a mile wide and about 2000 ft higher in elevation than any other large cirque on Rainier. The cirque headwall begins at 12,500 ft, then maintains a constant angle to Liberty Cap, the upper slopes of Sunset Ridge, and the ice cap at the W edge of the upper Tahoma Glacier. It is characterized by conspicuous furrows carved by ice and rock avalanches that have crashed down its steep slopes.

Although the cirque is similar to that resulting from glacial erosion, studies indicate it is a scar probably largely formed by repeated landslides. Its ice reservoir descends as the South Mowich Icefall, a narrow reach, then divides to send a portion of its volume to the Puyallup Glacier. In spite of this loss, the South Mowich Glacier attains a length of nearly 4 mi. The Puyallup remains on a higher bed and expands to a width of one mi.

MOUNT RAINIER from west
AUSTIN POST, U.S. GEOLOGICAL SURVEY

LIBERTY CAP

Success Cleaver

SOUTH
TAHOMA
GLACIER

Glacier Island

Rock Step

11,700' Gendarme

Tahoma
Cleaver

Red Tower

The Sickle

Sunset Amphitheater

TAHOMA GLACIER

Upper
Lower
St. Andrews Rocks

1939

9,063'

1958

Sunset
Ridge

SOUTH
MOWICH
GLACIER

Puyallup
Cleaver

PUYALLUP
GLACIER

8,000'

Gibraltar Rock

Nisqually Icefall

KAUTZ GLACIER

Success Cleaver

POINT SUCCESS

Black Buttress

South Tahoma Headwall

Tahoma Cleaver

11,700' Gendarme

COLUMBIA CREST

East Crater

West Crater

Register Rock

TAHOMA GLACIER

The Sickle

TAHOMA GLACIER ICECAP

Upper St. Andrews Rock

1937

LIBERTY CAP

exit gully

upper ramp

Sunset Amphitheater Headwall

1937

Sunset Amphitheater

The rugged W flank of Rainier, N of the Tahoma Glacier, was virtually unexplored until the late 1930s. The first ascent of the Sunset Amphitheater by J. Wendell Trosper and Fred Thieme on July 13, 1937 was a spirited effort involving unusual problems.

Use the approach as for the Tahoma Glacier to the 9200-ft campsite on the Puyallup Cleaver. Take the upper Puyallup Glacier to its head, then climb over lower St. Andrews Rock (easy but loose) and continue on the edge of the South Mowich Glacier around the N side of upper St. Andrews Rock; if crevasses bar the way, climb over its crest. Ascend the slopes of Sunset Amphitheater to the bergschrund at the foot of the final wall. Cross the schrund and ascend across the steep slope above (original party crossed schrund on a tilted ice plug, then cut steps and used ice pitons for protection). Climb and traverse steep ice to the N end of the upper Tahoma Glacier icecap at 12,500 ft. In 1937 this was climbed via stemming of a huge longitudinal crevasse to reach the surface of the upper Tahoma Glacier S of Liberty Cap. From here continue E to Columbia Crest. Grade III. Take ice screws. Time: 12 hours from St. Andrews Rock. References: *A.A.J.*, 1954, p. 23; *Mountaineer*, 1937, pp. 22-25.

SUNSET AMPHITHEATER HEADWALL: This headwall is the gullied cirque beneath Liberty Cap. First ascent by Gene Prater, Dave Mahre, Don McPherson, James Wickwire, and Fred Stanley on July 24, 1965.

Some difficulty may be experienced crossing the headwall bergschrund. This is done while still beneath the great ice cliff (S of 1937 route), then a traverse left is made along the schrund's top on rock and ice. A hard move on rock leads around a corner to the deep couloir separating the ice cliff from the headwall (considerable avalanche hazard en route). Cross the couloir to the open face. Climb diagonally up face across two large snow patches, then cross left to a third one and up a long snow ramp for several hundred ft to the steep rock buttress which lines the headwall's crest (ramp is safe). At upper end of the ramp, cross right to a narrow twisting 500-ft gully between two rock walls; it allows an exit from the headwall. The route ends about 200 ft below the top of Liberty Cap. Some rockfall was encountered on the first climb. Grade III. Take ice screws. Time: 7 hours from camp at 9200 ft. References: *A.A.J.*, 1966, p. 128; *Summit*, July-August 1966, pp. 8-11.

SUNSET RIDGE: This prominent spur, rising as a long serrated ridge, extends from opposite the 8500-ft confluence of the Puyallup and South Mowich glaciers and terminates at Liberty Cap. It is flanked on the N by the Mowich Face and on the S by the Sunset Amphitheater. Sunset Ridge broadens below 12,000 ft and is actually composed of two ridges separated by a steep snowfield and gully, and lower by a lobe of the South Mowich Glacier.

That such a prominent route was not attempted before 1938 is surprising. It was first climbed by Lyman Boyer, Arnold Campbell, and Don Woods on August 27-28, 1938. During the ascent the trio had to chop a bivouac platform at 11,000 ft. While the climb is long and has several steep sections, its angle has been quite exaggerated in some accounts. The route to about 12,000 ft is up the steep snow and gully slopes on the N of the main ridge crest (near the center of the broader lower half of Sunset Ridge). A direct ascent variation would be much longer.

From the 8000-ft notch on Puyallup Cleaver (see Tahoma Glacier route) traverse the Puyallup Glacier (at the same level) to the upper end of Colonnade Ridge (between the Puyallup and South Mowich glaciers) where a high camp can be made at 8300 ft (5-7 hours); alternate camp is at 9200-ft rock divide between South Mowich and Edmunds glaciers. Then descend to and cross South Mowich Glacier; turn the lowest cliff corner of Sunset Ridge, then climb the steep side-lobe of the glacier to its upper bergschrund. Cross it and ascend the long steep central snow/ice gully; gain the ridge overlooking Sunset Amphitheater at 12,000 ft. Traverse the rotten ridge crest (most crumbling and delicate about 12,500 ft) to a small saddle, then climb the steep upper 1000 ft of the ridge to the final broad névé slope leading to Liberty Cap. Grade III. Time: 9-12 hours from high camp. References: *Mountaineer*, 1938, pp. 30-32; 1949, pp. 4-7; *A.A.J.*, 1939, pp. 310-315; 1950, pp. 503-504; 1957, pp. 24-25; *Mazama*, 1967, pp. 68-70.

Variation: Sunset Amphitheater — Sunset Ridge: By J. Wendell Trosper and Hans Grage, early August 1939. Reach the head of the South Mowich Glacier via the Sunset Amphitheater approach or by climbing the South Mowich Icefall. From above St. Andrews Rock traverse N below the Sunset Amphitheater cliffs, then climb the steep snow slope which joins the glacier with Sunset Ridge at 12,000 ft. Time: 7 hours from high camp. References: *A.A.J.*, 1957, p. 23; *Cascadian*, 1961, pp. 51-52.

Variation: South Flank of Edmunds Glacier Headwall: By Gene Prater, Dave Mahre, James Wickwire, Fred Stanley, and Fred Dunham on May 31, 1963.

This variation stays left of the lower portion of the Sunset Ridge route, and climbs on the S flank of the Edmunds Glacier Headwall. Access is gained by a saddle on the lower left edge of Sunset Ridge, above the bergschrund at the head of the side-lobe of South Mowich Glacier. From the saddle angle diagonally up and left across rock on the edge of lower Edmunds Headwall (onto face only slightly off the ridge crest); numerous gullies and some rockfall may be encountered. Climb upward on edge of headwall to bear back to original route just below where it meets actual crest of Sunset Ridge. Reference: *Cascadian*, 1963, pp. 43-45.

MOWICH FACE

The upper North Mowich and Edmunds glaciers adorn the NW face of Mount Rainier's Liberty Cap, between Sunset and Ptarmigan ridges. The North Mowich Glacier is fed by two lobes above 8000 ft; one heads at 10,500 ft against Ptarmigan Ridge and the other heads centrally under Mowich Face. The Edmunds

COLUMBIA CREST

POINT SUCCESS

LIBERTY CAP

Sunset Ridge

Ptarmigan Ridge

Upper St. Andrews Rock

Lower St. Andrews Rock

PUYALLUP GLACIER

9,200'

Colonnade Ridge

8,300'

SOUTH MOWICH GLACIER

9,200'

EDMUNDS GLACIER

9,600'

9,200'

1

2

3

4

5

NORTH MOWICH GLACIER

Routes

1. South Flank Edmunds Glacier Headwall
2. Edmunds Headwall
3. Central Mowich Face
4. North Mowich Headwall
5. North Mowich Face Icefall

Glacier heads on the S half of the Mowich Face, N of Sunset Ridge.

The Mowich Face forms a roughly triangular incline that rises 4000 ft to its apex at a snow dome (13,500 ft) W of Liberty Cap, above these glaciers. The mile-wide face is characterized by steep ice slopes above which are several thick ice cliffs; one immense ice cliff hangs halfway on the central-right part of the face, while another caps the N half of the face. In addition, there is a long, precipitous icefall on the N end of the face. The apparent steepness of the Mowich Face, as it has come to be known after the first climb in 1957, undoubtedly discouraged earlier attempts. In reality, most of the face is not over 40 degrees in angle and only short stretches exceed 50 degrees; still the face is an exceptional climb. Because of its span, three parties have been able to find new routes to the N of the original line, and for the sake of clarity, these will be treated as separate routes. Because rock bands can create dangerous stonefall, climbs are best done in early summer and during cold conditions. Descents are generally made via Tahoma Glacier.

EDMUNDS HEADWALL: This was the original route on the Mowich Face, climbed by John Rupley, Don (Claunch) Gordon, Fred Beckey, Tom Hornbein, and Herb Staley on June 23, 1957; because of an oncoming storm, the first ascent party descended the route immediately thereafter.

One can use the same general approach as for Sunset Ridge. Leave high camp at 8300 ft on Colonnade Ridge, make a slight descent and cross the South Mowich Glacier, then ascend lower ice lobe of the Sunset Ridge route to the rock divide at 9200 ft overlooking the Edmunds Glacier. Descend slightly, then contour below an icefall during a ½-mi. traverse N across upper Edmunds Glacier. Beyond a little icefall turn upward; a flat-topped rock island on the left at 9600 ft (separating Edmunds from North Mowich Glacier) offers an alternate campsite — allow 8 hours from road. Ascend to and cross bergschrund, then climb directly up snow and ice slopes to the upper part of Sunset Ridge and to Liberty Cap. Grade III or IV. Take ice screws. Time: 9-12 hours to Liberty Cap from Colonnade Ridge. References: *A.A.J.*, 1958, pp. 78-79; *Challenge of the North Cascades*, pp. 228-229.

CENTRAL MOWICH FACE: This route ascends above the North Mowich Glacier N of the original Mowich Face route; the party establishing the route camped at 9600 ft on the rock island (see Edmunds Headwall). First ascent by Dee Molenaar, Gene Prater, James Wickwire, and Dick Pargeter on July 24, 1966.

Reach the face as for the Edmunds Headwall route; from the rock island make a climbing traverse of the S edge of North Mowich Glacier, cross bergschrund if necessary and ascend 45-degree slopes to an alcove below the rock bands at 12,500 ft. Here the lower of three rock bands is climbed at a 15-ft cliff at the waist of an ice hourglass (a later party found this to be a 40-ft rock pitch). Then traverse N along a steep, narrow snow-covered ledge and around an exposed corner, where the ledge broadens to steep ice, then narrows to the ice chute that separates the rock bands from the icecap bulge on the N. The chute may need some step-cutting, depending on technique and conditions. It gives direct exit to the rounded crest on the upper part of Ptarmigan Ridge. Grade III or IV. Take ice screws. Time: 6 hours from camp to top of face, then 1 hour to Liberty Cap. References: *Mountaineer,* 1967, pp. 131-132; *A.A.J.,* 1967, pp. 348-349; *Summit,* March 1967, pp. 4-7.

Variation: Right Upper Section: By Del Young, Bill Cockerham, Bill Sumner, and Ed Marquart on July 4, 1967. Below base of rock bands make a diagonal traverse right below the system of rock bands, then climb directly up steep open ice slope at apex of face (possible extensive use of ice screw belays).

NORTH MOWICH HEADWALL: This route ascends the N third of the face; there is a significant rock cliff at the bottom and several more at the top, under the capping ice. This is a hard route and one should be prepared for technical climbing; it could be subjected to fall of some rock and ice. First ascent by Mike Heath, Dan Davis, Mead Hargis, and Bill Cockerham on July 22, 1968.

Approach as for Edmunds Headwall route. A short climbing traverse past the little icefall on the upper Edmunds leads to a good bivouac rock outcrop at 9200 ft between the Edmunds and North Mowich glaciers. Traverse the North Mowich about ½ mi., angling to a concave bowl at the route's start (bowl is directly below top ice cliff). Cross the bergschrund and then ascend a difficult "hourglass" of steep rock and ice which cuts through the lower rock band. Above it, continue directly up snow/ice to the rock cliff just below the right end of the ice cliff. Then traverse up and right to beneath right end of the ice cliff (ice steepens here). Then climb a 50-ft vertical rock band (hard class 5 or easy aid; solid base but loose higher) to the ice just to the right of the ice cliff. Final 600 ft of climbing on steep ice slopes until slopes round off onto upper Ptarmigan Ridge. Then follow easy slopes to Liberty Cap. Grade IV. Take ice screws and some rock pitons. Time: 12 hours from high camp. Reference: *A.A.J.,* 1969, pp. 384-385.

NORTH MOWICH FACE ICEFALL: This icefall forms the N extremity of the Mowich Face and heads the S lobe of the North Mowich Glacier. The route ascends alongside and on this prominent icefall. Primarily a snow and ice climb, there is some rock climbing in midface and in exiting at the top. The climb should be done no later than the end of June. First ascent by James Wickwire and Rob Schaller on June 26, 1970. Part of the icefall was descended by Bauer and Grage, September 1934.

Use same approach as for North Mowich Headwall. Traverse across the North Mowich Glacier to the base of a cleaver separating the icefall from the North Mowich Head-

Sunset Ridge

Mowich Face

Ptarmigan Ridge

LIBERTY CAP

NORTH MOWICH GLACIER

LIBERTY CAP GLACIER

Ptarmigan Ridge

1935

Liberty Ridge

Point 10,310

RUSSELL GLACIER

Curtis Ridge

CARBON GLACIER

wall. The bergschrund can be avoided by a delicate leftward ice traverse (two leads) above it, just below the cleaver's base. Climb the depression which parallels the lowest section of the icefall: several pitches on steep ice lead to a rock section which offers one 40-ft vertical pitch on surprisingly sound rock. Two moderate rock pitches above lead toward the snow/ice left and above the "hourglass" of the North Mowich Headwall Route. Ascend the left edge of the broad névé slope, parallel to the other route for 500 ft, then climb diagonally left through the upper icefall. A 45-degree slope is climbed to the large cliff band forming the uppermost portion of Ptarmigan Ridge. An obvious gully leads to a final steep 30-ft rock pitch (class 5) which exits onto the névé slopes of upper Ptarmigan Ridge at 12,700 ft. Grade IV. Take ice screws and rock pitons. Time: 9 hours on the face. Reference: *A.A.J.*, 1971, pp. 340-341.

PTARMIGAN RIDGE: One of Mount Rainier's most impressive spurs is Ptarmigan Ridge, which rises on the NW flank in a series of sharp rocky crests starting between the deep canyons of the North Mowich Glacier on the W and the broad surface of the Russell Glacier on the E. At 10,500 ft the ridge forms a steep face featuring the 300-ft ice cliff of the Liberty Cap Glacier. On the W side of Ptarmigan Ridge the North Mowich Glacier forms a headwall base near 10,500 ft. Above 12,500 ft broad open slopes lead S toward Liberty Cap.

The original Winthrop Glacier party of Fobes, James, and Wells ascended to about 10,000 ft on Ptarmigan Ridge on August 16, 1884, then came to an abrupt halt. In 1905 a Lee Pickett of Bellingham claimed to have climbed Ptarmigan Ridge with a companion, an adventure that no historian has accepted. L. A. Nelson had been on an early climb onto Ptarmigan Ridge, then in 1912 Dora Keen with two others tried it twice; she reached 9500 ft when one member of the group became ill, a high wind halted the second effort. Her account states "this side of the mountain was considered impossible because of the almost continuous avalanches." She felt that the steep ice slope was the only serious problem, and like other early climbers, that September was the best month for this route. The first pioneering onto the upper slopes was in late summer 1933 when Hans Grage, J. Wendell Trosper, and Jarvis Wallen climbed to about 11,000 ft to the right of the ice cliff; they did some cutting, to the limit of their time.

The following year Grage and Wolf Bauer made two attempts, the last one on September 2. They climbed to 12,500 ft, but ran short of time, then descended the edge of the Mowich Face. On a climb made hazardous by falling rock, the first ascent was made by Bauer and Jack Hossack on September 7-8, 1935, when they spent 12 hours cutting on ice and verglas. The use of improved crampons and cutting techniques were important reasons for the success of the first climbs on Ptarmigan and Liberty ridges. These ascents were both symptoms and catalysts of a developing trend toward bolder routes. The second ascent of Ptarmigan Ridge was

MOUNT RAINIER from northwest
AUSTIN POST, U.S. GEOLOGICAL SURVEY

made by Bill and Gene Prater on July 18, 1959, taking the lower principal snow/ice slope (now the normal way). First winter ascent was by Al Errington and party on March 7-11, 1972.

The major difficulties of the route lie between 10,500 and 12,500 ft where hard ice and sustained rockfall may be encountered; some rock belays may be needed. It is important to make the ascent during optimum surface and temperature conditions. An early start and good pace are equally important.

From Spray Park ◆ leave the trail at its high point (about 6400 ft) and gradually ascend parkland and Ptarmigan Ridge's lower slopes. Most parties cross SE, bearing to the saddle between Echo and Observation rocks, then continue near the right (W) edge of the Russell Glacier; when snow conditions are soft, it may be an advantage to follow pumice areas on the crest. A steeper slope leads to Point 10,310 ft. One can make a high camp just below the point (some water in midsummer) or follow the tottering, narrow crest (keep on E side to avoid the summit crag) to a small col at 10,200 ft just beneath the Liberty Cap ice cliff (room for high camp here).

From the narrow crest or the col, traverse downward W on the edge of the North Mowich Glacier. The usual swath of fresh litter is evidence of danger from the ice cliff (not an area to linger). Cross the bergschrund easily and make a long leftward ascent up the 40-degree principal snow/ice slope to the large rock band heading it. Cross a minor spur, then make a traverse closely under the rock cliff (sometimes icy; rock protection possible). Climb a steep shallow snow/ice apron (usually some ice) to the final rock buttress at 12,000 ft. Traverse left under the buttress for about three leads to the steep ice chute at the edge of the Liberty Cap Glacier. Ascend this chute (one pitch) on the E side of the buttress, then climb leftward the best way through the crevasse/serac pattern to the easier gradient above. Changing conditions may make climbing upward, not left, the best choice. It is best to keep near the crest of Ptarmigan Ridge and turn crevasses on the right. The ridge broadens, then merges with Sunset Ridge at 13,400 ft. Follow on or near the crest to Liberty Cap. Grade IV. Take ice screws and several rock pitons. Time: 6-12 hours from high camp. References: *Mountaineer*, 1912, pp. 37-39; 1933, pp. 14-15; 1934, pp. 3-5; 1935, pp. 3-6; 1972, p. 74 (winter); *A.A.J.*, 1957, pp. 19-21; *Summit*, May 1973, pp. 2-7; *Cascadian*, 1956.

Variation: (route of first ascent) Climb close to W base of the Liberty Cap Glacier ice cliff via snow/ice, then through a chute in the first rock band. Bypass a large rock step via the ice slope to its W, to join the normal route below the final rock buttress. This route is likely to involve more ice climbing and now appears to be subject to unnecessary dangers.

Variation: By James Wickwire and Rob Schaller in August 1969. Where the normal route is forced left by the major rock band heading the principal ice slope, make an eastward traverse past the snow/ice apron and beneath the two easternmost rock cliffs. From a belay recess at the edge of the Liberty Cap Glacier climb a 55-degree pitch (possibly black ice), then continue directly up to the chute at the E edge of the final rock buttress.

Variation: Climb the ice chute near 12,000 ft, then traverse right on slabby rock beneath the incipient ice cliff to the true crest of Ptarmigan Ridge. Difficulty and steepness depend on the condition of the ice cliff. Above, continuous snow/ice leads to easier slopes.

Variation: (route of 1934 attempt) From the base of the final rock buttress climb the snow/ice ramp on its W to a minor notch in the rock at its head. Then traverse snow above the upper edge of the Mowich Face; a narrow rock gully cuts into the band above. Exit to the upper glacier per the short, solid, but steep rock pitch of the North Mowich Face Icefall Route (can be climbed with crampons).

PTARMIGAN RIDGE — LIBERTY CAP GLACIER:
This climb has an inherent danger because of the threat of icefall while traversing beneath the major ice cliff. This traverse should be timed to proceed during ideal conditions so it can be done rapidly. First ascent by Fred Beckey, John Rupley, and Herb Staley on August 5, 1956.

From the Ptarmigan Ridge high camp ascend to the base of the great ice cliff (at about 11,000 ft) flanking the E side of the ridge. Traverse and diagonally ascend left (possibly some steep glazed rock) along an increasingly steep and narrowing sloping ramp (a few ice screws may be advisable) to around a slight corner. Ascend a 20-ft step onto a ledge, then traverse steep exposed ice to broad névé slope. Work up (original party did 50 ft of crampon rock climbing), then make a sharp cut back on a curved ice ramp through the cliff to the Liberty Cap Glacier. Then ascend the well-crevassed glacier to Liberty Cap. Grade III or IV. Take ice screws. Time: 10 hours high camp to summit. References: *Mountaineer,* 1956, pp. 122-123; Fred Beckey, *Challenge of the North Cascades,* pp. 224-228; *Appalachia,* December 1956, p. 240.

LIBERTY WALL TO LIBERTY CAP GLACIER:
First ascent by Paul Myhre, Don Jones, and Roger Oborn on June 30, 1968. Make approach as per Liberty Ridge or from Spray Park and via the glacier ramp between the Russell and Carbon glaciers to reach the large schrund at the western head of the Carbon. Ascend the slope of Liberty Wall, first on the long snow/ice area, then through the cliffs by a gully and a long, continuous rib. The succeeding ice slope leads to rock bands, where there is mixed climbing leading to a ramp onto the Liberty Cap Glacier. One should be aware of the objective dangers. Take ice screws. Grade IV. Time: 6 hours from 8300-ft camp on edge of Carbon to 12,300 ft on Liberty Cap Glacier. References: *A.A.J.,* 1969, pp. 305-306; *Mountaineer,* 1969, p. 112.

LIBERTY WALL — DIRECT:
This route ascends E of the 1968 route, near the longest part of the headwall west of Liberty Ridge. The ice cliff of the headwall, 150-250 ft high in the area of the climb, should be considered a most dangerous objective hazard. First ascent by Dusan Jagersky and Gary Isaacs on September 19-20, 1971.

On the original ascent, the route followed was from high camp on Curtis Ridge near 7500 ft to the bergschrund at the base of the avalanche chute (3 hours). The chute crossing should only be used if necessary. Bear left to minimize avalanches, and stay just right of a broken-up ice ridge. A 45-degree slope of snow/ice continues to some solid rock bands that lead to the 150-200-ft ice cliff. One lead of difficult free climbing was the crux, with use of about ten ice screws. From a good belay atop the ice cliff ascend a 45-degree+ snow/ice slope, working around crevasses up the fall line of Liberty Cap; original party made bivouac in a crevasse beneath its top. Grade IV or V. Time: 13 hours.

LIBERTY RIDGE:
One of the earliest references to Liberty Ridge was from the early geologist, F. E. Matthes, who wrote "The Carbon Glacier's amphitheatre . . . consists really of two twin cirques, separated by an angular buttress. But this projection, which is a remnant of a formerly long spur . . . is being eliminated by the undermining process." The base of Liberty Ridge is 8600 ft, about 1000 ft lower than the bergschrunds on adjacent Willis Wall and Liberty Wall. The ridge climbs at a constant angle to about 13,100 ft near Liberty Cap, being Mount Rainier's steepest major cleaver. The remarkable profile and protrusion from its flanking walls gives Liberty Ridge a purity of line. The flanking upper Carbon Glacier steepens at 9000 ft and merges with the upper ice cliffs of Liberty Cap Glacier at about 12,000 ft.

Liberty Ridge apparently was not attempted before the first ascent in late September 1935, when the climb was done under very icy conditions, slowing the party so they had to bivouac at 11,000 ft and again on the summit. The route has become popular for parties not objecting to continuous exposure and the possibility of stonefall. The climb should be done in early season (before August) to minimize icy conditions and rockfall. Conditions on Liberty Ridge are generally best in May and June, although the approach then may be on soft snow. High camps or bivouacs are usually made on Curtis Ridge at 7500 ft (on the Carbon's edge) or at the small saddle above Thumb Rock (10,775 ft); where there is space for several tents.

Depending upon conditions, the ascent of the ridge (above the Carbon) may take from 6 hours to more than one day. Liberty Cap is the logical conclusion of the route; most parties descend by another way — usually the Emmons Glacier or Disappointment Cleaver. The first ascent was made by Ome Daiber, Arnie Campbell, and Jim Borrow on September 29-30, 1935. The ascent was not repeated for twenty years (Dave Mahre, Marcel Schuster, Mike McGuire, and Gene Prater on August 21, 1955). The first winter ascent was made in January 1976.

Lower Curtis Ridge at 7500 ft is the highest location from which to make an easy entry onto the Carbon. This location can be reached from (1) Moraine Park (see East Wonderland Trail ◆) by leaving the trail just W of Mystic Lake and climbing gradual slopes southward, or (2) White River Campground and Glacier Basin ◆ by taking the trail to St. Elmo Pass (the pass was named by Major E. S. Ingraham after a fine exhibit of St. Elmo's fire one night), then crossing the Winthrop Glacier at the 7500 ft level to the broad slopes

UPPER PTARMIGAN RIDGE (September 11)
AUSTIN POST, UNIVERSITY OF WASHINGTON

Sunset Ridge

To LIBERTY CAP

LIBERTY CAP GLACIER

North Mowich Face
Icefall Route

exit gully

1934

snow/ice apron

major rock band

Ptarmigan Ridge Route

ice chute

final rock buttress

1969

Ptarmigan Ridge–Liberty Cap
Glacier Route

LIBERTY CAP GLACIER
ICE CLIFF

Ptarmigan Ridge

LIBERTY CAP

Liberty Cap
Glacier

1956

1968

Liberty
Wall

1971

1955

1955

1935

Thumb Rock

Liberty
Ridge

1976

1963

1965

buttress

band

Traverse of Angels

frosty cliff

gray buttress

1961
1970

1971

WILLIS WALL

1965

Curtis Ridge

boulder
field
cliff

1971

buttress

buttress

1974

1963

1962

CARBON GLACIER

of lower Curtis Ridge. Parties often make their first camp in Glacier Basin, then ascend to Thumb Rock for their second camp.

Descend onto the Carbon (often heavily crevassed) and ascend it to the base of Liberty Ridge. Most parties climb toward Willis Wall, taking the easiest line through glacier breakups, then bear W above crevasse mazes, finally descending slightly to the toe of the objective. A direct route is faster, crevasses permitting. Most parties attain the ridge crest from the E flank several hundred ft above its base (snow may provide an entry ramp) and make a steep traverse to a location slightly W of the crest.

Short cliffs pattern the route, which climbs the right flank to the saddle above Thumb Rock. Then climb rightward on firn or ice to the narrow gully that breaks a rock step. Ascend the gully, then continue upward to reach the ridge crest. Cross leftward and ascend the slope to the top of the formation known as Black Pyramid. Continue the ascent until Liberty Ridge merges with the edge of Liberty Cap Glacier. Then climb westward over a bergschrund to bypass the upper ice cliffs for the final trudge to Liberty Cap. Grade III to IV (IV if very icy). Take ice screws and hard hats. References: *Mountaineer*, 1935, pp. 7-9; 1955, p. 57; *A.A.J.*, 1936, pp. 475-478; 1957, pp. 21-23; *Off Belay*, December 1980; *A.N.A.M.*, 1982, pp. 48-49, 52-54, 57-60; 1985, pp. 61-62.

Variation: West Flank: By second-ascent party. The route starts W, below the toe of Liberty Ridge, then works over bergschrund to where snow/ice slopes permit an upward climb (just left of several small icefalls), to meet the normal route near the ridge crest. Follow normal route (or just right of narrow gully) to near 12,000 ft; here bear W to keep right of the prominent isolated rock outcrop. Ascend snow/ice slopes to meet normal route higher.

Approach Variation: This is quite feasible but has not become popular. From Spray Park ◆ ascend N of Echo Rock to the Russell Glacier. Cross it on a rising traverse to the western portion of the Carbon Glacier, work through crevasses to the base of Liberty Ridge.

WILLIS WALL

Willis Wall, named for the distinguished geologist Bailey Willis to honor his extensive explorations on the flanks of Mount Rainier in 1883, rises some 3600 ft at the head of the Carbon Glacier in a sweeping 45-degree face of lava and rock-strewn ice. It is Willis Wall, beset by avalanches, that gives the northern facade of Mount Rainier its awesome character. The Wall, bound on the E by Curtis Ridge and on the W by Liberty Ridge, rises from about 9700 ft to 13,500 ft, where it is capped by 300-ft ice cliffs at the rim of the summit dome. These cliffs have one exit ramp, which breaks into them about one-third of the span from their eastern edge.

Willis Wall has three incomplete spur ribs, which,

while rising slightly above the cirque level, offer only token protection from objective hazards. The dangers of ice fall on any route on the Wall should be recognized as a constant threat, day or night. Vast ice avalanches have littered the Carbon Glacier's cirque, and in an episode from the early 1920s, the Wall apparently discharged an immense rockslide. Most ice avalanches follow couloirs parallel to the ribs, but they may spill over the crests.

Willis Wall, with its scores of thin lava flows and interlayered breccia, is surfaced with unstable rock and is covered with varying amounts of snow, according to time and season. Optimum circumstances for ascent are ample consolidated snow on the Wall (as during early season) and well-frozen conditions (as after several fine days with very cold nights). Then loose rock will be frozen into the slope and the icy rocks covered with hard snow. The Wall is the source of great barrages of rockfall when thawing diminishes the holding power of snow and ice. An early observer, J. B. Flett, likely mistook this rock dust for "steam" (*Mountaineer*, 1912, p. 61).

Four routes have been climbed on Willis Wall and another on its eastern flank to the top of Curtis Ridge. The first climb of the Wall proper was in 1961 and generally followed the line of the westerly of the three spur ribs; the second route followed the eastern of the three; the third route took the central rib. Reference: *Mountaineer*, 1971, p. 73.

WILLIS WALL — WEST RIB (BRUMAL BUTTRESS): This area of Willis Wall has a distinct rib, but its upper portion flattens into a broad face 500 ft below the summit ice cliff. There may be some protection where the rib (sometimes called Damocles Rib) protrudes; the objective danger of falling ice is most prevalent on the lower portion and in the area directly above the rib's termination. One should allow one to two days for the climb (bring bivouac gear). Many sources credit Charles Bell with the first ascent on June 11-12, 1961, although there is still the disturbing question of whether he crossed the bergschrund under the face, and not near the toe of Liberty Ridge as he did in 1962. Alex Bertulis and James Wickwire made the ascent on February 10-11, 1970; they reached the base of the highest ice cliff, then angled across to upper Liberty Ridge. Actually the West Rib was not completely climbed until the ice cliff was surmounted in 1976.

Approach as for Liberty Ridge, but bear to the upper right portion of the glacier cirque. Cross schrund below icefield that breaks cliffs here and ascend directly upward. After climbing the snowfield (icefield) work over several rock bands and a difficult, wide 75 ft cliff band (hardest move here). The crest of the buttress is followed higher. However, most vertical rock steps are circumvented by traversing

WILLIS WALL
ED COOPER

under and left of the cliffs and climbing gullies back to the crest. A "second step" is bypassed on the left. Generally continue on crest until the buttress terminates into a steep snow slope leading to the final rock bands below the ice cliff. Circumvent another prominent buttress on its left and climb over small bands. A snow terrace leads upward to the ice cliff corner. Now the route angles steeply rightward beneath the sickle-shaped curve formed by the ice cliff (where hardest ice pitches are encountered) and rounds a corner. A difficult steep traverse (possible ice) leads to upper Liberty Ridge. Grade IV or V; class 5.7. Bring ice screws and a selection of rock pitons. Reference: *A.A.J.,* 1971, pp. 288-291.

Variation (Upper Ice Cliff): An ascent of the West Rib was made by Tomas Boley and Jack Lewis on February 7, 1976, then climbing from a saddle beneath the ice cliff up "salt and pepper" rock bands to the capping ice cliff. Two pitches of 45-50-degree ice were climbed on a leftward slant through the cliff. On the main portion of the rib the party climbed a leftward ramp some distance above the bergschrund, then found open snowfields just left of the rib crest. Climbing time: 10-12 hours.

THERMOGENESIS ROUTE: First ascent by Steve Doty, Jerome Eberharter, and Jon Olson on May 20, 1978. This route follows the 55-degree couloir to the right of the West Rib. The initial party encountered firm snow, water ice, and some loose rock, taking seven hours to the end of the couloir at 12,500 ft from a crevasse bivouac at 10,000 ft. This route is undoubtedly best under cold conditions, for it is in a hazardous situation. References: *Mountaineer,* 1978, p. 104; *A.A.J.,* 1979, p. 184.

WILLIS WALL — CENTRAL RIB: This rib lies about midway between Curtis Ridge and Liberty Ridge and has a slightly leftward bearing. The first party reported the slope to be usually about 40 degrees; few steps were cut and cramponing was generally good. The second party reported hard ice on the upper 2000 ft of the wall below the exit ledge. Rock areas may be verglassed. Where the Central Rib ends to merge into the Wall, the first ascent party followed the 1963 route (upper third of route), but made a different exit from the summit icecap arm. First ascent by Dean Caldwell and Paul Dix, June 20, 1965. Second ascent by James Wickwire and Ed Boulton, May 12-13, 1971. First winter ascent by Dusan Jagersky and J. Reilly Moss, February 27, 1965.

Approach as for Liberty Ridge and continue to the base of Willis Wall. Cross the schrund and climb onto snow immediately E of rib terminal. Climb directly to its crest (rockfall experienced here). Above are four arching bands of rock that cross the rib (each about 30 ft high). Cross them on the left side of the crest. The second party crossed the bergschrund on the W of the rib terminal and thereby avoided the arches by climbing on continuous snow near the rib's crest.

After the fourth arch climb up and right on a snow slope for several hundred ft to where it is feasible to traverse left (60 ft) on a crumbling ledge to the top of short cliffs.

Directly above is a gray buttress (about halfway on rib); climb directly to it, around left side on snow, then gain its top. Above and slightly left, climb a short, narrow snow or ice chute. Traverse right to slabby rock, then climb to an extremely steep "frosty cliff" of snow and rock. Make a difficult leftward bypass traverse on rock (class 5; frozen mud) for about 40 ft. A moderate 20-ft vertical pitch and a groove in the cliff face lead to a snow slope. Ascend it, then mixed cliffs and gullies to juncture with East Rib Route. The second-ascent party avoided this rock climbing by ascending directly above the ice chute to a 65-degree ice pitch (3 screws) leading to route juncture. Climb to ice terrace and summit exit as per description of prior East Rib Route. From the terrace the Central Rib Route varied by an ascent of the final ice wall by climbing into a crevasse, then chimneying. Grade IV or V. Take ice screws and some rock pitons. Time: 1-2 days, depending on conditions. References: *Mazama,* 1965, pp. 43-44; *Mountaineer,* 1971, pp. 74-75; *A.A.J.,* 1972, p. 114; 1974, pp. 141-142.

Variation: By Dusan Jagersky and Greg Markov, May 1973. From about halfway up the Central Rib, they made an ascending traverse to the eastern side of Willis Wall to the final pitches of Curtis Ridge. The party experienced rockfall and avalanche hazard.

WILLIS WALL — EAST RIB: Of the three ribs on Willis Wall, the eastern is the best protected from objective dangers; the route has its hazards, including stonefall on the lower portion of the rib. This feature has a leftward trend and flattens into the Wall about two-thirds of the distance to the icecap; here a traverse is made to the Central Rib. Some 1500 ft higher, the only break in the Wall's icecap is climbed via a terrace-ramp to the summit slopes. First ascent by Dave Mahre, Fred Dunham, James Wickwire, and Donald N. Anderson on June 8, 1963. First winter ascent by Matt Christensen, Craig Eilers, Dale Farnham, and David Rowland on March 17-22, 1980.

Approach as for Liberty Ridge. From the schrund beneath the East Rib, cross its left end (varying difficulty) and work out on snow/ice slopes, taking a rightward arc until the crest of the rib is attained. Continue up to its end as a buttress at est. 1500 ft up the wall. The completion of this section involves about 100 ft of climbing over very rotten and steep rock (difficult with crampons). From the top of the buttress climb to the head of a small ridge and make a rising right traverse on the sloping snow/ice band to the central avalanche couloir (polished ice-coating needed chopping — too thin for pitons). Cross to another short ridge, then ascend trough on its right (Central Rib Route joins here).

Here about three leads up the snow/ice slope lead to steep rock (three bands) at the base of the summit ice cliff. A full pitch begins up rock about 60 ft left of a conglomerate cliff with a snow ledge atop; a rotten ledge leads up and right to a 10-ft section of near-vertical "steep frozen mud impregnated with large rocks and glued bowling balls." A short traverse left on steep dirt is followed by a hard 20-ft vertical step on solid rock (class 5 — protect pitch with an angle piton and a sling on horn); pitch ends on 8-ft-wide ledge (may be overlain with 45-degree ice) between the first and second band. Here begin the "traverse of the angels." Turn right and in a narrowing 40 ft, crawl 8 ft under a roof. (The crawl is outward-sloping, snow-covered, loose, and unprotected.) Beyond, the ledge widens to a larger snow ramp, and at 200 ft a thermal moat under a rock band provides an emergency bivouac site and protection from avalanche hazard. Moderate slopes bear up and right, then climb through a gap behind a group of seracs formed by a split in the icecap. Reach summit by traversing snow slopes to the W just below the final bergschrund until it ends; then climb directly up and left to the crater rim. Grade V. Take ice screws and some rock pitons. Time: 1-2 days, depending on conditions. References: *A.A.J.,* 1964, pp. 169-170; 1972, p. 114; *Summit,* June 1964, pp. 9-11; *Cascadian,* 1963, pp. 51-53.

Variation: By Lee Nelson and Rob Schaller, June 15-16, 1971. This party reported considerable difficult water ice on the East Rib. They made a leftward traverse of 400 ft to join the Curtis Ridge Route just below its final exit gullies. Reference: *Mountaineer,* 1971, pp. 72, 74.

EAST WILLIS WALL: This route climbs the eastern flank of the Wall, then merges into the upper part of Curtis Ridge at about 12,500 ft. The first ascent was made by Ed Cooper and Mike Swayne on June 26, 1962, and met with the disfavor of the Park Service because permission had not been obtained. The party bivouacked on the upper Carbon Glacier, just beneath the Wall, then spent 8 hours on the final climb.

Approach as for Liberty Ridge. Continue up to upper eastern section of glacier headwall. The route crosses the schrund where it curves around left from Willis Wall, then climbs the steep snow slope on the Curtis Ridge flank. Ascend broken rock and snow to a key ramp, then take it right on a long traverse to bypass cliffs. Near the end of the traverse ramp, climb the long rock band above at "100-ft boulderfield cliff" (initial party did not rope due to hazard of loose rock; estimated treacherous class 4) to reach the ice slope above. Then climb mixed snow and rock until slope eases to ice toe crowning upper Curtis Ridge. Grade IV. Take ice screws.

CURTIS RIDGE: Curtis Ridge is the very prominent spur on Mount Rainier's northern face which separates Willis Wall from the Winthrop Glacier. Lower Curtis Ridge sweeps broadly to an apex rock point at about 10,300 ft; here there is a level section, succeeded by a gap, then a series of vertical cliff bands separated by slopes of steep snow and loose rock.

Attempts on this ridge date back to the 1930s, but were hampered by problems of loose rock in overcoming a prominent 75-ft vertical step at about 10,800 ft and the anticipated danger of rockfall higher. Joe Halwax, Arnie Campbell, and Jim Borrow made attempts, reaching the narrow section of the ridge. Tom Campbell did some exploring on an overhanging crack at this step; his piton may have

been that found on the first ascent, which was made by Gene Prater and Marcel Schuster on July 21, 1957. The climb was made a week after a snowstorm, with cool temperatures; the loose area had not yet thawed so they did not experience the anticipated rockfall. One should wait for similar cool conditions. The second ascent was made by Patrik Callis, Steve Marts, Bill Dougall, and Paul Williams in May 1964.

Emphasis should be placed on fast party movement on Curtis Ridge above the bivouac site chosen. Of all the major routes on Rainier, Curtis Ridge probably has the highest potential for rockfall. With this in mind, speed is of the essence and therefore direct-aid sections should be avoided if possible. An example of the need for speed on Curtis Ridge is illustrated by the 1969 tragedy in which valuable time was lost in surmounting the 75-ft vertical step, thereby placing the party beneath the highest rock band in the warm late afternoon. The 1965 and 1969 variations are faster, and therefore recommended.

Approach from White River Campground (see White River Road ◆), over St. Elmo Pass, and across Winthrop Glacier. Campsite can be found on Curtis Ridge at 8500 ft (6-8 hours). From here ascend to apex of gradual snow slopes at the 10,284-ft rock point shown on the map. There is a good camp platform about 10 minutes below, on the N side; this is the last really comfortable site, but it is far from the climbing problems. Climb down and rappel 50 ft off the SW corner of the buttress point onto a steep snowfield on W side of the Ridge.

Ascend and traverse the snowfield to the narrow rock crest. Follow it to the giant rock thumb (a small drop-off near the end of the crest may require a jump or short rappel to snow on W). Alternately, the steep snowfield has been traversed on a rise for several leads, then an open snowslope climbed to the crest N of the thumb.

Skirt the thumb on its E via a bench at ridge level (possible bivouac here and also beyond the prow-gendarme). Continue onward, passing a prow-gendarme on its W (or follow the prow, then make a short rappel on its W). This brings one to the small saddle beneath the 75-ft "vertical step."

There are several ways to negotiate the step, but avoid going too far E. The original route is the aid crack about 100 ft W of the ridge. The rock can be quite rotten (up to 4 hours has been spent here); second party used about seven aid pitons, finding a block had fallen out to lengthen the overhang. Above the aid, some loose, steep rock leads to a belay spot. The general line now follows open snow slopes just W of the crest to the base of the second major rock step. Traverse right some distance on a snow band until it narrows (at about 11,500 ft); here about 50 ft of low-angle rock climbing with possible ice coating (est. class 5.5) gains access to the largest snowfield on Curtis Ridge.

Diagonal left across the snow slope to again reach the crest. Ascend to a final ice or snow-filled exit gully E of the crest; at the mouth of the ice gully (12,500 ft) there may be a short pitch of sloping rock (class 5). Front-pointing or

LOWER CURTIS RIDGE
AUSTIN POST, U.S. GEOLOGICAL SURVEY

cutting may be required in the 20-ft-wide gully. The gully's continuation (steep icy snow) exits to the crest of upper Curtis Ridge. Ascend the easy glacier ice toe to the summit. Grade IV; class 5 and aid; take pitons or chocks and a few ice screws. Time: allow a full day from high camp to summit. References: *Mountaineer*, 1958, pp. 9799; *A.A.J.*, 1958, pp. 79-80; 1965, p. 407; *Cascadian*, 1957, p. 3-6.

Variation: By Dan Davis, Mark Fielding, Curtis Stout, and Don McPherson on May 30, 1965. At the foot of the "vertical step" angle up, right, on ice below the rock band for about 200-300 ft to a narrower part of the band where the rock looks both sounder and easier. Here is a shallow open book (vertical about 10 ft, then rounding off). Use several pitons or chocks for aid (angles to horizontals), then climb upward-left on slabs to a platform for a scramble to the original route.

Variation: By James Wickwire, Del Young, and Ed Boulton on November 2-3, 1969. This variation turns the first rock band some distance — perhaps 200 ft W — of the 1965 variation. Continue beyond the open book used on the above variation to where it is feasible to climb the band on broken rock (two slabs and a short class 3 pitch over the top of the band), then bear left and upward. This party turned the second step with ice climbing, using a frozen waterfall (difficult, three ice screws); but this provided a quicker way than the rock pitch (probably closely left).

UPPER CURTIS RIDGE
GENE PRATER

Variation: By Tom Stewart, Mike Heath, Gary Glenn, Gene Ohlson, and Bruce Loughlin in June 1967. From the base of the second rock step climb directly up a 100-ft gray rock pitch closely right of the true crest. (First part solid class 5, last part rubbly class 4.)

RUSSELL CLIFF — UPPER CURTIS RIDGE: The reddish beetling cliff bands named for the noted geologist I. C. Russell rise above the upper Winthrop Glacier's N margin from about 11,000 ft to 13,400 ft. On the lower flanks (beneath Curtis Ridge) this wall is extremely steep and

rotten. Higher, a shallow bowl framed by Curtis Ridge on the right and a rock spur adjacent to the upper Winthrop Glacier provides an indentation and route access to upper Curtis Ridge. First ascent by Dave Mahre, Gene Prater, Jim Kurtz, and Don Jones in July 1960.

From Camp Schurman at Steamboat Prow (see Emmons-Winthrop Glacier Route) work up and across the Winthrop Glacier's trough between crevassed areas to 11,000 ft. Then ascend the snow/ice below the shallow bowl. The route here traverses to the N and climbs a 600-ft snow slope ending at the far right extension of the snowfields in the bowl. Follow a snow band N across the cliffs, then ascend a gully or break in the rock to the crest of Curtis Ridge at about 12,500 ft. Grade II. Time: 10 hours from camp. Reference: *A.A.J.*, 1963, p. 471.

Variation: Direct Russell Cliff: By Dean Bentley, Jim Springer, and John L. Thompson on July 8, 1973. From the bowl, proceed directly up the snow face to three prominent rock bands. The original party found unstable snow atop thin water ice while climbing through breaks in the bands. Narrow snow ledges were traversed on the upper portion of the rock bands. Grade II. Time: 8 hours from Camp Schurman to the summit. Reference: *A.A.J.*, 1974, p. 142.

EMMONS — WINTHROP GLACIER: The combined ice streams of the Emmons and Winthrop glaciers blanket the NE flank of Rainier and form what is easily the largest ice expanse in the conterminous United States. The Emmons supplies the White River, largest stream emanating from the mountain. (Samuel Emmons, for whom the glacier is now named, called it the "White River Glacier.") The glacier has a length of nearly 5 mi.; it becomes littered with morainal debris at its lower end, but normally has a clear central lane nearly to the snout. Its crevasse patterns, configuring to the rock bed, are perhaps the most interesting on Mount Rainier: between 7000 and 9000 ft the pattern conforms to an echelon system trending downward, slightly E. The Emmons and Winthrop, flowing from a common source at the crater, are separated at 9500 ft by the rocky wedge of Steamboat Prow (9720 ft). F. E. Matthes wrote that the "descending névés part . . . like swift-flowing waters upon the dividing bow of a ship."

The Winthrop Glacier, which was named for the early writer Theodore Winthrop, flows past the Prow as it separates from the Emmons, and drains into the timber-lined valley of White River's W fork. It ends with a low surface gradient as a massive rock-covered stagnant terminus, with debris extending down to nearly 4700 ft. Probably due to the great supply of loose rock at the edge of Russell Cliff, it competes with the Carbon as the glacier carrying the largest volume of rock.

The ascent route of the Emmons-Winthrop glaciers is long, due to the low start at the 4500-ft White River Campground, but, because of its simplicity has become the second most popular route on the mountain. The only usual problem on the climb involves routefinding on the crevassed slopes above Steamboat Prow. The ascent generally is made from the campground, then along Inter Fork to Glacier Basin, and to the Prow for high camp. The crater rim then is reached along the divide between the Emmons and Winthrop glaciers. Some parties elect to take a more modest pace and make initial camp in Glacier Basin.

The first substantiated ascent of the route was by a party from Snohomish on August 20, 1884: Rev. J. Warner Fobes, George James, and Richard O. Wells. Hiking from the town of Wilkeson, they ascended the Winthrop from near 9000 ft on Curtis Ridge. On July 24, 1896 Bailey Willis, I. C.

Russell, George Otis Smith, F. H. Ainsworth, and William D. Williams of a U.S. Geological Survey party followed the same route, experiencing a notable shock when two of them fell into a crevasse. The first winter ascent of this flank of Rainier was made by Delmar Fadden, climbing solo, in late January 1936.

From Glacier Basin ◆ continue on the trail along the N flank of the White River's Inter Fork to the lower portion of Inter Glacier (about 7000 ft). Ascend about 1500 ft, either near its center or by bearing to the right portion; parties should be roped on the glacier — minor rockfall can be experienced near its right margin in late summer.

Then angle toward the bare ridge on the glacier's SE rim at 9000 ft. In earlier times Camp Curtis (on the rim) was a popular high camp, but most parties now camp near the Camp Schurman hut (9500 ft) at the base of Steamboat Prow. From the rock rim traverse a pumice scree slope eastward onto the edge of the Emmons Glacier and ascend it to the base of the Prow. An alternate route is the climb nearly to the Prow's summit, then traverse left across the S slope to the first feasible gully on the Winthrop flank. Time: 6-8 hours from the road. Note: the hut is closed except for emergency. In winter, digging may be necessary to enter.

The usual route from the Prow follows a long and smooth snow slope (the "Corridor") above and slightly left (E) to about 12,000 ft, where it fades to more crevassed slopes. Among many variations on this wide glacier expanse, the customary method is to bear right to the final crevasse of the Winthrop, then walk into the broad saddle between Liberty Cap and Columbia Crest. Then bear left on gentle snow rising to the crater rim. Grade I or II. Time: 5-8 hours from the Prow. References: *Mountaineer*, 1909, pp. 6-9; 1912, pp. 28-36; 1939, pp. 30-31 (ski); 1948, pp. 37-38 (ski); *A.A.J.*, 1957, pp. 13-14; *Summit*, May 1962, pp. 6-9; *A.N.A.M.*, 1984, pp. 51-53.

LITTLE TAHOMA   11,138 ft/3395 m

This high, crumbling satellite of Rainier stands as an erosional remnant from the formerly larger Rainier volcano. It forms a wedge between the Ingraham and Emmons glaciers. On its back slope Little Tahoma contains the Whitman, Fryingpan, and Ohanapecosh glaciers. On an early visit to study glaciers, and before the peak was named, I. C. Russell observed, "This spur . . . has the shape of a triangle whose apex is formed by a huge pinnacle of rock, which as its bedding indicates, once formed part of the crest of the mountain, but now stands isolated, a jagged peak rising about 3000 ft above the glaciers at its foot." Little Tahoma is formed of andesite lava flows. From a southern vantage one can see mudflow breccia formed from thin lava flows shattered by steam explosions as they glided down steep slopes and mixed with meltwater.

MOUNT RAINIER from northeast
AUSTIN POST, U.S. GEOLOGICAL SURVEY

LIBERTY CAP

COLUMBIA CREST

Curtis Ridge

Willis Wall

WINTHROP GLACIER

St. Elmo Pass

Russell Cliff

Camp Schurman

Steamboat Prow

INTER GLACIER

Glacier Basin

Camp Curtis

The Corridor

Disappointment Cleaver

EMMONS GLACIER

Gibraltar Rock

North Face

LITTLE TAHOMA

K's Spire

Northeast Face

The flanking glaciers are vigorously eroding the crumbling walls of Little Tahoma. In December 1963, massive rockslides on the N face, possibly caused by a volcanic steam vent, shed the debris of a weakened section of the face for over 4 mi. down the Emmons Glacier. Cushions of compressed air buoyed the debris, so that now masses of broken rock lie on the valley floor beyond the glacier terminus.

A relatively simple ascent, Little Tahoma is popular because of its height, alpine setting, and superb location on the flank of Mount Rainier. Its first ascent was made by J. B. Flett and Henry H. Garrison on August 29, 1894 from Summerland, using the E shoulder. The first ski ascent was made by Paul Gilbreath and J. Wendell Trosper in April, 1933. References: *Mountaineer,* 1931, pp. 12-15; *Summit,* May 1966, pp. 15-21; *A.A.J.,* 1957, p. 17; *A.N.A.M.,* 1984, p. 56; D. R. Crandell, and R. K. Fahnestock, "Rockfalls and Avalanches from Little Tahoma Peak on Mount Rainier, Washington," U.S.G.S. Bulletin No. 1221-A (1965).

EAST SHOULDER: This is the "sloping" side of Little Tahoma, cradling the Whitman Glacier, and is the route adopted by nearly all climbing parties. From Summerland (see Wonderland Trail ◆) at 5400 ft skirt rocky cliffs to right and ascend S up a rounded slope to Meany Crest (7000 ft) and then SW (heading SW at 235 degrees onto the Fryingpan Glacier; 7500 ft); at 7580 ft go W 260 degrees on flat terrain. Ascend glacier SW to the 9000-ft (low point) notch connecting Whitman Crest to Little Tahoma (this notch is W of the 9364-ft high point on Whitman Crest; in late summer it can become icy). Contour SW around the first rock outcrop and then climb Whitman Glacier to its head at about 10,500 ft. Climb loose rock and snow slopes through the rocky gully on the left side of the crest to within 200 ft of the summit, then bear left through a rock break. Ascend rightward to the crest; follow it to a small notch. A rope is advised in crossing the exposed notch 15 ft below the summit (otherwise class 3). Grade I. Time: 6 hours from Summerland.

Approach Variation: From Paradise ◆ follow the Skyline Trail ◆ toward Camp Muir to about 8500 ft (below Anvil Rock). Then traverse at 8600 ft, crossing the Cowlitz Glacier (be careful to stay above the major crevasse field below that level), to the 8400 ft notch in Cathedral Rocks ridge (make a slight descent to it); cross Cathedral Rocks and traverse directly across the Ingraham Glacier to below a prominent notch (est. 8800 ft) leading to the Whitman Glacier. Ascend loose, down-sloping slabs to this notch, then ascend Whitman Glacier to join the main route. Time: 9-11 hours from Paradise.

WEST RIDGE: First ascent by Paul Cook and Matt Christensen, December 31, 1980-January 1, 1981. This is an excellent route with some spectacular climbing, but has poor rock with high objective hazard. Despite winter conditions, the first party encountered rock and ice fall when forced to the S side of the ridge. The first party belayed on 18 pitches and placed 25 pitons or chocks, and three ice screws; three 75-ft rappels were made. Crampons were worn on all but two pitches.

From Camp Muir traverse the Ingraham Glacier to gain the ridge via a snow and ice chute (some rock climbing). On the ridge steep snow and ice slopes are traversed on the N face just below the crest (one rappel in this section). Near midpoint of the ridge, vertical rock walls force one to the crest. A ramp leads onto the S face for 1½ pitches. Climb a 40-ft vertical rock wall to gain a snowpatch below the first of two large vertical rock steps. Gain the ridge crest by this snow. Climb the vertical step in 2½ fairly easy leads (good rock). Rappel from the top of the step to a snowfield at the base of the last rock step (bivouac).

The final rock step includes four difficult and serious leads. First traverse right on a ramp from the notch at the head of the snowfield (walls above and belay overhangs). The crux move could only be protected by a half-driven knife blade with no more protection for 40 ft (poor rock and serious for both leader and second). The next lead climbs up from a good belay (good rock and well protected class 5.6). Then bear right to a snowpatch on the S face; climb diagonally left to the crest on a snow/rock ramp (rock and ice fall encountered). From the ridge crest at the ramp's end climb a vertical wall (class 5.7) for 80 ft to the top of the second step. A short rappel and one difficult rock pitch lead along the very narrow ridge to the summit. Grade V; class 5.7.

NORTH FACE: This steep face heads directly above the Emmons Glacier. The route crosses over the Northeast Face Route and finishes on the East Shoulder on its final portion. The route may be subject to rockfall, and may now be altered by the 1963 rockslide. The safest climbing period would be under cold conditions; hard hats, crampons, and rock and ice pitons should be taken. First ascent by Gene Prater and Dave Mahre in June 1959.

Travel to the gap in the N cleaver of Little Tahoma just above K's Spire; possible camp spot here. (See Northeast Face Route.) Drop onto the Emmons Glacier via steep snow chute and ascend the glacier to 9000 ft at the base of a large ice/snow apron on Little Tahoma. Ascend the left end of the bergschrund apron (it triangles W of center-face); upper wall of schrund was on rotten rock (difficult and hard to protect; climbed with crampons). Traverse back right to the apron, then climb steep snow (or ice), and rotten ledges up and left to the E end of prominent rock band in midface. Then climb up and left over snow terraces and rock bands to the pinnacle at base of summit cliff. The E end of the summit ridge (about 300 ft below the summit) can be attained up a vertical pitch of loose rock, starting from the notch between the pinnacle and summit ridge; then work around to complete climb on normal route. Grade III or IV; class 4 and 5. References: *A.A.J.,* 1960, pp. 114-115; *Mountaineer,* 1960, pp. 76-77.

MOUNT RAINIER and LITTLE TAHOMA from east
AUSTIN POST, U.S. GEOLOGICAL SURVEY

COLUMBIA CREST
East Crater

Ptarmigan Ridge

Camp Schurman

Steamboat Prow

EMMONS GLACIER

K's Spire

Summerland

Meany Crest

GLACIER

FRYINGPAN

Northeast Face

LITTLE TAHOMA

9,000' notch

Whitman Crest

Gibraltar Rock

Cathedral Rocks

Camp Muir

INGRAHAM GLACIER

COWLITZ GLACIER

WHITMAN GLACIER

OHANAPECOSH GLACIER

Variation: By George Dunn and Eric Simonson, January 8, 1980. A winter ascent was made by a route to the right of the original line. Excellent ice conditions were found on the high central icefield. Reference: *A.A.J.*, 1980, p. 537.

NORTHEAST FACE: This face rises out of the upper Fryingpan Glacier to the N of the East Shoulder, then on to the summit. There is potential rockfall danger; safest period is early morning. It is advisable to have hard hats, crampons, and ice screws. First ascent by Lex Maxwell, Dave Mahre, and Bob McCall on August 23, 1959.

From Summerland ascend Meany Crest directly above to reach Fryingpan Glacier at about 7500 ft. Traverse it in a NW direction to beyond K's Spire at the northeastern foot of Little Tahoma. A number of crevasses may have to be crossed or detoured. The route then climbs the Northeast Face, climbing through the major rock band at the 9500 ft level to a hanging ice patch. On the NW skyline (above) are two small towers: these may be passed on either side to reach a difficult 80 ft rock pitch leading to the E summit ridge. Make a 300 ft traverse on the S flank of the ridge; three small pinnacles are climbed directly to reach the summit. Grade III; class 4. Time: 9 hours. References: *Mountaineer*, 1960, p. 78; *A.A.J.*, 1960, pp. 115-116.

K'S SPIRE   8849 ft/2697 m

This thumblike rock stands on the cleaver between the Emmons and Fryingpan glaciers (on NE flank of Little Tahoma). First ascent by Cornelius ("K") Molenaar and Dave Bodenburg in 1951. References: *Summit*, January 1957, pp. 8-11; *Cascadian*, 1956, pp. 28-29.

ROUTES: From Summerland (see Wonderland Trail ♦) proceed SW to Meany Crest and Fryingpan Glacier. Traverse the glacier westerly to meet the spur ridge bearing N from Little Tahoma to K's Spire (study the glacier to avoid crevassed sections). Begin the climb on friable rock from the SW side, and diagonal up a wide crack toward the summit (class 4), then from a ledge ascend directly (class 5). A rappel can be made to the E, from 20 ft below the summit. Time: 6 hours from road.

Another route, via the S face, was climbed by Gene Prater, Lex Maxwell, and Bob McCall on September 23, 1956. Ascend the S-facing crack just right of the sharp S edge, then climb right to a ledge via a traverse and a flake lieback (class 5). The final 20 ft is climbed on the opposite side of the spire. Reference: *Summit*, January 1957, pp. 8-11.

TATOOSH RANGE

This prominent subrange is located near the Park's southern boundary. The capping rock of the Tatoosh Range is Fifes Peak Andesite. This rock is composed of lavas and mudflows removed by erosion from most of the Park. The range is alpine in nature, and includes ice patches on Pinnacle, Unicorn, and Boundary peaks.[46]

The summits are popular because of quick accessibility and for the remarkable perspective of Mount Rainier. Spring and early summer is a good time for ascents, but be prepared for a snow approach. Records are incomplete regarding early ascents, but the peaks must have been among the first scaled in the Park area. Although the rock is relatively stable, the steeper routes present some hazard from party-inflicted rockfall (hard hats suggested on rock routes). The various peaks are listed from E to W. Reference: *Sierra Club Bull. 6*, no. 1 (1906), pp. 15-21.

BOUNDARY PEAK   6720 ft/2048 m

A satellite peak of Unicorn on a spur ½ mi. to its SE. Follow Unicorn Peak direct approach to just underneath Unicorn's final horn. From here angle downward in a southeasterly direction for a short distance. Travel SSW to a saddle between Boundary and Unicorn (about 6500 ft). The summit is easily reached from this point.

An alternate approach to Boundary Peak is via the trail along the crest of Tatoosh Ridge (see Tatoosh Peak).

STEVENS PEAK   6510 ft/1984 m

An isolated peak (named for Hazard Stevens) at the eastern end of the Tatoosh Range, slightly over 1 mi. E of Unicorn. Follow the Unicorn Peak direct approach. From below the horn of Unicorn traverse downward in a southeasterly direction to the saddle between Boundary Peak and Stevens Peak at the head of Maple Creek. Climb the long ridge crest NE to the summit. Allow a full day.

TATOOSH PEAK   6310 ft/1923 m

Tatoosh Peak stands near the SE end of Tatoosh Range and has a 6-mi. trail (No. 161) to the former summit lookout. This is a rewarding trek to view the Muddy Fork of the Cowlitz, a name derived from a tribe of Indians who once inhabited its valleys.

From the N end of Packwood on U.S. Hwy No. 12 ♦ drive W on Skate Creek Road No. 52. Cross the Cowlitz River bridge and drive to Road No. 5290; follow for 9 mi., turn right on No. 5292 for 1.2 mi. to the trailhead. Note: One could follow Skate Creek Road from near Ashford (see Berry Creek Road ♦).

UNICORN PEAK   6917 ft/2108 m

The highest Tatoosh peak, located 2 mi. SE of Reflection Lakes. Unicorn is a good early season ascent on a continuous snow approach. One can see remnants of the Fifes Peak Formation up to 1000 ft in thickness.

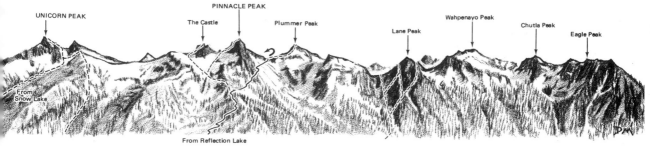

TATOOSH RANGE from north

On Unicorn, lava flows form cliffs alternating with less resistant volcanic sedimentary rocks. Along Stevens Canyon one can see remnants of an intracanyon flow. Stevens Creek is entrenched below the base of the flow at The Bench.

ROUTE: Leave the Stevens Canyon Road ◆ at the Bench Lake Trail (about 2 mi. E of Reflection Lakes at 4500 ft) and follow it past Bench Lake to Snow Lake (1 mi.; 4678 ft). Pass it on the right and climb S up steep slopes into the basin to where it narrows into a steep snowfield. Continue up the snow slope to a saddle at about 6500 ft. (When snow is gone a climber's route is marked out.) Cross the saddle to the S side of the ridge, then ascend NE up heather slopes and a rock ridge to the base of the summit tower. The final 50 ft of the tower may be ascended on the S (solid rock) or SE sides. Class 3. Time: 4-5 hours.

Approach Variation: From the ridge on the E side of The Castle, follow the crest SE to the base of Unicorn's S peak. Contour around the lower peak on its N side and follow the snow slope as in the normal approach.

NORTH FACE: From Snow Lake continue up Unicorn Creek to the steeper rock of the N face. It is climbed over moderately difficult loose rock (class 4) to a notch just below the summit on the E side. From this point the final horn is easily climbed by the SE side.

THE CASTLE   6440 ft+/1963 m+

Box-shaped Castle on the immediate E of Pinnacle Peak has a uniquely craggy silhouette; it is a short rock scramble, often done in conjunction with Pinnacle. Take the trail to the central saddle (see Pinnacle Peak), then traverse the volcanic scree (or snow) on the S slope to Castle's SE face. A short pitch leads to the summit (several variants).

When the terrain is snow covered, the preferable route from the road is to ascend directly to the ridge crest E of the summit formation. Time: 2-3 hours from road.

PINNACLE PEAK   6562 ft/2000 m

Although not the highest of the Tatoosh peaks, Pinnacle's central position and attractive form have made it the most popular ascent in the Park. When the Mazamas climbed it on July 26, 1897, they dubbed it the "Matterhorn of the Cascades." Just who made the first ascent is uncertain. Reference: *Overland Monthly,* vol. 32, 2nd series, p. 117.

SOUTH ROUTE: From Reflection Lakes (4854 ft) on the Stevens Canyon Road ◆ take the trail to the Pinnacle-Plummer saddle (5900 ft — 1.3 mi.). Follow the loose talus slope E, then ascend the western portion of the S face up an easy gully to the ridge crest just below the summit. There is some exposure, as the route lies near the edge of the face. Time: 2 hours (maximum difficulty: scrambling).

Approach Variation: From the Pinnacle-Castle saddle (6200 ft) traverse the S slope to the S face gully.

NORTH RIDGE: This somewhat treacherous and steep, though short, ridge was first climbed by John R. Glascock and Ernest Dudley on July 28, 1905, the day after they ascended Success Cleaver. The first winter climb was made by Ed Cooper, Eric Bjornstad, and John Holland on January 1, 1965.

Ascend a steep gully on the lower W side of the ridge; then up the ridge for the final 200 ft, where it has short vertical steps; the last portion is done on the left-outward edge; the last 125 ft are the hardest. Class 3-4. References: *Sierra Club Bulletin,* 1906, pp. 15-17; *Summit,* September 1965, pp. 20-23.

EAST RIDGE: This short rock route offers some problems. Begin at Pinnacle-Castle saddle; at about 200 ft higher traverse right on small ledge (can use slings on trees). At a dead-end by a tree with three trunks, ascend 30 ft of solid rock (class 4) to top of ridge. Then hike to top.

OTHER ROUTES: The W face and NE face offer interesting belayed climbing and are occasionally done.

PLUMMER PEAK   est. 6370 ft/1942 m

A rounded summit, just SW of Pinnacle, Plummer is

a ¼-mi. heather scramble from trail's end at the saddle. In winter it appears as a white pyramid from the N, with easy slopes that provide a pleasant ski tour.

LANE PEAK   est. 6012 ft/1833 m

This is a small peak on the Tatoosh crest ½ mi. W of Pinnacle Peak. As seen from the N it is rocky, with chutes in view.

ROUTES: Ascend from Stevens Canyon Road (see Nisqually Entrance Road ◆) at the road bend SE of Narada Falls. Cross the creek and ascend an avalanche fan, then a basin, to the 5400 ft + saddle E of Lane. Note: In winter or spring one can walk the road beyond the falls to where it turns SE, then continue SW for ½ mi. The final ascent is made by gullies (one scrambling pitch).

More direct routes are up the steep, N-side couloirs; be sure snow conditions are firm during early-season ascents.

From the Pinnacle-Plummer saddle (5920 ft +), traverse ¾ mi. W to above Cliff Lake; from here scramble NW to the summit.

Peak 5810 (1771 m) is a small peak on the crest 0.4 mi. SW of Lane. From the saddle E of Lane, make a descending traverse to the objective, and traverse around its E flank to the S saddle. There are interesting snow ridges in winter on this peak.

WAHPENAYO PEAK   6231 ft/1899 m

Located about 2 mi. E of Longmire, where the range crest takes a curve to the S. Sluiskin, Stevens, and Van Trump nearly climbed it en route to the Pinnacle-Plummer saddle and Mount Rainier on August 14, 1870.

Leave the Eagle Peak Trail in the meadow area (near 4800 ft) and traverse beneath Chutla Peak on its southerly slope to gain the ridge crest; follow it SE to the summit rocks, passing several rocky outcrops (no difficulties).

Variation: Go through the Chutla-Wahpenayo pass, then climb the broad gully on the easy N side of Wahpenayo.

CHUTLA PEAK
est. 6000 ft +/1829 m +

Chutla, an Indian term meaning "rock," is a short, easy rock scramble from the Eagle-Chutla Peak saddle (see Eagle Peak). The ascent can readily be combined with that of Wahpenayo Peak.

EAGLE PEAK   5958 ft/1816 m

Eagle is a small peak marking the western end of the Tatoosh Range; it presents a cliffy facade on the N but is not steep elsewhere.

Approach from the Nisqually River bridge at Longmire (2761 ft) via the trail (3½ mi.) to just above the Eagle-Chutla Peak saddle (5720 ft +). Follow the ridge; at 100 ft before reaching the summit there is a short face. One can climb this (class 4) or turn left to a bypass gully.

HIGH ROCK   5685 ft/1732 m

The highest point on Sawtooth Ridge, an area of small peaks and attractive lakes largely uncut by loggers, to the SW of Longmire. The summit lookout is reached by a 1½-mi. trail No. 922 from Berry Creek Road. This can be a superb viewpoint.

MOUNT WOW   6040 ft +/1841 m +

Mount Wow lies in the SW corner of Mount Rainier National Park and offers a grand view of Mount Rainier. From 1½ mi. up the West Side Road ◆ at 2500 ft take a 2-mi. trail to Lake Allen (4596 ft) and from there follow a rudimentary trail (about 1 mi.) to the top. Reference: *Mountaineer,* 1917, p. 67.

PYRAMID PEAK   6937 ft/2114 m

This prominent satellite peak of Mount Rainier is located at the base of Success Cleaver. It is known that members of the 1915 Mountaineer outing climbed it, as well as Copper and Iron. Dr. William Tolmie noted: "two large pyramids of rock arose from the gentle acclivity at the southwest extremity of the mountain."

From Indian Henrys Hunting Ground (see Tahoma Creek Trail ◆) travel NE, past Mirror Lake, skirting Copper Mountain on its left and descend into a meadow at Pyramid's base; then walk eastward to the top. Time: 5 hours from West Side Road ◆.

COPPER MOUNTAIN
6280 ft +/1914 m +

Formerly called "Crystal Mountain," it slopes NE of Indian Henrys Hunting Ground. The ascent is a walk via the notch (est. 6000 ft) between Copper and Iron mountains.

IRON MOUNTAIN   est. 6283 ft/1915 m

From the notch (see Copper Mountain) the summit is a walk, southward.

TOKALOO SPIRE   7480 ft +/2280 m +

A tower ranging from about 70 to 150 ft high on the Puyallup Cleaver 1½ mi. above St. Andrews Park, adjacent to Tokaloo Rock (7684 ft), it has vertical side

Summits in northwestern Mount Rainier National Park

walls as seen from the E. The first ascent was made by William Herston, Karl Boyer, and Mrs. Karl Boyer in 1943.

Approach is from St. Andrews Park (6000 ft) via Klapatche Park ◆ by taking the cleaver to the spire. Climb directly up the E ridge to a large iron spike, then descend 10 ft to a crack leading across the N face to an open chimney. The remainder is easy. Class 4. Time: 4 hours from the West Side Road ◆.

Tokaloo Rock's summit is a short, easy scramble.

ECHO ROCK   7870 ft/2399 m

A craggy, notable outcrop on the flank of lower Ptarmigan Ridge, nearly surrounded by the Russell Glacier. Echo Rock has a lava conduit, once a separate vent. From the trail in Spray Park ◆ hike SE through the subalpine landscape, crossing the broad ridge and snowfields to the foot of the W tongue of the glacier (inactive and safe). Ascend easy snow and pumice to the broad col between Echo and Observation rocks. Scramble leftward, keeping near the far W side of the crag (hands may be needed, but easy loose volcanic rock). Time: 3 hours from Spray Park.

Reference to peaks in the northwestern portion of the Park: *Mountaineer,* 1931, pp. 56-58.

OBSERVATION ROCK

8364 ft/2549 m

This prominent rock on lower Ptarmigan Ridge has a sloping form, with a short cliff facing E. First ascent by a "Henderson" in 1885. Echo and Observation rocks are dissected remnants of two satellite cones that erupted floods of olivine andesite after Mount Rainier was nearly fully grown. These flows banked against older lava of Ptarmigan Ridge and built up the plateau of Spray Park.

From the broad col between Echo and Observation, traverse SW; climb snow slopes to the ridge just SE of the easy rocky grade (scree) to the summit.

Another approach from Spray Park is to cross snowfields and the Flett Glacier on the W side of the rock, then finish via the easy S or SW side.

HESSONG ROCK   6385 ft/1948 m

Hessong is just NW of Spray Park, the summit being 0.3 mi. NE of the map's name legend. William Tolmie neared the summit on September 2, 1833 on his exploration of Mount Rainier; the ascent was definitely made on the 1915 Mountaineer outing. References: *Mountaineer,* 1931, p. 57; 1967, pp. 61-71.

From Spray Park ◆ at an area of small ponds (5700 ft) ascend a grassy, herbaceous slope leading NW to a col between Hessong and Pleasant. From the col traverse the basin on the NW side of Hessong and ascend to summit via the NW ridge. Gullies on the S side offer steeper but more direct routes; a chimney route distinguished by a tall slender tree at its top is now perhaps the standard route (class 2).

MOUNT PLEASANT   6454 ft/1967 m

From the col between Hessong and Pleasant ascend NE up easy rock to the summit. Pleasant can also be reached via an easy traverse from Knapsack Pass, or from Fay Peak. Pleasant, Fay, and Hessong are often done on 1-day traverses.

FAY PEAK   6492 ft/1979 m

Named for Fay Fuller, the first woman to ascend Mount Rainier, the peak is located only ½ mi. SE of Mowich Lake (see Mowich Lake Road ◆). The summit offers grand views of Mount Rainier and its northern and western glaciers. First ascent by J. Warner Fobes, George James, and R. O. Wells on August 15, 1884.

Take a hiker's path from the lake past the ranger's cabin toward Knapsack Pass. Below the pass take a right fork to Fay's E ridge; follow this, avoiding a false summit (minor scrambling). Time: 1½ hours from the lake. Reference: *Mazama,* 1914, pp. 51-53.

An alternate route is to leave the path at about 5400 ft, bear S, then ascend the easy W ridge.

MOTHER MOUNTAIN

Mother Mountain is a 3-mi. subrange E of Mowich Lake, the name originating from the outline of a female figure on the northeastern summit, as seen from the Carbon River Trail. The highest of the three principal summits (First Mother Mountain) is the western. Less than 25 m. y. ago the formation was built from successive lava flows erupting from broad, low volcanos. The large empty cirques on the N of the subrange, dating to the Pleistocene, once cradled voluminous glaciers. Reference: *Mountaineer,* 1931, p. 57.

FIRST MOTHER MOUNTAIN

6480 ft+/1975 m+

From the ranger's cabin at Mowich Lake (see Mowich Lake Road ◆) take a 1.5-mi. trail leading E to Knapsack Pass (6160 ft+). Then ascend easy slopes NNE and follow the ridge a short distance to the summit.

SECOND MOTHER MOUNTAIN

6375 ft/1943 m

First ascent by Maynard Miller and H. Kinzner in 1938. Begin as for Castle Peak. Hike to the saddle NE of Mowich Lake, then drop E toward the small lake at 5100 ft. Start a long rising contour on grassy benches to above 5500 ft, then bear for the skyline E and cross the ridge (est. 5900 ft). Continue to the meadow and talus cirque on the NW flank of Second Mother, then bear toward a broad gully that ascends the W flank of the castle-shaped summit (a short scramble).

Another route is from Knapsack Pass: descend eastward, then make a 1-mi. traverse across alp slopes to beneath the objective summit. A scrambling ascent can be made.

THIRD MOTHER MOUNTAIN

5804 ft+/1768 m+

Located 1 mi. NE of Second Mother. From the latter descend its NE flank and from 5300 ft contour to under the S rib. Ascend through a col and ascend E, scrambling through cliffy trees to the summit. The summit could also be reached from Ipsut Creek.

CASTLE PEAK   6110 ft/1862 m

Located 1 mi. NE of Mowich Lake, Castle is a flat-topped summit on a spur coming NW off Mother Mountain. Reference: *Mountaineer,* 1931, p. 56.

The most direct route is to ascend through open timber due E from the N end of Mowich Lake. Follow a faint trail northerly from the ridge top to easy scrambling on the SW slopes. This ridge may also be reached from timberline on the Knapsack Pass Trail by ascending N up a grassy hillside.

TOLMIE PEAK   5920 ft+/1804 m+

Named for Dr. William Tolmie, this small peak is located 2 mi. NW of Mowich Lake. It stands above Eunice Lake, which is in a bedrock basin scoured out by ice 15,000 to 20,000 years ago. A 3.5-mi. trail from Mowich Lake leads to the summit lookout, from which the summit is an easy 600-ft scramble along the ridge to the E. Reference: *Mountaineer,* 1931, p. 56.

HOWARD PEAK   5683 ft/1732 m

A small peak NW of Tolmie; reach it by following the easy meadowed ridge from Tolmie Peak lookout (low point is 5600-ft ridge saddle).

FLORENCE PEAK   5508 ft/1679 m

Just before reaching the Tolmie Peak lookout, leave the trail and descend N to Alki Crest. Follow it NW 1½ mi. to Florence, over a small false summit.

Variation: from the West Side Boundary Trail at the Carbon River Entrance (1750 ft) follow the trail to the saddle (4520 ft +). Turn SE onto Alki Crest, then follow the ridge to Florence Peak.

ARTHUR PEAK   5465 ft/1666 m

From Howard Peak descend to a notch on its N, then W to large rockslides at 4800 ft. Then contour NE and E until nearly NW of the summit; here ascend a rockslide to the grassy summit knoll.

Another route is via Green Lake Trail from Carbon River Road ◆. Leave the trail at 2500 ft and ascend W to the N ridge; follow this to the summit.

GOVE PEAK   5320 ft+/1622 m+

Located 2 mi. NE of Ipsut Pass. From Mowich Lake take the Eunice Lake Trail 2 mi. to Ipsut Pass. Here a way trail leaves the main trail and ascends the steep hillside to the N. After ¼ mi. descend to a cirque on the E and then climb northeasterly through steep timber to the alpine ridge crest at 5650 ft. Go NE along the wooded ridge crest for 2 mi.

From Green Lake one can ascend on forest slope to a SW-bearing ridge; the narrow ridge leads to the summit.

OLD BALDY MOUNTAIN
5795 ft/1766 m

Located 2 mi. NE of the NW corner of Mount Rainier National Park. At 4.1 mi. up Coplay Lake Road ◆ at 3200 ft, a logging spur goes left (N). Ascend this road, up switchbacks, to its end near a cliff on the left (W). Climb left from here, to the ridge crest through a burned area with slash, rockslides, and rocks, to emerge on the false summit. From here it is an easy hike along a goat trail right (N) to the summit, about ½ mi. distant. Summit has a huge rock cairn and three VABM markers. Time: 2-3 hours.

PITCHER PEAK   5933 ft/1808 m

On Carbon Ridge, 2 mi. NE of Old Baldy Mountain.

About 5½ mi. up the Coplay Lake Road ◆ is a sharp switchback. An abandoned logging spur goes northwesterly from this switchback. Hike to a switchback, turn W into timber to find the McGilvery Creek Trail. The old cabin is encountered in ½ mi. Continue straight on, ascend a brushy steep hillside to a notch which is left (SW) of Pitcher's summit. Descend 200 ft down the other side of the notch. Contour to the right through steep timbered slopes on Pitcher's N side to the NE ridge. Turn up the ridge and follow it to the timbered summit. Time: 2 hours.

A somewhat steeper but more direct route is to ascend directly from the notch.

BEARHEAD MOUNTAIN
6089 ft/1856 m
and EAST BEARHEAD   6052 ft/1845 m

The Bearhead summits are the highest in the new Clearwater Wilderness. They provide fine views of Mount Rainier and the NW portion of the Park. From the end of Coplay Lake Road ◆ (4200 ft) take Summit Lake Trail No. 1177 a short distance to Twin Lakes, then keep right on the branch trail leading to Bearhead. On the ridge shoulder below Bearhead, the trail forks: the left one leads to Bearhead's summit (3¼ mi. total), and the right one contours on to East Bearhead. Time: 2 hours.

It is possible to traverse the ridge to East Bearhead, but due to intervening knobs it is simpler to descend to the trail, which traverses the hillside; where it rounds the ridge end, ascend grassy slopes to the rocky outcrops that form East Bearhead's summit. Time: 1½ hours from Bearhead.

CLEAR WEST PEAK   5644 ft/1720 m

Clear West is a huge plug of welded tuff and flow bands. There is a 1 mi. trail to the summit lookout. Follow the West Fork White River Road ◆ approximately 10 mi., then turn left at Viola Creek on Road No. 7430. This leads to the road's end and trailhead at the top edge of a large clearcut. Reference: *Trips and Trails, 2.*

TYEE PEAK   6030 ft/1838 m

Tyee is the highest point on Chenuis Mountain ridge. At 5850 ft, just below Windy Gap, leave the Northern Loop Trail ◆ and ascend N up the hillside, E of the Yellowstone Cliffs, to the broad ridge top. The summit of Tyee is a few hundred yards W along the ridge, just above the Yellowstone Cliffs.

SLUISKIN PEAKS from northwest (near Windy Gap)
ROBERT GUNNING

CRESCENT MOUNTAIN

6715 ft/2047 m

The culmination of the ridge to the N of Elysian Fields, 1 mi. W of Sluiskin Peak. From a level area just below Windy Gap (est. 5½ mi. — see Northern Loop Trail ◆), note a ridge parallel to the trail, directly S. Ascend to the top, turn SW, follow it a few hundred yards to the summit.

SLUISKIN MOUNTAIN

The high crest of Sluiskin, carved from pre-Mount Rainier rocks, is located between Windy Gap and Vernal Falls. The Chief, the castellated-tower high point, is located at the E end of the mountain. The pyramidal Squaw and smaller Papoose rise to the W. The 1909 climb by The Mountaineers was probably the first ascent. References: *Mountaineer,* 1931, p. 58; *Mazama,* 1914, pp. 37-38.

THE CHIEF   7026 ft/2133 m
From Windy Gap (see Northern Loop Trail ◆), de-

scend slightly and contour SE 1 mi. to the N side of the peak. Ascend a broad gully to the 6500-ft saddle separating the Chief on the E and the Squaw on the W. Ascend E from the saddle up the W ridge of the Chief; one short class 3 pitch. A variation is to ascend some scree and rock ledges to the base of the cubical summit, then swing left on a wide ledge at the base of cliffs, around to the N ridge. Exposed but firm rock leads to the summit. The 1914 Mazama party found a record of the 1909 ascent; they circled around the N side to the E face for 100 ft of rock climbing.

An alternate approach is from Moraine Park (see Wonderland Trail ◆) and then across Elysian Fields and Vernal Park to the S side of the peak (hiking), then to the central saddle.

THE SQUAW   6960 ft+/2130 m+
From the saddle between the Chief and the Squaw it is an easy scramble to the summit of the latter.

Several small pinnacles (The Papooses) on the ridge W of the Squaw offer easy scrambling. These may be reached by traversing over the Squaw or by traveling cross-country from Windy Gap.

REDSTONE PEAK   5680 ft + / 1727 m +

Redstone is a small, isolated, and attractive rock peak located about 1 mi. NE of Sluiskin Mountain, between Windy Gap and the West Fork of the White River. There are two approaches to the peak, one from the W within the Park and one from the N outside the Park.

If making the approach from the Northern Loop Trail ◆, leave the trail about 1 mi. E of Windy Gap, then contour SE above timberline to the col SW of the summit of Redstone. Bypass a first summit, then make the final climb, which is a steep but short scramble.

The shorter northern approach uses West Fork White River Road ◆ and branch No. 7550. Hike the final portion of the road (about ¾ mi.), then continue S about 100 yards through forest to reach the old trail on the right; follow this on a descent to the river. Continue on the trail on the E side of the river into the Park; reach the Northern Loop Trail in about 2 mi. Cross the river and climb the switchbacks to Lake James (about 2 mi.), then continue S to the ranger station (about 3 mi. from the river). Leave the trail and hike SE, cross Van Horn Creek and ascend diagonally left up a rockslide. When about halfway up, turn left to a second and third rockslide. Ascend the latter, then bear right to a saddle. Continue to a gully on the upper W side of the summit. Ascend the grass-and-rock gully to the ridge crest just N of the summit block. Follow the ridge, then contour and drop slightly on the E side. Make the short summit scramble from here. Both routes are class 3. Time: 2 hours from Windy Gap or Lake James.

OLD DESOLATE   7137 ft / 2175 m

Located 1½ mi. N of Mystic Lake. Take Wonderland Trail ◆ to Moraine Park. At 5700 ft, about ¼ mi. before Mystic Pass, exit at the stream gully coming down from the E. Ascend it to a large flat area of rock-glacier deposits at 6400 ft. Cross the flat in an easterly direction and, turning slightly right, ascend to the ridge crest. The summit is just NE along the ridge, over weathered and shattered rock. The route up the ridge from Mystic Pass traverses over numerous small, shattered false summits.

MINERAL MOUNTAIN

6500 ft / 1981 m

Situated ½ mi. S of Mystic Lake. Just before reaching Mystic Lake from the W (see Wonderland Trail ◆) a grassy draw leads S up to the Mineral Ridge. On the ridge crest, turn left (E); a short scramble leads to the rocky summit.

BURROUGHS MOUNTAIN

7828 ft / 2386 m

Burroughs Mountain is a prominent remnant of an ancient intracanyon lava flow from Mount Rainier. The flow partly filled the former canyon of White River. The river re-established along the S margin of the flow is entrenched 1300 ft below its former level opposite Yakima Park.

Reach the mountain by trail in 2½ mi. from Sunrise (see White River Road ◆). The unique alpine tundra is easily destroyed: stay on the trail. In 1½ mi. the trail crosses First Burroughs, then Second Burroughs (7402 ft). Third Burroughs is beyond the saddle through which the trail passes. The high point is at the S end, where views are superlative. One can scan large moraines adjacent to the Winthrop Glacier; one moraine was pushed up by ice 300 ft.

SKYSCRAPER MOUNTAIN

7078 ft / 2157 m

Skyscraper, W of Berkeley Park, is carved from pre-Mount Rainier rocks. Hike to the top along an easy crest from Packtrain Ridge, 3 mi. from Sunrise on the Wonderland Trail ◆.

MOUNT FREMONT   7317 ft / 2230 m

The Mount Fremont lookout (7181 ft) is reached by a 2.8-mi. trail leading W from Sunrise (see White River Road ◆). The S summit point is the highest. Patterned ground in the alpine landscape here includes stone nets and stripes. The cirque on the E flank of Fremont has blocky debris left by a former rock glacier. Reference: *Trips and Trails, 2*.

SOURDOUGH MOUNTAINS

The northern portion of the Sourdough ridge (Sourdough Mountains) can be reached by Palisades Lakes Trail ◆. One can hike the crest line and upper slopes quite readily; there are small summits but no outstanding peaks. The western portion of the ridge is a melange of intrusive rocks that make a complex contact with the Ohanapecosh Formation. One of the largest rock glacier deposits in the Park occupies the E-facing cirque midway between Hidden Lake and The Palisades (E of Peak 7040 ft +). The rock glacier deposit, which covers about 100 acres and is 100 to 300 ft thick, is derived from talus debris from cliffs of The Palisades.

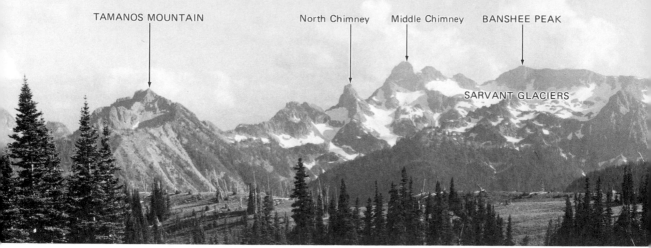

TAMANOS MOUNTAIN   North Chimney Middle Chimney BANSHEE PEAK

SARVANT GLACIERS

COWLITZ CHIMNEYS from Yakima Park
JACK BOUCHER, NATIONAL PARK SERVICE

GOAT ISLAND MOUNTAIN
7288 ft/2221 m

This is a massive, rounded formation located between the White River and Fryingpan Creek. It probably is the summit called "White River Peak" by Samuel F. Emmons and Allen D. Wilson when on October 9, 1870 they climbed to its summit and counted eight glaciers.

Follow the trail along Fryingpan Creek for about 3 mi. (see Wonderland Trail ◆), then ascend wooded and open slopes N to the summit; there may be some brush on the lower portion. Time: 4 hours.

BANSHEE PEAK   7400 ft+/2262 m+

Banshee Peak is the high remnant of bedded Ohanapecosh Formation lava flows trending E to W between Cowlitz Chimneys and Panhandle Gap. A series of summit rim cliffs and the Sarvant Glaciers extend broadly on the northern slopes. The planed southern slopes feature a pumice and arctic-alpine slope. A large herd of goats has been in residence on these slopes and nearby crags.

From Panhandle Gap (see Wonderland Trail ◆) traverse the easy slopes on grass and pumice for about 1¼ mi. to the summit point.

COWLITZ CHIMNEYS   7605 ft/2319 m

The very prominent Cowlitz Chimneys are remnants of a rhyolite plug that overrides the nearly horizontal bedded rocks of the Ohanapecosh Formation. Francois E. Matthes described the chimneys as "a group of tall rock towers that dominate the landscape on the east side of Mount Rainier." Sarvant Glaciers lie on the NW flank, draining to Fryingpan Creek; only the largest ice segment is active, but the glaciers have interest because of the annual bands displayed.

There are three principal chimneys, all on the N-S-trending crest between the Ohanapecosh River, Needle, and Fryingpan Creek drainages. The main (southern) chimney is remarkably sheer except on its S ridge. The S flank of the Chimney flares outward, truncating and overriding the nearby horizontal bedded Ohanapecosh rocks. It was known to have been climbed during the 1915 Mountaineer outing when "two of our men made the difficult climb of Cowlitz Chimneys." The central chimney is high and bulky, and the northern chimney, while lower, is quite sheer and striking.

ROUTE: From Panhandle Gap (see Wonderland Trail ◆) make a long but easy rising traverse across the arctic-alpine southern slopes of Banshee Peak, then at about 7000 ft angle downward, rounding the basin to just SW of the summit formation of the Main Chimney. A herd of goats frequents the traverse area.

The major object of the rather curious rock route is to reach the hanging gully immediately right of a right-leaning pinnacle identified above a broad, whitish overhanging headwall near the Chimney's base. Where the basal scree turns to a rocky slope directly beneath the distinctive U-shaped gap S of the Chimney's southern crest, sight a spiry solitary fir. From this tree ascend heathery rock about 100 ft toward the gap, but do not ascend to this feature.

Turn left at the right-hand edge of a horizontal fence of small evergreens, traversing the short alp slope above them,

COWLITZ CHIMNEYS and GOVERNORS RIDGE from east

and beneath the rockwall of the S ridge, to the last tree clump (a thick hemlock cluster). Traverse northward on a big ledge for about 100 ft, then continue at this level on rounded and solid rock for 30 ft to a small hidden cave with scrub trees (the traverse is class 3, moderately exposed, although not far above the basal scree). Move left from the cave and climb a short rock slot (about 15 ft) to a clump of krummholz in the gully adjacent to the aforementioned leaning pinnacle.

Ascend the shallow rock gully (scree and numerous scrub trees) to the ridge crest. Easily scramble the left side of the ridge northward. One of several gullies can be taken to the summit. An obvious central gully with dead snags at its top is a certain route (solid class 2 rock at a narrow spot). The Chimney's summit offers great views from Mount Stuart to Mount Adams, and with binoculars one might see Mount Rainier summit climbers high on the Ingraham Glacier. Time: 3-4 hours from Panhandle Gap.

Approach Variation: This is a shorter route, proven useful in the month of June, when a thick snow bridge crosses Fryingpan Creek opposite the trail at about 2½ mi. Here a long snow chute between cliffs descends from the basin near Banshee Peak's summit rim. Ascend the chute, which narrows and steepens near the 5100 ft level. A level niche atop a small rock outcrop at about 5400 ft just W of the top of two waterfalls provides a fine bivouac site (water nearby).

Ascend open slopes leftward toward the highest cliffs, hiking along the fringe of small evergreens. Complete the leftward ascent by a goat path through scrub trees to a notch (about 6720 ft) on the crest of a lateral ridge of crags. Descend a moderately steep snow gully until it is possible to traverse onto the Sarvant Glacier snowfields. Traverse and ascend SE about ¾ mi. to the prominent gap W of Central Cowlitz Chimney. Cross the gap, descend scree and traverse ¼ mi. to the Main Chimney.

Central Cowlitz Chimney is a hike and rock scramble from its southwestern base.

NORTH CHIMNEY   7015 ft/2138 m

This rock formation, set NE and apart from the other chimneys, is one of the more inaccessible points in the Park. The chimney is best seen from ½ mi. along Fryingpan Creek on the trail to Summerland. First ascent by Calder Bressler, Ralph and Ray Clough in 1941.

From the head of Needle Creek (use Owyhigh Lakes ◆ approach) climb the gully to the small notch immediately S of the objective. Then climb and traverse out on the sloping W rock face. There is an awkward move after about 150 ft (class 5). Continue upward, later bearing left on easier climbing to the summit area. The climb ranges from scrambling to class 4 or 5. Note: one could reach the small notch by ascending Wright Creek, but there may be a moat above the steep snow; not recommended in late season.

A route along the narrow crest from the small notch was climbed by Jim Yoder, Mike Adams, and Quinn Conan in May 1975. There were three pitches, one being a difficult step (class 5.8).

THIRD CHIMNEY   est. 6600 ft/2012 m

Stands closely NE of North Chimney. Reach by ascending W from head of Kotsuck Creek.

TAMANOS MOUNTAIN
6790 ft/2070 m

A broad and gentle lava flow remnant, extending N of

Cowlitz Chimneys at about ⅔ mi. NW of Owyhigh Lakes ◆. Ascend W from the lakes, then turn S to avoid cliffs and gain the ridge. Follow the bare crest northward to the summit (scrambling). Time: 3 hours from the road.

GOVERNORS RIDGE
6600 ft+/2012 m+

This ridge is a N-S-trending crest of jagged rock points between Cayuse Pass and Owyhigh Lakes. The coarse mudflow breccia of the Ohanapecosh Formation is prominent on this crest. Two rock spires, a few hundred ft apart, are the most obvious features.

Governors Peak, the pyramidal southern one, is the highest and the one usually climbed. The northern spire has a small knob, seemingly balanced, atop its blocky shape. One mi. N is a rounded and prominent 6566-ft point, an extension of the ridge.

Governors Needle (est. 6500 ft) is the slender S-leaning pinnacle S of Governors Peak. The apparent route is from its northern notch. No climbing information known; possibly class 5 on friable rock.

Barrier Peak (6521 ft) is a rounded form anchoring the S end of the Governors Ridge crest.

WEST ROUTE: From Owyhigh Lakes ◆ ascend SE to the high col between Governors and Barrier peaks. Cross and traverse, then make a rising northward ascent to S of the highest summit. Follow the rocky crest to the top (class 3).
EAST ROUTE: A longer and more cumbersome route is

GOVERNORS RIDGE from Owyhigh Lakes Basin
HERMANN F. ULRICHS

possible from Cayuse Pass (4694 ft). First ascend W via a canyon to a 5200-ft gap, traverse along the ridge past Sheepskull Gap, then descend and traverse S across Boundary Creek's basin to reach the slope above the W fork; ascend to the crest S of the summit.

Another route to the summit of Governors Peak, using this approach, is to ascend a gully to the notch N of the summit spire; steep rock leads to the top (class 4). This gully also offers a route to the N spire. The 6566-ft point can be hiked directly from the ridge joining from Cayuse Pass.

DOUBLE PEAK   6199 ft/1890 m

The double summits are the SW peak (higher) and the NE peak. Leave State Hwy No. 123 ◆ about 6 mi. S of Cayuse Pass (parking area is 1 mi. S of Kotsuck Creek Trail at about 3100 ft). Drop 300 ft and cross log bridge on Chinook Creek to trail on W side; walk S ¼ mi. and cross northern of three creeks that drop from basin E of Double Peak. Climb forest near the S side of this creek (keep high). Enter large open E basin at 4400 ft (can see NE peak here). Cross basin WSW and climb slopes to crest of SW ridge of Double Peak (some scrambling). Ascend ridge to top of SW peak; a traverse to NE peak involves a rappel and rock work. Total of 3 mi. Time: 5 hours.

One could climb the NE peak directly from a scrub-tree shoulder near its N side. The left side of the NE face offers a route with first talus, then scrub trees mixed with moderate rock.

SHRINER PEAK   5834 ft/1778 m

This is a small peak which provides a fine viewpoint in the SE portion of Mount Rainier National Park, E of Chinook Creek and W of the main divide.
ROUTE: The best route is to follow an old unmaintained trail that begins off State Hwy No. 123 ◆ at the first road corner W of Deer Creek (facing Kotsuck Creek at about 3200 ft), at 2 mi. NNW of Shriner Peak's summit. The trail can be followed up forest slopes and the subalpine N ridge. The marked trail route to the summit from the SW, beginning at about 2400 ft, is much longer.

DEWEY PEAK   6710 ft/2045 m

Located on the Cascade Crest 2⅜ mi. SE of Chinook Pass, and ¾ mi. S of Dewey Lakes. A fine high viewpoint with a rocky summit. The peak provides an excellent 1-day winter or spring climb via Dewey Creek; snowshoes or skis can be used to within ¼ mi. of the top.
ROUTES: The easiest gradient is to leave the Crest Trail ◆ at about 5440 ft, about 1 mi. N of Anderson Lake.

From State Hwy No. 123 ◆ at Dewey Creek crossing (1½ mi. S of Cayuse Pass) follow Dewey Creek cross-country to

the 6000-ft saddle between Dewey and Seymour Peaks. Climb E to Dewey's N ridge and continue along it to the first pinnacles (bypass easily on SW). Climb a gully to the notch below the main peak and ascend 75 ft of class 3 rock to the top. Time: 5 hours.

SEYMOUR PEAK   6337 ft/1932 m

Seymour Peak is easily reached from the saddle between it and Dewey Peak.

NACHES PEAK   6452 ft/1967 m

The rock of Naches and nearby peaks along the crest are in the Ohanapecosh Formation. Popular Naches Peak is a remarkable viewpoint for a Mount Rainier vista. From Chinook Pass (State Hwy No. 410 ◆) ascend the green-toned N ridge, generally keeping just on its W flank; foot tracks are in evidence most of the way.

Another route is to take the Crest Trail ◆ to the peak's S ridge; there is a short scramble at the final rock rise.

YAKIMA PEAK   6226 ft/1897 m

A popular meadowed ridge summit ½ mi. W of Chinook Pass (see State Hwy No. 410 ◆). From the pass one can hike up easy grass slopes and ascend a gully on the E side, turning left at top to follow ridge to summit (1 hour). Or, from the Tipsoo Lake parking lot, hike up the heathery S slope, taking care to keep left of a southeastern rock outcrop well up on the peak.

CRYSTAL PEAK   6595 ft/2010 m

Crystal Peak is a subsidiary point about 1 mi. W of the Cascade Crest. The corresponding high point on the Crest (6904 ft) is ¾ mi. to SE. Crystal Peak has a 3.8-mi. summit trail which leaves State Hwy No. 410 ◆ at about 4½ mi. S of the Park boundary (alt. 3300 ft); lower branch trail goes to Crystal Lake (2.7 mi.).

Point 6904 can be hiked up from the Crest Trail.

CUPALO ROCK   est. 6600 ft/2012 m

An interesting outcrop about 3 mi. NE of Chinook Pass. It offers a number of 1-2 pitch routes on good rock.

Follow the Crest Trail ◆ N from Chinook Pass past Sheep Lake. The peak is the one about ¼ mi. E of Sourdough Gap. The E face routes are most easily reached by descending from the notch on the E side of the peak. The descent route is a class 3 gully on the SW side.

The following routes are known:

BROTTEM'S ROUTE: By John Brottem, 1965. Easy class 5; an outside corner, starting near notch.
EAST CHIMNEY: By Jim Langdon and Ron Fear, July 1967. Class 5.7. Three leads (second route from notch).
NORTHEAST CHIMNEY: By Jim Langdon, Roger Stenbak, and Rusty Engle in July 1966. Class 5.7. Three leads (third route from notch).
EAST FACE DIRECT: By Tom Hargis and Mead Hargis in 1966. Class 5.6 and A2. Hanging belay at bolt (fourth route from notch).

THREEWAY PEAK   6796 ft/2071 m

One of the high points on the Morse Creek rim. Ascend by a short summit hike or ski climb directly from the Crest Trail ♦, or hike NE from Sheep Skull Gap.

SILVER KING   6998 ft/2133 m

Silver King stands high on the White River-Silver Creek crest at about ¾ mi. NW of Threeway Peak. There is an easy ridge hike or ski tour connection. One could continue N along the divide via The Throne, and Silver Queen (6960 ft+) to Crystal Mountain (6872 ft) at the top of the ski area chair lift. Hiking routes are obvious and easy, and there are numerous way trails.

NOBLE KNOB   6014 ft/1833 m

Noble Knob is reached from Corral Pass (5600 ft) (see Corral Pass Road No. 185 ♦) via Trail No. 1184 in 3.6 mi. A ridge crest by the trail about ½ mi. S of the Knob peaks out at 6205 ft.

FIFES PEAKS   6917 ft/2108 m

The Fifes Peaks group is a complicated cluster of andesite outcrops N of the Chinook Pass highway, on the American River-Crow Creek divide. On their N they actually form a circling watershed around the head of Falls Creek, a fork of Crow Creek. The Fifes Peaks are the remnants of a large composite volcano of early Miocene age, with a basal diameter of about 5 mi. Successive lava streams once flowed from broad, low volcanos to build the rock formations less than 25 m. y. ago. Spectacular outcrops and towers were eroded from the lava for some 2 mi. along this divide. The peaks were named for Robert and Thomas Fife, early placer miners who held the Blue Bell claims at the head of Union Creek.

The bulkiest and most impressive summit is the centrally-located East Peak (6793 ft), located 2¼ mi. N of the American River at Pleasant Valley. This peak has a "citadel" appearance, with very sheer walls on its S and E.

Fifes West Peak (6880 ft) is on the same crest at 0.3

mi. distant. It is a flat-topped summit, with short walls on all sides except the E slope, which runs gradually to the summit.

The highest peak, logically called the Northwest Peak (6917 ft), is located about ¾ mi. NW of the continuing watershed around the head of Falls Creek. It has a detached crag (6880 ft+) on its E. Topographically it is part of the Fife's group, although the maps do not identify this clearly.

About ½ mi. E of the East Peak is a rather massive and rocky "Far East Peak" (est. 6320 ft), with a curious rock tower (Teddy Bear Pinnacle) high on its W face.

Between this peak and the East Peak are a number of rocky outcrops and sharp pinnacles; the most spectacular of these is the Masthead, the first pinnacle E of the sheer E face of East Peak. The complexity of the area is such that all of the many towers and crags along the crests, and on the N slope, have not yet been fully catalogued; some are likely unclimbed. The one other major identifiable summit is Cannonhole Pinnacle, located just E of the main gap between East Peak and West Peak.

ROUTES: Approach routes vary a good deal depending on the nature of the objective. Three basic routes are feasible:

(a) Follow Crow Lake Trail ♦ to Grassy Saddle; here one is SW of the West Peak. Make a rising traverse across meadowed hillsides to the E, to reach the gap between Cannonhole Pinnacle and West Peak (it is U-shaped, with a tiny pinnacle in center).

(b) From about ½ mi. uptrail follow E branch of Miner Creek for a distance, then slopes (game trails) and a vale directly to notch between the East Peak and Mainmast. This route avoids cliffs if care is taken; the route is almost in a straight line to the notch.

(c) Take the Fifes Ridge Trail for about 2½ mi. to where it crosses the divide to the N (est. 5200 ft); one may have to descend some on the N. Hike about ⅔ mi. W, across slopes to the basin beneath the various peaks. This basin can be followed to a waterfall: turn left up a steep gully to the gap between Cannonhole Pinnacle and the West Peak.

To reach the Northwest Peak, whose final portion appears easy on the W side, it would be easiest to make a rising NE traverse from the N side of Crow Creek divide (about 5600 ft) where a stream heads in a pond. Pond to summit about 0.8 mi.

To reach the West Peak, approach (a) is shortest. The climb is done on the E (simple scrambling). However, there is much loose scree below the peak and friable rock up to the summit.

The approach to the East Peak is more of a problem. One could use approach (c) to beneath the N side, or use (b), then contour W on the N slope for about ⅔ mi. to below center face. If using (a) one would have to descend and traverse around below the cliffs of Cannonhole Pinnacle. It appears

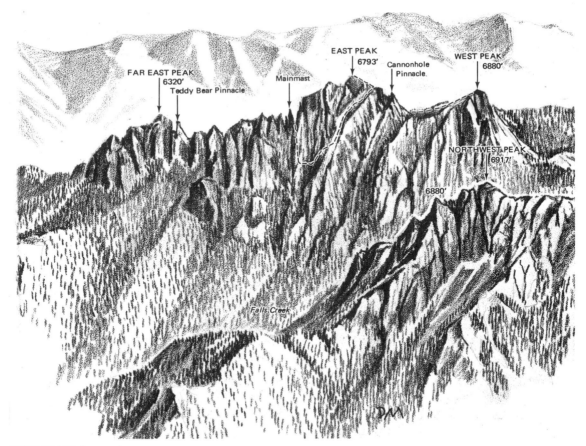

FIFES PEAKS from north

that the most feasible summit route lies on the N face, a bit right of center; here a snow gully and a rightward-slanting depression work to just W of the highest point.

CANNONHOLE PINNACLE
6560 ft+ / 1999 m+

Cannonhole Pinnacle is identified by a large hole on its W side, where it appears as though a tower has fallen across to close a gap. Approach (a) seems shortest. The final climb is on the N; one bolt for safety used on pitch alongside the hole. Class 4. First ascent by Rudy Miller and Fred Beckey on September 17, 1950.

MASTHEAD est. 6400 ft/1951 m

The Masthead, the sharpest of the Fifes Peak needles, was first climbed by Pete Schoening and Don Wilde in 1950. Use approach (b). The first lead is the hardest: begin on the W and circle to a belay ledge on the N. Ascend the steep wall to the small summit. Pitons and bolts were used for both safety and aid; rock tends to be brittle.

BUFFALO HUMP 6960 ft+/2121 m+

The Boy Scouts' name for a pointed peak E of Mount Aix. From the Fifes Peak area it resembles a dinner plate on edge but from the opposite quarter is very gentle.

Follow Bumping Lake Road ◆ about 10 mi., to the first crossing of the river above Goose Prairie. Dirt roadway turns left to reach Richmond Mine Trail No. 973 in ½ mi. Follow trail about 3½ mi. up Thunder Creek to a pass. Turn left on ridge; peak is ½ mi. to the N and is ascended by this ridge on the SE side; hardly more than a scramble.

MOUNT AIX 7766 ft/2367 m

Mount Aix is the dominating mountain in the region E of Mount Rainier and the Cascade Crest. The mountain is located 4½ mi. SE of Bumping Lake. The bared area above timberline features talus ridges, boulderfields, and nivation hollows. Goats are frequently seen on the high slopes. A trail climbs to the summit,

135

which has excellent views of Mount Adams, Goat Rocks, Mount Rainier, and the Cougar Lakes area.

From Deep Creek Road (see Bumping Lake Road ◆) at 5 mi. beyond Bumping Lake Dam (3800 ft), turn E up a hiking roadway. Trail No. 982 extends 7.3 mi. to the summit. The trail climbs the long W slope to the W summit of Aix, then follows the crest to the highest point. There is a grassy bench campground at about 6400 ft.

Nelson Ridge is a high N-S crest trending N of the W summit of Aix; the high point is 7537 ft — merely a ridge hike.

The summit can also be reached via a 10.8 mi. hike on Trails No. 981 and 982 from Bethel Ridge Road ◆ via the lush valley of Hindoo Creek. Leave the road at 11.6 mi. from State Hwy No. 410 ◆ (elevation 3400 ft).

NELSON BUTTE   7160 ft + /2156 m +
This is a large mass between Rattlesnake Creek and its N fork (3 mi. NE of Mount Aix). One could reach this objective by Windy Ridge Trail No. 985 from Clover Spring and the N fork of Rattlesnake Creek. This trail climbs to 6360 ft + on the divide W of the summit; the final part is a hike.

BISMARCK PEAK   7585 ft/2312 m
Bismarck is a gently-sloping, bald peak 2 mi. SW of Mount Aix, and quite prominent because of its height. The summit is an easy ridge hike on the SE flank from the Rattlesnake Peaks Trail ◆ , which traverses the S flank at about 6600 ft. Trail distance is

about 8.7 mi. if approaching from the W, and about 14 mi. from the E. Elk are occasionally seen in the area. Reference: *Cascadian,* 1961, pp. 12-14.

OLD SCAB MOUNTAIN
6608 ft/2014 m
This summit offers a good viewpoint in the area E of the Cascade Crest. Approach via Little Bald Mountain Road ◆ . At 1.8 mi. SW of the lookout junction follow the trail bearing NW past Flat Iron Lake. From about 5600 ft SE of the objective, leave the trail and hike to the summit.

BOOTJACK ROCK   est. 6000 ft/1829 m
Two wild-looking, loose-rock towers on Russell Ridge, N of Rimrock Lake. Approach as for Russell Ridge ◆ . Ascend about 150 ft on "back" side. Class 3.

SPECTATOR SPIRE
est. 4200 ft/1280 m
A crumbling 150-ft tower set off from the cliff adjoining the N side of the highway at 3.3 mi. E of White Pass. The name was derived from a sidelight of the first ascent, when motorist-spectators quickly dispersed as a climber-loosened rock crashed on the roof of a Buick parked below.

The ascent was made by tyrolean traverse from the adjoining cliff by Fred Beckey, Richard Berge, Jim Henry, Richard McGowan, and Tom Miller on October 27, 1951. References: *Mountaineer,* 1951, photo p. 60; 1952, p. 82; *Appalachia,* June 1952, pp. 36-37.

SECTION III

North-Central Cascades (West Side)

STAMPEDE PASS TO DECEPTION PASS

GEOGRAPHY

The rich and varied region of peaks, rivers, lakes and forests included in this arbitrary sectional breakdown is perhaps the best known to the public of any in the Cascades. It is traversed by two major cross-state highways and two railway routes. Once the domain of a variety of explorers, miners, hikers, climbers, and loggers, its periphery has now become familiar to mass recreation.

Snoqualmie Pass (only 3004 ft and the lowest of the Cascade passes) and Stevens Pass (4056 ft) are today's best-known trade and travel routes. Stampede Pass and Green River are traversed by railway, but not wholly open to the public since much of the valley lies within a restricted watershed. The principal west-side drainages are the Snoqualmie River (with its three branches), the Tolt River, and the Skykomish River (with such branches as the Foss and Miller). These main valleys are extremely heavily forested (now much-logged) and have noticeably very low gradients until nearly their headwaters. Shorter secondary streams generally exhibit a steep gradient and often have impressive cascades and waterfalls.

The present trunk streams have been incised thousands of feet below the old erosion surface uparched by the Miocene and Pleistocene growth of the Cascade Range. The valleys were excavated within belts of erosionally weak rock, whose structure generally trended northwest. During and after the Cascade Range uplift, many streams (including the Skykomish, Snoqualmie, Yakima, and Wenatchee rivers) exploited these weak-rock belts.

Erosion of the principal southern drainages, the Yakima and Cle Elum river valleys, has been along zones of weakness created by faulting. Pleistocene alpine glaciation followed the courses of these drainages, deepening and widening them. Except where removed by erosion, unconsolidated alluvial and glacial deposits cover bedrock in the valleys of the Yakima, Cle Elum, and their tributaries.

The virtually solid complex of mountains extending from the foothills east of Puget Sound Basin to the Cascade Crest, contains a great variety of peaks and alpine ridges. The highest and most majestic peaks are on the Cascade Crest near Dutch Miller Gap; such summits as Chimney Rock, Overcoat, Lemah, Summit Chief, and Bears Breast stand like a desolate row of ancient sawteeth, averaging about 7500 ft in height and offering magnificent alpine adventure. High summits Daniel and Hinman provide easy yet picturesque glacier climbing.

The colder climate of the Pleistocene resulted in extensive glaciers and a lower snowline. During Fraser glaciation (19,000 to 13,000 years B. P.), the colder climate is estimated to have resulted in a regional snowline as much as 900 m lower than today's. During Pleistocene time there were icecaps on the high mountain surface and great glaciers in distributary valleys. Confluent glaciers brought ice to the trunk glaciers, which carved and smoothed out the valleys. The erosional activity of the large glaciers severely modified the youthful topography of the Late Tertiary Cascade Range uplift.

There were scores of local cirque and valley glaciers in the Snoqualmie-to-Skykomish and Yakima-Cle Elum alpine areas, all terminating in outwash streams. The high mountain surface was carved into many U-shaped valleys headed by large cirques. Today, morainal deposits of gravel and other glacial debris are found along edges and on the bottoms of these valleys.

Late Pleistocene glaciers that formed at the head of the South Fork Snoqualmie River bifurcated at Snoqualmie Pass, then flowed west down the South Fork valley and east down the Yakima River valley. Glaciers scoured out Gold Creek and Kachess valleys, merging in a massive Yakima valley glacier. The glaciers that formed in the upper Yakima drainage basin were among the largest east of the Cascade Crest, and the record of their fluctuations extends more than 40 mi. downstream from the drainage divide.[47] The glaciers in the Yakima valley left bulky moraines, which mark the former positions of the glacier termini, and they deposited massive bodies of drift. Typically, the moraines are progressively older with increasing distance from valley heads. Modern Keechelus, Little Kachess, Kachess, and Cle Elum lakes are all contained behind prominent morainal dams.

Evidence shows that at the Pleistocene maximum the Puget Lobe of the Cordilleran ice sheet pushed into the Cascade Range, impounding long lakes in mountain valleys. During this maximum, the eastern margin of the lobe lay along the range front. Tongues of ice flowed eastward up mountain valleys freshly vacated by the large valley glaciers. These glacier tongues formed moraine embankments that blocked the mouths of the Skykomish, Snoqualmie Middle and South forks, and Cedar River valleys. All of the principal valleys along the Cascade front from the Sultan to the Middle Fork Snoqualmie are obstructed by large, flat-topped morainal wedges of till and waterlaid sand and gravel.[48]

Meltwater from the Puget Lobe built delta-like outwash plains into the Cascade valleys and formed glacial lakes in them. In the South Fork Snoqualmie Valley (near I-90) the postglacial stream has cut a deep gorge in the delta moraine.

Glacial Lake Skykomish contained thick, heavy deposits that now form conspicuous terraces. The silt and clay that accumulated in this lake buried all valley-floor evidence of previous alpine glaciers.[49] The gravel, sand, and mud deposited by meltwater and lakes during glacial retreat mantle much of the bedrock terrain in the lower ends of mountain valleys west of the morainal embankments, and along the western Cascade front. Studies indicate that the lakes dammed by ice tongues drained south and west. After its maximum stand about 14,000 years b. p. the Puget Lobe receded northwest, and the ice-dammed lakes merged with lakes in the lowland.

A cluster of modern glaciers lies between Chikamin and Overcoat peaks along a sector of the Cascade Crest. A grouping of larger glaciers occupies the gentle high slopes of mounts Hinman and Daniels, where the highest summit elevations are located on an east-west crest line.

The fresh, rubbly, sharp-crested moraines of coarse rock waste that front existing glaciers along the Cascade Crest extend as much as 1 km beyond present termini. Such deposits also are found in cirques and valley heads now devoid of ice, lying at altitudes equal to or only slightly lower than nearby glaciers.

Cirques are distributed through a wide range of altitude in the Cascades, but there is a progressive rise in average cirque-floor altitude eastward across the range. Floors of cirques near the western front of the Cascade Range stand as low as 3000 ft, whereas at the eastern limit of glaciation in the central Cascades they average about 5700 ft.[50] Some of the lowest cirques have been so altered by headward erosion and valley fill that they are in the form of elongated basins.

Lakes formed from glacial scouring are often dammed in structurally oriented rock basins, the lakes lying mostly between 3300 and 6000 ft elevation. Tributary valleys of the Middle Fork Snoqualmie, Miller, Foss, and Cle Elum rivers have numerous cirque lakes near their headwaters. Such magnificent bodies of water as lakes Waptus and Cooper are set in open timbered valleys, while high lakes such as Venus and Spade are set in pocket cirques beneath Mount Daniel. No other section of the Cascades is so blessed with lakes: in an area of roughly 700,000 acres, there are 130 wilderness lakes of over ¼ mi. in length — all evidence of a youthful landscape. The entire 393,000-acre Alpine Lakes Wilderness is wildly picturesque, not only with lakes, cirques, and waterfalls, but with small glaciers, perennial snowfields, wet meadows, and exotic heather hollows set among bare knobs and sharp rock horns.

Weathering has fractured granites and metamorphic rocks to create extensive talus slopes. At the higher elevations talus, glacial and mountain-stream deposits typically merge into one another. Some talus and moraines merge downslope into coarse fans of debris that are scantily vegetated.

By accepted nomenclature, the main Yakima River heads near Snoqualmie Pass and runs through Lake Keechelus, but the Cle Elum is the longer and larger stream. Both rivers and such branches as the Cooper and Waptus are deeply excavated glacial troughs that maintain nearly flat gradients far into the interior of the range. Lakes Keechelus, Kachess, and Cle Elum are natural bodies of water on the Yakima-Cle Elum system, raised by storage dams and used as irrigation reservoirs.

Mean annual precipitation ranges from about 120 inches near Snoqualmie Pass to about 180 inches in the vicinity of Mount Index. Mean annual snowfall recorded for Snoqualmie Pass is 398 inches; mean annual temperature is 51° F. Heavy winter snows accumulate on countless avalanche slopes and the resulting slides often spread out to cover flat valleys and meadows with debris. The traveler should be especially wary of avalanche danger after heavy snowfall and during any unstable conditions.

On the west side of the main divide, western hemlock (*Tsuga heterophylla*), western red cedar (*Thuja plicata*), and Douglas fir (*Pseudotsuga menziesii*) are the dominating evergreens in the montane (Canadian) zone. In the subalpine (Hudsonian) zone are Alaska yellow cedar *(Chamaecyparis nuthana)*, mountain hemlock *(Tsuga mertensiana)*, and scattered subalpine fir *(Abies lasiocarpa)*. The heavy vegetative cover begins to thin near the 4800-ft level; higher there is less tree-cover and more talus areas and alpine meadowlands characterized by heather, huckleberry, and flowers. Most talus slopes are stable, and can support trees and vegetation.

East of the main divide Engelmann spruce *(Picea engelmanii)* is common (particularly in the Cooper, Pete, and Waptus Lake basins). Whitebark pine *(Pinus albicaulis)* is picturesque in high basins (Spectacle Lake). Many mountain meadows are lush with floral exhibits. A report from Cathedral Rock lists Indian paintbrush *(Castilleja)*, tiger lily *(Lilium columbianum)*, larkspur *(Delphinium xantholeucum)*, columbine *(Aquilegia flavescens)*, lupine *(Lupinus laxiflorus)*, squaw grass *(Xerophyllum tenax)*, saxifrage *(Saxifraga)*, shooting star *(Dodecatheon conjugans)*, and phlox *(Phlox)*. In the upper Cle Elum Valley, the giant hellebore *(Veratrum viride)* and cow parsnip *(Heracleum lanatum)* are evident.

GEOLOGY

The geology of the southern Cascade Range of Washington between the Snoqualmie, Skykomish, and Yakima rivers, with its Tertiary volcanic and sedimentary cover, is highly complex. The principal structural feature, the Straight Creek fault, is a right-lateral displacement strike-slip fault; it trends north-south between Skykomish and Kachess Lake. The fault forms a boundary between fundamentally different geologic terranes: chiefly high grade regionally metamorphosed rocks to the east and low-grade metamorphic rocks to the west.

South of Kachess Lake, the Straight Creek fault intersects a major lineament in a complex of curving faults and folds. This lineament, which stretches from the Wallowa Mountains in Oregon to the Strait of Juan de Fuca, traverses the central Cascade Range from southeast to northwest. The lineament is most strongly expressed in the faulted and folded rocks of the Manastash River area, where the lineament meets the Straight Creek fault. The lineament appears to be expressed in broad northwest-trending folds and faults in Miocene volcanic rocks between the South Fork Snoqualmie and White Rivers, southwest of Snoqualmie Pass (Frizzell, 1984).

North of the Skykomish River and west of the Straight Creek fault, the oldest rocks are diverse types of Paleozoic and Mesozoic ages. They are overlain unconformably by the volcanic rocks of Mount Persis. The latter consist mostly of andesite flows and tuffs, and form a west-descending upland surface located south of the Skykomish River and generally west of the Mount Index and Snoqualmie batholiths. These volcanic rocks, radiometrically dated at 38 m. y. in age, may have erupted during the same Eocene interval as the volcanic rocks in the Naches Formation.

A widespread unit associated with the terrane west of the fault is the Easton Schist. Near Snoqualmie Pass thermally metamorphosed chert, basalt, and marble are exposed on peaks and ridges.

By early Tertiary time the Cretaceous and older rocks had been uplifted and partly eroded. To the east of the Straight Creek fault the sandstone and conglomerate of the early Eocene Swauk Formation, and some volcanic rock, were deposited unconformably on the pre-Tertiary rocks. The tightly folded and faulted Swauk Formation is cut by many northwest-trending faults and is faulted against the Easton Schist in the Straight Creek fault zone.

Peaks of the Swauk Formation, such as Bears Breast and Summit Chief, have steeply-dipping rock strata resulting from severe deformation. These sedimentary rocks, altered by heat, form a very hard, fine-grained arkose sandstone with numerous beds and lenses of coarse pebbles.

The more recent volcanic rocks of Tertiary age are widespread, with andesite predominating. Following deformation and erosion of the Eocene rocks, a variety of volcanic rocks and sandstones of the Naches Formation (upper Eocene to Oligocene) were deposited west of the fault; they extend southward of Kachess Lake. The Naches Formation consists mostly of steeply dipped to overturned rhyolitic and basaltic lava flows and interbeds of sandstone, recrystallized by the nearby Snoqualmie batholith. The Chimney Rock-Lemah Mountain-Chikamin Ridge portion of this formation lies in a narrow north-south band in fault contact with the Easton Schist and the Swauk Formation.

Guye Peak is a sedimentary member of the Naches Formation; the rock consists of sandstone, shales, and conglomerate. The Denny Peak-Tooth ridge is mostly andesite, with unusual hardness probably due to recrystallization during intrusion of the Snoqualmie batholith.

The massive rocks of Mount Garfield comprise an isolated volcanic group. Breccia, tuffs, and ash flows at this location are highly recrystallized by thermal metamorphism.

The western slope of the Cascades between Puget Sound and the Naches Formation is covered by mildly deformed volcanic rocks that predominate the range southward. The well-bedded volcanic rocks of Huckleberry Mountain are an extensive cover west and south of Snoqualmie Pass. Deformation continued in the mountainous regions here and southward. Deformed Naches and volcanic Ohanapecosh formations are overlain unconformably by the Stevens Ridge and Fifes Peak formations (Oligocene to Miocene) to the south of this section.

The volcanic rocks of Mount Daniel and Goat Mountain are a prominent accumulation east of the Straight Creek fault. They are an outlier of the volcanic cover of the main southern Cascade volcanic terrane. The main mass of these volcanic rocks are ash flow tuffs and breccias, intruded on the west by the Snoqualmie batholith.

The various pre-Tertiary rocks and Tertiary sedimentary and volcanic rocks in this section were intruded by the Snoqualmie, Mount Index, and Grotto batholiths during Tertiary time. The Mount Index batholith cooled about 34 m. y. ago and the Snoqualmie and Grotto batholiths about 25 m. y. ago. Much of the Alpine Lakes area was carved from the Snoqualmie Granodiorite, and many peaks, including Big Snow, Snoqualmie, Granite, Lennox, and Hinman, stand within this intrusive granite.

Several bodies of mafic rock, mostly metamorphosed gabbro, are near or at the margin of the Snoqualmie batholith and were thermally metamorphosed by it. One gabbro crops out along the north valley wall of Money Creek. Rocks forming the Mount Index massif are a metagabbro. These rocks and the adjacent volcanic unit are intruded and thermally metamorphosed by the Mount Index batholith.

In the Alpine Lakes area, a zone of disseminated copper and molybdenum deposits in mineralized rock extends from the area of the Middle Fork of Snoqualmie River southward through Gold Creek to Mineral Creek, and there are veins of copper ore near LaBohn Gap. The area has some 137 patented claims; a recorded total of about 500 tons of gold, silver, and copper has been produced.

References: R. W. Tabor, et al., *Preliminary Geologic Map of the Skykomish River 1:100,000 Quadrangle, Washington*. U.S.G.S. Open-File Map QF 82-747 (1982). Virgil A. Frizzell, Jr., et al., *Preliminary Geologic Map of the Snoqualmie Pass 1:100,000 Quadrangle, Washington*. U.S.G.S. Open-File Map QF 84-693 (1984).

HISTORY

Indians once roamed the region freely, leaving little but names to commemorate them. "Snoqualmie" is modified from a complicated native word having reference to the legend that the tribe's people came from the moon and settled the mountains in the area. "Cle Elum," derived from "Tlee-al-lum," means "swift water." Many of these names were altered to their present form: the 1903 U.S.G.S. map shows the "Clealum" River, but the spelling of "Kachess" is today's. Fortunately such derivations as Skykomish for "Sky-wha-mish"[51] (meaning river people) prevailed. The topographic report of Lt. J. K. Duncan (for Captain McClellan) in the summer of 1853 described the "Yahinese" River heading in "Lake Kitchelus," near Snoqualmie Pass. Duncan explored Lake Kachess and a double-lake 1 mi. above called Pilwaltas . . . where he reported the mountains are "needle-shape in structure"[52] (likely he saw Three Queens). McClellan probably gave the first description of the "Snoqualmie Peaks" from near Naches Pass in 1853, when he wrote "to the northward there is a vast sea of bare, jagged, snow-crowned ranges extending as far as the eye can reach."[53]

Hudson's Bay Company trappers explored the Snoqualmie and Yakima valleys in the early 1800s. A well-known Indian trail extended from the south end of "Lake D'Wamish" (Washington) to Snoqualmie Falls, then via the "Nook-noo" (Cedar) River across Yakima Pass to the Yakima Valley. In a search for a better railroad route across the Cascades than the Naches Trail, both Capt. George B. McClellan (September 1853) and Lt. Abiel W. Tinkham (January 1854) carried exploration from the east through Yakima Pass.[54]

McClellan, a West Point graduate who served in the Mexican War, and geologist George Gibbs with a horseback party came close to Yakima Pass on September 6 and camped "at the summit of the pass . . . . To the northward of the pass the mountains are very lofty, generally bare at the top . . ." Tinkham continued down the Cedar River on his winter trek to study snow depths and railroad possibilities, making the first reliably documented Cascade crossing in this region. McClellan was discouraged about examining Snoqualmie Pass because of unfavorable reports from Indians.

Both Indians and Hudson's Bay Company trappers knew of Snoqualmie and Yakima passes, but the earliest use of them is vague. It is possible that one of the passes was the "Sinahomish Pass" supposedly used by

Dwarfed, wind-bent alpine zone conifers. Looking across Necklace Valley: MALACHITE PEAK (far left) and BALD EAGLE PEAK (far right) ED COOPER

A. C. Anderson during a cattle drive in 1841. Major J. H. H. Van Bokkelen of the Washington Territorial Volunteers crossed the pass in 1856 while scouting for military fortifications. In 1858 several large pack trains crossed Snoqualmie Pass to east-side mines. In July 1865 Seattle citizens (including A. A. Denny) spent two weeks exploring Cedar River, Snoqualmie, and Naches passes; on returning they reported favorably for Snoqualmie Pass compared to the old Indian trail along the Cedar River to Yakima Pass. Within two years a wagon road was built over the pass and down the Yakima Valley by community action, but the road for some years was only suitable for pack trains and cattle drives because of an inability to keep it in repair. Tolls were inaugurated in 1867.[55] The Chicago, Milwaukee, St. Paul, and Pacific Railroad completed its line over Snoqualmie Pass March 29, 1909, the original grade going over the pass without a tunnel.

Miners made their mark in such valleys as Gold Creek, where intense prospecting began in 1890. Most of the activity was in the Ptarmigan Park area. Dutch Miller Gap was named for Andrew Jackson Miller's "Dutch Miller Mine." Miller prospected the La Bohn Gap copper deposits in 1896.

Prospecting began in the Miller River area in 1892 when the Great Northern was being constructed in the Skykomish River valley. In Money Creek the Apex Ledge was the first property to be developed, and from which ore was shipped. A wagon road and tram were built to the property. The name "money" came into use because of large sums sent by Eastern stockholders for mine development. Many claims were staked in nearby valleys, the Coney Basin mine on the slopes of Mount Lennox with its buildings and tram being of importance.

Geologists and surveyors explored this entire region before and at the turn of the century. Bailey Willis traversed the west slope from Snoqualmie Pass to beyond the Skykomish in 1895. G. O. Smith, A. H. Sylvester, F. C. Calkins, and G. C. Curtis were important pioneer surveyors. Early miner-blazed rudimentary trails were tramped out by hikers, climbers, fishermen, and sometimes goats. Groups from The Mountaineers have thoroughly explored and climbed the Snoqualmie Pass region since early in the century; now the high country is reached by a network of good Forest Service trails. Additionally, cross-country routes in this region are extremely appealing because of the many meadowed ridges and hidden lakes that can be visited in this adventurous manner.

After Washington's statehood in 1889 administra-

tive areas were defined, and in 1908 Snoqualmie National Forest was established.

The Snoqualmie Pass area has had a functional unity from the hiking and mountaineering standpoint since the early 1900s. The summit groupings, particularly the Snoqualmie Pass and Gold Creek peaks, offer moderate and scenic climbing opportunities. Because these attractive peaks are quite accessible, they have long been popular. Relief on the approaches is not great, and there are only minor amounts of understory brush travel. Connecting ridges permit traverses and combination ascents in a day's time. The peaks provide excellent schooling for larger climbs in other portions of the range.

General references to the Snoqualmie Pass and Gold Creek areas are: *Mountaineer,* 1916, pp. 70-79; 1920, pp. 54-56; 1922, pp. 53-57; 1931, pp. 58-66; Vicky Spring, Ira Spring, and Harvey Manning, *100 Hikes in the Alpine Lakes.*

References to the area east of the Cle Elum River and the Alpine Lakes are: *Mountaineer,* 1925, pp. 21-27; *Summit,* July-August 1969, pp. 18-25; *Living Wilderness,* vol. 32 (Spring 1968), pp. 21-31; *Mountaineer,* 1966, pp. 123-132; 1971, pp. 19-25; Brock Evans, *The Alpine Lakes,* Seattle, 1971; David Knibb, *Backyard Wilderness: The Alpine Lakes Story,* Seattle, 1982; University of Washington, Department of Geological Sciences, *The Alpine Lakes Environmental Geology,* Seattle, 1972; H. J. Foster, "Tertiary Geology of a Portion of the Central Cascade Mountains," *Bull. Geol. Soc. Amer.* 71 (February 1960): pp. 99-126; *20th Annual Report,* U.S.G.S., part 2, pp. 80-310; G. O. Smith and F. C. Calkins, *Snoqualmie Folio, No. 139* (1906), U.S.G.S. Atlas; Yvonne Prater, *Snoqualmie Pass: From Indian Trail to Interstate,* Seattle, 1981.

LAND MANAGEMENT

Ranger Stations:

North Bend: 4204 North Bend Way
North Bend, WA 98045
(0.6 mi. E of mid-town)
(206) 888-1421
Open daily 7:30 to 4:30 except holidays

Skykomish: Skykomish, WA 98288
(1 mi. E of town)
(206) 677-2414

Cle Elum: Cle Elum, WA 98922
(On Roslyn Road at W side of town)
(509) 674-4411

Ellensburg: Ellensburg Information Office
(509) 962-9813

Salmon la Sac: Salmon la Sac Forest station
(Summer)

Lake Kachess: Lake Kachess Forest station
(Summer)

Campgrounds

Numerous forest camps are located throughout the
Mt. Baker-Snoqualmie and Wenatchee National
Forests on I-90 and U.S. Hwy No. 2 and roads lead-
ing off these two major highways. Consult Forest
Service maps (can be obtained at ranger stations) for
up-to-date information on fees and facilities.

Alpine Lakes Wilderness: note camping and fire
restrictions as shown on maps and signs. There is a
12-person group limit.

MAPS

Topographic (U.S. Geological Survey)

Grotto (1965)	1:24,000
Skykomish (1965)	1:24,000
Scenic (1965)	1:24,000
Mt. Daniel (1965)	1:24,000
Big Snow Mtn. (1965)	1:24,000
The Cradle (1965)	1:24,000
Snoqualmie Lake (1965)	1:24,000
Bandera (1960)	1:62,500
Index (1957)	1:62,500
Mt. Si (1960)	1:62,500
Kachess Lake (1961)	1:62,500
Snoqualmie Pass (1961)	1:62,500

Planimetric (U.S. Forest Service)

Mt. Baker-Snoqualmie National Forest Map
Wenatchee National Forest Map

Private

Alpine Lakes Wilderness Area, 1:100,000 topographic
map. Seattle: The Mountaineers, 1981
Weyerhaeuser Recreation Map

BESSEMER MOUNTAIN
5166 ft/1575 m

Located 2 mi. E of Lake Hancock, a moderate hump-
shaped peak, largely subalpine. New maps correctly
show its location in Section 13; previous maps placed it
between Sections 22 and 23, and at 5022 ft, a really
lesser summit.

ROUTES: There appears to be no brush-free route to the
summit. The shortest is to skirt the N side of Lake Hancock
(see Lake Hancock Trail ◆), then ascend Hancock Creek
easterly to the NW flank of the peak; the distance is about 3
mi. from the lake. There are no technical difficulties.

Another possible route is from the W end of Quartz Creek
Road, which exits from Taylor River Road at about 1 mi.,
but is currently not driveable because of a bridge washout
(see Middle Fork Snoqualmie River Road ◆). The road
ascends to the 3000-ft level in about 4 mi. One could hike
cross-country SW for 1 mi. to Lake Blethen (3198 ft), then
on for ½ mi. to the upper lake. Ascend S about ½ mi. to just
W of Bessemer Mountain; ascend bushy rock terrain and a
steep gully to the ridge between the two highest summits.

MOUNT SI   4167 ft/1270 m

Because of its proximity to urban growth and a freeway, Mount Si, closely E of North Bend, has become
very popular. Named for early settler Josiah Merritt,
the mountain is dominant because of its great W-side
fault scarp. The S and SW flanks display the contrast
between ice-scoured lower slopes and the higher un-
glaciated terrain.

The summit "haystack" has three chimneys splitting the S face, popular for rock climbing. Members of
a Mountaineers trip climbed here as long ago as 1923.
A prominent gendarme several hundred yards N of the
summit is often scaled. The State Department of
Natural Resources has developed a new parking area
and relocated the trail, which now crosses the old trail
at 3150 ft. Stay on trails and do not take shortcuts
(numerous individuals have become lost while descending). References: *100 Hikes in the Alpine Lakes;*
Footsore 2; Mountaineer, 1907, pp. 49-51; 1910, pp.
64-66; 1923, p. 56; 1977, pp. 3-6.

ROUTE: Take exit 31 on I-90 ◆ into North Bend and
follow through town eastward. At 1.3 mi. from the main
stoplight turn left on Mount Si Road (432nd Ave. SE) to
cross the river bridge, then drive about 2 mi. to the parking
area at the 700 ft level. The summit is 4 mi. distant (with an
18-percent grade); the final part of the "haystack" is a short
scramble on its E side.

EAST ROUTE: A private logging road leaves Mt. Si Road
at 3.3 mi. from the bridge. This road of about 4 mi. is steep
and probably rough (may be gated). One could leave at
between the 3800 ft and 4000 ft level, then hike cross-
country westward about ½ mi. to the Haystack or hike E to
Mount Teneriffe (4788 ft). This peak is also accessible via the
N-side jeep road (Spur No. 12C of the Tree Farm system).
Expect brushy travel on these routes.

RUSSIAN BUTTE   5123 ft/1562 m

Located S of the Middle Fork of the Snoqualmie River,
this is a rugged series of rock peaks, well cliffed and

forested. The lower N peak is an estimated 4880 ft, and the S summit about 4960 ft. Gifford Lakes are just SW of the summit. The summit juts high above the Middle Fork valley; views here to Mount Garfield and a vista of clearcut logging. The Butte was climbed by a U.S.G.S. mapping party in 1960.

ROUTES: Because of the relief and rugged terrain, the summit would be a trying adventure from the valley of the Middle Fork.

A more feasible route would be to take Granite Creek Road and jeep trail from about 4 mi. on Middle Fork Snoqualmie River Road ◆, then hike cross-country to the saddle W of Thompson Lake (est. 4250 ft). Hike N for 0.8 mi. to Point 5124 on the ridge, then follow the crest NE for ⅔ mi. to beyond Point 5454. Descend on the E slope and contour at about the 4400-ft level; easy hiking leads nearly to the S summit in 1¼ mi. Bypass steeper terrain near this summit at about 4600 ft, then continue to the little saddle just S of the true summit (a scrambling finish).

MOUNT DEFIANCE   5584 ft/1702 m

This moderately sloped peak is nearly climbed by the Mount Defiance Trail (see Pratt Lake Trail ◆). From the alpine meadowland at about 3 mi. (5250 ft) hike to the summit via either the S or W slope.

A shorter approach is via the 2½ mi. Mason Lake Trail (see Bandera Mountain). From the lake ascend to the Mount Defiance Trail, then westward.

BANDERA MOUNTAIN

5240 ft/1597 m

Bandera can be reached from Rainbow Lake (see Mount Defiance Trail); go S cross-country to N end of Island Lake (¼ mi. distant; 4240 ft); then hike S to the top (easy).

Another approach is via Look-Out Point Road No. 9031: Exit from I-90 ◆ at Exit 45, then cross N of the highway. Drive 3.8 mi. to a gate (2,100 ft), then hike the roadway ½ mi. to Mason Creek; about 100 yards farther pass the Mason Lake Trail (gate to end of roadway is 1½ mi.). Scramble a fire trail to the top of the old burn, then follow paths to the mountain's W ridge crest (about 4700 ft). Ascend E on the crest through the subalpine terrain, across boulders to the first summit, then to Bandera's highest point. Reference: *100 Hikes in the Alpine Lakes*.

PRATT MOUNTAIN   5099 ft/1555 m

Pratt Mountain is merely a bouldery hike from the Mount Defiance Trail ◆, which crosses its S side through meadows at about 4500 ft, 1 mi. along trail.

GRANITE MOUNTAIN

5629 ft/1716 m

The Granite Mountain Trail branches from Pratt Lake Trail ◆ in 1 mi. and reaches the summit in another 3½ mi. From the lookout atop the granite floral garden on the broad summit one can see Mount Rainier, Glacier Peak, Mount Stuart, and many nearer summits. Crystal Lake and Denny Lake nest high on the N and SE slopes.

In winter or spring there may be avalanche danger in the gully at 4000 ft, where the trail veers E; avoid this situation by hiking up Granite's rocky but easy SW ridge. References: *Mountaineer*, 1931, p. 64; *100 Hikes in the Alpine Lakes; A.N.A.M.*, 1984.

McCLELLANS BUTTE   5162 ft/1573 m

This pointed summit is a prominent landmark midway between North Bend and Snoqualmie Pass. The peak is part of a Tertiary volcanic rock coverage between the South Fork Snoqualmie and White rivers. It is a popular hike and winter ascent because of easy access and the trail approach. References: *Mountaineer*, 1923, pp. 58-59; *100 Hikes in the Alpine Lakes; Summit*, July-August 1970, pp. 24-25.

ROUTE: Leave I-90 ◆ at Tinkham Road (exit 42), then bear S on Road No. 55 to the trailhead in about 100 yards (altitude 1500 ft). The trail (No. 1515) first ascends various marred areas (railroad grade and tracks, clearcut, logging spur), then switchbacks up attractive forest terrain to reach the S summit ridge at 3.3 mi. (4300 ft); the trail crosses to the W flank of the ridge, then permits an easy summit scramble (4 mi.). Time: 4 hours.

Note: in winter and spring an ice axe should be taken. Beware of avalanche danger in gullies and slopes of the steeper sections.

Variation: East Spur: Leave trail at the top of the E-slope switchbacks; then ascend directly to the rocky spur leading to the top. Some scrambling (class 2 and 3).

NORTH BASIN: This route is popular in winter and spring, when the basin is largely snow-filled; variations in the form of short rock routes can be made on the upper N face, which is steep for a short distance, but can be readily bypassed by contouring W.

Reach the basin by leaving I-90 ◆ just W of bridge crossing of the main river (9.3 mi. E of North Bend). Park on a short gated spur. Climb up cat tracks, cross the railroad, and pick up a short trail through brush at the high point of the cleared area. Time: 4-5 hours.

SILVER PEAK   5605 ft/1708 m

This traditional summit, visible from the freeway, is located 4½ mi. SW of Snoqualmie Pass. The peak is largely subalpine, but has open meadow slopes and

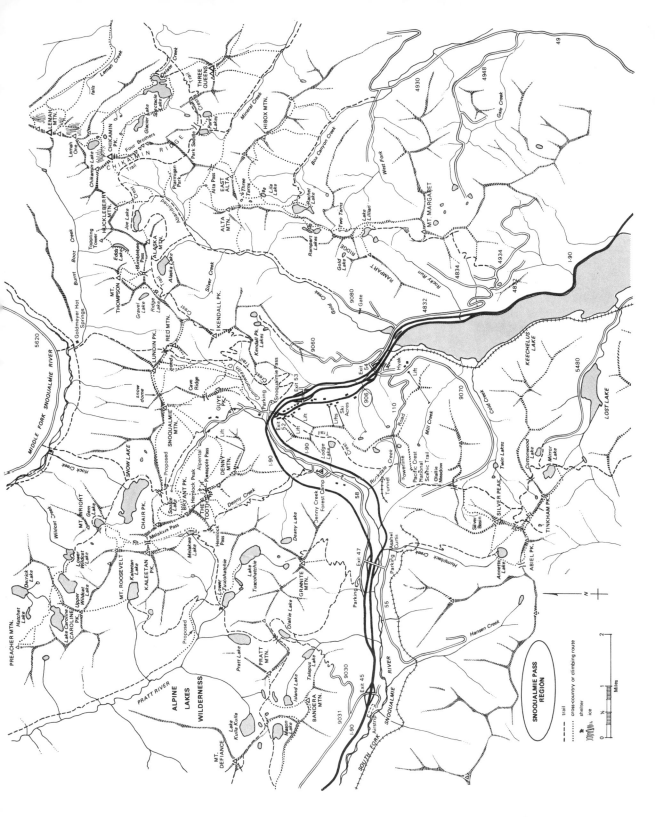

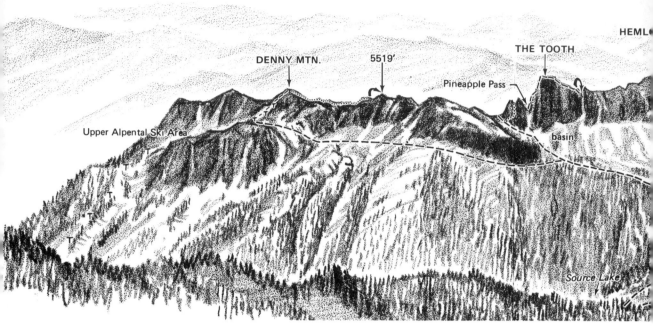

HEML

THE TOOTH

DENNY MTN. 5519'

Pineapple Pass

Upper Alpental Ski Area

basin

Source Lake

DENNY MOUNTAIN to SNOW LAKE from northeast

exposed rock near the summit. Silver was probably climbed by Frank Calkins on August 29, 1902; his report mentions the Keechelus volcanic rocks. Long popular as a winter route, the peak was climbed on skis in 1918. Reference: *100 Hikes in the Alpine Lakes; Mountaineer,* 1918, pp. 52-53; 1920, p. 51; 1931.
SOUTH SPUR: Leave the Crest Trail ◆ S of Olallie Meadow (about 4400 ft) via an unmarked branch path climbing W about 0.6 mi. to reach the Silver-Tinkham saddle (4925 ft). Then ascend the gradual, broad South Spur; this is talus and a grassy crest.

Alternate approaches: use Mirror Lake Trail, then follow Crest Trail NW, or approach via Cold Creek Road ◆ and trail.

A more direct but less pleasant summit route is to ascend the SE slope from the Crest Trail N of the branch path.

Olallie Meadow can be reached by hiking the Crest Trail from Cold Creek Trail or Cold Creek Road ◆. The 2½ mi. Cold Creek Trail reaches the Crest Trail about ½ mi. N of the branch path and the road crosses about 1 mi. farther N.
WEST ROUTE: From Annette Lake (see Annette Lake Trail ◆) ascend directly E, via slopes of mixed small timber and talus; no difficulties, but beware of avalanches in early season.
NORTHEAST ROUTE: Leave Crest Trail ◆ S of Olallie Meadow and climb by way of Silver Basin; either arm of basin is sound travel (good ski route). Avoid direct summit rocks at top by veering to ridge on either flank.

TINKHAM PEAK   5360 ft + / 1634 m +
Named for surveyor Abiel W. Tinkham, this small peak is 1 mi. SE of Silver Peak. The highest point is on the W end of the flat summit ridge; the E summit is listed as 5395 ft.

Tinkham must have been one of the earliest climbs in the region, and even was ascended on skis in the early 1900s. Reference: *Mountaineer,* 1931, p. 66.
NORTHWEST RIDGE: Leave the Crest Trail ◆ at about 1 mi. NW of Mirror Lake (est. 4400 ft) N of the peak; closest approach is Mirror Lake Trail ◆. Turn SW to the 4720-ft saddle on its NW side. Keep on the S side of the crest and follow to the summit area; no difficulties.
Approach Variation: From Annette Lake (see Annette Lake Trail ◆) via the Silver-Abiel saddle (est. 4880 ft), then along the slope to the Tinkham-Abiel saddle.
SOUTHEAST SPUR: From the Crest Trail ◆ at the S end of Mirror Lake climb SW and then W and NW; only ¾ mi. to the summit; no difficulties.

ABIEL PEAK   5365 ft / 1635 m
One mi. NW of Tinkham, it can be reached from the 4720-ft saddle on the NW side of Tinkham. Contour W across a basin above Abiel Lake to avoid a 5040-ft hump (keep on its S), and go to the 4880-ft saddle just E of Abiel's top; then up its short E ridge.

From Annette Lake (see Tinkham Peak) two ways exist: (1) The 4880-ft+ saddle is SE of the lake, and can be readily reached; to avoid thick brush leave trail 200 yards N of Annette Lake, climb rockslides toward Silver Peak, then work S along ridge bearing S of Silver Peak. (2) From W side of the lake reach the W ridge of Abiel via a 4480-ft+ saddle at ½ mi. W of the summit; the ascent is then straightforward.

DENNY MOUNTAIN

5520 ft+/1683 m+

Denny is a small, craggy and wooded peak 1½ mi. NW of Snoqualmie Pass, its highest point is a small horn N of the first summit crags. The peak was climbed by General James Tilton and his railroad survey party in August 1867 and called Mount Gregory Smith. G. O. Smith and W. C. Mendenhall climbed it during an 1899 survey.

The peak is named for Arthur A. Denny, who made the first mineral discovery in this district in 1869. Unfortunately the surroundings of Denny Mountain barely resemble the scene of his day; the only saving grace is the winter snow mantle, which seasonally disguises most of the blight and building of the Pass area. A chairlift of Alpental reaches to within a short distance of the summit on the SE flank. The peak therefore has little reward as a climb, but can be used as a viewpoint and a springboard to traverse the Denny ridge N to The Tooth (this traverse was first done by Don Blair and Art Winder on July 9, 1932). References: *Mountaineer*, 1920, pp. 53-54; 1923, p. 57.

EAST ROUTE: The shortest summit route is to follow service roads under the chair lifts (or ski tour) through the saddle (4320 ft+) SE of the summit. Continue on the upper SE slope to the summit. The final rocks (andesite breccia) are a short easy scramble from the upper Edelweiss lift terminal.

NORTH ROUTE: This route, which terminates on the 5519-ft N summit, about ¼ mi. N of the true summit, is a good ski touring route to the Denny-Tooth ridge saddle (5200 ft+) in winter or spring. There are four methods of reaching the large upper basin beneath The Tooth's East Face: (1) Follow the Snow Lake Trail ◆ until nearly above Source Lake, descend the short forest slope to cross the stream below the lake, then ascend SW and S up the open and obvious principal gully in the forest; this leads into the objective basin. (2) From the end of the long switchback above Source Lake, make a slight descending traverse, aiming for a small cliff band. A path crosses under the cliff; continue to a mossy talus gully, then ascend its left side. (3) From the upper Alpental parking lot follow the valley bottom on the SW side of the stream (a good route when terrain is snow-covered) nearly to Source Lake, then either ascend the forested slope or the gully to the upper basin. (4) A good winter ski tour or spring and early summer snow approach is directly from Alpental. Ascend the Lift 18 service roads westward, then continue upward, bearing slightly right into the slope beneath the true summit. Climb rightward to the crest of a broad granitic spur ridge at about 5000 ft, then make an easy traverse of about 1 mi., keeping beneath the upper rampart wall. Round the subalpine ridge at the end of the wall at about 4900 ft and make a minor traverse into the basin.

Ascend the basin to the tree-lined ridge saddle connecting the Denny and Tooth formations. Cross and traverse toward Denny on the W-facing slope. Once on the ridge, the completion to the N summit is a short rock scramble.

THE TOOTH   5604 ft/1708 m

This prominent rock pyramid on the Denny-Chair Peak ridge, about 2½ mi. NW of Snoqualmie Pass, is a quite popular climb. The Tooth is formed of Tertiary andesite breccia thermally metamorphosed by the Snoqualmie batholith (the short faces of The Tooth offer generally sound climbing rock). Its historic names have included Denny Horn and Denny Tooth. First ascent by Charles Hazlehurst and C. G. Morrison on June 25, 1916. References: *Mountaineer*, 1920, pp. 52-53; 1931, p. 62.

NORTH RIDGE: Leave Denny Creek Trail ◆ at about 3 mi. (est. 4200 ft) just before the trail crosses the creek westward. A path of sorts ascends (rockslides and open forest) to the western base of The Tooth. Skirt the base rock leftward and ascend to a notch (est. 5400 ft) in the North Ridge (best keep right of saddle and ridge N of The Tooth). Cross notch via a short rock pitch (class 4) and follow a ledge to the right. Slabby and broken rock (class 3) provides an easy route just W of the ridge crest. Few parties stay precisely on the ridge crest, which can be followed, but is longer and more exposed. Time: 4 hours.

EAST FACE: This 500-ft face is The Tooth's steepest, and was attempted as early as 1940, when Ed Kennedy took a serious fall after entering the final chimney. Don (Claunch) Gordon and Bill Niendorff on September 9, 1951 ascended the lower center face, but were forced left on steep rock to reach the upper South Face. The first direct climb was done by Roger Jackson and Mike Kennedy in September 1959; from the top of the prominent slab they climbed about 20 ft left of the final chimney. First winter ascent by Jim Nelson and Scott Fisher in December 1984. References: *Mountaineer*, 1978, pp. 31-32, 37-38; *A.N.A.M.*, 1982, p. 60.

Use one of the approaches given for Denny Mountain, North Route, to the base of The Tooth's East Face.

From below center face ascend a steep and obvious gully with some loose rock to the lower right corner of a large sloping slab in midface. Traverse obliquely left past a narrow spot and ascend another slab. Climb heathery and steep rock to the final wall, then climb about 50 ft to reach the deep chimney that leads directly to the summit. It is a full pitch: on the first ⅓ one may need to climb out on the right margin

to pass overhangs in the chimney; the final section becomes a steep gully. Grade II or III; class 5.6 or 5.7.

Winter Route: There is a route of about 4 pitches to the right of the central wall. Snow and ice tend to form here, permitting a steep route to the upper North Ridge; some tree belays.

SOUTH FACE: This face is about 330 ft high, above "Pineapple Pass" (est. 5280 ft), the small notch between the South Face and a southern pinnacle. While the steps on the narrow, solid face are steep, they are interrupted by good belay ledges with stunted evergreens. The popular climb has become the traditional classic of the area. The first ascent was done by C. L. Anderson and Herman P. Wunderling on September 1, 1928 in just 4 hours from the old Mountaineers Lodge; they stated "no rope was used as there was no place to tie a rope." In their account "those attempting it are urged to take along a rope and a couple of lightweight strong iron hooks with rings in them, in the event it is necessary to back down for lack of holds, using the hook to hook over a slab or crack and the ring for the rope tie." *Mountaineer*, November 1928. The following day Hans-Otto Giese repeated the climb. The first winter climb was done by Vic Josendal, Dick McGowan, and Pete Schoening in March 1952.

The shortest route to the face is via the basin beneath the East Face (see Denny Mountain, North Route). When closely below the ridge saddle, climb snow or talus into the narrow notch between the first pinnacle adjacent The Tooth's South Face and a lesser crag on its S. Cross the notch, descend a few feet, then scramble through trees around the pinnacle's rock corner into the W-facing gully leading to "Pineapple Pass." A quick scramble leads to the "pass" and the first pitch.

If making the approach from Denny Creek, ascend to the western base of The Tooth, then skirt the rock base rightward.

There are three methods on the 60-ft first pitch. The easiest is to take a ramp leftward to a tree, then climb rightward along in-cut holds on the left-outside corner of a slot to reach a large ledge. The central, more classic route (solid and easy class 5) ascends rightward on whitish rock, closely right of a slanting crack. An alternate but less attractive route is to take the rightward ramp around the corner and climb to small evergreens.

Climb 20 ft to the E edge of the ledge, then up big solid blocks and cracks on the corner to a ledge with a wedged block. Climb the corner immediately above, then move left on the face by climbing left-slanting thin ramp holds steeply to a ledge; this 15-ft section is the crux. Work left to where the ledge becomes a block: make a short upward move, then climb rightward easily to a prominent tree (tree normally used on rappel).

Climb rightward on a ramp to small trees, then up a ledge face with small trees. From a dirt ledge climb rightward on an easy little face, then up and left on dirt ledges to the final 50 ft headwall. At the highest whitish broken rock reach the right edge of the obvious and classic "catwalk." Good holds

THE TOOTH — south face
SYBIL GOMAN

The Catwalk →

apple Pass

EAST

FACE

gain the needed footwalk, then traverse carefully leftward across the face to its SW edge; easy rock leads to the summit.

A more direct route on the headwall climbs a succession of flakes (solid, class 5) to an evergreen patch at the summit. Class 4 to 5, depending on variations. Time: 1-2 hours from Pineapple Pass.

Descent: The route is frequently rappelled. There is a horn just below the summit, solid tree anchors, and the wedged block.

Variation: By Charles Kirschner and Tom Myers, about 1938. Take an angular chimney on the right side of the Southwest Face to connect with the South Face Route at about 50 ft beneath the summit. Class 4 or 5.

SOUTHWEST FACE: First ascent by Fred Beckey, Helmy Beckey, and Louis Graham on October 25, 1942.

From just N of the gully to Pineapple Pass, ascend a series of open books. Angle left on a slab to three parallel cracks on an overhanging crest high on the face. Ascend left side of these cracks by a vertical pitch, then cut left back to easier rock just W of the summit. Class 5.5. Time: 2-3 hours from base.

WEST FACE: This slabby face offers interesting variations: one can climb almost anywhere (ranging from class 4 to 5.2); face is about 400 ft high; because of the many possibilities, no set route description is given. Approach as for North Ridge or South Face. First ascent by Ray Clough and Charles Kirschner, July 10, 1938. Time: 2 hours.

BRYANT PEAK   5801 ft / 1768 m

Sometimes called "Hemlock," this small, pyramidal andesitic rock peak 0.7 mi. S of Chair Peak, was named for Sidney V. Bryant of The Mountaineers. It is frequently climbed in combination with The Tooth or Chair Peak. A certain confusion arose because the name Bryant was once used for Chair's S shoulder and a register left there. *Hemlock Peak* (5560 ft), the minor summit several hundred yards SE of Bryant, offers a hiking ascent. Bryant was first climbed by C. L. Anderson, Walter C. Best, W. J. Maxwell, Paul Shorrock, Hubert West, and H. P. Wunderlung on October 17, 1926. References: *Mountaineer,* 1924, p. 73; 1925, p. 23; 1926, p. 45; 1931, p. 65.

NORTH ROUTE: Leave Snow Lake Trail ◆ at 4200-ft switchbacks and ascend NW up talus, then W through timber clumps to rockslides bearing toward Chair Peak. Head left of the buttress forming the left basin wall and skirt S below cliffs; cross to a shallow basin beneath the col that forms the S end of Chair's S ridge. Ascend W on the last rockslide to beneath Bryant's summit, then angle to the N saddle (5,440 ft).

Alternate approaches to the saddle are (1) directly from beneath the E face (see Southwest Route); (2) from Denny Creek Trail at same departure per Southwest Route. Travel NE, then N at the lower edge of a mossy rockslide to the W flank of Bryant, about 400 yards. Continue along the base of the cliff, dropping 20 ft down steep dirt, until feasible to

climb NE up a rockslide basin to the N saddle. A broken face offers an easy summit completion. Time: 5 hours from road.

SOUTHWEST ROUTE: This tree-dotted slope has Bryant's lowest angle. From 150 ft beyond Hemlock Pass (see Denny Creek Trail ◆) turn up to a meadow. Continue NNE to a gully, then ascend it and a rockslide; keep left and close to trees. An easy ridge (scrambling) leads to the summit.

An alternate approach is from Source Lake (see Denny Mountain, North Route). Ascend SW into the basin beneath the E face, then climb the narrow defile in rock ramparts to the skyline tree-notch (may be steep snow). Time: 5 hours from the road.

One can also make a rightward-traversing ascent from the eastern basin by the obvious sloping bench/ramp (with small tree clumps) to reach the northern saddle.

CHAIR PEAK   6238 ft / 1901 m

Chair is among the highest and best-known of the "Snoqualmie Peaks," and the culmination of the crest of summits beginning with Denny Mountain. Its name is derived from the resemblance to an armchair, as seen from Kaleetan Peak, or the SE vantage. Chair has a high rounded shoulder coming S; this drops to a lower area of the crest before reaching Bryant Peak. The rock on Chair is partly a pre-Tertiary melange and partly a sedimentary member of the Naches Formation.

First ascent by Hec V. Abel and L. F. Curtis on May 30, 1913. References: *Mountaineer,* 1916, p. 74; 1920, p. 53; 1931, pp. 59-60; *Summit,* March 1965, p. 33; *Off Belay,* December 1976, pp. 111-112; *A.N.A.M.,* 1979.

SOUTHEAST ROUTE: This is the route generally used; it connects the lower SE face with the upper southern rocks.

Take the Snow Lake Trail ◆ to the rockslide about ½ mi. short of the Snow Lake divide (est. 4200 ft). Ascend NW up one of the stream beds to the upper basin (keep right of cliffs); then bear W to a large rockslide basin (usually has large snowpatch and finger) SE of the summit. Near its head are twin, deep rock chimneys. Note: there is considerable loose rock in each chimney.

The left chimney is the standard route (some stemming — class 4); right chimney has two short sections with awkward roofs; these are strenuous (class 5). One can bypass both sections of the right (recommended). This involves steep face climbing for 15 to 20 ft — the rock is solid and holds are small but good.

From the ridge crest, descend a short distance, then turn N to ascend the broad, loose summit gully. Time: 5 hours.

On descent: After rappels down the left (S) chimney, beware of steep snow and the moat; this is an accident-prone area.

Variation: "Tooth Face": From above the base of the left chimney, ascend the broad tree and heather-covered shelf leftward across the face of the "Tooth." Proceed diagonally up

CHAIR PEAK from east

and left above the shelf over slabs to a bush, then up heather to its summit. Then continue to the upper southern rocks of the true summit.

A variant is to bypass the "Tooth" by ascending the depression and couloir on its S, to reach the crest of the South Shoulder.

Variation: South Shoulder: This variation is actually the easiest summit route (but longest). Bear S in rockslide basin. Keep under the toe of protruding spur, then work on a left rise to the SE slopes of the South Shoulder. Scramble easily to the ridge crest N of the shoulder's high point, then follow closely below the broad S crest of Chair (on its W), to meet the summit rocks.

The South Shoulder can also be reached from the saddle N of Bryant (see Bryant Peak, North Route), or from Melakwa Lake via a steep scree slope to the col which forms the S end of the Chair Peak massif (done by Bill Degenhardt and Chris Lehmann, July 24, 1927). If traveling from the saddle joining Bryant, continue northerly, dropping onto the E side

of the ridge and contour N to the basin (mossy slab descent) beneath the ridge col. Keep below the buttress leading to the South Shoulder by ascending northerly to beyond its high point.

The South Shoulder's high point (est. 6050 ft) is erroneously identified as "Bryant Peak" by a metal monument. It is often climbed as an objective (or en route to Chair Peak using a version of this variation). One can ascend its E flank to a notch closely N of its top. The S buttress and numerous gullies along the E face, leading to the crest, offer class 3 to 5 rock climbing.

WEST FACE: First ascent by Charles M. Farrer, Frank Lee, C. G. Morrison, Dean Morrison, and Hunter Morrison, on August 4, 1928.

From upper Melakwa Lake (see Denny Creek Trail ◆) go N about ¼ mi.; ascend a long gully (steep and loose) which terminates on the S ridge. Just below its top traverse left along heather to where the slabby West Face drops steeply. Ascend over harder but solid rock ("30 ft of small holds"), then an easy scramble to the summit. Class 4. Reference: *Mountaineer,* September 1928.

NORTHWEST RIDGE: This is an indirect route, slightly more difficult than the Northeast Buttress, first climbed by Roger Jackson and Bonnie Krook on July 3, 1965. Traverse across cliffs above the S flank of Snow Lake (snow slopes, scrub trees, and rocks), then climb a wide, broken crack on the E side of the ridge objective; several pitches of moderate rock climbing continue (some looseness; class 3 and 4).

NORTH FACE: The upper 400 ft of this face are quite steep, with somewhat treacherous rock. It rises immediately above the broad, flattish sloping alpine bench (usually well snow-covered) above the cliffs S of Snow Lake. First ascent unknown.

Approach the steep portion by a traverse W from the base of Northeast Buttress on slabby rock (or snow). Class 4.

NORTHEAST BUTTRESS: This prominent rock corner divides the East and North faces, and is really a continuation of the Snow Lake divide. The route is popular, and sought in winter during good conditions. The climb is exposed and the rock solid.

Follow the trail to just before the divide, then turn left up an obvious talus slope. Head for a minor notch in the divide; cross to the N flank, then hike along the divide. An alternate approach (best when snow covered) is to ascend from the basin on Chair's E flank (see Southeast Route).

Ascend a crooked chimney that angles up and right, then head to easier rock at a small tree patch at about the 175-ft level; keep right of trees. On the final 300 ft, keep generally left of the crest by going up an open book; work left on a broken horizontal ledge 50 ft above the tree patch, then up broken slabs to an obvious tree 130 ft higher. Work left to a depression between the sub-summit (on left) and the true summit, then climb easily over the sub-summit. Class 4. Time: 4-5 hours from road. Reference: *A.N.A.M.,* 1985, p. 62.

Variation: At the final 300 ft angle up and left about 100 ft to the edge of the short band that crosses the East Face (left of the open book). Climb the edge of the band, through a heather patch, and then up to the summit.

EAST FACE: This slabby 400-ft face offers Chair Peak's best rock climbing (mostly class 4). There is a noticeable overhanging band about 150 ft below the sub-summit. The probable first ascent was made by Don Blair and Art Winder on September 30, 1933; however a summit entry by Scott Osborn and Don McClellan on June 28, 1930 may relate to an earlier climb.

Near the base of the wall under center-face is an obvious groove. One can climb rock on either side, to the band. Climb this via a cleft; begin near the lower right part of band and climb 45 degrees left for about 10 ft (loose), then 5 ft of vertical (class 5.5). Above is easy, heathery rock, leading to the sub-summit. Time: 5 hours from road.

Winter Routes: There are good ice route possibilities on the North Face in the winter season, ranging from 4 to 6 pitches. Kit Lewis and companions have done several routes here, one being a gully near center face.

Two winter routes have been done on the East Face — one goes through the band and the other is along the Northeast Buttress.

KALEETAN PEAK   6259 ft/1908 m

Prominent and triangular Kaleetan is located 3.7 mi. NW of Snoqualmie Pass. Once it was known as "The Matterhorn;" fortunately this appellation was replaced by the Indian name for "arrow," as suggested by The Mountaineers. Kaleetan's rock is part of a pre-Tertiary melange. The first ascent was made by Sidney V. Bryant and two companions in 1914. Ten years later, Harold B. Sparks, a prominent climber, was killed in a fall on the peak. The first winter ascent was made by Hermann Ulrichs and Paul Cope on February 12, 1929. References: *Mountaineer,* 1916, pp. 71-72; 1920, p. 52; 1931, p. 60.

SOUTH RIDGE: From Melakwa Lake (see Denny Creek Trail ◆) make a contour left of the rock face to the W, then ascend to the ridge top. Continue N along the ridge and an easy open gully to the summit, or bear left at the top. Class 2. Time: 3 hours from lake.

EAST FACE: The first climb was made by Art Winder, Merritt Corbin, and James Robertson on June 26, 1932. From the base of the final rise of the large talus basin to Melakwa Pass, turn left and follow a route featured by a gully and tree strip to the rocky upper S slope; then continue to the summit.

NORTH RIDGE (Roosevelt-Kaleetan traverse): This exposed, narrow ridge traverse was first made by Cal and Herb Magnusson in 1960. The scrambling traverse, beginning from the summit of Roosevelt is generally on sound rock, although just beyond the lowest section, there is some loose, exposed climbing. The most difficult section is about one-third of the distance on Kaleetan's ridge. Here is a rock step; climb around on the left (class 5.2).

MOUNT ROOSEVELT   5835 ft/1779 m

This small, rocky peak is located between Snow and Kaleetan lakes, ½ mi. N of more prominent Kaleetan Peak. When viewed from Snow Lake flank, Roosevelt has three rocky points N of the true summit; there is a snowy basin cupped beneath. The Bandera Mountain quadrangle shows the peak's location incorrectly, as do other maps. Reference: *Mountaineer,* 1931, p. 66.

SOUTHEAST ROUTE: From the outlet of Gem Lake (see Snow Lake Trail ◆) follow the lightly wooded ridge SW, then climb the left edge of a big talus slope to rock headwall. Make a leftward traverse several hundred ft on a scree bench above lower eastern cliffs. At the SE base of summit rocks ascend a gully about 200 ft to the top (class 2). Time: 2 hours from lake.

Another approach is via Chair Peak Lake (see Variation). Continue about ¼ mi. N from the lake to the summit gully.

Variation: South Ridge: From Melakwa Pass (see Denny

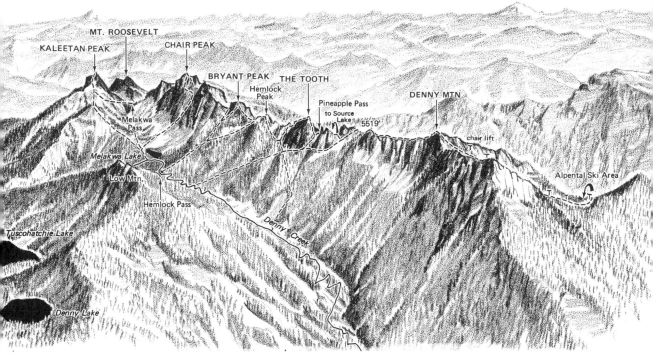

KALEETAN PEAK to DENNY MOUNTAIN from south

Creek Trail ♦) descend 300 ft to Chair Peak Lake. From its SE side contour N and up gully with loose scree. Reach base of ridge cliffs under low-point and traverse right until opening is visible to the ridge. Scramble up ridge; last 100 ft is class 3. Time: 5½ hours from road.

MOUNT WRIGHT 5430 ft/1655 m

From the trail on the N side of Gem Lake (see Snow Lake Trail ♦) ascend directly up gentle slopes to the summit.

CAROLINE PEAK 5885 ft/1794 m

Caroline Peak, marked "Roosevelt" on maps, is located just S of Lake Caroline, with a connecting ridge to Preacher Mountain. It is not a rugged peak.

ROUTES: Several approaches and routes appear: one could ascend from Lake Kaleetan (see Pratt Lake Trail ♦); ascend slopes 1 mi. NW (easy). Also the W ridge is easy. (Use same trail approach.)

A route appears feasible from Upper Wildcat Lake (see Snow Lake Trail ♦). Ascend to ridge N of the lake (about 4600 ft) from E end, then follow it SW to the peak (keep N of steepish area on upper E side of summit).

PREACHER MOUNTAIN
                                     5924 ft/1806 m

Located 3½ mi. SE of the Taylor-Middle Fork Snoqualmie River junction. Preacher has low-gradient slopes, but is massive because of low valley footings of the Middle Fork Snoqualmie and Pratt rivers.

SOUTH RIDGE: From Upper Wildcat Lake (see Snow Lake Trail ♦) ascend to ridge N (about 4700 ft), then traverse W on N slope (above Derrick Lake). Go to the E end of Lake Caroline (4720 ft) — this is about 1 mi. from E end of Upper Wildcat Lake. Hike through the low gap N into the Hatchet Lake drainage and make a traverse to the W, then NW, around the basin about ½ mi. Then either work to the 5200-ft saddle at ½ mi. S of the summit (S ridge), or work NW closer up the broad, open talus and snow basin toward the summit; no difficulties.

OTHER ROUTES: An adventurous approach exists via Rainy Lake on the NW flank of the mountain, a slope that is generally very moderate. The problem here is that a former trail to the lake cannot be located (4½ mi. distance to the 3764-ft lake). One could approach the route from Camp Brown on the Middle Fork Road ♦ (about 1½ mi. W of the Taylor junction); one would have to raft or locate logs to cross the Middle Fork.

GUYE PEAK 5168 ft/1575 m

Guye is the prominent thimble-shaped rock peak located close to Snoqualmie Pass. Guye's face and summit area, which can be scrutinized from the highway, are composed of rhyolite, which overlies Tertiary sedimentary rocks of the Guye Formation (the latter crops out on the lower West Face). Much of the steep

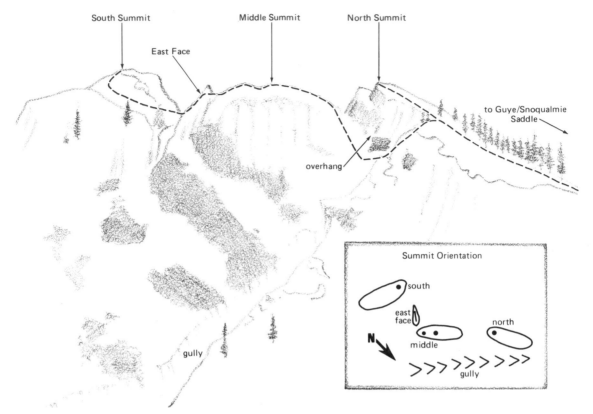

GUYE PEAK from Red Mountain

rock on the S and W faces is brittle, therefore treacherous to the climber.

Early geologists identified the summit as Slate Peak, but the name Guye prevailed — in honor of F. M. Guye, who held twelve patented claims on the lower slopes. Prospectors, who intensively explored the Pass area before the turn of the century, probably climbed Guye Peak as early as 1891. References: *Mountaineer,* 1920, p. 54; 1931, p. 60.

NORTH ROUTE: The easiest method of reaching the broad Guye-Snoqualmie saddle (4600 ft +) is from Commonwealth Basin ◆. One can use the trail system into the basin, but a more direct approach is to begin from Alpental Road, across Commonwealth Creek at a parking lot. Hike the track-roadway on the left side of the ski slope, then the cat track-trail toward Guye Peak and its S flank. Traverse around the flank for nearly ¼ mi. in forest, cross Commonwealth Creek, then hike upstream until nearly beneath the saddle. Cross the creek, then ascend the gullied forest slope rightward. A path leads to the saddle. Note: In winter or spring, when leaving the basin for the saddle, the lower area may be a dangerous avalanche slope.

Western approach: The saddle is often reached from near Alpental; this is a shorter route, but the rocky terrain is generally brushy and unpleasant for travel.

There are three rock points on Guye Peak's summit area; the S summit is the usual destination.

From the Guye-Snoqualmie saddle circle left (S) and ascend through trees to small knobs and pinnacles to the N summit (class 2). To reach the middle and S summits: descend the steep gully directly N of the N summit for about 70 ft (to just below a large overhang). Turn right and ascend directly to the notch between the N and middle summits. Walk left up and over the middle summit, then right onto its steep but easy E face (class 3). Descend this face (50-degree snow in winter and spring) to the notch and walk S, then up to the S summit (class 3). Beginners may want a rope for the gully and E face descents. Note: the gully beside the N summit and the E face of the middle summit are avalanche prone and caution should be exercised during winter and spring climbs. Time: 4 hours from road.

Descent Route: From the N summit take a path among rocks and small trees to the Guye-Snoqualmie saddle, then descend a path to the E (see North Route).

EAST GULLY: A very direct route from Commonwealth Basin is to climb the steep, narrow gully that follows a shear zone in rock on Guye Peak's E face, slanting from the basin northward to just N of the N summit. The gully is a good winter and spring climb, when snow-filled. Be certain the route is safe from avalanche danger. See North Route for details concerning continuation to the S summit.

SOUTH GULLY-SOUTH SPUR: Take Alpental Road ◆ to just across the Commonwealth Creek bridge. Park, then hike the roadway up the Sahale Ski Club slope; from the top of the cleared area, a track leads up the rib to the base of Guye Peak's South Rib. Just before reaching the heavy timber, ascend. The South Gully is just right of the South Rib and near the South Spur.

Ascend the gully (minor rock scrambling); from small trees at its head traverse right to the South Spur. Ascend easy rock with small trees on the rib of this spur to reach the S summit. Class 3. Time: 3 hours.

SOUTH RIB: This obvious rib on Guye Peak is located on the W side of the South Gully. The rib, long a popular practice route, begins lower and S of the West Face. Sustained, interesting climbing can be found at the rib's toe, at about 3600 ft.

The rock is generally solid (although friable), and provides opportunity for class 3 and 4 climbing, with latitude for variety. There are variations on the rib and on the wall area to the E. One can also reach the rib from the gully on the right. Approach per South Gully-South Spur route.

WEST FACE: The complexity of Guye Peak's broad 1000-ft West Face is due to the configuration of slabs, discontinuous ramps, overhangs, and rock planes of varying angle. Small evergreens grow on isolated ledges and ramps. The spalling of friable rock has created a concave, partly-overhanging central wall directly above the tip of Guye Rockslide — itself a reminder of a disintegrating wall. The comparative solidity of some portions of the face has guided the pattern and character of climbing routes, which follow modes of least resistance in a sometimes zigzag and crisscross manner. The feeling of insecurity some parties have experienced has given some routes a serious air. Much of the climbing can be enjoyable, but one should be aware that there has been rockfall, and handholds have broken.

To aid in route description the West Face has been divided into N and S sections, roughly separated by a sheer central wall and a slight protrusion, which break the face into two portions. The N section, not generally as steep as the concave S section, features tree-dotted slabs and ramps above the scree and talus scarp at its base.

Not all of the routes and variations on the West Face are known, because of incomplete reporting. The climbs here described, with the probable exception of the 1940 route,

GUYE PEAK — west face
TOM MILLER

have been repeated, some of them frequently. Some of the exploratory climbing on the central wall is omitted because of incomplete reports.

The first climb of the face was made by Don Blair, Forest Farr, Norval Grigg, Jim Martin, and Art Winder on May 24, 1931. They wore tennis shoes and climbed without a rope. Their exact route on the face is not known, but it apparently took place on the N section.

WEST FACE, NORTH SECTION: There are several routes and variations on the N section, one being the Northwest Chimney and another being the more popular ramp and slab route to the S (right).

From Alpental Road ◆ at 0.5 mi., park in a lot and walk up a roadway past new buildings to the foot of Guye Rockslide. Ascend its left side to the base of the West Face, then skirt leftward under the central protrusion and buttress (left of the major gully that slices into the central face). Ascend the scree gully that breaks into the face. The *Northwest Chimney* is a steep chimney-gully (deep and very obvious) that leads to slabs NW of Guye's summit; climbing in the chimney varies from scrambling to class 4. Time: 3 hours.

Northwest Ramp: The very prominent tree-dotted Ramp-Slab Route S of the chimney route involves the scrambling and climbing of broken rock areas, slabs, ledges, and gullies to the right-bearing, sloping ramp. From the base of the West Face, ascend the scree slope toward its left side, heading for a tall, white dead fir. At the tree, bear diagonally rightward through light brush to the rock. Contour left on the first ledge above the scree slope, traversing around a bulge, to a wide gully. Follow the gully to a belay ledge with trees on the outside; a class 4 pitch bears upward and right. Then scramble up and left, following a ledge past a gully to trees. Here a crack leads rightward toward the gully (the crack into the gully is a long pitch). At the top of the gully is some loose rock and the surface may be slippery with tree needles.

Several routes can be taken to the summit area. One can turn up the face (exposed class 4), then continue via a gully to the summit area. Another method, from the upper right portion of the ramp, is to follow the boot track northward to the S summit. See North Route for continuation to Guye-Snoqualmie saddle.

Improbable Traverse: This is an exposed and fairly popular route that begins at the edge of the S section of the West Face; the route ends on the upper N section, cleverly avoiding overhangs by a zigzag pattern. First ascent by Dave Hiser and Mike Borghoff in 1960. From the rockslide tip ascend a ramp leftward (class 3), then climb several pitches (up to 5.5) up a broken wall to Lunch Ledge (under the smaller overhang). Now climb rightward to a ledge belay (class 5.5). The "traverse" begins here. First follow a ledge that ends; then climb steep friction steps (class 5.7) to reach another ledge. From a belay a short easy lead bears right to a prominent ramp. Turn left to its end in one or two pitches (class 3 and 4). Grade II; class 5.7-5.8. Time: 5 hours from

road. References: *A.A.J.*, 1961, p. 369; *Mountaineer,* 1961, p. 103.

Variation: From the belay at the traverse, climb a chimney and crack system for one pitch; the lower portion overhangs slightly (class 5.8). Variations above and left of the Lunch Ledge can also be done. An apparent variation (reported by Bruce Thayer and Penny Williams, 1974): From Lunch Ledge climb up and right 65 ft, then from a belay ledge continue up and right of a large roof into a broken, dirty chimney; climb this to the large ramp. Two leads; class 5.6 (hard to protect at times).

A route near the central portion of the West Face, probably S of the Improbable Traverse, was climbed by Leo Scheiblehner and [?] Sullivan in 1962. This was a difficult route, with some direct aid.

WEST FACE, SOUTH SECTION: There are several routes and route variations on this steep portion of the West Face. Documentation has been difficult due to imprecise descriptions and possible route overlaps. The Ramp Route and Beckey's Chimney are climbs that have been repeated a number of times. The Crooks-Kennedy climb was the first technical route pioneered on the face: the route keeps right of the partly overhanging central triangle, then climbs to near the top of the S section before bearing right to the upper South Rib.

Crooks-Kennedy Route: First ascent by Jim Crooks and Ed Kennedy on September 22, 1940. From the rockslide tip climb rightward on the steeply sloping apron for two pitches, then ascend a vertical open book that opens to a wide ledge on the right. To the left is a blank face: traverse left on a ledge (class 5), then downclimb slightly and up to a foot-wide pedestal on a steep face (this section is difficult class 5 — the original pitons may still be in place). The 1940 party made a shoulder stand at the pedestal belay, finding this the hardest portion. The pitch is vertical for about 12 ft (possibly an aid piton used), then tapers to a steep gully that leads to a large tree. Climb an open book with an overhang (one pitch); this ends most difficulties.

Ramp Route: A route that takes the lower apron slabs of the 1940 climb, then bears rightward; there are several variations. First ascent unknown; first winter ascent by Jim Madsen, Dan Davis, Don McPherson, and Curtis Stout in February 1968. Slabs on the lower portion naturally lead to a right-angling and exposed ramp. A pitch (about class 5.4) of about 100 ft is climbed until a vertical rock area blocks movement. Two continuations are known: (1) Exit right via a short tricky downward finger traverse (class 5.7-5.8 or pendulum from a piton) to a ledge with a thick fir tree; this traverse has been reported as being as short as 8 ft and as far as 40 ft. Now climb steeply about 40 ft (class 5.5), keeping just right of a pretzel-shaped evergreen shrub, to a broken gully. Proceed on a curved trend to the upper right portion of the S section. (2) The alternate is to climb a very shallow chimney (class 5.7 or more difficult) which begins as a dihedral; this variation leads upward to easier climbing.

With either variation, one can climb rightward to the

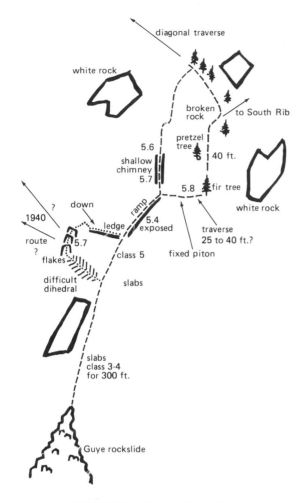

GUYE PEAK - West Face (Ramp Route)

upper South Rib at a minor notch. The exposed leftward-diagonalling traverse leading underneath the summit is more challenging; the traverse is reported as not being especially difficult, but has mossy and heather-covered spots (traverse first climbed by Don [Claunch] Gordon and Paul Salness on May 5, 1951). Grade II or III (entire route); class 5.7 (possibly more difficult).

Note: A variation on the lower portion of the route: From slabs, climb a difficult, rounded dihedral with thin, friable flakes (10 ft of 5.7); this may be same as the 1940 party's open book. Then make a slightly downward traverse on a ledge (rightward).

Beckey's Chimney: First ascent by Fred and Helmy Beckey, Tom Campbell, and Walt Varney in 1941.

From the rockslide head climb diagonally right (sloping slabs). A left-opening crooked crack (just left of a white snag) cuts the face from a buttress on the right. From a small spruce climb a vertical start (class 5.7); after 20 ft the crack veers back, continuing to a narrow alcove. From a pedestal climb onward (off-width) for 25 ft, then in 20 ft reach a belay ledge. Take a ledge around a rib to the right. Easier pitches with variations lead to the upper South Rib. Class 5.7; take protection for thin cracks. Time: 5 hours.

A chimney S of this route has been climbed from slabs above the rockslide. A report terms it class 5.1. Eventually a band of loose rock is traversed to the South Rib.

SNOQUALMIE MOUNTAIN
6278 ft/1914 m

This is the bulky, amorphous massif 2½ mi. directly N of Snoqualmie Pass. The summit is the rounded western uplift, not the rocky granitic E crest. There is a curious overhanging crag which juts W of the summit. On the NW flank there is a steep hidden face. The mountain has had various names, including Kate's Peak. The probable first ascent was by A. H. Sylvester and a U.S.G.S. party in 1897 or 1898 (a bronze tablet was set in the summit rock). There exists a possibility that the Tilton-Jared S. Hurd party climbed the mountain during an 1867 railroad survey. First winter ascent by Hermann Ulrichs and Jeffrey Cameron on February 5, 1928. References: *Mountaineer*, 1920, p. 54; 1931, p. 61; *Snowshoe Hikes*.

Warning: *In winter and spring the Forest Service may be sending artillery fire for avalanche control on the large slide path on the SW slopes. It would be extremely hazardous for anyone to be in this area or on Cave Ridge during such control action. Before climbing verify with the Ranger Station at North Bend (phone 888-1421). Keep alert for notices or check with ski patrol at Alpental.*

SOUTH SHOULDER: From the Guye-Snoqualmie saddle (see Guye Peak-North Route) hike northward up Cave Ridge, then work westward into a minor basin. Now ascend the easy South Shoulder through boulders, scrub conifers, and broken rock. Caution: Cave Ridge develops a large cornice through late spring. Time: 4 hours from road.

SOUTHWEST SLOPE: Hike directly to the summit via this slope, which is forested in its lower portion and then becomes subalpine. Leave the Snow Lake Trail ◆ in old timber shortly after the waterfall cliff. This is a non-technical route. Time: 3-4 hours to the summit.

WEST RIDGE: Leave the Snow Lake Trail ◆ at the divide. This is a long ridge, about 1½ mi., with some minor points and occasional scrambling on its S flank to avoid cliffs (keep S of the two steep crags above timberline).

NORTHWEST FACE: First ascent by Dan Davis on September 29, 1968. First winter ascent by Dan Cauthorn and Greg Collum in January 1984. Take the West Ridge Route (or a more direct access from the trail) to about 5250 ft, then descend to the basin on the N flank (head of Thunder Creek).

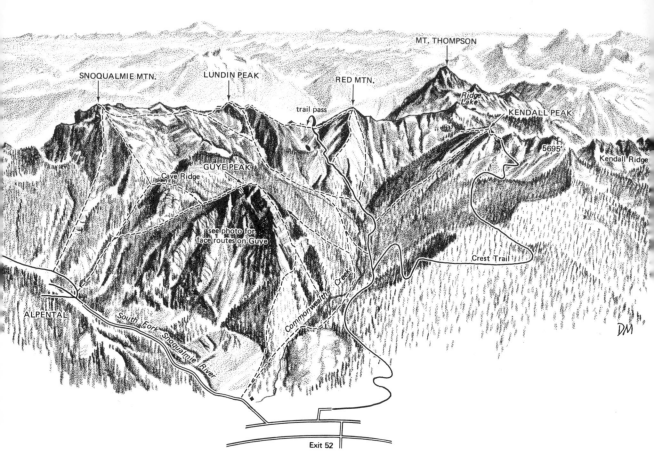

SNOQUALMIE PASS PEAKS from south

Traverse under most of the Northwest Face to a steep, narrow scree and snow couloir near the left portion of the face. Ascend this couloir to a "Y," then the easier right branch to the ridge crest at the top of the face. A short, easy scramble leads to the summit. Grade II; class 4. Take ice axe and crampons. Reference: *A.A.J.*, 1969, p. 386.

A route termed "New York Gully" was climbed by Bob Cotter and Jim Ruch on March 3, 1985. A snow ascent was made into the large gully bisecting the main summit from the western satellite peak. Gain the main face by climbing a groove, then a rising traverse (down-sloping slabs), then up a gully. Ascend into an obvious right-slanting box-gully, then follow it to the shoulder of Snoqualmie Mountain near the summit. The climbing as done on the winter ascent was mixed: The pitch into the gully to a hanging belay was difficult; the fourth pitch surmounted a large chockstone (difficult). The fifth pitch took a dihedral that turns into a chimney before ending at a dwarf fir. The next pitch climbed a slab to an overhanging flake (difficult off-width and aid on knife blade pitons in the left wall). Continue up the dihedral and snow gully toward the top of the face. Grade III; class 5.8 and A1. Suggest ice tools, KB, angles, Friends; beware

of avalanche hazard. Time: 18 hours round trip from road.

EAST SHOULDER: From Commonwealth Basin (Commonwealth Creek Trail ◆) climb to near the base of Lundin Peak (see Lundin Peak, West Ridge); make a traversing ascent or follow the ridge W to the snow dome (6160 ft) at 0.3 mi. from the summit. Then keep S of the sharp E rock summit; this climb can readily be combined with that of Lundin.

LUNDIN PEAK   6057 ft/1846 m

A satellite peak of Snoqualmie, located at the head of Commonwealth Basin halfway between Red and Snoqualmie mountains. It is a very narrow spine of rock, with steep but short S and N faces; the summit is at the E end. Rock is part of the Snoqualmie Granodiorite. The peak was once known as "Little Sister" (of Snoqualmie), then renamed to honor J. W. Lundin, a pioneer forest ranger of the district. First ascent by Harry Morgan and Art Winder in 1930. References: *Mountaineer,* 1931, p. 65; *A.N.A.M.,* 1981, pp. 53-54.

SOUTHEAST RIDGE: Take the Crest Trail ◆ and Commonwealth Creek Trail ◆ to the Red Mountain saddle, then follow a climbers' path W to the first false summit. Drop 30 ft down a gully on the W side and contour N on heather 50 ft to a notch. Then contour around the E side of a second false summit and then up heather to its top. Drop 100 ft down easy gully and contour to the major saddle SE of summit rock. Then up final ridge and easy smooth slab to the summit. Class 3. Time: 4 hours. On descent, a 30-ft rappel is frequently made.

Approach Variation: If trail is snow-covered, either leave it at about 4000 ft (where it begins to climb), and contour W on the S slope to the broad snow gully leading up to the South Face. By climbing to the saddle close to the summit, one can avoid the ridge points. This is a more direct route. One can also follow the W side of Commonwealth Creek to a clearing in the upper basin. Here the snow (or talus) gully leads to the South Face; watch for avalanche danger in spring.

SOUTH FACE: This short, but very steep rock wall was first climbed by Jim Crooks and Ed Kennedy in 1941.

Use the approach variation, then climb several hundred feet of rock to a steep slab in line with the summit. Face climbing leads to a steeply sloping ledge, then a short vertical section (one aid piton on original); one ends between the two summit points.

SOUTH FACE-WEST SIDE: First ascent by Barry Briggs, Kenneth Small, and Lee Whiteside on July 31, 1975. Begin at the lowest point between the summit and the West Ridge start. Climb an obvious right-facing dihedral 40 ft to a pillar top, then up a short dihedral to a ledge. Bear left, then ascend to a dihedral (has small roof at top). Climb right on the face, turning a roof on the right, then continue to the upper ridge. The first and third pitches offer sustained climbing. Class 5.7; 12 nuts used. Reference: *Mountaineer,* 1975, p. 102.

WEST RIDGE: A fine, though short climb on superior rock, which has purity. Reach as for South Face. Contour beneath it and ascend to the West Ridge just W of its steep portion (about 5760 ft+). Ascend to a rocky point and descend 6 ft at a minor notch; ascend a face on the N side of the steep step in the ridge, then follow the crest to the top. Class 4. Time: 1 hour on the ridge.

RED MOUNTAIN   5890 ft/1795 m

Located 3 mi. NE of Snoqualmie Pass, Red is a rounded summit of loose, reddish rock, with the usual name given to a peak of such surface color. A 5720-ft+ hump ½ mi. to the E is located at the head of the upper E fork of Commonwealth Creek. East of this hump the ridge is flat, then rises NE to a 5851-ft point just SW of Ridge Lake. The new Crest Trail ◆ passes closely S of the hump.

Climbing parties often do a multiple-peak traverse, beginning with Red and continuing to Thompson.

Prospectors probably climbed Red in the 1890s. Surveyor W. C. Mendenhall and others were on the summit September 13, 1898. References: *Mountaineer,* 1920, p. 54; 1931, p. 60.

ROUTES: Hike the Commonwealth Creek Trail ◆ to about 4900 ft. Ascend the prominent spur on Red's SW slope (above the pond) which bears to the summit at a constant angle of about 40 degrees.

Alternately one can climb the snow gully from the trail on the W slope. Time: 3-4 hours from the road.

Another route is to leave the trail lower and ascend the southern (red) face. This is a pleasant scramble on solid rock. Class 3.

The climb can be made on the NW spur, from the Red Mountain saddle; slopes are more crumbly here, but gullies frequently contain hard snow well into summer.

Now that the new Crest Trail ◆ is completed, one can readily leave it on the divide near the 5720-ft+ hump; hike over it, then follow the E ridge to the summit (minor scrambling). There is an area of unpleasant loose rock at the 5400-ft low-point on the ridge.

KENDALL PEAK   5784 ft/1763 m

Located on the E side of Commonwealth Creek, about 2 mi. NE of Snoqualmie Pass. Kendall is drained by Commonwealth Creek and the Silver Creek branch of Gold Creek.

Kendall has four small and nearly equal rocky summits closely spaced, over the 5600-ft level on the rim above Kendall Peak Lakes. These three lakes are located between about 4400 ft and 4800 ft in the basin to the SW of these summits. The true summit is N of this rim and ¾ mi. N of the central lake. Maps do not mark the name at correct highest summit, but place it at the 5441-ft rock hump 1 mi. SE. Surveyor W. C. Mendenhall climbed to one of the summits on August 4, 1898. On August 25, 1902 geologist Frank Calkins climbed to a knob at 5456 ft and wrote, "The Kendall group of peaks show very regular bedding, their form being determined by erosion along bedding planes." The first winter ascent of the summit was made by Hermann Ulrichs and Kathleen Ortmans in February 1931.

The new Crest Trail ◆ crosses the ridge saddle about ½ mi. N of the summit; the saddle lies between Kendall and Point 5699 on the connecting ridge to Red Mountain. References: *Mountaineer,* 1920, p. 55; 1931, p. 60.

ROUTE: Follow the Crest Trail to the first switchback after the long northward traverse (est. 5100 ft). Ascend the wide couloir through the large tree clump to the summit ridge. Make a short ridge scramble or traverse left under the

MOUNT THOMPSON from south

rock rib, then bear up on heather and easy rock. Time: 3 hours total.

MOUNT THOMPSON   6554 ft/1998 m

Mount Thompson is the prominent bell-shaped rock peak located NE of Snoqualmie Pass, on a ridge spur N of the Gold Creek-Burnt Boot Creek divide. The upper portions of the mountain are steep on all faces, and the S face has massive blank portions. The rock is andesite of the Naches Formation, typical of the region. The mountain was named for Seattle city engineer R. H. Thomson, who is not remembered by a correct spelling. The new Crest Trail ◆ makes the climb quite feasible in one day; the mountain is sometimes climbed in combination with Kendall Peak or Huckleberry Mountain.

The first ascent was made by Joe Hazard and Boyd French on September 2, 1917; the first winter climb was done by Greg Markov and Jim McCarthy in February 1975. References: *Mountaineer, 1920,* p. 54; 1931, p. 61; *Mazama, 1966,* p. 32.

EAST RIDGE: Follow the Crest Trail ◆ to the stream coming from Ridge Lake. Make a rising NE traverse to a sharp, 5400-ft notch (Bumblebee Pass) ½ mi. from Ridge Lake.

Drop 400 ft N into the basin S of Mount Thompson. Ascend ramp between rocks and trees to the NE shoulder; (best to go to far left-hand notch in ridge); follow East Ridge or its N side on heather and easy rock. Time: 6 hours from road; 3 hours return.

SOUTHEAST FACE: First ascent by Don Blair and Art Winder on August 11, 1934. This steep route begins near the 5800-ft level just E of the center of the S face (in a slight hollow, left of a small buttress). There is a vertical nose about 100 ft below the summit; the final portion was partly a steep gully. The initial party reported some difficult climbing on poor rock. Class 4.

WEST RIDGE: This is a steep 600-ft face and ridge. On its left it corners sharply with the N face. First ascent by Fred Beckey, Helmy Beckey, Robert Craig, and William Ford in 1940.

From Bumblebee Pass (see East Ridge), contour NW, then climb to the 5960-ft saddle inside a small rock horn at the ridge's foot. Ascend a 60-ft pitch on a right diagonal via steep rock to a tree. Work left on a ledge, then climb back to the ridge crest over broken rock. Climb up and right, then back left to a great slab. Ascend slab to the W corner near summit, then keep to the N flank and ascend an easy gully. Note: loose move at final notch. Climb reports indicate one can keep on the ridge all the way except at the base. Grade II; class 4 and easy 5. Time: 3 hours. The approach can be varied from Ridge Lake by hiking N and crossing the divide E of Gravel Lake, then contouring on the E-facing slope.

Variation: A direct route from the base of the W corner begins by traversing on the N side to a chimney, then climbing to the second of two horizontal ledges. Work

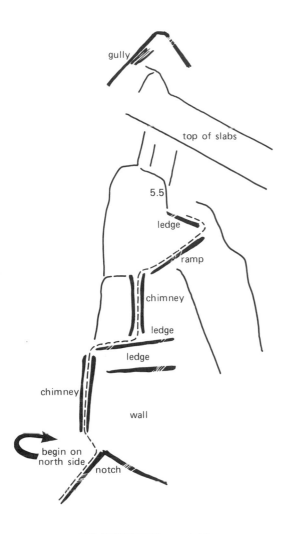

MT. THOMPSON - west ridge

right, then ascend another chimney. Above, take a ramp right to meet or come close to original route at left-leading ledge; report estimates class 5.5 on section above.

ALASKA MOUNTAIN 5745 ft/1752 m

Alaska Mountain is located between Alaska and Joe lakes; follow along near ridge crest from Bumblebee Pass (hiking) to the top; or ascend SW from Joe Lake.

TOPPLING TOWER

est. 4800 ft/1463 m

This is a 250-ft tower on the valley spur of a cliff face just NE of Edds Lake between Thompson and

Huckleberry. First ascent by John Holland and Dan Davis in July 1963.

ROUTE: Reach Edds Lake as per Mount Thompson (East Ridge). From the tower's upper notch, climb a short, slightly overhanging pitch to a narrow tree band and follow to W ridge. Climb to a step by steep slab, then a vertical jam. From the W summit point rappel to a notch, then climb the higher E summit. Class 5.5. Time: 2 hours. Reference: *A.A.J.*, 1964, pp. 172-173.

HUCKLEBERRY MOUNTAIN

6320 ft + /1926 m +

Huckleberry is a curious little rock thumb atop the W corner of a ridge hump on Gold Creek rim at ½ mi. N of Joe Lake. Rock is a solid example of andesite of the Naches Formation.

First ascent made in May 1915, an early date for rock climbing, by Charles Hazlehurst and Thomas Acheson. They doubted they might survive the descent and one of them wrote his will on shirt cuffs. The peak was not climbed again for nine years. The only known route is still the original one.

A passage in the 1920 *Mountaineer* says: "a difficult overhanging rock cornice near the top should be attempted only by those with steady nerves and sure feet shod with plenty of number seven calks." Reference: *Mountaineer,* 1931, p. 64. First winter ascent by Donald J. Goodman, Allan Albright, John Marconi, and Paul Wagonaar on January 30, 1977.

EAST FACE: From Crest Trail ◆ E of Joe Lake ascend the alp slope, passing the large final tree to a clump on the SE slope at 5200 ft. Follow game paths into the small basin SE of the summit, then heather slopes to the rock's base at 6000 ft. Climb gully to notch E of summit.

From the notch climb to a ledge with a small dead tree and then up a 12-ft face to another ledge. Slant left for 30 ft and ascend an easy face to the top. Class 4. A 100-ft rappel usually handles the descent. Time: 6 hours from road.

CHIKAMIN PEAK

7000 ft + /2134 m +

The summit of Chikamin is a solitary rock point, the highest on the Gold Creek rim. Its slope above the creek is scored by long gullies. The peak's N slope contains remnant snow and ice patches. The true summit's position is not shown correctly on the Snoqualmie quadrangle, which lists the name at a 6926-ft hump that terminates Chikamin Ridge. The first ascent was possibly made by C. G. Morrison and I. J. Kohler on May 30, 1915; evidence points to a U.S.G.S. ascent prior to 1902.

Four Brothers (6485 ft) are picturesque rock points

HUCKLEBERRY MOUNTAIN from Joe Lake
BOB AND IRA SPRING

GOLD CREEK AREA from south

on the ridge about 1 mi. SE of the summit. Four Brothers were named during the 1890s by early miners working and living at the head of Gold Creek. References: *Mountaineer*, 1920, p. 56; 1931, p. 64.

SOUTH RIDGE: From Crest Trail ◆ at Ptarmigan Park ascend E side of talus and steep bushy slopes to timberline, then alp slopes to the western base of Four Brothers. Contour ledges and broken slopes along their N flank to Chikamin's South Ridge saddle (est. 6250 ft), then continue as per Southwest Slope.

Approach Variation: Reach from Glacier Lake (Pete Lake Trail ◆). From above the N side of the lake (or from the upper lake) ascend gentle barren slopes W to Chikamin's South Ridge above the saddle (about ½ mi. from the lake).

SOUTHWEST SLOPE: Leave the Crest Trail ◆ just E of Joe Lake, then traverse into the head of Gold Creek. An old route to timberline is the main gully (usually snow-filled: beware of undermined snow). Ascend this, then steep grass/talus slopes above in a NE direction to reach the ridge crest just S of the pointed summit; follow ridge to summit rock left on easy ledges to a gully that leads to top. Class 2. Time: 2½ hours from trail.

One could also leave the Crest Trail ◆ where it crosses the Gold Creek slope beneath the summit, or from Chikamin Pass.

NORTH ROUTE: From Chikamin Lake (Pete Lake Trail ◆) ascend a perennial snowfield or bedrock to high under the summit horn. An arm of snow extends left to the final rocks. This is a moderate route, but more alpine than the others.

RAMPART RIDGE   5870 ft/1789 m

The highest point of Rampart Ridge is about ⅔ mi. N of Lake Lillian. It has a prominent point (5680 ft) at ½ mi. W of the lake. An extensive cliff of andesite closely below the ridge top forms a palisade high above Gold Creek.

ROUTE: Hike uphill directly N from the W end of Lake Lillian (see Rampart Ridge Trail ◆). The slope becomes a ridge crest near 5500 ft. A path can be taken to the short area of slabby rock ledges at the summit. Slab-scramble to the top. Class 2.

Variation: From S end of Rampart Lakes (see Rachel Lake Trail ◆) the highest summit is at 200 degrees. Ascend the gully underneath the cliff line that runs down from the ridge saddle S of the summit to find the climber's path.

ALTA MOUNTAIN   6250 ft/1905 m

Alta is the gentle but prominent summit between Gold Creek and Box Ridge. The ascent is frequently combined with that of Hibox. Among panoramic views are the peaks across Gold Creek. Frank Calkins climbed Alta on August 22, 1902, via Gold Creek; he mentions the well-jointed volcanic rocks. References: *Mountaineer*, 1920, pp. 55-56; 1931, p. 62.

SOUTH RIDGE: From the saddle above Rachel Lake (Rachel Lake Trail ◆) take the N path (toward Lila Lake) until it goes to the E side of the South Ridge. Ascend the gentle nose and walk to the summit (1¼ mi. from Rachel Lake).

The approach could be varied by coming from Lake Lillian and Rampart Lakes (Rampart Ridge Trail ◆). Time: 5 hours from road.

WEST ROUTE: Leave Gold Creek Trail ◆ just W of where it crosses Gold Creek (near center of Section 36). Cut up hillside in series of wooded and bush strips. Gain 1000 ft to a cliff, then traverse right along a heavily wooded ledge, then reach open slopes and the South Ridge of Alta. Time: 5 hours from road.

NORTH SPUR: From about 4½ mi. up Gold Creek Trail ◆ (near 3100 ft) at a timber cluster (past Alaska Lake turnoff), turn S and ford Gold Creek; then begin to follow an eastern branch (keep to slope on right) to Alta's N spur. The spur is forested, but does provide some easy scrambling near the top (avoid cliffs on E). Time: 6 hours from road.

A similar route is to leave Gold Creek where a stream from the E side of Ptarmigan Park enters. Follow to first big waterfall, then climb the right-hand slope (some brush) and later take the open slope to the summit.

HIBOX MOUNTAIN
est. 6560 ft+/2000 m+

Hibox is the summit of Box Ridge, which trends NW for over 4 mi. between Box Canyon and Mineral Creek. The Mineral Creek slopes are cliffy and gullied. The upper W and E faces are rocky and steep, with extensive scree beneath. Hibox has a decided Southeast Peak at 6032 ft at 1 mi. distant. At ½ mi. SE of Alta Pass there is a 6242-ft Northwest Peak (½ mi. distant from the summit). First ascent by Harry R. Morgan and Art Winder on September 21, 1930. First winter ascent by Donald J. Goodman and Rick Knight on January 8, 1977. Reference: *Mountaineer*, 1931, p. 64.

NORTHWEST RIDGE: From the upper part of Box Canyon (Rachel Lake Trail ◆) (about 2½ mi. uptrail, near 3300 ft), follow a stream-draw NE to a saddle (est. 5880 ft) on the NW side of the summit (between the Northwest Peak and the summit); follow the rocky ridge to the top. Class 2 or 3. Time: 6 hours. Note: the Northwest Peak would be a mere hike from the saddle.

Variation: From Lila Lake (Rachel Lake Trail ◆) travel N

and drop slightly to avoid cliffs. Contour around the head of Box Canyon and below the W extremity of Box Ridge. Gradually climb to a small park in basin between Hibox and the Northwest Peak; then climb to the 5880-ft saddle. This variation could be used if combining the ascent with that of Alta.

SOUTH ROUTE: One could leave the trail at 2.3 mi. (near 3200 ft); then simply go upslope; this route can be seen from the first view of the peak. Just after passing the dense brush above trail turn right and head for the cliff. Easy route on left of cliff; once atop go through open wedge-shaped timber area to its end at base of second cliffs. Pass these on right (last water); from here it is open meadow over and up to the right side of the SE summit ridge (heathery and rocky). Near summit keep to right to avoid final cliff (large talus boulders). Time: 5 hours.

SOUTHEAST RIDGE: Leave trail at about 1.7 mi. and follow a creek bed; below a waterfall, traverse out and follow timber on side to reach Southeast Ridge, then ascend the moderate gradient of the Southeast Ridge to summit. If one wishes to follow stream draw to the area of the 5200-ft saddle between the Southeast Peak and summit, leave trail near the 1-mi. point. The Southeast Peak could be ascended from the saddle.

THREE QUEENS   6687 ft/2038 m

This distinctive triple-peaked rock formation, once known as Mineral Mountain, is located 3 mi. NE of Little Kachess Lake and 4 mi. W of Cooper Lake. The main portion of the peak is part of the Naches Formation, the same as nearby Chikamin Peak and Lemah Mountain, but on the E flank there is a stock which is part of the Snoqualmie batholith. Of the three individual summits, the East Peak is highest and bulkiest; the Middle Peak (6600 ft +) and the needle-like West Peak (6400 ft +) are less massive.

The first ascent was made by eight Mountaineers led by Glen Bremerman and C. A. Fisher in August 1925. Reference: *Mountaineer*, 1925, p. 25, 63.

SOUTHEAST SHOULDER: Hike Mineral Creek Trail ◆ to an open talus slope (2.3 mi. — 3500 ft). Ascend directly to the obvious notch on the SE ridge, above. Cross the notch through a pass, then continue around the back side (N) for about ¼ mi. to a class 3 ledge. Ascend to the rock ridge, then SW to the summit. Time: 5 hours from trail.

An alternate route is to ascend 80 ft of steep rock on the SE face. Here follow an obvious ledge to the S face, where the first gully is taken 300 ft to the summit ridge near the summit (possibly some class 5).

An alternate approach is to leave the trail near the creek ford (est. 3000 ft) at about ¼ mi. above the old minesite. Ascend N up obvious spur ridge (some brush at beginning) to the Southeast Shoulder.

Another approach is via the road through Cooper Pass:

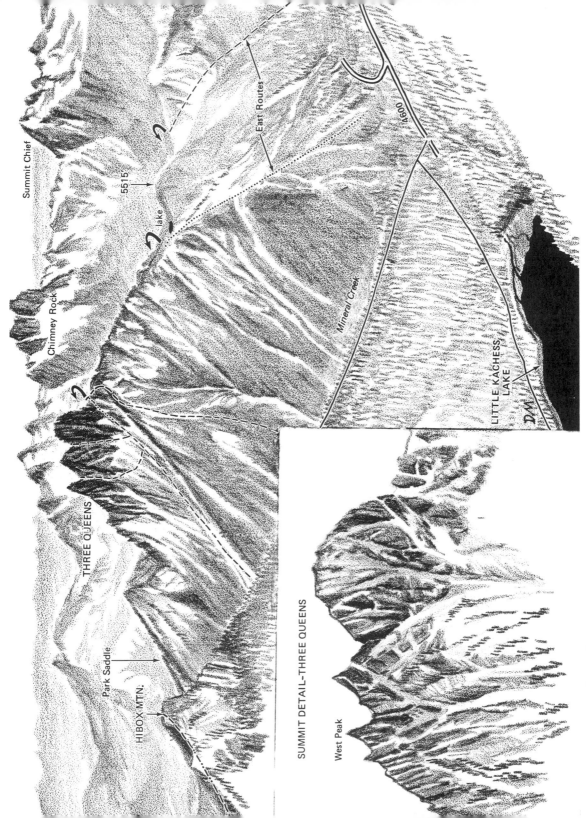

Summit Chief

Chimney Rock

5515'

lake

East Routes

4600

Mineral Creek

LITTLE KACHESS LAKE

THREE QUEENS

Park Saddle

HIBOX MTN.

SUMMIT DETAIL—THREE QUEENS

West Peak

THREE QUEENS from southeast

ascend the lightly forested spur between Mineral Creek and Kachess River.

EAST ROUTE: After driving to Cooper Pass (via Cle Elum River Road ◆) take the first logging spur on the right (No. 126) to its end. A path from the top of the clearcut leads to a timbered ridge. Follow to a cirque N of the small lake; ascend the rockslide in the cirque, then follow the main ridge to where one can traverse to an expansive bench system on the N side of the summit. A rock route can be taken to the summit; a short scramble of class 3-4. The final portion of this route could also be reached from Spectacle Lake.

Another approach is to leave the road earlier and ascend the basin E of this approach. Cross the ridge and make a long traverse on the N slope to the bench system.

From near Spectacle Lake (see Pete Lake Trail ◆ and Crest Trail ◆) a northern route can be taken to the summit of Three Queens. A broad snow or talus slope can be ascended to the notch between the East and Middle peaks. This is the least technical route on the mountain, and the one likely used on the first ascent.

MIDDLE PEAK

There appear to be no special problems from either of the adjacent notches. One could traverse the upper S slope from the Southeast Shoulder Route, or ascend the long talus slope from Mineral Creek.

WEST PEAK

The first climb was made by Pete Schoening, Don Wilde, and Phil Sharpe in August 1950 via the S face. Begin at the E notch of the peak, some 250 ft steeply under the summit (reach from Mineral Creek approaches or gully on N side). The route works around to the S; the initial party used three pitons plus tree anchors. Class 5. Reference: *Mountaineer*, 1950, p. 42.

LEMAH MOUNTAIN
7480 ft + /2280 m +

Lemah, whose name is an Indian term for "fingers," is comprised of five pointed rock summits whose relative height physically caricature human fingers. The massif's vertically dipping, hard, dark, contact-metamorphosed lavas and breccias are interspersed with occasional lighter colored sedimentary interbeds. The Main (central) Peak is the outstanding one, and has the appearance of a true pyramid, with a long rock face falling on the Burnt Boot Creek flank. It is located at 1.4 mi. NNE of Chikamin Peak and 1.1 mi. S of the Main Peak of Chimney Rock, on the divide between Burnt Boot Creek and Lemah Creek branch of the Cooper River. The topographic map is misleading in placing the name adjacent to the second summit.

The first summit (Lemah One, 6960 ft +) is located just ⅞ mi. NE of Chikamin Peak. Just over ⅓ mi. N

is Lemah Two ("Lemah Middle"), at about 7280 ft; the Main Peak is less than ¼ mi. N. Lemah Four (7200 ft +) is ¼ mi. N of the Main Peak, and Lemah Five (7040 ft +) is midway between Lemah Four and the 6480-ft gap which separates the Lemah and Chimney Rock massifs.

Two rock towers stand on the pronounced rocky spur trending SE, dividing the Lemah Creek and Spectacle Lake drainages. The lower tower is much more massive than the upper (6360 ft +) — which has been dubbed Goatshead Spire.

The Lemah Glacier on the E slope of the mountain is now nearly divided into three remnants, totalling 0.5 km² (less than a quarter sq mi.). The median level averages from about 6600 ft to 5840 ft, though it reaches higher (to 7000 ft) into pockets under each of the summit-ridge gaps. The northern remnant is a narrow 0.6 km ice couloir in the upper Lemah Creek depression, beneath the 6480-ft gap.

The Main Peak was climbed by Wallace Burr and party on July 7, 1923. Lemah One (also called Lemah Thumb and Iapia Peak) was climbed on the 1925 Mountaineer outing. References: *Mountaineer Bull.*, August 1923, p. 4; July 1925, p. 5; *Mountaineer*, 1925, pp. 24-25, 63.

APPROACH ROUTES: (1) See Pete Lake Trail ◆. From meadows at the Lemah Creek valley head, climb the ice gully of the creek to 5500 ft (take crampons). Traverse S out of the gully onto the upper glacier; there may be some scoured rock. From the lower pocket glacier, turn a cliff band on the left to reach the upper snowfield between Lemah Two and the Main Peak. (2) Hike around the N side of Spectacle Lake and follow the flat valley leading NW to where the gradient steepens. The most direct way is to ascend NW on scree and heather through a steep rock gully, keeping S of the SE towers. Cross to the N by a rock scramble, then make a short easy descent on the opposite slope and bear onto the glacier.

A longer but somewhat easier route is to climb NE up the scree, later diagonalling E on talus and heather benches (goat trails helpful in locating best way) to the ridge crest approximately ½ mi. SE of the towers. Descend the crest a short distance until descent can be made to the moraines and snowfields below the glacier. Make a rising traverse around the NE side of the towers, then continue on snow/ice ¾ mi. until below the Main Peak or objective summit. Time: allow about 5 hours to summits from Spectacle or Glacier Lake.

CLIMBING ROUTES: Lemah One is done on the S ridge (hike and easy scrambling); reach the ridge crest via an obvious gully from the S end of the glacier or from the pass just above Chikamin Lake (a southern route; only about ⅓ mi. to the summit). Some rock climbing; last pitch has a steep crack (class 3).

Lemah Two, the most difficult of the summits, is prefera-

CHIKAMIN PEAK and LEMAH MOUNTAIN from southeast
BOB AND IRA SPRING

CHIKAMIN PEAK

BIG SNOW MTN.

BURNT BOOT PEAK

LEMAH ONE

LEMAH TWO

LEMAH MTN.

LEMAH FOUR

CHIKAMIN LAKE

S.E. Towers

to
LEMAH FIVE

GLACIER LAKE

SPECTACLE LAKE

LEMAH MOUNTAIN (left) and CHIMNEY ROCK (right) towering above Cooper Lake
ED COOPER

bly done by the short N ridge (class 4). The S side has less angle, but is craggy and longer.

Lemah Main Peak: the normal route from the glacier is to climb snow and easy rock to the gap between Lemah Two and the Main Peak. Continue on the E flank of the crest, then N on the generally easy and broad rock slope; there is a final short class 3 rock pitch. A ridge of rock is surmounted by a small room-size cap about 30 ft high (can be done several ways). At the final portion, keep on the S skyline to the summit. The route via the N ridge involves about 400 ft of climbing (class 3) from the ridge gap, after ascending the névé finger from the glacier.

Lemah Four is climbed most easily via the S ridge (class 3). Lemah Five is done from its S notch (class 3).

The two SE towers provide some interesting rock climbing. The lower tower is the greater challenge (first ascent unknown). The W ridge, from the inside notch, provides two pitches — one of 90 ft and one of 100 ft (both class 5.5); one finishes by working E around the back side.

Goatshead Spire was climbed by Donald Goodman and John Mason on August 8, 1982 (low class 5 for one lead).

CHIMNEY ROCK

est. 7680 ft+/2341 m+

Chimney Rock, with its two principal summits striking a sharp pattern in the sky about 3 mi. SW of Dutch Miller Gap, is the most distinctive peak in this section. Rock is vertically dipping, hard, dark, contact-metamorphosed breccias with occasional lighter colored sedimentary interbeds (Naches Formation). The entire western faces of Chimney Rock are quite steep rock from the 6000-ft level up, perhaps more typical of the North Cascades than this region.

The highest summit forms a boxlike tower atop a distinctive rock formation between Burnt Boot and the Chimney Creek branch of Lemah Creek. Maps had long listed Chimney Rock at 7727 ft; its height is probably close to 7700 ft. It is misleading that the Big Snow Mountain quadrangle has the name placed adjacent the lower North Peak. This summit, really a NE peak, has been triangulated at 7634 ft. It has a very long and steep rock face on its S and E, and on the NE flank the walls fall sheerly to about 6000 ft. Above the dividing col with the main peak some vantages make its profile quite vertical; actually this eases farther W, above the actual col. The walls on the Main Peak's East Face begin at about 6600 ft, then rise very steeply to a summit overhang. The less important South Peak, on the same divide, is shown at 7440 ft +. It spurs out closely to the main peak much like the seat of a chair.

The lowest point between the Lemah Peaks and the Chimney Rock formations is a gap at the head of the main fork of Lemah Creek (est. 6480 ft), which is ½ mi. from the main summit. The S point of the Chimney Rock formation is about ¼ mi. NE of the gap, a sharp point (7240 ft) with a sheer W face. This point is the apex of the long, rocky and very rugged spur ridge separating the drainages of Lemah and North Fork Lemah Creek.

Chimney Rock has three glaciers: The Overcoat Glacier on the N side, which reaches to the Main-North Peak gap; the Chimney Glacier on the S and E sides, rising from near 5000 ft to 6600-6800 ft against the rock walls of the peaks (it has a steep 600-ft icefall-snout); and an unnamed glacier on the E side of the North Peak, which drains E from about 5960-5080 ft. Here is a narrow connection on the N to the higher Overcoat Glacier. The periglacial area has a well-preserved series of moraines.

The Main Peak, once a much sought-after objective, has an interesting climbing history. An account in 1923 stated that a party of seven reached the summit, but this proved to be an error in geography (the climb made was Lemah). In 1925 Joe Hazard and C. A. Fisher made a reconnaissance of Chimney Rock, then described its summit as probably impossible. But the summit was reached in what was a remarkable achievement of the time by Forest Farr, Art Winder, and Laurence Byington on August 27, 1930. Taking bivouac rations, the party found the vital ledge which leads from the S to the East Face, where they found a short but "extremely difficult chimney, blocked by an overhang." Farr and Winder first made the climb unroped, wearing tennis shoes on "smooth, outsloping walls," then returned to the ledge to escort Byington (who climbed barefoot) to the summit with a rope. The climb was not repeated until the 1940 ascent by Jim Crooks and Fred Beckey; first winter ascent (Main Peak) was made by Greg Collum, Dan Cauthorn, and Pat McNerthney on December 28, 1985. Any route on Chimney Rock is a unique experience. References:

Mountaineer, 1919, p. 46; 1925, p. 25; 1930, pp. 44-47; 1970; *Summit,* May-June 1965, pp. 38-41; *Cascadian,* 1963, pp. 25-27; 1964, pp. 45-47.

EAST FACE: Instead of following a route along the wooded ridge between Lemah Creek and its N fork (Chimney Creek) to reach the glacier beneath the East Face of Chimney Rock, it is more prudent to follow an established route near Chimney Creek.

Take the Pete Lake Trail ◆ to the intersection of the trail with Lemah Creek. Take the way trail (No. 1323B) for 0.8 mi. on the NE side of the creek (marked "bridge crossing") to the Crest Trail ◆. Follow the latter NW to the first switchback, then leave the trail and descend along a faint path in an upstream direction to Chimney Creek. Cross the stream about 200 ft upstream from the edge of the large, brushy avalanche path which is visible from the switchback. Ascend the slope approximately 200 ft to the right of the edge of the slide path on a game and climber's trail which becomes well defined several hundred yards from the creek. Ascend toward the NW, approximately parallel to the slide path, through forest, fern-covered talus, and a short brush patch to a small bench near the first significant stream. This bench is located just above a rock outcrop with views of waterfalls of the stream draining Chimney Glacier and flowing through the avalanche slope.

Change direction and ascend toward the NE until the slope flattens and the forest opens. Traverse NW to reach the stream and then ascend a gully to where it flows from the base of a cliff. Continue up the broad gully to the crest of the spur ridge (about 5800 ft) E of Chimney Rock. Descend 100 ft to a perennial snowfield, then ascend snow below rock ribs, gendarmes, and cliffs to the glacier.

Ascend the lower section of the glacier, to a break in cliff leading to upper glacier; (best is a loose rock gully veering just right of stream coming from upper glacier, and ending above the icefall).

Ascend the glacier to big chimney at base of the S face of Main Peak (possible schrund in late season; in early season it may be a steep snow couloir). Ascend left chimney of this system for 600 ft to the South-Main Peak notch (scrambling) at 400 ft below the summit. Climb around the E side of a rock point and descend about 60 ft to a blind chimney at the edge of the main wall. Climb an easy debris-covered ramp to the big obvious key ledge (about level of last notch). Traverse it rightward to the E face.

The final portion of the climb is done via several leads of steep and slabby rock. One method is to take a chimney from the ledge, then ascend a heathered rock area to a pitch on the right. This is exposed with small holds for 15 ft, then leads to an adequate ledge and the final pitch — a 50 ft chimney (stemming); work right near the summit. Grade II; class 4. Time: 4 hours from timberline; road to summit: 10 hours. On descent: first rappel one rope length, then down-climbing feasible.

Variation: From timberline, climb the left snow/ice finger to the upper glacier, then ascend wide snow gully to

NORTH PEAK

Southeast Face

Finger of Fate

East Face of Chimney Rock Col Route

MAIN PEAK

Chimney Glacier Headwall

1st ascent

Direct Route

2nd ascent

SOUTH PEAK

East Face Route

Icefall

U-Gap

CHIMNEY GLACIER

SOUTH POINT

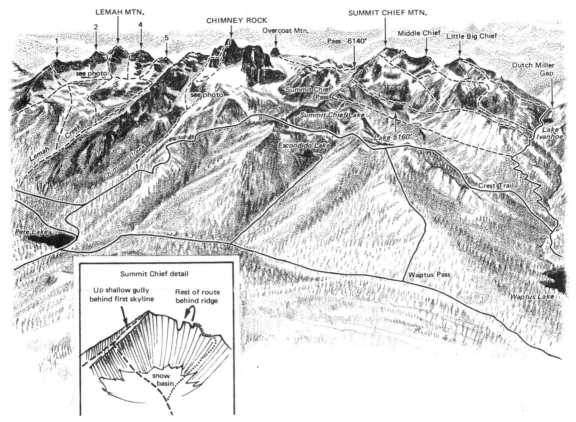

NORTH CENTRAL CASCADE CREST PEAKS *from south*

the U-gap (cst. 7000 ft+) S of the South Peak. From just beneath the gap, leave the gully via a large bench that swings around to the E; make a N-traverse on it, then a rising traverse to the South-Main Peak notch (largely heather benches). Note: this variation is easier than the normal route except under early-season conditions.

Variation: Instead of traversing on the key-ledge, climb directly up (about 3 leads) to the final chimney. This is more difficult than the normal method.

EAST FACE DIRECT: This is an exposed, continuous, and exhilarating climb. There are nine pitches of largely class 4, with intermittent easy class 5 on generally sound rock. The belay ledges are good. First ascent by Cornelius (K) Molenaar and Elvis R. Johnson in July 1954.

From the glacier directly beneath the summit, climb two pitches to an obvious heather incline. Access to the rock on the first pitch may be blocked or made difficult by a large moat (first 20 ft may be class 5.3). Ascend right on the incline to a leftward-sloping heather-covered ledge; this leads to a shallow gully near the left corner of the face. Climb two pitches by small gullies and on the face to a belay ledge below a headwall. The fifth pitch is the most difficult: a 40-ft northward traverse avoids very difficult climbing, and leads to a short crack which is climbed to the outside corner on the face (class 5.2). Scrambling leads to a 30-ft steep gully (class 5.3), continuing to a belay ledge above a small gendarme. The next pitch (class 3-4) leads to the "key ledge" of the normal East Face Route. Continue directly upward for three class 4 pitches leading to the summit. Grade II; class 5.3.

Variation: From the incline, one can take a route farther N (right) (see photo).

NORTH FACE: First ascent by Roger Jackson and Ernest White in 1957.

Ascend to Chimney Rock col (see North Peak — West Face). Continue on névé right to its termination at the notch W of Finger of Fate. Cross to the E side and traverse to prominent narrow notch beyond a "boxlike" formation on the ridge. Cross again to the N face and contour on steep, broken rock below crest to an inconspicuous gully below the big overhanging band of the N-horn of the summit formation. Climb a 20-ft class 5 wall to the right of a gully. Then make a short traverse to the gully below the prominent chimney that splits the N face. Stem or jam the deep 4-ft chimney to a large slab, then scramble to the summit (hardest pitch is slab crossing and climbing to the chimney). Grade II; class 4 and 5. Time: 7 hours from Middle Fork Trail.

Variation: Via Easternmost Chimney: By Mike Anthony and Lawrence Nielson, August 10, 1974. This 320-ft chimney cuts steeply into the face. Class 5.8; some ice encountered.

Variation: Chimney Glacier Headwall: By Gene and Bill Prater, August 13, 1964. Cross schrund and climb eastern rock face via class 4 pitches. Then take ledges and minor gullies directly to N edge of the overhanging band; the route can be identified by a minor depression in the wall. Class 4.

NORTH PEAK   7634 ft/2327 m

First ascent by Larry Strathdee and Jim Beebe on July 11, 1944. The route used on this climb was on the S or adjacent face, and may have preceded one of the later routes; it is known that the party used 14 pitons. Reference: *Mountaineer*, 1945, p. 25.

WEST FACE: Use approach as for Overcoat Peak; from Overcoat Glacier ascend its high névé arm SW to Chimney Rock col (est. 7240 ft). Climb an obvious shallow rock gully from the W edge of the col (the upper part may be class 5). Face climbing leads to a second gully. Then traverse left on a heather bench, then a steep rock pitch leads to an easy area near the summit (total of four pitches). Grade II.

Variation: East Face of Chimney Rock Col: By James Wickwire, Fred Dunham, Dave Mahre, and Tom Hargis on October 9, 1966. (Possibly preceded by the first ascent party.)

This 700-ft rock wall leads to the notch between the Finger of Fate and the North Peak. The first three pitches are hardest and the last five pitches are class 3 and 4; the second pitch is a short ascending-traverse to the right; the third pitch — hardest — includes getting from a dihedral left to slab below an overhang. Grade II; class 5.7 or 5.8. Time: 3 hours on rock.

SOUTHEAST FACE: First ascent by Fred Dunham, Barry Prather, James Wickwire, and Don Jones on September 15, 1962.

From high camp on bench above North Fork Lemah (Chimney) Creek, ascend to Chimney Rock cirque bypassing icefall on left side via ice couloir. Once on the upper glacier, traverse right (E) to base of North Peak's SE face, just under a large patch of yellow lichen. Climb three easy but exposed leads toward lichen (class 4) nearly to gnarled pine tree on ledge 300 ft above glacier. Traverse right on ledge 100 ft — here are two alternatives: climb directly up steep slab (class 5.6) or traverse a lead farther right on ledge, then climb a difficult pitch until overlooking a deep gully (joins first alternative above). Five leads on steep, very exposed groove in face. Absence of cracks precludes adequate piton or chock protection, but belay platforms readily available. On this section of the route, fourth lead with slight overhang is most difficult. Two steep parallel gullies are then climbed diagonally to right. Four easy leads on arete to right of second gully leads to last hard obstacle — a 40-ft buttress. This can be climbed head-on (class 5.7) or circumvented on left via

strenuous chimney (class 5.5). Two leads to the summit ridge. Grade III; class 5.7 (17 roped leads; small piton and chock selection). Time: 7 hours on face. References: *A.A.J.*, 1963, p. 474; *Cascadian*, 1962, pp. 11-12.

Note: Can approach from canyon of Chimney Creek by light bushwhacking up the steep hillside just N of the large tributary emanating from Chimney Glacier.

Finger of Fate (est. 7320 ft): This is the prominent tower on the crest, on the S side of the Chimney Rock col.

First ascent by Larry Strathdee and Jim Beebe on July 11, 1944. From the N side of the col, this one-lead climb works around to the W, then to the NE (class 4). Reference: *A.A.J.*, 1968, p. 131.

Chimney Glacier Icefall: First ascent by Gene and Bill Prater on August 13, 1964. The icefall usually becomes hard alpine ice after firn disappears in late summer. Short pitches up to 55 degrees were found on the original, which went from lower right to upper left. Reference: *Cascadian*, 1964, pp. 40-41.

SOUTH PEAK   7440 ft+/2268 m+

First ascent was made by Hugh McKenzie, Earl Smith, and Robert Schellin on August 27, 1928.

The route used by the initial party was up the long chimney to the Main-South Peak notch (some loose rock). Easy scrambling on or near the ridge leads out to the summit. From the traverse area on the face of the South Peak, simply scramble upward. It is equally feasible to make the climb using the first variation, Main Peak. References: *Mountaineer Bulletin*, October 1928, p. 4; *Sunset*, May 1923.

OVERCOAT PEAK   7432 ft/2265 m

Overcoat is a rocky castellated peak of the Naches Formation located ½ mi. N of Chimney Rock. The parallel dipping ramps are very noticeable. The peak's faces, while short, are all steep.

Overcoat Glacier begins against the peak's E face and almost wraps around it; the glacier's SW head is the Overcoat-Chimney Rock saddle (6760 ft+). The main body is about 1¼ mi. long, terminating near 5600 ft (Middle Fork Snoqualmie drainage). A large and gentle snow-dotted amphitheatre of similar size and shape lies to its N, high above the valley. The first ascent was made by Albert H. Sylvester and John Charlton in July 1897, probably via the W side. Sylvester named the peak after the overcoat he left atop while surveying. References: *Mountaineer*, 1925, pp. 23-25, 63; 1958, pp. 105-106; 1970, pp. 105-106.

NORTHEAST FACE: Approach via Overcoat cross-country route (see Dutch Miller Trail ◆). From the 6120 ft+ pass, follow the approach suggestion for ½ mi. to the eastern edge of the Overcoat Glacier at about 6600 ft; most of this route is a rising SW traverse over intermittent snow

*NORTH CENTRAL CASCADE CREST PEAKS from north. Exposed rock is Swauk Formation,
Naches Formation, and Snoqualmie batholith*
WALLACE C. GUY, U.S. FOREST SERVICE

ALTA MTN.

HUCKLEBERRY MTN.

BURNT BOOT PK.

CHIKAMIN PK.

WILD GOAT PK.

LEMAH MTN.

CAMP ROBBER PK.

TOURMALINE PK.

PURVIS LAKE

CHIMNEY ROCK

MALACHITE PEAK

SUMMIT CHIEF MTN.

IRON CAP MTN.

ANGELINE LAKE

MIDDLE CHIEF

North Peak

LITTLE BIG CHIEF

BEARS BREAST MTN.

OTTER LAKE

OTTER POINT

LA BOHN PK.

LA BOHN GAP

and gentle rock outcrops with heather-ledge systems. Cross névé about ¼ mi. in a W direction to below Overcoat Peak. Just W of the steep portion of the Northeast Face is a prominent left-angling 40-degree snow finger; this feature leads to the summit crest just W of the highest point.

Various completions can be made via steep rock and broken ledges. One can first make a traverse on the W side, then ascend. An alternative is to drop down the SW face about 100 ft, then turn 90 degrees and ascend class 3 slabs to a notch facing Chimney Rock. Take the right hand of two grassy ledges to the summit. Time: 7 hours from the road.

Variation: By circling the glacier around N, beyond the sharp NW nose, the first slanting rock ramp can be taken up and right. This leads to the upper NW summit ridge or the above alternate.

EAST FACE: First ascent by Wayne Swift, Fred Beckey, Joe Barto, and Campbell Brooks in August 1939.

Begin from glacier edge (see Northeast Face), then ascend leftward on a band of broken rock and heather which bears to just S of the summit. The face is about 500 ft high; largely ascended by this band. Class 4.

SOUTH ARETE: This narrow crest has numerous short steps formed by the rock bedding. First ascent by Franz Mohling, Richard McGowan, and Tim Kelley in July 1954.

Beginning from the snow, the original party ascended two short leads in a chimney to near the top of the first step, then descended onto the W face to a steep slab; a rock pitch and the arete led to the summit. It is possible to vary the route: one can climb ledges just below the arete on its W until a gully bears right onto the crest at the base of the summit block. Class 4. Reference: *Mountaineer,* 1954, p. 64.

BURNT BOOT PEAK
6520 ft + / 1987 m +

A light-colored grey crest, its summit forms the top of the divide between Burnt Boot Creek and the Middle Fork at 1.8 mi. SW of Overcoat Peak; highest point of three summits is the eastern. The S face is rocky and steep, marked by deep parallel ribs and gullies. First ascent by Phil Weiser and Clarke Stockwell in August 1963. Reference: *Mountaineer,* 1966, p. 203 (under "Keechelus Peak").

ROUTE: From the Middle Fork Snoqualmie Road ◆, travel S to the river (here W of Hardscrabble Creek). Cross on log jam and go downstream about ¼ mi., then up hillside cross-country. Ascend timbered rocky rib toward prominent couloir NW of the main peak. At timberline angle W to saddle about ½ mi. SW of the top. Ascend ridge E to false summit (6400 ft). Make a short rappel into the notch, then ascend (class 2) to the true summit. Time: 6 hours.

Variation: Where trail leaves the river at about a mi. beyond Hardscrabble Creek ascend generally southward to reach open area W of the lower summits. Ascend NW-facing couloir (possibly snow) to the notch between the W and main summits.

NORTH RIDGE: First ascent by Don Williamson, Tom Oas, and Bill Bucher, June 6, 1971.

This climb involves three class 5 pitches on good granitic rock. Use either approach to where the ridge steepens (est. 6000 ft). A 5.8 pitch leads to a large down-sloping slab. A following pitch is rated 5.5, then one along a sharp crest. The final three pitches are class 3 and 4. The route ends on the northern point, surveyed at 6480 ft. Grade II; class 5.8. Time: 7½ hours from road. Reference: *Mountaineer,* 1972, p. 116.

SUMMIT CHIEF MOUNTAIN
7464 ft / 2275 m

The western and highest of the "Chief" peaks, located about 1½ mi. SW of Dutch Miller Gap. It has an immense dark wall on the N; the western side has a corrugation of moderately steep ridges and gullies; these continue around to the S above North Fork Lemah (Chimney) Creek, where steep rock extends below timberline. The triangular-shaped SE side is largely talus and scattered snow patches below the summit rocks. First ascent on the 1925 Mountaineer outing by a Glen Bremerman-led party. References: *Mountaineer,* 1925, p. 25, 63; 1945, p. 25.

SOUTHEAST FACE: Leave the Waptus River Trail about ⅓ mi. S of Lake Ivanhoe, S of where it crosses the creek near 4500 ft. Bear to the SW up an easy spur (some timber) to about 5400-ft level, then begin a traverse to above the lake on the N fork of Chief Creek; keep crossing W to the next basin (or, make the traverse slightly lower, to reach the 5160-ft lake SE of Middle Chief). Much of this terrain is heather, semi-barren, with talus leading to the snowy basin SE of the summit. Summit Chief appears as a three-pronged ridge. Ascend to a point just below and S of the most westerly of these spurs. Climb snow gully to base of summit rocks. Then scramble to ridge on left. Ascend, then climb into gully behind skyline ridge. A scramble leads to the summit (loose rock). Class 2. Time: 5 hours.

Variation: Climb up and right for two leads; here a small chimney (with tree) appears to the NW. Climb it (moderately difficult for 30 ft) and then keep high on leftward traverse (class 3) to summit.

Variation: Make a rightward traverse up broken rock to the E summit ridge. Traverse the exposed ridge toward summit; at one place drop down on S side 40 ft to a small notch. A one-lead level traverse on the N side is followed by a final summit lead. Class 4.

A N-side approach to the ridge can be made by ascending a talus and snow couloir route on Summit Chief's NE flank, approaching from the hanging valley and then climbing to the Summit Chief-Middle Chief notch (route detail not known). The final climb would be by way of the E summit ridge (this appears feasible). See Middle Chief for approach.

Approach Variations: (1) One could also reach the basin SE of the summit by using the cross-country route to Sum-

CHIMNEY ROCK-SUMMIT CHIEF GROUP from east
U.S. GEOLOGICAL SURVEY

BIG SNOW MTN.

CHIMNEY ROCK
Main Peak
North Peak
OVERCOAT MTN.
Overcoat Glacier
SUMMIT CHIEF MTN.
Middle Chief
LITTLE BIG CHIEF
Dutch Miller Gap
Lake Ivanhoe

Woodedridge
Vista Lakes
Summit Chief Pass
Pass 5680'
Summit Chief Lake
Lake 5160
Escondido Tarns
Crest Trail
Chief Creek

mit Chief Pass or bearing N to the 5160-ft lake en route (see Waptus River Trail ◆). (2) There is also a higher-level approach; from ¼ mi. S of Lake Ivanhoe take "way trail" W for ¼ mi. to a flat basin surrounded by cliffs (good high camp, est. 4800 ft). Climb left of two rockslides, proceed across a flat, then follow the right flank of the ridge for ½ mi. to base of a 500-ft buttress of Little Big Chief. Make a short drop, then plan route to traverse W closely below Middle Chief. (3) A route from Escondido Lake (see Pete Lake Trail ◆ and Crest Trail ◆) to the summit is about 2½ mi. (shortest approach from a road). See Summit Chief Pass-Escondido Ridge High Route, Waptus River Trail ◆ for hike to Summit Chief Pass, reversing the directions. Then head toward the upper SE basin to meet the normal route.

See Middle Chief Route for another approach variation.

MIDDLE CHIEF   7120 ft+/2170 m+

This is the smaller of the "Chief" formations, located nearly midway between Summit Chief and Little Big Chief. It is rocky and fairly steep on all sides. References: *Mountaineer*, 1945, p. 25; *A.A.J.*, 1970, p. 117.

First ascent by Jack Schwabland and William Granston in 1945. On August 13, 1969 Kenn Carpenter, Ron Miller, and Frank Dallman made an exposed traverse 75 ft S to a point that appeared to be 2 ft higher.

ROUTE: Ascend a 1500-ft talus and snow couloir that rises from the side valley on the NW flank of the Chief group (see Overcoat Cross-Country Routes, Dutch Miller Trail ◆). This leads to the saddle (6680 ft) between Little Big Chief and Middle Chief (there is a tiny lake just E of this saddle). Note: The approach could also be made as for the Southeast Face of Summit Chief.

Ascend toward the triangular E face. Then angle right to the low point of the NE ridge. It is gentle, but slabby and about 30 ft wide; follow to apparent summit (unstable rock near top; class 3). To reach the S point, two runners and four chocks were used.

LITTLE BIG CHIEF MOUNTAIN
7225 ft/2202 m

This is the rocky, prominent peak just ¾ mi. SW of Dutch Miller Gap; it forms the eastern anchor of the "Chief" group. The actual summit is a narrow rock crest, atop a sheer NW face. Rock is sound. Proximity to the Gap makes it moderately popular. It was named for Lorenz (L. A.) Nelson on the 1925 Mountaineer outing. First ascent by Fred Beckey, Wayne Swift, Joe Barto, and Campbell Brooks in August 1939.

NORTHEAST FACE: From Dutch Miller Gap (via Dutch Miller Trail ◆ or Waptus River Trail ◆) contour 100 yards SW and then climb steep heather slopes through short, broken cliffs for 500 ft to a basin (usually snow). Ascend the basin to where it broadens out into a large snow cirque below

the upper E face. Turn right and traverse to the N ridge (est. 6500 ft). Follow its crest a short distance, cross an exposed rock notch, then traverse left (talus and heather) to the snowfield directly beneath the summit. At its S end, climb a 60-ft pitch, take a short left traverse, then climb 60 ft of rock to the summit. Class 3-4. Time: 3 hours.

Variation: Center of East Face: By Jack Schwabland and William Granston on July 31, 1945. The route was on polished slabs on left side of face to the summit area snowfield; four leads (class 4).

BEARS BREAST MOUNTAIN
7197 ft/2194 m

An elongated rocky, alpine massif just E of Dutch Miller Gap. It trends NW-SE, rising out to promenade between the upper Waptus River and the valley of Shovel Creek. There are a number of individual crags and spires, with the summit tower near the SE end of the high crest. There are three distinct crags N of the summit and the two smooth horns to its SE.

The massif shows steeply inclined Swauk sandstone beds thermally altered by intrusion of the nearby Snoqualmie batholith. On the Waptus Lake side, there is an immense dipping slab of remarkable smoothness descending to far below the regional timberline. From this vantage the formation gives the possible appearance of a bear on hind legs. Bailey Willis, and other early geologists, called the mountain "Wapitas Needle." Bears Breast was scouted by the 1925 Mountaineer outing and first climbed by Fred Beckey, Joe Barto, and Wayne Swift on August 8, 1939. References: *Mountaineer*, 1939, pp. 29-30; 1945, p. 24.

SOUTHWEST FACE: From Lake Ivanhoe (see Waptus River Trail ◆), follow the wooded ridge leading N, to avoid a band of cliff. Work into the shallow draw which heads the stream flowing S, at about ¼ mi. E of the lake. Head for the major gully that rises and curves right, to reach the notch (est. 7000 ft) just N of the summit tower (some scrambling en route). Note: the key gully begins near the base of the main talus chute leading N below cliffs of the N ridge (green patch and cliffs on its right). Note: one may depart from gully higher for scree and heather.

Then ascend steep rock to a slab in midface, to where it corners in a deep chimney, with a grey, smooth wall on left. Climb to belay spot at right of overhanging chockstone (piton protection often used below chimney and at chockstone). A continuing ledge (loose rock) leads across the upper W face to the summit. Grade II; class 5.4-5.6. Time: 5-6 hours.

Variation: By Fred Hart and Norm Winn, August 1971. Begin 75 ft below and right of standard route at summit tower base. Traverse a prominent slab below a horizontal crack to reach a steep gully. Climb this to a broad sloping

MOUNT DANIEL-WAPTUS LAKE AREA from south
U.S. GEOLOGICAL SURVEY

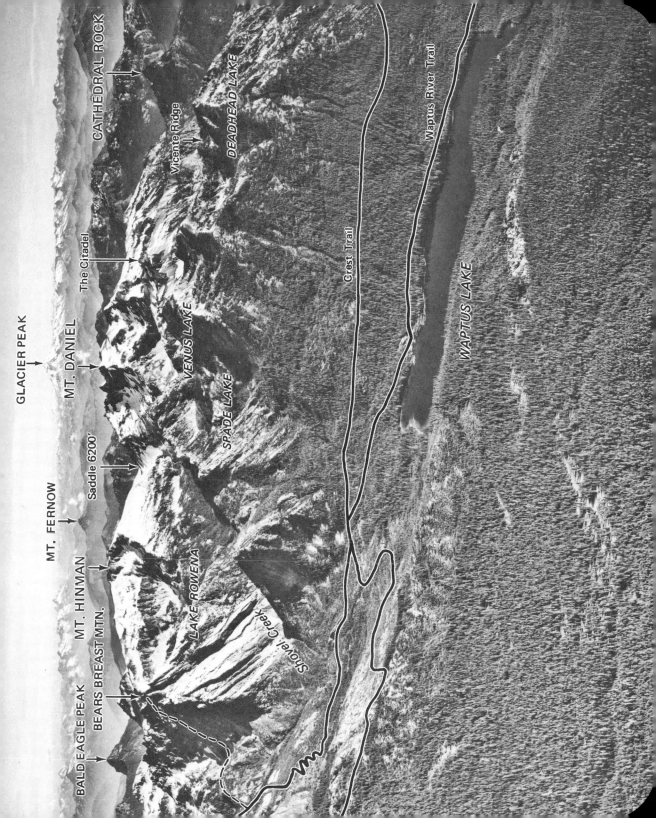

GLACIER PEAK

CATHEDRAL ROCK

Vicente Ridge

DEADHEAD LAKE

The Citadel

MT. DANIEL

VENUS LAKE

Saddle 6200'

SPADE LAKE

MT. FERNOW

Waptus River Trail

Crest Trail

WAPTUS LAKE

MT. HINMAN

LAKE ROWENA

BALD EAGLE PEAK

BEARS BREAST MTN.

Shovel Creek

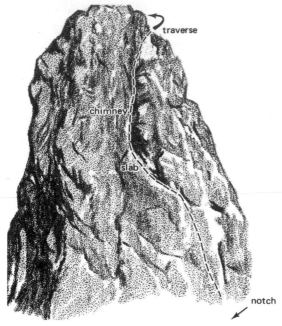

BEARS BREAST MOUNTAIN — summit tower from northwest

ledge, then continue vertically up gully or exposed pitch to its right to easier climbing. Three leads — up to class 5.4; good chock placements.

MOUNT HINMAN   7492 ft/2284 m

Hinman is located midway between La Bohn Gap and Mount Daniel. It is unusually massive, and perhaps the gentlest peak of its size in the Cascades. Lake Rowena hides in the deep cirque on its S, with the S spur and W ridges forming almost a perfectly shaped outline around it. The highest point on the summit rim is nearly at its true center, with a lesser point (7480 ft +) at 300 yards E.

The 2.4 km Hinman Glacier on the NW slope is the largest glacier between Mount Rainier and the White Chuck on Glacier Peak. It extends from 7315 ft to 5510 ft. The 1.1 km Foss Glacier on the N slope is nearly as large, and covers an extensive area from the summit to about 6200 ft. The two glaciers are separated by only a narrow, nearly level rock cleaver that comes to a minor hump N of the summit. Twin tarns carved out of bedrock just below the Foss Glacier still have ice remnants on their upper sides. The very narrow Lower Foss Glacier at the head of the central upper fork of the East Foss is 1.1 km long; it extends from about 6200 ft at the Daniel-Hinman saddle to

5440 ft. In earlier times an extensive icecap covered almost all of Hinman's W, N, and eastern exposures. The three La Bohn Lakes nest on a bench to the W of Hinman. The ascent of Hinman could be the highlight of a pleasant alpine high route from La Bohn Gap to Marmot Lake. The mountain is named for Dr. Harry B. Hinman, who led the Mountaineer outing to Mount Stuart in 1914. The Forest Service climbed Hinman in 1928, calling it the West Peak of Mount Daniel. First ski ascent by Dwight Watson, Dave Lind, Charles Cehrs, and Gene Paxton on May 7, 1944.

WEST ROUTE: From La Bohn Gap (see Dutch Miller Trail ◆ or East Fork Foss Trail ◆) ascend talus and slopes (keep left of broad W ridge) ½ mi. E to the ridge which runs NE at 6600 ft. Ascend this easy ridge (it crests along the top of the Hinman Glacier) and then E to the summit. Time: 2 hours. Note: the approach would require more cross-country work, but the ascent of the Hinman Glacier would be straightforward.

EAST ROUTE: From Lynch Draw (see Mount Daniel, Lynch Glacier Route) travel westward to cross lower edge of Lower Foss Glacier. Then begin a rising traverse above the two tarns, bearing directly for the summit via the Foss Glacier.

SOUTHEAST SLOPE: From Shovel Lake (see Waptus River Trail ◆) travel N through forest and later ascend NW up talus and snow slopes. At the top of the slope, travel westward along the crest, or on its N side above the Foss Glacier, to the E summit. Continue easily to the true summit. Time: 3 hours.

Note: One could vary the approach from Lake Rebecca or Rowena, then work E to the gentle S spur; no difficulties either route.

An ascent of the SW slopes is possible, but there is a cliff band above the lower talus slopes, and beneath the summit there is a short, steep cliff (this could be circumvented on the W).

MOUNT DANIEL   7960 ft +/2426 m +

Daniel is a massive complex whose volcanic rock is composed of andesite, dacite, and rhyolite inflows, breccia, and tuff; locally it is interbedded with volcanic sandstone. The Mount Hinman plutonic stock is located closely to the W. Writer L. K. Hodges called Mount Daniel "a huge bank of glistening snow, backed by a line of dark saw teeth, of equal height with Grieve's peak." Early geologists (1898) identified the formation as Mount Dewey. From most vantages Mount Daniel is a triple-crowned mass, but there are five summits. Old topographic maps listed the highest at 7986 ft; field reports read the western of two summits shown on the Mount Daniel quadrangle (at 7960 ft +) as highest. The middle summit is 250 yards to

KALEETAN PEAK →

LABOHN PEAK →

HINMAN GLACIER

LABOHN GAP

SNOQUALMIE MTN. →

BURNT BOOT PEAK →

MT. THOMPSON →

MT. HINMAN

FOSS GLACIER

LEMAH MTN.

CHIMNEY ROCK →

SUMMIT CHIEF MTN. →

tarns

MOUNT RAINIER

CHIKAMIN PEAK →

ALTA MTN. →

HIBOX MTN. →

BEARS BREAST MTN. →

MT. DANIEL
(Northwest Peak)

LOWER FOSS GLACIER

WEST LYNCH GLACIER

DIP TOP PK.

LYNCH GLACIER

MOUNT DANIEL from east (OCTOBER 2)
AUSTIN POST, UNIVERSITY OF WASHINGTON

the NE, and closely to the N is a rock smokestack.

The summit just NW of the highest summits (about 0.2 mi. NW of true summit) is listed at 7880 ft+; it is called "West Pyramid." It drops off sheerly several hundred ft on the W, and has a longer near-vertical S face on the Shovel Creek drainage.

The Northwest Peak (7686 ft) is 0.45 mi. NW of the true summit. It has a steep and rugged NW wall which toes down to 6500 ft on its N. This wall lies above the hanging glacier (West Lynch Glacier), which once was a segment of, but now is divided from, the main body of the Lynch.

The East Peak (7899 ft) S and above the Daniel Glacier, is located at 0.4 mi. SE of the Middle Sum-

mit. There is a prominent rock spire 180 yards down-ridge eastward.

The 1.6 km Lynch Glacier on the NW slope of Mount Daniel is its largest, and the second largest in the area. It extends from 7800 ft to impounded Pea Soup Lake (6220 ft); drainage is to the East Fork of the Foss. Its upper portion is quite active. When larger, it spilled E to the Cle Elum drainage through 6240-ft Lynch Draw (almost a "flat") E of its terminus. There is a fresh set of crescentic moraines by the lake; one mi. W (near head of East Fork of Foss) are additional Neoglacial moraines.

The Lynch's sources are connected to a nearly-separate glacier on Daniel's NE slope, heading against

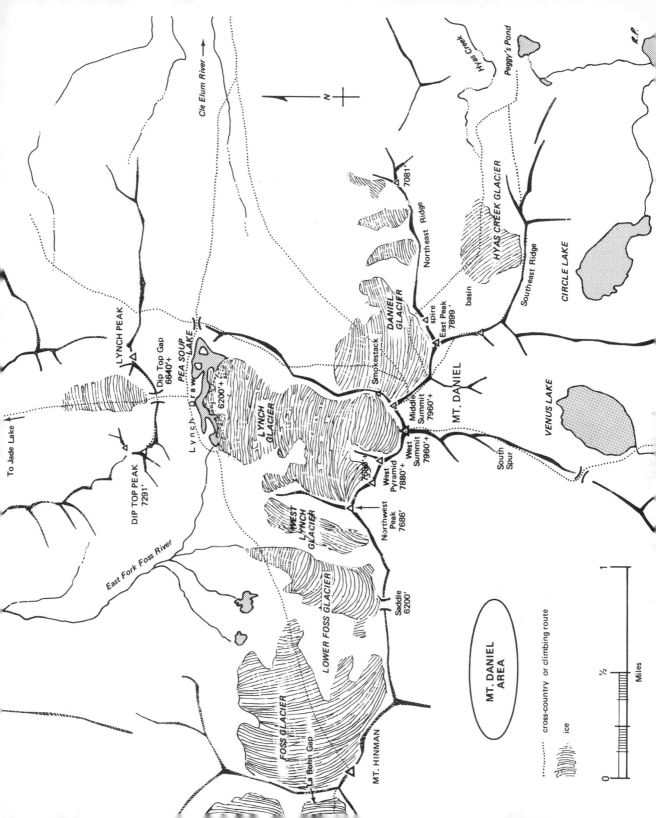

MT. DANIEL AREA

- ·········· cross-country or climbing route
- ice

Cle Elum River →

Hyas Creek

Peggy's Pond

Northeast Ridge

7081'

DANIEL GLACIER

HYAS CREEK GLACIER

basin

spire

East Peak 7899'

Southeast Ridge

CIRCLE LAKE

LYNCH PEAK

Dip Top Gap 6640'+

PEA SOUP LAKE

Lynch Draw

6200'+

Smokestack

MT. DANIEL

Middle Summit 7960'+

West Summit 7960'+

VENUS LAKE

To Jade Lake

DIP TOP PEAK 7291'

LYNCH GLACIER

7880'+

West Pyramid 7880'+

South Spur

East Fork Foss River

WEST LYNCH GLACIER

Northwest Peak 7686'

LOWER FOSS GLACIER

Saddle 6200'

FOSS GLACIER

La Bohn Gap

MT. HINMAN

Miles

0   ½   1

WEST LYNCH GLACIER →

NORTHWEST PEAK →

WEST PYRAMID →

WEST SUMMIT
(True Summit) ↓

LYNCH GLACIER

MIDDLE SUMMIT ↓

EAST PEAK ↓

The Citadel →

spire →

DANIEL GLACIER

PEA SOUP LAKE

Middle Summit and East Peak, which descends to about 6400 ft on the Cle Elum drainage. Given the tentative name "Daniel Glacier," it is losing mass, but is still a crevassed living glacier nearly 3000 ft across and 3500 ft in downslope extent. Several remnants, now merely perennial snow accumulations, rest against the high N slope to the glacier's E.

The Hyas Creek Glacier (6960 ft to 6240 ft) nests against a cirque headwall in a basin on the SE side of the mountain, with drainage running past the N side of the flat holding Peggy's Pond. It is now just an isolated small ice mass, a remnant of a larger glacier which at maximum Neoglacial advance reached 5520 ft and was 1.6 mi. in length.

The separate West Lynch Glacier hangs on a sloping bench between the walls of the NW face. (It is very broad, and barely connected on the N; the broad steep W face is just above it.)

The Lower Foss Glacier lies in a basin to the N of the Daniel-Hinman saddle, heading at 6200 ft (see Mount Hinman).

Mount Daniel's southern flanks are uniquely adorned by alpine cirque lakes whose waters drain to Waptus Lake. The most striking examples are the combinations of Venus and Spade lakes, and that of Circle and Deep lakes.

No climbing records prior to the 1925 Mountaineer outing have been located, but it seems probable that surveyors had already ascended Daniel. The 1925 party climbed the Middle Summit or East Peak via Lynch Glacier. Reference: *Mountaineer,* 1925, p. 26, 63.

EAST ROUTE: From the saddle area adjacent to Peggy's Pond (see Peggy's Pond Route, Cathedral Rock Trail ◆) climb W up talus and névé, keeping right of bedrock hump in basin center. Head upslope over the Hyas Creek Glacier toward the East Peak or follow the gentle SE ridge to left of upper basin (this easy ridge has a small rock outcrop to bypass or cross). Skirt S of summit of East Peak on talus (keep closely under top) to the 7600-ft saddle between it and the Middle Summit. Follow the gentle crest above the Daniel Glacier to the NW. Then climb either the Middle Summit or follow a plateau just to its S to reach the true (western) summit. Time: 5 hours. Note: The East Peak is merely a hike-scramble from the high point on the SE ridge, or from the Middle-East saddle.

Variation: Via E side of Daniel Glacier: From Hyas Creek Glacier turn NW and ascend moderately steep snow to the crest of the major ridge (at about 7200 ft) which extends E from the East Peak. From just below the spire of East Peak traverse W between crevasses on Daniel Glacier, then ascend SW to reach the Middle-East saddle. Note: Distance is minimized by keeping close to East Peak on moderately steep slopes; a gentler route stays N farther. Take ice axe and rope for this variation.

SOUTH SPUR: From Venus Lake's W side (see Waptus River Trail ◆) ascend the S slope of Daniel; keep right of a ridge with a western face and left of low cliffs above the lake (between 6000 ft and 6600 ft). On the upper half of the spur one may find snow. Follow along the spur to the true summit or via the slight depression to its right. Time: 3 hours.

Note: Some parties continue a climb of Hinman from the La Bohn Gap area by traversing about 1 mi. SE from the Hinman-Daniel saddle; one can then reach the S spur at about 6500 ft above Venus Lake.

SOUTHWEST ROUTE: From Shovel Lake (see Waptus River Trail ◆ and Crest Trail ◆) ascend to the basin (est. 5100 ft) at the valley head (est. 1 mi.). Climb NE up rocky slopes and gullies; likely some rock scrambling (one could work over to the S spur). The upper SW slope of Daniel is sufficiently steep to require selective climbing, and the rim W of the true summit has steep cliffs. Time: 5 hours from the trail.

LYNCH GLACIER: The entire glacier is low gradient, but crevasses exist at breaks, becoming open in late season. An ascent via the glacier was made by The Mountaineers on August 10, 1925.

The approach can be made from Marmot Lake (see Marmot Lake Trail ◆) and Lynch Draw. Recent recession of Lynch Glacier has resulted in an enlarged Pea Soup Lake, whose waters now loop back to the cliffs. Unless this situation changes, this is not a practical summer route, especially from an eastern approach.

DANIEL GLACIER: Take the Deception Pass Trail ◆ and Crest Trail ◆ to the N side of Daniel Creek (or ascend directly from pass trail). In about 1½ mi. reach the upper basin and then ascend SW to the glacier; it reaches to the Middle Summit's E side at its very highest point (slopes are moderate, but some crevasses exist). The Middle Summit is just a short rock hike; or work around the S slopes to the true summit.

Variation: On the approach, hike into Lynch Draw (see Lynch Glacier). Then ascend the gentle bedrock crest between the Lynch and Daniel glaciers, later bearing up the western edge of the Daniel. This leads to a level area on the crest just E of the Middle Summit.

West Pyramid: Can be climbed readily from the upper Lynch Glacier or the connecting ridge to other summits; but

MOUNT DANIEL from north
AUSTIN POST, UNIVERSITY OF WASHINGTON

the faces to the NW are challenging. A first climb of this peak was reported by Gene and Bill Prater (1950, from the E side); one lead of class 3.

THE CITADEL   7020 ft/2140 m

This is a rock outcrop located 1.1 mi. SE of Mount Daniel, standing atop a long spur ridge, and flanked by four magnificent high lakes: Circle, Vicente, Spade, and Venus. The Citadel has short rock faces on all flanks. First ascent by C. L. Anderson and Bernard Larson, August 10, 1925.

ROUTE: From Spade Lake (see Waptus River Trail ◆ and Crest Trail ◆) a trail ascends to the 6280-ft saddle just SW of Lake Vicente, and then contours above the W side of the lake. Leave the trail S of the summit and climb rockslides to the ridge crest (considerable snow E of ridge until midsummer). Ascend the snow finger atop the scree slope (pointing to the summit) to within 200 ft of summit. The short final climb to the flat summit area is done on the SE face; use a depression (steep and loose for a short distance). Class 3. Reference: *Mountaineer,* 1925, p. 26, 54.

Approach Variation: The Citadel could readily be approached from Lake Vicente (see Crest Trail ◆) on its S; or any of several ways from Circle Lake or Venus Lake; midaltitude slopes flanking the formation are moderate and allow simple traversing (such as from Peggy's Pond; see Cathedral Rock Trail ◆). The climb could be combined with that of Mount Daniel.

CATHEDRAL ROCK   6724 ft/2050 m

Located between Hyas and Deep lakes, W of the upper Cle Elum River, Cathedral Rock is an intrusive andesite volcanic complex. This prominent formation with its vertical E face forms a striking contrast with the massive snow-clad slopes of nearby Mount Daniel. The first climb was made by James Grieve between 1882 and 1896; an early description termed it "a great knob of rock ... named Grieve's peak" (*Seattle Post-Intelligencer,* September 6, 1896, p. 6). Another rock formation near Deep Lake known as The Buttress was first climbed by C. A. Fisher and seven Mountaineers on August 6, 1925. Reference: *Mountaineer,* 1925, pp. 26-27, 63.

SOUTHWEST FACE: Follow the Cathedral Rock Trail ◆ to Cathedral Pass on the flattish spur S of the Rock. (A shortcut is an old "way trail" beginning at Squaw Lake and climbing sharply to the crest of this spur.) Ascend the rounded spur to where it meets the summit formation (about 6400-ft level); climb the obvious gully to the left of the S buttress (loose). Then climb the SW face to ridge crest; scramble on to summit. Class 3 or 4. Time: 4 hours from road.

NORTHWEST COULOIR: From Peggy's Pond (see Cathedral Rock Trail ◆) skirt lake and ascend brushy cliffs to large talus corral (or snow) on NW side of Cathedral. Climb short narrow gully at its head to small upper corral. Turn right and traverse, ascending broken slopes to base of NW couloir. This couloir is not visible from the lake and may be difficult to find. Couloir is identified by 50-ft rock spires on either side of its base and trees in between. Ascend through trees and loose rock in a SE direction to head of couloir, turning slightly left (E) at top to a cul-de-sac. Turn left (N) and ascend a chimney by climbing under a massive chockstone. Beware of party-inflicted rockfall below the chockstone. Turn right (E) and ascend broken slopes to summit. Class 3. Time: about 2-3 hours.

Variation: Couloir can also be reached by skirting right (S) side of large rock corral and then circling back to the left over easy, open slopes.

SOUTHEAST FACE CHIMNEY: First ascent by C. M. Holt, Randy Johnson, and Terri Van Hollebeke on July 1, 1973. Begin at an obvious chimney: the first lead is a mossy dihedral extending from a cave to a tree. Continue for two leads (class 3) and one lead (class 4) to the summit ridge. Class 5.6. Reference: *A.A.J.,* 1976, p. 442.

NORTHEAST BUTTRESS: This feature of Cathedral Rock is about 900 ft in height. First ascent by Paul Bellamy and Gary Speer on September 17, 1984.

From meadows SE of the objective, traverse N over scree slopes, then climb a perennial snowfield to the E face (about 100 ft S of the objective buttress). Climb the apron below the vertical E face to a large ledge (class 4 — about 70 ft), then make a rightward traverse to an obvious small tree on the buttress (class 5.3). From a tree belay, move up the buttress in a generally leftward direction (good protection) to a loose 30 ft dihedral (class 5.7). Continue on easier rock to a large, loose block. The fourth and fifth pitches are low class 5: follow the buttress crest to a dead tree at a gap. Take an obvious narrow ledge to a questionable block; ascend the block for access to a vertical crack (class 5.7) — long pitch leading to a small belay ledge. The seventh pitch follows a prominent gully leading toward the ridge crest to near the gully end (full pitch). Climb to the left (20 ft — middle class 5); this leads to easy scrambling and the summit. Grade III; class 5.7 (wear helmets). The rock quality is variable (shallow angled ledges tend to be shattered andesite; steeper pitches tend to be solid). Time: 6 hours. Reference: *A.A.J.,* 1985, pp. 189-190.

DAVIS PEAK   6426 ft/1959 m

This is a summit of moderate elevation, long used as a lookout site, on the W flank of the Cle Elum River valley. Trail No. 1324 ascends 5.4 mi. to the lookout on the eastern summit, then continues about ½ mi. to the highest point. Begin the trail route via spur road No. 134, about 1 mi. NE of Salmon la Sac (see Cle Elum River Road ◆). The trail crosses the river, then switchbacks steeply up the pine-forested slope.

Northwest Couloir

CATHEDRAL ROCK from northwest
WILLIAM A. LONG

GOAT MOUNTAIN

6600 ft+/2012 m+

An extended ridge continues NE from Davis Peak to Goat Mountain, whose highest point is 2 mi. from the summit of Davis Peak.

DIP TOP PEAK   7291 ft/2222 m

Two peaks not officially named, just N of the Lynch Glacier, are designated as Dip Top and Lynch Peak; a central saddle (Dip Top Gap, est. 6640 ft) offers a good cross-country route via Jade Lake and a small glacier on the N.

Both peaks have ridges extending due N, keeping over the 7000-ft level for ⅜ mi., with the effect of forming a N-facing horseshoe. Traverses to the high points near the ends of the horseshoe seem feasible. Dip Top Peak has a curious summit saddle with two rock horns; the southwestern is the true summit. The peak has steep W and SW faces. Rock is highly folded, with considerable talus, and therefore is not especially attractive for technical climbs. First ascent by Bill and Gene Prater, August 1950.

ROUTES: Reach Dip Top Gap from Jade Lake (see Marmot Lake Trail ◆) or from Pea Soup Lake (see Mount Daniel,

Lynch Glacier Route). A moderate ridge bears W (easy scrambling), then curves to the first of the summit horns. Loose but easy rock climbing appears to lead to the lower second horn.

A route from the NE appears feasible (unverified): from Jade Lake ascend rubble and bedrock slopes SW, then bear S below ridge crest to snowpatch and tiny saddle between summit horns.

LYNCH PEAK   7280 ft+/2219 m+

See description of Dip Top Peak. Lynch is rather gentle, except on the NW. The glacier is named for John Lynch, a prospector of the late 1800s, who worked a mine near Hyas Lake.

ROUTE: From Dip Top Gap a moderate ridge leads NE to the summit (class 2). Routes from the E and N appear equally moderate.

TERRACE MOUNTAIN

6361 ft/1939 m

A secondary, pointed peak located in the attractive meadowy high country between Deception Creek and the East Fork of the Foss, at 4 mi. NNW of Mount Daniel. Except for its N flank, slopes are not steep. The ridge on the S connects to a rim of 6000-ft+ summits ringing the W and S slopes of Marmot Lake.

SOUTH SPUR: From the N side of Marmot Lake on Marmot Lake Trail ◆ merely hike NW uphill.

NORTHEAST RIDGE: The peak is only 2½ mi. from the junction of Deception and Fisher creeks (near end of Tonga Ridge Road ◆). Simply ascend semi-open ridge to S, keeping on or near the easy crest between the two creeks. Near the 5800-ft level (W of Lake Clarice) the NE ridge begins to rise (probably class 2).

BALD EAGLE PEAK   6259 ft/1908 m

From the deep valley of the Foss, Bald Eagle Peak appears as a twin to Silver Eagle, which is 1.1 mi. SW. The lowest area on their connecting ridge is 5200 ft. Maps have incorrectly placed the name "Bald Eagle" at its companion's position. First ascent by Hermann F. Ulrichs and Ben Falkenberg in May 1933, via North Ridge.

SOUTHEAST SHOULDER: From the East Fork Foss Trail ◆ at about 6 mi. (est. 3200 ft) ascend timbered slopes W to the low point on the connecting ridge between the "Eagle" peaks. Follow the ridge NE then N about ½ mi. to treeline as it curves left to the foot of the summit rock pyramid (est. 5800 ft). Take the S ridge; broken rock — class 3. Note: Lower E slopes are very brushy; therefore it is prudent not to leave trail until slide paths passed. An approach variation via Bald Eagle Lake appears feasible, but has not been verified.

NORTH RIDGE: This is a more direct route to the summit, but less attractive because of longer and more taxing forest travel. Leave Foss River Road ◆ about ½ mi. S of the Tonga Ridge junction, then ascend through second growth forest toward the objective's North Ridge. Once virgin forest is attained, the ascent becomes easier, and the terrain becomes open at the subalpine level. There are no technical difficulties, but near the summit, reports state that one should keep left of the ridge.

SILVER EAGLE PEAK   6241 ft/1903 m

Located between the forks of the Foss River and 2 mi. NW of Necklace Valley. Because of considerable local relief on the N, it stands out attractively. In early summer its upper E side has a white snow plume. The Big Snow Mountain quadrangle has "Bald Eagle" incorrectly marked at its location. First ascent by Hermann Ulrichs, Dan O'Brien, and two companions on March 29, 1934.

SOUTHEAST RIDGE: From the East Fork Foss Trail ◆ at about 3600 ft (at 6½ mi. uptrail) where trail crosses creek, climb W up brushy slopes and a talus basin to a saddle between the peak and a subsidiary hump to the E (about 5440 ft). Continue NW about ¾ mi. up the SE ridge to the summit; class 2 and 3. The 1934 party climbed from the E to a sub-summit; here they made a rappel into a deep notch and continued easily to the summit.

Approach Variation: From Otter Lake (see West Fork Foss River Trail ◆) it would be a long traversing ascent to the N, but quite feasible. There is a good camp spot at W side of Nazanne Lake, then ascend NE to the upper ridge.

NORTHWEST RIDGE: From Trout Lake on the West Fork Foss River Trail ◆ ascend cross-country up the wooded ridge; no special difficulties aside from brush; this is the shortest route to the summit. It also appears possible to start up a timbered ridge from the road at just S of the vale that comes down between Silver and Bald Eagle; keep in tall timber at the start, then a broad timber shoulder which leads to a moderate rocky ridge higher.

OTTER POINT   6359 ft/1938 m

Otter Point gives a fine view of the entire Alpine Lakes region.

ROUTE: Approach from Necklace Valley (see East Fork Foss River Trail ◆). Reach it by a stroll 1 mi. NW along the gentle, beautiful divide leading to the summit. The actual highest point is the N end of the long, nearly-level summit crest.

LA BOHN PEAK   6585 ft/2007 m

This is a small summit 0.4 mi. W of La Bohn Gap. Below its NW face there are remnants of the Pendant Glacier; there are steep cliffs on the peak and its adjoining ridges to the NW. There is a gentle W ridge curving from the peak to the southernmost of the Tank Lakes.

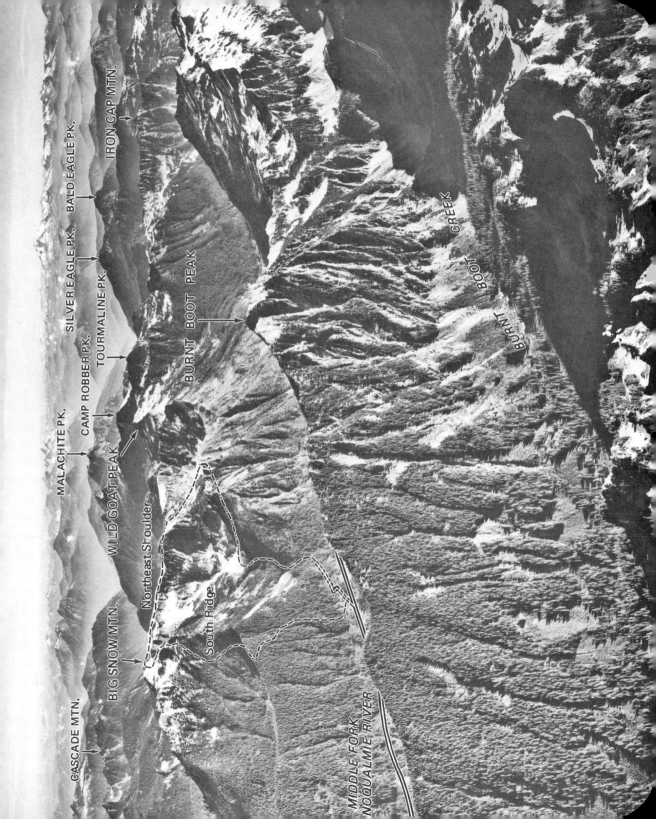

CASCADE MTN.

MALACHITE PK.

SILVER EAGLE PK.

BALD EAGLE PK.

IRON CAP MTN.

CAMP ROBBER PK.

TOURMALINE PK.

BIG SNOW MTN.

WILD GOAT PEAK

Northeast Shoulder

BURNT BOOT PEAK

South Ridge

BURNT

BOOT

CREEK

MIDDLE FORK
SNOQUALMIE RIVER

ROUTES: There are several non-technical summit routes. One can hike and scramble up talus slopes from Williams Lake on the S flank (see Dutch Miller Trail ◆). From La Bohn Gap one can scramble bedrock (or ascend snow) on the peak's E flank to reach the pointed summit. For another approach, see Alpine Lakes High Route, Lake Dorothy Trail ◆ .

IRON CAP MOUNTAIN
6347 ft/1935 m

A small peak located on the Middle Fork Snoqualmie-Otter Lake divide. There is a small ice remnant on the E flank and ice in a northwestern cirque. The gentle N spur is almost entirely talus and snow. A party under Joe Hazard climbed the peak in 1925 (*Mountaineer*, 1925, pp. 23, 25, 63).

ROUTES: From Chetwoot Lake, Azurite Lake, or the S end of Otter Lake (see West Fork Foss River Trail ◆ or Alpine Lakes High Route, Lake Dorothy Trail ◆) one could ascend the relatively easy N or NW slopes with a wide choice of bedrock or névé routes; two possible parallel snow gullies on the NW (above glacier) run to the pyramidal summit. The same approaches could be used to reach the moderate W ridge.

From the vicinity of Iron Cap Pass on the E flank of the peak, a simple route would be to ascend the snow basin, bearing to a gap in the left skyline. Bypass the rock cliff on its left by following a right-slanting ramp to reach talus just NE of the summit. Reach Iron Cap Pass via either of the above approaches or from Williams Lake (see Dutch Miller Trail ◆).

The broad southern scarp of the peak features extensive cliff ramparts. The most feasible southern approach from the trail would be to ascend to the W ridge, outflanking the cliffs, at least ¼ mi. from the summit.

MALACHITE PEAK   6261 ft/1908 m

This small but interesting alpine rock peak is located on the East Fork Miller River-West Fork Foss divide, about 1 mi. N of Malachite Lake. Malachite has a sharp 6208 ft N summit, about ½ mi. distant. There are several craggy minor points outside and between principal summits. The S side of the main summit is short but steep. Malachite is virtually surrounded by attractive small, high lakes and glacier remnants; ice feeds into Panorama Lake (5262 ft) on its E side; Purvis Lake lies cradled high in the rocky western summit cirque. The peak is an ideal spring and early summer ascent, especially on the NW route, when snow will cover brush.

The only early climbing record is the 1937 ascent by the U.S. Geological Survey.

SOUTH ROUTE: From Malachite Lake (see West Fork Foss River Trail ◆) ascend NW (from outlet) up woods to open hillside with meadow-talus; here is a broad swath with pygmy evergreens. Ascend it via slight gully on left, to end of trees. Then climb open talus to little step-saddle (left) S of summit rock step. Go behind to rock horn (class 3). Follow ridge short distance N and keep on E side. Scramble about one lead up to top along crest (steeper). Class 2 and 3.

Alternate Route: Ascend talus, bearing right to defile in rock structure to right of summit. Work up to ridge SE of true summit; from small tree area on summit ridge walk to whitish gully heading just left of highest crag (it is to right, with grey wall to N). Then climb to top. Class 3.

Note: It would be possible to traverse to the N summit; a short rappel, snow slopes and scrambling should be anticipated; a 5840-ft saddle is the low point.

NORTHWEST ROUTE: Take the Miller River Road ◆ about 1½ mi. past the bridge over the E fork, where an old spur turns E to a logged area. Hike up and left to ridge crest. Stay on the narrow crest going SE until it begins to steepen quite abruptly (past lower brushy area of streamdraw on left). From a big rock atop the narrow ridge, make an angling descent to the draw. Ascend it (a talus corridor or snow-filled) to Purvis Lake (5280 ft). Time: 3 hours to lake; about 3000 ft altitude gain.

Take the left-most gully going NE (easy) and work above a low rock knob which rises directly above the E lake shore. Climb to the notch just S of the most prominent pinnacle between the two main summits, and continue up its far side. At a steepening of rock, traverse around the first pinnacle on its W side at the rock/snow junction to a steep gully. Climb this to a notch and repeat; go around the next group of pinnacles on an ascending traverse on steep snow to the flat space on rocks just S of the summit. Time: 2 hours from lake.

Variation: (harder) Instead of leaving the narrow ridge, continue up crest (some pinnacles and cliffs). If this is done, make a traverse into Purvis Lake under the NE side of the prominent point on the ridge apex.

NORTH ROUTE: An interesting alpine cross-country route, ending on the N peak only 2 mi. away, is possible via Maloney Ridge Road (see Foss River Road ◆). Follow Maloney Ridge Road for about 3 mi.; here a spur (No. 6846) enters sharply from the S; follow it an estimated 2 mi. to clear-cut in Section 19, just E of Lake Evans.

Continue on a SW pattern to Rock Lake (4546 ft); ascend the rocky shoulder (with scattered trees) that leads up from the outside of the lake, then ascend SW up the rocky N summit. A rappel and traverse on to the highest summit is certainly possible, but specifics are lacking.

CAMP ROBBER PEAK   6286 ft/1916 m

The high point of the divide between Camp Robber Valley and Big Heart Lake, it is located about 1 mi. from the N end of Big Heart Lake and is about ¾ mi. NW of Tourmaline Peak, with a high continuous connecting ridge.

The peak's expansive western facade presents a con-

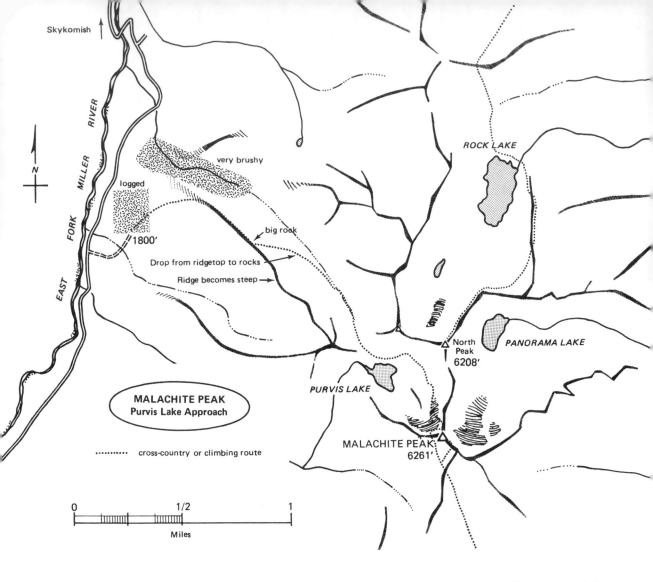

Skykomish ↑

EAST FORK MILLER RIVER

very brushy

logged

1800'

big rock

Drop from ridgetop to rocks

Ridge becomes steep →

ROCK LAKE

North Peak 6208'

PANORAMA LAKE

PURVIS LAKE

MALACHITE PEAK 6261'

MALACHITE PEAK
Purvis Lake Approach

·········· cross-country or climbing route

0   1/2   1
Miles

---

tinuous series of steep gullies and cliffs above the basal talus fan. The E side is gentle, as is the N side, except a steep band of rock from 5200 to 5600 ft (considerable permanent snow on the N).

ROUTES: One could make a traverse from Tourmaline Peak, or climb from either end of Big Heart Lake; if approaching from the N end, it is best to detour the cliff band on the lake side. One could also ascend the talus and snow area W of the NW bay of the lake, then work to upper slopes.

TOURMALINE PEAK   6245 ft / 1903 m
Located to the NW of Chetwoot Lake, this informally named summit, once called Interlake Mountain, is just ¼ mi. N of Chetwoot Pass.

ROUTE: The peak is a simple ascent from Chetwoot Lake (see West Fork Foss River Trail ♦ or Alpine Lakes High Route, Lake Dorothy Trail ♦). Ascend any slope from the N around to the SE, but avoid the steep cliffs on its S, just above the pass.

WILD GOAT PEAK   6305 ft / 1922 m
Once called "Little Snowy," this is the high point between Gold and Chetwoot lakes. The peak has a rock wall on its W and there is a cliff belt on the Gold Lake slope. First ascent by Hermann Ulrichs and Dwight Watson in spring 1937 via NW slope and W ridge.

ROUTE: If making the ascent from Gold Lake (see Lake Dorothy Trail ♦) keep left of these walls and work beneath the N side of the summit to the little high notch on the E ridge close to the summit.

If making the ascent from Chetwoot Lake or Chetwoot Pass (see West Fork Foss River Trail ♦ or Alpine Lakes High Route, Lake Dorothy Trail ♦) on the NE (³/₅ mi.), simply ascend the divide, keeping right of the rocks of the eastern sub-peak to reach the little high notch; then scramble the short E ridge.

BIG SNOW MOUNTAIN
6680 ft/2036 m

Located closely N of the Middle Fork of the Snoqualmie River, Big Snow is well named, for its expansive, rounded summit area and gentle northern slopes keep a white cover much of the summer. The mountain's steep section is the upper E flank, where a granitic wall stands above an ice remnant.

It is known that a climb was made by a group of Mountaineers on July 20, 1917; in view of several simple routes available, one could assume the mountain had already been climbed by then. It is an excellent ski tour from Lake Dorothy. The summit view is truly remarkable, showing to great advantage most of the widely scattered summits in the North-Central Cascades. Reference: *Mountaineer*, 1917, p. 72.

NORTH SLOPE: From S shore of Myrtle Lake (Dingford Creek Trail ♦) contour ¼ mi. SE through woods to a prominent talus area, then ascend it to Big Snow Lake (4940 ft); bypass cliffs above lake by traversing right around the far shore of adjacent Snowflake Lake, then ascend short brushy slopes above (best to angle left to a little spur). Climb SE on easy slopes directly toward the summit. At first rock outcrop detour right to easier terrain, then bear left, again SE. Expect snow climbing until late summer.

NORTHEAST SHOULDER: This long, broad shoulder provides an easy hiking or ski ascent of Big Snow, and may be largely a snow climb until late summer. There are two usual approaches, neither being short: (1) From the S end of Gold Lake (see Alpine Lakes High Route, Lake Dorothy Trail ♦) hike southward up a draw, then later ascend SW past an area of ponds toward the summit shoulder. (2) Ascend from the Middle Fork Snoqualmie River Road ♦ via the W side of Hardscrabble Creek to Lower Hardscrabble Lake (4059 ft); on the final portion of this cross-country ascent, the E side of the creek is the best choice. Then take the gully right of the stream to the upper lake; keep right, then ascend NW via a gully toward the Northeast Shoulder. Traverse westward on its N flank to bypass a hump, then follow the shoulder.

EAST BUTTRESS: First ascent by Don Williamson and Jeff Dial on May 11, 1971. At about 0.4 mi. before reaching the end of Middle Fork Snoqualmie River Road ♦ an overgrown logging roadway climbs and switchbacks about one mi. to come close to Hardscrabble Creek. Ascend near the W side of the creek until about ⅔ of the distance to Lower

Hardscrabble Lake, then cross to the E side. Round the lower lake on its W. To reach the buttress and the E face, do not hike to the upper lake, but follow the principal stream gully NNW to the small glacier located on a shelf under the summit of Big Snow. Traverse the glacier S to the objective route.

This buttress of Big Snow Mountain is characterized by a prominent dihedral and some overhangs on its crest. The first serious pitch (class 5.7) leads to easier climbing above. Higher, climb up and left around a slight corner to break through a steep section to a broad ledge system halfway up the buttress. Move right to the northern side, then up, bearing left to the crest and top of the buttress. Grade III; class 5.7 (three pitons for aid on original); ten pitches on very firm granite. Time: 12 hours from road. Reference: *A.A.J.*, 1972, p. 116.

PROMINENT DIHEDRAL: Lies to the S of the East Buttress. First ascent by Pete Doorish and Russ Devaney in 1979. Begin at the far left corner of the lower face and climb a crack/chimney fault to brushy ledges. Continue up to just below the dihedral. A short aid pitch leads to two free pitches in the dihedral. Grade III; class 5.10 and A1. Recommend a few pitons up to ¾-inch, plus a 4-inch Friend or bong, and small stoppers.

LOWER RAMP ROUTE: Was also climbed by the above party. Begin per the Dihedral Route, then follow a ramp system up and left to the large ledge system halfway up the face (class 5.8).

SOUTH RIDGE: From 0.4 mi. before reaching the end of Middle Fork Snoqualmie River Road ♦, hike the overgrown logging spur switchbacks to the NW corner of an old clearcut (est. 3200 ft). Ascend the brushy slopes NW to a saddle at about 4300 ft. Traverse NNE about ⅜ mi. around a basin to reach a wide avalanche gully that bears N to timberline; ascend broad open slopes (or snow) to the summit. Time: 6 hours.

SOUTHWEST RIDGE: Head NE from Hester Lake Trail about 1 mi. after leaving Dingford Creek (see Dingford Creek Trail ♦) and just before crossing branch of Hester Lake Creek. Head NE going easterly around rock escarpment up ridge. Follow ridge easterly and northerly directly to the summit.

MOUNT PRICE 5587 ft/1703 m

This seldom-visited peak, mostly forested, abuts the Middle Fork Snoqualmie River for 5½ mi. The summit offers splendid views of neighboring peaks such as Mount Garfield, Big Snow Mountain, and the Lemah Mountain-Chimney Rock group. Despite the mountain's modest altitude, a climb from the Dingford Creek trailhead involves an elevation gain of over 4100 ft. The mountain's complex form provides interesting cross-country approaches.

NORTHEAST ROUTE: From Hester Lake outlet (see Dingford Creek Trail ♦) follow the N and W shorelines on a faint trail through forest to the base of rockfall, then ascend SW up a forested spur to Little Hester Lake. From the S shoreline, and southward on rockfall, turn W at 4750 ft and scramble a short slope to the cliff base below a minor summit. Contour W through boulders to the saddle just E of the main summit. Continue to the top via a short path, then scramble up the S slope (some exposure). Time: 3 hours from lake outlet.

OTHER ROUTES: The North Ridge can be climbed from the W end of Little Hester Lake. Ascend NW through boulders and open forest to the saddle just SW of Point 4892. Turn SW and follow the ridge route (grassy plateaus and minor brush). Zigzag along the ridge to avoid cliffs; class 2-3. Reported by Dave Beedon (1985).

Note: a springtime ascent could be made directly from Dingford Creek to the saddle NW of Little Hester Lake.

The West Ridge Route can be climbed from the road immediately S of Dingford Creek bridge. Probable first ascent by Dave Beedon, August 18, 1984. Ascend through forest at a bearing of about 95 degrees. Reach a bouldery, forested N-S ridge at 3900 ft. Scramble this ridge to avoid a steep slope on the W flank. At the top of a boulderfield, ascend to a plateau (4460 ft), then drop into a little basin (possible last water). Continue ascending SE to reach a saddle at 4940 ft. Then follow the ridge, traversing under Point 5341 on its E side, and regain the ridge near 5280 ft. Continue on the ridge or its N flank (class 3 at times). Time: 10 hours.

TREEN PEAK   5763 ft/1757 m

A seldom-visited peak of volcanic rock, similar in type to that of Mount Garfield, which is 1½ mi. to the SE; the name is for early forest supervisor, L. A. Treen. The pyramid-shaped peak is quite rocky on its upper eastern flank, and there are steep sections on all flanks; a snow gully splits into the peak on the NE. The probable first ascent was not made until April 1974, by Jan Anthony, Mike Bialos, and Joan Webber.

ROUTE: From the end of the Taylor River Road (hiking required — see Middle Fork Snoqualmie River Road ◆) take the 2 mi. trail to Nordrum Lake. A difficult cross-country trek in brushy subalpine terrain of about 2 mi. can be taken to the objective. The final ascent of Treen Peak is made from the SE flank (scrambling). The cross-country route keeps just N of Nordrum, Judy, and Carole lakes. Then the route bears SW, climbs W, then NW to cross the ridge NE of Charlie Brown Lake.

MOUNT GARFIELD   5519 ft/1682 m

The massive rock of Garfield is a Tertiary volcanic, which includes andesite, dacite, and breccia flows. The rock is highly recrystallized by thermal metamorphism. Garfield is a hazardous enigma. It is an extremely complex formation located within the diverging angle of the Middle Fork Snoqualmie and the Taylor River, extending some 3 mi. from W to E. It is massive, and because of very low footings, has great local relief despite moderate altitude.

As has been reported elsewhere, Mount Garfield offers the mountaineer more than a climb, for it is also a physical and orienteering challenge. In climbing Garfield, it is important to get a very early start. While a 12-hour round trip is generally a minimum, only during the long days of summer will there be sufficient daylight for what is a long, steep climb, with some very exposed areas. During this season one can make a snow-free ascent of the upper gullies, but rockfall, and a possible lack of water above the small basin are negative factors. Light bivouac gear is suggested. A few pieces of protection for the three pitches of class 4 climbing in the No. 2 Gully, and ample webbing for rappels, is suggested.

The stream from Garfield Mountain Lakes, to the E of the massif, flows to the Taylor. The highest and most-climbed summit (*Main Peak*), located about 1 mi. W of the upper lake, is a large rocky pyramid with a vast and slabby S face.

The *West Peaks,* located on the main ridge some 0.9 mi. W of Main Peak, are composed of four principal summits in a ¼-mi. span; their altitudes range from about 4800 ft to 4896 ft. The southern rock walls of these peaks feature vast slabs of a very spectacular nature. The distance from the Middle Fork-Taylor River junction, only 1.2 mi. to the highest peak, is an indication of the steepness of this flank of Mount Garfield.

The very prominent *Leaning Spire* (5240 ft +), located only about 300 yards W of the higher Main Peak, has a spectacular tilt toward the latter. Despite the rough approach, this objective has become a classic ascent — one of sustained exertion, but with scenic and technical reward.

Courte Echelle is the prominent, narrow wedgelike spire (5400 ft +) located about 300 yards NNE of Main Peak. Because of the difficult northern approach, this summit has seen few ascents.

Little Flat-Top (est. 5200 ft) is a slender pinnacle located between Courte Echelle and Main Peak.

East Peak (5480 ft +) is a craggy summit on the Garfield massif's crest line at 0.4 mi. E of Main Peak; there is also a slightly lower summit 200 yards northward.

Outrigger Spire (4960 ft) is a lower and isolated rock formation, about 0.3 mi. to the N at the end of a spur ridge.

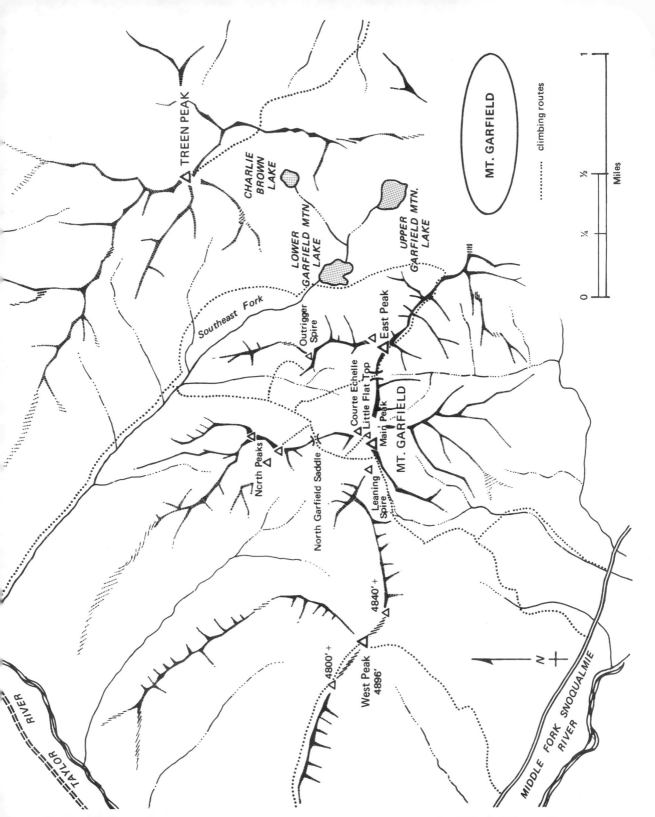

TAYLOR RIVER

TREEN PEAK

CHARLIE BROWN LAKE

LOWER GARFIELD MTN. LAKE

UPPER GARFIELD MTN. LAKE

Southeast Fork

Outrigger Spire

East Peak

Courte Echelle
Little Flat Top

Main Peak

MT. GARFIELD

North Peaks

North Garfield Saddle

Leaning Spire

4840'+

4800'+

West Peak
4896'

MT. GARFIELD

climbing routes

Miles

1   ½   ¼   0

N

MIDDLE FORK SNOQUALMIE RIVER

EAST PEAK

COURTE ECHELLE

MAIN PEAK

LEANING SPIRE

GOAT MTN.

WEST PEAK

Little Flat Top

key ledge

glade

razorback

Great Canyon

rock outcrop

slabs

dirt gully

wrong canyon

waterfall

lower west variation

path

overgrown road

reach creek

gravel wash

The *North Peaks* lie on the "Courte Echelle spur" that begins some 300 yards E of Main Peak. Summits are about ½ mi. N (two summits at 5000 ft +); the highest point (5101 ft) is at the NE side of the cluster. To the SW and below the North Peaks are one or more spires.

It should be emphasized that any and all routes to the summits are long, due to the low-altitude starts; they are strenuous masochistic undertakings because of brush, windfalls, slabs, and rock gullies. It is advisable to limit size of groups to avoid party-inflicted rockfall in gullies. A history of numerous accidents has included a fatal slip from the "key-ledge" in April 1965, a double fatality on the No. 1 Gully's steep snow in May 1972, and a serious fall in 1983.

Experience has shown the described route and variations on the Main Peak, South Route the wisest. Innumerable variations are possible here, many with misleading cairns. Water and snow can be a problem on this route (too much or too little); various gullies may be snow-filled until summer, and moats and wet rock may be a hazard. It is advisable to get a very early start. Helmets and bivouac gear are advised. In some late seasons there may be no water above the lower slabs. References: *Mountaineer*, 1952, pp. 79-80; *Mazama*, 1966, pp. 44-45; *A.N.A.M.*, 1984, pp. 47-51.

MAIN PEAK

First ascent by Jim Crooks and Judson Nelson, August 27, 1940 by South Route.

SOUTH ROUTE: From Middle Fork Snoqualmie Road ◆ at 2.6 mi. from Taylor River junction (alt. 1000 ft) find a gravel outwash, then follow the dry stream bed to a blazed path on the E; follow path in woods parallel with water chutes to a small deep basin (45 minutes); snow here in early season. Angle down left to stream (the chutes to this position are a satisfactory alternate when dry). Ascend the prominent dirt and rock-filled gully which enters the basin from left (one can avoid the lower half by going up onto ridgetop to its N). After leaving the gully, follow the slab-grass boundary up and left until it is easy to climb over slab. Ascend directly about 100 ft and then bear right on small ledges to the crest of the rim (edge of the "Great Canyon") at a short rock outcrop. Move over its crest for about 100 yards to the base of the "Razorback" rock formation. Follow its crest until its end at a tiny notch at a headwall. Traverse left and slightly down a brushy slope (turning a corner) into the first gully (about 150 ft). Note: this is the gully W of "Great Canyon"; it continues to the crest between the West Peaks and Leaning Spire. Ascend it about 300 ft and keep right, bearing up short right-branch that leads to a minor tree-covered saddle (glade) on the canyon's edge (giant cairn).

Climb rightward up a steep rock gully (about 50 ft), continuing into a tree-covered slanting ramp. Continue E along a cliffy forest-ledge (at 4100 ft). *This key-ledge is an obscure, exposed traverse* of 100 yards to the "Y," ending at the cliff edge atop the "Great Canyon" headwall. Note: beware of treacherous footing on traverse.

Reach the base of No. 1 Gully (left branch of the "Y"). Descend 10 ft from the level of the ledge-traverse, then traverse exposed rock across the top of the "Great Canyon" to base of No. 2 Gully (E fork of "Y," leading to Main-Leaning Spire col). In about 500 ft reach a level with the basal wall of the Spire. Ascend two gully steps, each of about 20 ft (watch loose rock), then long slabs to a spur ridge; then N 200 ft via a series of slabby chimneys (stemming class 4) toward the col (5080 ft +). The summit is a scramble over easy rock and steep heather. Grade II. Time: road to "Y" — 5 hours; then 3 hours to summit. Descent: 4 hours. One can use small trees for rappels.

Lower West Variation: Begin on road exactly 2.2 mi. from Taylor junction, at an overgrown clearing 100 yards W of old gravel pit. Walk uphill about 200 ft to a faint logging road. Follow it, turning right at large boulder, and continue toward the slabby watercourse which cascades down the W side of the lower cliff band. Ascend beaten path on crest left of water. Atop cliff (2300 ft) cross watercourse on flat polished slabs; continue through brush about 200 yards, past two steps, then take smaller watercourse (usually dry), coming in from right. Continue on its right side, angling up-right (moderate brush) about 500 vertical ft to a grassy-brushy slab. Ascend slab, angling right to the "rock outcrop" on the canyon rim.

Gully Variation: Take left branch of "Y" (No. 1 Gully) to a level with base of Leaning Spire (about 500 ft up). Scramble right-hand gully fork to intervening tree-covered rock ridge on E. Cross, then scramble down across to No. 2 Gully, near base of the slabby chimneys.

Chimney Variation: One can avoid the chimney leading to the col by climbing above it; two leads easy class 5 (a diversion if chimney is wet).

Leaning Spire Variation: Reach the col by rappels from the summit of Leaning Spire.

NORTH ROUTE: This seldom-used route is best done in spring, when snow covers the extensive shrub and brush slopes. First ascent by Richard Berge and Pete Schoening in 1950 or 1951.

Hike or possibly drive the Taylor River Road for 2.4 mi. (see Middle Fork Snoqualmie River Road ◆). Here a road spur exits to the river. Make a ford (treacherous in early season) and continue inland to an overgrown roadway, then bear W to the gravel bed parallel to the creek. After ¾ mi. the creek forks and the valley narrows (the main stream branch, from Garfield Mountain Lakes, enters from the chasm).

Cross the stream and ascend the underbrush slope right (W) of the S fork to the cirque between Outrigger Spire and the North Peaks; this traversing ascent is difficult travel — it

MOUNT GARFIELD from south
BOB AND IRA SPRING

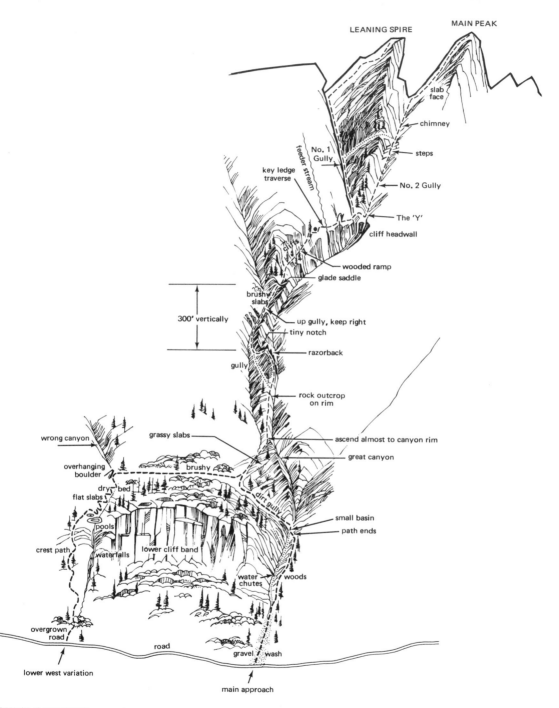

LEANING SPIRE

MAIN PEAK

slab face

chimney

steps

No. 1 Gully

No. 2 Gully

feeder stream

key ledge traverse

The 'Y'

cliff headwall

cliffs

wooded ramp

glade saddle

brushy slabs

300' vertically

up gully, keep right

tiny notch

razorback

gully

rock outcrop on rim

wrong canyon

grassy slabs

ascend almost to canyon rim

great canyon

overhanging boulder

brushy

dry bed

flat slabs

dirt gully

small basin

path ends

pools

crest path

waterfalls

lower cliff band

water chutes

woods

R.P.

overgrown road

road

gravel wash

lower west variation

main approach

MOUNT GARFIELD — south route

196

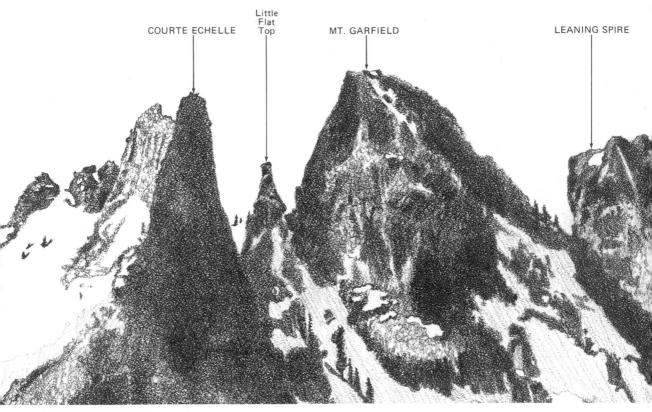

COURTE ECHELLE   Little Flat Top   MT. GARFIELD   LEANING SPIRE

MOUNT GARFIELD from north

is best to keep away from the stream. Ascend to the N of Courte Echelle, crossing westward over a sub-ridge via North Garfield Saddle at 4800 ft+. Then descend slightly into the next cirque. The final ascent takes a steep 300-ft gully to the Main-Leaning Spire col (the gully is reported easy if snow-filled, but difficult after melt-off). Reference: *Mountaineer,* 1952, p. 79.

LEANING SPIRE   5240 ft+/1597 m+

First ascent by Fred Beckey, Louis Graham, and Walt Varney on November 9, 1941 by West Route.

WEST ROUTE: From the "Y" (see Main Peak, South Route) ascend the No. 1 (left) Gully, which leads to the notch in the main Mount Garfield ridge immediately W of Leaning Spire. Short gully walls on this route create minor climbing or bypass problems. At the junction 500 ft farther upslope, take the left fork (this has a rock step). Two vertical steps of 20 ft each (about midway to the notch) can be avoided by climbing a steep dirt gully and brushy rock on

the left flank, then bearing back into the gully; moats at the steps may cause additional difficulty.

From the notch climb on the right flank of the arete to a tree belay (about 90 ft — parties here used two safety pitons). Then climb the West Face to the ridge crest (one method is to use a sloping crack which broadens into a shallow chimney). Grade II or III. Class 5.2. Time: 4 hours from "Y." Descent: 5 rappels and some scrambling reach "Y." Descent to Main Peak-Leaning Spire col: short rappel E to exposed horn for sling; 120 ft free rappel to col.

Variation: Upper South Ridge: From 100 ft below W notch, diagonal right through broad rotten face to S ridge at some scrub trees. Follow nearly vertical crest on solid rock for two leads (class 5).

NORTH FACE: First ascent by Klindt Vielbig, Anthony Hovey, Don Keller, and Cal Magnusson on May 26, 1958.

From Main-Leaning Spire col (see Main Peak, South Route) descend about 300 ft in steep gully (optimum when snow-filled). Cross W below a rock buttress and climb a steep 250-ft gully and slabs on the N face, heading for the W

West Peaks   Leaning Spire
MAIN PEAK
No. 2 Gully

MOUNT GARFIELD from southwest
ED COOPER

notch of the Spire. A giant chockstone prevents direct access; exit left at some dense trees, then scramble up easy rock to summit. Note: alternate approach is that of Main Peak, North Route. Descent from Main Peak col is steep and treacherous except when snow-covered.

EAST FACE: First ascent by Tom Miller and Pete Schoening, September 1950.

Begin the route on the S side of the Main-Leaning Spire col, some 200 ft below the Spire's summit. The route involves broken chimneys: first work up-left, then up again. Work right of an obvious steep crack; a hard move for 10 ft working right on a slab brings one about 30 ft right of pitch-start. Scrambling on a ridge crest leads to the summit; class 5.7 (used 8 pitons on original). Time: 2 hours.

WEST PEAKS

First ascent by Tom Campbell and Stan Garson, August 1940, via the W ridge. Route details are unknown. Extensive brushy scrambling should be expected.

It should be possible to reach the West Peaks by bearing left from the Leaning Spire approach, climbing to the main ridge, then scrambling westward.

SOUTH FACE: First ascent by Gerry Roach, Dick Springgate, and John Wells on February 22, 1963.

Leave the Middle Fork Snoqualmie River Road ◆ about 1 mi. from Taylor junction. Climb N through brush and pick a line to the base of the face via brushy class 3 rock. Engage the main rock face near its low point, just right of a very smooth white base slab. Climb straight up the face toward a discontinuous, tree-speckled ledge system that arches across the face like an inverted "U" (this system separates the lower face from the slightly steeper upper third). Climbing to here is enjoyable 4th class. Reach the ledge near its high point under an overhang. The first lead off the ledge is class 5.5. Work generally left, well across the upper face (several class 5 leads mixed with class 4 leads), then ascend rock on a spur to the highest W summit. Descent can be made to the N, then W down shoulder to the Taylor River. Grade III; class 5.5. Note: the W shoulder could be used as an ascent route, but appears brushy and rocky.

NORTH PEAKS

There are several peaks; the one nearest Garfield saddle

is fin-shaped. The best approach is from the NW flank of the first cirque (see Main Peak, North Route). First ascent by Richard Berge and Pete Schoening in April 1951 (it is not known if they climbed more than one summit; route details unknown).

LITTLE FLAT-TOP   5200 ft + /1585 m +
First ascent by Richard Berge and Pete Schoening, 1951.

Approach as for Main Peak, North Route. From the cirque below the Main-Leaning Spire snow gully make the ascent by the NW side. Details are lacking; probably one class 5 pitch.

COURTE ECHELLE   5400 ft + /1646 m +
First ascent by Richard Berge and Pete Schoening, 1951.

NORTHWEST RIDGE: Approach via North Garfield saddle (see Main Peak, North Route). The final climb of this wedge-shaped rock formation is an exposed edge (class 5.4 or more difficult); one can rappel the opposite crest and continue eastward.

SOUTH RIB: History uncertain, but route reported. Using same approach, work S of the saddle to E side of the spire. Climb 250 ft up-face to the E of the S rib. Ascend the rib from the S notch. Probably class 5.

EAST PEAK   5480 ft + /1670 m +
First ascent by Richard Berge and Pete Schoening in April 1951, probably traversing the crest from Courte Echelle and climbing the W ridge of the East Peak.

There appear to be two routes from the fork of Garfield Mountain Lakes Creek (see Main Peak, North Route). From the cirque at the head of the S fork, ascend to the gap (est. 4950 ft) between Courte Echelle and the East Peak. This route appears to offer no problems other than some brushy travel and scrambling.

The E ridge appears to be a feasible scramble (history unknown). One could take the SE creek fork cross-country and ascend above the brushy cascade to reach the lower lake (about 3600 ft). From here ascend southward to gain access to the ridge.

OUTRIGGER SPIRE   4960 ft/1512 m
Follow the North Route nearly to the chasm of the S fork. Cross the creek and ascend cliffs and a long cedar jungle for about 1000 ft to a headwall. Here bear left on small talus slope and manage a crossing of the stream. Ascend a gully to the SE, then make the climb of the spire by a slanting ramp on the E; there are about three pitches (class 3 and 4) on the SE arete. First ascent by Fred Beckey and Phil Leatherman.

CASCADE MOUNTAIN
5591 ft/1704 m
This formation is a little-visited crest bearing SW-NE, between the upper portion of the Miller River forks. The highest point is near the S end, to the NE of Dream Lake. The main summit has some cliffs on the E and N portions of the mountain, but is gradual on the W flank; rock is of the firm Snoqualmie batholith.

ROUTES: Take Miller River Road ◆ for 3.7 mi. to the West Fork Road; this is a mine-to-market road (not open to the public). One could hike (perhaps bicycle) to near the Cleopatra Mine. Ford the river and ascend cross-country (bearing SE) along a side stream; this stream enters the W fork between sections 30 and 31, at about 2600 ft altitude.

A means of reaching the northeastern and central summits of the mountain, or traversing high points to the true summit from the N, would be to plan a route via Francis Lake (good camping by outlet). The approach would be via the same road, then cross-country across the river and up the drainage stream to the lake.

The ascent could also be done from the East Fork Miller Road, from Smith Creek (all cross-country).

The SW flank could be done from Dream Lake (3451 ft) by ascending NE from its W end to Smith Lake (4800 ft), and then NE to the summit. Reach Dream Lake by ascending cross-country up Big Creek, off the Taylor River Road ◆ at about ¾ mi. W of its end. A technical route has been done on the 800-ft wall near the Snoqualmie Lake outlet by Steve Brien and Bruce Garrett in August 1971 (four leads; class 5.6). Reference: *Mountaineer*, 1971, pp. 75-76.

GOAT MOUNTAIN
5560 ft + /1695 m +
A very gently-sloping but rather individual mountain located between Lennox and Sunday creeks, about 5 mi. SW of Lennox Mountain. While largely forested, Goat has extensive open upper slopes.

ROUTES: One could readily make the ascent from the Sunday Creek Trail ◆ at about the 2-mi. point. Hike cross-country up the easy W slopes.

One could leave from near the end of the Lennox Creek Road ◆, where it makes an elbow into the valley of Cougar Creek, in Section 27.

An old trail led about 1 mi. along Cougar Creek (probably overgrown); one could ascend to Goat Mountain Lake and easy upper slopes. Then ascend W to the upper area.

LENNOX MOUNTAIN
5894 ft/1797 m
Lennox is a massive locally-high formation extending NW-SE for about 1 mi.; it is located at about 7 mi. S of

LENNOX MOUNTAIN from west
U.S. GEOLOGICAL SURVEY

Baring on the Money Creek-North Fork Snoqualmie and West Fork Miller River divide. Rock is Snoqualmie batholith. Coney Lake (5161 ft) rests on a rocky open low-gradient slope high on the E side of Lennox; Lake Kanim (3941 ft) is SW of the mountain. The polished cirque floor of Goat Basin is an unusual example of a well developed low-level cirque.

Lennox was climbed by a party under H. B. Hinman in May 1915, using a northern route. Reference: *Mountaineer,* 1915, pp. 83-84.

NORTHWEST ROUTE: Approach from North Fork Snoqualmie River Road ◆. A spur road (not driveable) can be hiked eastward to Bare Mountain Trail. Ascend E up steep timber N of the North Fork (1½ hours) to the NW ridge of Lennox. Traverse SSE, keeping on the left side of the ridge. The summit can be reached in 4 hours, despite the long upper ridge. The trail is in good condition at present.

SOUTHEAST ROUTE: See Cascade Mountain. At about 3 mi. up the W fork road (about 2000 ft) a trail (condition unknown) leads to a mine near the 3100 ft level (about 1.7 mi.). Ascend a gully to bedrock at Coney Lake, then ascend westward to the SE summit. The area is open and attractive, the ascent merely a hike.

SOUTHWEST ROUTE: Take Lennox Creek Road (see North Fork Snoqualmie River Road ◆) about 3 mi. to where an old spur leads E to Bare Mountain Trail (about 2100 ft altitude). Follow the trail to a fork at about 3560 ft; take the lower trail to the basin of Bear Creek. A fisherman's trail climbs past mining relics and along the left side of a waterfall to Bear Lake (possibly brushy). Ascend N to the ridge saddle (5320 ft+), then skirt the N flank of Point 5706. Continue NE along the mile-long ridge to the SE summit of Lennox (5695 ft); a largely level and easy crest continues 0.3 mi. to the true summit.

MOUNT PHELPS   5535 ft/1687 m

The rounded hump of Mount Phelps can be seen from the Seattle area. It is a rocky peak, though scrub trees grow almost everywhere amid outcrops, which are steep except on the S. Maps currently call the summit "McClain Peaks." The Webster Brown map of 1897 labels the mountain as Phelps (see L. K. Hodges, *Mining in the Pacific Northwest*).

First ascent by Laurence D. Byington, J. B. Spellar, and Harry Morgan on August 14, 1932.

SOUTH ROUTE: Take the North Fork Snoqualmie River Road ◆, then fork on Road No. 5736 for about 1 mi. to an old log dump (2650 ft). Follow the abandoned roadway on the right to the old Blackhawk mine, located on the N side of the stream draining the basin between Phelps and Lower Phelps. A trail ascends the ridge here. At 3800 ft, below rock outcrops, traverse left into the basin. Cross, staying below 4200 ft to the opposite ridge, then ascend the ridge, traversing rightward to the summit. Note: In spring there is

MOUNT PHELPS from east
JOHN V.A.F. NEAL

Little Phelps

MT. PHELPS

NORTH FORK SNOQUALMIE RIVER

LAKE KANIM

avalanche potential high in the basin. Under good snow conditions one can climb directly by the narrow chute from the basin, then traverse left onto steep snow to the summit. Time: 4 hours.

LITTLE PHELPS   5162 ft/1573 m
This summit, labeled "Phelps" on maps, is located 1 mi. SW of Phelps' true summit. The rocky peak has a hornlike shape (the summit sheers off on the N). One could climb it by ascending ½ mi. to the SW from the saddle area; rocky places on the final NW side force the route around to the S.

RED MOUNTAIN
(Mount Rudderham)   5576 ft/1700 m
The correct summit is located 1 mi. N of Lake Elizabeth, between Money Creek and branches of Index Creek. The summit marked "Red" on recent maps (5447 ft) is 1½ mi. westward, on the edge of the City of Seattle watershed. The 1923 edition of the Sultan quadrangle placed the name lettering midway between the summits. The 1897 Webster Brown map inscribes the highest peak as Rudderham.
ROUTES: Reach by ascending N from Money Creek Road ◆ closely E of Lake Elizabeth (some shrubs). Semi-open forest travel leads to just left of the rocky upper portion of the mountain; no technical difficulties. Time: 4 hours. The western summit could be reached by a ridge traverse.

MOUNT CROSBY   5520 ft+/1683 m+
Crosby is a largely forested peak with a rocky summit, located N of upper Money Creek and about 6 mi. W of Skykomish. The summit is at the NW end of the massif. Pinnacles on the summit ridge offer climbing. First ascent unknown; first winter ascent by Ralph James and Hermann F. Ulrichs in 1932.
SOUTH ROUTE: Take Money Creek Road ◆ about 6 mi., about ¼ mi. past second road switchback. Ascend forest just E of the creek draining the slopes of Crosby, then bear for an area of dead timber and grassy slopes (this appears as summit from below; keep right of rocky spur.)
SOUTH ROUTE: Leave the road about ½ mi. after the second switchback (est. 2500 ft), then follow the main streambed. Bypass a 100-ft waterfall on its left. Ascend the stream course (several class 3 pitches) to a basin at 4400 ft, then ascend to the 5000-ft crest W of the summit. Very little brush reported on this route. Time: 5 hours.
NORTHEAST ROUTE: From Money Creek Camp on U.S. Hwy No. 2 ◆, cross the road bridge and take Lowe Creek Road No. 6030 westward about 2½ mi. An old road built into Lowe Creek drainage to access mining claims (now abandoned and overgrown) can be hiked to beyond a switchback at about 2200 ft. Ascend the timbered shoulder of Crosby, then follow the ridge SW to the summit (some brush).

PALMER MOUNTAIN
5043 ft/1537 m

Largely wooded with some rocky points on summit ridges; located about 1 mi. N of Mount Crosby, and 2 mi. W of South Fork Skykomish River.
EAST SHOULDER: Hike the old logging road into Lowe Creek drainage (see Mount Crosby) to about 2600 ft (about 2 mi.); then ascend cross-country on the wooded E ridge of Palmer about 1 mi. to the summit. A rocky step must be passed near the top. Note: Lowe Creek Road is a forest road on the E end to Lowe Creek (bridge at creek crossing washed out). W of the creek, the road is on private land. Logging spurs E of Index Creek that offer possible entry to the N flank of Palmer are on private land.

MOUNT CLEVELAND
5287 ft/1612 m

Because of its proximity to the Skykomish River Valley, Mount Cleveland is a good regional viewpoint; its summit was once the site of a fire lookout. The mountain is easily approached, but one would have to hike an unused logging road (No. 6422) switchbacking S in Section 32, from about 1 mi. up Money Creek Road ◆. Currently one can drive the first mi. — on the flat. From the last clearcut hike to the ridge, then SW to the summit.

MOUNT INDEX   5979 ft/1822 m
Because of their public prominence, the Index peaks need little introduction. The three striking peaks, in descending progression the Main, Middle, and North, form a spectacular rock palisade between Lake Serene and Anderson Creek fronting the Skykomish River. The opposite slope, facing the Tolt River drainage, is seldom seen by comparison.

The romance of the Index area is derived from the achievements and mishaps of the prospectors who explored the area's rough subalpine slopes. Miners termed the mountain massif "West Index"; railroad surveyors had used the name Mount Index for the present Mount Baring, but in 1913 the name was transferred.

Of the three Index peaks, only the Main Peak has a relatively simple route. Index rock is brittle and hard, a metamorphosed gabbro that is massive and foliated. The Mount Index batholith that forms the Index Town Wall terminates near the altitude of Lake Serene.

The nearness of the peaks to civilization has con-

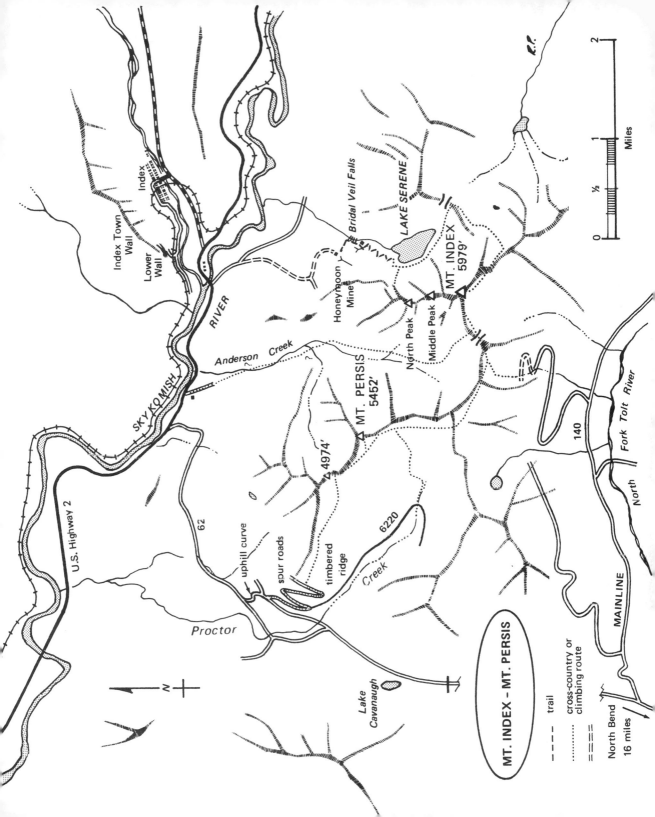

MT. INDEX – MT. PERSIS

trail
cross-country or climbing route

North Bend
16 miles

NORTH PEAK

North Rib

North Face

notch

crossing

East Face

1971

1971

False Summit

Winter 1978

MIDDLE PEAK

East Face Route

notch

North Norwegian Buttress

Wedge Gendarme

South Norwegian Buttress

MAIN PEAK

tributed to accidents; there have been falls from rock faces in summer and steep snow gullies in winter. The low-level cliffs above Lake Serene are an invitation to a slip from the slopes above, and the difficult travel near the lake has led to tragedy.

MAIN PEAK

The spectacular portion of the Main Peak is the great eastern cliff above Lake Serene, which features the Norwegian Buttresses. The N face above and below the Middle-Main Peak notch is very steep, and corrugated with ribs and chimneys.

Since goats have often been seen near the summit, they should be credited for the first ascent. Mount Index lacked a documented human history until October 29, 1911, when H. B. Hinman, Ernest Martin, Lee Pickett, and George E. Wright, ascending from Anderson Creek, found a flagpole on the summit (*Mountaineer Bull.,* November 1911, pp. 1-2). Probably the first climb via the normal Lake Serene Route was made by Charles K. Browne and Leo Gallagher, who made the ascent on August 31, 1924. A winter climb was made by Cecil Bailey, Stan Jensen, and Jim Pritchard in 1963, possibly the first in that season.

The upper N face was climbed at the end of the long alpine traverse from the North and Middle peaks by Fred Beckey and Pete Schoening on August 13, 1950 (see Middle Peak for route description). The first winter traverse was made by Larry Cooper, Mike Marshall, Don Page, and Byron Robertson during January 29-30, 1977.

EAST ROUTE: At Lake Serene (see Lake Serene Trail ◆) skirt the W side (start by rough rising path), then ascend rockslides SE; keep just above and right of the saddle (3040 ft) SE of the lake. Follow just right of center of brushy and rocky ridge crest SW to where it broadens at 4000 ft, and then bear left below rock cliffs about ¼ mi. to obvious gully to summit ridge. (Note: There may be snow moats and large schrund at 5400 ft in the gully; in late summer it may be impassable without technical climbing.) Watch for cornices in spring and early summer. Mount a ridge, then pass left of two rock masses while ascending NW to the summit. Time: 5 hours from lake. Reference: *A.A.J.,* 1948, pp. 92-93.

SOUTHWEST ROUTE: (From North Fork of Tolt River) This has road closure problems, but a short route; advised for May or June. Proctor Creek Road ◆ is the shortest approach. Also see Snoqualmie Tree Farm Roads ◆. Ascend through slash at 2800 ft, keeping in open timber and left of creek. Stay first below and to the right of the first sharp ridge at about 4400 ft (it directs toward the southernmost point of the Index-Persis ridge); then traverse right up to a low point on ridge ahead (5100 ft) from which the summit can be seen.

Drop 250 ft to a saddle and ascend the W ridge about

1200 ft to the summit. Some scrambling (class 3) and some moderately steep snow traverses likely. Time: 5 hours.

ANDERSON CREEK ROUTE: This feasible route, good for early season, is probably the safest on Mount Index. There is some brushy cross-country travel unless there is a good snowpack.

See Anderson Creek Route ◆; beyond the cabins, the old roadway must be hiked (overgrown at times). After crossing Anderson Creek at about 1½ mi., keep on succeeding right branches and follow the stream to near the head of the basin. Ascend gullies on the far W flank of Mount Index. As a variation, one could climb S and reach the ridge connecting Mount Persis. Time: 7 hours. Note: Expect some shrubs and brush travel in the lower basin once the spring snow melts.

NORTH NORWEGIAN BUTTRESS: This very imposing feature on the Index Peaks is separated from the South Norwegian Buttress by the deep cleft leading to the Main-

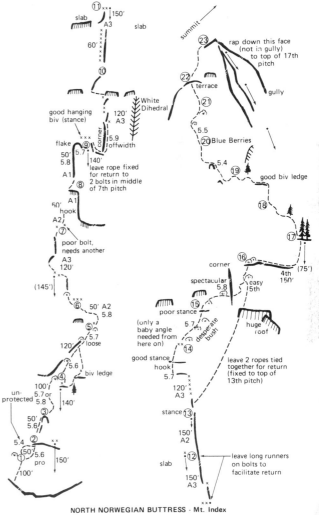

NORTH NORWEGIAN BUTTRESS - Mt. Index

source: Pete Doorish

INDEX PEAKS from east
ED COOPER

Middle Peak notch. The buttress terminates at a prominent sharp wedge high on the E face of the Middle Peak. First ascent by Pete Doorish, Dale Farnham, and Charles Hamson July 15-20, 1985 (with additional earlier route preparation); there were several earlier attempts on this buttress, all frustrated by continuous difficulties and blank sections. There are some loose blocks and sharp corners that can cause rope damage on the climb.

The first four leads reach an obvious brushy ramp leading up and right (up to class 5.8). From its top, the sixth lead works back left to three bolts. Nail up and left, then upward, turning a roof on the eighth pitch. Fifty feet above this (and right) is a semi-hanging belay alcove. Drop down and right, then up an off-width crack to a bolt (5.9). Nail up and leftward to a belay below a bolt ladder. The eleventh pitch turns the overhang above, then there are three long pitches up a dihedral, working left near the end of the fourteenth pitch to reach a good stance. Climb up and right one pitch to a poor stance (5.7). The sixteenth pitch is a spectacular 5.9 traverse rightward around a corner to easier climbing. The seventeenth pitch bears right, then the remaining six pitches work up and back left across the upper face of the buttress to its top. Grade VI; class 5.9 and A3 or A4. Bring a few ¼-inch nuts and hangers, plus tie-off loops. Selection: Friends (one 4-inch, double others), chocks, 12 LA, three bugaboos, two 1½-inch, two 1¼-inch, three 1-inch, three ¾-inch, six baby angles, seven KB's, two rurps, hooks, bashies.

SOUTH NORWEGIAN BUTTRESS: This is the southerly of the great twin elongated, triangular buttresses forming the lower NE face of the mountain. The South Buttress climaxes at a sharp point, then a near-level, narrow arete leads to a gendarme on the N face of the Main Peak — closely S of the Main-Middle Peak notch. The only ascent of this difficult problem was by Eric Bjornstad and Alex Bertulis, when on September 3, 1964 they climbed through the principal difficulties on the South Buttress to the sharp culmination point; they elected not to complete the traverse to a juncture with the Main Peak, but rappelled back to the base.

Approach via the steep snow chute between the South Buttress and the Main Peak walls. Cross the moat, gain the rock, then make a rising right-traverse up steep slabs, behind trees, and through vertical brush patches to a position well above the steep lower cliff and onto the left portion of the wall. Ascend to the N of a chimney (class 5.4, brushy) to where the steep wall forces a leftward traverse. Aid around a detached flake; the traverse (mixed aid and free on brittle rock) reaches an exposed belay (straddle a pinnacle); 150 ft, A3.

The following crux pitch (A4) has some poor protection and ends in a sustained 5.7 overhanging jam crack (good belay). Then climb a ramp on the left side of the buttress (some steep brush). Ascend leftward to a sloping bench just S of the final sheer wall (original party bivouac). Climb a maze of gullies and ledges to the culmination point. Grade III or

IV; class 5.7 and A4. Reference: *A.A.J.*, 1966, pp. 129-130.

MIDDLE-MAIN PEAK GULLY: This is the deep gully S of South Norwegian Buttress. First ascent by Fred Dunham and Bill Sumner on January 20, 1984. The route consists of several steep steps separated by lower angle sections. When done in winter these sections were snow and ice; the crux was a 70-ft vertical and overhanging waterfall about midway on the climb. This is a potentially dangerous route, with avalanche hazard in winter and spring, and stonefall at other times. Reference: *A.A.J.*, 1985, p. 186.

MIDDLE PEAK　5440 ft + / 1658 m +

The extremely rugged Middle Peak of Index, so striking from Lake Serene but nearly invisible from the highway to the W because it is slightly recessed from the North Peak, is certainly one of the most inaccessible spots in the Cascade Range. A direct ascent was not made until 1960. Only a very competent team should consider the climb by any route; the consequences of either accident or bad weather could be serious. Warning: After the last accessible snow patches disappear, there is no water on the entire traverse. Take bivouac gear.

The first ascent was by Pete Schoening and Fred Beckey on August 12, 1950 as part of the first "Index Traverse"; an effort a week earlier was halted by weather. The second climb of the Middle Peak was by Ed Cooper on a S-N traverse July 5-6, 1960.

TRAVERSE ROUTE: Begin the North Peak descent over steep and somewhat loose rock. Use the SW corner for about 150 ft, then traverse W into the deep gully below the first horn (rappels can be made). Descend gully to below the second (lower) horn until possible to traverse to the North-Middle Peak notch (4880 ft +). Alternate: one can rappel and down climb the W side of the second horn.

The crux first pitch is on the E corner of the sharp step on the Middle Peak. It is exposed with meager protection (class 5.6 — three pitons used). This is followed by a somewhat easier pitch to the narrow crest of the N ridge. Follow this to the false summit, keeping on or just W of the ridge. One can make a short rappel here, or bypass the top by dropping down slightly and traversing around its E side. Scramble to true summit. Note: snow patches for water may remain on steep heather down on E.

Descend easily to the Middle-Main Peak notch (4960 ft +). Climb a short difficult wall (class 5.5 or 5.6) to the crest of a wedge-gendarme, which is actually a continuation of the South Norwegian Buttress. This is hardest at its base, then bear left to the crest. Follow the sharp wedge's crest to its top. Then make a one-lead descent into minor notch behind it. Work W via a rising crossing and across a steep gully that comes from upper face (class 4). An obvious ledge system leads W under another upper wall. Traverse it around

NW corner. Ledge and heather scrambling bear up and right (easier); scramble SE to the summit. Grade V. Time: Minimum 16 hours total climbing, allowing 6 hours from lake to summit of North Peak. References: *Mountaineer*, 1950, pp. 39-40; 1952, p. 80; *A.A.J.*, 1951, pp. 175-176; 1961, pp. 363-364.

Variation: Descent from North Peak: Scramble W down to first pointed horn. Make a short steep rappel. Downclimb and traverse on W face, then two rappels to notch (bypass no. 2 horn on W).

Variation: North-Middle Peak Notch: Ascend up and right (N corner). Class 5.7 with poor protection (1967 party).

WEST FACE: An exposed wall of about 2800 vertical ft of precipitous rock, much of its lower portions brush-covered. The several ribs patterning the wall tend to veer to the right. The climb is long and arduous; a bivouac should be anticipated. The first ascent was made by Fred Beckey and Don (Claunch) Gordon on June 12, 1960.

From Anderson Creek (see Main Peak, Anderson Creek Route) climb a sharp and steep wooded ridge on the S extremity of the North Peak for about 600 ft. Then work right to another ridge and the main gully separating the North and Middle peaks. Stay on crest of brushy ridge right of gully until forced right on a section of loose, reddish rock. From a sub-rib climb left on a steep friable wall (class 5) to another bushy ridge crest; this is a jungly, vertical and difficult pitch. Eventually this merges into a face with a long rock gully (with a big wall to right). Keep in gully (which hits a snow patch and a few small trees) except on the last lead, which is done to left, ending in a tree clump.

On the final slabby rock wall (leading to notch NW of false summit) ascend a slab wall left of a deep chimney. Continue slabby climbing to the ridge curving to the false summit. Grade III or IV; class 5. Time: 11 hours from road. Descent: either use same route, or climb on via North or Main Peak. References: *Mountaineer*, 1961, pp. 102-103; *A.A.J.*, 1961, p. 363.

NORTH FACE: This route climbs the E face gully between the North and Middle peaks. Route by Doug Klewin and Dan McNerthney in December 1978, climbing the entire route on snow and ice. The route began in the gully, then climbed the face toward the Middle Peak's summit; the climb could be subject to rockfall and otherwise questionable except in good winter conditions. The party traversed to the Main Peak (two bivouacs). Reference: *A.A.J.*, 1981, p. 172.

EAST FACE: The wall above Lake Serene, about 2500 ft in height, was first ascended by Ed Cooper and Eric Bjornstad on August 18 and 19, 1961; they completed the climb to the Main Peak, making the second of two bivouacs on its N face. Allow a full day or more to the top of the Middle Peak.

From talus slopes, scramble up the S edge of E face of North Peak, then two class 5 pitches to reach the deep couloir between the North and Middle peaks (stay alert for rockfall).

Cross the couloir and then ascend rock buttress to left. Climb into a secondary couloir on the left and then traverse out onto the main buttress crest (the portion after the deep couloir involves some 600 ft of brushy, but easy-to-moderate rock). Attempt to keep to the main buttress/rib: a 140-ft vertical step on the rib (which drops off on both flanks) is difficult, with brittle rock, poor cracks — some aid. The original party bivouacked on alternating sloping ledges.

At 500 ft higher, reach giant steps and towers on the rib. Pass the first 300 ft tower on the right, and while regaining the far notch, climb a quite difficult aid pitch (loose). Another tower is bypassed on the right (this portion includes a delicate traverse). Regain the crest, then climb the final 500 ft to the summit (class 4). Grade V; class 5.7 and A3 (hardware should include KB's). References: *Mountaineer*, 1962, pp. 97-98; *Summit*, September 1962, pp. 10-11; *A.A.J.*, 1962, pp. 203-204.

NORTH PEAK   5357 ft/1633 m

The North Peak is the most legendary of the Index trio, and rightly so. Located ½ mi. N of the Main Peak, it rises in a sheer rock wall from the 2800-ft level of the Lake Serene cirque, from even lower on the N and W, where three main ribs and numerous steep gullies rise from the basin of Anderson Creek. A deep and knifed notch connects the North Peak to the Middle Peak. The actual summit is a massive pointed rock spire. On its N is a wedge with small horns. South of the summit is no. 1 horn (small and pointed) at about 150 ft below summit level. Then about 100 ft S at the same level is the giant no. 2 horn (it has a steep S face dropping to Middle-North Peak notch).

Because of their visibility to the highway and railroad, the Index peaks have captured the imagination of the public. In particular the diminutive yet formidable North Peak has come to embody the savagery of the Cascades. Its climbing demands effort and route-finding skill. The lower section has some brushy rock, but is not really unpleasant if dry; the three leads on the upper N rib are enjoyable and exposed. It is a climb for good judgment, weather, and a team in good condition: it should be remembered that there is no quick descent in case of poor weather; rain will start stonefall. Bushes and small trees are generally reliable for protection — often more useful than pitons or chocks. Be prepared for a bivouac on this climb.

Lionel Chute, a climber rather unknown to his contemporaries, persevered through four attempts in two years before making the first ascent with Victor Kaartinen of Boy Scout Troop 263 in 1929. During the successful ascent they only had a 40-ft manila rope, which nearly broke after being cast over a rock horn

False Summit of Middle Peak   MIDDLE PEAK   MAIN PEAK

NORTH PEAK →

Traverse Route

North Rib

Climb Behind Buttress

Wedge Gendarme

1946 →

Gendarme

North Face

West Face

and then hand-climbed. Apparently Chute's verbal account was not widely accepted and the party that had a near-fatality on July 11, 1937 hoped to make the first ascent. Joe Halwax, Scott Osborn, and Stanley King were within 600 ft of the summit when Halwax took a 60-ft leader fall and suffered a broken leg; fortunately he was held by the rope snubbed around a rock. In an unprecedented rescue, nineteen Forest Service men and Index loggers worked all night to evacuate him. In 1940 Otto Trott and Erick Larson reached the summit to find proof of Chute's climb. The third ascent, the first without a bivouac, was made by Fred and Helmy Beckey on July 1, 1945. The first winter ascent was made by Patrik Callis and Dan Davis between January 3 and 6, 1963. References: *A.A.J.*, 1946, pp. 43-44; *Off Belay*, October 1979, pp. 10-12.

NORTH FACE: This, the original route and the one followed by all but a few of the parties to reach the summit, actually begins from a broken, bushy spur on the NE, which rises from a wooded ridge above Lake Serene. The route stays on NNE exposure, rather than true N until reaching the upper N rib.

From the rockslide on the W side of Lake Serene, ascend talus and grass slopes leading to the NE spur. Begin by scrambling several hundred ft on the brushy spur to the first slab. Keep just right of the crest to the base of a vertical face. Ascend left sharply and then to the crest on the left. Climb an exposed corner pitch and traverse left 15 ft to a gully just above a sheer wall. Climb about 50 ft up a rock bowl, then cut sharply right (behind a block) around the skyline via a hidden ledge. The ledge traverse develops into an exposed slab (has a short section of small holds). Round a corner to the base of a steep, brushy, shallow gully. Turn up it and climb two leads to the slanting ramp system which bears right about 400 ft to the large open basin on the true N face (may have snow to mid-season). Ascend (either snow or rock) for three-four leads up the right-curving, steep gully rising above the left side of the basin. Note: when free of snow it is made more difficult by slabby rock (hard to protect), can be marginal when wet.

As the gully ends, ascend a broad, right-slanting ramp to the sharp N rib. Ascend it for three leads (first two leads are class 5.5 on solid, exposed rock) to an open grassy bench (end of rib). Follow it left around corner toward the E face. The bench ends abruptly at a prominent gully leading up-face. Ascend this, largely scrubs and brush for 100 ft. When it forks, follow left branch through larger trees for two leads to a steep heather slope just below the crest. Follow the crest right on easy rock to the first false summit. Following a little depression climb SW to the second point, then drop 50 ft to avoid a cliff. Final summit is done by heather and broken rock on its N side. Grade III; class 4-5.6. Time: 6-8 hours

up; 5 down. References: *A.A.J.*, 1946, p. 43; *Mountaineer,* 1946, p. 44.

Variation: On the lower portion of the climb, from the "hidden ledge" ascend a steep rock wall to a large hanging brush patch. Imitate a gorilla through the brush and bear right along the oblique slab and ramp system several hundred ft to the open basin.

Variation: Ascend the headwall of the "rock bowl" to the next ledge system (a slower option; class 5.5 with poor protection). Then work right to N-face basin.

Variation on North Rib: From the "open basin" on the N face, make a rising traverse (right) to the N rib. Gain the crest and ascend it directly. The final obstacle is a near-vertical gendarme, which is ascended directly (good rock). This variation is steep and exposed, with enjoyable rock, but not difficult.

Variation: By Wesley Grande and Jack Kendrick on August 2, 1947. From the rock bowl climb brushy rock to a gully. Climb to the base of a small gendarme; possibly climb a gully behind. Ascend mossy, dirty ledges on a face, bearing somewhat right. The face is wide at first, then narrows. The route description is not well recalled. The ascent and descent on the original was made unroped, and as a route this is likely more difficult than the normal route.

EAST FACE: This 2200-ft face was one of the early "big problems" solved in the Cascades. It is a major undertaking, a route of character with continual exposure, consecutive pitches, often with poor protection because piton or chock cracks are scarce. Rock is variable in soundness, ranging from solid to shattered; there can be some stonefall.

The first climb was completed in one day, but had the benefit of some ropes and previous reconnaissance; about ten pitons were used and many runners on the vegetation. Small bushes eliminate aid in some spots. First ascent by Fred Beckey, Richard Berge, Jim Henry, and Pete Schoening on July 1, 1951. The second ascent was not made until May 31, 1967 by Chris Chandler, Dan Petersen, Heinz Graupe, and Mike Berman.

Scramble the standard route on the NE corner for about 300 ft, then work left to a sloping ramp. Two exposed leads reach a shallow open book (protection bolt at its lower left; thin climbing with poor protection for about 50 ft, class 5.7). A continuing section (knobby rib) is hard but clean; climb slightly left on rounded, brushy steps to a headwall. After climbing a chimney, traverse S. Gain 100 ft by a narrow brushy gully, then climb a headwall with face climbing and a difficult leftward traverse made possible by overhead hanging brush (class 5.7) to the top of a step (several variations have been done on this section). One should reach a rib near midface, parallel to the deep canyon to the S. Climb the rib, then a right-slanting mossy slab/ramp system to an outcrop on the canyon edge (moderate climbing). Traverse left around a corner to the left arm of an obvious "V" formation.

This arm is a steep ramp/dihedral (just left of the great wall that makes up the main part of the face) that bears

INDEX PEAKS from northwest
ED COOPER

Photo labels: MIDDLE PEAK, NORTH PEAK, Gendarme Notch, West Face

NORTH and MIDDLE PEAKS of MOUNT INDEX from northwest
TOM MILLER

slightly left for three-four pitches. Many tree and shrub runners are used, as cracks are scarce; several of belays straddle small trees on overhangs. When the dihedral ends there is a steep, loose reddish wall and slab that bears to the edge of a great ramp (est. 700 ft below summit). Follow the rising ramp northward nearly to a corner with trees. Ascend a brushy hidden and slanting crack/chimney (maximum class 5.7) that leads to a grassy platform in 200 ft.

Here are two alternatives. (1) Climb a series of ledges and cracks (some trees), then a buttress. A blind traverse right takes one across a crux. Then bushes and rock pitches: there is an 80-degree moss pitch and an open gully bearing to a meadow patch on the N ridge near the summit (1941). (2) Angle left through a cliff (possible waterfall) and up a brushy

gully. At a key final bush (hand over hand) bear right on a ledge, then take a rib as rock gets easier and grassier near false summit (1967). Grade IV; class 5.7. Selection: an assortment of 12 pitons, including KB, chocks and wire stoppers; many tie-off loops and runners (1941 used runners about 50 times). Time: minimum one long day for ascent; allow ½ day descent. References: *Mountaineer,* 1952, pp. 80-81; *A.A.J.,* 1952, pp. 344-345; *Appalachia,* June 1952, pp. 77-79; *Challenge of the North Cascades,* pp. 175-186.

SOUTHEAST BUTTRESS: The buttress forms the left flank of the E face. First ascent by Garrett Gardner and Bill Lingley in August 1971. From Lake Serene angle up and left to gain the buttress, then climb upward for about eighteen pitches, generally keeping right of the crest. Near the top it is necessary to traverse left for two leads before continuing upward for another three leads. Here the climb joins the normal route's final three leads. About ⅓ of the route is class 5, with much of the terrain brushy class 4 (one short section of aid). Grade IV; class 5.7 and A2.

WEST FACE: This is a long, remarkable route with continual exposure. Problems are similar to those of the East Face. Brush anchors supplement occasional piton usage. First ascent by Don (Claunch) Gordon and Pete Schoening on July 5, 1954.

Take Anderson Creek Road ◆ to crossing of the creek. Follow overgrown logging spurs to a point near the base of the peak's NW corner (spurs may be difficult to find). Traverse through brush, then timber, for about ¼ mi. to the base of the W face. Ascend, bearing to the main ridge on the face nearest the North-Middle Peak couloir. Climb steep brush and cliffs, then work left to open brush/trees. First party made a bivouac in trees about ⅓ distance to the summit.

Ascend steep brush to an intermediate rock ridge that traverses up-right; here is end of brush except for anchor bushes. Ascend ridge that starts to right, but curves left and becomes sensationally narrow. At one spot the route enters a narrow chasm. Exposed stemming-chimneying leads toward the top of a prominent gendarme (about 500 ft below summit); descend its opposite side about 50 ft to a wide ledge. Work S to bypass a vertical wall, then climb a steep broken face. Climb to a notch in the crest S of the summit. Grade IV; class 4 and 5. Time: allow 1-1½ days for ascent and descent. References: *Mountaineer,* 1954, p. 62; *A.A.J.,* 1955, pp. 150-151.

MOUNT PERSIS   5452 ft/1662 m

Persis, a forested mountain with large rock cliffs facing the Skykomish River valley and located 2 mi. NW of Mount Index, is named for the wife of Amos Gunn, the pioneer Index settler and prospector. The massive rock on Mount Persis is composed of andesite flows, tuffs, and breccia, combined with sandstones and conglomerate. It is a hard rock that forms resistant cliffs. Recent logging roads extending high on the mountain's W slope have changed the environment and shortened the ascent. The first ascent was made by Harry B. Hinman and party in 1917, or earlier. References: *102 Hikes,* 1st ed.; *Snowshoe Hikes.*

WEST RIDGE: Follow Proctor Creek Road ◆ about 3½ mi., then hike the lesser left fork about 1½ mi. Keep left again to reach the highest clearcut on the W ridge. The summit is some distance, but there are no technical difficulties. Note: logging may change the nature of the spur roads.

SOUTHWEST ROUTE: Take the approach road as per West Ridge, but follow logging road (No. 6220) into Proctor Creek to where it crosses the creek at the sharp hairpin. Ascend upstream about ⅓ mi. to a narrow chasm 50 yards before reaching a waterfall. Exit left on a short class 4 rock wall, then traverse N several hundred yards. Angle right and go up ledges that lead to a large basin SW of the summit of Persis. Keep right in the basin and ascend to the S ridge. This is an easy and scenic route.

Ascend the steep timbered W ridge of Mount Persis to the 4974-ft NW summit. Cross and descend S to a minor saddle, then hike the meadowed ridge crest eastward to the true summit. Time: 3 hours.

A traverse to Mount Index can be made: generally follow the crest or slightly down on the S flank to avoid minor outcrops and obstructions. The lowest areas on the traverse are about ½ mi. S of the summit of Mount Persis (est. 4800 ft) and at the southern head of Anderson Creek (est. 4880 ft).

"The highest peaks of the range, Tacoma, Adams, and Baker, rear dazzling summits of perpetual snow into the firmament. These magnificent peaks have an apparent altitude much greater than that of the highest Alps, from the fact that they are seen from the sea level towering above the forests and reflected on the calm waters of the Sound."
EUGENE V. SMALLEY, 1883
History of the Northern Pacific Railroad

SECTION IV

North-Central Cascades (East Side)

CLE ELUM TO STEVENS PASS

GEOGRAPHY

The Wenatchee Mountains, a major subrange with summits higher than most west flank Cascade peaks, extend eastward 50 mi. from the Cascade Crest and separate the Yakima and Wenatchee River drainage basins. Their monarch is Mount Stuart, the second-highest non-volcanic peak in the state of Washington, standing well above the regional alpine summit accordance and 15 mi. east of the Cascade Crest. George Otis Smith described the Wenatchee Mountains in U.S.G.S. Professional Paper No. 19 as "a secondary range in the general trend of the Cascades, but are characterized by the same rugged topography. The mountain crests are deeply carved into spires and crags, while precipitous slopes descend into glacial amphitheatres where remnants of glaciers still persist."[56] Captain George B. McClellan of the Corps of Engineers observed the mountains from the vicinity of Yakima Pass: "I saw the rough mountains in which the Pisquouse heads . . ."[57] George Gibbs, with the Pacific Railroad exploration in 1853, referred to "the craggy sierra of the Cascades" in contrast to the mountains west. Noting a change in geologic character here, he commented, "sharp peaks, rising singly or in groups, some of which seem to be the skeletons of mountains."[58]

The exploration's topographer Lt. Johnson K. Duncan, while near the Yakima-Columbia divide, observed "a sharp angular range of snow mountains is seen off to the left of the trail . . . Mount Stuart is the most prominent." This impressive and dominating mountain, which rises to over 9400 ft, is the second highest non-volcanic summit in the Cascade Range and possibly the largest single granitic mountain in the United States.

Landscape diversity is the main characteristic of the Wenatchee Mountains. The region's unique characteristics include deep U-shaped valleys, picturesque rock spires and massive peaks, steep-walled cirques, small glaciers, rock-basin lakes, and alpine meadows culminating in a spare tree cover of alpine larch. Much of the high country is barren, with perennial snow-banks and little soil. Frost-wedging on headwalls and rocky spurs has left extensive talus; some of these rock fields extend from ridges to heavily forested valley bottoms.

The high peaks were first mentioned by David Thompson on July 7, 1811 as "high rocky mountains to the south-west" (Tyrrell, p. 48). The noted geologist, Israel C. Russell, called the area centering around Mount Stuart the "Wenache Mountains"[59] in 1897, and described results of weathering, which "produced numerous tapering pinnacles and spires . . . . The light color of the naked granite gives the precipices and crags a seemingly white color when seen from a distance."

Indeed the amazing array of light-hued spires informally called the "Cashmere Crags" everywhere overlook the polished granite basins, brilliantly clear lakes, and gnarled trees that decorate this isolated upland now popularly known as the "Lost World Plateau." Erosional surfaces such as "Edward Plateau" and "Dragontail Plateau" seem misplaced among the spires and jagged peaks of the Stuart Range. The upland is reminiscent of ancient felsenmeer-mantled surfaces of the Wind River Range. In some places converging glacial cirques have divided surfaces, creating precipitous walls and serrate crests; some crests (such as Pennant Peak) are associated with this accordance and not remote from them.

Russell did not overlook a unique slope of this upland, "the precipitous granitic escarpment bordering Ingalls Creek on the north." He added "it is so slightly trenched by gorges that the heavy snows of the glacial period, like those of the modern winters, must have fallen in large part as avalanches."[60] Though the entire Stuart Range was extensively glaciated, it is now in about the same condition as when the last of the Ice Age glaciers departed. One of the most marvelous examples of an ice-sculptured wilderness in the Cascade Range is the Enchantment Lakes Basin on this upland.

Though Russell did not mention the system of some fourteen lakes, he described this region in detail. Four miles east of Mount Stuart he examined a glacier, one of four small ones he observed. It "lies like a blanket on the broad surface of the mountain top at a elevation of between 8000 and 8500 feet, but slopes eastward . . . the waters formed by its melting descend a steep glaciated slope of bare granite and supply the Twin Lakes" (i.e., Snow Lakes).[61]

The ice, now called Snow Creek Glaciers, is a post-Ice Age body with an area of ¾ mi.[2] (about 7000 ft wide) melted into five separate patches of ice from the slope of Little Annapurna to Dragontail Peak; ice exists on the cirque floor from 7700 ft to a maximum altitude of 8600 ft (the highest mean altitude — 2493 m — of any glacier in the North Cascades). A horseshoe-shaped and relatively unweathered recession moraine extends near Brynhild Lake at the foot of one ice section; the moraine may be less than a century in age. A study has shown glaciers in this area have decreased 40 percent during the first half of this century.

Most glaciated valleys of the Wenatchee Mountains head in cirques now devoid of ice, but some modern glaciers lie in sheltered recesses beneath steep north-facing headwalls. The most prominent glaciers are the Stuart, Ice Cliff, Sherpa, and Colchuck. Small glaciers in protected cirques exist below the regional snowline on the flanks of the Chiwaukum Mountains. The largest rock glacier lies in a high cirque on the northwest flank of Mount Stuart; it terminates as an elongate tongue of coarse rubble nearly 3000 ft long, which has advanced into a moraine-dammed lake. Topographically, as elsewhere in the Cascades, the Wenatchee Mountains are largely a function of bedrock structure and lithology, which also plays a role in the orientation of cirques. Underlain by granitic and metamorphic rocks, cirques have distinct bedrock thresholds that impound tarns. But in more erodible sedimentary-rock terrain, cirque floors tend to erode away from headwalls and lack closed depressions.

A striking geomorphic feature of many ridge flanks of the Wenatchee Mountains is a magnificent array of well-developed and for the most part ice-abandoned cirques, many in tandem. The significance of the cirque sequence lies in an apparently close relationship between cirque floor elevations and mean freezing levels (elevations of maximum snowfall) during sequential stages of the Wisconsinan. The frequency distribution of these abandoned cirques suggests that their levels relate to a former regional snowline.

The mean altitude of ice-free cirques through this section of the Cascades lies some 1600 ft below the mean altitude of existing small glaciers. An impressive glacial feature of the area is the well-preserved lateral moraine that begins where the Leavenworth Glacier debouched from the mouth of Icicle Canyon (the moraine abuts the south side of the canyon mouth and then sweeps east and north in an arc to Leavenworth — like a railroad embankment). Evidence points to three successive Pleistocene glaciations, each less extensive than the preceding.

Many of the other cirques in the Wenatchee Mountains head tributaries of Icicle Creek. Icicle Creek, in one of the deepest valleys in the Cascades (a narrow U-shaped trough over 6000 ft deep), emerges from cirques near the Cascade Crest to flow across the Mount Stuart batholith. It emerges from Icicle Canyon at the base of the fault scarp to meander across the flat Leavenworth basin, joining the Wenatchee River at the mouth of the Tumwater Canyon.

Ingalls Creek is deeply excavated and for most of its length has a well defined U-shape in profile. The ice streams that once fed it by spilling down steep troughs have left low headwalls; these all show scouring and the lichen-trimline. All five southern tributaries to Ingalls Creek head in cirques whose floors lie between 5600 and 6200 ft.

Throughout this section, small steep-gradient fans of angular debris at the mouths of small tributaries are differentiated from the more gently graded valley floor alluvium of the trunk streams. In formerly glaciated valleys such as Ingalls Creek, late glacial fans typically coalesce into continuous aprons along lower slopes of the valley. An unusual, winding gorge cut by the Wenatchee River, Tumwater Canyon, displays hard granitic rocks behind a foreground of soft sandstones (the Chumstick Formation). At the base of the Wenatchee Mountains near Tumwater Canyon is the Leavenworth fault line scarp.

Gullies which are the geomorphic effects of snow avalanches are particularly well displayed on the southern walls of Mount Stuart and also in Tumwater Canyon and other deeply-incised valleys such as Ingalls, Mountaineer, and the South Fork Chiwaukum creeks in this region. At the downslope ends of scores of chutes in bedrock on valley walls are tongue-shaped deposits of rubble called avalanche boulder tongues.

One of the most striking features of the Stuart Range are the abundant fingerlike avalanche tracks that reach from the forest line down to elevations as low as 4500 ft. Most of the tracks head in bedrock chutes and widen downslope through alp slopes and the forest terrain. They are often brush-filled at the lower altitudes. Piles of dirty snow and freshly broken

ENCHANTMENT LAKES BASIN near the outlet of Rune Lake
ED COOPER

trees are common at the downslope ends of these tracks, to indicate that avalanches have run down them nearly every year. The non-forested tracks have few trees growing in them and are covered dominantly by grasses and shrubs. Because of frequent winter and spring snow avalanches, many nearby trees have their tops sheared off. Large snow avalanches that extend to valley bottoms sometimes impact the trees on the opposite slope so violently with wind blast that they are broken, with their trunks or tops pointed upslope.

The forested tracks are covered with young, living trees and are outlined by distinct trimlines that separate them from the adjacent older forest. Such forested tracks can be seen at a number of locations in the Wenatchee Mountains, as well as elsewhere in the North Cascades. The floors of the forested tracks are littered with broken trees, whose tops generally point downslope; these tracks are the result of infrequent avalanches that run into the forest.

Western white pine *(Pinus monticola),* Ponderosa pine *(Pinus ponderosa),* and Douglas fir *(Pseudotsuga menziesii)* grow in relatively open stands on the broad valley floors. A typical valley is upper Ingalls Creek, where the north-facing slopes have dense tree stands; the south-facing slopes contain meadows and scattered brush between strips of trees. The dominant trees near the forest line are whitebark pine *(Pinus albicaulis),* subalpine fir *(Abies lasiocarpa),* and Lyall's or alpine larch *(Larix lyallii).* Groves of these specimens can be found magically blended amid meadows and along rocky crests. The rare alpine larch is sometimes found in pure stands on rocky soils. The Engelmann spruce *(Picea engelmannii),* more common in ranges east of the Cascades, also makes its appearance in this section, east of the range crest line.

However, trees often do not occur on ultramafic outcrops, steep talus and exposed ridgetops. Soils derived from ultramafic rocks such as peridotite are typically low in calcium, and this affects plant growth. Serpentine areas are characterized by unusual plant communities and floras. Vegetation is invariably stunted in such sites.

The patterns of vegetation reflect present climatic and soil characteristics and also the legacy of past events. The characteristics of forests and vegetation vary according to the extent of avalanche zones, bedrock outcrops, slope exposure, length of snow-free period, and the texture, depth, and stability of the soil. The water-holding capacity and texture of soils is related to its source — bedrock decomposition or water and glacier transport. Due to cooler tempera-

tures that occur with increasing elevation, the vegetation on the mountain slopes exhibits strong vertical zoning between valleys and the permanent snowline.

The Lost World Plateau hosts a truly unique plant community. Dwarf conifers and miniature plants coexist at the fringe of life zones. Lyall's larch, which in the fall turns a bright gold, grows here. The abundant floral life includes many species of *Erigeron,* phlox, heather, purple saxifrage (which forms pink-flowered mats on slabs), Indian pipe, fireweed, and goldenrod.

There are some 150 species of birds and 50 species of mammals in the Wenatchee Mountains and nearby Alpine Lakes area to the west. Black bear, mule, and blacktail deer are natural, but elk are introduced (herds are in Ingalls and Icicle valleys). The mountain goat may be seen in the high crags.

The prevailing southwesterly winds bring maritime Pacific air; annual precipitation, which falls mostly as snow, is 40 to 80 inches. Clear skies are far more common here than on the west Cascade slopes. Insolation is high; diurnal and seasonal temperature variations show stronger contrast than on the west slopes.

GEOLOGY

The area between the Wenatchee and Yakima rivers and Stevens Pass, which Mount Stuart dominates, embraces a unique and varied terrane of rocks. The base rocks of the area form a structural block between the Leavenworth fault zone and the fault zone of the Cle Elum River. The major depression of the area is the Chiwaukum graben, which includes the town of Leavenworth.

In the early Tertiary, differential uplift and erosion of the older rocks produced basins, and the graben rapidly filled with fluvial rocks of the Swauk, Teanaway, Chumstick and other formations. Deformation and erosion continued until the eruption of Yakima Basalt in Miocene time.

The oldest units in the uplifted block east of the Straight Creek fault are the Chiwaukum Schist (north of Mount Stuart) and the Hawkins Formation. The Hawkins unit, consisting mostly of greenstone, lies to the south and southwest of Mount Stuart.

The Ingalls Tectonic Complex (late Jurassic in age), a wide belt that wraps around the south end of the Mount Stuart batholith, contained the most important of the Blewett gold deposits. The Ingalls belt was thrust over the Chiwaukim Schist, part of the Cascade crystalline core. The metamorphic units (Chiwaukum, Hawkins, Peshastin) were intruded by the

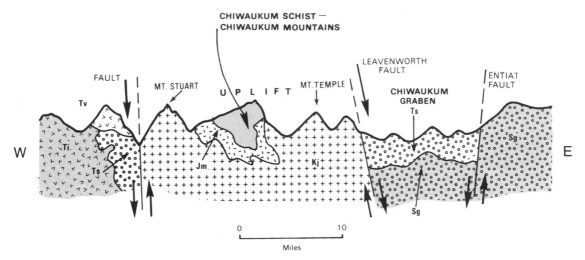

Structure-section across the Mount Stuart batholith and vicinity at approximately 47° 30' N. latitude. Sg = Swakane Gneiss, Kj = Mount Stuart Batholith, Ts = Tertiary sedimentary rocks, Tv = Tertiary volcanic rocks, Jm = Ingalls Tectonic Complex, Ti = Tertiary igneous rocks.

Source: Erikson, E.H., Jr. General Geologic Setting of the Stevens Pass-Leavenworth-Swauk Pass Area. In Brown, E.H., and Ellis, R.C., Geologic Excursions in the Pacific Northwest: Department of Geology, Western Washington University, Bellingham, WA (1977).

Ingalls Complex, which is a batholith of peridotite partly altered to serpentinite, and later deformed and faulted. At Paddy-Go-Easy Pass the Ingalls Complex has been metamorphosed and tectonically mixed. Components of the complex have been recrystallized by the Mount Stuart batholith.

The crowning geologic feature of the region, the Mount Stuart batholith, which is about 13 by 16 mi. in extent, underlies a substantial portion of the Wenatchee Mountains. There are two plutonic masses, separated by a thin screen of Chiwaukum Schist and rocks of the Ingalls Complex. The eastern pluton is dated at about 93 m. y. in age; the western was intruded between 83 and 86 m. y. ago. Where cut by intersecting vertical and horizontal jointing, the rock tends to weather and erode into sawtoothed ridges and monolithic needles. Although quartz diorite predominates, a considerable amount of granodiorite crops out. Of interest to the climber, pegmatite and aplite dikes cut the granodiorite near the summit of Mount Stuart.

This batholithic intrusion thermally metamorphosed the massive serpentinite and serpentinized peridotite of the earlier Ingalls Complex.

The Mount Stuart block and metamorphic rocks were uplifted and eroded before the Tertiary sedimentary and volcanic rocks were deposited. After the Cascade uplift, millions of years passed before erosion and weathering removed the overlying rocks to expose the batholith.

Exposed sandstone of an age younger than the batholith dominates much of the remainder of the Wenatchee Mountains. The thickly bedded Eocene Swauk Sandstone, the oldest of the stratified rocks of Tertiary age, occurs in a broad belt extending east and west. It can be commonly seen in the Swauk Creek and upper Teanaway drainage areas. The Cle Elum River above Salmon la Sac is cut in this sandstone. The age of the Swauk Formation, along with volcanic rocks at Silver Pass (east of Lake Kachess), is about 50 m. y. The similar but younger sandstones of the Chumstick Formation (Eocene age) crop out in the Chiwaukum graben, bounded on the east by the Entiat fault. The formation, a 5000-ft sequence of interbedded sandstone, shale, conglomerate, and tuff, was deposited and preserved within the boundaries of the graben. On the west, the Chumstick Formation is bounded by the Leavenworth fault zone, where rocks are commonly sheared.

The blocky jointed Teanaway Formation (Eocene age) of basalt, andesite flows, and other volcanics unconformably overlies the Swauk in the southern part of the region. This basalt is black, but contains interbedded sedimentary rocks which weather to yellow and red-brown. Along a ridge at the head of Paris Creek (Cle Elum River-Middle Fork Teanaway River divide) prominent basalt dikes cut the Swauk sandstone.

The later Roslyn Formation (Eocene age), to the north of Cle Elum, is a thick-bedded non-marine sandstone that overlies the Teanaway.

During Miocene time, the Yakima Basalt flows erupted east of the Wenatchee area and lapped up on the early Cascade Range. These basalts and sedimentary rocks were tilted eastward, folded and faulted as the range later rose and the Columbia Plateau subsided.

Reference: R. W. Tabor, et al., "Geologic Map of the Wenatchee 1:100,000 Quadrangle, Washington." U.S. Geol. Survey Misc. Investigations, Map I-1311 (1982).

During the Pleistocene Epoch an icecap occupied the summit portion of the Stuart Range, being centered in the Enchantment Lakes area. Outlet glaciers flowed down Mountaineer, Rat, and Snow Creek valleys to join the trunk glacier in Icicle Canyon. Ice spilled down the trough of Crystal Creek to join another trunk glacier in Ingalls Creek.

Ice Age glaciers seemingly were too short-lived to sculpt all the high regions into sharp crests and steep-walled troughs; the glaciers did not encroach on each other to remove all the preglacial upland surfaces. Surviving patches (called erosional surfaces) remain along the tops of high divides. In contrast to the sharp-crested glaciated ridges, these patches form gently sloping tabular surfaces. The erosional surfaces are deeply covered with coarse sand derived from the disintegration of the underlying granodiorite. Where the upland surfaces slope gently toward steep walls of modern stream valleys, the topographic break is often so uniform that the distinctive character of the area is really due to its abruptness, rather than to exceptional height. Remnant benches left from broader, higher glacial profiles represent valleys occupied by earlier glaciers. In Upper Rat Creek valley an almost continuous remnant bench is prolonged in two-story U-shaped profile, decreasing in altitude to the brink of Icicle Canyon.

HISTORY

Early explorers of this region were prospectors, topographers, and geologists. Professor I. C. Russell made a high-level traverse along the Teanaway divide from Blewett townsite to Mount Stuart in 1897. He also ascended the Ingalls Creek rim to overlook Snow Lakes. Mount Stuart was included as one of five peaks in the Cascades marked on the earliest state and geological survey maps. The Mount Stuart area was surveyed in the late 1890s by G. E. Hyde, S. S. Gannett, and F. L. Cole, but the resulting map did not show the Enchantment Lakes and it is not known what summits were attained. George Otis Smith's geologic atlas (1904) of the Mount Stuart quadrangle map was the only study done for many years.

Miners prospected extensively (but extracted little ore) in this section of the Cascades, the best-known areas of their activity being those along Swauk and Peshastin creeks, where placer gold was found in 1860. Liberty was the center of the Swauk placer mining district. Lode gold was found in 1881, years after the old Blewett townsite built an arrastra operation.

Mining in the Cle Elum River valley included a stamp mill at Fortune Creek and "Galena City" near Camp Creek. The high regions of Fortune and Van Epps creeks were heavily prospected. The valuable King Solomon ledge of galena ore was discovered by an Indian (see L. K. Hodges, *Mining in the Pacific Northwest*). Mount Hawkins had a claim mirthfully called I-I Ass, which incidentally was the name for Hyas Lake at an earlier period. Though some trails are still rudimentary, the miner-pioneered trail network extends well throughout the high country.

Stevens Pass was named for John F. Stevens, explorer for the Great Northern Railroad, who recommended the pass as a route for the railway in August 1890 after months of exploration. Track was completed in 1893, when it crossed the crest by a series of switchbacks; the first tunnel was completed in 1900.

It was on this route that the Wellington disaster, the worst train catastrophe in the Pacific Northwest, occurred on February 22, 1910, when slides struck two stalled trains in Tye Canyon. To avoid avalanches a lower tunnel was built.

Feature names were originally applied by miners, topographers, and Indians. Some surviving Indian names are Swauk, Chiwaukum, Teanaway, Cle Elum, and Icicle (a derogation of *Nasikelt,* meaning narrow bottom canyon). Indian trading and hunting trails were certainly the first routes in this region. The map of George Gibbs in 1860 shows a trail from the "Winitsha" River to "Ketatas."[62]

It is interesting to note that the tribes near Puget Sound applied "mish" to many endings for stream names, while the Wenatchee and northern tribes applied "qua," and Yakima tribes "um."

Albert H. Sylvester, pioneer explorer and surveyor of the Wenatchee Mountains and forest supervisor from 1918 to 1931, named many of the area's features. Many names were for prospectors (such as Van Epps and French), and many for family and friends.

General references to this region include: *Mountaineer,* 1914, pp. 57-61; 1925, pp. 28-37; *Summit,* June 1963, pp. 18-22; December 1964, pp. 8-13; November 1967, pp. 16-21; *Cascadian,* 1957, pp. 75-80; *100 Hikes in the Alpine Lakes;* U.S. Geol. Survey, Folio No. 106; *Northwest Science,* vol. 25.

Selected references to the geology of the area are:

Foster, R. J. "Tertiary Geology of a Portion of the Central Cascade Mountains, Washington," *Geol. Soc. Amer. Bull.* 71 (1960), pp. 99-126.

Hopkins, K. D. "Glaciation of Ingalls Creek Valley, West-Central Cascade Range, Washington," M.S. Thesis, Univ. of Washington, 1966.

Page, Ben M. "Multiple Alpine Glaciation in the Leavenworth Area, Washington," *Jour. of Geol.,* vol. 47, no. 8 (1939), pp. 785-815.

Plummer, C. C. "Geology of the Crystalline rocks, Chiwaukum Mountains and Vicinity," Ph. D. Dissert., Univ. of Washington, 1969.

Porter, S. C. "Pleistocene Glaciation in the Southern Part of the North Cascade Range, Washington," *Geol. Soc. Amer. Bull.* 87 (1976), pp. 61-75.

Pratt, R. M. "The Geology of the Mount Stuart Area," Ph. D. Dissert., Univ. of Washington, 1958.

Tabor, R. W., et al., "Geologic Map of the Wenatchee 1:100,000 Quadrangle, Central Washington," U.S. Geol. Survey, Misc. Inv. Series, Map I-1311 (1982).

LAND MANAGEMENT

Ranger Stations:

Wenatchee National Forest

Cle Elum: Cle Elum, WA 98922
(N of town on Roslyn Hwy)
(509) 674-4411

Leavenworth: Leavenworth, WA 98826
(509) 782-1413

Salmon la Sac: Salmon la Sac
(Summer)

Campgrounds

Numerous campgrounds are located along the highways fringing this section and on the major forest roads. Increasing usage has taxed their capacity during peak periods. For locations see campground directories or Wenatchee National Forest Map.

Alpine Lakes Wilderness: note camping and fire regulations. There is a 12-person hiking group limit.

MAPS

Topographic (U.S. Geological Survey)

Scenic (1965)	1:24,000
Stevens Pass (1965)	1:24,000
The Cradle (1965)	1:24,000
Chiwaukum Mountains (1965)	1:62,500
Kachess Lake (1961)	1:62,500
Leavenworth (1964)	1:62,500
Liberty (1961)	1:62,500
Mt. Stuart (1961)	1:62,500
Wenatchee Lake (1965)	1:62,500
Wenatchee (1971)	1:250,000

U.S. Forest Service

Wenatchee National Forest

JIM HILL MOUNTAIN

6765 ft/2062 m

The mountain is named for James J. Hill, the Great Northern empire builder. It is located 3.7 mi. E of Stevens Pass on the Mill-Whitepine Creek divide. While prominent as a summit, the mountain is not rugged, providing a pleasant hiking or ski ascent from the southern flank.

SOUTH ROUTE: Whitepine Creek Trail ◆ passes the mountain's S flank at about 3800 ft in altitude. The ascent is straightforward from here.

NORTH SPUR: Take Lanham Lake Trail from the Sno-Park area on Hwy No. 2 ◆ (just E of where highway divides) to Lanham Lake (4143 ft), 1.6 mi. From the lake, hike and scramble cross-country due E, ascending a steep ridge (some brush). Note: keep directly E to avoid a tendency to contour

CHIWAUKUM MOUNTAINS from northeast
WALLACE C. GUY, U.S. FOREST SERVICE

N where there are cliffs. From the top of the ridge the true summit is the westerly one (to the right). Turn S and ascend to a large basin. Traverse W and ascend into the notch. Class 3. Time: 4 hours. Note: Heavy pants are recommended due to some devil's club.

Note: currently there is a slide over a portion of the approach using the Mill Creek Road ◆ to the powerline spur; this route connects with the jeep trail and trail to the lake.

BULL'S TOOTH   6840 ft+/2085 m+

A small, rocky uplift N of Icicle Creek at 5½ mi. SE of Stevens Pass. The highest peak of the uplift has two small high points close together. The Stevens Pass U.S.G.S. quadrangle places the name at a rocky ridge point (6807 ft) to the SW across a minor col.

The actual "tooth" (a rock horn likely suggesting the name) is 6800 ft+, just SW of the listed name. There is a 6680-ft summit SE of the 6200-ft trail pass between Chain and Doelle lakes.

NORTHWEST ROUTE: Leave the Doughgod Creek-Chain Lakes Trail (see Icicle Creek Trail ◆) just W of the trail pass (at 6000 ft). One could ascend SE up a small basin and with a final scramble reach the top of the highest peak of the uplift.

To reach Point 6807 and the "tooth," ascend to the little col at head of the basin, then follow the ridge SW (difficul-

ties uncertain).

CHIWAUKUM MOUNTAINS

The Chiwaukum Mountains subrange is a pronounced high crest some 6 mi. long, forming the eastern boundary of the Wildhorse-Whitepine watershed. Chiwaukum and Glacier creeks drain the E flank of the mountains. The highest summit (Big Chiwaukum) is not officially named. There is no precise southern boundary but Ladies Peak is the last summit of importance. The subrange extends N to Nason Creek, and is of geologic interest (the Chiwaukum Schist is a metamorphic unit). The area has typical slopes of talus blocks characteristic of schist.

Remnant glaciers lie at the head of Glacier Creek, on the E side of Big Chiwaukum, the N side of Snowgrass Mountain, and the N side of Ladies Peak.

BIG CHIWAUKUM   8081 ft/2461 m

This broad summit at the head of Glacier Creek, the highest of the Chiwaukum Mountains, is readily identified from the E by its long southern rock rim and the broad ice remnant on the low-angle bedrock slope. Its E and lower W slopes offer fine skiing terrain. Extensive talus slopes with minor cliffs which are easy to bypass lie below at the head of Glacier Creek; climb out of the basin via a long snow gully on its left side.

Make the easy but alpine ascent from the head of Glacier Creek (see Glacier Creek Trail ◆) or from the Wildhorse Creek Trail (see Whitepine Creek Trail ◆). A N spur is feasible from Deadhorse Pass; when reaching gentle slopes of the ice remnant keep E of the rocky crest.

Summits N of Deadhorse Pass are Point 7534 (close to pass), Point 7377, and Point 7423 (about 1½ mi. NW of the W end of Chiwaukum Lake). These northern summits offer no climbing problems.

SNOWGRASS MOUNTAIN
7993 ft/2436 m
The second-highest peak of the Chiwaukum Mountains, located at the head of the South Fork of Chiwaukum Creek about 2 mi. N of Ladies Pass, with a rugged, multiple-summit area and a small, steep glacier under the summit on the N. It is known to have been climbed on July 27, 1914, during a Mountaineer outing. Reference: *Mountaineer,* 1914, pp. 62-65.

There are high points on the ridge between Glacier Creek and the South Fork of Chiwaukum Creek to the E of the summit. Point 7680 and Point 7502 are the principal ones; the N side of Point 7694, just S of Lake Charles, is short and steep.

Snowgrass could readily be climbed via the W side from Wildhorse Creek Trail (see Whitepine Creek Trail ◆); the E side from the upper part of South Fork Chiwaukum Creek (see Chiwaukum Creek Trail ◆).

An ascent from the head of Glacier Creek via Lake Charles is possible, but involves rock scrambling to the subsidiary E summit, then along the rock ridge to top.

LADIES PEAK   7708 ft/2349 m
Less than 1 mi. NW of Ladies Pass. It stands out distinctly and has a rocky appearance.

The climb is an easy hike via the SE ridge from Ladies Pass (see Icicle Creek Trail ◆ and Icicle Ridge Trail ◆); or climb from the trail saddle (6800 ft) ½ mi. S of Lake Mary.

BIG JIM MOUNTAIN   7763 ft/2366 m
A relatively gentle peak but outstanding since there are no summits of its height to the E. It once harbored three glaciers, each flowing to Tumwater Canyon.

Make the easy ascent via spur ridges or open basin from Big Jim Lakes (see Hatchery Creek Trail ◆); these are set in an attractive timberline meadow on the NE side of the peak. The climb could be done from any side, but other approaches are longer.

GRINDSTONE MOUNTAIN
7533 ft/2296 m
A moderately important peak in the Wenatchee Mountains located 2 mi. N of Icicle Creek, opposite the entrance of Jack Creek. It has a rocky summit crest coming out from the NE. The alpine NW flank of the mountain has twin snow/talus basins with summit rock rims. Spanish Camp Mountain is to the W of Grindstone.

ROUTES: One could approach via Chatter Creek Trail (it continues off a road spur at 12½ mi. on Icicle Creek Road ◆) near 5600 ft at NE of the mountain; ascend W to the N shoulder, then up its final portion.

From Lake Edna on Icicle Ridge Trail ◆ one could ascend the N shoulder to the summit (snow, with some outcrops). One could also ascend the NW cirque.

A route has been done on the Northeast Face to the E of a tree-covered ledge by Gordon Briody on July 14, 1985. The five-pitch climb begins from a steep ramp, then follows quartz dikes to steep blocks (class 5.4).

CASHMERE MOUNTAIN
8501 ft/2591 m
Cashmere is the highest and most massive mountain in the Wenatchee Mountains except for the major Stuart Range peaks. It is located in the center of lower Icicle Basin, with N-facing slopes of considerable relief; its eastern flank drains to Eightmile Creek. Cashmere's summit tops a profusion of deep-walled valleys and small meadowed basins on the mountain's N slope; here Lake Victoria (5662 ft) nests in a deep cirque.

Cashmere's western shoulder (8250 ft) is a craggy rock area above the W basin, which is broad with lovely scalloped meadowed cirques. The mountain has a rocky East Pyramid (8055 ft) at 0.4 mi. E of the true summit; this feature has a short rock wall on its N flank. Cashmere Mountain offers ski touring terrain from an altitude of 8200 to 4000 ft, particularly in the basin of Doctor Creek, the western basins, and SW slopes. The mountain is also a natural for spring mountaineering.

ROUTES: Cashmere can be climbed from any direction; the easiest way is to use the high trail to Windy Pass (see Eightmile Creek Trail ◆). There is a campsite at an open area about ¼ mi. past Lake Caroline (5½ mi.), near the base of a ridge. This ridge faces S and terminates at a notch on the upper W ridge. This ridge is a hike, but the final portion to the summit is exposed scrambling for several hundred ft; one can traverse on the N side to avoid rock crags. Note: Watch for avalanche hazard in gullies during the winter and spring season.

From Lake Victoria one could ascend the long snow trough that ends at the notch W of the summit.

The NW ridge of the Northeast Pyramid has been climbed by Gordon Briody and Ron Aschoff in June 1984. Approach from the logging road bearing N off Eightmile Creek Road. Hike the closed road for over 1 mi. to a stream ravine. Ascend a game trail to the saddle NE of the pyramid, then descend around to the NW ridge. There are six pitches (class 5.6), with the route being mostly on the ridge, but traversing off and bearing to the N ridge near the top.

EIGHTMILE MOUNTAIN
7996 ft/2437 m
Eightmile Mountain is located 3 mi. SW of Cashmere Mountain and NW of Eightmile Lake. There are slopes good for spring skiing.

ROUTES: From Eightmile Lake (see Eightmile Creek Trail ◆) hike around to its W end, then N up the entry creek that veers W. Ascend upper E side of the mountain. An alternate route is to continue farther up Eightmile Creek, then ascend the S slopes.

CANNON MOUNTAIN
8638 ft/2633 m
Located immediately W of Coney Lake at the head of W fork of Rat Creek, Cannon is the massive point on the long bedrock divide between Rat and Mountaineer creeks. A large upland surface (Druid Plateau) about ½ mi. long lies on its gradual slope W of Shield Lake (at about 8300 ft); the W and N sides slope off with moderate abruptness, with high local relief. A long and gradual sloping crest runs to the summit from the col N of Enchantment Peak.

ROUTES: (1) From Shield Lake (see Rat Creek Route ◆) merely choose the easiest uphill hike to the W.

(2) From Coney Lake (7401 ft) ascend SW; go up an easy snow gully between cliffs to Druid Plateau E of the summit.

A hiking route from the Eightmile Creek Road's logging extension can be taken, bypassing Cannon Mountain by first ascending the mountain's lower N ridge, then the slopes along the W fork of Rat Creek and keeping E of the mountain to climb to the Lost World Plateau; one can descend to the Enchantment Lakes Basin.

(3) From Lake Stuart Trail ◆ at 1 mi., ascend due S, bearing left under cliffs into open rocky hillside. Ascend through a saddle and enter a broad basin leading to the summit; a long altitude gain.

CASHMERE CRAGS

The name applies to the nearly countless outcrops and pinnacles of quartz diorite between Ingalls, Icicle, and Mill creeks, and the Snow Creek Glaciers. The Crags (including the Edward Plateau) are an upland within the Stuart Range and part of the large Mount Stuart batholith. The geologist I. C. Russell, who scanned the Crags in 1897, later wrote of "a great cathedral-like mass of clustering granite spires rising within the amphitheatre."

On September 12, 1898 Bailey Willis hiked to the ridge above Snow Lakes, where he saw the glacier at the head of Enchantment Lakes. His journal mentions the nunatak beyond Snow Lake with its flanking canyons cut by glaciers. He described the glaciated slopes of the basin ". . . with needles standing boldly out on the crests."

This upland of the Stuart Range, with its wryly imaginative names, has become a haven for the hiker and rock climber. It is hoped that the users of this beautiful area will continue to respect its unspoiled and very fragile nature.

References include: Fred Beckey, *Challenge of the North Cascades,* pp. 154-172; *A.A.J.,* September 1949, pp. 248-255; 1951, pp. 173-174; *Summit,* November 1967, pp. 16-21; December 1968, pp. 16-21; July-August 1970, pp. 15-23; June 1963, pp. 18-23; *Mountaineer,* 1943, pp. 18-20; 1948, pp. 24-29; 1952, pp. 82-83; 1967, pp. 41-48.

Individual approaches can be varied in many ways, although the routes from Snow Lakes and the one from Colchuck Lake to Aasgard Pass are the most popular. Once the plateau uplands are reached, cross-country travel is generally easy. Because the rock ridges and outcrops of The Crags are so diverse and geographically scattered, concise groupings are limited. However, some definitions, with recommended approaches, are given here.

RAT CREEK GROUP: Located at the northern extremity of the Lost World Plateau and on the N slope, high above Icicle Creek. Approach using Rat Creek Route ◆ (Eightmile approach), or Hook Creek.

THREE MUSKETEERS RIDGE: Approach from Toketie Lake or Nada Creek (see Snow Creek Trail ◆).

MOUNT TEMPLE RIDGE: This is the 2-mi. ridge of towers immediately N of Upper Snow Lake and Snow Creek. Approach via Nada Creek (see Snow Creek Trail ◆). The Enchantment Lakes Route is equally good for summits near the western end of the ridge. West of Mount Temple there are numerous notches where the ridge can be crossed.

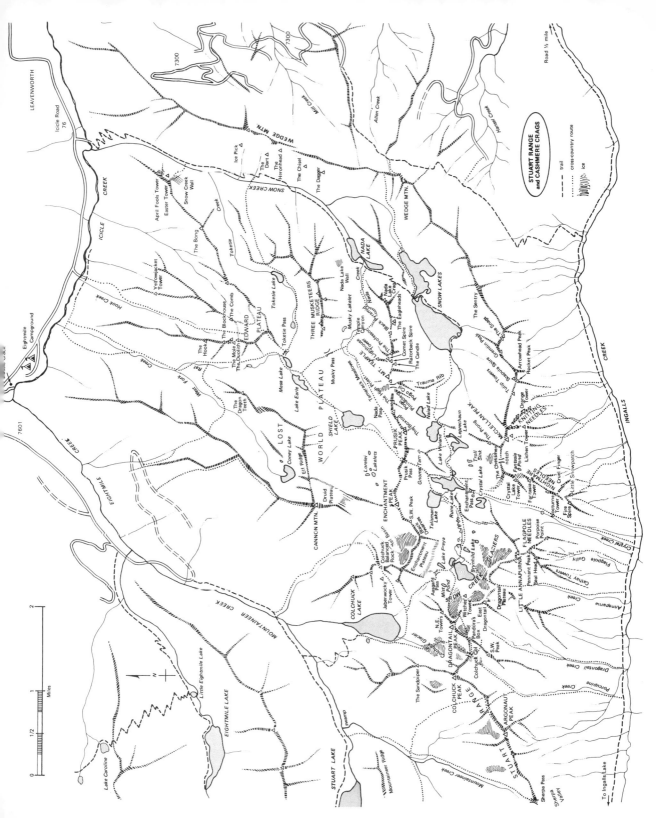

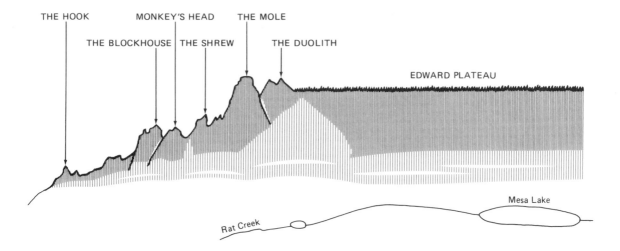

THE HOOK   THE BLOCKHOUSE   MONKEY'S HEAD   THE SHREW   THE MOLE   THE DUOLITH   EDWARD PLATEAU

Mesa Lake

Rat Creek

McCLELLAN RIDGE: The long divide between Snow Creek-Snow Lakes and Ingalls-Mill Creek. Approach via Snow Creek Trail ◆ and Enchantment Lakes Route.

INGALLS SLOPE: Pinnacled spurs are basically divided into the Knitting Needles, Nightmare Needles, and Flagpole Needles. Reach from Ingalls Creek Trail ◆; good campsite at 5 mi.

The Knitting Needles adorn the slope above the 5-mi. point, and about ½ mi. SW of Rocket Peak.

The Nightmare Needles crown a spur edge E of Crystal Creek (runs N to S). One approach is to leave the trail at 6¾-7 mi., climb 500 ft to pass cliffs, then work up and right on game trails on a forested rib to reach an open gully and basin below the Lizard Wall. Some of the towers are best reached from Crystal Creek.

The Flagpole Needles are on the spur W of Crystal Creek, to run to the northern high point at Pennant Peak. Reach via Crystal Creek Route, Flagpole gully, or Annapurna Creek. The row of towers E of Annapurna Creek are known as the Cathay Towers.

YELLOWJACKET TOWER
est. 4500 ft/1372 m
(Rat Creek Group)
This is a solitary tower on the longitudinal spur E of Hook Creek (use Hook Creek approach; see Rat Creek Route ◆). First ascent by Pete Schoening, Fred Beckey, and Herb Staley on September 1, 1948.
ROUTE: Make the ascent of two gullies on the E flank (up to low class 5). Climb the final 15-ft summit block on its W. Reference: *Mountaineer,* 1948, p. 27.
OTHER ROUTES: The South Face was climbed by Stella Degenhardt and Frank Fickeisen in 1962. From the ridge at

the southern base of the tower, traverse W on practical ledges to the base of a chimney; ascend this to the summit block (there is a chockstone two-thirds of the way up the chimney). Class 5 (take protection to 2 inches). Reference: *Mountaineer,* 1962, p. 102.

The Northwest Face was climbed by Dave Anderson and Ed Gibson in July 1971. This fivedpitch route includes cracks, slabs, and ledges. Begin to the right of a large chimney near the left side of the face; use a lieback flake to reach a tree. Grade II; class 5.8. Reference: *Mountaineer,* 1973, pp. 75-76.

The West Face was climbed by David Collins and Ray Smutek in August 1972. The route climbs a gully (easy class 5).

THE HOOK   6160 ft + / 1878 m +
(Rat Creek Group)
The lowest tower on the Rat-Hook Creek spur, readily identified by its thin tip. First ascent by Pete Schoening, Fred Beckey, and Herb Staley in 1948.
ROUTE: Approach from upper Hook Creek; ascend through broken rock and scrub trees to its S ridge. Climb to top of blocks below final smooth wall; a piton and bolt anchor used here. By a rope throw, the final flawless 30 ft was done by prusik ascent to within several ft of the tip. Reference: *Mountaineer,* 1948, p. 27.

THE BLOCKHOUSE
6960 ft + / 2121 m +
(Rat Creek Group)
The Blockhouse has been described as "a huge cube of granite which drops off almost vertically on all sides."

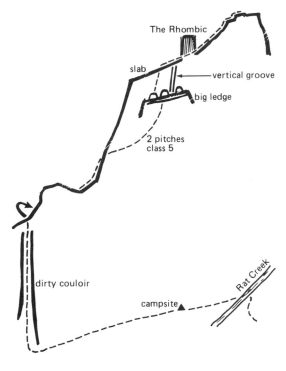

The Rhombic

slab

vertical groove

big ledge

2 pitches
class 5

dirty couloir

Rat Creek

campsite ▲

THE BLOCKHOUSE - Northwest Face

It is located on the Hook-Rat Creek spur and is the largest rock formation N of The Mole. First ascent by Pete Schoening and Ralph Turman in 1949.

NORTHWEST FACE: One approach is Hook Creek, then to the ridge S of The Hook. A better approach is from the Eightmile Creek Road (see Rat Creek Route ♦). From the slopes of Rat Creek take a final loose couloir to the ridge N of The Blockhouse. It is necessary to bypass a large rock hump by using a broad ledge on the E side of the ridge. The base of roped climbing begins from the ridge crest about 400 ft below the summit.

The first lead goes up and right across the Northwest Face; the second lead ends on a spacious ledge (boulder-strewn and 30 ft from N skyline) about 70 ft below the base of The Rhombic (lead is moderate class 5 but took some aid on first climb). Climb a steep "V" chimney on a vertical wall with a 2-inch crack, for 40 ft. The remainder of the pitch can be climbed via an overhanging, shallow 7-inch groove; or by free or aid in an overhanging, straight-in crack 15 ft to the left. The original party climbed the groove by starting from an exposed 1-ft projection, gaining 8 ft via shoulder stand, then using a poor aid pin on flake, a finger-hold move, and another aid pin to reach the sloping slab above. Scramble onward to the true summit block, where there are a short,

tricky slab and a few moves. Grade II; class 5.8-5.9, original party used horizontal and angle pitons. Time: 3 hours on rock. References: *Mountaineer,* 1948, p. 59; 1949, pp. 33-35; *A.A.J.,* September 1949, p. 343; 1950, pp. 504-505.

Descent: Three rappels; first from tree, then bolt, then a tree.

Variation: North Ridge: First ascent by James Mitchell and Al Errington on September 1, 1968. Begin at the steepening of the Northwest Face Route. Climb ridgeline (three pitches, mostly aid) to rejoin route for final pitch to summit rim. Class 5.7 and A2. Reference: *Mountaineer,* 1970, p. 107.

The Rhombic **(Rectiloid Tower):** This block stands 40 ft high, about 150 ft NW of the summit (about 35 ft lower in altitude). First ascent by James Mitchell and Al Errington on September 2, 1968. The climb involves 30 ft of nailing (A3), then two bolts. Reference: *Mountaineer,* 1970, p. 107.

SOUTH FACE: First ascent by Fred Beckey, John Brottem, and Dave Beckstead on September 21, 1966.

Approach from Hook Creek. Climb rotten gully on E side to just SE of uphill notch. Use aid (3 bolts) and free to notch. Two pitches on good rock (mixed free and aid) on or barely left of the crest, then make an exposed piton traverse left to an overhanging traverse on a corner. The final pitch is largely an open book (5.7), then a left exit to an open chimney. The original climb used 36 pitons and seven bolts (hangers in). Grade III; class 5.7 and A2, or 5.10 (left traverse is crux). Time: 5 hours. Reference: *A.A.J.,* 1967, pp. 349-350.

WEST FACE: Two difficult grade III routes have been climbed, both starting at near the same location and crossing at a pine tree beneath an overhang. Make the approach from Eightmile Creek Road (see Rat Creek Route ♦), then ascend a right slanting gully (class 3-4). Todd Bibler and Doug Klewin climbed a four-pitch route in August 1982, first bearing right, then reaching a ledge and the pine tree. Higher, the route works leftward. There are some obvious hard off-width cracks; class 5.10 and some aid.

Dan Cauthorn and Pat McNerthney climbed the other route in July 1982. This route bears right of the pine tree and ends on the last pitch of the South Face Route (four pitches, class 5.10).

An off-width crack just left of a prominent dihedral was climbed in 1983 by Pete Doorish and Charles Hampson. The route begins per the Bibler route, then bears left as a variation. Grade III; class 5.9.

MONKEY'S HEAD   est. 6950 ft/2118 m
(Rat Creek Group)

A fist-shaped tower immediately SW of The Blockhouse. First ascent by Pete Schoening and Dick Widrig in 1949.

SOUTH FACE: Reach via an exposed traverse from the N side of The Shrew (to gap between latter and objective). Aid up an overhanging nose leads to summit slabs (one-two leads to top; class 4). Reference: *Mountaineer,* 1949, p. 55.

- — — CAUTHORN-McNERTHNEY
- - - - - BIBLER-KLEWIN

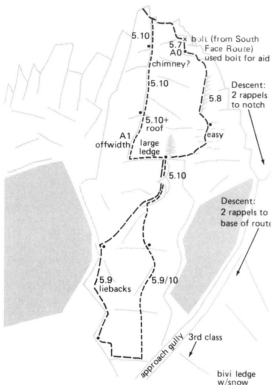

BLOCKHOUSE - West Face

WEST FACE: First ascent by Jim Jones and Jim Stoddard on June 4, 1968.

Start from right side of gully between Blockhouse and Monkey's Head. Bear right up slabs to right side of face. The major problem is a vertical dihedral about midway up the climb. It has a thin crack which can be done free by a 10-ft fingertip lieback (class 5.8), but poorly protected. Continue upward directly to an overhang one-half lead below the summit; bypass it by a right traverse to a short jam crack (class 5.6) which leads to the top. Grade II; class 5.8. Time: 3 hours.

CROCODILE FANG

est. 6700 ft/2042 m

(Rat Creek Group)

A tower between The Shrew and The Blockhouse, on the Hook Creek side of the spur. First ascent by Dave

Beckstead and Paul Myhre on June 18, 1970.

NORTH FACE: From the base of the gully on the E side of The Blockhouse, traverse left through slabs and trees; then work up left side of mossy cracks, and move diagonally left toward cleaner left side of face; second lead is hardest. From a ledge on the corner, climb a series of small faces and ledges to the right side of the summit. Grade II; four leads; class 5.8. Note: It is estimated that the easiest route (probably class 4) is to ascend the western gully (adjacent to The Blockhouse), then climb final rock on S.

THE SHREW   est. 7100 ft/2164 m
(Rat Creek Group)

A striking, angular spire closely N of The Mole, whose narrow tip points S. First ascent by Dick Widrig and Pete Schoening in 1949.

ROUTE: Reach from Rat Creek flank. The climb is done via cracks on the W face and along the N ridge. Class 4. Reference: *Mountaineer*, 1949, p. 55.

THE MOLE   7240 ft+/2207 m+
(Rat Creek Group)

The Mole is a steep-walled, bulky granite citadel rising above upper Rat Creek, just N of the northwestern rim of Edward Plateau. The formation, separated from the other large towers and rock masses of the upland, is one of the most important summits in the Crags. All routes involve 400 ft or more climbing. First ascent by Fred Beckey, Wesley Grande, and Ralph Widrig on May 23, 1948 (via South Face).

Note: there is a rappel route on the E face; down-climb, then make two rappels from bolts to reach the E couloir N of the great chockstone.

SOUTH FACE: Begin in the narrow gully slicing from SW to NE against The Mole's face (below the giant chockstone). Climb a slightly overhanging, left-trending 30-ft lieback crack to a pine tree. Take easy ledges a short distance left, then climb a series of cracks on a steep, broken 100-ft depression. Continue up a narrowing fissure to a nearly invisible flake that is split off from the overhanging wall. Climb the flaring crack at the flake's right edge (aid on original, but will probably be feasible free). Traverse left behind the flake for 50 ft (a squeeze) to an alcove; climb a short unpleasant gully. Squirm up a narrow "keyhole" tunnel inside the S rib's capstone. Then scramble about 300 ft on the well-broken upper South and Southwest faces. Class 5.7 and A1 (original rating). Time: 2 hours. References: *Mountaineer*, 1948, p. 25; *A.A.J.*, September 1949, pp. 251-252 (photo p. 248); *Challenge of the North Cascades*, pp. 159-160.

SOUTHWEST FACE: The Mole has steep and solid rock between the South and West faces. First ascent by Pete Doorish and Kent Stokes in 1980. Begin about 80 ft right of the Southwest Rib, climbing a prominent crack splitting the slab above. Continue mostly straight up through a steep section. Grade II; class 5.9.

SOUTHWEST RIB: First ascent by Pete Doorish and Bob Crawford in 1980. Begin at the base of the rib in a dihedral. Higher, keep mostly on the right side of the rib. Grade II; class 5.9.

A route has been done on the large black triangular slab to the S of The Mole (Pete Doorish and Kent Stokes, 1980). Follow the crack system to the right on the obvious dihedral. Grade II; class 5.7.

WEST FACE: First ascent by Patrik Callis, James Fraser, and Gerry Honey on September 15, 1957.

Ascend steep broken spur ridge on left of face for three leads (class 5.3); keep N of lower, mid-face hollow. Then traverse S across nearly vertical face (one or two pitches of 5.7, including an exposed finger traverse); this is at top of hollow but beneath big jumble of overhanging blocks. Then a vertical but well broken crack leads to easier SW ridge about a half lead distant. Several moderate leads (5.3) continue to the summit. Grade II; class 5.7. Time: 5 hours. Reference: *A.A.J.*, 1965, p. 408.

Variation: By Fred Beckey and Don (Claunch) Gordon, June 1962. On finger-traverse, continue level out S to corner. Other routes and variations have been done on this face.

NORTH FACE: This face is about 500 ft high (four leads), very smooth, and high-angled; rises at head of Hook Creek; can be plainly seen from the Icicle Road.

First ascent by Don (Claunch) Gordon, Patrik Callis, Eric Bjornstad, and Dan Davis on August 20, 1962.

Best approach is Hook Creek. From head of a gully start at lower right-center side of face at a clump of scrub pines. Take a mossy class-5.6 crack system (grey rock on left and white on right); in 80 ft it branches. Take grassy left fork (class 5.6 or 5.7) to a ledge with bush about midway up face (near left edge of face). This lead is 150 ft.

Then climb the wall on the left portion of the face — generally small holds (class 5.6-5.7 moves for about 20 ft) above the platform. Pass a dead white tree; follow the upper left portion of the face to the summit (the final pitch becomes class 4+). Grade II or III; class 5.7. About 10 pitons, one for aid, were used on the original climb. Reference: *Mountaineer*, 1963, p. 95.

Variation: Take a shallow jam crack (class 5.8), starting about 30 ft above the platform. After about 25 ft one can work right on chickenheads (class 5.6) to small flakes, then up to a traverse ledge.

EAST CORNER: First ascent by Fred Beckey and Bob Lewis August 7, 1957. The route begins just N of the giant chockstone adjacent to The Duolith. There are two aid pitches — ending in an overhanging narrow chimney (need some large chocks or pitons). The final pitch is easy. Grade II; class 5.8. Reference: *Mountaineer*, 1958, p. 107.

Variation: By Mike Waddell and Bill Powell on July 5, 1969. The second aid pitch can be bypassed on the bounding

right-hand face. Angle up and right via obvious small ledges to the corner overlooking the SE gully. Class 5.7.

THE DUOLITH   7280 ft+/2219 m+ (Rat Creek Group)

This double-tower crag is located on the N edge of Edward Plateau, closely E of The Mole. The southern crag is slightly the higher. First ascent by Fred Beckey and Ralph Widrig on September 19, 1948.

ROUTE: Climb the E face via a deep chimney to the notch separating the two summits (class 4). Climb the S summit crag via the steep slab facing NE (keep on the N edge); class 5. Climb the N crag from the notch (class 4). Reference: *Mountaineer*, 1948, p. 28.

SOUTH CRAG, WEST FACE: Climbed by Joe Catellani, Marty Gunderson, and Tom Townsend on August 29, 1982. Begin in the center chimney; it steepens and narrows to off-width and fist size, exiting left below a chockstone; there is a crux traverse. Traverse around a corner and follow a dihedral to a notch. Join the regular route or traverse right to a tunnel chimney leading to the summit block's edge; class 5.8.

THE COMB

est. 7000 ft to 7126 ft/2134 m to 2172 m (Rat Creek Group)

The Comb is located at the N edge of Edward Plateau, about ¼ mi. E of The Duolith. All summits were climbed by Fred Beckey and Ralph Widrig on September 19, 1948.

The SW sides of both the middle and northern pinnacles are done by chimneys and face climbing (class 4). Reference: *A.A.J.*, September 1949, p. 342.

BONG BUTTRESS: This rock formation, very visible from the lower Icicle Creek valley, has a steep N face. The Bong is located on a high ridge over ½ mi. SW of Snow Creek Wall. The best approach is from Toketie Lake. The face was climbed by Dave Stutzman and Doug Klewin in June 1982. Three of the pitches were roped climbing (class 5.7).

THE DRAGON TEETH   7051 ft/2149 m (Rat Creek Group)

Three striking rock needles W of The Mole stand on a N-S spur ridge W of Rat Creek. The northern two teeth are the smallest; the S tooth is unusually thin. First ascents by Ralph Widrig and Fred Beckey, May 22, 1948.

ROUTES: Northern teeth are short, exposed climbs. Class 4.

The S tooth is climbed via the E face. Begin up a white

overhang, climb a groove on a steep slab; some aid on original, now rated class 5.8.

There is a class 5.8 route on the NW slab, via a prominent left-facing dihedral. There is a route up the prow of the N face (Grade III; class 5.10). The latter routes were climbed by Pete Doorish and Bob Crawford in 1981. References: *Mountaineer*, 1948, pp. 24-25; 1982, p. 84.

THREE MUSKETEERS
7680 ft + / 2341 m +
(Three Musketeers Ridge)

The fictional characters created by Alexandre Dumas name a ridge of E-W pinnacles between Nada Creek and upper Toketie Creek, NE of Mount Temple. First ascent by Fred Beckey, Jack Schwabland, and Fred Melberg on August 14, 1948. References: *Mountaineer*, 1948, p. 27; *A.A.J.*, September 1949, p. 341.

ROUTES: Individual climbs vary in difficulty — generally short, interesting problems (class 4 and 5). A shoulder and difficult lieback were used to gain the base of the three main pinnacles. The lowest is easiest. The two higher ones are quite flawless; it is possible to stem the intervening space. In October 1951, Richard McGowan and Tim Kelley repeated the climbs and possibly made some firsts. The left side of the S face of the highest pinnacle was climbed by Greg Ball and Bill Fryberger in July 1971 (two pitches — class 5.6); finishes in short flaring chimney.

D'Artagnan Tower, South Face: This is a name given to the largest gendarme, in about the central part of the ridge. The relatively large and obvious S face was first climbed by Dave Anderson and John Teasdale on June 30, 1971.

From a start at cracks on the left side of the triangular slab at the face's base, follow a rather direct line. There are four pitches composed of a variety of liebacks, jamming, and friction. A 20-ft stem between two summit blocks ends the climb. Class 5.8. Reference: *Climbing,* September-October 1971.

TOKETIE WALL: This steep granitic wall, rather hidden on the eastern edge of the Lost World Plateau, is located closely S of Toketie Lake. There are a number of routes, all on firm rock. Make the approach via Snow Creek Trail ◆ (Toketie Lake Route).

The prominent buttress on the wall was first climbed by Jim McCarthy and Carla Firey in June 1974. From the base of the N-facing prow, climb crack systems up the slight prow, turning the steep white headwall on the left. The route is six pitches, varying from class 5.7 to 5.9. Grade III.

A multi-pitch route on the right (W) flank of the prow was climbed in the summer of 1981 by Jim Donini, Bob Plumb, and Antoine Savelli. The route begins about 100 ft right of the prow, at a recess. Begin at its left side. The first pitch is a very obvious left-facing corner (stemming and chimneying — class 5.8-5.9). This is followed by two pitches (class 5.8-5.9), then a crux right-slanting finger crack on a steep wall (class 5.10+). Another pitch climbs

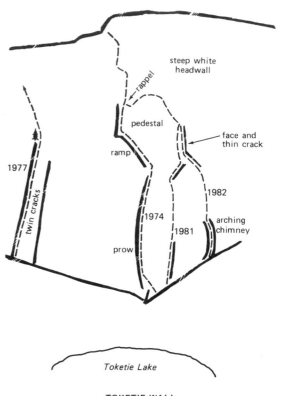

TOKETIE WALL

the final pedestal; here make a short rappel to the left and join the 1974 route. The final two pitches follow the latter.

A variation of the above route was climbed by Dan Cauthorn and Wayne Kamera in 1982. The climb begins about 100 ft right of the left-facing corner, climbing a wide, left-arching chimney. Stem and use cracks in its rear to the top of the chimney, where it narrows; a steep, difficult crack continues to the belay (class 5.10). Continue on steep cracks with steps, which lead to a squeeze chimney. End the pitch on a ledge (class 5.9). A difficult left-slanting finger crack features the next pitch (discontinuous and thin cracks — class 5.10); end at a ledge that is below a short flared chimney. Climb the chimney; one is forced right by blocks at the top of the chimney (the climb probably joins the 1981 route near this point). Climb the right side of the pedestal via a ramp (class 5.8) leading to the top of the pedestal.

There is a route on the left of two prominent parallel cracks. Follow the crack to a tree and then continue up and slightly left (first climbed by Pete Doorish and Neil Rockwell in 1977; grade III; class 5.10).

The dome to the W of the lake has one-pitch climbs (done by Pete and Judy Doorish, 1977); left-side route rated class 5.7 and center route 5.8.

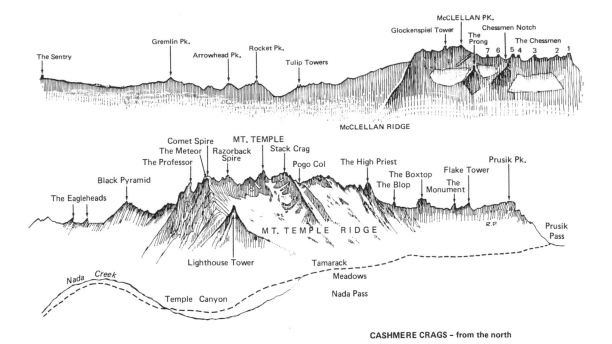

CASHMERE CRAGS – from the north

A triangular face above and E of the lake outlet was climbed by Pete and Judy Doorish in 1977. The route takes the jam cracks on the left side. Grade II; class 5.7.

Two pinnacles high on the ridge S of the lake and E of Toketie Wall were climbed by Pete Doorish and Neil Rockwell in 1977. The left pinnacle is an off-width climb on the S side (class 5.6); the right pinnacle is climbed on the NE (class 5.7); both are one pitch.

NADA LAKE CRAG
(Mount Temple Ridge)

Rock climbing opportunities exist on or near this ragged crag, which is the eastern anchor of Mount Temple Ridge. Two of these are worth mentioning here.

NADA LAKE WALL: This is a clean slab-wall above the N section of Nada Lake; it has numerous possibilities for good, short rock climbs. A route following the obvious line traversing below the prominent black overhanging section was done by Jim Langdon and Bruce Garrett in July 1967. Grade II; class 5.7.

BOOT CRACK: This is the obvious wide crack leading to the ridge between Snow Lake and Nada Creek, and is approached from Upper Snow Lake. First ascent by Mead Hargis and Jay Ossiander in 1970.

An initial 4-inch crack climbs to a ledge; a second ledge holds a dead tree. Higher, a 4-inch crack continues. About 200 ft of broken rock continues to the ridge. Class 5.9 (two pitches). Bring protection for cracks to 4 inches.

THE EAGLEHEADS   est. 6700 ft/2042 m
(Mount Temple Ridge)

These are two small but striking needles with beaked tips, located on the Nada Creek-Upper Snow Lake crest. They are about 200 ft apart, with the western needle about 200 ft from the upthrust of Black Pyramid. First ascents by Jack Schwabland and Fred Beckey in September 1948.

The routes are on the E sides; class 4.

The E face of West Eaglehead was climbed by Doug Bond and Jason Edwards in May 1980 (crack systems, class 5.7).

BLACK PYRAMID   7400 ft+/2256 m+
(Mount Temple Ridge)

This rock formation, about ½ mi. E of Mount Temple, can be identified by the spectacular sweep of dark lichen on its N face; it rises just above a miniature timberline bench, E of the talus below the Professor-Comet face. First ascent by Jack Schwabland and Fred Beckey on September 6, 1948, via West Ridge.

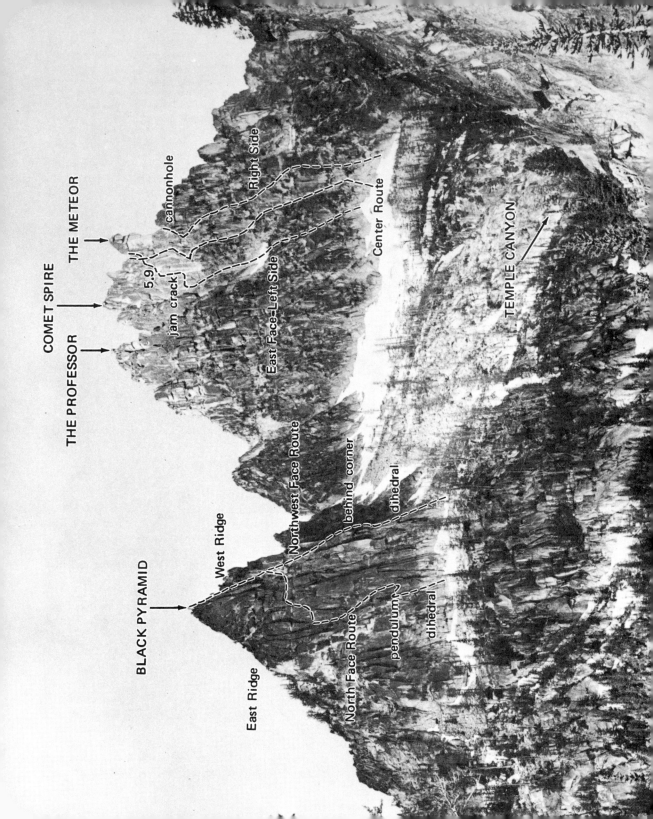

COMET SPIRE

THE METEOR

THE PROFESSOR

BLACK PYRAMID

cannonhole

Right Side

Center Route

5.9

jam crack

East Face—Left Side

TEMPLE CANYON

Northwest Face Route

West Ridge

behind corner

dihedral

East Ridge

North Face Route

pendulum

dihedral

WEST RIDGE: Reach via a gully from the talus/larch slope S of Nada Creek, or via the S-facing slope from Upper Snow Lake. From the W col, ascend cracks, then veer right to above the S drainage (class 4). Finish by working down and right behind a big block, then climb through blocks and cracks to the summit (class 5).

Variation: By Roger Jackson and Mike Kennedy in 1964. Via chimney and through large blocks on the right side of North Face to meet the summit ridge 200 ft W of the top (at a small notch); some loose rock. Class 5.

NORTHWEST FACE (Dihedral): This dihedral can be identified as being at the right edge of a very white rock patch one pitch above the face's base. First ascent by Bill Lingley and Jim McCarthy on July 4, 1969.

Start 100 ft below the dihedral. This pitch (class 5.7) involves some hard routefinding up cracks and ramps. Then a 5.7 pitch in the dihedral ends in a chimney. The next pitch (class 5.2), and a class 4 pitch, up the dihedral lead to a notch closely W of the top. Drop onto the S side and traverse E to join the West Ridge Route. Grade II; class 5.7. Selection: up to 2 inches. Time: 4 hours.

NORTH FACE: This route begins in the major right-facing dihedral which rises to the summit crest E of the summit; it is an enjoyable climb, mixed free and aid. First ascent by David Beckstead and James P. Stuart, on June 3, 1964.

Climb the dihedral to a slab, then make a rightward tension traverse to the main dihedral crack. Aid climbing passes a small roof, then a poor crack (loose rock) leads to a small ledge with a tree. A 30-ft pitch leads to a larger tree ledge. Traverse this right one-two pitches to a broken area. Here it is feasible to continue up on easy to moderate class 5. At the top, circle right around the summit block and up the opposite final few feet. Grade II; class 5.6 and A1 or 5.10. Selection: 15 pieces, up to 4 inches suggested. Time: 3 hours. Reference: *A.A.J.*, 1965, pp. 407-408.

NORTHEAST FACE: By Dave Davis and Greg Markov in June 1974. Begin just left of the North Face Route, climbing behind a 10-ft pedestal. Continue up a steep rib, passing right of a large bulge. Continue up a dihedral system. On the fifth pitch climb obliquely up and right to the summit via cracks and knobs. Grade II; class 5.6 (solid rock).

Another route was done on this face, by Dave Anderson and John Teasdale in 1973 (details unknown). The climbing includes a deep chimney and a rightward rising traverse to the summit ridge; the rock is quite lichen encrusted.

EAST RIDGE: First ascent by Ed Cooper on June 22, 1960.

Climb a slab (class 3) to gain the ridge where it steepens. Near its top make a traverse on the S side; then 150 ft of climbing (class 4) leads to the summit. Reference: *Mountaineer*, 1961, p. 108.

LIGHTHOUSE TOWER
est. 7680 ft/2341 m
(Mount Temple Ridge)
This celebrated rock tower is located ¼ mi. NE of

MOUNT TEMPLE RIDGE from east
WILLIAM A. LONG

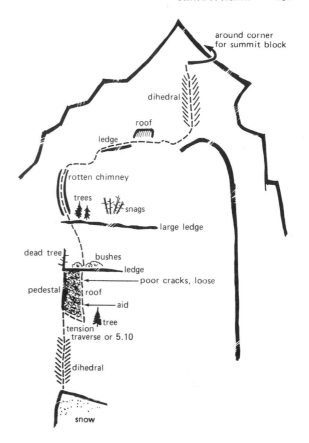

BLACK PYRAMID - North Face 1964

Mount Temple on a spur biting into upper Nada Creek basin. It is so named because it stands out like a beacon. First ascent by Pete Schoening, Fred Beckey, and Ralph Widrig on August 29, 1948.

WEST FACE: From the S notch traverse W face to small platform where flake with a solitary crack rises to within 15 ft of the summit. Free climb (possibly one or two aid moves) to a depression at N side of summit block. A line can be thrown over the summit to pull a spare rope to prusik the last portion. Class 5 and A1 (large chocks or pitons). Reference: *A.A.J.*, September 1949, pp. 253-254. An aid crack on the S side of the summit has been climbed.

EAST FACE: A fine 400-ft route on good rock; jam cracks with good protection. First ascent by John Marts and Jan Starwich in May 1966.

To begin this four-pitch route, start on a scrub-pine ledge on the lower right portion of the face (beneath the large midface pillar). Climb various cracks, flakes, and chimneys to a ledge (class 5.7). Move right, then up a crack: climb

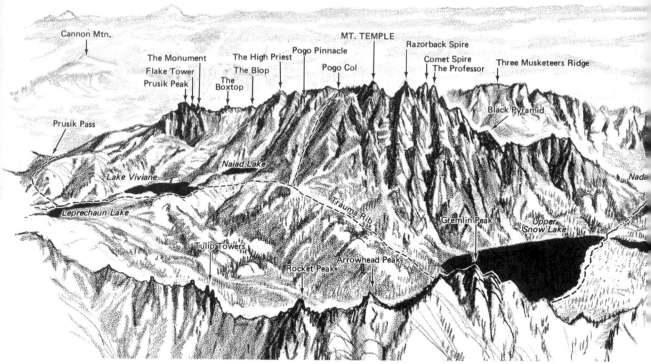

CASHMERE CRAGS (Mount Temple Ridge) from south

right around the corner and ascend an easy jam crack to a ledge (class 5.7). Make a short leftward traverse to the pillar's base (20 ft), then climb the chimney on its right (class 5.8-5.9) until a hand traverse left and a mantle leads to the top half of the pillar. Move left and climb the left-hand crack to a belay perch atop the pillar. Climb steeply (aid or class 5.9) and ascend the left-hand jam crack. In about 50 ft, move right on a crack (around the NW corner) to reach the beginning of the normal route. Grade II or III; class 5.9.

Other variations are possible.

One variation from the lower right side of the face is to scramble up to an evergreen tree on a small ledge. Move right, then directly up to the base of the pillar (one pitch — class 5.7). Step right around a small corner into a crack, then climb a hand crack for 30 ft that leads onto the tower's NE side to reach a ledge. Follow this ledge to cracks and blocks that bear left to the top of the pillar (one long pitch).

THE PROFESSOR   est. 8000 ft/2438 m
(Mount Temple Ridge)
The Professor stands off the cliff E of Comet Spire. It is so named because of an odd slab, projecting like the nose of a dignified professor. First ascent by Ralph Widrig, Fred Beckey, and Pete Schoening on August 29, 1948.
ROUTE: From the Comet-Razorback col, rappel or

downclimb to the gap on the W side of The Professor (original party descended E face of Comet to gap, then did a steep traverse to reach objective). Work right, then ascend a near-vertical pitch (60 to 100 ft) that includes a right-facing book. From a high ledge, a shoulder was used to surmount a slight overhang on summit block. Class 5. Reference: *Mountaineer,* 1948, p. 27.

THE METEOR   est. 8050 ft/2454 m
(Mount Temple Ridge)
This is a whitened, isolated block jutting N of Comet Spire's summit. First ascent by Ralph Widrig, Fred Beckey, and Pete Schoening on August 29, 1948.
ROUTE: Reach the block by traversing the W face of Comet to the tiny notch on its S. The short but exposed route involved two shoulder stands to gain a lichened slab (class 4 or 5). Reference: *Mountaineer,* 1948, p. 27.

COMET SPIRE   est. 8080 ft+/2463 m+
(Mount Temple Ridge)
Located on the N end of the high ridge extension E of Mount Temple, its principal attraction is the major E face rising above Temple Canyon. First ascent by Pete Schoening, Fred Beckey, and Ralph Widrig on August 29, 1948 (via SW face).

SOUTHWEST RIDGE: From the basin N of Mount Temple, ascend snow, talus, and broken rock toward the Comet-Razorback col. The Southwest Ridge of Comet Spire is a rounded edge featuring a series of parallel cracks; the edge drops off on both flanks to provide exposure. The climb is class 4 or easy class 5. Variations on the SW face are feasible; the climb is often done by a traverse from Razorback Spire.

Note: Bring ample webbing for rappel rope retrieval.

EAST FACE — RIGHT ROUTE: This 700-ft face is a continuous exposed climb on good rock, with good ledges and scrub pines for belaying. First ascent by Don (Claunch) Gordon, Dave Collins, and Paul Salness on June 3, 1951 (the original climb done on the East Face).

Begin the route at the right end of the lichen trimline (whitened) and climb toward The Meteor. In its upper part, the route uses a hard lieback crack. Traverse right beneath a chockstone just below The Meteor, then climb through it to the W side of the arete. Traverse around the W side of The Meteor, then follow Comet's N crest to the summit. A final pitch has short jam cracks. Grade II or III; class 4-5 sustained and difficult with optional use of some protection. Time: 5 hours.

EAST FACE — CENTER ROUTE: First ascent by Tom Hornbein and Dick Emerson in September 1964.

Start up shallow gully; climb sandy ledges and short pitches to work to about 100 ft right of midface basin (close to original route); class 4. Climbing then becomes class 5 (can use some runners on scrub trees). Then climb free or about 20 ft of aid, using about seven pitons (or chocks) in a left-leaning wall crack. Then climb a long hard lead into the Comet-Meteor notch (jams and small holds, with good protection). Now climb the edge of the crest to the top of Comet: the first pitch used a dihedral ending in a mantle onto a loose flake (can flip rope over flake for protection). Grade III; class 5.7. Time: 6 hours.

EAST FACE — LEFT ROUTE: This route is to the S of the other. First ascent by Mark Weigelt, Chris Chandler, and Steve Beck on July 4, 1969.

Start from the highest finger of snow below and slightly right of the basin in midface. Three leads end at the top of the basin (second lead was class 5.9, but can be bypassed). Then a lead (class 5.7) ends at the base of a classic chimney (to right of the huge Professor gully). Then a full lead right-traverse (class 5.7) ends below a good class 5.8 jam crack. The next lead is the crux: two sections of class 5.9 unprotected on a right-traversing ramp (cannot be nailed) end in a belay below an overhang. An easy left traverse, then some moves (class 5.8) to the right lead to the Comet-Meteor notch (part of last lead may be same as center route). Continue as per latter. Grade III; class 5.9. Selection: 12 chocks.

SOUTH FACE: A route was done by Dave Anderson and John Teasdale in 1971. This is a short wall, approached from the Comet-Razorback col. One long pitch of cracks, near center (class 5.7).

RAZORBACK SPIRE
est. 8160 ft / 2487 m
(Mount Temple Ridge)

Located on the ridge extension E of Mount Temple, immediately S of Comet Spire. It is quite rugged on the S. First ascent by Pete Schoening, Fred Beckey, and Ralph Widrig on August 29, 1948.

SOUTHWEST FACE: From the basin NE of Mount Temple, climb a snow tongue to the S of the Comet-Razorback col (or take a ramp to the Temple-Razorback col, and then follow the ridge and broken rock to the upper SW face). The final climb is up broken rock; climb through the last whitish section to the level summit crest. Class 4. Reference: *A.A.J.*, September 1949, p. 252.

Variation: From Comet col ascend the wide N corner; it has a low profile with long wide cracks (reported as five leads on solid rock, from class 4 to low class 5, beginning from the NW flank).

Approach Variation: Traverse about 0.3 mi. E from Naiad Lake to bypass slabs, then ascend to the Temple-Razorback col.

THE CANDLE   est. 7900 ft/ 2408 m
(Mount Temple Ridge)

A needle jutting atop a promontory S of the Temple-Razorback col. First ascent by Tim Kelley, Richard McGowan, and Betty (Woodward) McGowan in October 1951.

ROUTE: From the col walk the promontory slabs to the right margin where the slab narrows (at large block). Climb friction to the base of the final flawless 20-ft summit block where there is a knob near the right corner. Two bolts used here. References: *Mountaineer*, 1952, p. 83; 1955, p. 57.

MOUNT TEMPLE   8292 ft/ 2527 m
(Mount Temple Ridge)

This impressive tower is the highest point on the Mount Temple Ridge; some parties confuse it with a gentler, but rocky crag several hundred yards W, of almost equal height. First ascent by Keith Rankin, Ken Prestrud, and William Herston on July 6, 1946.

ROUTE: From the head of Nada Creek and the high basin W of Lighthouse Tower, climb the prominent left-slanting snow finger and continue to the notch immediately W of the summit tower. Climb a stone-choked crack to a platform (50 ft) and a 30-ft slab to a belay. Traverse left, then take a short chimney (possible loose blocks) to summit notch; a mantle and narrow block edge leads to the summit. Class 5.3. Time: 1 hour on rock. Reference: *Mountaineer*, 1946, p. 29.

Approach Variation: From Naiad Lake on the S, make a rising easterly traverse; ascend the gully immediately W of a large slab-pillar, to reach the notch W of the summit tower.

EAST FACE: First ascent by Don (Claunch) Gordon and Fred Beckey on June 7, 1959. From the base of the N face, climb a left-slanting ramp to the V-notch on the Razorback-Temple crest. Climb broken rock on its S flank to the final pitch of the East Face. This is a steep crack on center-face (a jam crack with black lichen on its right). Class 5.5 or 5.6. Time: 3 hours. Reference: *Mountaineer,* 1960, p. 89.

SOUTH FACE: First ascent by Dan Davis, Stan Gregory, and Fritz Zimmerman on September 3, 1961.

From the W end of Upper Snow Lake ascend a long system of slabby easy gullies to the SW corner of the summit tower. At the base of the South Face is a large flake separating from the summit tower by a narrow cannonhole. This is a key crawl-through to the opposite end; climb up onto a spacious ledge formed by the flake's top. Aid was used (five pitons) up a vertical crack above the right side of the ledge to a smaller ledge about 30 ft higher; then climb wider cracks and broken rock to the top. References: *Mountaineer,* 1962, p. 102; *A.A.J.,* 1962, p. 202.

Stack Crag (Velikovsky Stack — Northwest Face: This is the crag several hundred yards W of Mount Temple (est. 8280 ft). A new route by John Bonneville, Mark Weigelt, and Julie Brugger done in June 1970 climbs the obvious dihedral system on the final steep portion. From the dihedral's base climb a class 5.8 pitch to a large broken ledge. Then climb leftward to a small roof; the rightward move under the roof is class 5.8. A hidden lieback to the right (class 5.6) is made, then a scramble to a squeeze chimney; climb this and continue to a ledge, then scramble leftward to the top. Class 5.8 (bring chocks). Time: 2 hours. Reference: *Mountaineer,* 1971, p. 77.

POGO PINNACLE   est. 8000 ft/2438 m
(Mount Temple Ridge)

A striking 130-ft tower located on the S side of the Mount Temple Ridge, some 300 ft from the crest, about midway between Mount Temple and High Priest. First ascent by Tim Kelley and Art Maki on August 31, 1955.

ROUTE: Reach it from Pogo Col (est. 8160 ft) at head of large snowfield W of Mount Temple; cross to S slope and traverse short distance W to the NE corner of the tower. It can also be reached from Naiad Lake by ascending NE; when talus slopes become gullies, take right-hand one to the uphill notch.

From the NE corner climb a 50-ft crack (class 5.6), then a 20-ft exit left (class 5.6) to a small stance. A long pitch via grooves leads to a platform 40 ft below the summit (easy class 5). Continue 40 ft to the summit (six bolts and one piton used for aid). Note: Report of original party indicates a partially different route: from the corner they took a difficult 30-ft crack (free and aid), then a 10-ft S traverse on a one-inch ledge, then a crack and chimney stem to the platform. Reference: *Mountaineer,* 1955, pp. 57-58.

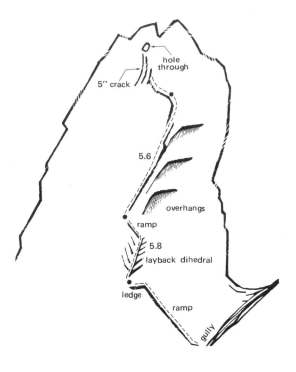

THE HIGH PRIEST—south face

Al Givler

THE HIGH PRIEST
(west peak of Mount Temple)
                    est. 8240 ft + /2512 m +
(Mount Temple Ridge)

This E-leaning, prominent white tower on the main Temple crest is about 0.3 mi. W of Mount Temple. It appears to be the result of a giant's play with building blocks. Rappel pitons are 40 ft down the W side, to allow a 75-ft ground rappel to the NW couloir.

First ascent by Fred Beckey, Melvin Marcus, and Bil Dunaway in May 1947 (via W face). Reach the tower from Naiad Lake by ascending uphill to the 7920-ft W col. Or from the Nada Creek Route traverse W across the Tamarack Meadows bench until beneath the NW side of the tower, then ascend to the col. Or from Mount Temple traverse high around the N side of Stack Crag to Pogo Col; then cross W over the head of the N snowfield and scramble the ridge or just N of it to the high E notch of the tower.

WEST FACE: This 300-ft route with its large blocks gives a forbidding appearance, but is maximum class 4 on good rock with a variety of cracks, slabs, and small ledges. Reference: *Mountaineer,* 1947, p. 51.

NORTH FACE: First ascent by Richard McGowan, Don (Claunch) Gordon, Tim Kelley, Paul Salness, Ron Bucklin, and Ted Lundberg on June 10, 1951. Begin directly above Tamarack Meadows, where there is a rock rib from the face; the route is on broken, sound rock with considerable jamming. Generally keep left of the rib; the final part of last lead bears right under a horn, then up a wide jam that flares. Class 5.5.

EAST FACE: First ascent by Richard Berge, Ray Secoy, Dick Hill, and Eric Peterson in 1951. This narrow face begins slightly overhanging for about 50 ft. The original climbers used some aid — now rated class 5.9; the last portion of the face is much easier.

SOUTH FACE: This face has weathered to a curious sequence of joints and blocks, with small overhangs. First ascent by Al Givler, Jim Langdon, Mike Langdon, and Steve Ansell on July 3, 1969.

From the gully below E notch work left 100 ft on sloping ramp (class 4); round a corner and then climb strenuous lieback dihedral (class 5.8) to a ramp. Work left to belay under a roof. Climb right, upward (class 5.5), then ascend a long dihedral which traverses above prominent overhangs (class 5.6). Ascend looser rock to belay. Then 40 ft of class 3

leads to the top (ascend a crack, then crawl from a chimney through a hole). Class 5.8. Selection: protection up to 2½ inches.

Hepzibah Blop (est. 8000 ft): A name given to the first prominent point W of High Priest. The 200-ft N face was climbed by Mike Kennedy and John MacDonald in August 1960. Cracks, an ice patch, then a class 5.6 jam crack led to the top.

THE BOXTOP 7960 ft/2426 m
(Mount Temple Ridge)

This large, curious rock tower is located on the ridge crest ½ mi. W of Mount Temple. The Boxtop appears to list uniquely to both the N and E. The formation is adorned with picturesque overhanging blocks, a result of ancient jointing in the batholith and more recent frost wedging. Although a short climb, The Boxtop has an aspect of novelty, with no simple route. The rock is unusually sound, and delightful for climbing. First ascent by Fred Beckey and Pete Schoening on September 25, 1948.

ROUTE: Reach notch between a flat western rampart and "Little Boxtop," the western crag of the formation, from

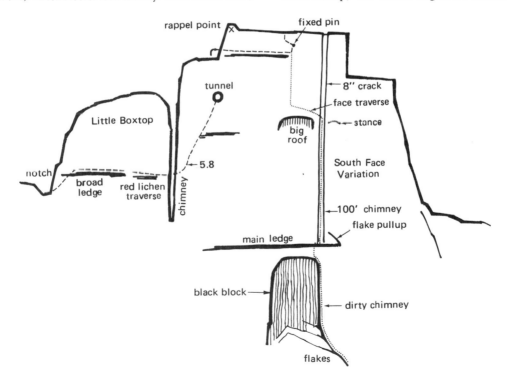

THE BOXTOP– south view

either N or easy S slopes. Climb to a platform on the ridge, then traverse around the corner of the S face on a broad ledge, past a small tree. Ledge ends at a broad pedestal 15 ft from a large chimney. Make a delicate "red lichen" traverse to the chimney.

Climb the chimney to where it opens to a gap, then up the right wall (class 5.8). Continue up and right on easier rock to a large belay ledge beneath a tunnel. Climb a narrow chimney into the hole, then through to the steep N face. About 40 ft of chimney climbing brings one to a splendid platform at the W edge of the last summit block. Traverse the ledge on the S side; go around a blind corner with a loose block. Then climb directly upward; start up a groove by stemming (to a fixed pin); halfway up, climb left on a diorite knob, reach up and get feet onto a higher one; holds improve to summit crest. Grade II; class 5.7 or 5.8. Time: 3 hours. Note: a horn at W end of summit edge can be used for a 150-ft rappel to bottom on N face. References: *Mountaineer,* 1948, p. 29; *A.A.J.,* September 1949, p. 342.

Variation: Little Boxtop: By Mike Kennedy, Bill Blair, and David Mitchell about 1964. Climb a 50-ft chimney from the W notch (class 4) to gain the top of Little Boxtop. Rappel 90 ft into the gap between the summits. Climb 20 ft on the main formation's SW corner to the ledge beneath the tunnel (class 4).

From W notch, traverse left on a ledge. Then climb a small vertical crack to top of ridge (about 15 ft, class 5.7 or 5.8). Then follow ridge E until reaching headwall. Make short drop to right to meet normal route above red lichen.

SOUTH FACE: By Dan Petersen and Bruce Schuler in September 1969. Flakes on the lower S face lead to a big black block against the face (class 4). A dirty chimney is climbed behind the block (40 ft, class 5) to main cross ledge. A flake pull-up (class 5.8) leads to a 100-ft chimney (class 5.6). Come to a stance just past major roof on the left. Make a left traverse on knobs, just above the roof (about 15 ft, class 5.6). Then reach the crack continuing through the final ledge (at about 20 ft) of the normal route. Class 5.8; can be done on jam nuts and slings. The 8-inch crack can be finished directly (class 5.10b).

EAST FACE: First ascent by Mike Heath and Tom Oas on July 6, 1969.

Scramble to crest E of Boxtop. From right-hand base of face lieback and jam steep crack and block system leading up and left 50 ft to a wide mantle shelf. Climb over an awkward bulge above a sharp-edged block at left edge of the shelf. An easy jam crack above leads 25 ft to a large platform. Shoulder stand to enter right-hand of two overhanging jam cracks at inside corner of platform, then stem a wide chimney for 30 ft to the summit. Grade II; class 5.8. Take protection to 1½ inches. Time: 3 hours. References: *Mountaineer,* pp. 106-107; *A.A.J.,* 1970, pp. 117-118.

THE MONUMENT   est. 7920 ft/2414 m
(Mount Temple Ridge)

This white monolith is located about 150 yards W of

The Boxtop. It has a four-sided, flawless summit block. First ascent by Ralph Widrig and Pete Schoening in May 1948.

WEST FACE: At 200 ft below the summit on the SW side, take a class 4 chimney to a large ledge with a huge boulder (80 ft from summit). Climb to the W face of the monolith. Ascend the left-hand crack (next to north corner); it can be jammed free (class 5.7 or 5.8) but was nailed on the first climb (six pitons). Throw a spare rope over the summit block, then follow a ledge around the N corner to reach it for a prusik ascent. Take protection for sizes between 1 and 2 inches. References: *Mountaineer,* 1948, p. 26; *A.A.J.,* September 1949, pp. 249-250.

EAST FACE: First ascent by Fred Beckey and Dan Davis on June 26, 1962. From the NE ridge crest climb the left of three prominent parallel cracks to the summit block ledge. Then throw rope for prusik ascent. Class A2, using a number of Friends or bongs. References: *Mountaineer,* 1963, p. 95; *A.A.J.,* 1963, p. 472.

FLAKE TOWER   7920 ft/2414 m
(Mount Temple Ridge)

This is a lichen-covered, W-pointing rock crag W of The Monument. First ascent by Ralph Widrig and Pete Schoening in May 1948.

ROUTE: Approach as for The Monument, W face. From the ridge notch the climb is a short route on sloping ledges, slabs and two steep cracks. Class 5. Reference: *Mountaineer,* 1948, pp. 26-27.

NORTH FACE: By Fred Stanley and James Wickwire on July 21, 1963. This 400-ft route begins as an easy left-slanting ramp. Then climb right a few ft on a smooth slab until a traverse can be made to the difficult crack on the left. A lead then continues over easier rock to a short, harder pitch (possible aid). The next lead diagonals left to where the notch adjacent to The Monument can be reached. Complete the ascent by traversing around the N of the summit block; there is easier rock to the NW. Class 5.7 and A2. Take protection up to 1½-inch sizes. Reference: *Cascadian,* 1963, p. 22.

PRUSIK PEAK   8000 ft+/2438 m+
(Mount Temple Ridge)

Prusik Peak is the western outpost of Mount Temple Ridge, ¾ mi. W of Mount Temple. The rock on this often-photographed peak is unusually solid and clean. The first ascent party named the peak for Dr. Karl Prusik because their climb was completed by means of a prusik ascent of the summit horn.

A good rappel route should be noted: from bolt at E edge of summit block rappel N face 150 ft to broken rock, then scramble down N, later W to Prusik Pass.

First ascent by Fred Beckey and Art Holben in May 1948 (via East Route).

ENCHANTMENT LAKES BASIN from east
WASHINGTON STATE DEPT. OF GAME

MT. STUART

ENCHANTMENT PEAK

HIGH PRIEST

DRAGONTAIL PEAK

Enchantment Plateau

Prusik Pass

BOX TOP

Aasgard Pass

PRUSIK PEAK

ARGONAUT PEAK

POGO PINNACLE

East Dragontail Plateau

Witches Tower

TALISMAN LAKE

Pogo Col

Dragontail Plateau

SNOW CREEK GLACIERS

BRYNHILD LAKE

RUNE LAKE

LITTLE ANNAPURNA

CRYSTAL LAKE

LAKE VIVIANE

NAIAD LAKE

LEPRECHAUN LAKE

Labels on image: notch, FLAKE TOWER, WEST RIDGE, chimney, THE MONUMENT, chockstone, Snafflehound Ledge, gully to East Ridge, Burgner and Stanley, Beckey and Davis, 1977, trees, ledge, deep chimney

PRUSIK PEAK from south
BOB AND IRA SPRING

EAST ROUTE: Climb gully system (white rock on left, black rock on right) at far E side of S face to a 50-ft crack (possible minor aid). Climb it to narrow E ridge between a jutting flake and the first vertical ridge step. Climb ridge step (aid), then traverse N side on ledges to base of overhanging summit block. This can be climbed three ways:

(1) Aid 20-ft crack on facing side of block (medium chock size).

(2) Lasso summit horn and make prusik ascent.

(3) Climb from final notch to N (variation by Callis, Honey, and Fraser in September 1957); descend on N several ft and step right onto a two-ft ramp. Sneak up ramp (in 5 ft can put in a ⅝-inch angle). Then a class 5.7 or 5.8 move (delicate friction traverse) ends at a corner; ascend via good

jam crack to summit. Reference: *A.A.J.,* September 1949, pp. 249-250.

Variation: Route to area of final notch on E can be made from N (class 4).

SOUTH FACE: An old classic, this fine face route climbs the scenic wall that rises about 600 ft above the Lower Enchantment Lakes basin. First ascent by Fred Beckey and Dan Davis on June 26, 1962; first free ascent by Mike Heath and Bill Sumner on July 5, 1969; first winter ascent by Alan Kearney and Les Nugent in December 1976.

Start in deep chimney left of two prominent "V"s. Body jam the chimney (class 5.6 or 5.7, unprotected); near its top move left, then climb rightward on knobs. Climb onward diagonally right up a steep slab to a long chimney-gully,

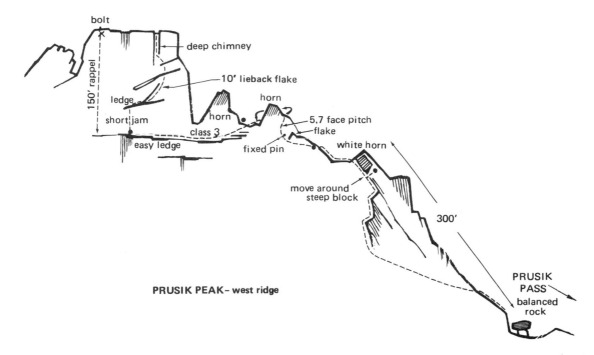

PRUSIK PEAK– west ridge

then ascend it two leads. Eventually climb out of its right side and then traverse right on major ledges ("Snafflehound Ledge") one short lead. Then climb up a short lead to a small tree. A steep crack system reaches up and slightly left toward the cleft on E side of summit block. Just above, climb crack system (free or aid for one long lead — use large stoppers). Continue up system (almost a steep gully now), bypassing large chockstone on left, to the tiny notch E of the summit horn. Continue as for East Route options. Grade III (10 leads); class 5.7 and A2 (or 5.9). Take a selection of Friends and chocks to 1½ inches. Time: 6 hours. References: *Mountaineer*, 1963, p. 95; 1970, p. 106, *A.A.J.*, 1963, pp. 472-473.

Variation: By Bill Sumner and Mike Heath on July 5, 1969. From the base of the giant chockstone of the South Face-West Side Route, this party abandoned an attempt on it, to make a difficult right exit into a slanting crack leading to a long traverse E to "Snafflehound Ledge." Follow original route to "small tree." Then climb shallow diedre on thin holds (class 5.8) until forced to step out right on outside corner. Climb alongside 8-ft partly detached pillar. When an overhang forces the route left, place a chock in a vertical crack, and make a step across into a rounded crack and move over the bulge (class 5.9); meet original route again.

SOUTH FACE — WEST SIDE: First ascent by Ron Burgner and Fred Stanley on June 12, 1968.

Climb 50 ft up the initial chimney of the South Face Route, then make a left exit into a crack and block system leading past a small pine (class 5.7). Climb up and behind small trees, then right over awkward blocks to a steep gully. Ascend by hand jams and a toe-to-heel squeeze chimney. Continue and enter a wide chimney bearing up the W side of the face; climb to beneath the giant chockstone blocking it. Squirm behind the chockstone (class 5.7) and continue up the chimney (class 5.9 — can protect this with No. 2 and 3 Friends and small stoppers). In about 100 ft reach a prominent right-slanting ledge. From its right corner climb the final and obvious left-facing dihedral (class 5.9) leading to a break in the summit rim; the original party made a belay under the roof near its top, then used several bongs for aid. Grade III; class 5.9 (sustained chimneys and cracks). Protection is good on the route. Selection: No. 1, 2, 3, 4 Friends, hexes No. 1-10, stoppers No. 3-10. Time: 6 hours.

WEST FACE, LADY GODIVA ROUTE: By Alan Kearney, Stephen Mitchell, and Charles Sink on May 28-29, 1974. Begin climbing in cracks on the right side of the face (2½ leads). Dihedrals on the right side lead to a good ledge two pitches from the summit. Traverse right and ascend a dihedral, then a crack and chimney system. Grade IV; class 5.9 and A3 (about 40 percent aid). Take 40 chocks up to No. 8 hex size. Reference: *A.A.J.*, 1975, p. 125.

SOUTH FACE OF WEST RIDGE: First ascent by Paul Boving and Matt Christensen in July 1977. The route climbs the steep face, beginning with a 5.9 pitch. Bear slightly left (5.7, 5.10a lieback, 5.10a), climbing cracks to the first level edge of the W ridge. Grade II; class 5.10b; chocks ³/₁₆-inch to 2 inches.

WEST RIDGE: This is the classic, sharp arete leading up

from Prusik Pass. It is a route of purity on marvelous granite. First ascent by Fred Beckey, John Rupley, Don (Claunch) Gordon, and Fred Ayres in May 1957. First winter ascent by Dave Anderson, Cal Folsom, Tom Linder, and Jim McCarthy in January 1975.

From Prusik Pass climb up to where the ridge steepens; one pitch leads nearly to the crest (class 4 or easy class 5). Traverse upward on the N flank for about one lead to the actual crest. Continue on crest until a tricky 12-ft slab is met (unprotected; class 5.7). Climb it and move on (becomes easier) to the slab's top at the crest. Make an exposed traverse on the S side to a belay. Scramble left via ledges to N side of summit structure. From highest easy ledge climb up and lieback a steep corner for about 10 ft (or jam and mantle onto ledge) (class 5.6 or 5.7) to another large ledge which leads out onto ridge crest. Now climb a right-facing thin flake (lieback) off the ledge to another ledge. Then squeeze a narrow chimney (class 5.3) to the summit. Grade II. Time: 3 hours. References: *Mountaineer*, 1958, p. 107; *A.A.J.*, 1958, pp. 81-82.

Variation: An easy traverse can be made from below final summit structure to the upper E notch; then climb one of the E route completions.

WEDGE MOUNTAIN   6885 ft/2099 m
(McClellan Ridge)

Wedge Mountain forms the backbone of the divide E of Snow Lakes and Snow Creek. Maps show the summit about midway between Icicle Creek and Nada Lake, at about 5840 ft. However, popular terminology and logic makes the choice the 6885-ft summit 1 mi. SE of Nada Lake, between Snow Creek and the heads of Allen and Hansel creeks. This summit's N ridge slopes gently, but the S ridge is a rocky crest. As the northeastern terminus of the Stuart Range, the Wedge Mountain divide circles on to McClellan Peak. Wedge is a good winter or spring trip and offers a marvelous vista of the Cashmere Crags.

ROUTES: The lower eastern slope of Wedge Mountain is laced with roads that climb upslope; roads climb higher than 4500 ft, but may not always be driveable, and gates may close approaches (reach from Swauk Pass Hwy ◆). Both the Hansel and Allen creek branch roads can be used as a basis for easy cross-country routes to the summit of Wedge via the N ridge crest. Hansel Creek Road begins at Ingalls Creek approach road, climbing NE to a switchback (may be gated), then continuing W to about 4200 ft. Allen Creek Road is a southern branch of Mountain Home Road (Mill Creek Road) that branches W off Swauk Pass Hwy. The Ingalls-Mill Creek Trail climbs to about 6000 ft roughly ¼ mi. NE of the summit.

Three climbing routes have been done on the East Face of Wedge. The Couloir Route, taking the couloir that climbs to just S of the summit, was done by Jim Yoder and Pete Austin in Spring 1983 (crampons used). A face route, about

one pitch rightward from the couloir, and climbing almost directly to the summit, was done by the same party in July 1983; class 4 to 5.8.

A direct route, to the N of the other routes, was climbed by Jim Yoder and Kevin Buselmeier in January 1984 as a winter ascent. The route took very steep ice on a granite slab, then climbed a steep ice couloir. There was an ice bulge on the fourth pitch, then the route was completed by a steep snow couloir (6 hours of climbing).

THE ICE PICK   est. 5000 ft/1524 m
(McClellan Ridge)

The northern of small prominent towers on the E valley wall of Snow Creek. It is located approximately above the 3-mi. point on the trail.

THE DART   est. 5200 ft/1585 m
(McClellan Ridge)

A pointed spire about 1000 ft up and slightly N of the 4-mi. point on Snow Creek Trail ◆ (where it crosses creek). First ascent by Don Wilde and Pete Schoening on April 10, 1949.

From a good wide ledge, work up an overhang from the W. Reach a thin "straddling" crest. Then climb the steep S portion; some aid and possible one or two bolts used.

THE HERONHEAD
                              est. 6000 ft/1829 m
(McClellan Ridge)

A descriptively named tower, located near the crest of the Snow-Mill Creek ridge, above and slightly S of The Dart. First ascent by Pete Schoening and Don Wilde on April 10, 1949. Reference: *A.A.J.*, September 1949, p. 342.

Approach as per Wedge Mountain, then Allen Creek Road. Follow the Mill Creek Trail westward about 1½ mi., then hike cross-country to the divide. The objective is not far across the ridge, being located N of and higher than The Chisel. The original route details are scant, but a current report indicates one should climb a chimney (inside a flake) on the tower's NE corner, then traverse to the ledge that crosses the W face (class 5.7). Make a shoulder stand and a hard move to gain the summit.

THE CHISEL   est. 5500 ft/1676 m
(McClellan Ridge)

The Chisel is a rectangular tower on the E valley slope of Snow Creek above and slightly S of the 4-mi. mark on the trail. First ascent by Joe Hieb, Fred Beckey, and Pete Schoening on May 21, 1949.

ROUTE: The 75-ft route begins on a ledge and ascends a N-facing crack near the tower's eastern edge. Some aid and two bolts used on original. The standard route is now rated at class 5.8-5.9, and there is a class 5.7 direct finish variation. The W face is rated at class 5.9 — a crack pitch. Take Friends or large hexes. Time: 4 hours from trail. Reference: *A.A.J.*, 1950, photo opp. p. 506.

One can also make the approach as for The Heronhead. The Chisel is not far below the ridge of Wedge Mountain.

THE DAGGER   est. 5800 ft/1768 m
(McClellan Ridge)

The Dagger is a pointed tower about ¼ mi. S of The Chisel — a short but interesting climb. First ascent by Fred Beckey, William Fix, Joe Hieb, and Graham Matthews on September 4, 1949.

Leave Snow Creek Trail ◆ at 4-mi. bridge crossing and continue ¼ mi. along the E valley slope. Ascend gullies to the S flank of the tower, then cross to the N side of the upper notch. The climb is class 5, with one aid move and a shoulder stand used on the original. Time: 3 hours from trail. Reference: *Mountaineer,* 1949, p. 55.

THE SENTRY   est. 7000 ft/2134 m
(McClellan Ridge)

The Sentry is the 75-ft rectangular isolated tower on the ridge crest above Upper Snow Lake. First ascent by Jack Schwabland and Fred Beckey on September 4, 1948.
ROUTE: From the neck between the two Snow lakes, hike and ascend about 1 mi. due S. The route is via a 50-ft inside corner on the SE (can be done free or aid), to a small ledge on the E edge, 20 ft below the summit. This was climbed by a head-stand and lassoo on first ascent. Now it can be climbed with the aid of a bolt, followed by hard free climbing. Bolt atop for rappel.

THE SNAGS   est. 6920 ft/2109 m
(McClellan Ridge)

The Snags are the two similar blocks atop the flat ridge crest closely E of Gremlin Peak, where it begins its rise westward. First ascent by Jack Schwabland and Fred Beckey in September 1948.
ROUTE: From the level ridge between the blocks, they are climbed from the S or W — each a short class 3 pitch. Reference: *Mountaineer,* 1948, p. 28.

GREMLIN PEAK   7250 ft/2210 m
(McClellan Ridge)

The first prominent peak on the crest W of The Sentry

(est. 0.4 mi. NE of Rocket and ⅜ mi. S of Upper Snow Lake). First ascent by Jack Schwabland and Fred Beckey on September 5, 1948.
ROUTE: From level ridge on E (6800 ft) traverse across S slopes to the SW, and then up. The climb is class 2 except for the summit shoulder stand.

ARROWHEAD PEAK
7240 ft+/2207 m+
(McClellan Ridge)

Arrowhead Peak is a small summit on the ridge crest 200 yards E of Rocket Peak. First ascent by Jack Schwabland and Fred Beckey in September 1948.
ROUTE: Reach from Snow lakes by ascending through the saddle on the N. Traverse to the SW side, then climb up. The ascent is trivial except for the shoulder stand at the summit block; there are three summit blocks.

ROCKET PEAK   7375 ft/2248 m
(McClellan Ridge)

Rocket Peak is the outstanding crag on the crest E of McClellan Peak; it is about ¾ mi. SW of the W end of Upper Snow Lake. First ascent by Jack Schwabland and Fred Beckey on September 5, 1948.
ROUTE: Make the approach from Upper Snow Lake to the saddle (7080 ft) on the W of Rocket. Climb over a subsidiary rock hump to a gap with a large chockstone, just SW of the summit. Work up and right across the S face to high on the E ridge, then around to a ledge on the N face; follow this to the notch at the NE base of the summit block (35 ft below the top). Here an awkward shoulder and hand stand is used to gain a sloping ledge; friction to the top. The climb is maximum class 4 except for the aid and harder moves on the final block. There is a crack for a piton rappel on the summit. References: *Mountaineer,* 1948, p. 28; *A.A.J.*, September 1949, p. 391.

Scapula Spire (est. 7200 ft) is the large, detached gendarme on Rocket Peak's NE face. The first ascent was made by Richard Berge and Eric Peterson in 1951 by a spectacular open chimney; class 5. Reference: *Mountaineer,* 1952, p. 82.

TULIP TOWERS   est. 7350 ft/2240 m
(McClellan Ridge)

These are the two small but prominent towers on the crest, on the opposite side of the saddle W of Rocket Peak. First ascents by Ira Spring and Fred Beckey on May 30, 1949.
ROUTE: From the saddle, traverse the S slope around the towers. Climb the W tower from the NW side (class 4). Climb the E tower by making a traverse of the N side of the W tower to the dividing notch; continue up the NW side via steep cracks. This is the better climb of the two (class 4 and 5).

McCLELLAN PEAK   8364 ft/2549 m
(McClellan Ridge)

The highest summit on McClellan Ridge; it is located 1¼ mi. SW of the W end of Upper Snow Lake. First ascent by Ken Prestrud, Keith Rankin, and William Herston on July 5, 1946. First winter ascent by Bill Prater and Cecil Ouellette in March 1958. References: *Mountaineer,* 1946, p. 28; *Cascadian,* 1960, pp. 26-27; 1962, p. 19.

ROUTES: The easiest way to the summit is from Lower Enchantment Lakes. Ascend southward, keeping W of The Prong. Climb a narrow snow finger or easy rock slopes to the summit's W ridge; the final ascent involves only easy scrambling.

The 1946 party climbed the N face (class 4), weaving between large gendarmes to the eastern ridge crest; there is steep broken rock and intermittent snow in this area. Follow the ridge or its S flank to the summit.

A long ascent from Ingalls Creek Trail ♦, using the approach for Knitting Needles, can be taken to the crest of the E ridge.

Bloody Tower is a jagged crag on the S slope of McClellan Peak, not far below the summit. A 60-ft route has been done via the western crack (class 5.6).

Tiresome Tower is possibly a small pinnacle just SE of McClellan's summit, climbed by Richard Berge's party in 1951.

Glockenspiel Tower was named and first climbed by Richard Berge, Dick Hill, Eric Peterson, and Ray Secoy in 1951. Its precise location has not been established, but it may be the tower near the ridge crest about 800 ft E of McClellan's summit. The capping block resembles a bird's beak; the route is a short pitch on the W (class 5).

Nubby Needles stand below to the W of McClellan's summit (the climbs are class 4); another needle just NW is a class 5.5 climb on the SE flank.

The Hand is most prominent from the basin to the W: it has a skeletal appearance. Routes have been done by Pete Doorish and Franci Ries in 1984: on the SE, a crack is climbed, then one tunnels through to the top (class 5.6); the northern face is class 5.7.

THE PRONG   est. 7800 ft/2377 m
(McClellan Ridge)

The Prong is the very prominent N-tilting needle on a pronounced spur running down and N of the McClellan-Chessmen Ridge. The E spur face below The Prong drops sheerly to a perennial snow patch. First ascent by Richard Berge, Ray Secoy, Dick Hill, and Eric Peterson in 1951.

ROUTE: Begin via a 35-ft overhanging crack on the outer face. There are short vertical steps with separating ledges. On the original climb, there were three short pitches with aid. Reference: *Mountaineer,* 1952, p. 82.

THE CHESSMEN
8080 to 8200 ft/2463 to 2499 m
(McClellan Ridge)

The Chessmen are the seven final (western) towers crowning the high spur ridge W of McClellen Peak. Their northern sides slope to Lower Enchantment Lakes, and the S sides drop to a sloping talus basin. Chessmen Notch is between the fifth and sixth towers, a good place to cross the ridge.

Three towers on the W end of the ridge were climbed by Phil Sharpe and Alan Lambuth in 1950 (class 3 and 4). The three eastern towers were climbed by Herb Staley and Fred Beckey on July 27, 1952, and named "Knight," "Bishop," and "Pawn." The easiest approach is to cross from the N through Chessmen Notch, then traverse the talus under the towers. It is also feasible to come up the long straight gully from Crystal Creek to the S edge of the western towers. The first tower (western) has a blocky shape; it appears short but steep (probably best on final E side). The second tower is really a crag, broken in two by a sharp notch; it is likely best from the S, then ridge scrambling. The third tower is a pyramid.

The fourth and fifth towers stand close, nearly leaning together, with a short steep N wall. Climb from respective outside edges. The pyramidal sixth tower has a face on the W; climb it on the E. The seventh tower is a small upright block at the W end of the highest N-facing snow basin; climb from the E. Reference: *Mountaineer,* 1952, p. 83.

ORANGE TOWER   est. 6800 ft/2073 m
(Ingalls Creek Slope — Knitting Needles)

This massive orange-toned tower is the most noticeable on the row of towers and nearby outcrops that comprise the Knitting Needle group. The first ascent was made by Pete Schoening and party in 1950; the route was from the W (class 4).

Cigar Tower (est. 7200 ft) is a monolith located on the spur above Orange Tower. First ascent by Richard Berge and party in 1951; climbing details unknown.

WINDOW TOWER   est. 6900 ft/2101 m
(Ingalls Creek Slope — Knitting Needles)

This is a small but striking tower in the Knitting Needles, located on a rib to the E and higher than Orange Tower. First ascent by Fred Beckey and John Parrott on April 24, 1954.

From the cliff on its W, descend to the tower's inside notch. The final 150 ft lead is on the SW, ending

INGALLS CREEK SLOPE from south (east end)

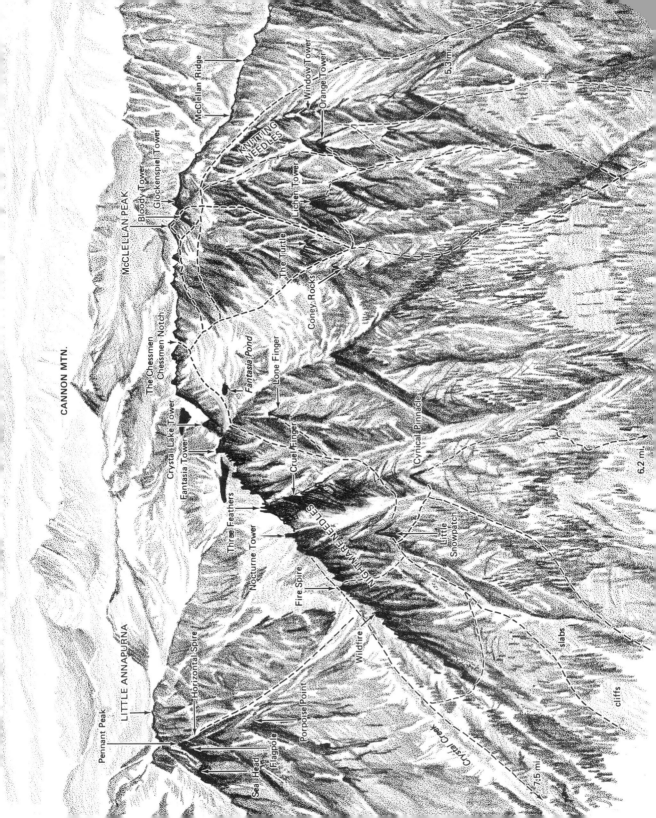

via a vertical crack on the S skyline; class 5.8 (minor aid on original). Rappel bolt on summit. Reference: *Mountaineer,* 1954, p. 63.

The smaller tower below, on the ridge, is a class 5.7 climb.

LICHEN TOWER   est. 7000 ft/2134 m
(Ingalls Creek Slope — Knitting Needles)

This dark-toned pyramidal feature is the most prominent in the Knitting Needles. It is located W of Orange Tower, across a bowl. First ascent by Fred Beckey and Phil Sharpe on June 24, 1951. The route involves three pitches on the E face, bearing to the NE corner at times; class 4. Reference: *Mountaineer,* 1952, p. 82.

There are three routes on Lichen Tower's South Face: (1) Left side crack route, by Pete Doorish and Ellie Brown, 1972 — two pitches, class 5.9. (2) Center chimney route, same party — class 5.8. (3) Right-side dihedral, Pete and Judy Doorish, 1985 — class 5.6. These are all excellent climbs on firm rock.

CONEY ROCKS   est. 6800 ft/2073 m
(Ingalls Creek Slope — Knitting Needles)

These twin monoliths, slightly lower and several hundred yards W of Lichen Tower, were climbed by the original Lichen Tower party. The eastern Rock is highest.

Begin from the NE corner. A hard traverse gains the central notch. A shoulder stand, pitons, and rope throw were used to gain the highest summit. Reference: *Mountaineer,* 1952, p. 82.

Gray Tower (est. 6800 ft) is located on a minor crest and across a gully from Coney Rocks. Early history unknown. A route was done by Pete Doorish and Franci Ries in 1984 on the W side (5.7).

Black Lamb and *Grey Falcon* are two small but prominent towers above Lichen Tower (at about 7400 ft). The lower tower (Black Lamb) has a split top; the climb was done by Pete Doorish and Ellie Brown in 1972 (an off-width crack on the E). Gray Falcon has a flared chimney (class 5.9) on the NW side (climbed by Pete and Judy Doorish, 1985).

THE TURTLE   est. 7200 ft/2195 m
(Ingalls Creek Slope — Knitting Needles)

The Turtle is a massive rock crag located on the Ingalls Creek valley slope above Lichen and Gray towers. First ascent by William Fix and Will Murray in 1963. The route taken began on the E, then went coun-

ter-clockwise to finish on approximately the E side. Class 4.

RFK TOWER   est. 7900 ft/2408 m
(Ingalls Creek Slope — Knitting Needles)

This is the uppermost of the Knitting Needles, and quite prominent. The climb (from the inside notch — class 5.3), may have been done by Richard Berge and party in 1951 under another name. Approach by descending the upper slopes of McClellan Peak.

CYNICAL PINNACLE
est. 6400 ft/1951 m
(Ingalls Creek Slope — Nightmare Needles)

This is a small but noticeable pinnacle at the lower eastern area of the Nightmare Needles, located about 200 yards E and below (across a gully) from Little Snowpatch. First ascent by Fred Beckey, Joe Hieb, William Fix, and Jack Schwabland on May 27, 1950.

To approach, follow the route to the base of Little Snowpatch, traverse beneath, then eastward. The route is on the NW: climb a chimney, then work right. Class 4.

LITTLE SNOWPATCH
est. 6600 ft/2012 m
(Ingalls Creek Slope — Nightmare Needles)

Distinctively shaped Little Snowpatch is one of the largest towers in the Nightmare Needles; in early season there is a snowpatch ledge on its E face. Distance from the inside notch to the top is about 140 ft. The tower is located at the upper right end of the shallow basin below Lizard Wall. First ascent by Joe Hieb, Pete Schoening, and Fred Beckey on June 25, 1950.

EAST FACE: From the inside notch walk out on the E-side tree-covered ledge, then climb a series of steep bathtubs. Climb the 60-ft crack to the "snowpatch ledge" (some aid on original), then a long leftward offset crack to its end at a ledge on the upper SE corner about 30 ft from the summit. Work S to scale a block: the summit is a small horn. Class 5.8 (bring large chocks, Friends, or piton sizes). Time: 2 hours. Reference: *A.A.J.,* 1951, p. 173.

SOUTHEAST RIB: This is actually the easiest route to the summit. First ascent by Pete Doorish and Ellie Brown in 1972. Climb the first 40-ft lead of the South Face Route, then continue directly up a curving dihedral to the ledge on the upper SE corner (class 5.7).

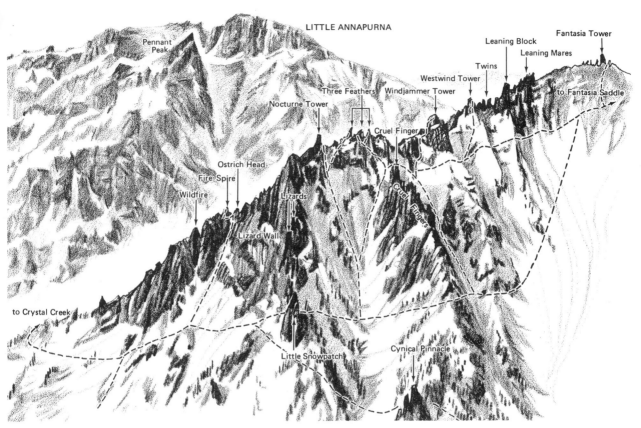

NIGHTMARE NEEDLES from southeast

SOUTH FACE: First ascent by Jim Langdon and Ron Fear in July 1967.

From E-face ledge a 40-ft lead on small holds (class 5.7) rises leftward to a large ledge on the South Face. Walk about 30 ft along the ledge to a bush. Ascend a steep crack to an overhang; aid this, then free up another crack (becomes a dihedral). Some aid is used at a steep corner on a rightward traverse, to end lead at upper SE corner ledge (this pitch was rated class 5.6 and A1).

NORTHEAST RIB: First ascent by Pete Doorish and Alex Cudhowicz in June 1985. From the "snowpatch ledge," walk to the right (N edge), then climb a long class 5.9 crack system to the top.

LIZARD WALL
(Ingalls Creek Slope — Nightmare Needles)

This steep feature, directly above Little Snowpatch, was climbed by Pete Doorish and Don Leonard in May

1978. The route involves six pitches up the center of the wall. Grade III; class 5.8-5.9.

THE LIZARDS est. 6750 ft/2057 m

Two towers detached from the Wall. The upper tower was climbed by Pete Doorish and Ellie Brown in 1972 from the inside notch: traverse left to finish up the chimney on the SE (class 5.7). The lower tower was climbed by the Lizard Wall party. Reach the tower's inside notch from the W (a class 5.4 gully), from the E (a short class 5.9 face), or the S face (four leads, class 5.7). From the notch work up and right to the ledge just below the top on the upper S face, where an aid move (bolt in place) finishes the climb. Class 5.6 and A0.

OSTRICH HEAD est. 6700 ft/2042 m

A tower in the gap between Lizard Wall and Fire Spire,

climbed by Fred Beckey and William Fix on May 27, 1950. Climb the E side (class 4).

FIRE SPIRE   est. 6650 ft/2027 m
(Ingalls Creek Slope — Nightmare Needles)

Fire Spire is a major rock fin with a series of pinnacles, located at the upper W end of Lizard Wall basin. The summit is at the N end of the fin. First ascent by Fred Beckey and Arthur Holben on June 10, 1950, via East Face.

ROUTES: The easiest route to the summit is on the West Face; first ascent by Pete Doorish and Ellie Brown in 1972. From the northern notch, traverse S across the face, then up a chimney to the summit jam crack (class 5.6).

The East Face (the original route) can be reached by the SE gully and broken rock leading to the northern notch. Traverse the vertical upper face, then ascend slanting cracks (two aid pitons on original). From a cheval belay on the summit ridge the final 15-ft block was climbed by lasso. Grade II; difficult class 5 (bring Friends and large chocks). Reference: *A.A.J.*, 1951, p. 173.

The Southeast Face was climbed by Pete Doorish and Don Leonard in May 1978. Begin at the lowest left side of Fire Wall: follow crack systems up and right to where one can begin climbing a steep gully. Higher, work right around a corner to a crack that leads to a notch on the S side. The final pitch is a long crack (5.9) above the notch. Grade II; class 5.9.

FIRE WALL (Southeast Rib): First ascent by Pete Doorish and Karin Malmberg in August 1983. From slabs below the S face of Fire Spire, climb a 5.9 pitch to gain the crest of the rib to the E. An easier pitch leads to a jam crack system on the left side of Fire Wall. Several leads continue to the notch on the ridge atop the wall. Grade II; class 5.9.

Two of the lower (southern) pinnacles of Fire Spire were climbed by Dan Davis and Norm Webber in 1964. One (called "Wildfire") is easily identified as a sharp spike on the lower ridge crest. The climbs were approached from Crystal Creek basin; both were one pitch (class 5). One climb was very unprotected; one was done by working around to the E side.

NOCTURNE TOWER
est. 7200 ft/2195 m
(Ingalls Creek Slope — Nightmare Needles)

One of the outstanding towers in the Nightmare Needles, Nocturne Tower stands closely N of a rounded promontory culminating the Lizard Wall. First ascent by John Rupley and Louis Pottschmidt in June 1956.

ROUTE: The best approach is from Crystal Creek at the 6000-ft level. From depression and broken rock at W side of summit tower, slant left up steep cracks (class 5) to a ledge on NW corner. Final block is done on bolt ladder; nine bolts in place; bring hangers and nuts for ¼-inch Rawl drives.

An alternate approach is from the Little Snowpatch area (see approach for Three Feathers); one should be able to climb to the inside notch from rock at eastern base of final tower. Reference: *Appalachia,* December 1956, p. 240.

There is also a variation from the E. Climb the center rib for three leads to a final crack (class 5.8) leading to the ridge S of the summit block. Descend to join the W-side route.

THREE FEATHERS
est 7200 ft+/2195 m+
(Ingalls Creek Slope — Nightmare Needles)

Three Feathers are a needle trio on the Nightmare Needle crest just N of Nocturne Tower. First ascent of the western needle (White Feather) by Fred Beckey, John Parrott, and Robert Lewis on June 27, 1955. First ascent of the Middle and East Feather by Fred Beckey, Joe Hieb, and Dick Irvin on September 26, 1953.

ROUTES: From Little Snowpatch traverse E a short way to bottom of main gully. Ascend it about 400 ft, then bear left up steeper gully branch to rocks at E base of Nocturne Tower. Climb rock wall to ridge between Nocturne and White Feather (class 4), then follow ridge to White Feather. This point can also be reached by rappel from near Middle Feather. To reach the Middle and East Feather more directly keep in the curved main gully and ascend on the S side of Cruel Finger ridge; then up through rocks to East Feather. Or, reach these from above the N side of Cruel Finger.

The basic route on East and Middle Feather is from the gap next to Cruel Finger. The East Feather has a short aid pitch and Middle Feather is class 4.

On White Feather, follow an airy crest to the base of the 45-ft monolith, where there is a belay ledge just W of the S face. Ten bolt studs are left from the original climb (bring nuts and hangers for ¼-inch Rawl drives). References: *Mountaineer,* 1955, p. 56; *A.A.J.,* 1956, p. 122.

CRUEL FINGER   est. 7100 ft/2164 m
(Ingalls Creek Slope — Nightmare Needles)

Cruel Finger is a spectacular tower located to the E of the main Nightmare Needle crest. From some appearances, the tower seems to grope inchoately toward expression. There are a number of lower towers on the Cruel Finger spur crest. First ascent by Fred Beckey and Don (Claunch) Gordon on May 18, 1958.

ROUTE: From Little Snowpatch cross first gully E and across first ridge (at last trees below Cruel Finger spur) to next gully; it leads steeply along the N side. Start in a partial chimney and climb a 50-ft crack on N face to notch adjoining summit tower (between summit and block on W). From the notch (about 60 ft below the top), make a left traverse to a good crack; climb to a ledge 15 ft under the top, then climb the steep face up and right to the summit (2 bolts and some aid on original; now rated class 5.9 and A0 — one aid bolt). Reference: *Mountaineer*, 1960, p. 89 — photo opp. p. 93.

The lower Cruel Finger towers, in ascending order, have been named Cruel Thumb, Beatrice, Cruel Shoes, Francesca, Paolo, and Chiron.

Cruel Thumb was climbed by Pete Doorish and Dale Farnham in July 1984. Begin below the southern notch. Climb three leads to a tree ledge (the third lead is an obvious class 5.6 dihedral left of a curving chimney). Above, two parallel cracks lead to the notch. Follow the right crack (class 5.10) to a belay tree just right of the notch. A final crack (class 5.9) leads to the top. Grade II.

Beatrice (a sharp spike) was climbed by Pete Doorish, Franci Ries, and Alex Cudcowicz in June 1985. Begin on the N side of the spur, reach the right (upper) notch; two leads — class 5.6. Then climb a short jam crack (class 5.8) to the top. Another route begins from the N side. Climb a face (class 5.8) to the spur crest left of the final tower. Climb the final crack from this side (class 5.10); route done by Pete Doorish and Greg Stan in September 1984.

Cruel Shoes has a route that begins from the tree ledge on Cruel Thumb (climbed by Pete Doorish and Alex Cudcowicz in June 1985). Climb the left of two parallel cracks to the notch (class 5.9 or 5.10), then hand traverse left (class 5.8) and climb a flake/chimney to the final crack of the summit spike.

The ascents of Francesca, Polo, and Chiron were made by Pete Doorish and Greg Stan in September 1984. *Francesca:* Approach from the N flank of the spur. Climb a pitch past a tree (class 5.7) to the notch on the right; easy from here. *Paolo:* From the notch on Francesca, climb jam cracks on the S side (class 5.7). *Chiron:* Approach from the N side of the spur. Climb a class 5.6 pitch to its crest (left of the final tower). Work left around the S face to the opposite side, then ascend.

Sticky Finger is located NE of Cruel Finger, across the gully on a parallel spur. This is a two-pitch climb on the NE (Pete Doorish and Ellie Brown, 1972 — class 5.7).

Butterfinger is the upper of two small towers on the rib below Cruel Thumb. There is a two-pitch route on the NE side (class 5.8) climbed by the Beatrice party.

THE TORTOISE   est. 7400 ft/2256 m
(Ingalls Creek Slope —
Nightmare Needles)

This is a massive crag to the E of the main Nightmare Needle crest, higher than Lone Finger.

The East Face was climbed by Pete Doorish and Greg Stan in 1984. Begin on the lower left of the face;

climb up and right to make a rightward traverse, then climb past small conifers to a broken area one pitch beneath the top; class 5.8.

The South Face was climbed by Pete Doorish and Alex Cudcowicz in 1985. Take a prominent dihedral to a roof, then the cracks above. Grade II; class 5.10.

The West Face was climbed by Pete Doorish, Alex Cudcowicz, and Franci Ries in 1985. Climb the crack arching upwards and left; its top is the crux (class 5.9).

The Hare (est. 7500 ft) stands above and slightly W of The Tortoise. The South Face was climbed by the above listed party; three leads — class 5.4.

WINDJAMMER TOWER
est. 7400 ft/2256 m
(Ingalls Creek Slope —
Nightmare Needles)

A large, square-topped tower N of Three Feathers on the main Nightmare crest. Summit is split longitudinally; E block is higher. First ascent by Pete Schoening and Fred Beckey on June 25, 1950.
ROUTE: From the N flank of Cruel Finger ascend rightward across a basin and spur, then NW to the lower E face of Windjammer. Keep left of the steepest part and climb to the notch to the S of the final block. A shoulder stand and aid piton were used on the original climb to begin the summit pitch (now rated class 5.7). Time: 2 hours or less. Reference: *Mountaineer*, 1950, p. 41.

The West Face of Windjammer was climbed by Pete Doorish and Greg Stan in September 1984. The climb uses an off-width crack on the left side of the concave center portion of the face. Class 5.9.

The NW chimney is an easy class 5 climb (done by same party).

WESTWIND TOWER
est. 7400 ft/2256 m
(Ingalls Creek Slope —
Nightmare Needles)

Located just N of Windjammer Tower. First ascent by Pete Schoening and Fred Beckey on June 25, 1950.
ROUTE: From the base of Windjammer Tower traverse and cross a spur rib into the next gully. Ascend to the eastern base of the objective. Climb the right-hand of several crack series to the top of a flake (on original climb a shoulder stand and several aid pitons used). Climb a difficult slab; a protection bolt is in place on the slab below the summit. Class 5 and possible aid (large angle sizes used on original). Reference: *Mountaineer*, 1950, p. 41.

On the Nightmare crest N of Westwind Tower there are numerous blocks and needles. The "Leaning Mares" is the formation with an inward-tilting block and a slim tower.

The Twins were climbed by Pete Doorish and Greg Stan in September 1984. Both are easy class 5 on the E sides.

Leaning Block was climbed by Pete Doorish and Dale Farnham in 1984 by a flake route on the E side (class 5.7).

The *Leaning Mares* have a route from the S (class 5.6); climbed by above party.

FANTASIA TOWER   7876 ft/2401 m
(Ingalls Creek Slope — Nightmare Needles)

Fantasia Tower is the culmination of Nightmare Needles. The tower is just SW of Fantasia Pond, a 7600-ft tarn closely E of the ridge. First ascent by Fred Beckey and Herb Staley on July 27, 1952; adjacent N and S pinnacles also climbed.

ROUTE: Approach as for Windjammer Tower and continue up along E side of the crest. From near Fantasia saddle climb from E to the upper NE face in two leads; class 4. Reference: *Mountaineer,* 1952, p. 83.

The North Face was climbed by Dan Stage and Martin Woodruff on August 2, 1977. Ascend to the notch between the summit and E pinnacle, then make a traverse to a ledge on the W. Climb atop a block, then a tricky summit move. Class 5.6.

CRYSTAL LAKE TOWER
est. 7800 ft/2375 m
(Ingalls Creek Slope — Nightmare Needles)

A sizable tower with a summit-thumb, located closely W of the Nightmare Needle culmination point; it actually rises from the Crystal Creek trough, with a long western wall. First ascent by Fred Beckey and Herb Staley on July 27, 1952.

ROUTES: Reach by rappel from the ridge above Fantasia saddle (see Fantasia Tower). Climb up slabs and blocks on the E side; class 4.

The South Face was climbed by Alan and Shari Kearney, and Steve Mitchell on July 4, 1976. Take the obvious jam cracks up the center of the face; class 5.8.

The Southwest Rib is a long, involved route climbed by Pete and Judy Doorish in September 1982. Follow the rib crest, keeping just left at the steep white wall in the center portion. Climb the final part of Crystal Lake Tower, drop down to the notch, and follow the ridge to the summit of the westernmost Chessman. Grade III; class 5.8 (19 pitches).

CRYSTAL LAKE WALL
(Ingalls Creek Slope — Nightmare Needles)

This is the prominent rock wall located above the dry tarn in Crystal Creek basin. First ascent by Pete Doorish and Dale Farnham in July 1984. The route follows the prow (a slight nose) and finishes in the vicinity of Leaning Block and Leaning Mares. Grade II; class 5.8.

PENNANT PEAK   8080 ft+/2463 m+
(Ingalls Creek Slope — Flagpole Needles)

Pennant Peak is the large rock peak at the head of the Flagpole Needles. A deep gap separates it from Little Annapurna, about 400 yards away. There are two summits, with the southern one higher by a few feet. First ascent of both summits by Fred Beckey, Phil Sharpe, and Pete Schoening on July 15, 1950.

ROUTE: Climb the major gully W of the dry pond in Crystal Creek for about 1000 ft to the level of the shelf system leading S. A step is managed via the right edge of a rib dividing the gully. Traverse S some 800 ft along ledges to the SE side of the peak. Work right, up the divide and keep climbing in zigzags on the E side to a lower summit (which is the ridge N of Horizontal Spire). Traverse and drop W into a subsidiary gully and climb it to the notch between the N and S summits of Pennant. S summit is done on the NE side (class 4). N summit is done from the notch (short, class 3). There is likely a route from the gap adjacent to Little Annapurna, but it is not verified. Time: 4 hours. Reference: *Mountaineer,* 1952, p. 83.

Note: Reported time for the combined climbs of Pennant and Flagpole, and return to Crystal Creek varies from 7 to 15 hours.

THE FLAGPOLE   est. 7900 ft/2408 m
(Ingalls Creek Slope — Flagpole Needles)

The Flagpole is certainly the most bizarre of the many needles and towers on the broad Ingalls Creek slope. The needle defies probability because of its slender profile. The Flagpole is located on the crest of the sharp southern ridge of Pennant Peak. First ascent by Fred Beckey and Pete Schoening on July 16, 1950.

ROUTE: The simplest way to reach the base of The Flagpole is to make a tricky ridge traverse from the S summit of Pennant Peak (class 4). Stay on the ridge to a tiny notch between a block and a rock sliver just N of The Flagpole; using the rope on the opposite sides of the sliver, rappel to the inside notch of The Flagpole. The route, on the W face, begins with incipient cracks, then two bolts. Tension right (subsequent party placed two more bolts) to bolts and work up to a slight depression in middle of face. A crack leads up past a hole (a Friend or bong is handy) to just left of the top; one can lasso a knob on the crest, pull up, then straddle the final edge. Nine or more bolts in place (hangers in — bring tie-off loops). To descend from Flagpole notch: rappel the lower SW face, then return via another route. References: *A.A.J.,* 1951, photo p. 172; *Mountaineer,* 1950, p. 41; 1952, p. 83; *Cascadian,* 1960, pp. 4-5.

Variation: Lower Southwest Face: First ascent by

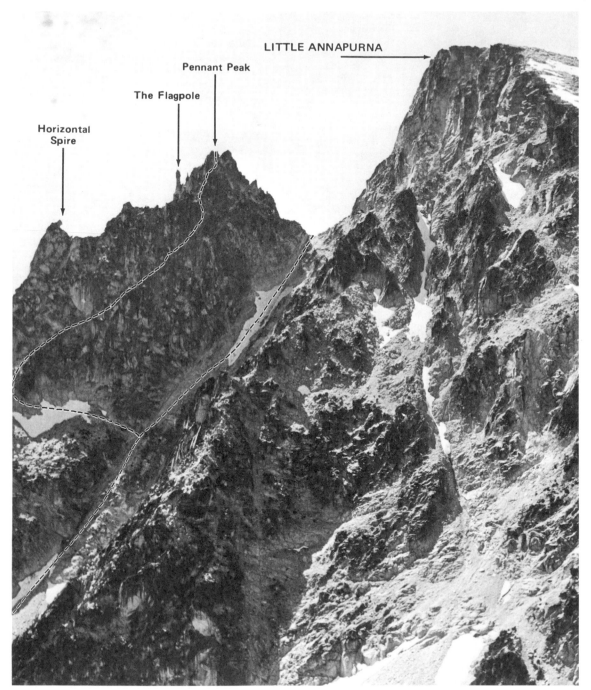

LITTLE ANNAPURNA

Pennant Peak

The Flagpole

Horizontal Spire

THE FLAGPOLE and PENNANT PEAK from east
WILLIAM A. LONG

Donald N. Anderson and Arnold Bloomer on May 30, 1959. The route is three short leads, ending at the final notch; one pitch used a bolt and two poor aid pitons.

The base of this face can be approached three ways (also useful for Pennant Peak and other spires in the area): (1) ascend Annapurna Creek from Ingalls Creek Trail; when almost under the walls of Little Annapurna take a subsidiary gully working right, directly toward The Flagpole; (2) from upper Flagpole gully; (this gully is the first continuous drainage W of Crystal Creek and ends against the S face of The Flagpole walls) one could ascend the gully by working left from low on Crystal Creek; (3) a direct approach from Crystal Creek (see Horizontal Spire, then traverse W).

SEAL HEAD   est. 7650 ft/2332 m
(Ingalls Creek Slope — Flagpole Needles)
A crag located SW and lower than The Flagpole (W, across Flagpole gully). First ascent by The Flagpole party. Approach per the direct route to the SW base of The Flagpole, or from upper Annapurna Creek. The final route is short, on the NE edge. Class 4.

HORIZONTAL SPIRE
est. 7700 ft/2347 m
(Ingalls Creek Slope — Flagpole Needles)
Horizontal Spire is SE and about 200 ft below The Flagpole (the second very white point below The Flagpole, with a summit block tilted sharply N). First ascent by The Flagpole party.
ROUTE: Reach the spire by approaching from Crystal Creek toward the E-facing cliff below it, then circling to the S (some scrambling). It is also feasible from Flagpole gully (the first drainage gully W of Crystal Creek). The climb is done via a ledge on the E side, then up a slab to the summit. Class 4.

PORPOISE POINT   est. 7300 ft/2225 m
(Ingalls Creek Slope — Flagpole Needles)
This prominent rock outcrop is located on the rocky spur below Horizontal Spire, dividing Crystal Creek from Flagpole gully. The East Face falls steeply to Crystal Creek's basin. First ascent by The Flagpole party.

One can ascend per Horizontal Spire Route to the flat N ridge, or reach the objective from upper Flagpole gully's far right side.

The East Face was climbed by Pete Doorish and Karin Malmberg in August 1983. Ascend the long face directly below the Point. The first pitch reaches the slab through overhangs (one chock for aid) and ends at a semi-hanging belay. A difficult jam crack and a mantle reach a good ledge. Climb left around the next steep section to the final upper headwall. Grade III; class 5.10 and A0.

A chimney route was also done on Porpoise Point by Pete and Judy Doorish and Karin Malmberg, August 1983. Follow the obvious fault line left of the East Face Route, finishing on the shoulder below and left of the final point.

CATHAY TOWERS
(Ingalls Creek Slope — Flagpole Needles)
There are several towers on the spur E of Annapurna Creek, between about 6000 and 7000 ft in altitude — considerably lower than The Flagpole.

T'ang Tower is the lowermost tower, which is quite prominent. The inside notch route is class 4. The South Face Route (three leads) finishes on the upper right side of the face in a steep crack (class 5.8).

Higher, the towers form three distinct subridges. The prominent upper needle on the farthest W ridge is *Ming Spire.* Climb the inside notch (class 5.7).

The uppermost ridge of the center subridge (*Manchu Tower*) is identified by a huge slabby chockstone between its dual summits. From atop this objective (class 5.7) the northern and highest summit is easy class 5; the S summit is a class 5.6 off-width crack. All climbs were first done by Pete and Judy Doorish in September 1985.

LITTLE ANNAPURNA
8440 ft+/2573 m+
The Little Annapurna-Dragontail Plateau is a gently-sloping tabular surface of coarse bedrock blocks, a remnant of an ancient preglacial upland. Little Annapurna, a pyramidal peak with a steep South Face, and so named because of its fancied resemblance to Annapurna in the Himalaya, is a most prominent feature on the S rim of Upper Enchantment Lakes Basin. The eastern section of Snow Creek Glaciers lies to the N of Little Annapurna. The first ascent was made by Melvin Marcus, Art Holben, Dick Merritt, and a companion in 1947.
NORTH ROUTE: This route is merely a hike (or ski trip) from Upper Enchantment Basin or Crystal Lake (approach via Snow Creek Trail ◆). The NE snowfields offer good glissading.
SOUTH FACE: This route is about 500 ft high, on good rock. First ascent by Eiichi Fukushima and Laurence Campbell on September 6, 1969.

INGALLS CREEK SLOPE from south

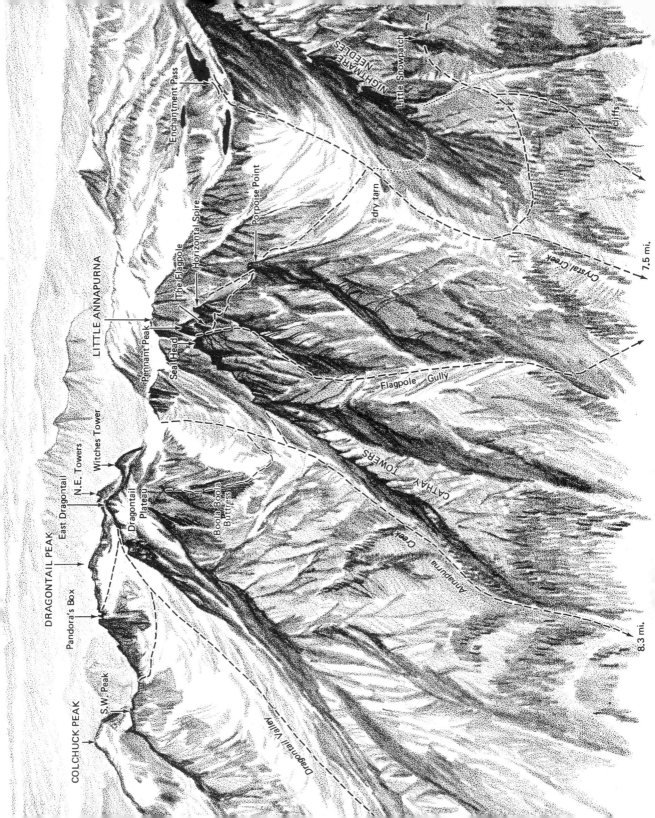

Reach the col (7840 ft) S of Little Annapurna; one can descend about 300 ft from Crystal Lake, then traverse scree W to a system of gullies and then ascend to this col in 3 hours (some scrambling on loose and steep rubble). Another approach is from Crystal Creek, using the beginning of the approach to Pennant Peak, then continuing upward.

Near the middle of the lower face is a SW-facing furrow; start about 20 ft right at a group of thinner cracks leading to a ledge near the E end of the face. Ascend a crack, which curves right to a ledge. The next pitch (a dihedral) is short, but the crux: climb to the end of the crack, then up to a long grassy ledge with a bush; to reach the ledge squirm up a steep, strenuous 15-ft inside corner; an alternate is to climb an exposed friction section around the bulge. Now bear left 40 ft, then up to a platform on the right of a squat tower. Two leads end directly at the summit edifice. Grade II; class 5.6. Time: 3 hours on face. Reference: *Mountaineer,* 1970, pp. 107-108.

There is another route about 100 ft to the right (E) starting in a chimney; climbed by Pete Doorish and Ellie Brown in 1971. Grade II; class 5.8.

SOUTH FACE GULLY: This gully is W of the original route. First ascent by Donald Goodman, Diane Elprekamp, Al McGuire, and Roger Pates on July 1, 1984. From the 7840-ft col scramble 100 ft to the base of the prominent, smooth white gully that splits the W side of the South Face. Two long leads (class 4) end at a narrow blocky ledge on the W face. A 130-ft lead ends at a small notch near the N edge of the W face (class 4 with two 5.5 moves). The final pitch is sustained class 5.7 (90 ft) on the NE corner; the route ends on the ridge crest 200 ft W of the summit.

SOUTHWEST SUMMIT, OPEN BOOK: This is a steep route, taking the obvious large open book and its left flank. First ascent by Jim Yoder and Gordon Briody in August 1983. One can reach the route by descending from the col W of West Annapurna, then traversing. Enter from the lower right side, below and right of the open book. Ascend the gully one pitch (class 5.4), then climb a pitch traversing on a face (class 5.6) to the large ledge at the base of the book.

Climb cracks closely left of the open book to a hanging belay (class 5.8). Follow the same crack system (class 5.8-5.9) for one or two pitches. Here make a leftward traverse on a small ledge, then angle up on small ledges and overhanging blocks (class 5.10 at the crux); a pendulum may be done here.

The final pitch becomes easier (class 5.7) and leads toward the top.

WEST ANNAPURNA, SOUTH FACE: First ascent by Fred Beckey and Dave Beckstead in June 1984. The approach was made via Annapurna Creek. Climb a rocky crag adjacent to a gully at the right-hand base of the face (optional). The route climbs blocky terrain on a rib (class 4), then on the last pitch a right-bearing chimney (class 5.7) leads to easy summit terrain. The highest point of the formation is a curious, perched block.

DRAGONTAIL PLATEAU, SOUTHEAST FACE

There is a steep face and a significant buttress on the SE flank and a steep wall on the eastern flank of Dragontail Plateau. Because these features face Annapurna Creek and are not visible from most of the Cashmere Crags upland, there has been little climber visitation.

ROUTES: Two routes have been climbed on the Southeast Face, both to the S or left of Boola Boola Buttress. The 1985 route is about 100 ft left of the latter, and the 1971 route about another 100 ft farther left.

The 1985 route was done by Pete Doorish and Ellie Brown. The route takes a steep rib on dark rock just left of an apron of light-toned rock, and ends climbing a final headwall. Grade II or III; class 5.9. The obvious chimney system left of this route, climbed by Pete and Judy Doorish, finishes on the shoulder midway up the face (class 5.6).

BOOLA BOOLA BUTTRESS: This distinct buttress, facing SE, rises from Annapurna Creek to the upland crest of Dragontail Plateau. The climbing route, which is slightly on the right flank of the buttress, was climbed by Lee Cunningham, Jim Yoder, and Bill Crawford in August 1971.

Follow a ramp system on the right to the bullet-shaped formation on the buttress. Easy cracks lead to a right-facing corner. Then climb cracks right of the bullet formation for one-half pitch (class 5.10c). Face climb rightward one-half pitch to a hanging belay. The second pitch begins with a short crack to a roof (class 5.10). Lieback around the left side of the small roof and continue upwards 30 ft on a class 5.7 crack. When the crack seams out, traverse right for 40 ft to non-obvious face cracks (class 5.10+). Protect with knife blades (possibly aid) and climb upward (class 5.11) through another small roof to an alcove (belay). The third pitch begins with class 5.9 climbing, then about four pitches in chimneys (class 5.4). Now climb a headwall with cracks (class 5.7). A big crack leads through an overhang (class 5.9), then the summit overhangs are climbed on their right (class 5.10a). Grade IV; class 5.11 (original party used Friends, stoppers, and two KB's). Total of 11 pitches.

WITCHES TOWER
8520 ft+ /2597 m+

A steep, rounded rock crag that nearly splits two portions of Snow Creek Glaciers, located 0.2 mi. W of the W shore of Brynhild Lake. It has a steep wall of about 400 ft on the N flank, starting from the E edge of the western ice section.

ROUTE: Approach as for Little Annapurna (North Route). From the inside col (8360 ft) climb up talus to beneath the summit on its S side. Broken slabs lead to the summit. Class 3.

WEST BUTTRESS: By Charles Sink and Eric Gerber on July 4, 1971.

Begin about 100 yards N of the inside col. Ascend easy slabs on lower portion (one class 4 lead). The next pitch enters an 80-ft chimney and continues out of it onto slabs. A class 4 lead goes to the top. Class 5.4.

NORTHWEST BUTTRESS: By Bradley Albro and Rick Piercey in September 1976. Begin at NW notch, 20 ft right of the buttress. Climb obvious twin cracks, then left to buttress. Climb a jam crack to a ledge, then slabs. Grade II; class 5.7 (rock is solid).

NORTHEAST FACE: By Duane Constantino, Dave Fox, Bob Gundrum, and Paul McKnight in August 1976. Climb from the lower left of face, later crossing to central depression. Higher, cross to left (class 5.8), then climb dihedral (class 5.8). Grade II.

ENCHANTMENT PEAK
8520 ft+/2597 m+

This small but high peak tops the sloping bedrock plateau ½ mi. to ¾ mi. W of Prusik Pass. The NE summit, which leans N, is merely a little rock pyramid, and is the highest point. Here a NW face with a steep rock wall contains gullies, snow, and ice patches. The SW summit is a split, block-like ridge tower. First ascents by Fred Beckey, September 20, 1948.

ROUTES: From Prusik Pass, hike W of the broad talus ridge; from beyond Aasgard Pass scramble northward. The NE summit is a scramble on its S side. The SW summit involves a short class 4 climb. The span between the summits is composed of broken bedrock blocks; if hiking, keep E of the crest.

The ridge continuing W forms a row of small rock crags called the **Black Dwarves.** The northern face contains two large ice patches, in addition to couloirs and a large deposit of moraine rubble.

A new route to the highest tower was done by Richard McGowan and Steve Trafton in September 1975. From the col to its E traverse a southern ledge to an 80-ft crack leading from a dance floor to the summit. Climb for 25 ft and enter a chimney that splits the summit tower; climb the chimney. Class 5.

COLCHUCK BALANCED ROCK
8200 ft+/2499 m+

This feature of the Stuart Range is a prominent and isolated rock peak, located on a spur crest midway between Enchantment Peak and Colchuck Lake. Positioned only about ½ mi. E of the lake, the sheer western face is quite noticeable from that vantage. The peak is capped by a huge block (about 15 ft in height) that appears to balance on the summit — seemingly placed there by a playful demon.

COLCHUCK BALANCED ROCK from west
JEFF SMOOT

The flanking crests of Colchuck Balanced Rock have other points, including a prominent one on the N (about 7800 ft in altitude). The S end of the crest terminates at the Black Dwarves section of the bedrock upland of Enchantment Peak. First ascent by Gene Prater and Thomas Quin in October 1958.

ROUTE: Approach from the E side of Colchuck Lake (see Colchuck Lake Trail ◆), ascending the obvious gully to the notch above Jaberwocky Tower. From the N side of the notch, climb eastward on talus and broken rock slopes to the ridge saddle on the S crest of the Rock. Scramble on talus around to the E flank, then climb rock to the summit area. Cracks lead to the final block, which is a bouldering problem (one can throw a rope over the top for protection).

WEST FACE, DIRECT ROUTE: First ascent by Jack Lewis and Tomas Boley in July 1980. Second ascent by Mark

Twight and Mark Johnston in August 1983 (reported as first climb). This 12-pitch route follows cracks and corners to an obvious roof high on the sheer face. The crux pitch is the long, right-facing book. The route turns the roof leftward (Friends and hooks — A2 or A3). Above the roof, a hand crack (class 5.9) leads to a smaller roof, a loose squeeze chimney, and another roof. Two easier pitches follow.

Several variations have been made, both on the lower cracks and the portion above the large roof (see topo for details). Grade IV; class 5.10 and A3. References: *A.A.J.*, 1984, p. 162; *Climbing*, June 1984, p. 10.

Variation: Starting from the angling gully beneath the face, a major variation features the climb of a right-facing corner on an orange-toned (lichened) wall about 300 ft N of the original route. Climbed by Lee Cunningham and Monte Westlund in July 1984. Begin with a crack and face climbing (class 5.10) to the obvious corner (has an orange streak on its right). Climb the corner (class 5.10) to a ledge. Continue 20 ft (class 5.9), then turn a 20-ft roof on the left (class 5.9) and mantle into a chimney behind a flake. The variation joins the 1975 route (Northwest Buttress). Grade III or IV; class 5.10 (six pitches).

NORTHWEST BUTTRESS: First ascent by Al Givler, Jerry Barnard, Jim McCarthy, and Carla Firey in June 1975. The route begins at the base of the lower NW pillar, which is separated from the West Face by a gully (see topo). On the pillar portion of the climb there are five pitches (some class 5.8, followed by pitches of 5.5). From the top of the pillar five more pitches lead to the top of the Balanced Rock. On this section, first traverse around the corner to a chimney (left of big roof), then climb upward and right. The rock on the route is solid, with good cracks. Grade III; class 5.8.

NORTH FACE: Approach from Stuart Lake Trail ◆ and ascend to Hel Basin. Climb left of obvious narrow couloir to rock buttress and snow gully (six pitches to ridge). The ridge leads to the lower W pinnacle; there are about four pitches of class 3-4 to the summit of Colchuck Balanced Rock. Route done by Dan Cauthorn and Tobin Kelly, April 1983.

JABERWOCKY TOWER   est. 6840 ft/2085 m

This tower, located between Colchuck Balanced Rock and Colchuck Lake, tends to blend into its precipitous surroundings. The western face, about 500 ft in height, is located close to the lake; the short side is about 100 ft high. From the SE end of the lake, ascend eastward, then take the prominent gully (and its left fork) to reach the inside notch of the tower. First ascent by Dave Beckstead and Paul Myhre on July 13, 1970.

Two routes have been climbed (both by the original party). The East Face: from the NE corner make a short ledge traverse leftward, then climb a flaring chimney (class 5.6). The North Ridge: from the NE ridge, traverse right, then climb a tilting dihedral to a large roof. Traverse right under the roof (class 5.6-5.7), then take a short crack to the top.

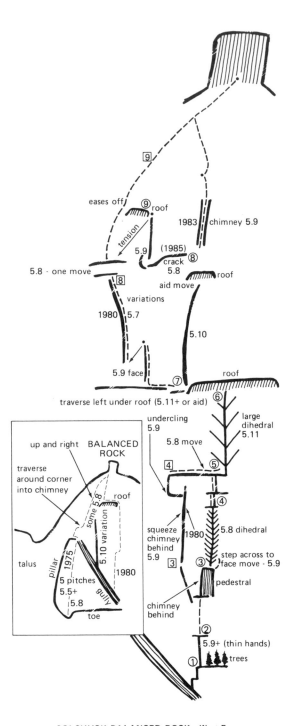

COLCHUCK BALANCED ROCK · West Face

Source: Jim Nelson and Chuck Gerson

ROSEBUD SPIRE   est. 7700 ft/2347 m
Located SW of Colchuck Balanced Rock on the lake slope of the jagged ridge descending from the Rock. First ascent by Colchuck Balanced Rock party. Climb from the upper notch: two leads (class 5 and some aid).

AASGARD PASS SENTINEL
This is a pinnacle E of the pass, above the heather cirque on the E end of the col (est. 8200 ft). First ascent by Dave Anderson, Steve Barnett, Bruce Carson, and Donn Heller in June 1972. The route follows a large 200-ft left-facing open book for one pitch, climbs a lieback on a short headwall, then climbs through a cannonhole to the ridgetop. Grade II; class 5.9.

SPINELESS PROW

This formation is a S-facing prow about 200 yards below Aasgard Pass (est. 7900 ft). First ascent by Dave Anderson and Julie Brugger in June 1973. Begin the climb in a chimney on the Prow's right. From its top make a left traverse onto the Prow. Here are five pitches of interesting and solid crack climbing. Grade III; class 5.9.

DRAGONTAIL PEAK
8840 ft+/2695 m+

The large granite massif of Dragontail is the second-highest peak in the Stuart Range. The name originates from the miniature "tails" or rock needles on the thin crest SW of the summit. Rock on the peak is unusually sound. Its expansive Northwest Face, rising above the moraines and ice of Colchuck Glacier, is one of the finest walls in the Cascades. It continues impressively as a North and also Northeast Face where it corners toward Aasgard Pass. Dragontail is becoming very popular with climbers because of its accessibility, sound rock, and grand appearance.

While the North Face is very visible on approach, located just S of the terminal moraine above Colchuck Lake, the Northeast Face is less noticeable because of its orientation toward the broad couloir leading to Aasgard Pass. Dragontail has a well defined summit ridge that extends about ½ mi. in length, and on this ridge the several summit towers are located. The jagged crest extending NE of the summit terminates in three towers W of Aasgard Pass. The highest of these Northeast Towers (about 8520 ft) is the third from the termination.

Lateral ridges extend out from the spine. The two most prominent ridges, Serpentine Arete and Backbone Ridge, project in a northwesterly direction on the Northwest Face. The long Northeast Buttress projects from the Northeast Towers toward Colchuck Lake.

Dragontail Peak's summit is located ¾ mi. S of the S end of Colchuck Lake. The peak's southern ramparts slope toward Ingalls Creek and its NE to E flank holds a remaining portion of the Snow Creek Glaciers.

The high crest to the SE of Dragontail's summit culminates in a mass of coarse bedrock blocks at East Dragontail (8760 ft+) and the craggy upland of Dragontail Plateau — which divides the high cirque containing the Snow Creek Glaciers from the long scarp of Ingalls Creek.

There is a wedge-shaped Southwest Peak of Dragontail (est. 8400 ft) located at 0.6 mi. distance from the main summit (between Porcupine Creek and the next creek eastward, Dragontail Creek). The Southwest Peak is connected to the upper SW ridge of Dragontail by a quite distinct U-shaped col.

Dragontail's first ascent was probably made by William A. Long and Dudley Kelly in June 1937; the first winter climb was by Gene Prater, Barry Carlson, and Ralph Uber on March 3, 1957. The Southwest Peak (Norma Spire) was climbed by Long, and Elvin R. Johnson on September 11, 1948. References: *Cascadian*, 1956, pp. 22-23; 1957, pp. 21-22; 1963, p. 33.

EAST ROUTE: From near Aasgard Pass or Brynhild Lake (see Snow Creek Trail ◆) bear SW and ascend the glacier section to climb through the obvious saddle in the crest above. Here a gentle rock spur with ice on its N side leads to the summit rocks some 300 ft above. The highest point is a small bedrock clump that drops on the N. Class 2.

SOUTH ROUTE: From Ingalls Creek Trail ◆ about 1½ mi. W of Crystal Creek (4100 ft) ascend near a small tributary (Dragontail Creek) that descends from NNE. Near timberline the valley forms a large open basin between Dragontail's Southwest Peak and the Dragontail Plateau (basin usually has snowfields). Here ascend directly N to the final summit rocks (scree or snow); easy. One could vary the route by ascending first to the saddle immediately E of the summit.

WEST ROUTE: From Colchuck Col (see Colchuck Peak) climb the easy gully on the S drainage to a summit ridge notch left of Pandora's Box (gully is closely S of Rooster Finch Tower). Cross the notch, then complete as for final portion of South Route.

COLCHUCK COL BUTTRESS: This is the rugged rock buttress at the southern end of the Northwest Face; it begins N (and below) the Dragontail-Colchuck Col. Both Rooster Finch and Bull Durham towers are located on the slopes of this buttress. First ascent by Steve Barnett and Keith Hansen in July 1974. The route has five pitches, up to class 5.6. Grade II.

Summit

Serpentine Arete

Rooster Finch

Bull Durham

Boxing Route

Pillar

COLCHUCK GLACIER

steep headwall

5.8 chimney

Serpentine Arete

5.7

4th class ledge system

Ball Bearing Amphitheater

5.9

Backbone Ridge

top of tower

lieback

5.7

5.8

5.7

couloir

5.9 (The Fin)

Triple Couloir

hidden couloir

Northeast Towers

N.E. Couloir Route

Northeast Buttress

rappel

Dragonfly

Dragonfly Madness

North Face Route (June 1971)

On the Dragontail crest (between the Southwest Peak and the summit of Dragontail Peak, about 0.3 mi. SW of the true summit) is a significant tower: *Pandora's Box* (8720 ft+), a short but prominent fork-shaped tower. First ascent by Bill Prater and Tom Lyon in 1957, via the N side: one lead, including a shoulder stand, then class 4 climbing. The 50-ft S side was climbed by Jim Wickwire and Fred Stanley in August 1963; aid to the fork, then stemming.

There are two towers on the slope of Colchuck Col Buttress. They are *Rooster Finch Tower* (est. 8550 ft) and *Bull Durham Tower* (est. 8430 ft). The upper tower was climbed by Jim Wickwire and Fred Stanley in August 1963; a jam crack on the E face was rated class 5.5. The lower tower, about 100 ft in height, is climbed from the upper notch (same party). The route is located on the S face, and done in two leads: Begin with class 4 climbing, then minor aid on a short crack and an overhang.

BOVING ROUTE: This is a difficult route on the smooth, solid face to the W of Serpentine Arete. First ascent by Paul Boving and Matt Christensen in August 1977. The route begins off the Colchuck Glacier about 100 ft W of a large corner (at a set of double cracks about 8 ft apart closely above the glacier), then follows discontinuous cracks on the left side of the gray slabs. The first five pitches are class 5.10 on excellent glacier-polished granite; the remaining 1200 ft climbs broken rock (class 4 to 5.7).

The first pitch starts from ledges just above the moat, taking the right-hand finger crack (class 5.10a) to a small overhang. Now make a class 5.10 move to the left crack, then ascend the broken dihedral to a ledge belay. The second pitch traverses up and right via cracks and face climbing to a dihedral; follow this about 40 ft to a ledge. The crux pitch takes the crack system to a small roof (class 5.10c), which is passed by finger jams and face climbing. Another 40 ft leads to a ledge. Pitch four continues for 70 ft up the previously used crack system, then moves right 8 ft to another crack which becomes an overhanging flake. Undercling this and turn the corner to gain a belay stance 30 ft higher (large dihedral on right). Pitch five moves right to the classic dihedral: ascend to its top and move left to a slot (class 5.10), then up to a semi-hanging belay. Now traverse left on easy ledges about 250 ft until able to ascend on broken rock to the ridgetop. Grade IV; class 5.10c. Take a standard chock rack ⅛-inch to 3-inch, including RP's and a No. 4 Friend for first pitch (KB's for belay spots are optional). Note: before mid-July there may be some running water.

SERPENTINE ARETE: This is the distinctive arete W of Backbone Ridge, one that emerges from the Dragontail face a few hundred ft above the glacier and emanates at the true summit. The climb is becoming popular because of its sound granite rock and general quality. First ascent by Tom Hargis and Jay Ossiander on July 1, 1973.

From the large boulders at the S end of Colchuck Lake (see Colchuck Lake Trail ♦) ascend the old ground moraine slopes and then higher bear left to the northern lateral moraine. Follow its crest to below the orange-toned wall

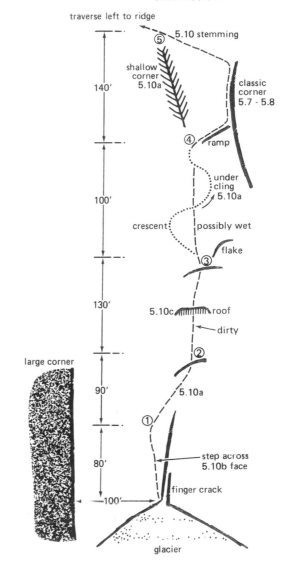

DRAGONTAIL PEAK - Boving Route
source: Larry Kemp

beneath the Northwest Face's depression (this is where the lower left edge of the glacier terminates against a steep whitish wall). The easiest start, directly below the Arete, is to ascend snow or boulders to the wall, then scramble up and leftward on ledges to where an obvious pitch of moderately broken rock (class 3 and 4) leads to a sandy ledge (a part of the depression). Climb easily up and slightly right on bro-

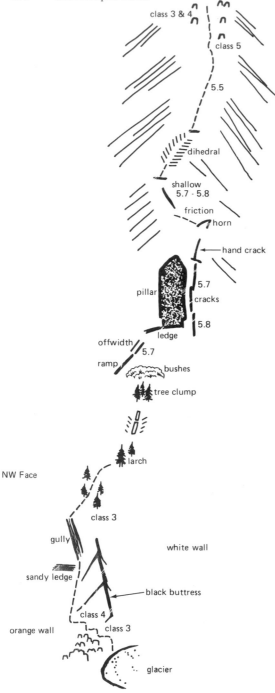

class 3 & 4

class 5

5.5

dihedral

shallow
5.7 - 5.8

friction

horn

hand crack

pillar

5.7

cracks

5.8

ledge

offwidth

5.7

ramp

bushes

tree clump

larch

NW Face

class 3

gully

white wall

sandy ledge

black buttress

class 4

orange wall

class 3

glacier

DRAGONTAIL PEAK - Serpentine Arete

ken dark rock toward the prominent pillar on the Arete. At the location of several small larches, a large larch tree will be seen on a ledge to the right (beneath a headwall). Turn the corner 15 ft to a small fir, then climb cracks along the left side of a 40-ft pillar in a dihedral (class 5.5-5.6) to a ledge with small tree clumps. Climb up and left (bushes) and then to a large ledge. Now climb a ramp rightward with an off-width crux to reach the left end of the ledge at the foot of the Arete's pillar. Traverse the ample ledge (about 30 ft) to a belay spot at its right side.

Step down and start up the thin crack about 15 ft right of the inside crack of the pillar. Begin this with finger locks (class 5.8), then continuing face cracks (class 5.7): the last part of the pitch is a hand crack (protection is good on the crack system). Belay on a small slanting ledge with a horn on the right (can use long runner). Now friction left easily to a shallow groove-dihedral. Climb an awkward finger crack (thin climbing for a few moves — class 5.7-5.8) to a small platform; here one can look directly down to the top of the pillar. Make a move right and then up the right-slanting dihedral (jamming, liebacks, and face climbing on chickenheads) to a belay spot where another dihedral joins from below.

Blocky climbing continues on the summit, generally taking a route along the arete. Most of the climbing is moderate and solid (class 3 to lower class 5) and enjoyable (six to eight pitches). The last pitch to the summit is a short face of about 20 ft (class 5.7). Grade IV; class 5.8. Time: 7 hours from base. Note: numerous variations can be taken on the route; some parties have climbed cracks farther right from the ledge at the base of the pillar.

The left side of the pillar provides a variation (class 5.8). The inside crack on the right side of the pillar provides a variation (class 5.8 — jams and liebacks).

Lower Variations: A western start, climbing the large dihedral right of the black buttress, from the glacier edge (by C. M. Holt and Keith Boyer in 1975) is more difficult than making the leftward traverse on ledges, but a reasonable route. Parties have also made a more direct and difficult entry to the sandy ledge.

Winter Variation: By Tim Wilson and John Wesson, April 1983. Begin right of Serpentine Arete via thin ice. Four ice pitches lead to snowfield; one mixed pitch and then up and left to meet the normal route.

The route line takes a depression between the Arete's normal route and the Boving Route, leading to the upper wall of Dragontail. The lower portion of the climb was made on a series of spring ice runnels. Grade IV, with difficult technical ice pitches under winter conditions. The route would probably not be feasible in summer.

NORTHWEST FACE: This is the steep face directly above Colchuck Glacier. The original 1700-ft route climbs largely in a wide, shallow gully between Serpentine Arete and Backbone Ridge. One should beware of rockfall in gully sections. First ascent by Fred Beckey and Dan Davis on June 28, 1962.

DRAGONTAIL PEAK from northwest
WILLIAM A. LONG

COLCHUCK PEAK

Northwest Route

Boving Route

DRAGONTAIL PEAK

North Buttress

The Sandpiper

Northwest Face Route

Serpentine Arete

The Fin

Backbone Ridge

Northeast Towers

Northeast Buttress

North Face Route

Hidden Couloir

Spineless Prow

Aasgard Pass

COLCHUCK LAKE

DRAGONTAIL PEAK — northwest face
U.S. GEOLOGICAL SURVEY

Reach from Colchuck Lake (see Colchuck Lake Trail ◆), then ascend closely left of the glacier terminus. Climb directly left into the gully depression and continue up its left flank until about ¾ of the distance to the summit; the hardest pitch is on slabs about midway up the depression (some of the friction climbing is hard to protect). Climb rightward and into a chimney, crossing a ridge on the right to another depression. Ascend the broken area of its left side to emerge closely N of the true summit. Climb a short vertical pitch to the left of a pinnacle; circle left to the summit. Grade III (class 5; most of climb is class 4). Note: depending on the season, there may be snowpatches in the depressions, with resulting wet rock. References: *Mountaineer*, 1963, p. 96; *A.A.J.*, 1963, p. 472.

BACKBONE RIDGE: This is the steep rock crest left of the white slabs (and left of original route) on the Northwest Face. The route's length of 21 pitches will possibly force a bivouac before return to a base at Colchuck Lake. Subsequent parties have intersected the route in its upper sections and found easier completions. First ascent by Mark Weigelt and John Bonneville on August 5, 1970.

Start at the lowest point of the ridge, which here toes into the snow. After two leads, traverse right; some hard climbing (lieback to a shallow chimney) gets one to class 3 rock. Work up and right on this easier ground for 500 ft, bearing toward the ridge crest. Here is a crux dihedral: a 90-ft 6-inch crack (class 5.9 — only protected by questionable chockstones). Then ascend right and up to a belay on a ledge. Traverse left (face climbing), then up. Easier climbing (two pitches) takes one to base of a white wall ("Ball Bearing Amphitheater" — has water). Continue up the ridge (easy for several hundred ft) to a steeper section. Traverse left around ridge (class 5.8 unprotected) to a belay around corner. Climb upward on "The Fin" (class 5.9 face climbing) (left into a gully is optional). Ascend to the ridge, then S to the summit. Grade IV; class 5.9; take protection up to 2 inches. Reference: *A.A.J.*, 1971, p. 342.

Variation: A variation was done by the thin crack system near the left edge of The Fin by Dave Anderson, Julie Brugger, and two others in June 1974. Class 5.9. The last of the three pitches were done on rightward trending cracks.

NORTH FACE: This route on the North Face begins W of the Hidden Couloir, climbing the slabs and face to the N of Backbone Ridge until near the N summit ridge. First ascent by Eric Gerber and Charles Sink on August 1, 1971.

Begin at the lowest apron of the North Face and generally climb right of a central spur for about 900 ft (largely class 3-4 on ledges and minor gully systems). As the angle increases, follow chimney systems for several leads (up to class 5.7), then an easier section of the face. Continue to a shallow amphitheatre below and left of The Fin (a major smooth, large rock protrusion); this portion of the route is class 4-5. Now traverse snow or rock to a gully leading toward Backbone Ridge (class 5.7). Climb a minor ridge near the edge of The Fin, then ascend the steep ice couloir (same as Triple Couloir Route) left of The Fin to the summit ridge.

Grade III; class 5.7 (about four pitches of class 5 — the remainder is easier). Take ice axe and crampons. Time: 6 hours.

NORTH FACE: This route climbs the Hidden Couloir on the lower half of the North Face, then crosses Backbone Ridge to the left flank of a major depression and leading to the summit ridge; there are 10 rock pitches. First ascent by Jim Wickwire and Fred Stanley on June 7, 1971. First winter ascent by Skip Edmunds and Dick Heffernan, February 1976. This is a fine route in early season if the snow is firm.

Begin the climb on snow/ice in the deeply recessed 45-degree Hidden Couloir, which angles rightward for 800 ft to near midface. Exit onto steep slabs (or snow, early season) which are climbed for about 300 ft; the route crosses the Gerber-Sink Route. Climb rightward on an easy buttress (one lead). Cross Backbone Ridge here, then ascend an easy ledge system on the left side of a prominent indentation beyond Backbone Ridge. The crux of the route is the final headwall: one makes three leads across this wall (one lead is a delicate traverse — class 5.7). A final lead on 50-degree snow/ice takes one to the upper rocks below the summit ridge closely E of the true summit. Grade III; class 5.7. Take ice axe and crampons. Time: 9 hours. Reference: *Mountaineer*, 1971, pp. 76-77.

TRIPLE COULOIR: This is a 2500-ft snow and ice route that has become relatively popular. It can be a fine winter or spring route, but beware of avalanche danger and rockfall. First ascent by Bill Joiner, Leslie Nelson, and Dave Seman in May 1974. Begin the ascent via the Wickwire-Stanley Hidden Couloir, then traverse left into and up the prominent couloir in center face: this portion is the crux and its difficulty depends upon the amount and type of snow cover. There may be ice. Then climb the couloir N of The Fin (same as August 1971 route). Grade II or III; class 5 (up to 5.8 if conditions are difficult). Bring ice screws, rock pitons, ice tools, hard hats. Time: 4-7 hours.

DRAGONTAIL MADNESS: This long route on the North Face is located in the area of rock between Hidden Couloir and the Northeast Buttress. The route ends at the notch between the Northeast Towers and the summit ridge of Dragontail Peak. Due to loose rock, it is suggested to climb during winter or frozen conditions. First ascent by Michael R. Croswaite and Thomas A. Stanton on April 3-4, 1978.

Begin in the first major gully left of Hidden Couloir. Traverse left across a ledge until just below three small trees, then climb directly to the base of a chimney (a cave permits an excellent bivouac site). Climb the chimney and directly over two minor overhangs (this is the crux due to loose rock). Once into the avalanche chute, exit right to an exposed ridge, then continue to the notch. Grade IV; class 5.9 (22-25 pitches). Bring chocks to 2 inches; one ice screw used. Crampons used entire climb on original.

DRAGONFLY: NORTH FACE OF NORTHEAST BUTTRESS: This route takes a very sheer and difficult face, beginning on the lower Northeast Buttress (see topo). There are 12 pitches to the ridge crest. The route connects to the

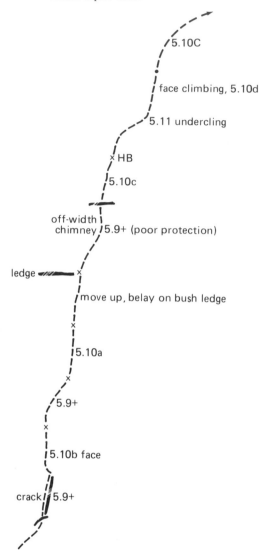

DRAGONFLY ROUTE
Northeast Buttress of Dragontail Peak

The route begins from slabs (or snow) at edge of stream descending from Aasgard Pass (at 6800 ft). Climb slabs with intermittent ledges on right side of first open book (closely) W of the Northeast Couloir. After several leads (class 3-4) reach a rib (right outside corner). Bear left and climb class 4 cracks on corner (which flattens into face). In about 150 ft one meets the narrow gully of the book. Climb a 20-ft wall (class 5.5) on right side, then scramble leftward up broken rock 100 ft. Now, three pitches of delightful class 5 climbing up cracks and small holds, well on the right flank of the enlarged book lead to the right corner again. Scramble right into adjacent gully, then shortly left again to belay ledge on corner. A steep pitch (deep cracks) on corner is done by a short delicate left traverse, then squeezing up a deep chimney (hard to start). Broken rock leads to a long but easy gully-book scramble, ending on a corner below the giant square-topped tower on the buttress crest. One pitch up whitish cracks (class 4) leads to the crest right of the blank tower; from fixed pins on W side of crest rappel 200 ft to ledge system on this exposed face. Follow this rising system S, parallel to the ridge crest (numerous class 3-5 leads) until reaching the large ledge one pitch before notch in Dragontail

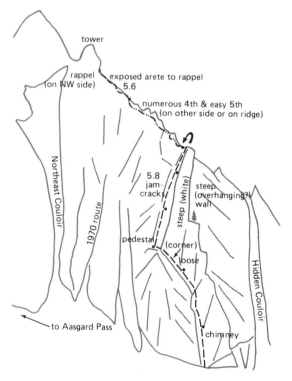

DRAGONTAIL - **Complete Northeast Buttress**

source: Dan Cauthorn

upper portion of the buttress (1971 route). First ascent by Jim Yoder and Bob McGown in July 1985. Grade V; class 5.11 (include Friends, RP's, stoppers, four KB's).

NORTHEAST BUTTRESS: This long buttress is not as continuously steep as Serpentine Arete, but the total climbing distance is greater due to the long knife-edged section in the middle, and several steps. Rock is overall sound. First ascent by Fred Beckey, Ron Burgner, and Thom Nephew on September 14, 1971.

DRAGONTAIL PEAK from northeast
FRED BECKEY

Witches Tooth

1962

1972

Northeast Towers

Northeast Buttress

Aasgard Pass

Northeast Couloir

meet ridge crest

1971

1984

Dragonfly

Hidden Couloir

crest W of the third NE tower. One can traverse to this notch (rotten) or climb solid rock (class 4) to notch between second and third towers. From the E flank of the crest a tree fixes the first of two descent rappels to easy slabs. Grade III or IV; class 5.7 or 5.8. Time: 9 hours. References: *Mountaineer,* 1971, p. 77; *A.A.J.,* 1972, p. 114.

Variation: The complete Northeast Buttress was climbed by Dan Cauthorn and John Stoddard in July 1984 (probable first party). Begin at the lowest point of the buttress, at a prominent chimney system. The first six pitches were good cracks on the lower steep portion (class 5.6 to 5.8); the route kept on the crest or just to its right for eight pitches, meeting the rappel point of the original route. The entire climb is grade IV and quite long.

NORTHEAST COULOIR: First ascent by Dave Beckstead and Paul Myhre on July 12, 1970. First winter ascent by Cal Folsom and Donn Heller in February 1975.

This is the principal couloir entering the NE face between Hidden Couloir and Aasgard Pass; the couloir begins at about 6800 ft, is long and narrow, steepening to 40 degrees in places (possible ice at times). From its end, keep right and climb two pitches of shattered rock to the sharp crest of the upper Northeast Buttress (the second lead is class 5.7); considerable loose rock has been experienced here in late season. Follow the exposed crest about 200 ft southward, then make a broad ledge traverse to the notch between the Northeast Towers and the jagged ridge leading to Dragontail Peak's summit (the last pitch to the notch is loose). Grade II; class 5.7. Take ice axe and crampons.

Variation: Couloir Right Wall: By Jim Yoder and Bob Shonerd in July 1985. The first two pitches are class 5.6 rock climbing, followed by six pitches of chimneys (averaging 5.4). A pitch rated class 5.6 and one of 5.7 lead to a hanging belay. This is followed by a chimney pitch (class 5.8); the route continues to the upper Northeast Buttress. Grade III; class 5.8. Take chocks to 3 inches.

NORTHEAST TOWERS   8520 ft+/2598 m+

ROUTE: The easiest route to their summits is from the W section of Snow Creek Glaciers, then to one of the notches in the Dragontail crest. The towers offer various means (class 4) on solid rock. The lowest notch is W of the third (highest) tower. The eastern crest beginning near Aasgard Pass, and leading to the towers, offers climbing opportunities.

EAST FACE OF NORTHEAST TOWERS: First ascent by Dan Davis and Fred Beckey June 28, 1962.

Approach from Colchuck Lake. Begin the route about 500 ft below Aasgard Pass. Ascend a long rock gully on white right side of large open book heading directly for the pointed first summit tower, until it meets the NE ridge. Slabby rock may contain snow patches and some loose rock. Near the top bear left to reach the easternmost point of the Northeast Towers, then scramble and climb to the highest tower over a crest of blocks. Grade I or II; class 5 (two pitons used); remainder class 3 and 4. Reference: *Mountaineer,* 1963, pp. 95-96.

NORTHEAST ARETE: There are three distinct crests that lead to the Northeast Towers' summit ridge. The eastern crest rises from near Aasgard Pass. The quite distinct NE Arete begins lower, from just above the Northeast Couloir; the less prominent NNE Arete begins still lower, with a cliffy beginning.

The NE Arete was climbed by Dave Anderson, Steve Barnett, Bruce Carson, and Donn Heller in June 1972. Begin about 100 ft left of the toe, then climb on or near the crest for 4-5 pitches (good rock — class 5.6-5.8). Near the junction with the larger crest above, traverse left and up for two pitches (very loose) to the crest. Then traverse to the jagged pinnacled ridge leading to the summit. Grade III; class 5.7 (take moderate chock selection).

The N face of the upper portion of the Arete was climbed from where the Northeast Couloir widens near its top (Bob Cotter and Jim Ruch, October 1985). There is one pitch of class 4 to easy 5, then left and upward on a hand traverse to left-bearing cracks and dihedrals (class 5.7). Traverse sharply rightward on a snow ledge to a steep ice patch (this ice is higher than the couloir top). Continue up to ledges leading around to the gully and summit of the Northeast Towers. Grade II or III; class 5.7.

A route reported as the NNE Arete was climbed by Tom Michael and Brian Povolny in June 1980. This may be the same as the 1972 route, or a different route.

COLCHUCK PEAK   8705 ft/2653 m

Colchuck is the high, rugged granitic peak located SW of Colchuck Lake, with an alpine flank above the Colchuck Glacier. The glacier, which occupies the spectacular cirque between Colchuck and Dragontail peaks, terminates at about 6400 ft, but ground moraine and talus extend downward to the lake. The glacier ice has now largely broken into twin lobes, and has receded considerably from the nicely-formed prominent terminal moraine, with its fresh, sharp crests. Colchuck Peak is quite rugged everywhere, though less so on its southern flank. The western summit is the highest of several points. First ascent by Elvin R. and Norma Johnson, William A., and Kathy Long on August 11, 1948 (via the glacier and E col). First winter ascent by Gene Prater and party, February 21, 1960.

SOUTH ROUTE: Take Ingalls Creek Trail ◆ about 9 mi. to Porcupine Creek (4160 ft). Be certain you are W of Dragontail Ridge. Follow drainage to about 7000-ft level, then keep on its W side (polished slabs) on a simple, direct ascent to summit; or at 7600 ft where valley splits at a monolith, bear right to Colchuck Col (see below).

EAST ROUTE: Use above route to Colchuck Col (8000 ft+) at head of Porcupine Creek; or from Colchuck Lake (see Colchuck Lake Trail ◆) climb up talus and glacier slopes to

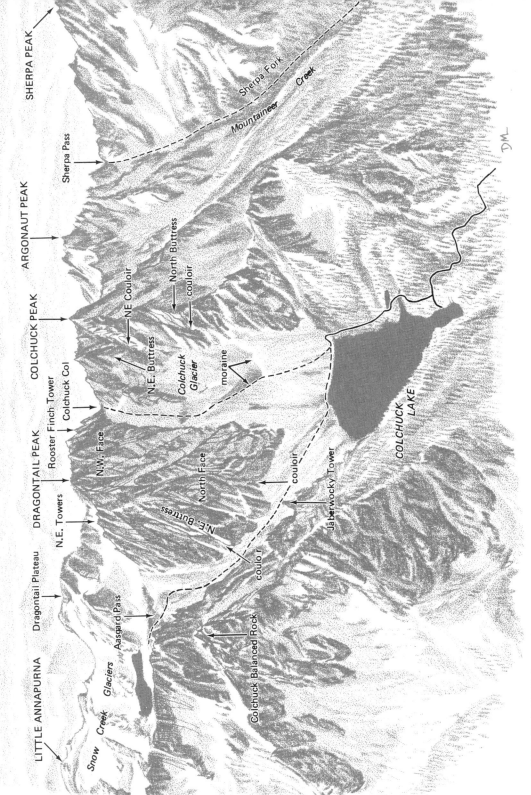

LITTLE ANNAPURNA

Snow *Creek* *Glaciers*

Dragontail Plateau

Aasgard Pass

N.E. Towers

DRAGONTAIL PEAK

Rooster Finch Tower

COLCHUCK PEAK

Colchuck Col

ARGONAUT PEAK

Sherpa Pass

SHERPA PEAK

N.W. Face

N.E. Buttress

North Face

N.E. Buttress

couloir

Colchuck Balanced Rock

Jaberwocky Tower

couloir

Sherpa *Fork*

Mountaineer *Creek*

NE Couloir

North Buttress couloir

N.E. Buttress

Colchuck *Glacier*

moraine

COLCHUCK *LAKE*

DM

STUART RANGE from north

COLCHUCK PEAK — northeast face
FRED BECKEY

the col (⅞ mi. S of lake shore). From col, the climb is a rock scramble to summit (keep just S of crest). Time: 4 hours from lake, or 5 hours from Ingalls Creek.

NORTHWEST ROUTE: From beginning of Mountaineer Creek cross-country route (see Stuart Lake Trail ◆), hike uphill in woods into basin S of Point 6991. Ascend basin rightward under rock band to its head. Exit on left onto broken rock (scrambling). Then up toward summit (snow in early season). Reach N summit ridge (scrambling) just N of top.

NORTH BUTTRESS: To reach this prominent buttress ascend from the S end of Colchuck Lake to a col on the lower portion of the formation (about 6760 ft). The first portion of the buttress is largely scrambling, and the upper portion becomes blocky face climbing (class 3-4) with snow sections in gullies and pockets in early season. On the upper portion it is easiest to climb about 200 ft right of the crest. One can

bear right on easier terrain (snow or talus). Grade II. Reference: *A.A.J.*, 1971, pp. 341-342.

NORTH BUTTRESS COULOIR: First ascent by Ray Lilleby and James Wickwire, July 15, 1962. From the lower W extremity of Colchuck Glacier (est. 7200 ft) and just E of the prominent lateral moraine, gain entry to the narrow 45-degree snow couloir (can be icy or difficult at entry). A rock step about 200 ft on the route may cause a problem. Ascend the couloir to the upper North Buttress, then make an upward traverse W of the crest; a gully can be taken to a summit scramble. Grade II. This is a good winter route. Reference: *A.A.J.*, 1963, p. 471.

NORTHEAST FACE: This route begins at the center of the face, directly beneath the summit (between the deep couloir on the left and the shallow gullies leading to the N ridge). Route by Jim Carlson, Eric Gerber, Bill Herman, and Charles Sink in June 1971. The first 600 ft follows chimneys

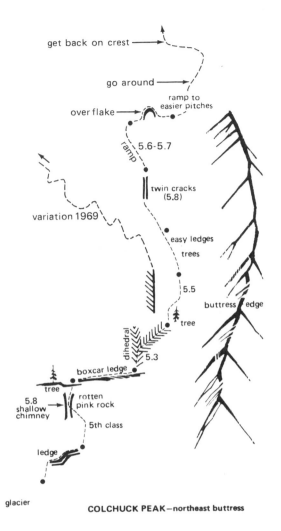

get back on crest →

go around →

ramp to easier pitches

over flake →

variation 1969

5.6-5.7

twin cracks (5.8)

easy ledges

trees

5.5

buttress edge

tree

dihedral

5.3

boxcar ledge

tree

5.8 shallow chimney →

rotten pink rock

5th class

ledge

glacier

COLCHUCK PEAK—northeast buttress

Mark Weigelt

and ledges (class 3 and one short class 5 area). At about 1000 ft up the route, ascend a snowpatch left onto a ridge. Climb rock to another snowpatch (below the false summit), then take a narrow ridge to the main summit. Grade II; class 5.2.
NORTHEAST COULOIR: This is the deep couloir N of the Northeast Buttress; it was climbed by Skip Edmunds, Clark Gerhardt, Paula Kregel, and Greg Markov in January 1975. The most difficult portion is a 60-degree headwall and rightward traverse on steep flutings at the couloir top. Recommended only as a winter climb. Grade II or III.
NORTHEAST BUTTRESS: This buttress is the arcing crest left of the central NE depression. This route of some 18 pitches requires a variety of techniques on occasionally sound rock (also some snow). Some parties have experienced much

loose rock. If planning descent via Colchuck Glacier ice axes (and crampons in late summer) will be needed. First ascent by Mark Weigelt and Julie Brugger, July 1970.

From Colchuck Lake ascend the glacier to left of buttress toe. Gain the rock by climbing right to a ledge below a rotten pink dike left of the crest; the objective is to gain access into a major dihedral on the lower portion of the buttress. Climb directly up a shallow chimney (class 5.8; good protection) on left of pink rock to a boxcar ledge with a tree. (Note: variation to right via rotten rock to same ledge not recommended).

Cross ledge rightward to base of a groove (now on good rock); third pitch ascends groove 60 ft; then right up an easy dihedral (class 5.3) to belay at a small tree on its right face. Ascend slightly right via class 5.5 face climbing to a huge left-slanting ledge. Follow this ledge (has some trees) for 160 ft to its end; then climb a series of shallow twin cracks (class 5.8) to a belay. Diagonal left on a ramp (class 5.6-5.7) until one reaches a large ledge with a short lieback on the right. Climb the lieback rightward, then down the opposite side. Follow a rightward catwalk around the buttress crest; bypass the crest, then climb back in about two pitches. The best rock is on the crest rather than to the right. There is a class 5.7 jam crack about one pitch from the summit. The original party traversed to the right after the catwalk, reaching the central depression (much loose rock). Note: A variation can be done directly from the catwalk (class 5.11). There have been some more direct starts that are more difficult. Grade III or IV; class 5.8 (take protection for cracks up to 2 inches). Time: 10 hours lake to summit. Reference: *A.A.J.*, 1971, p. 341.

Variation: Upper East Face: By Manuel Gonzales and Don Williamson on September 15, 1969. From beyond the boxcar ledge (but before the buttress steepens) follow a prominent left-diagonalling ledge system E of the buttress. The route with this variation included 16 pitches of class 4 and 5 (occasional aid); some ledge debris creates stonefall hazard. Grade III (entire route); class 5.8 and A1. Reference: *A.A.J.*, 1971, p. 300.

ARGONAUT PEAK 8453 ft/2577 m
Argonaut is a prominent rock citadel in the Stuart Range, somewhat box-shaped from most vantages. The peak is located on the main crest between Colchuck and Sherpa peaks. The SE and W summits are of almost equal height, with the latter being the true summit. Argonaut features a very noticeable SE spire. Ingalls Creek is located at the base of the long southern scarp. The North Face and Northeast Buttress stand boldly above a branch of Mountaineer Creek. First ascent by Lex Maxwell, Bob McCall, and Bill Prater, September 1955 (via South Route).
SOUTH ROUTE: From Ingalls Creek Trail ◆ at about ½ mi. W of Porcupine Creek, ascend the semi-brushy slope to reach a gully (some loose rock) which reaches the sum-

Northeast Buttress

Northwest Buttress

open book

ramp

7100 ft.

ARGONAUT PEAK — northeast buttress
RICK LA BELLE

mit ridge E of the highest point. Turn left and follow ridge. Class 2.

SOUTH FACE: This face is a steep 300-ft wall beneath the summit tower's western flank; the rock is solid for climbing. First ascent by Ed Cooper and Ron Niccoli on August 7, 1958.

One can make the approach by the long curving gully on the Ingalls Creek slope. Climb several hundred ft of steep granite to a sloping platform. Bear to the left up a chimney; higher make a hand traverse to the right, then continue upward. Class 5.3. Reference: *A.A.J.,* 1959, p. 302.

WEST RIDGE: This is a long traverse. First ascent by Rick La Belle, Glen Sterr, and Pat Carney on July 18, 1971.

Reach Sherpa Pass from Mountaineer Creek or Ingalls Creek Trail ♦. From the pass scramble along or near ridge crest for about ¾ mi. Just below the summit, traverse for several class 4 and 5 pitches over the crest spires to avoid gullies below. Cross beneath the summit tower's S side for a scrambling finish to the summit ridge. Grade I or II; low class 5.

Variation: Direct West Ridge: By Mark Wiegelt and party in 1972. Climb six pitches up ridge and onto edge of S face. On third pitch make a class 5.6 right traverse. Some difficult routefinding.

Northwest Arete: By Pat Carney, Pat Derr, Rick La Belle, and Glen Sterr on July 5, 1972. Eight pitches. Reference: *Mountaineer,* 1977, p. 75.

NORTH FACE: First ascent by Fred Beckey, Anthony Hovey, Ed Cooper, and Ron Niccoli on August 17, 1958.

Reach the northern basin via Mountaineer Creek (see Stuart Lake Trail ♦); can camp at creek forks. Ascend a right-bearing ramp to the main N face buttress, then climb a complex 300-ft face with steps and gullies. Grade II; class 4. References: *Mountaineer,* 1959, p. 111; *A.A.J.,* 1959, p. 302.

A probable new route was done on the North Face of Argonaut Peak (E of the 1958 route) by Jack Lewis and Tomas Boley in May 1980. From an approach via Mountaineer Creek, the climbing began at the lowest portion of the face. Two steep pitches (class 5.8) led to more broken rock, eventually continuing to the summit.

NORTHEAST BUTTRESS: First ascent by Rick La Belle, Tom Ormond, and Glen Sterr on August 8, 1971.

Use same general approach as for North Face. From the base of the NE buttress (7100 ft) climb several hundred ft of loose rock (becomes solid after 200 ft). Two pitches of moderate class 5, including a leftward ramp, lead to a series of tree-covered ledges about ⅓ of the distance up-buttress. Scramble 200 ft up the ledges to the base of a prominent open book that splits the buttress center. Three pitches (class

5.7, 5.8 — 5.5, A1) lead to the book's top; last pitch has been done free. Follow easy ledges E around a corner, after which the last 500 ft are class 4 and scrambling along the right edge of the broken slope leading to the summit ridge. Grade II; class 5.8 and A1. Time: 6 hours.

NORTHEAST GULLY: This is an obvious approach which starts from the ridge connecting Argonaut and Colchuck. Reach the northern basin via Mountaineer Creek cross-country route. From the forks head SE to the avalanche area (many downed trees). Proceed up through brush in the avalanche cone and attain the wide, flat connecting ridge midway between the two mountains. An easy walk leads to the Northeast Gully after crossing the rock spur trending N from the Southeast Spire; the gully may have hard snow until late season. One route involves a half-lead of class 5.4 directly to the lower corner of the easy upper slope — or climb from top of gully (class 5.4). Descent: rappel into gully top from bolt. Note: if snow fills the gully it would permit one to bypass all technical portions on rock, providing an easy route.

SOUTHEAST RIDGE: This is an interesting rock route by way of the Southeast Spire (the false summit), continuing to the highest point. First ascent by Robert Loomis, Will Parks, Dan Schnell, and Dave Seman on May 30, 1977.

Begin the climb by an easy left-trending ramp leading to the ridge from the E flank. Climb mostly moderate class 5 on the ridge, to reach the false summit; there is a class 5.6 roof (the hardest portion); five pitches to this point. Traverse behind the notch, then make two rappels into the notch. Continue climbing (two pitches) to the next summit. The crux on this portion is a 2-inch jam crack (class 5.6).

One can descend by rappel to the NE snowfield, then walk off in a NE direction. Grade II; class 5.6 (take protection to 3 inches). Reference: *A.A.J.,* 1980, p. 537.

LOWER ARGONAUT SPIRES: The spires are located on the crest W of the summit. The lower three were climbed from Sherpa Pass by Fred Dunham and Gene Prater on September 4, 1961 by their W sides (class 5, two pitches each). The first spire involved a hard lieback and rightward traverse to the summit ridge; the second spire began with a traverse around a corner, then a pendulum and a crack to a cannonhole; the third spire took the W side (class 4). Note: the E sides of the spires would be scrambles.

Three other spires were climbed from the upper direction by Fred Stanley and Jim Wickwire on July 28, 1963 (class 3 and 4). References: *Cascadian,* 1961; 1963; *Mountaineer,* 1962, p. 103.

SHERPA PEAK   8605 ft/2623 m

Sherpa is a stately peak, the first summit E of Mount Stuart (about 0.7 mi. distant). Sherpa is particularly distinct because of its curious balanced rock resting on the SE portion of the rocky summit mass, seemingly ready for an outer space launching.

The Sherpa-Stuart col (8160 ft+) is located at the head of Sherpa Glacier on the northwestern cirque, between the Ice Cliff spur of Mount Stuart and the North Ridge of Sherpa Peak. First ascent by Dave Mahre, Bill and Gene Prater on July 1, 1955.

SOUTH ROUTE: From the area of Ingalls and Turnpike creeks (see Turnpike Creek Trail ◆ and Ingalls Creek Trail ◆) ascend the semi-open grassy slope, then bear rightward across minor gullies and talus to reach the right side of the basin just SW of the summit area of Sherpa Peak. Ascend the broad gully that bears to the notch several hundred ft E of the balanced rock; then follow the summit ridge past the balanced rock to the top of the peak. Class 3-4. Time: 5 hours from valley. Note: variations have been done, including the upper SW face. One could reach the route by traversing eastward from the standard route on Mount Stuart.

WEST RIDGE: First ascent by Fred Dunham, Ray Lilleby, and James Wickwire on August 13, 1961. Ascend to the Sherpa-Stuart col (see South Route) or ascend per Mount Stuart's normal route, Variation No. 1, then at 6000 ft enter a gully that leads to the ridge crest. The route on Sherpa Peak follows the West Ridge or closely on either flank. After a 200-ft section of blocks and horns on the crest, or just to its left, reach a small notch. Continue on the crest (class 3-4), then when it becomes jagged, traverse on the right (S) flank about 50 ft via a large ledge. The next face section is the crux (one to 1½ pitches to a notch in a subsidiary ridge to the right); one report describes a move left from a belay recess on small face holds, then a hard mantle into a gully. Beyond the notch keep right of the crest (class 4 and easy 5), at one place traversing S on a narrow ledge. Exposed and pleasant climbing leads to the summit. Class 5.4 to 5.5. Time: 2 hours on the ridge—7 hours from Ingalls-Turnpike Creek. Reference: *Cascadian,* 1961, pp. 23-24.

NORTH RIDGE: First ascent by Rick La Belle and Pat Derr on July 5, 1971.

From S branch of Mountaineer Creek (see Stuart Lake Trail ◆) ascend Sherpa Fork to beneath the NE face, then rightward to prominent narrow lower notch (est. 7200 ft) on ridge (two pitches of class 5 onto ridge). Traverse along E side below crest to a second major notch at 8100 ft. From here the climb consists of five class 5 pitches directly up the ridge crest to the summit. Grade II or III; class 5.8.

NORTHEAST FACE: The steep portion begins at the 7600-ft level at the head of Mountaineer Creek. First ascent by Fred Beckey and Ed Cooper on July 20, 1958.

Reach from head of S branch of Mountaineer Creek (see Stuart Lake Trail ◆) or from Ingalls Creek ascend to Sherpa Pass (6960 ft+) and drop 750 ft on N side. Then work up (mostly talus) to climb a 45-degree right-angling snow gully to an indistinct ridge. Pass a major ledge under final rock wall (class 3, 4 to here); steeper climbing for 200 ft (class 5) reaches summit crest between balanced rock and the top. Grade II or III. Reference: *Mountaineer,* 1959, p. 111.

Sherpa Rock (balanced rock): First ascent by Dave Mahre, Gene and Bill Prater in 1955. Stem a crack, traverse left to S corner, then climb a passage over several chockstones to the

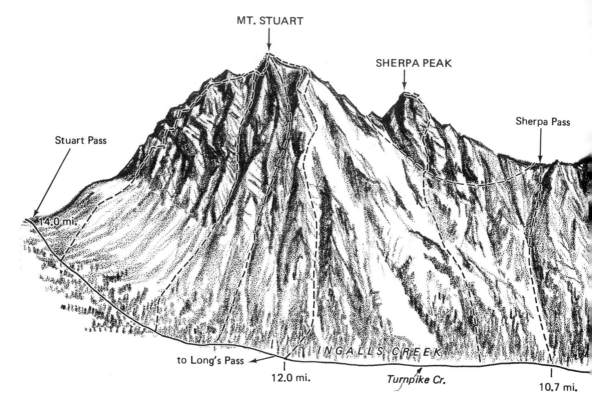

MT. STUART

SHERPA PEAK

Sherpa Pass

Stuart Pass

14.0 mi.

to Long's Pass ←

12.0 mi.

Turnpike Cr.

INGALLS CREEK

10.7 mi.

STUART RANGE from south

base of the Rock. Shoulder stand or rope throw over pedestal point gains E side pedestal, then with bolt protection, frictioning gains the top. Class 5.7; rappel bolt atop. References: *Cascadian,* 1956, pp. 24-26; 1962, pp. 19-21.

MOUNT STUART   9415 ft / 2870 m

Without a rival as the crown peak in the central Cascades of Washington, Mount Stuart has been pronounced the single greatest mass of (exposed) granite in the United States. Professor W. D. Lyman called Stuart a "dizzy horn of rock set in a field of snow." Certainly its northern and eastern faces are the alpine climax of the Wenatchee Mountains. They make a powerful impact on first sight. This aspect of the mountain is only available to hikers and climbers, but a fine tourist view of the southern flank can be obtained from Indian John Hill on I-90 between Cle Elum and Ellensburg.

The structure of Mount Stuart requires some description: the upper portion consists of a gigantic E-W wedge, 1½ mi. long, the summit centrally placed.

Three principal ridges support this wedge: (1) The East Ridge, which rises from the Sherpa-Stuart col (8160 ft) to the eastern false summit at about 9160 ft.

(2) The West Ridge, which begins near Stuart Pass and extends due E as a watershed to the summit. It rises irregularly in a series of steps to the West Ridge horn, then descends about 150 ft to a notch before continuing to the summit. A less pronounced Northwest Buttress shoulders the lower West Ridge NW of the horn. A large triangular facet, a NW face, stands between the lower West Ridge and the Northwest Buttress.

(3) The North Ridge (which really trends NE) splits the broad N and E expanse of alpine faces. It descends from the summit as a buttress, then a ridge to the topographic break at terminal moraine slopes (6600 ft) between the Stuart and Ice Cliff glaciers.

The N and E faces are structurally complex and pillared by steep spur ridges. Professor I. C. Russell

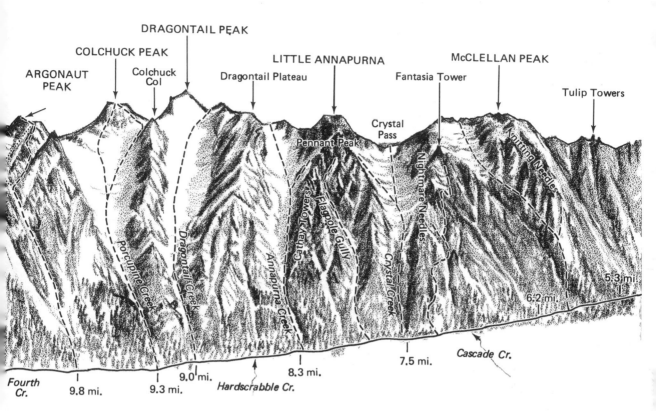

ARGONAUT PEAK — COLCHUCK PEAK — Colchuck Col — DRAGONTAIL PEAK — Dragontail Plateau — LITTLE ANNAPURNA — Pennant Peak — Crystal Pass — Fantasia Tower — McCLELLAN PEAK — Tulip Towers — Knitting Needles — Nightmare Needles — Porcupine Creek — Dragontail Creek — Annapurna Creek — Cathworts Creek — Flagpole Gully — Crystal Creek — 5.3 mi. — 6.2 mi. — Cascade Cr. — Fourth Cr. — 9.8 mi. — 9.3 mi. — 9.0 mi. — Hardscrabble Cr. — 8.3 mi. — 7.5 mi.

wrote "on the north side of Mount Stuart and 1000 ft below its summit ... there are three small glaciers situated in steep gorges or clefts in the granite and sheltered by outstanding cliffs."[63]

The N face is bound on the W by the Northwest Buttress and on the E by the North Ridge. The intervening area is filled by less prominent spur ridges and headwalls above the Stuart Glacier, which hangs on a steeply sloping shelf. There is a rock glacier, an elongate tongue of coarse rubble, in the cirque beneath Mount Stuart's Northwest Face. The distribution of such rock glaciers is controlled by periglacial climatic conditions.[64]

On the E flank of the North Ridge is the slabby Northeast Face, falling to the deep chasm of the Ice Cliff Glacier. The headwall directly above the glacier is the precipitous Northeast Face of Mount Stuart's eastern shoulder, rising to the False Summit at 0.2 mi. E of the summit.

The Stuart, Ice Cliff, and Sherpa glaciers are post-Ice Age, perhaps 3500 years old. The Ice Cliff Glacier, which heads at about 7800 ft and terminates near 6400 ft, is cradled much deeper than other cirques on the mountain. As ice spills out, a cliff of about 100 ft is formed. Lower, there is a steep trough and a broken glacier tongue. Perhaps as recently as the 18th century all three glaciers were coterminous, covering the denuded slopes above the present timberline. Sharp-crested moraines mark an earlier modern terminus of both the Stuart and Ice Cliff glaciers. The prominent end moraine of the Ice Cliff Glacier is now 500 ft below its terminus.

The rocky spine of the Ice Cliff spur bears NE to divide the Ice Cliff and Sherpa glaciers; the latter glacier heads in the cirque between the spur and the North Ridge of Sherpa Peak.

The entire southern flank of Mount Stuart is combed by gullies leading at intervals to the sum-

GLACIER PEAK

MT. STUART

False Summit

SHERPA PEAK

Sherpa Pass

Ice Cliff Glacier
route end

Variation No. 2

Variation No. 3

Variation No. 1

Ulrich's Couloir

Cascadian Couloir

mit ridges. They are separated and interspersed by complex and precipitous merging subridges and headwalls.

Strong winds blowing predominantly from the SW redistribute the fallen snow on Mount Stuart and the other high peaks of the Stuart Range. As a result, while SW- and S-facing slopes are often bare in late winter, wind drift and avalanching may produce snow depths in excess of 20 ft in some N- and NE-facing cirques.

Because of its height and alpine nature, Mount Stuart has dangers unique to peaks in this section. Early mountaineer Claude E. Rusk aptly alluded to it as "the mountain of thrills." A 1930 Mazama group, getting off-route, told of a hard "angleworm wiggle" in a narrow chimney. That the peak can be a dangerous lightning target was shown in August 1952 when Paul Brikoff was fatally struck.

The mountaineering problems are magnified by the mountain's massive dimensions and its complexity. A commentary by J. A. Laurie appearing in the *Mountaineer* (1914) is enlightening: "Mount Stuart is most deceptive as viewed from the base, there being many ridges radiating to the south and southeast from the summit, almost any one of which appears to extend clear to the top. The key to the ascent, however, is a certain gulch opening almost opposite the mouth of Turnpike Creek . . ."

Regardless of the ascent route taken, the descent of Mount Stuart is generally done by the Southeast Route or Ulrich's Couloir. The couloir is a good early-season descent (ice axe needed, crampons optional) but very tedious after the snow melts, because of the couloir's blocky bedrock. Snow and manageable scree make the Southeast Route preferable when the couloir is not in its best condition.

Mount Stuart was named by Capt. George B. McClellan on September 30, 1853 during scouting for the Pacific Railroad Survey, for his best friend Jimmie Stuart, who died during a military mission. McClellan observed "there was nothing to be seen but mountain piled on mountain . . . . About west-northwest was a handsome snow-peak, smaller than Mount Baker; as it is not to be found on any previous map that I know of, and had no name, I called it Mount Stuart."[65]

Rusk, uncertain who made the mountain's first climb, was told by Frank Bryant of Yakima about finding a stick at the summit bearing the name "Angus McPherson — 1873." A. H. Sylvester, who climbed to the summit in 1897 and 1899 for triangulation, be-

lieved the first ascent was made by Richard U. Goode and Frank Tweedy during the Northern Pacific land survey about 1890 (possibly 1885).[66] Dr. H. B. Hinman, W. E. Doph, and Redick McKee, as scouts for the 1914 Mountaineer outing, reached a position 100 ft beyond the West Ridge notch; their verdict was "only from the south side was the ascent feasible" (*Mountaineer*, 1914, p. 69). First winter ascent by Bill and Gene Prater, Everett Lasher, Dave Mahre, and Don Torrey on February 14, 1955.

References: C. E. Rusk, *Tales of a Western Mountaineer*, pp. 196-230; *20th Annual Report*, pt. 2, U.S.G.S., pp. 89-210; *Mountaineer*, 1914, pp. 69-75; 1925, pp. 28-32; *Mazama*, 1930, pp. 29-33; *Summit*, June 1963, pp. 18-22; November 1967, pp. 16-21.

SOUTHEAST ROUTE: There are four distinct approaches to this, the normal summit route; these approaches can apply to other S- and W-side routes:

(1) Long's Pass Trail (continue to Ingalls Creek Trail near 4800-ft level at old outing campsite).

(2) Ingalls Lake Trail ◆ (descend Ingalls Creek Trail about 1 mi. to 4800-ft level).

(3) Beverly-Turnpike Pass Trail ◆ (continue to juncture of trail with Ingalls Creek Trail).

(4) Ingalls Creek Trail ◆ (to about 12 mi.).

From Ingalls Creek Trail at large clearing E of Long's Pass Trail juncture, ascend "Cascadian Couloir" (narrow bottom, then widening) to its end on a moderately sloped ridge with scrub trees at left side of a major talus basin.

Ascend basin's upper left side to a boulderfield (8000 ft) and big sloping shoulder which converges from the E. A steep 1000-ft slope (usually snow) leads to the eastern false summit. Now traverse along S side of E arete through broken rock, then ascend directly to the summit. Note: *be prepared for moderately steep snow if in early season.* Time: 5 hours from trail.

Variation 1: This is the easier route, long the traditional way. There is a lesser gradient than "Cascadian Couloir" and this is the safest early-season route.

From the same clearing on Ingalls Creek Trail one can make a rising traverse of about ½ mi. on semi-open slopes to the pronounced gully which becomes the talus basin to the E of "Cascadian Couloir."

One can also begin from the trail where this gully crosses (about 4840 ft) and ends in a large alluvial fan. The valley of Ingalls Creek is devoid of timber here and a tongue of buck brush extends into the gully mouth. The start should be made on the ridge just W of the gully; when part-way on the ridge, drop into the gully and continue into the talus basin at about 7000 ft.

Variation 2: From trail ½ mi. farther E (4560 ft) ascend to large basin between Sherpa Peak and gully of Variation 1. Where route steepens (est. 7800 ft) ascend one of several

MOUNT STUART from southeast
WALLACE C. GUY, U.S. FOREST SERVICE

ARGONAUT PEAK

SHERPA PEAK

MT. STUART

Southwest Face of Summit Pyramid

West Horn

South Headwall

Variation No. 1

Cascadian Couloir

Ulrich's Couloir

Ingalls Pass

South Rib

West Ridge Couloir

Long John Tower

West Ridge

Goat Pass

Stuart Pass

gullies (likely snow) then work left on a rising ledge system to the 1000-ft slope.

Variation 3: At 8200 ft bear left of rock outcrop left of 1000-ft slope; a scrambling route first left then back up spur ridge to right leads to the False Summit.

ULRICH'S COULOIR: This prominent couloir, about 4000 ft high, bites into the S slopes of Stuart, and higher curves westerly to reach the summit in an uninterrupted sweep. A principal difficulty is the selection of the proper couloir (it is the first major couloir W of "Cascadian Couloir"). This is a good early-season route when snow-filled (may be frozen); bring crampons. The couloir is loose and not recommended when snow melts in late summer. First ascent by Louis Ulrich, Lex Maxwell, and Joe Werner in July 1933.

Approach as for Southeast Route (leave trail about 5100-ft level at small clearing where couloir's streambed descends). Route ascends couloir entire distance. Class 2 and 3 (when snow-free). Time: 5 hours from trail. References: *Cascadian,* 1961, pp. 31-32; *A.N.A.M.,* 1985, p. 68.

SOUTH HEADWALL AND UPPER SOUTH RIB: This headwall is at the head of the first major couloir W of Ulrich's Couloir. The S rib flanks the couloir's W side and continues above to the summit. First ascent by Paul Myhre and Darrell Sorenson on May 30, 1966.

Ascend from trail at a clearing W of Ulrich's Couloir to the lower part of the West Ridge Couloir (it slants right). When it forks (est. 7000 ft) keep right beneath huge black slab and ascend, crossing rock into couloir on right, flanked on right by 200-ft cliffs. Ascend to headwall of large cirque with nearly vertical walls (8700 ft). Ascend at center of headwall, then diagonal left (class 5.0 to 5.7) via open books, chimneys, and large flakes in a straight line onto the upper S rib (near top of headwall work left and climb hidden gully to bypass a difficult chimney). Ascend rightward across short slabs, then up the easy broken upper rib to the summit. Grade II or III; class 5.7 (20 pitons used). Time: 7 hours. Reference: *A.A.J.,* 1968, pp. 130-131.

Variation: From about 8000 ft in West Ridge Couloir climb the W edge of S rib via ramps, ledges, and a final wall (class 5.6) to meet the route over halfway up the headwall.

Variation: By Rick La Belle, Glen Sterr, and Bob Deltete, July 1969. Shortly above headwall base, cross its face via a prominent ledge to the right skyline (three pitches; second pitch has a 20-ft jam crack — class 5.6). Then 500 ft of scrambling to summit.

WEST RIDGE COULOIR: This route ascends a couloir system to the West Ridge notch. In early season the route is largely snow up to 35 degrees.

From open slopes on Ingalls Creek Trail ◆ climb N up the entrance couloir to about 7000 ft. Bear left here; the system leads to the obvious notch. Finish via one of West Ridge completions, or one of several variants on SW face of summit pyramid. Time: 5 hours via easiest route.

Variation: Southwest Face of Summit Pyramid: First ascent by Paul Myhre and Don Cramer on May 30, 1965.

Where the couloir heads against the summit pyramid's rock face (about 400 ft below the West Ridge notch), follow the large ledge which trends diagonally from the main ridge for 200 ft. Begin here, climbing for the summit: the route consists largely of short pitches interspersed with large and small ledges. Grade II; class 5 and aid. Time 7 hours total. References: *A.A.J.,* 1966, pp. 128-129; *Mountaineer,* 1966, pp. 202-203.

WEST RIDGE: This long and jagged rock ridge is one of Mount Stuart's most prominent topographic features, and the western culmination of the immense mountain massif. The ridge steepens its gradient from Stuart Pass at about 7200 ft and rises sharply to the West Ridge horn (9160 ft), then knifes to a 9000-ft notch before continuing as one edge of the summit pyramid.

As a climb the ridge is exposed, athletic, yet not continually hard. Many difficulties of the West Ridge can and usually are circumvented: few parties stay precisely on the ridge. Innumerable variations are possible, and it is needless to catalog them all. The route provides interesting climbing on generally solid granitic rock — with many blocks from the rock's jointing, and small ledges.

First ascent by Lex Maxwell, Fred Llewellyn, and John Vertrees in August 1935.

From the meadows of upper Ingalls Creek (see Ingalls Lake Trail ◆) ascend steep grassy slopes rightward into the first deep, continuous gully of the lower West Ridge. One can also enter the gully from the left by following the West Ridge to a ledge at the base of a triangular rock face.

Continue to gully head, then cross E via broken ledges over a rock separation to the next gully. Ascend to near its head below a cliffy area, then traverse right (at the foot of a steep chimney) via a broken ledge leading around a corner toward the notch behind Long John Tower (est. 8700 ft). One can (1) from the notch, making a slightly rising traverse, cross gullies on irregular ledges to just beneath the West Ridge notch (9000 ft); or (2) continue up the next gully system to the ridge crest, to the W of the West Ridge horn (est. 9000 ft); traverse on a broad ledge about 200 ft beneath its top (S) under a scissorlike formation on the skyline; this is followed by a slight descent and continued traverse across minor ribs on easy systems to the West Ridge notch.

Continue just S of the ridge crest, (a short distance), then cross to the N flank on a ledge; continue about 60 ft (exposed class 4), then when climbing becomes difficult, climb back to the crest at a tiny notch.

Continue toward the summit pyramid for about one lead. Here a ledge bears downward, then across the SW face (about 1½ leads total) to the ledge ending near the upper South Rib. Just before the ledge end cracks curve upward to easy rock on the rib (about 1½ leads), in the direction of the West Ridge crest. An alternate method is from the ledge end, to climb a vertical crack (lieback) up to the rib crest and toward the summit (more strenuous, class 5). Grade II; class 5.4. Time: 6 hours from meadows.

MOUNT STUART from southwest
LYNN K. BUCHANAN

West Horn

MT. STUART

Long John Tower

Northwest Face of
Lower West Ridge

West Ridge Route

MOUNT STUART from west
WILLIAM A. LONG

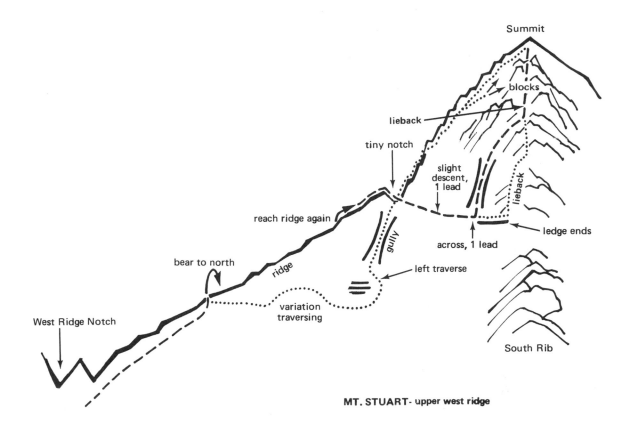

MT. STUART- upper west ridge

Variation: North Side of Lower Ridge: From N side of Stuart Pass or from lower West Ridge before its NW face traverse and climb scree NW, then into the large gully at the head of the rock glacier. Ascend this system, which bears rightward to a notch in the West Ridge (est. 8240 ft). Then cross to the S side of the West Ridge. A more difficult continuation would be to proceed on the N side of the ridge.

Variation: South Side Bypass: Beyond West Ridge notch (where usual crossing made to N side), make a rising southward traverse over a minor spur (one-two leads). Make a short left traverse (class 5) to a gully parallel to the West Ridge; ascend it to the ridge crest.

Variation: West Ridge of Summit Pyramid: From West Ridge notch, route remains mostly on the corner. Total of four-five pitches can be run this way (class 5.3-5.6). Numerous interesting possibilities, including steep cracks near the summit.

NORTHWEST FACE OF LOWER WEST RIDGE: This 600-ft triangular face rises above the rock glacier between Stuart Pass and Goat Pass. First ascent by Ron Burgner and Don McPherson, August 1968.

From Stuart Pass, make a rising northerly traverse until below the face; possible bivouac on large ledge with protecting roof. From here walk S (right) about 100 ft to a mid-face chimney. Climb it to a tree (class 5.7; A2). Rappel or nail a short distance left to a ledge. From its left end climb to big bench with trees. Climb interesting 5.7 chimney (used chocks) to belay stance up and right from its end. Climb back down to top of chimney, then climb up left. A few jam moves (class 5.7) lead to class 4 and a belay on a "wide-mouthed" dihedral slab.

Climb the steep chimney above to top of huge block forming one wall. Next lead (seventh) begins loose and involves tricky routefinding; climb up and slant left from block, then zigzag right until reaching horizontal crack leading around corner (class 5.7). From end of crack climb the difficult vertical jam crack (need 3-inch Friend or bong to protect last 30 ft; hardest move early in lead — class 5.9). This crack ends on large ledge; follow for three leads to reach crest of West Ridge (class 4 and easy 5). Grade III or IV; class 5.9. Selection: 20 pieces for protection up to 3 inches. Time: 8 hours.

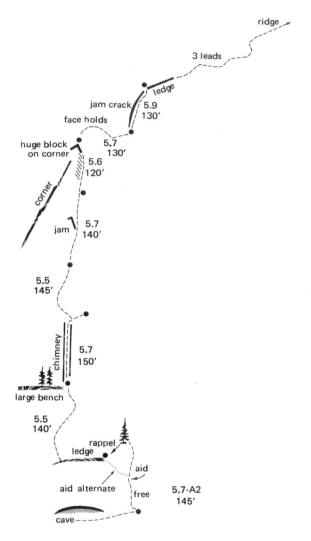

ridge

3 leads

ledge

jam crack   5.9
130'
face holds

5.7
130'

huge block
on corner

5.6
120'

corner

jam   5.7
140'

5.5
145'

chimney   5.7
150'

large bench

5.5
140'

rappel
ledge

aid

aid alternate   free   5.7-A2
145'

cave

MT. STUART—northwest face of lower west ridge

NORTHWEST BUTTRESS: This route begins well W of Razorback Ridge, but tops out very near (W) of it, on the crest of the West Ridge. First ascent by Louis Ulrich, Edward Rankin, and John Riley in August 1937.

From Stuart Pass make traversing ascent across the rock glacier (talus or snow) to Goat Pass (7640 ft +). Descend 200 ft or more and cross remnant ice of Stuart Glacier to the small rock spur that breaks glacier. Ascend it to the lower face of the buttress. Ascend generally good rock, with sandy

ledges and chimneys, bearing left across gullies and broken rock just W of the West Ridge notch. Then follow one of West Ridge routes to summit. Grade II; class 3 and 4.

Variation: From Goat Pass climb up the rock spur S, keeping right of the remnant ice. Ascend largely broken rock on the spur, then mixed snowpatches and rock on a leftward course to the buttress, to arrive at the W side of the West Ridge horn. Cross its W face, then meet the higher alternate of the West Ridge Route. Class 4. The buttress is sufficiently broad to allow numerous courses. The ascent was done by Dave Mahre and party in 1958, but may have an earlier ascent. Reference: *Cascadian,* 1964, pp. 10-11.

RAZORBACK RIDGE: This is the sharp ridge immediately W of the Stuart Glacier Couloir, which tops out on the West Ridge just W of the West Ridge notch. The ridge is shorter than the North Ridge and very direct; at one point the rock forms a perfect knife-edge. Climbing is interesting and varied on solid rock (12 leads). The route is relatively safe because of moderate slabs to its left; although these slabs have loose rock, they would provide an escape to the West Ridge. First ascent by Scott Davis, Al Givler, and Doug McGowan on August 27, 1967.

Reach route as per Stuart Glacier Couloir. The route stays largely on the crest, with the lower third hardest (maximum class 5.8 at several spots). Most of the pitches are class 4 or easy class 5 (easing higher on the ridge). Grade III; class 5.8 (original party used six pitons). The rock is solid but large lichens present. Time: 7 hours from glacier. Reference: *Mountaineer,* 1968, pp. 204-205.

STUART GLACIER COULOIR: This extremely alpine route should only be done under ideal conditions. In early summer, under warm conditions, soft surface snow could slide away. In late summer there may be much blue ice and treacherous loose rock exposed (possible rockfall). Crampons, hard hats, and ice screws are recommended. First ascent by Helmy Beckey and Larry Strathdee in June 1944. First winter ascent, then traverse to upper North Ridge, by Paul Ekman and Joe Weis in 1976.

Reach Stuart Glacier as per Northwest Buttress Route or from Stuart Lake (see Stuart Lake Trail ◆) by following the valley onward 1 mi. to rubble under glacier; then ascend to terminus at about 6500 ft. Climb to head of the main portion of the glacier. Cross the bergschrund (7800 ft) on its right, then ascend ice up the 50-degree couloir to its tip. A narrow portion at about midway is only 8 ft wide and in excess of 60 degrees (expect water-ice here). The final portion of the couloir leading to the West Ridge notch (9000 ft) may be eroded rock. Grade III; class 5; bring ice protection.

Variation: By Del Young and Bruce Schuler on June 4, 1968. From just above the narrow portion of the couloir, climb left. Eight leads then ascend directly to small notch E of main West Ridge notch. Two of leads encountered class 5.6 climbing, and a lieback going to notch, class 5.7.

NORTHWEST FACE: This is the 1500-ft rock face of the summit structure between the North Ridge/Buttress and Stuart Glacier Couloir (also called Valhalla Buttress).

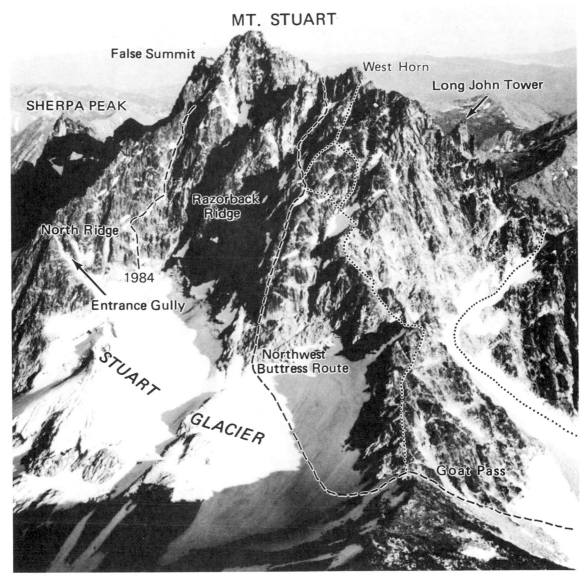

MOUNT STUART from northwest
DON J. EASTERBROOK

First ascent by David Beckstead and Paul Myhre on July 20, 1970.

Approach as for Stuart Glacier Couloir, and ascend the glacier to the schrund at about 100 ft E of the couloir. Cross the schrund, then climb an open book for about 50 ft (several aid pitons on original, and hard free climbing) to a ledge.

Climb 10 ft left to another book, the top of which is vertical; this 80-ft pitch ends at a big ledge (mixed free and A1).

The next three pitches are easier (mostly class 4), and follow a curving pattern on broken rock first left, then up, then right to the edge of the first "half moon" (large white rock face). Keeping to its left, climb one lead to a ledge.

MT. STUART

West Horn

Northwest Buttress Route

West Ridge Notch

Stuart Glacier Couloir

Razorback Ridge

STUART GLACIER

West Ridge Notch

Northwest Face

Great Gendarme

North Ridge

Lower North Ridge— West Side

Lower North Ridge— East Side

1960

Northeast Face

1985

False Summit

Girth Pillar

Northeast Face of False Summit

ICE CLIFF GLACIER

SHERPA GLACIER

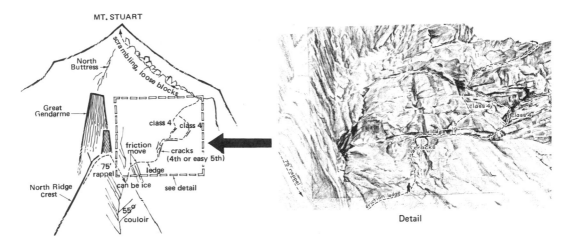

MT. STUART-upper North Ridge route

Detail

Traverse it right about 60 ft to reach a left-leaning open book (class 4), then up the latter to a good ledge. Now climb a prominent crack on slabs to the right of the base of an overhang (class 5.8 and A1). Climb left to it, then aid (A1) up the overhang to a ledge at the base of the second "half moon" (about four leads from summit). Follow this ledge to its right side, then turn a corner which veers left. Then ascend a rotten gully and broken rock toward the summit. Grade IV; class 5.8 and A1 (original party used 35 pitons and six chocks).

NORTHWEST FACE COULOIR: This is the narrow couloir located between the Northwest Buttress and the upper North Ridge. The optimum time to make the climb is spring, when ice builds up over down-sloping slabs at the route's base. The route consists of thin ice covering rock slab, and connecting snowpatches. The first pitch above the Stuart Glacier may be very difficult, with verglas or thin ice covering steep rock (a small right-facing corner on the left was used).

First ascent uncertain. Take crampons and ice tools. The climb crossed the North Ridge Route at the traverse, then kept in the continuing gully; variations are possible in this section. Grade III to IV; class 5.4 plus ice climbing. Time: 9 hours moraine to summit.

NORTH RIDGE: This classic rock spur which divides the Stuart and Ice Cliff glaciers is not only an exceptional alpine route, but has become moderately popular. The normally used route only climbs the upper half of this long ridge and buttress. Two direct routes have been made from its base, to offer a more complete route. Rock is generally excellent. First ascent by John Rupley and Don (Claunch) Gordon on September 9, 1956. First winter ascent by Craig McKibben and Jay Ossiander in March 1975. The route bypasses the

Stuart Glacier's crevasses via its W side, then traverses at about 7600 ft to the eastern edge. Climb sharply left up the steep, obvious gully (snow or scree) to the ridge crest notch just S of a prominent point. Here one should decide whether to follow the crest or continue about 100 ft lower (on the W ledges), then join the slab some three pitches below the Great Gendarme; the ridge difficulty in this section is class 5.6-5.7 and the lower variant is under class 5.5.

The classic route now is to follow the jagged crest until it narrows to nearly a knife-edge just below the final buttress (the Great Gendarme). When almost against its wall, look for a bolt on the crest. Rappel 75 ft to a ledge on slabs, then traverse the slab on an exposed corner (reach in 20 ft) to enter a 55-degree couloir (this can be icy). Ascend about 30 ft, then cross to the right side (ice can inhibit right exit). There is a crux friction move over a rounded face, and leading to sandy ledges (class 5.4, but harder with verglas). Climb a right-diagonalling crack system for 100 ft to a small tan saddle behind the terminus of the Northwest Face. Then bear left on broken rock and sandy scrambling to the summit (watch for loose blocks). Grade III; class 5.7. Time: 10 hours from upper Ingalls Creek or 7 hours from glacier. Bring crampons and include 3 small wired stoppers with chock selection. References: *A.A.J.*, 1957, pp. 144-145; Steck and Roper, *Fifty Classic Climbs of North America*, pp. 129-132; *Cascadian*, 1960, pp. 30-31; 1963, p. 34.

Variation: Lower North Ridge, West Side: This original complete route climbs the entire ridge to join the normal route at the notch just S of the prominent point on the lower ridge. First ascent by Steve Marts and Fred Beckey on July 14, 1963. This party made a bivouac, then continued on the normal route.

Approach as for Ice Cliff Glacier (or descend E from

MOUNT STUART from northeast
ED COOPER

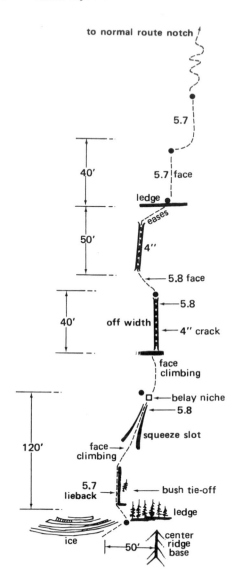

MT. STUART—lower north ridge (east side)

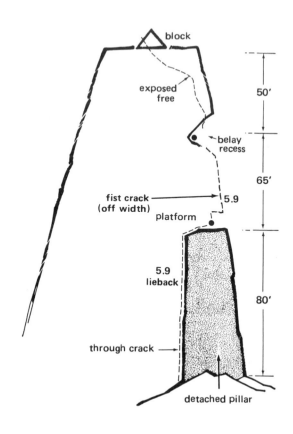

MT. STUART—great gendarme on north ridge

beneath Stuart Glacier). Begin on W side, near base of the ridge (est. 6600 ft). Climb up a steep snow finger until practical to exit left to slabby rock. Ascend a slab near the ridge crest (three pitches, hard class 5). Then ascend on or near the crest to meet the normal route. Grade IV if complete to summit; class 5. Reference: *A.A.J.*, 1964, p. 171.

Variation: Lower North Ridge, East Side: This difficult rock climb with six class 5 leads begins at the edge of the Ice Cliff Glacier at the center and at the lowest point of the North Ridge. The variation ends at the notch in the ridge where the normal route reaches it. Recommend boots for wide cracks. First ascent by Mead Hargis and Jay Ossiander, July 1970.

Approach as for Ice Cliff Glacier. First 100 ft of class 3 leads to a broken ledge which crosses the bottom of the ridge. Start to the left of some trees, climbing via a lieback to a prominent right-leaning slot which becomes a 5-inch crack (class 5.8) at the top (120 ft lead). From a belay niche the next lead involves face climbing, then a 4-inch crack (class 5.8). Then face climbing (class 5.8) is followed by a 4-inch crack to a ledge; the next 40 ft completes the third lead: the first 25 ft are the hardest (class 5.7 face climbing). A fourth lead (class 5.7) is followed to three easier leads (class 5.0) to a prominent ridge notch (joining the W-side variation). About six more leads continue to the notch of the normal route. Grade IV; class 5.8. Take a varied selection of protection for cracks up to 4 inches. Reference: *A.A.J.,* 1971, p. 341.

Variation: Great Gendarme: This "direct" route on the final buttress ascends the 200-ft "gendarme" located about 500 ft below the summit. First ascent by James Wickwire and Fred Stanley in July 1964. Use the crack system formed by the left side of the detached 80-ft pillar (liebacks, up to class 5.9). From a belay atop the pillar climb to a recess in about 65 ft (class 5.9); this pitch is the hardest because of off-width. An exposed 50-ft lead (class 5.5) reaches the top of the gendarme. Follow the ridge crest (or its right side) and bypass a grey horn on the right (largely class 4; on original climb; one short aid pitch done). Except for one step this portion is moderate, but there is some instability. On the original climb about 25 pitons were used. The route can be done free; take protection for wide and medium cracks. Reference: *A.A.J.,* 1965, p. 409.

NORTHEAST FACE: This is a demanding route, since it involves ascent of the Ice Cliff Glacier, then considerable rock climbing to the N edge of the face where it meets the North Ridge. At this juncture the original party elected to complete the climb as per North Ridge Route; to be a separate complete route one should finish as completion E and below the "Great Gendarme" (by Gene Prater and Dave Mahre, from North Ridge in 1958). Take crampons and ice screws. The great slabs on the left-center of the face look intimidating because of possibly dangerous remnants of perched snow and ice.

First ascent by Dave Mahre, Gene Prater, Richard Hebble, and Donald N. Anderson, August 1959.

Reach route as for Ice Cliff Glacier. Climb the glacier to its upper section, then leave its right side via a steep ice pitch onto rock slabs at the bottom/center of the face. Traverse right, then a short hard pitch tables up to a ledge; ascend slabs traversing right and up on a ledge to bypass a recess. Climb up, then traverse down and right to a sandy platform (possible bivouac site). Now a very steep open book offers an aid route (A1) (can be strenuous handjams and counter pressure for 50 ft, class 5.8).

From top of open book climb to a ledge: here a 3 inch ledge leads left around corner past a small tree to a short overhang. Walk around corner to a chimney; higher, slabs lead left to a difficult dirt-filled crack. Climb for several low-angle pitches to a difficult 200-ft inside corner (starts as a class 5.8 off-width crack, then becomes a chimney; aid used on first two ascents).

A strenuous chimney leads to sloping, dirt-covered ledge. From its highest point climb one lead, then move up and left around corner to a ledge with a large flake (first party bivouacked here). Around corner (left) more slabs lead up to where North Ridge becomes a buttress. Traverse great undercut slabs on E side of "Great Gendarme." Follow a wide crack one lead; next a ledge that widens. At end of the slab

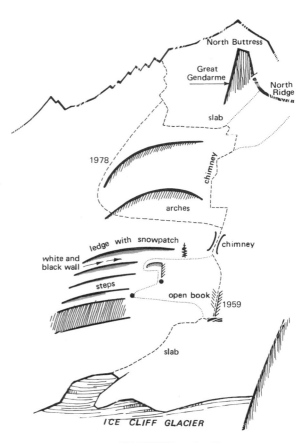

MT. STUART- northeast face

about 500 ft horizontally from the buttress, climb up onto a scree ledge (possible snow patches); various summit finishes possible from here. Grade IV; class 5.7 and A2 or class 5.9. References: *Mountaineer,* 1960, pp. 80-81; *A.A.J.,* 1960, pp. 111-117.

Variation: By Dave Mahre and Gene Prater on original ascent. At the "downward traverse" work left several leads. Difficult climbing leads to overhanging bands. Climb these: there is some aid on two short pitches; the second pitch has a 6-ft roof — aid left with white wall on the left. A long traverse right leads past a tree to the first chimney.

Variation: By James Wickwire, Dave Mahre, and Fred Stanley in September 1963. This variation (used on the second ascent) departs just below the bivouac spot of the first

MOUNT STUART from east (Northeast Face)

Ice Cliff Glacier
route end

East Ridge

Northeast Face
of False Summit

Winter 1978

MOUNT STUART from east
ED COOPER

climb. An ascending right traverse to the ridge crest is made in five leads, class 4 with some class 5.

Winter Conditions Variation: By Doug Klewin and Jim Nelson in May 1978. Climb the lower portion of the route to above the chimney, but not as high as the inside corner. Make a long leftward traverse to the first large snowpatch on the slabs. Climb an ice pitch to the snowpatch on the second slab, then traverse left. Climb snow and rock to join the original route.

Variation: Ramp Route — Ice Cliff Glacier to Northeast Face: By Phil Boyer and Michael Yokell, June 18, 1976. From the head of the glacier follow the ramp of the Northeast Face of False Summit Route, then continue. Climb a 45-degree snow/ice gully to above the North Ridge notch.

LEFT SIDE ROUTE: Starting from the Ice Cliff Glacier at about the same elevation as the Northeast Face Route, a slabby face with sloping ledges was climbed for five pitches to the level of the base of Girth Pillar, here joining an earlier route. The climb was made by Jim Nelson, Bill Pilling, and Bob Cotter in September 1985.

The hardest portion is the face gaining a ramp; there are a few aid moves. Several pitches on the ramp continuing beyond the False Summit Route permit one to reach a snowfield on the Northeast Face. Traverse the snow rightward to a small buttress (on the right of the snow). One can climb left of the buttress, entering a corner system where there is some ice; three additional pitches lead to the summit ridge. Grade IV (entire route); class 5.10 and A2.

NORTHEAST FACE OF FALSE SUMMIT: This face is the direct headwall above the Ice Cliff Glacier; and was originally called Stuart's "east face." The route basically ascends the Ice Cliff Glacier to its upper section, then the steep 1400-ft rock headwall to the false summit, closely E of the true summit. The route was conceived on a high reconnaissance, then done on the second attempt by Fred Beckey and Ron Niccoli on August 20, 1960. Take crampons and ice screws.

Ascend Ice Cliff Glacier to right side of bergschrund beneath the upper ice couloir. Climb slabby rock, bearing rightward on an obvious ramp which spirals above the edge of great NE face slabs. The first three leads above the ice are class 5 (10 pitons used). Continue on the ramp system to beyond Girth Pillar near the center of the headwall. Then climb directly up the wall via steep but well-jointed solid rock. Higher on the wall, follow a slight indentation, then bear right to the crest between the false and true summits. Grade IV; class 5.6. Time: 11 hours from valley. References: *Mountaineer*, 1961, pp. 101-102; *A.A.J.*, 1961, pp. 362-363.

GIRTH PILLAR: This feature is the obvious pillar near the center of the False Summit's face. First ascent by Kit Lewis and Jim Nelson on July 15-16, 1983. First winter ascent by same party, February 1985; four days were spent on the climb, with descent by Ice Cliff Glacier (8 days to and from Leavenworth).

The route begins at the entrance to the Ice Cliff Glacier's couloir. Climb four pitches on the obvious ramp system to the pillar's base (good bivouac ledge here). The crux of the route consists of four pitches of very steep rock. Begin on the pillar's right (N) wall and finish on its left side. Five to six moderate pitches continue to the False Summit. Grade V; class 5.10 and A1; the rock is excellent. Considerable aid was used on the first ascent due to crack cleaning. Reference: *Climbing*, December 1985, pp. 42-43.

ICE CLIFF GLACIER: This spectacular glacier offers a N-facing route to high on Stuart's E shoulder. Proper conditions should be chosen; the route could be dangerous when too warm, or the glacier too split, as late in the season. The second ascent party found it practical in the month of April to climb over the major icecliff on the glacier. However, by summer there may be a wide wall-to-wall crevasse above the icecliff; it may require technical ice climbing to surmount it. Take crampons and ice screws. First ascent by Bill and Gene Prater, and Dave Mahre on August 5, 1957. First winter ascent by J. Reilly Moss in March 1975. Approach via Mountaineer Creek cross-country route (see Stuart Lake Trail ◆) or by a descent from Goat Pass along the terminal moraines of the Stuart Glacier.

Climb lower E side of the glacier, leaving the ice below the ice cliff. Most parties climb polished rock (unprotected class 4 — may be wet) for about 200 ft near the ice, then return to the gentler gradient of the upper glacier. The final couloir leads directly to the crest on the E shoulder. Bypass schrunds on rock and snow to the W for about 300 ft. Then ascend the long snow/ice couloir; its upper portion is about 45 to 50 degrees. Beware of late-season rockfall when lower ice cover exposes unstable rock. Grade II or III, depending

upon conditions. Time: 7-9 hours from timberline. Note: a good return route to Mountaineer Creek is to traverse the S flank of Sherpa Peak, then cross the pass to Sherpa Glacier. Reference: *Cascadian*, 1957, pp. 7-9 and 75-80.

SHERPA GLACIER: First ascent by Bill Prater, Gene Prater, Don Torrey, and Nelson Torrey in June 1956. Approach via Mountaineer Creek cross-country route (see above). It may be prudent to first ascend talus, then bear right on polished slabs to avoid any sliding ice danger, then ascend to the lower W portion of the glacier. The original party climbed the left side of the glacier to the right-hand of the two couloirs (at est. 8000 ft); large schrunds are likely in late season. A long chute (to 40 degrees) leads to the E ridge crest at a tiny notch (about 8700 ft). Grade II. Take crampons. Time: 6-8 hours from valley. Reference: *Cascadian*, 1956, pp. 20-21.

INGALLS PEAK   7662 ft/2335 m

Ingalls is a triple-summit peak of generally sound peridotite 2 mi. W of Mount Stuart. Massive red cliffs of this rock are well exposed on the high glaciated surfaces at the head of Ingalls Creek and on the peak itself. The North (main) Peak is the highest, and is more rugged than the South Peak (7640 ft +). The East Peak (est. 7500 ft), a classic horn shape, is directly E of the North Peak.

The popularity of Ingalls has developed because of good rock and easy access. The view of Mount Stuart and of the Dutch Miller Gap peaks is remarkable. Some of the early climbing history is unknown. A group from The Mountaineers made the ascent of either the South or North Peak on August 12, 1925. Surveyor G. C. Curtis and G. O. Smith in 1898 dubbed the massif "Three Sisters." Curtis described the glaciated bedrock, boulderfields, and Ingalls Lake in his field journal.

NORTH PEAK

SOUTHWEST FACE: From rim crossing just before Ingalls Lake (see Ingalls Lake Trail ◆) ascend easy slabs, then bear right under cliffs to the broad basin and couloir. Ascend snow or scree to the North-South Peak col (7320 ft). Descend W a short distance to a light-toned slab. Ascend by friction to a ledge (rock shoes recommended), then move left and up into a shallow gully. Ascend past chockstone to a small sloping terrace. Pass a rappel tree, climb about 40 ft, then follow a ramp left. This leads to an exposed but easy traverse of several hundred ft on small ledges to just below the W skyline notch. The climb is completed by scrambling along boulders and scree of the broad W ridge; the far summit point is highest. Class 4. Time: 4-5 hours from road.

Variation: Southwest Gully: Instead of traversing W on the ramp and ledges, continue directly up the steep SW

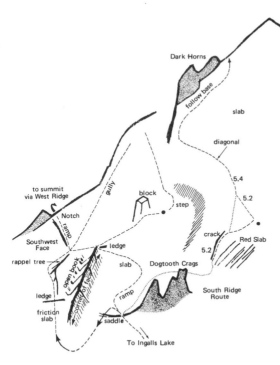

INGALLS PEAK (North Peak) - south ridge and southwest face

of the dark horn crags (fixed piton). A short class 4 pitch along the crack at the right base of the crags leads to the ridge edge; scramble on to the farthest rock point, which is the summit. Take a small selection of stoppers. Note: variations have been made in the slab center (central crack, 5.6). Time: 1 hour. Reference: *Mountaineer,* 1954, p. 66.

SOUTHEAST FACE: First ascent by Lex Maxwell and Bob McCall, June 1956.

Reach the prominent slanting shelf on the face from the couloir leading to North-East Peak notch. Traverse S on the

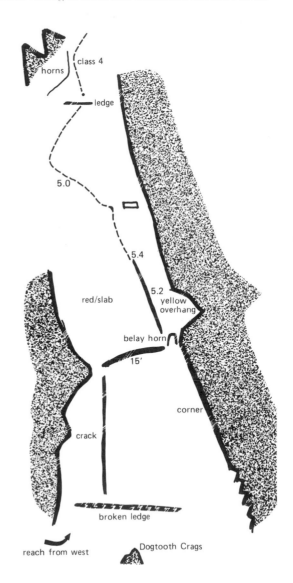

INGALLS PEAK - South Ridge

gully. When it merges into the face, continue up slabs near the dark horns. Class 4.

Variation: From closely W of the Dogtooth crags in the col, scramble to a slab-ramp; in about 50 ft climb left across a narrowing slab, then make an ascending traverse to the left corner of the S face below a large rectangular block. The climb continues around the corner to a ledge, then meets or crosses the SW gully. Class 4; rock is solid.

Variation: By Eiichi Fukushima and Philip Spence on July 23, 1966. From the rectangular block, climb right 10 ft, then move up a trough. Climb left above the block and leftward up cracks to the corner (80 ft, class 5.4). Climb up and right on the slab under the dark horns.

SOUTH RIDGE: This is the shortest route to the summit; a recommended route on solid rock. The first ascent was probably made by Keith Rankin and Ken Solberg on May 30, 1941 (a 1949 party found pitons en route).

From the North-South Peak col drop slightly W and bypass Dogtooth Crags to gain the notch behind them. Ascend the South Ridge slab to where it steepens and becomes smooth. From a broken ledge climb the obvious crack near the left edge of the red slab for 40 ft (class 5.2), then traverse right easily for 15 ft to the corner (edge of yellow overhang); one can belay at a horn. Climb the left-angling crack in the slab center (class 5.4 maximum) to a small ledge with two fixed pitons (optional belay) and continue leftward (class 5.0), then up to a small ledge 15 ft right

INGALLS PEAK from southeast
WILLIAM A. LONG

shelf about 400 ft, then climb an open book (120 ft to belay atop a minor buttress; probably class 5.3). Ascend up and right on easier rock leads to the upper East Ridge; follow this to the top. Note: slanting shelf can also be reached from left through break in face.

EAST RIDGE: First ascent by Don Jones and Barry Prather in June 1957. Ascend talus, then rock couloir toward North-East Peak notch. About 200 ft below the notch scramble left onto rock to bypass chimney. Then regain the gully above; continue to beneath the notch chockstone. Then climb the East Ridge. Pass N of the ridge gendarme, then scramble over blocks. Near the summit is an exposed 50-ft pitch (class 5); most of the climb is solid, class 4. Time: 3 hours from lake. Reference: *Cascadian,* 1962, pp. 16-17.

SOUTH PEAK   7640 ft+/2329 m+
ROUTE: From the North-South Peak col, the ascent is made by hiking and scrambling along the crest. Other slopes of the peak offer moderate scrambling routes; rock is not

steep, but is badly fractured. Reference: *Mountaineer,* 1925, p. 28 and 63.

EAST PEAK   est. 7500 ft/2286 m
First ascent by Gene and Bill Prater, and Stan Butchart in November 1952.

SOUTHWEST FACE: Climb to North-East Peak notch (see North Peak, East Ridge). Climb above chockstone in notch and proceed to a good ledge on slabs above. Follow ledge and gully to a big ledge. Work right and follow rotten ridge to the highest point on E. Class 4 to easy class 5. Time: 3 hours from lake.

SOUTH FACE, LEFT SIDE: First ascent by Gene Prater, Donald N. Anderson, and Jim Richardson in September 1959.

Ascend couloir leading to North-East Peak notch to about 200 ft below notch (until a right-traverse leads up behind a prominent gendarme). From halfway between the gendarme

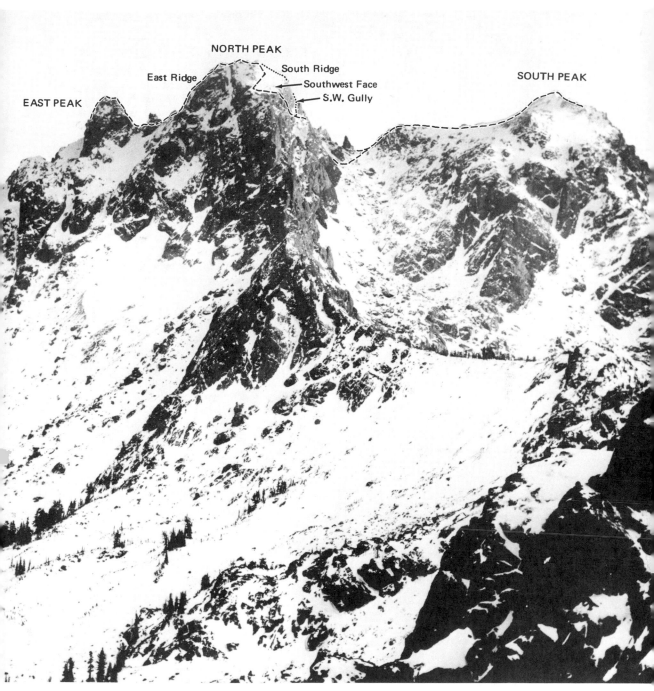

INGALLS PEAK from northwest
LYNN K. BUCHANAN

and a smaller one farther right climb up and left on the steep wall to a ledge. Move left on the ledge and then up easy broad slabs to the upper E ridge. Follow this to summit block. Class 4 with one class 5 move on first pitch. Time: 4 hours. References: *A.A.J.*, 1960, p. 119; *Mountaineer*, 1960, p. 90.

SOUTH FACE, RIGHT SIDE: Rock on this route ranges from quite good to poor. First ascent by Dave Hiser and Hal Lee on September 9, 1961.

Reach lower part of face beneath the two chimneys crossed by a white dike. Original party began in left chimney, then bore to right one (both chimneys reported suitable). Above, traverse 200 ft obliquely left to prominent midface gendarme (some looseness), then climb an extremely loose overhang. Scramble to broad slabs that slope to join the E ridge. Cross slab ledge and then climb up and left to gully leading to summit block. Class 5.2 — most of climb is class 4. Reference: *Mountaineer*, 1962, pp. 89-90.

DIKE CHIMNEY AND EAST RIDGE: This SE-facing chimney formed by the prominent colored dike (actually a deep gully) can be clearly seen from Ingalls Lake. First known ascent by Donald N. Anderson, Dee Molenaar, Gene Prater, and Barry Prather on October 1, 1960; previously done, unknown party.

From talus above the lake, climb about 400 ft up chimney to its intersection with upper E ridge (class 3-4). Once on E ridge, several leads to top (last pitch is class 5). References: *Mountaineer*, 1961, p. 102; *A.A.J.*, 1961, p. 365.

JACK RIDGE   7893 ft/2406 m

A long and high crest flanking Jack Creek valley on the E. The highest point is about 1 mi. NW of Mount Stuart, and only ¼ mi. N of Goat Pass.

Point 7492 just NW of Horseshoe Lake is prominent, as are several points above 7000 ft to the N. The highest of these is Point 7828 (in Section 36), which is 1.3 mi. SW of Eightmile Mountain. The old Jack Ridge lookout is burned down.

ROUTES: Point 7893 is a mere hike from Goat Pass (reach from Stuart Pass). The northern summits could be reached from the head of Trout Creek (reach by trail from Icicle Creek Road ◆); trail end is at Trout Lake, 5 mi. from the road. A trail over Jack Ridge is no longer maintained. Enormous rockslides choke the valley of Trout Lake beneath cliffs at the head.

Point 7828 could be reached easily from near the head of Eightmile Creek.

DUDLEY SPIRE   7492 ft/2284 m

The prominent thimble-shaped rock knob on the ridge spur just NW of Horseshoe Lake (see Stuart Lake Trail ◆). First ascent by William A. Long, Kathy Long, Elvin R. Johnson, and Mrs. E. R. Johnson in September 1948.

Hike upslope from Horseshoe Lake to the summit

scramble. The original ascent was done from the N, which is steeper.

YELLOW LICHEN TOWERS
est. 7000 ft/2134 m

There are three towers located on a spur ridge at 0.3 mi. NW of the North Peak of Ingalls. First ascent by Fred Dunham, Gene Prater, and Jim Wickwire on September 24, 1961. References: *A.A.J.*, 1962, p. 208; *Mountaineer*, 1962, p. 103.

One reaches the towers by a ½-mi. scree descent from Main-South Ingalls Peak col; or from the trail to Lake Ann (see Fortune Creek Jeep Trail ◆), continue ½ mi. N and then bear uphill.

Climb the E tower on the W (from notch adjacent to middle tower); it is 50 ft high here; class 3.

Climb middle tower on E side; it is 60 ft high; class 4; rappel bolt on summit.

Climb W tower from SW side; it is 90 ft high; class 4. Traverse across lower face to large chockstone in a wide crack. Another crack runs up gently on the E, and a wide crack continues up to the ridge above. Holds are generally good, but rock tends to fracture.

NADINE SPIRE   est. 5600 ft/1706 m

This spire is located directly above the Teanaway Road ◆ at ½ mi. S of road end (on rocky slope below Dissension Peak). First ascent by Bill Prater and Barry Carlson on July 3, 1957. Climb and traverse from uphill notch to sloping ledge on N side. Then work to the rib above. Class 5 — shattered rock. Time: 2 hours from road.

VOLCANIC NECK   6600 ft+/2012 m+

A 200-ft fin on the Hardscrabble-Fourth Creek divide, at ½ mi. N of Bean Peak. First ascent by Gene Prater and two companions in May 1952.

Take County Line Trail about 3 mi. W from Stafford-County Line Trail junction (see Stafford Creek Trail ◆) to the 6400-ft saddle at 200 yards S of the Neck. Traverse W and climb gully on NW corner (poor rock) to summit ridge, or climb from E end of ridge. Class 3. Time: 5 hours from road.

ESMERELDA PEAKS
6480 ft+/1975 m+

The Esmerelda Peaks, located E of Hawkins Mountain in the angle between DeRoux Creek and the upper North Fork Teanaway River, have two principal summits: the higher East Peak (which rises steeply from about 4400 ft on its E scarp), and the West Peak (6477 ft).

There are two higher summits (6765 ft and 6760 ft+) at 0.7 mi. to the W, and about ½ mi. from Gallagher Head Lake.

ROUTES: One could leave Boulder-DeRoux Trail ♦ above the 5200-ft level, then make a scrambling ascent to either summit group. Another possible approach is from the County Line Trail on the northern flank.

The rock gully on the E side, facing the parking lot at end of North Fork Teanaway Road, was ascended by Gene and Bill Prater, and Les Miller in June 1949. Cross creek from parking lot and enter bottom of gully, which continues to right of apparent summit. Several pitches are climbed, the lower of which are harder (class 3 and 4).

HAWKINS MOUNTAIN
7160 ft+/2182 m+

Hawkins is a large mountain located on the Big Boulder-South Fork Fortune Creek divide. There are two main summit formations: the West Peak (the highest), the East Peak or Thimble is lower (7080 ft+). Generally the S and W slopes are easiest; the broad ridges are mostly basalt scree.

The West Peak is largely a hike, but the East Peak involves some scrambling near the summit. There are splendid summit views of the Dutch Miller Gap and Mount Stuart areas. The name is for prospector S. S. Hawkins. The rock of the mountain is volcanic, intimately associated with serpentine. The journal of Bailey Willis indicates his party made the ascent on September 8, 1899. The Willis and Frank Calkins survey party used the summit for triangulation on September 22, 1902.

ROUTES: The ascent can readily be made from near Gallagher Head Lake, using either road approach to Boulder-DeRoux Trail ♦. Follow a short jeep road spur (No. 209) westward to a mine site at about 5900 ft. Ascend scree and easy slopes NW to the 6800-ft central saddle.

Another route is to hike 2 mi. on Big Boulder Creek Trail until just past the junction with a branch (about 4600 ft). Cross the creek to the N and ascend the ridge that is W of the creek draining the southern flank of Hawkins. Ascend N until this ridge intersects the main summit ridge; follow it to the summit. Occasional traverses to the W may be needed to avoid steep loose rock and/or cornices on the crest and eastern flank of the ridge.

Variation: Hike the trail about ½ mi. past the open scree slopes (about 3800 ft). Go NE up a gully or through forest to gain the broad SW ridge of Hawkins (5200 ft). Ascend the ridge NE until it intersects with the main summit ridge at about 6400 ft. Continue as above.

EAST PEAK, NORTH ROUTE: Via South Fork Fortune Creek Jeep Trail (see Fortune Creek Jeep Trail ♦); route by Gene and Bill Prater, and Ron Bissemette in 1950. Leave near 4600 ft NE of the mountain; cross creek and bear SW to broad slanting ledge that crosses the peak (easy). Rock above is class 4; N buttress leads to 7000-ft rock point NW of summit (Thimble). Rock is loose.

HARDING MOUNTAIN
7173 ft/2187 m

A rugged, bulky mountain located in the diverging angle of Meadow and Jack creeks at 2½ mi. N of Van Epps Pass. Harding is connected to the Wenatchee Mountains crest line by a ridge to Point 7095. The mountain is an isolated knob of granodiorite, part of the Mount Stuart batholith. The mountain was named by A. H. Sylvester for President Harding.

SOUTHEAST ROUTE: Take Jack Creek Trail ♦ to the 4000-ft level, where Solomon Creek enters. Ascend the latter cross-country 1 mi. and then ascend the long, but easy and open slope.

The W flank route could readily be climbed from the Meadow Creek Trail (see Jack Creek Trail ♦). If done this way, it appears best to climb into the basin W of the summit, then continue to the SW ridge.

HIGHCHAIR MOUNTAIN
7016 ft/2139 m

Situated about 2 mi. E of The Cradle, between Meadow, Black Pine, and Snowall creeks. Its S summit (6908 ft) forms the suggested shape. The ridge continuing northward is called Ridge 6600; its E slopes offer good skiing.

SOUTH RIDGE: From the trail at Cradle Lake (see Jack Creek Trail ♦, and French Creek Trail ♦) head NW to the 6480-ft saddle above the lake; then contour northward on the W slope to bypass the S summit, and follow the South Ridge to the top; generally easy.

OTHER ROUTES: From near the end of Icicle Creek Road ♦ one could take Blackjack Ridge Trail to just E of the summit, at the head of Ben Creek. The ascent would be simple from there.

The ascent could also be made from upper Black Pine Creek — an isolated hanging valley, or from the trail crossing on Ridge 6600; this ridge offers easy travel to the summit.

THE CRADLE   7467 ft/2276 m

The Cradle is one of the more notable peaks in the Wenatchee Mountains. Located about 8 mi. NW of Mount Stuart (and of the same granitic stock), it has a double summit that forms a perfectly shaped depression to lend reality to the name. Both N and S summits are rated the same altitude; however, the South

Peak seems higher; the saddle between the summits is 7280 ft+. There is a high continuing ridge both N and S of the summit uplift. The eastern slopes above timberline are talus, but snowcovered much of the summer. Long western scree slopes rise above light timber.

First ascent of the South Peak by Dwight Watson and Gene Paxton on August 6, 1944. First ascent of the North Peak by Gene and Bill Prater in July 1952.

SOUTH RIDGE: Take the trail to Paddy-Go-Easy Pass ◆ and then descend to French Creek Trail ◆ (1½ mi.); take it S about ¼ mi. to meadows, then ascend open slope and light timber and talus to the South Ridge at about 6800 ft. One could camp at Sprite Lake or at French Creek. Note: One could approach via French Creek Trail ◆ to SW of the peak, or reach via Snowall Creek, leaving the trail at about 4600 ft to ascend to the S shoulder.

Cross the ridge and travel N across the rockslides. Class 2; short rock scramble at top. Can be climbed from any direction.

The Southwest Buttress of the W face has been climbed; loose rock reported — class 5.1 by Lawrence Duff and Anthony Mendoza, July 1971.

NORTH PEAK: From the South Peak descend to the central saddle, then traverse on E side below gendarmes. Climb moderately steep ledge to the top (class 3). It appears the North Peak could be done from the W side directly; easy gullies lead to the central saddle.

GRANITE MOUNTAIN
7144 ft/2178 m

Located about 2½ mi. SE of Deception Pass, just SE of Robin Lakes (the NW summit is ⅜ mi. from the upper lake). Granite is the highest point on the Hyas Lake-French Creek divide, at the western edge of the Wenatchee Mountains — a mass of granodiorite some 3 mi. long. The South Peak (7080 ft+) is ½ mi. distant; it has a distinctively steep wall on its E flank.

The entire ridge from Trico Mountain to Paddy-Go-Easy Pass rises easily on the SW flank. There are a number of minor summits on the crest SE of Granite Mountain; one could readily traverse from this crest to Paddy-Go-Easy Pass and beyond. Attractive peaks on this spur crest are "Deceptive Peak," with a face on one side, and "Boulder Top Spire," with a long unusual summit block. The spire is most easily climbed from the W. Boulder Top and Flat Top were climbed by Bill and Gene Prater, and Frank Markey in 1979. Reference: *A.N.A.M.*, 1985, p. 66.

ROUTES: The long ridge from Paddy-Go-Easy Pass ◆

could be traversed to Granite Mountain. About ½ mi. N of the pass is a sharp contact between granite and peridotite.

From the S end of upper Robin Lake (see Tuck and Robin Lakes Route ◆) one can ascend S to a draw, then E to the true summit. One can traverse the high W slope of the connecting ridge to the South Peak.

One could climb the easy NE flank from the W end of West Klonaqua Lake (see French Creek Trail ◆); take the trail to the E lake and hike cross-country around the lakes.

It would be feasible to reach the mountain from French Potholes (highest is 5680 ft), then climb NW to the S summit and the peaks on the SE crest. To reach the true summit from here would first involve a loss in altitude. Reach French Potholes from French Creek Trail ◆ by ascending cross-country up sidestream (about 1½ mi. to upper lake).

French Ridge is a timberline ridge spur NE of Granite Mountain, between Leland and French creeks. The highest point is 6767 ft, due N of the ithsmus between the Klonaqua Lakes (a hike from the lakes). There is a 6748-ft peak at ¾ mi. to the W and a 6600-ft peaklet just E of the highest summit. It is a gentle ridge with a number of points barely rising into the alpine zone.

TRICO MOUNTAIN   6640 ft/2024 m

Trico, whose name is derived from the three-county junction, is located 2 mi. N of Hyas Lake and to the NW of Robin Lakes. The mountain is steepest on the E, where it presents a broad, rounded shape, with a short summit-ridge rock wall.

ROUTES: From Deception Pass (see Deception Pass Trail ◆) the ascent is largely subalpine travel, following the watershed. The ascent can also be done from Tuck Lake, a route mostly in timber (see Tuck and Robin Lakes Route ◆).

It is also feasible to make the ascent from upper Robin Lake: hike over a low saddle (6240 ft), then NW to Granite Mountain Potholes (average 6000 ft). Trico is ¼ mi. NW of the upper pothole. Ascend the easy SE spur.

MAC PEAK   6859 ft/2091 m

One mi. S of Square Lake, the peak is of importance in the area because its height tops those of nearby summits; S and W slopes are gentle and the pyramidal E side has a short rock wall.

ROUTES: From Square Lake (see Leland Creek Trail ◆) walk around the E side, then hike up to timberline just E of the summit; a short scramble to the top.

From Deception Lakes (see Surprise Creek Trail ◆) ascend gentle basin to the SE. The ascent offers no difficulties from here.

The S and W slopes could readily be climbed to the summit from the Deception Pass Trail ◆

THUNDER MOUNTAIN
6556 ft / 1998 m

A moderate peak located on the Cascade Crest between Square and Glacier lakes, about 1 mi. S of Trap Pass. Its upper E side is rocky.

ROUTES: The W ridge offers a hiking ascent. Begin from midway along Glacier Lake or at the shelter there (see Surprise Creek Trail ◆ and Crest Trail ◆).

The SE flank offers a simple route from Square Lake (see Leland Creek Trail ◆). Begin from the lake's NW corner.

The 600-ft granitic N face was climbed by Bruce Garrett and Dennis Nelson on July 6, 1972. Three leads of class 5 and some aid. Reference: *Mountaineer,* 1972, p. 77.

UNNAMED PEAK   6711 ft / 2046 m

The peak, which has a double summit, is ½ mi. NE of Thunder Mountain and just N of Upper Thunder Mountain Lake. The climb would be simple from the lake (see Leland Creek Trail ◆). A ridge N of the peak continues to Trap Pass, with two lower rocky intermediate points. The rectangular tower is Slippery Slab.

SLIPPERY SLAB TOWER
est. 6400 ft / 1951 m

This 250-ft rock tower is perched on the high ridge E of Surprise Lake, extending N of Peak 6711. It is the first major tower S of Trap Pass. First ascent by Dave Harrah, William Herston, and Keith and Ruth Ran-kin in May 1947 (via Southeast Face). Reference: *Mountaineer,* 1947, pp. 49-50.

NORTHEAST FACE: This has become the favored route. Take Surprise Creek Trail ◆ and Crest Trail ◆ to Trap Pass. On E side of ridge take a goat track leading S to talus slopes below the eastern foot of the tower (est. ¼ mi.). About four sling runners can protect the climbing, using horns and scrub trees (class 4). Time: 6 hours from road. *Descent:* The pine near the top of the last pitch is a good rappel anchor.

There is another route on the extreme N portion of this face. First ascent by Patricia (Malmo) Crooks, Jim Crooks, and Ray Rigg in 1948. A 60-ft slab, then a chimney is climbed to a minor notch on the N ridge; then scramble (two pitches).

EAST FACE: First ascent by Jack Schwabland and Fred Melberg on July 25, 1948. This route ascends the center of the face. It is shorter but more difficult than the Southeast Face; on the original ascent several pitons were used for aid. Reference: *Mountaineer,* 1948, p. 83.

SOUTHEAST FACE: From the eastern foot of the tower, climb to a large slab. Cross a ledge to the S face, and ascend a shallow chimney. Moderate class 5.

WEST FACE: First ascent by Gary Glenn and Mike Heath in July 1971. From ridge N of tower (at NW corner) descend a gully, then follow a ledge to the bottom center of W face. Climb prominent dihedral-gully 50 ft, then right to blocky ledge. Traverse right across smooth slab, then up steep chimney to belay ledge on right. An exposed traverse right leads up to an overhanging lieback-jam, then easy blocks to the summit. Total: 3 leads, each class 5.7. Good rock, good protection; small chock or piton selection to 1 inch. Time: 2 hours.

"Going down the Columbia, the reason of the Cascade mountains being so named becomes apparent from the steep sides of that tremendous chasm through which the gathered waters seek the ocean . . . . beautiful little falls which pour from every crevice, at every height, and frequently from the very mountain top."

LT. JOHN LAMBERT, 1855

NOTES

[1] R. G. Thwaites (ed.), *Original Journals of the Lewis and Clark Expedition 1804-1806* (New York, 1905), vol. 4, pt. 2, p. 226.

[2] George Vancouver, *A Voyage of Discovery to the North Pacific Ocean,* vol. 1 (London, 1798), p. 235.

[3] Henry R. Wagner, *Spanish Explorations in the Strait of Juan de Fuca* (Santa Ana, 1933), map p. 82. The map was drawn by Gonzales López de Haro.

[4] David Douglas, *Journal kept by David Douglas during His Travels in North America* (London, 1914), pp. 221, 252, 256, 257.

[5] John Lambert, "Report of the topography of the route from the Mississippi River to the Columbia," *Reports of explorations and surveys to ascertain the most practicable and economic route for a railroad from the Mississippi River to the Pacific Ocean* (33rd Congress, 2nd sess., *House Exec. Doc. 91*), vol. 1, part 2 (Washington, 1855), p. 176.

[6] Charles Wilkes, *Narrative of the United States Exploring Expedition during the years 1838, 1839, 1840, 1841, 1842* (Philadelphia, 1844).

[7] J. Quinn Thornton, *Oregon and California,* vol. 1 (New York, 1849), pp. 255-261.

[8] F. P. Farquhar, "Naming America's Mountains — The Cascades," *Amer. Alpine Jour.,* 1960, p. 49.

[9] Map of British Columbia, Lands and Works office (under Hon. J. W. Trutch), 1871.

[10] I. C. Russell, *North America,* 1904.

[11] Stuart S. Holland, *Landforms of British Columbia,* B. C. Department of Mines and Petroleum Resources, Bull. 48 (1964).

[12] Bauerman, *Report on the Geology of the Country near the 49th Parallel of North Latitude.* Report of Geological Survey of Canada, 1882-4.

[13] G. O. Smith and F. C. Calkins, *A Geological Reconnaissance Across the Cascade Range near the 49th Parallel.* Bulletin of the U.S. Geol. Survey, No. 235 (1904).

[14] Spelling of Indian names became a phonetic interpretation; established forms took long to settle.

[15] In 1813 the Corps of Topographic Engineers was created, and it was this branch of the Army that conducted much of the exploratory work in the American West prior to the Civil War. The overall mapping achievement was that of Lt. Gouverneur K. Warren. Congress had directed the War Department to make preliminary railroad surveys along different latitudes, and in early 1853 these enterprises were placed in the hands of military engineers. Captain McClellan was directed to survey the Cascades and construct a military road from Walla Walla to Fort Steilacoom.

[16] The Wilkes map was the beginning of accurate western cartography. Strangely, much information about the West coming from the Hudson's Bay Company, Mackenzie, Lewis and Clark, Ogden and others was transmitted to Aaron Arrowsmith in London, and this cartographer (who kept pace with maps) was the basis for the maps prior to Wilkes and those of Army explorers and railroad surveyors. Albert Gallatin's 1836 map, like others of his time, presents an idea of the West based largely on reports of explorers, and was devoid of detail. The Tapetete River (Yakima) was the only river in the Cascades shown on some maps of the early 1800s. In Major Benjamin Bonneville's 1837 map, one not based on astronomical observations for positions of latitude and longitude, the Cascades are only a single narrow chain and there is no Coast Range in any of the West. A map, "Territory of Oregon," made by Captain Washington Hood of the Topographical Engineers in 1838 perpetuated major myths and errors. Maps made by Capt. McClellan and his topographer suffered in accuracy because they were based on compass courses, without observations made for longitude. One result was that Mount Rainier was placed 15 minutes too far E.

[17] I. C. Russell, "A Preliminary Paper on the Geology of the Cascade Mountains in Northern Washington," *20th Annual Report, U.S. Geological Survey, 1898-1899,* pt. 2 (Washington, 1900), p. 146.

[18] Inventory of Glaciers in the North Cascades, Washington. *Geological Survey Prof. Paper 705-A* (1971).

[19] George Gibbs, "Physical Geography of the Northwestern Boundary of the United States," *Bull. Amer. Geog. Soc. of N.Y.,* vol. 4 (1873), p. 353.

[20] "Loowit" is an anglicized version of longer Indian names for Mount St. Helens, as settled on by early writers.

[21] Vancouver; see note 2.

[22] Thwaites, vol. 3, pp. 195-196; see note 1.

[23] W. G. Steel, "Mountain Lore," *Oregon Native Son,* vol. 1 (May, 1899), p. 21.

[24] Capt. J. C. Frémont, "Report of the Exploring Expedition to the Rocky Mountains in the Year 1842 and to Oregon and North California in the Years 1843-'44," 28th Cong., 2nd sess., *Senate Exec. Doc. 174,* serial 461 (Washington, 1845), pp. 193-194.

[25] Elliott Coues, *The Manuscript Journals of Alexander Henry and of David Thompson 1799-1814,* vol. 2 (Minneapolis, 1897).

[26] Frémont's entry of October 29 stated: "In the course of the day Mount St. Helens, another snowy peak of the Cascade Range, was visible. We crossed the Umatilah at a fall . . ." (Frémont, p. 184).

[27] Gibbs observed, "It is not a little singular that neither Lewis and Clark, nor Lieut. Wilkes, distinguished Mount Adams as a separate peak from St. Helens; for although they resemble each other considerably in general form, their positions and range are very different. Mount Adams alone is visible from the Dalles; but both of them, as well as Rainier, can be seen from a slight elevation at the mouth of the Willamette." Report of George Gibbs upon the Geology of the central portion of Washington Territory. *House Exec. Doc.*

129, 33rd Cong., 1st sess. (Washington, 1854), p. 497.

28 *Steel Points,* vol. 1 (July, 1907), pp. 134-135. See also Elva C. Magnusson, "Naches Pass," *Wash. Hist. Quart. 25,* no. 3 (1934), pp. 171-181.

29 *Mazama,* 1896, pp. 124-125.

30 *Mazama,* 1903, p. 168. Professor W. D. Lyman estimated 200,000 sheep pastured on the slopes of Mount Adams, to virtually make Bird Creek Park a desert.

31 James Longmire, "Narrative of James Longmire, a Pioneer." *Wash. Hist. Quart.* 23 (January 1932), p. 59. The Naches "road" was very primitive. Longmire wrote that his party followed the Naches River 4 days and made 68 river crossings. Some 38 wagons crossed the pass, where on the W side they were lowered by ropes belayed around trees.

32 Lieutenant Richard Arnold's Report on the Military Road from Wallah-Wallah to Steilacoom. *Sen. Exec. Doc. No. 1,* 34th Cong., 1st sess., pp. 532-538. During this project Lt. Arnold visited Mount Ikes and later submitted a map. This minor peak just N of Naches Pass, far out of relevance, was also shown on various maps as Mount Aiks (*Harpers Magazine,* April 1884, map p. 706).

33 Eugene V. Smalley, *History of the Northern Pacific Railroad.* New York, 1883.

34 Vancouver, p. 235; see note 2. The publication of Vancouver's work placed the name "Mount Rainier" on British maps, from which it was copied in America. Captain J. C. Frémont alluded to the mountain as "Regnier," believing it had been named for Lt. Regnier of Marchand's 1791 expedition to the Northwest Coast.

35 Eliza R. Scidmore, *Appleton's Guide-Book to Alaska and the Northwest Coast.* New York, 1898, p. 7.

36 *The Journals of William Fraser Tolmie: Physician and Fur Trader.* Vancouver: Mitchell Press Ltd., 1963, p. 397. This was the first account reporting the existence of glaciers in the United States.

37 *The Columbian,* September 18, 1852. See also George H. Himes, "Very Early Ascents," *Steel Points,* July 1907, p. 100. An interview with Himes many years later makes it unclear how high the men climbed. There is no valid reason to believe they were successful.

38 Saluskin's account, given 62 years later, is subject to senility and vagueness. There is little reason to believe surveyors engaged in determining the boundary of the Yakima Indian Reservation could have made the long N-side ascent and descent in one day. The quite experienced, well-equipped, and competent Russell party of 1896 took two days to reach the summit via Steamboat Prow. See L. V. McWhorter, "Chief Sluskin's True Narrative," *Wash. Hist. Quart.* 8 (1917), p. 99, and J. A. Splawn, *Kamiakin, the Last Hero of the Yakimas,* Portland, 1917, pp. 343-345.

39 A. V. Kautz, "Ascent of Mount Rainier," *Overland Monthly* 14 (May, 1875), p. 400. German-born Kautz was a

West Point graduate. He was the first to use a metal-spiked alpenstock in the United States.

40 Hazard Stevens, "First Successful Ascent of Mount Rainier," *Atlantic Monthly* 38 (1876), p. 524. Stevens had been a Brigadier-General in the Union Army. Van Trump had come W from Ohio to prospect for gold.

41 Ingraham was one of the mountain's most active explorers. He named Columbia Crest during a July 1894 ascent. Included in his feature names is St. Elmo Pass, where in 1887 he witnessed the phenomena of St. Elmo's fire after the end of a thunderstorm.

42 Willoughby Rodman, "The Sierra Club in the Northwest," *Out West,* May 1906, p. 372.

43 S. F. Emmons, "Volcanoes of the Pacific Coast of the United States," *Jour. of the Amer. Geog. Soc. of N.Y.,* vol. 9 (1879), pp. 45-65.

44 R. S. Fiske, C. A. Hopson, and A. C. Waters, "Geology of Mount Rainier National Park, Washington," *Geol. Survey Prof. Paper 444* (1963), p. 36.

45 A deposit of pumice represents the only known eruption of new magma since the last major period of volcanic activity, estimated at about 2000 years ago. D. R. Mullineaux, R. S. Sigafoos, and E. L. Hendricks, "A Historic Eruption of Mount Rainier, Washington," *Geol. Survey Prof. Paper 650-B,* pp. B15-18.

46 Early surveyors noticed the Tatoosh peaks. "There are several sharp needle-points to the south of Mount Rainier, and the mountains in that vicinity are very irregular and thrown together in every variety of manner," was one comment. Topographical Report of Lt. J. K. Duncan, U.S.A., Olympia, Washington Territory; February 21, 1854. *Sen. Exec. Doc. No. 78,* vol. 1. 33rd Cong., 2nd sess.

47 S. C. Porter, "Pleistocene Glaciation in the Southern Part of the North Cascade Range, Washington." *Geol. Soc. Amer. Bull. 87,* no. 1 (1976), pp. 61-79.

48 R. W. Tabor, et al., "Preliminary Geologic Map of the Skykomish River 1:100,000 Quadrangle, Washington." *U.S. Geol. Survey Open-File Map 82-747* (1982).

49 *Ibid.*

50 Porter; see note 47.

51 The spelling shown on the 1870 map of Public Surveys in Washington Territory and other maps.

52 Report of Lt. J. K. Duncan. *Pacific Railroad Reports,* vol. I. *Sen. Exec. Doc. 78,* 33rd Cong., 2nd sess., p. 211.

53 Report of Captain George B. McClellan. *Pacific Railroad Reports,* p. 192; see note 52.

54 Both Indians and Lewis and Clark referred to the Yakima River as the Tapteel or Tapetett. Tinkham used Yak-E-mah. Tinkham camped at the foot of Lake Keechelus on January 20, 1854. The following day he snowshoed across the lake, then crossed Lost Lake to Yakima Pass. His descending route passed Nook-Noo Lake (Cedar Lake) to the Puget Sound area.

[55] J. O. Oliphant, "The Cattle Trade Through the Snoqualmie Pass," *Pac. Northwest Quart. 38* (July, 1947), pp. 193-213.

[56] G. O. Smith, "Geology and physiography of Central Washington," *U.S. Geol. Survey Prof. Paper 19* (Washington, 1903), p. 22.

[57] Pacific Railroad Reports, p. 196; see note 52.

[58] *Ibid.,* p. 431.

[59] This spelling is shown on the 1870 map: Public Surveys in Washington Territory.

[60] Russell, 20th Annual Report, p. 155; see note 17.

[61] *Ibid.,* p. 191.

[62] National Archives, Cartographic Branch.

[63] Russell, p. 191; see note 17.

[64] A rock glacier is a lobate body of angular blocks that resemble a small glacier. The slow-moving, ice-cored rock glacier has a debris mantle that is derived from cliffs. The rock glacier owes its existence to the accumulation of snow close to the cirque headwall, a large debris supply which moves into the ablation area, and the insulative properties of the debris mantle.

[65] *Pacific Railroad Reports,* p. 196; see note 52. Lt. Robert E. Johnson saw the mountain in 1841 from Naches Pass, well before McClellan. Johnson did not name the mountain, but clearly described it. On August 26, 1853, McClellan sketched Mount Stuart (McClellan Papers, Library of Congress).

[66] A. H. Sylvester Papers, Univ. of Washington Library. The geologist G. O. Smith ascended Mount Stuart on the S, August 15, 1898, and attempted in vain to descend into a northern cirque. He noted that "Perched blocks seemingly ready to fall at any time are to be found on the highest points" (U.S.G.S., Denver. Smith Book 1211, p. 23). Professor I. C. Russell must have made one of Stuart's earliest ascents, but his writings do not reveal locations reached. R. U. Goode and G. E. Hyde surveyed the Mount Stuart quadrangle in 1896.

"Mount St. Helena presented a conspicuous and romantic prospect — an immense cone enveloped in snow . . . tapering up to a point without any rugged irregularity."

HENRY the YOUNGER, January 11, 1814

APPROACHES

Roads and trails are described separately in alphabetical order. Cross-references to road and trail descriptions are marked with small black diamonds ♦.

ROADS

Most National Forest roads in the Cascades are low-standard, one-lane roads with occasional turnouts for meeting oncoming traffic. Many of these roads, especially on the east flank of the range, are not graded. Maintenance cannot be guaranteed, and there is always the chance of tree blowdowns.

Most roads are not maintained or cleared of snow during the winter; the exceptions are county roads and ski-area roads.

Encounters with logging trucks are likely, even on weekends. Food, gas, and lodging are seldom available along forest roads. The trunk and most collector roads have campsites and campgrounds; the latter are shown on National Forest maps.

Park well off the road, but do not block turnouts. For safety, do not drive in the dust of other vehicles (at times headlights are advisable).

Road route markers are posted at the entrance of primary and secondary routes; the signs use white numbers on a brown background and are posted at road entrances and intersections. New road numbers have as many as seven digits. Main (arterial) roads are signed with two-digit numbers (such as 16). Moderate-use secondary roads (collectors) are signed with four digits (such as 1610), the first two of which designate the arterial off which they branch. Local roads which branch off collectors, are identified by seven digits (such as 1610-232), the first four of which indicate the collector from which they branch.

Drivers should no longer anticipate road nomenclature or destination signs (such as Icicle Creek Road). The best tactic is to have a guidebook, map, or road-numbering list with you when driving. Local road numbers normally appear vertically on posts, with only the last three digits shown (the first four, designating collector roads, are understood). These are low-standard roads that probably are not maintained. Obstructions such as drainage ditches, washouts, or blowdowns may close these roads; wet weather and snowmelt may render them difficult or impassable because of deep ruts.

Alpental Road. See I-90 ♦.

Bald Mountain (Manastash Ridge). Take Rocky Creek Road No. 1701, which exits from State Hwy No. 410 ♦

about 11 mi. SE of Little Naches junction (junction is 35 mi. from Yakima). Follow uphill and continue on No. 1701-530 to Bald Mountain (12 mi. total); the road nearly reaches the top of the 5755-ft mountain — a scenic viewpoint, especially for the Stuart Range. Manastash Ridge is an uplifted block of pre-Tertiary volcanic rock of the Western Cascade Group.

Bear Creek Mountain Road No. 1204. See Bear Creek Mountain ◆ (Trails).

Berry Creek Road No. 84. This road provides an approach to Sawtooth Ridge and High Rock in the forested region SW of Mount Rainier. At 2.6 mi. E of Ashford (see Nisqually Entrance Road ◆) turn S on Kernahan Road and drive 1.4 mi. to Skate Creek Road No. 52. Turn E and reach Berry Creek Road (Towhead Gap Road) in 3 mi.

From this junction turn S. Locations of interest include branch road No. 8410 (extends 4 mi. to Teeley Creek Trail and Bertha May Lakes), branch road No. 8420 (1½ mi. to Big Creek Trail and Cora Lake), Towhead Gap and High Rock Trail (10 mi.). The road climbs through stands of Douglas and noble fir on this loop road, which can be continued NW around Sawtooth Ridge.

By using Skate Creek Road, the distance from Ashford to Packwood is 22.4 mi.

Bethel Ridge Road No. 1500. This mountain road crosses Bethel Ridge and the Rattlesnake Creek area, E of the Cascade Crest between the Naches and Tieton rivers. The road can be taken either from U.S. Hwy No. 12 ◆ at 17.5 mi. E of White Pass or State Hwy No. 410 ◆ at 28 mi. from Yakima.

Two branches of the Bethel Ridge Road lead to viewpoints and the backcountry: McDaniel Lake Road No. 1502 exits at 8.1 mi. from the Naches River end of the road and extends 7.6 mi. westward (past Meeks Table Natural Area). Timberwolf Mountain Road (No. 190) climbs almost to the top of the 6391-ft summit (the final portion may be 4-wheel); leave the main road at 13.6 mi. from Hwy No. 12.

BIA Road No. 285 (Yakima Indian Reservation — Bench Lake). From Trout Lake on State Hwy No. 141 the distance to Bench Lake on Indian Lands is about 16½ mi. Take roads No. 82 and 8290 to the BIA road; camping charge at Bench Lake.

To reach Bird Lake, fork W on Road No. 204 at about 14 mi. (car camping charge). Where the main road meets the ridge in another mile N, a branch bears upslope to a picnic area (meets Round-the-Mountain Trail ◆). Use permits for BIA lands may be purchased at Bird Lake during the summer season.

Bumping Lake Road No. 18. This important primary forest road leaves State Hwy No. 410 ◆ at American River (20 mi. E of Chinook Pass) and ends in 17 mi. *Deep Creek Road No. 1808* branches at 13.3 mi. (at Bumping Lake), ending at Deep Creek Campground (a total of 20.3 mi.). This road system provides access to the William O. Douglas Wilderness and other scenic mountain terrain E of the Cascade Crest.

Burley Mountain Road No. 77 (Pinto Rock, Greenhorn Creek). See Randle-Lewis River Road ◆.

Cabin Creek Road No. 41. This road connects the Yakima and Green River drainages in the timber harvesting region S of Stampede Pass. The road begins from I-90 ◆ at Easton Exit No. 71 and ties in with Stampede Pass Road ◆ about 1 mi. E of the pass. Tacoma Pass branch No. 5200 forks S at 0.5 mi. and connects with the Green River road system (private); the public can normally drive to Lester, but the road may be gated ½ mi. W of Tacoma Pass. The road crosses the Crest Trail ◆ at Tacoma Pass.

Carbon River Road (Mount Rainier National Park). The Carbon River entrance to the Park (about 55 mi. from Tacoma, 70 mi. from Seattle) is reached from Buckley on State Hwy No. 410 ◆. From Buckley drive S through Carbonado on Hwy No. 165. The Park entrance is 5.8 mi. from Fairfax; the Carbon River Road extends 5 more mi. to an end at Ipsut Creek Campground.

Carlton Creek Road No. 44. Leaves State Hwy No. 123 ◆ about 1½ mi. S of Ohanapecosh Hot Springs and extends about 5 mi. The Carlton Creek Trail is reached in about 4 mi.

Chiwaukum Creek Road No. 7908. Leaves U.S. Hwy No. 2 ◆ at 25 mi. E of Stevens Pass and extends 1½ mi. into the narrow stream valley to Chiwaukum Creek Camp and trailhead. There has been a property dispute that affects the road status; therefore one may have to walk a portion of the road.

Cle Elum River Road (Salmon la Sac Road). State Hwy No. 903 and Forest Road No. 4330 can be reached from I-90 ◆ at Roslyn Interchange (Exit 80), then driving 3 mi. to Roslyn. The alternate is from Cle Elum, taking Hwy No. 903 for 3 mi. to Roslyn. From either origin, distances to key junctions are French Cabin Road (15 mi.), Cooper Pass Road ◆ (17.5 mi.), and Salmon la Sac Campground (18.5 mi.). From Salmon la Sac to the road end in the upper valley S of Hyas Lake, the distance is 12.8 mi. See also Cooper Pass Road ◆.

Clover Spring Road No. 1600. Leaves the Nile County Road (a loop off State Hwy No. 410 ◆ at 28 mi. from Yakima). The distance westward to Clover Spring (6351 ft) is 18½ mi. Use either the E or W entrance of the Nile Road.

Clover Spring offers a trail approach to the N fork of Rattlesnake Creek. The rough jeep road that leaves to the SW as Trail No. 976 (Mud Springs Trail) has good vistas into the William O. Douglas Wilderness, but ORV usage discourages hikers.

It is possible to use Clover Spring Road, then branch No. 231 at about 14½ mi. to make an eastern approach to the summit of 6108-ft Little Bald Mountain (lookout station); there is a proposal to name this William O. Douglas Peak.

Cold Creek Road No. 9070. Leave I-90 ◆ at Hyak Interchange (No. 54). Turn right, then in 0.1 mi. turn left onto No. 9070. Continue 3½ mi. to Cold Creek Trail No. 1303. The road continues, crossing the Crest Trail ◆ in Olallie Meadow at 4200 ft; the road extends into a recent clearcut very visible from the highway W of Snoqualmie Pass. Shortly after crossing the Crest Trail the road is waterbarred;

during logging operations one may be able to drive farther.

Cooper Pass Road No. 46 and 4600. This scenic mountain-access road branches W from the Cle Elum River Road ◆ to reach Cooper Pass in 7 mi. The road continues to the Kachess River (access to Mineral Creek Trail ◆).

Cooper River Road No. 4616 branches N at 4.5 mi. (near Cooper Lake) and can be taken to Road No. 113, which leads into Owhi Campground and the Pete Lake Trail ◆ .

Coplay Lake Road No. 7810. Leaves Carbon River Road ◆ just short of the Mount Rainier National Park entrance. Cross the Carbon River; then drive 5.3 mi. to a "T" junction; keep left 1.6 mi. to Summit Lake trailhead.

Corral Pass Road No. 7174. Leaves State Hwy No. 410 ◆ at 31.8 mi. from Enumclaw. The steep and narrow road extends 6 mi. to Corral Pass (road end).

Cougar Valley Road. See Raven Roost Road ◆ .

Coulter Creek Road No. 6930 (McCue Ridge). Leaves U.S. Hwy No. 2 ◆ at 18 mi. E of Stevens Pass (18 mi. from Leavenworth). The road is closed to vehicles beyond gates. For the road route to McCue Ridge take the first left fork to the gate (1.2 mi.); one can hike 7 mi. on the road to 5000 ft, where there is a shelter. For the trail to Lake Julius, Lake Donald, and Loch Eileen and McCue Ridge, take the right fork and gate (4 mi.).

Crystal Mountain Road. This paved road leaves State Hwy No. 410 ◆ at 33.3 mi. from Enumclaw and extends 6 mi. to the ski area.

Denny Creek Road. Exits from I-90 ◆ at 17½ mi. E of North Bend (Exit 47: follow signs to Denny Creek Road — 2.2 mi. to campground). Turn left on next road, cross the river, and reach parking/trailhead area in about ¼ mi. This road is generally open in winter.

Eightmile Creek Road. See Icicle Creek Road ◆ .

Foss River Road No. 68. This is a well-surfaced, important access road to the Alpine Lakes area. The road exits from U.S. Hwy No. 2 ◆ at 2 mi. E of Skykomish. Reach East Fork Foss River Trail in 4.3 mi. and West Fork Trail at road end (6½ mi.).

Maloney Ridge Road No. 6840 branches W off the Foss Road at about 5 mi.; this road climbs to the Maloney viewpoint in 4.7 mi., then doubles back S around the E flank of Sobieski Mountain for about 2 mi.

Greenwater River Road No. 70. Leaves State Hwy No. 410 ◆ at 20.4 mi. from Enumclaw and gives access to the historic Naches Pass area. The Naches Pass Trail (at 2560 ft) can be followed E from Himes Camp, 7.6 mi. on the road. The wagon-road route, now a trail track, reaches Government Meadows in 3½ mi.

To reach Twin Camps turn N prior to Himes Camp on Road No. 7030 (4.4 mi.); the road has rough sections. From Twin Camps the road bears NW about 4 mi. to the Kelly Butte trailhead; here is a 1.3 mi. trail to the lookout. *Kelly Butte* (5360 ft +) is a dissected Miocene volcano with a barren summit area.

A branch road (No. 7032) continues about 1½ mi. W along the Green Divide. The Green Divide Trail begins at the end of this road on the S side of the ridge in an old clearcut. Scott Paper roads that bear N to Green River are restricted to the public.

From Twin Camps, Road No. 7036 bears E along the divide toward Windy Gap; the road becomes No. 7036-110 beyond a junction with No. 7038, and meets the Crest Trail ◆ at the gap. The road continues about 4 mi. to its end, which is approximately 2 mi. W of Blowout Mountain at Green Pass (road driveable, parallel to the Crest Trail).

I-90. The interstate highway from Seattle eastward provides basic access to the Snoqualmie River Valley roads, Snoqualmie Pass, Stampede Pass, Yakima River Valley roads, and Cle Elum River Valley roads. Key mileages are: Seattle to North Bend — 30 mi.; North Bend to Snoqualmie Pass — 21 mi.; Snoqualmie Pass to Cle Elum — 31 mi.

Distances eastward from North Bend (Exit 31):

Exit 32. North Bend. 2.4 mi.

Exit 34. Edgewick Road. 4.4 mi.

Exit 42. Tinkham Road. 12.2 mi.

Exit 45. Bandera Airfield. 15.6 mi.

Exit 47. Denny Creek Road. 17.5 mi.

Exit 52. Snoqualmie Pass (W Summit exit). 22.4 mi. Frontage road to Crest Trail ◆ parking lot and Snoqualmie Pass. Alpental Road bears N from the overpass and reaches parking lot for Snow Lake Trail ◆ in 1.2 mi.

Exit 53. Snoqualmie Pass (E exit). 23.1 mi.

Exit 54. Hyak. 25 mi. Frontage road No. 4832 to Rocky Run. Frontage road to Cold Creek.

Exit 62. Stampede Pass and Lake Kachess. 33.3 mi.

Exit 63. Cabin Creek Road. 34.4 mi.

Exit 71. Easton. 42 mi.

Exit 80. Roslyn (to Cle Elum River Road). 51 mi.

Exit 84. Cle Elum. 53.7 mi.

Exit 85. Swauk Pass Hwy junction. 56.6 mi. Hwy No. 970, leading to Hwy No. 97.

Exit 106. Ellensburg. 77 mi.

Icicle Creek Road No. 76. Leaves U.S. Hwy No. 2 ◆ on the W limits of Leavenworth and ends in 18 mi. at Blackpine Creek. This important road provides access to much of the Wenatchee Mountains.

Eightmile Creek Road No. 7601 leaves the Icicle Road at 8.6 mi. (campground) and climbs S about 3½ mi. to the parking area. An eastern continuation and logging spurs W of the road are closed.

Johnson Creek Road No. 21. Begin on U.S. Hwy No. 12 ◆ at 10 mi. E of Randle. *Chambers Lake Road No. 2150* branches E at 13 mi. and reaches Berry Patch in 3 mi. Walupt Lake Road No. 2160 branches E at 16½ mi., then extends 4½ mi. to Walupt Lake (campground).

The main road reaches Adams Fork in 22½ mi. (campground). From here one can drive about 4½ mi. W to meet the main Randle-Trout Lake Road ◆ . Another connection to the latter is to continue S on Road No. 5601 to Olallie Lake (campground).

Lake Kachess Road No. 49. Exit from I-90 ◆ at No. 62, then drive to Box Canyon Road No. 4930 (5.4 mi.). Rachel

Lake Trail is 4.1 mi. from the Kachess Campground entrance.

Lennox Creek Road No. 57. See North Fork Snoqualmie River Road ◆.

Lewis River Road No. 90. To reach this important forest road, one can leave I-5 at Woodland, taking State Hwy No. 503. At Yale (23 mi.) continue along Yale Lake and reach Cougar in 6 mi. and the Lewis River Forest Road in 8½ mi. The road follows the canyon of the Lewis River, cut in volcanic rock, eastward. There is a junction with Randle-Lewis River Road ◆ at 18 mi. from Cougar, with Road No. 88 (Trout Lake-Lewis River Road ◆) at 42 mi. from Cougar, and ends at the Randle-Trout Lake Road ◆ near Mount Adams (about 51 mi. from Cougar). At present, Road No. 90 is paved within 5 mi. of the No. 88 junction.

Road No. 88 can be taken to Trout Lake (not kept open in winter); the distance is 25 mi.

Pine Creek Visitor Information Station is reached on Road No. 90 at 17.6 mi. from Cougar. Campsites on the road include Beaver Bay and Swift Creek.

Little Naches River Road No. 19. Leaves State Hwy No. 410 ◆ at 23½ mi. from Chinook Pass (at Little Naches Campground junction; 30 mi. from Naches) and extends NW up the valley to near Naches Pass. From the main highway, the road distance via Road No. 19 and No. 1914 to Trail No. 941 in Section 25 (leading to the Crest Trail ◆ near Pyramid Peak) is 19.4 mi. Trail No. 941 heads W about ¼ mi. past Road No. 1914-787; the trail has been used mostly by ORV's.

The jeep trail to Naches Pass, which still retains some of its pioneer characteristics, is No. 942. From Road No. 1914 in Section 34 the distance is about 2.7 mi. to Naches Pass; it is an additional mi. to Government Meadow and the Crest Trail ◆. The Naches Pass Trail can be taken W to Himes Camp on Greenwater River Road ◆.

The Crest Trail can also be reached by a hike of about 5 mi. to near Blowout Mountain. Take Road No. 1911, forking N at about 11 mi. and extending to Section 30. Here Trail No. 943, continuing on No. 943A and No. 1388, or Trail No. 943, are routes to the Crest Trail.

Lost Lake Road No. 1201. Extends closely E of Kloochman Rock. Reach via Tieton Road ◆.

Merrill Lake Road No. 81. Can be used to reach Kalama Springs (campground) in 13 mi. from Cougar; leave State Hwy No. 503 about 1 mi. W of Cougar. Spur No. 8123 extends N from just W of Kalama Springs, leading to near the Goat Marsh Research Natural Area. From Kalama Springs the main road continues E to connect with Swift Creek-Muddy Road ◆ and formerly provided access to Mount St. Helens. Note: the final 2 mi. of the road (W of Swift Creek-Muddy Road) have been blocked most of the year by mudflows.

Warning: watch for closures on roads S and W of Mount St. Helens. Use permits may be necessary. Obtain from Mount St. Helens National Volcanic Monument.

Middle Fork Snoqualmie River Road. Leave I-90 ◆ at Exit 34, to the E of North Bend, and turn E on Edgewick Road. Follow this road 0.4 mi. to a stop sign, then right on SE Middle Fork Road, which becomes Forest Service Road No. 56. An alternate route is from North Bend, continuing eastbound on SE North Bend Way to the road end. Turn left at Edgewick Road (Trucktown).

The distance on Road No. 56 to the Middle Fork-Taylor River road junction is about 12.3 mi. Cross the Taylor River bridge and turn right on No. 5620, which ends at Hardscrabble Creek (25.7 mi.). At about 22.6 mi. there is a bridge and trail connection to Goldmeyer Hot Springs, which is on private land and currently closed. At 23.5 mi. a short spur bears toward the river; one can cross the river here and make a trail connection to the Commonwealth Basin ◆ (Red Mountain) Trail and the trail to Snow Lake.

There is a footbridge across the Middle Fork at Dingford Creek, and logs can be used to cross at Rock Creek. A new section of trail is planned from Dingford Creek to Rock Creek, giving a link to the Snow Lake trail. It is proposed to extend the trail eastward along the S side of the Middle Fork to bring a connection with the Dutch Miller Trail.

Taylor River Road No. 5630 is currently closed because of a burnt bridge; one can hike the 6 mi. span (see Snoqualmie Lake Trail ◆). The road will probably be open to auto traffic to Quartz Creek and possibly Marten Creek (about half-way) in the future.

Midway Loop Road No. 2329. This is a mountain loop road with one end beginning near the Cispus-Lewis River divide NW of Mount Adams, then bearing NE to Midway Camp, then W to Adams Fork. From the Randle-Trout Lake Road ◆ near Baby Shoe Pass on the divide, the Midway Loop Road trends NW for about 1 mi., then bears E to Taklakh Lake (camp) in another mi. Killen Creek Camp is reached in about 5 mi. and Midway Camp (to the N) in another 5 mi. The road then turns W for about 3 mi. and meets Orr Creek Road No. 56 in a continuation to Adams Fork (about another 4 mi. farther).

At a junction about 2 mi. S of Midway Camp, Spring Creek Road No. 5603 turns E (passing Potato Hill) into BIA lands. There is a parking area at the Crest Trail ◆ intersection. A permit is needed for continuation inside the reservation boundary. Potato Hill Road is No. 9115.

Another approach to the Midway Loop Road is via Johnson Creek Road ◆ to Adams Fork, then continuing on Road No. 5601 to just beyond Olallie Lake. Note: at the higher levels the winter snowpack may delay summer road openings.

Mill Creek Road No. 6960. Leaves U.S. Hwy No. 2 ◆ at 5.8 mi. E of Stevens Pass and meets the Crest Trail ◆ as a powerline road. The road becomes rough; it may be possible to drive for 3.8 mi. Be prepared to hike several miles.

Miller River Road No. 6410 and 6412. Exits from U.S. Hwy No. 2 ◆ at 3 mi. W of Skykomish (at Money Creek Campground). Drive SE about 1 mi. on the old Cascade Hwy (No. 6810), then drive S on No. 6410 for 3.7 mi. to the junction with No. 6412. The latter continues S another 5.8

mi. to the road end and Lake Dorothy Trail; 9.5 mi. total from the old Cascade Hwy.

The West Fork (No. 6410) is a private road, closed to the public. Distance is 3 mi. to Coney Creek, and another ½ mi. up the creek to mine workings.

Money Creek Road No. 6420. See Miller River Road ◆. Turn W off Road No. 6810. The Money Creek Road extends about 7½ mi. — about ½ mi. past Lake Elizabeth.

Mount Adams Timberline (S Side). From Trout Lake on State Hwy No. 141 drive N to junction with Road No. 80 (4.7 mi.). Follow No. 80 and 8040 to Morrison Creek Camp and upward to Cold Spring Camp at 5600 ft (15.2 mi. total). The last portion is a narrow roadway. Trail distance (No. 183) to old Timberline Camp, at 6240 ft +, is 1½ mi.

Also see BIA Road ◆ (Yakima Indian Reservation-Bench Lake) for the SE approach to Mount Adams.

Mount Index Road No. 6020 (to Lake Serene Trail). Begin on a gravel road leaving U.S. Hwy No. 2 ◆ at 12.8 mi. E of Sultan (just before Skykomish River bridge). At 0.3 mi. take the narrow uphill fork (before the powerline): walk or drive (depending on road condition and washouts) for 1.4 mi. to a fork. Traverse on the left fork another 0.4 mi. to the Honeymoon Mine at the 1200-ft level.

Mount Rainier National Park. See Carbon River Road ◆, Nisqually Entrance Road ◆, State Hwy No. 123 ◆, State Hwy No. 410 ◆, Stevens Canyon Road ◆, West Side Road ◆, White River Road ◆. In winter and spring, the park road is kept open to Paradise; other roads are only to entrance points. The road across Cayuse Pass may be closed, depending on policy.

Mowich Lake Road No. 165. Branches from Carbon River Road ◆ at 3 mi. S of Carbonado, then extends about 17 mi. to the lake. Note: the last few mi. are seldom open before mid-July. The Grindstone Trail is a 1-mi. hiker shortcut, eliminating the final two switchbacks; the trail is on upslope prior to the last northern switchback.

Nisqually Entrance Road (Mount Rainier National Park). This entrance, E of Ashford on State Hwy No. 706, can be reached from Tacoma and I-5 via State Hwy No. 7 in 55 mi., or from Seattle and I-5 via State Hwy No. 161 (about 80 mi.). From the Park entrance, Longmire (Visitor Center) is 6 mi. and Paradise is 19 mi. (open in winter).

North Fork Snoqualmie River Road. Take I-90 ◆ to North Bend. From Ballarat St. in the center of town follow the North Fork county road: keep generally right, but uphill and left at 3.8 mi. Cross the entry to Snoqualmie Tree Farm Roads (Spur 10) at 8 mi. Continue to the junction of Roads No. 57, 5731, and 5730 (20 mi. from North Bend).

The *North Fork Road (No. 5730)* begins just N of this junction (4.1 mi. in length). Branch No. 5736 exits W at 2.5 mi. and extends 1.4 mi. to near Mount Phelps.

Lennox Creek Road No. 57 extends from the junction for 6.7 mi. to end in Section 25 near the head of Lennox Creek.

Lennox Trail No. 1001 begins from a ½-mi. spur at 4.3 mi. on the road.

North Fork Tieton River Road No. 1207. This important forest road is reached by exiting U.S. Hwy No. 12 ◆ at Tieton Road ◆ and driving SW for 3.2 mi. Then continue on North Fork Road to its end in 5.2 mi. at Scatter Creek. Here are trail approaches to the Goat Rocks area and the Crest Trail ◆.

Packwood Lake Road No. 1260. Turns E at Packwood Ranger Station and extends 6 mi. to the lake trail.

Pinegrass Ridge Road No. 1205. See Bear Creek Mountain ◆ (Trails).

Proctor Creek Road No. 62. Leave U.S. Hwy No. 2 ◆ at 0.6 mi. E of Milepost 33 (about 6 mi. E of Gold Bar). The road continues across the low divide to the Tolt River drainage. An uphill fork (No. 6220) leading toward Mount Persis is at 3.6 mi. There is a gate at 6.7 mi. (may be open only weekends — see Snoqualmie Tree Farm Roads ◆); meet the tree farm mainline road at 7.8 mi.

Quartz Mountain. From Ellensburg take I-90 ◆ westward to Exit 101, where it goes under the old Thorp Hwy. The latter intersects the Taneum Road about 1 mi. NW of Thorp. One could also take the old Thorp Hwy from Ellensburg: From Ellensburg and the Taneum County road it is 15.1 mi. to the Forest Road.

Taneum Road (Forest Service) No. 33 to the junction of Gnat Flat Road No. 3330 is 6.8 mi. Climb on the latter southward for 8.2 mi. to Tamarack Springs Road No. 3120, then drive 6.1 mi. to Manastash Drive (Road No. 3100). Follow the latter 6.3 mi. to 6290-ft Quartz Mountain (total of 42.8 mi. from Ellensburg). Jeep roads extend both to the NW and SE along the ridge.

Randle-Lewis River Road No. 25. This paved road extends S from Randle on U.S. Hwy No. 12 ◆ to Lewis River Road ◆ near the E end of Swift Reservoir (46 mi.); campgrounds include Iron Creek. The fork to Windy Ridge (Road No. 99) in Mount St. Helens N. V. M. is 20 mi. from Randle.

One can drive W from the main road to Mosquito Meadows and the Pole Patch area by taking Pinto Road No. 28 at 22 mi. from Randle. Greenhorn Creek Road No. 77 continues N, passing Pinto Rock, French Butte, Pole Patch Camp, then connecting to Burley Mountain. There will be seasonal closures on these roads due to snowpack.

To reach Burley Mountain from the N, leave the main road at Iron Creek Campground (10 mi. from Randle) and drive E for 4.4 mi. on Greenhorn Road No. 76. A narrow dirt road (No. 7605) climbs to the crest of the mountain and connects with Greenhorn Creek Road (only open after winter snow melts).

Randle-Trout Lake Road No. 23. This is a scenic seasonal road flanking the W side of Mount Adams (usually not open until June). The road crosses the Cispus-Lewis River divide

MOUNT GARFIELD from south
ED COOPER

at Baby Shoe Pass — 31.2 mi. from Randle, then continues S to Trout Lake (23.6 mi.). Trout Lake can be reached from Hood River, Oregon, or State Hwy No. 14. Campgrounds on or near Road No. 23 include Blue Lake Creek, and Council Lake. The lower portion of Crofton Ridge can be reached by road fork No. 050, to the NW of Trout Lake. This fork offers a trail connection to Morrison Creek.

Raven Roost Road No. 1902. Extends from Little Naches Road ♦ at 2.8 mi. to near Raven Roost (14 mi.); at the final left fork the road continues 2 mi. to 5300-ft Cougar Valley. The right fork to Raven Roost (No. 856) climbs to the 6198-ft lookout, which provides a marvelous vista of Mount Rainier, Fifes Peaks, and a span from Kaleetan Peak to Mount Stuart.

Russell Ridge. This prominent ridge N of Tieton Reservoir is reached by road from U.S. Hwy No. 12 ♦. From Rimrock begin on Wildcat Road No. 1306 and follow to Russell Ridge Road No. 1362. Double back on No. 1362, drive SW on No. 1381, then W on Hart Creek Road No. 1384 and No. 1384-622 to the road end. Jeep road No. 622 is actually Trail No. 1111, which leads westward into the William O. Douglas Wilderness. Jeep Trail No. 1113, approached off the end of Road No. 1362, leads W to a mercury mine.

The western end of Russell Ridge can be reached by taking Indian Creek Road No. 1308 to Andy Creek Road No. 1382; this gives access to Andy Creek Trail No. 1110, leading NW into the wilderness.

Salmon la Sac Road. See Cle Elum River Road ♦.

Snoqualmie Tree Farm Roads. This is a private road system, with gated roads that are open to the public only at specific times. Most land at or near the road system is owned by the Weyerhaeuser Company or is on the Seattle city watershed.

The following regulations currently apply:

(1) Vehicles and their occupants are allowed on Snoqualmie Tree Farm roads on weekends and holidays only, from April 1 through December 15, from Friday at 6:00 PM until Sunday evening. During the balance of the period, the roads are closed. Gates are locked nightly. The weekend gate status may be checked by phoning (206) 888-4250 on Fridays.

(2) The Weyerhaeuser Company makes no guarantee that these roads will be open and reserves the right to close any or all portions at any time due to operations, fire hazard, or weather conditions. Roads are open all year to hikers unless fire closures apply. No overnight camping or campfires allowed.

To reach the mainline truck road, follow directions per North Fork Snoqualmie River Road to the Spur 10 gate. Turn left on Spur 10 for 0.1 mi., then right. The mainline road meets Proctor Creek Road ♦ at 16.3 mi. At 19 mi. the mainline bears right to cross the North Fork Tolt River. To reach the slopes of Mount Index continue ahead for 1.1 mi. to

a junction. Road No. 140 curves upward here and begins to switchback, climbing about 1000 ft through a clearcut. Present road condition good but may change.

South Fork Tieton River Road No. 1000. To reach this well-surfaced and important access road to the Goat Rocks area, begin on Tieton Road ♦ at 16.8 mi. E of White Pass. To reach Conrad Meadows follow Tieton Road for 4.8 mi., then the South Fork Road about 12½ mi. to private land in Section 23.

Stampede Pass Road No. 54. Turns off I-90 ♦ at Stampede Interchange (about 10 mi. E of Snoqualmie Pass) and reaches 3664-ft Stampede Pass in 5.1 mi. The road continues W as a private road to Lester and the Green River valley. Southern spurs from the pass lead ½ mi. to a campsite and ½ mi. to the weather station.

The Green River watershed is not accessible from the N or W. The main access route is over Stampede or Tacoma Pass, but many roads and private lands are restricted to public use. Generally those roads E of Lester are open to the public. All National Forest lands in the watershed are open to the public.

State Hwy No. 123 (Cayuse Pass). This is a connector passing through the eastern edge of Mount Rainier National Park between State Hwy No. 410 ♦ and U.S. Hwy No. 12 ♦. Stevens Canyon Road ♦ joins the highway at 11 mi. S of Cayuse Pass (Park entrance gate here).

State Hwy No. 410. This major highway joins the Tacoma area with Yakima, crossing the range at Chinook Pass (the pass is closed in winter and spring). The highway gives access to the White River Entrance of Mount Rainier National Park, State Hwy No. 123 ♦ at Cayuse Pass, and the Naches River drainage.

The highway can be reached from the Seattle-Tacoma area via I-5 or I-405 and State Hwy No. 167. The latter joins Hwy No. 410 near Sumner. From Enumclaw (junction of Hwy No. 410 and State Hwy No. 164) the White River Entrance is 38 mi. and Chinook Pass is 44½ mi. Yakima is 61 mi. from Chinook Pass.

Stevens Canyon Road (Mount Rainier National Park). The western end joins the Nisqually Entrance Road ♦ at 10.7 mi. beyond Longmire and passes Reflection Lakes in 1½ mi. The Stevens Canyon Entrance (near Ohanapecosh) is reached in 19 mi. (12 mi. NE of Packwood on U.S. Hwy No. 12 ♦). This road is closed in winter.

Summit Creek Road No. 4510. Leaves U.S. Hwy No. 12 ♦ about 1½ mi. E of its junction with State Hwy No. 123 ♦. Begin on Cartwright Creek Road No. 45, then follow Summit Creek Road to Soda Spring Campground (about 5½ mi.).

Swauk Pass (Blewett Pass) Hwy. From I-90 ♦ take Exit 85 (Cle Elum) and follow State Hwy No. 970, which becomes U.S. Hwy No. 97. Reach Teanaway Road ♦ in 6.6

mi., the junction with Hwy No. 97 in 10.2 mi., Mineral Springs Campground in 16.7 mi., Swauk Campground in 20.3 mi., Swauk Pass in 24.6 mi., Bonanza Campground in 29.7 mi., Ingalls Creek junction in 38.9 mi., and U.S. Hwy No. 2 ◆ in 46.1 mi. This junction is 17 mi. from Wenatchee.

At Ingalls Creek junction, a bridge and roadway lead 1.3 mi. to the Ingalls Creek trailhead.

Swift Creek-Muddy Road No. 83. See Lewis River Road ◆ and Merrill Lake Road ◆. The Swift Creek Road exits at 3½ mi. E of Cougar, to skirt the SE flank of Mount St. Helens. The road meets the Randle-Lewis River Road ◆ via Jack Pine Road No. 2588.

Ape Cave is a unique geological feature near the first portion of the Swift Creek Road. All roads in this area may be closed at any time due to snowpack, mudflows, and volcanic hazards.

Teanaway Road (County Road No. 970 becomes Forest Road No. 9737). This major access road to the upper Teanaway River area, Ingalls Lake and Creek, and Mount Stuart leaves the Swauk Pass Hwy ◆ at 6.6 mi. from I-90 ◆ and ends 23 mi. from the highway. From I-90, follow Hwys No. 10, No. 97 (toward Wenatchee), and No. 970 into the Teanaway River valley. Road No. 9737 ends at the parking area (4240 ft) on the Teanaway's N fork.

Stafford Creek Road No. 9703 branches at 15 mi. and extends E about 3½ mi.

Beverly Creek Road No. 112 extends N about 1½ mi., branching off the main road at 17 mi.

Tieton Road No. 1200. This forest loop road leaves U.S. Hwy No. 12 ◆ at 7.5 mi. and again at 16.8 mi. E of White Pass. The road encircles Rimrock and Clear lakes; camping at Clear Lake.

Tonga Ridge Road No. 6830. Leaves the Foss River Road ◆ at 3.5 mi. and climbs to Tonga Ridge, then eastward to the Deception Creek drainage. A short road spur leads S to Tonga Ridge Trail. At about 15½ mi. on the road, Trail No. 1059-A can be followed 0.6 mi. to a junction with Deception Creek Trail ◆.

Towhead Gap Road No. 8440. See Berry Creek Road ◆.

Trout Lake-Lewis River Road No. 88. This important connecting road (partly paved) begins at 1½ mi. W of Trout Lake on State Hwy No. 141. The distance to Lewis River Road ◆ is 23.6 mi. There is a fine view of Sleeping Beauty Mountain at about 6 mi.

The junction with Road No. 8851 (leading to Steamboat Mountain, Twin Buttes, and Tillicum Campground) is 12.8 mi.; the campground is about 5 mi. from this junction.

A southwestern approach to the Twin Buttes area can be taken from Wind River to Road No. 30, then Road No. 24. Another approach is from Swift Reservoir: use Lewis River Road ◆, then roads No. 3211, 30, and 24.

The Indian Heaven Wilderness Area's E side, with its many volcanic features and lakes, can be reached via Road No. 24, connecting Trout Lake and Tillicum Campground.

U.S. Hwy No. 2. Coincides with the northern boundary of this volume. The highway connects Everett on I-5 and Monroe on State Hwy No. 522 with Stevens Pass, Leavenworth, and Wenatchee.

There are important access roads branching southward: Proctor Creek Road ◆, Mount Index Road ◆, Miller River Road ◆, Foss River Road ◆, Mill Creek Road ◆, Whitepine Creek Road ◆, Coulter Creek Road ◆, Chiwaukum Creek Road ◆, Icicle Creek Road ◆, and Swauk Pass Hwy ◆.

U.S. Hwy No. 12 (White Pass). This highway connects I-5 just S of Chehalis with Yakima. The highway joins State Hwy No. 410 ◆ 34.7 mi. E of White Pass (the latter highway, which crosses Chinook Pass, is closed during the winter months).

To reach White Pass and Hwy No. 12 from the Seattle-Tacoma area, several road routes can be taken to Enumclaw on Hwy No. 410. Follow the latter highway to Cayuse Pass, then State Hwy No. 123 ◆ to reach Hwy No. 12 between Packwood and White Pass. Cayuse Pass is currently closed in winter.

West Fork White River Road No. 74. Leaves State Hwy No. 410 ◆ at 22 mi. from Enumclaw. In 7 mi. one can take a W branch for 1 mi., then Road No. 7430 winds S for about 6 mi. The main valley road continues to near the boundary of Mount Rainier National Park.

West Side Road (Mount Rainier National Park). Leaves the Nisqually Entrance Road ◆ at 1 mi. inside the Park entrance and ends at the North Puyallup River in 14 mi. (currently closed at Klapatche Point). This road is not open in winter.

White River Road (Sunrise Road) in Mount Rainier National Park. See State Hwy No. 410 ◆ for approaches. From the road fork (38 mi. from Enumclaw and near the White River Entrance) the road extends 16 mi. to Sunrise (Yakima Park at 6400 ft). At 5 mi. on the road a western fork extends 2 mi. to White River Campground. This road is closed at Hwy No. 410 in winter and early spring.

Whitepine Creek Road No. 6950. Leaves U.S. Hwy No. 2 ◆ at 13.7 mi. E of Stevens Pass. The gravel road is single-lane and moderately rough. Pass the forest camp, twist downhill, cross the railroad tracks, pass a summer camp and logging operation, and reach the trailhead (3.8 mi.) in the center of an active timber plantation.

Yakima Pass Road No. 5480. Begins on the Stampede Pass Road ◆ at 1.1 mi. from the I-90 ◆ interchange, then bears N for 4.3 mi. to Lost Lake. Continue on good gravel for 1.9 mi. around the lake to the Mirror Lake trailhead.

TRAILS AND ALPINE HIKING APPROACHES

Wilderness Information

Wilderness permits are not required in wilderness areas. Certain regulations have been issued for Mount Adams, Goat Rocks, William O. Douglas, and Norse Peak wilderness areas in order to protect the vegetation around lakes, streams, and meadows, to reduce soil compaction and erosion in heavily used areas, and to enhance the wilderness character within the Wilderness.

These restrictions include:

1. Entering or being in the Wilderness with a group consisting of a combination of persons and pack or saddle stock exceeding 12 in total number without obtaining a permit.
2. Short-cutting a trail switchback.
3. Camping within 100-ft slope distance of any lake.
4. Camping within 200-ft slope distance of the Crest Trail, except at Deer Lake, Sand Lake, Buesch Lake, Fish Lake, Dewey Lake, Arch Rock shelter, and Dana Yelverton shelter; camping within Snowgrass Flat and within Shoe Lake basin.
5. Building, maintaining, or using a campfire at Snowgrass Flat, Shoe Lake basin, or Dana Yelverton shelter.
6. *Crest Trail* (Pacific Crest National Scenic Trail): The use of motorized vehicles is prohibited.
7. *Covering all the wilderness areas* (including Alpine Lakes): It is prohibited to possess or use a motor vehicle, motorized equipment, or bicycle.

Mt. Adams Area:

Special permits from the Yakima Indian Reservation are needed for overnight trips in BIA lands to the E and NE of Mount Adams. There may be a trail fee, even for day use.

Alpine Lakes High Route. See Lake Dorothy Trail ◆.

Anderson Creek Route. This is a haphazard but possible entry to the basin between mounts Index and Persis. A logging roadway once provided a feasible entry to the basin, but currently the route is quite overgrown with brush. Timber cutting or development, of course, may change the nature of this route. At present, this non-maintained route is in its best condition when snow covered. Take note of private property signs off the highway.

Exit from Hwy No. 2 ◆ near Milepost 34 (Swanson's Cabins), 11.6 mi. E of Sultan. Because of private property, one should park off the highway, to the E. The old roadway crosses Anderson Creek at the 800-ft level (about 1 mi.).

Annette Lake Trail No. 1019. Annette Lake (3600 ft+) is nested in a crescent of cliffs on the W flank of Silver Peak. From I-90 ◆ (Exit 47) turn right 0.1 mi., then left onto Road No. 55 for 0.6 mi. to the parking area (2200-ft level). The trail ascends an old clearcut, crosses Humpback Creek, ascends to the railroad tracks, then bears across old forest slopes to the lake (3 mi. to the outlet).

Bear Creek Mountain (Pinegrass Ridge). This is an access road and hiking route to the eastern flank of the Goat Rocks. From Clear Lake Campground near Tieton Reservoir, follow Tieton Road ◆ S and E around Clear Lake to Pinegrass Ridge Road No. 1205. Turn left on Road No. 1205-742 and then drive 0.2 mi. to Bear Creek Mountain Road No. 1204. Turn right and proceed along Pinegrass Ridge to the road end at Section 3 Lake (9.2 mi. from Tieton Road and 15.7 mi. from Hwy No. 12).

Bear Creek Mountain Trail, No. 1130, climbs 4½ mi. to the 7336-ft summit. Here is a fine perspective of Goat Rocks and the volcanism of the High Cascade Group. A feasible cross-country route can be taken to the Conrad Glacier: Continue SW along the ridge, passing S and below the pyroclastic rocks of red-cragged Devils Horns (these form the base of the Goat Rocks volcanic complex) to the meadow fringe on the S slope of Tieton Peak; then hike open terrain 1 mi. to the glacier. References: *100 Hikes in the South Cascades and Olympics, Trips and Trails 2.*

Beverly-Turnpike Trail No. 1391. From Teanaway Road ◆ take the Beverly Creek spur to the trail. Reach Beverly-Turnpike Pass (5760 ft+) in 3.5 mi. One can descend to meet Ingalls Creek Trail ◆ near the 4800-ft level.

Teanaway Peak (6779 ft), on the N fork Teanaway-Turnpike Creek divide, is a summit that can be reached from Beverly-Turnpike Pass. Make a hiking scramble for about ½ mi. westward.

Big Boulder Creek Trail. See Boulder-DeRoux Creek Trail ◆.

Boulder-DeRoux Trail No. 1392. This can be taken from either the Teanaway Road ◆ or the Cle Elum River Road ◆. The span is 7.9 mi. The western start is called Big Boulder Creek Trail, beginning off road spur No. 138, at 5.4 mi. N of Salmon la Sac.

From the Teanaway at the old DeRoux Campground road spur (8.3 mi. inside the forest boundary) the trail ascends for 3.5 mi. to Big Boulder Creek Trail (5440 ft); open to motorbikes. At this junction, Jeep Trail No. 161 extends northward to Gallagher Head Lake; this route continues through a saddle to Fortune Creek's S fork (see Fortune Creek Jeep Trail ◆).

Carbon River Trail (Wonderland Trail). From the end of the Carbon River Road ◆ at 2300 ft, begin on the old roadway. At about ¾ mi. prior to reaching the Carbon Glacier one can see the end of the A. D. 1760 moraine near the trail. The trail bridges the Carbon River and at 3.6 mi. comes close to the advancing glacier snout.

Here the river emerges as a brown, roaring torrent from a cavern in the ice, which currently terminates at about 3520 ft. Moraine Park (5500 ft and higher) begins at 6 mi. from the road. Mystic Lake (5700 ft) is reached in 8.1 mi.; a tongue of the Carbon once pushed a terminal moraine to form this lovely lake. Note: This trail coincides with Wonderland Trail ◆ from the Carbon River to Mystic Lake.

Carlton Creek Trail No. 22. Extends from Carlton Creek Road ◆ to reach the Crest Trail ◆ at Carlton Pass in 3 mi. In August 1867 William H. Carlton crossed this pass while surveying for the Northern Pacific Railroad. The pass was in plans for a trans-Cascade road in 1922.

Castle Mountain Trail No. 1188. From Corral Pass at 5600 ft + (see Corral Pass Road ◆) the trail reaches the Crest Trail ◆ in 4.2 mi. at Little Crow Basin.

Cathedral Rock Trail No. 1345. Begin just short of the parking area at the end of Cle Elum River Road ◆; reach Squaw Lake in 2½ mi. and a good camp at Cathedral Pass in 4½ mi. (see Crest Trail ◆). One can follow the latter to Deep Lake (4382 ft — fire closure) with its waterfall dropping from 6014-ft Circle Lake (can reach latter by hiking W on S side of exit stream).

Peggys Pond Route, finds the Pond (5560 ft +) nesting in a meadowed hollow between Cathedral Rock and Mount Daniel, about ½ mi. N of Deep Lake. The Pond's sharply defined circular shoreline makes it a special gem. *Note: this is a very fragile area* (fire closure at Pond).

From the end of the first switchback W of Cathedral Pass, contour the W side of Cathedral Rock via goat path (3 hours road to Pond). An alternate is a path directly from Squaw Lake, leading NW to cross the ridge just S of the Rock's base.

Chatter Creek Trail No. 1580. This is a steep 5-mi. trail from Chatter Creek Campground on Icicle Creek Road ◆ leading to Icicle Ridge Trail ◆ E of Frosty Pass.

Chiwaukum Creek Trail No. 1571 and No. 1591. Begins from end of Chiwaukum Creek Road ◆ (2080 ft) and climbs to 5210-ft Chiwaukum Lake in 8 mi.

Chiwaukum is an Indian name meaning "many little creeks running into big one"; this is apparent, for five almost equal branches unite to form Chiwaukum Creek. The entire watershed affords fine examples of Ice Age glacial cirques. Chiwaukum Lake occupies the pit of a hanging valley; the lake is a mi. long, with timbered and rocky shores.

The N fork trail (No. 1591) continues from the lake through Ewing Basin to Larch Lake (10 mi. total), which is set in a timberline basin with a talus fan against its S side. To reach tiny Cup Lake (6443 ft) cross a meadow and an open talus draw. The lake, set in a snowy cirque, may have a floating "ice island" in midsummer. An old sheep trail crosses Deadhorse Pass (7200 ft +); keep to right side of Cup Lake.

South Fork Chiwaukum Creek Trail No. 1571 reaches Lake Flora (5680 ft) in 9 mi. from the road, continuing to Ladies Pass (6800 ft +) to connect with Icicle Ridge Trail ◆ near Cape Horn (12 mi. from road). Branch trails up Index and Painter creeks offer other connections to the ridge trail.

Colchuck Lake Trail No. 1599A. Drop left off the Stuart Lake Trail ◆ at about 2½ mi., cross Mountaineer Creek on a log and hike S along boulders at creek level before ascending. The trail switchbacks 1.6 mi. to the 5570-ft alpine lake in the cirque between Dragontail and Colchuck peaks.

To round the lake, follow the trail along the hogback near shore (many campspots) — an easy but uneven route amid terrain humps and rocks — to the large boulders at the S end of the lake.

To ascend Aasgard Pass, follow the path around the lake and a marked rockslide route on the SE corner of the stream dropping from a gully under the pass. Follow near this stream until a beaten path bears left of the first cliff; there are several routes upslope — the safest being to keep left into a basin containing a pond, then continuing SE up rock and heather to just NE of Aasgard Pass. A gentle talus or snow descent leads into the unique Enchantment Lakes Basin. *No fires permitted in the basin.*

There is a party size limit of 12 (no dogs permitted). Limit your camping to existing sites, such as at Freya, Reginleit, and Brynhild Lakes. Avoid the building of rock windbreaks, as this disturbs the porous soil and fragile alpine plant life.

Commonwealth Basin (Commonwealth Creek Trail No. 1033). Commonwealth Basin is an interesting example of a hanging valley, the steep exit stream descending to the South Fork of Snoqualmie River. The basin has long been a traditional hiking and snow-climbing area.

Because of private land, stream crossings, and non-maintenance of the old trail's lower portion, the best access is from the Crest Trail ◆ at 2.3 mi. before the end of the first long northern switchback. A new trail section connects with the old basin trail. At about 4000 ft the trail climbs steadily to Red Mountain Pass (5280 ft + — about 2¼ mi. from the Crest Trail). The steep slope here is prone to springtime avalanches. The northern flank of the pass is steep, with snow until midsummer. The trail descends to the Middle Fork Snoqualmie River Valley (not maintained) near Burnt Boot Creek, and will link with a new valley bottom trail.

The alternate entry to Commonwealth Basin is from Alpental Road just N of Commonwealth Creek; take the Sahale Ski Club hiking roadway up a bared spur ridge, then traverse in forest to the creek. Cross and look for the old trail. This approach is most useful in winter or spring when there is ample snowpack, or to reach Guye Peak. With ample snowpack, one could also begin on the S side of the creek, the location of the old trail.

Cougar Lakes. The two Cougar Lakes are a mystic highlight to the alpine meadows closely E of the Cascade crest line SE of Mount Rainier. The lakes, just over 5000 ft in altitude, form the heart of a unique wilderness area. They can be reached directly by trail using an eastern approach, or from the Crest Trail ◆.

From the end of Bumping Lake Road ◆ (3800 ft) take Swamp Lake Trail No. 970; reach the lake's shelter in 4 mi., then turn S in ½ mi. on American Ridge Trail No. 958. Reach the Cougar Lakes in 1½ mi. A continuing trail just W of Big Cougar Lake's upper end joins the Crest Trail in 1½ mi. (at about 6000 ft). The highest nearby summit is a

6624-ft crest S of the lakes — an easily hiked scenic viewpoint. References to the Cougar Lakes include: *100 Hikes in the South Cascades and Olympics; Summit,* October 1961, pp. 22-23; *Mountaineer,* 1966, pp. 133-137; *Living Wilderness,* October-December 1978, pp. 26-33.

Cougar Valley Trail No. 951. From the road end at Cougar Valley (see Raven Roost Road ◆) follow Crow Ridge westward to meet the Crest Trail ◆ on the Greenwater River divide (2.3 mi.).

Cowlitz Trail No. 44. The western approach is from Soda Springs Campground on Summit Creek Road ◆. The trail passes Penoyer Lake, meeting the Crest Trail ◆ near Cowlitz Pass (6 mi.). Trail No. 44 continues E to Tumac Mountain, then northward to Twin Sisters Lakes.

Crow Lake Trail No. 953. Leaves State Hwy No. 410 ◆ at 12.5 mi. E of Chinook Pass, climbing N from 3340 ft to 5680-ft+ Grassy Saddle (3 mi.), then traverses W to Crow Creek divide in 0.7 mi. The trail descends to 4971-ft Sheepherder Lake and Crow Lake shelter (4480 ft — 7 mi.). One can connect to Cougar Valley or hike W to reach the Crest Trail ◆ near Norse Peak.

Crest Trail No. 2000

Section I: Mount Adams area to White Pass. Part of the Crest Trail traverses high, treeless terrain: severe cold weather with high winds and sudden rain or snowstorms is possible. See "Approaches" (page 304) for camping and usage restrictions. Note party size limit of 12.

The high-country portion of the southern end of the Crest Trail in Washington State really begins at Stagman Ridge, where the ascending trail meets the Round-the-Mountain Trail (RTM) ◆ on the SW flank of Mount Adams. To reach this location one can drive E on a short road spur of 0.3 mi. (No. 521) from the Randle-Trout Lake Road ◆ at 14 mi. from Trout Lake. From this spur, the distance on the Crest Trail is 4 mi. to the RTM Trail junction (5680 ft+). Another hiking option is to follow either the Stagman Ridge Trail ◆ or the RTM Trail to upper Stagman Ridge. There are good campsites just E of the trail intersection at Horseshoe Meadow and W of the trail at Riley Creek.

As the Crest Trail traverses the scenic western flank of Mount Adams, there are several traditional campsites, including 6000-ft Killen Creek Meadows. The Crest Trail intersects Riley Camp Trail ◆, Divide Camp Trail ◆, and Killen Creek Trail ◆ (6.5 mi. from Stagman Ridge). Note: From Riley Creek to beyond Killen Creek one may find muddy glacial streams and high water in late spring and early summer.

The Crest Trail meets Highline Trail ◆ at the E edge of Killen Creek Meadows (7½ mi. from Stagman Ridge) and reaches Green Timber Camp (10 mi. from Stagman Ridge); the trail meets Spring Creek (Potato Hill) Road at 7.1 mi. from Killen Creek Meadows (4720 ft+). For road connection, see Midway Loop Road ◆. The trail meets Midway Lookout Road and follows it briefly to the W; here is a Forest Service station and shelter (Midway Campground is to the W); this crossroad is 8.8 mi. from Killen Creek Meadows and 16 mi. from Stagman Ridge.

From the Midway Lookout Road, the Crest Trail reaches Coleman Weed Patch at 4½ mi., Walupt Lake Trail (W) at 10.2 mi., Walupt Creek (campsite) at 13.5 mi., and Nannie Ridge Trail ◆ (5750 ft — campsite) at 14.2 mi. The trail traverses just below 6440-ft+ Cispus Pass at the southern foot of Goat Rocks: As the trail descends into Cispus Basin, there is a junction with the historic Klickitat Trail (long used by Indians) extending SE across Cispus Pass. Note: if one hikes into the Klickitat River drainage, a permit is needed to enter BIA lands.

The Crest Trail circles around Cispus Basin at about 6000 ft (18 mi. from Midway Lookout Road) and reaches the beautiful area of Snowgrass Flat (20 mi. from Midway Lookout Road and 20 mi. from White Pass); no camping at the Flat — use Alpine or Bypass camps. Beyond the Flat, meet Snowgrass Trail ◆ (W) in 0.4 mi. and Memorial Shelter (camping) in 1.6 mi.

The trail traverses above Packwood Glacier on its high-level traverse of the Goat Rocks area to Elk Pass. At 2.1 mi. from Snowgrass Flat the trail reaches 7620 ft near Old Snowy (highest point of the Crest Trail in the state). At 4.1 mi. from the Flat there is a junction with Coyote Trail to Packwood Saddle, and at 4.2 mi. Elk Pass (6640 ft+) is reached.

From Elk Pass, 5100-ft McCall Basin is reached in 2.8 mi. (camping); a way trail leads ½ mi. along the river to Glacier Basin. In 2 additional mi. reach 4720-ft+ Tieton Pass and junction with North Fork Tieton River Trail ◆. The Crest Trail crosses meadows above lovely 6134-ft Shoe Lake at 6½ mi. from White Pass (no camping in lake basin). The trail crosses the E shoulder of 6789-ft *Hogback Mountain,* which can be hiked easily by leaving the trail at a 6250-ft pass in the open area at 4.7 mi. from White Pass. The trail descends, crossing U.S. Hwy No. 12 ◆ at ½ mi. E of the 4470-ft pass. Distance from Midway Lookout Road to White Pass is 40 mi.

Section II: White Pass to Chinook Pass. This span of the Crest Trail is 25.6 mi. long. Much of the alpine crest was once ice-covered; the legacy of glaciation is the picturesque small lakes — especially those near Cowlitz Pass. Where the Crest Trail passes through Mount Rainier National Park, fire permits are required (not needed in national forest).

From ½ mi. E of White Pass on U.S. Hwy No. 12 ◆ a spur road extends to the trailhead at the E end of Leech Lake (4412 ft); campground here. In 3½ mi. reach Sand Lake Trail No. 60 (W), leading to the nearby lake (shelter and camping). Reach 5081-ft Buesch Lake at 5.8 mi. (camping), where the lake region begins. At 6½ mi. there is a junction with Cramer Lake Trail No. 1106, leading E to Dumbell Lake and Cramer Lakes; this trail can be followed for a scramble up 5992-ft *Cramer Mountain.*

The Crest Trail reaches 5191-ft Cowlitz Pass at about 7 mi. (camping). From just N of the pass, Cowlitz Trail ◆ bears eastward. The summit of 6340-ft *Tumac Mountain* (a peak of red volcanic ash) can be reached in 2 mi.

Reach Cowlitz Trail ◆ (W) at 8 mi. and the junction with Twin Sisters Lakes Trail ◆ (5030 ft) at 9.3 mi. Reach Carlton Pass (4160 ft — camping) at 13.4 mi. Reach Laughingwater

Creek Trail junction (5700 ft) at 15 mi. (trail W to Three Lakes and Sheep Lake). Meet the Cougar Lakes Trail ◆ at 18 mi. (2 mi. E to the lakes) and American Ridge Trail at 19 mi. (trail E to American Lake — 0.7 mi.). Reach Anderson Lake at 20.5 mi.

The Crest Trail reaches lovely Dewey Lakes (5140 ft, 5112 ft) at 23 mi. (horses and their droppings are currently permitted at campgrounds). The principal trail crosses the E-facing slope directly to 5447-ft Chinook Pass (State Hwy No. 410 ◆). An alternate trail crosses the SW slope of Naches Peak to reach Tipsoo Lake and the highway in 2.5 mi. The lake, formed by a cirque glacier that left a terminal moraine, lies in a glacially scoured bedrock basin of the Ohanapecosh Formation.

Note: Overnight camping in Mount Rainier National Park requires a backcountry camping permit.

Section III: Chinook Pass to Government Meadow. This section is 23.5 mi. in length. The first portion ascends gradually to Sheep Lake in 2 mi. (campsite), then Sourdough Gap (6450 ft) in 3.1 mi. At 3.2 mi. a connector trail leads to Crystal Lake via 6320-ft Sheep Skull Gap.

Reach Bear Gap (5882 ft) at 5.2 mi. (camping) and at 10 mi., Norse Peak Trail ◆ (6400 ft), which can be hiked W to 6858-ft *Norse Peak.* At ½ mi. N of the trail intersection, Big Crow Basin (5840 ft) offers shelter and camping. Reach Little Crow Basin at 11½ mi. (campsite), Mosquito Gap (6150 ft) at 14½ mi. (campsite), and Arch Rock Trail at 15 mi.

Reach Cougar Valley Trail ◆ (E) at 15½ mi. and Arch Rock shelter (camping) at 17 mi. The trail descends to Rods Gap (est. 4800 ft) at 21.2 mi. Reach Government Meadow (4880 ft) and Camp Urich at 23.7 mi. (camping and shelter). The historic Naches Pass wagon road crossed the Cascades here (for approaches to Naches Pass area see Little Naches River Road ◆ and Greenwater River Road ◆).

Section IV: Government Meadow to Stampede Pass. This 27.8-mi. section of timbered landscape is largely a scenic blight due to cut-over forests and intersecting roads. The railroad land grants, which gave alternating sections now in private ownership, have led to confusing ownership and usage patterns, as well as heavy timber harvesting. The trail nearly climbs 5715-ft *Pyramid Peak,* then descends to Windy Gap. A short branch trail climbs to the peak's summit.

A roadway spur leads to Windy Gap (5200 ft +) and the Green Divide Road. The main trail follows this road E for 4.2 mi. and then continues to Blowout Mountain and Green Pass at 10.5 mi. Reach Tacoma Pass (3320 ft) at 16.7 mi. (camping). There is a connection with Cabin Creek Road ◆ and branch No. 2019.

Snowshoe Butte (5135 ft) can be reached by a short branch trail from the Crest Trail at 6.7 mi. S of Stampede Pass. The Crest Trail meets a branch of the Stampede Pass Road ◆ at the 3963-ft weather station (camping at Lizard Lake, 0.3 mi. S of the pass).

Section V: Stampede Pass to Snoqualmie Pass. This 18½-mi. section is described from N to S because of greater use originating from that direction.

From Stampede Pass, Dandy Pass is 2 mi., Yakima Pass 8½ mi., the N end of Mirror Lake 9½ mi., and Olallie Meadow 14 mi. Because of intersecting roads and clearcuts, the route has limited rewards except for Crest Trail hikers and cross-country skiers.

From Snoqualmie Pass begin at the end of the ski area parking lot (W of the day lodge), following marked posts SW to Lodge Lake (camping) and Olallie Meadow (4½ mi.); camping here and intersection with Cold Creek Trail ◆. Reach 4195-ft Mirror Lake at 9 mi. (camping) and 3575-ft Yakima Pass and Twilight Lake at 10 mi. The Yakima Pass Road ◆ nearly meets the main trail; to the W there is a road to the Cedar River's N fork. Reach Meadow Mountain Trail No. 1022 at 11.7 mi. (side trail to the 5449-ft summit in 1½ mi.). The main trail reaches 3700-ft Dandy Pass at 16½ mi. (camping) and a Green River logging road; reach Stampede Pass at 18½ mi.

It is popular to reduce the initial distance by about 4 mi. and avoid the Snoqualmie Pass blight by taking a powerline road which intersects the main trail at ½ mi. N of Olallie Meadow. Take Hyak exit from I-90 ◆ and follow Road No. 9070-110, which climbs through the ski area; this becomes a powerline road and in 3 mi. (about 3400 ft) intersects the Crest Trail. The road is only seasonally open, and may be too rough for cars beyond Hyak Lake.

Section VI: Snoqualmie Pass to Deception Pass. This 49-mi. roadless section of the Crest Trail is particularly vulnerable to resource damage. Travel and camp in such a manner that impact will be minimal. Use only existing campsites and fire rings; use stoves instead of firewood (no fires permitted in fragile subalpine areas). Cutting of switchbacks erodes the trail and destroys vegetation.

The Snoqualmie Pass trailhead (3022 ft) is located on a paved spur just NW of the Exit 52 interchange off I-90 ◆. The trail climbs to a junction with Commonwealth Creek Trail (see Commonwealth Basin ◆) at 2.3 mi. (3950 ft) and at 4.9 mi. reaches its first high point (5460 ft). The trail crosses the rocky divide on the N side of Kendall Peak, and at 5.6 mi. reaches The Comb (5200 ft), the pass between Silver and Commonwealth creeks. Reach 5210-ft Ridge Lake at 7.3 mi. and Alaska Mountain saddle at 9.3 mi. The top of 5745-ft *Alaska Mountain* is a walk. Note: access trails extend from Gold Creek to the outlets of Joe and Alaska lakes.

Reach the Joe-Edds Lake saddle (5040 ft +) at 10.1 mi. (campsite), and Huckleberry saddle (5550 ft) at 11.4 mi. The gully of Chikamin Peak is reached at 12.5 mi.; this is an avalanche chute in winter and spring. At 12.9 mi. the trail is above Ptarmigan Park and at 14.4 mi. reach 5700-ft Watson Pass. Here one can hike over East Alta to Lila and Rampart lakes. There is a campsite at 14.9 mi.

Meet the route to the nearby Park Lakes at 15.8 mi. If camping at the lakes, respect the area's fragility (camp to the SW of the western lake; no fires permitted within ½ mi. of the lake). Here is the connection with Mineral Creek Trail ◆.

The trail crosses Chikamin Ridge (5310 ft) at 16.9 mi.,

then descends below rock-bound Spectacle Lake. There is an exit to Spectacle Lake at 18.8 mi. (Trail No. 1306 — ½ mi. to the lake). At 19.9 mi. meet the opposite loop of the Spectacle Lake Trail. Note: if camping at the lake, use the site to the NE of the E bay; no fires permitted within ½ mi. of the lake.

The Crest Trail meets Pete Lake Trail ◆ at 21.5 mi., Lemah Creek (camping) at 22.4 mi. and Chimney Creek (camping) at 23.4 mi. There is a hiker route up Lemah Creek: (see Pete Lake Trail ◆).

In a short distance the Crest Trail meets the Lemah Meadows Trail to Pete Lake, and in 0.4 mi. begins the first of 24 switchbacks to the alpine area. At 28.5 mi. the trail passes near Vista Lakes and then the five Escondido Ridge Tarns (no camping near the tarns). The trail reaches the ridgetop at 5600 ft and in 1 mi. an open basin (camping). At 30.2 mi. there is a junction to Waptus Pass; here the Crest Trail descends in 30 switchbacks to Waptus River at 3000 ft (camping) (see Waptus River Trail ◆). The trail crosses Spade Creek (camping) at 34.8 mi. and in another 1.3 mi. crosses the trail climbing to Spade Lake (see Waptus River Trail ◆).

The Crest Trail reaches Spinola Creek at 37 mi. (camping); here is a connection to Waptus Lake. Reach Deep Lake Meadows at 40.5 mi. In the valley head westward is Lake Vicente (5503 ft). The heavily forested valley of Vicente Creek steepens at meadows and avalanche chutes that fringe the base of the lake's bedrock barrier.

The Crest Trail passes the outlet of Deep Lake (camping), then climbs northward to 5560-ft + Cathedral Pass. The pass is crossed at 43.7 mi. (meet Cathedral Rock Trail ◆) to Hyas Creek (4800 ft) at 45.7 mi. (camping); this is a connection to Cle Elum River Road ◆ .

The trail crosses Daniel Creek (3900 ft) at 47 mi. (ford necessary). This stream is hazardous; it may be impassable in spring and after periods of heavy precipitation. Note: a bypass routing is planned. An alternate route via Hyas Lake may be necessary. Reach Deception Pass (4440 ft +) at 49 mi. (camping on Deception Creek, ½ mi. N).

Section VII: Deception Pass to Stevens Pass. This span of the Crest Trail is 19.2 mi.; N of Deception Pass there is a junction with Deception Creek Trail ◆ (W) at 3 mi. The first locality of interest is Deception Lakes (3½ mi.); camping and shelter. The original trail ascended Surprise Gap to reach Glacier Lake; the new section climbs NW, rounding Surprise Mountain to Pieper Pass (5920 ft +), then descends to Glacier Lake (7 mi., camping). Near the S end of the lake is an attractive basin of granite blocks and meadows.

The Crest Trail reaches Surprise Lake (camping) at 8 mi. and Surprise Creek Trail ◆ at 8.2 mi. Trap Pass (5800 ft +) is a mi. farther.

The trail meets a connector to Trap Lake (the lovely lake is ½ mi. to the E). Continue to 4360-ft Hope Lake at 12.2 mi. (junction with Tunnel Creek Trail) and Mig Lake at 12.7 mi. (camping). Reach Tunnel Creek (camping) at 13.7 mi.

There is a junction with Icicle Trail ◆ at 15.7 mi. and in

another ½ mi. reach Lake Susan Jane (camping). Continue to the powerline road, then ascend to a saddle at 5040 ft. Descend through the ski area to near the Forest Service station at Stevens Pass (4056 ft). See U.S. Hwy No. 2 ◆ .

Deception Creek Trail No. 1059. One can begin the trail at 7.8 mi. E of Skykomish on U.S. Hwy No. 2 ◆ (spur road E of Deception Creek). At 5 mi. there is a junction to Tonga Ridge Road ◆ , which provides a much shorter access. At 2 mi. above the junction a branch (E) leads to Deception Lakes. Reach Deception Pass in another 3¼ mi.

Deception Pass Trail. This trail begins at the 3300-ft level at the end of Cle Elum River Road ◆ . Reach the near end of Hyas Lake (camping) in 1.7 mi. (far end camp at 2.6 mi.). Reach Deception Pass (4440 ft +) in 5 mi. (campsite). See also Deception Creek Trail ◆ .

Denny Creek Trail No. 1014. This popular trail leaves from Denny Creek Road ◆ parking area at 2280 ft altitude. Denny Creek is a U-shaped glacial valley deeply incised by the present stream. Reach Snowshoe Falls in 2½ mi., after which the creek basin levels. The trail crosses Hemlock Pass (4560 ft +) (4 mi.) and reaches Melakwa Lake (4480 ft +) in a total of 4.5 mi. The lake's name means "mosquito"; good camping on W shore.

An easy cross-country hike leads N to Melakwa Pass (5280 ft +); take a faint trail around the lake's left side, then keep right of the upper lake. Ascend upvalley about 1 mi. Chair Peak Lake (4880 ft +) is just N of the pass, and is passed on a popular continuing trek to Snow Lake (¾ mi. from Melakwa Pass).

From Melakwa Lake, Trail No. 1011 extends W — a route to Pratt Lake.

Dingford Creek Trail No. 1005. Leaves the Middle Fork Snoqualmie Road ◆ at Dingford Campground (6 mi. from Taylor River junction at about 18.2 mi. — 1400 ft level). At 3 mi. there is a left fork to 3777-ft Myrtle Lake; camp on E shore (total 7 mi. from road). The right trail fork crosses Dingford Creek and climbs to 3886-ft Hester Lake (5 additional mi.).

Divide Camp Trail No. 112 (Middle Fork Adams Creek). Leaves Midway Loop Road ◆ at 1.7 mi. E of Takhlakh Lake road junction (4791 ft) and meets the Crest Trail ◆ at 6000 ft in 3½ mi. Divide Camp is located 0.2 mi. S on the old Crest Trail. This route is a good approach to the N- and W-side routes on Mount Adams.

Dutch Miller Trail No. 1030. Begins from the Middle Fork Snoqualmie River Road ◆ end (about 2950 ft). Trail distance to Dutch Miller Gap (4960 ft +) is 7 mi. This trail enters the subalpine area at about 4 mi. and follows a scenic valley to its head; at about 5.4 mi. the river flows swiftly over inclined slabs. There are campsites at about 1½ mi., 3.9 mi., 4.6 mi., 5.7 mi. (Pedro Camp); there are further campspots in the final 2 mi., but avoid camping at the fragile Gap.

Overcoat Cross-Country Routes. (1) At about 6.2 mi. (about 4200 ft) traverse several hundred yards off-trail to the river. Ford and ascend a steep forest ¼ mi. to the narrow, open hanging valley N of the Chief peaks. Ascend this about 1½ mi. to the meadowed 6120 ft+ pass at its head. A continuing hike leads to fabulous vistas and the Overcoat Glacier.

From the pass, hike upward (W) along the ridge flank. There is a deep gully at one point on this upward traverse; scramble down about 100 ft into the gully. The route, leading toward open slabs and the Overcoat Glacier, then becomes easier.

(2) Shortly after Middle Fork Trail crosses Crawford Creek (about 3300 ft) travel through light brush and cross the river on logs. Climb the timbered rib to the E of the open rockslide visible from the trail. Game paths lead to the lower part of the broad cirque NE of Overcoat Peak. Hike upward and left, then cross the rib to the cirque containing the Overcoat Glacier. This is a direct approach to Overcoat Peak and the N side of Chimney Rock. Reference: *Mountaineer*, 1970, pp. 105-106.

La Bohn Gap Branch Route. Near where the main trail crosses the river (est. 6.5 mi.) take a N-forking trail that passes above Williams Lake; this fades into the parkland and talus basins containing the 5500-ft tarns of Chain Lakes. The final slopes to the Gap (5840 ft+) often contain snow until midsummer; this branch route is about 2 mi. in length. Note: if making a continuing hike to Necklace Valley, be prepared for steep snow slopes N of the Gap. The Gap's location is shown incorrectly on the Mount Daniel map quadrangle (the 1905 Skykomish quadrangle is correct).

East Fork Adams Creek. This is an easy cross-country route to Adams Glacier high camp, and suitable for other N- and W-side routes on Mount Adams (slightly shorter than Killen Creek). Park at the bridge crossing the E fork of Adams Creek (about 3 mi. E of Takhlakh Lake); walk a faint trail on the E side of the creek about ¼ mi., then bear exactly SE. Keep E of the main stream, but well W of bouldery ridges.

East Fork Foss Trail No. 1062. Both the E and W forks of the confluent Foss River valley are U-shaped from glaciation and floored with drift. From the Foss River Road ◆ the trail passes through Necklace Valley; the route continues to La Bohn Gap (about 10 mi. total). If the stream ford at 5 mi. is difficult, detour to log jam downstream.

Reach Necklace Valley (a hanging valley) in 7.4 mi. (shelter at W side of Emerald Lake). The lovely valley has evidence of former glaciation, including a prominent series of moraines. The maintained trail ends at Opal Lake (8.3 mi.). The largest of the gem-like lakes is Ilswoot (4590 ft) — boxed in by a forested hump. To reach this lake either (1) hike N from Cloudy Lake and follow the stream to Ilswoot, or (2) walk E from the trail between Jade and Emerald lakes, over a minor timbered ridge. To reach Locket and Jewel lakes, cross a low saddle W of Emerald Lake (keep S of Point 5243).

Note: Necklace Valley and its grassy vales are very fragile. Camp only at existing sites. Be prepared for mosquitoes.

The valley continues S beneath a W-facing cliff. At the eastern head of the valley are the small La Bohn Lakes (about 5800 ft); they are generally frozen until midsummer. To reach La Bohn Gap, ascend a snow and talus corridor from the last grassy flat.

Inexperienced alpine hikers may want to avoid the snow slopes on the N side of the Gap, particularly on the descent. The alternative is to keep E to reach a bench, then traverse toward the Gap via the lakes.

Note: one can continue southward across the Gap to reach the Dutch Miller Trail ◆.

At the western stream branch near the valley head, Pendant Glacier (an ice remnant on the NW slope of La Bohn Peak, nearly reaches the valley floor). This stream heads at Foehn Lake, on a unique alpine table-land which includes the beautiful Tank Lakes. These lakes, which drain to the W fork of the Foss, rest on a rocky alpine flat with perennial snowfields and scattered evergreens.

Eightmile Creek Trail No. 1552. Leaves from Eightmile Road (see Icicle Creek Road ◆) at 3.1 mi. (3600 ft) and reaches Eightmile Lake (4641 ft) in 3.3 mi. (campsite). The trail has been intercepted by a logging road at about ¾ mi. Some hikers take the road, then meet the trail at a higher level.

Eightmile-Trout Lake Trail No. 1554 climbs N at Little Eightmile Lake, reaching the alpine basin of 6190-ft Lake Caroline in 5½ mi. from the road. The trail reaches Little Caroline Lake in ½ mi., then winds 2 mi. through meadows and larch groves to the shoulder W of Mount Cashmere at Windy Pass (7200 ft+). One can continue to the Icicle Creek Road via Trout Creek.

Enchantment Lakes Route. See Colchuck Lake Trail ◆.

Esmerelda Basin Trail No. 1394. Begins as a trail roadway from the end of Teanaway Road ◆. The trail climbs through Esmerelda Basin's rocky slopes between the Esmerelda Peaks and Ingalls Peak to a 5920 ft+ pass in 3 mi. A branch trail leads N to Lake Ann (6156 ft, 1 mi.); one can continue to Van Epps Pass. Trail No. 1394 continues W from the Esmerelda Basin pass to connect with Fortune Creek Jeep Trail ◆ and Gallagher Head Lake.

Fifes Ridge Trail No. 954. Leaves State Hwy No. 410 ◆ at 14 mi. E of Chinook Pass and climbs from 3200 ft to a ridge saddle (5120 ft+) E of Fifes Peaks (2.7 mi.). There are scenic views of the volcanic faces and crags of the Fifes Peaks.

Fortune Creek Jeep Trail No. 160. Leaves Cle Elum River Road ◆ at 7½ mi. beyond Salmon la Sac and climbs eastward to the divide just SE of Van Epps Pass (5840 ft+) in about 5 mi. The jeep trail descends N to the Van Epps Mine on the Jack Creek slope.

Near the head of Fortune Creek, on the final ascent to the divide, a branch jeep trail (No. 203) climbs E to County Line Trail No. 1394. This trail extends S to Lake Ann. At about 1 mi. S of the lake, Trail No. 1394-A makes a link westward with Fortune Creek's S fork.

The route into the S fork (Jeep Trail No. 161) exits from No. 160 at about 2 mi., then extends 4 mi. to Gallagher Head Lake in the alpine country. By continuing SW another 0.8 mi. from the lake, the route joins Boulder-DeRoux Trail ◆.

Foss River. See East Fork Foss Trail and West Fork Foss Trail ◆ .

French Creek Trail No. 1595. Exits from Icicle Creek Trail ◆ at 1.3 mi. (2960 ft) and extends up the valley bottom about 10 mi. to Paddy-Go-Easy Pass (6080 ft +) on the divide to the Cle Elum River (see Paddy-Go-Easy Pass ◆). An eastern trail fork extends to the head of the valley and crosses a 5320-ft pass, leading to Meadow Creek Trail (see Jack Creek Trail ◆).

From French Creek Trail a branch (No. 1564) climbs to French Ridge at 3.4 mi. Snowall Creek Trail No. 1560 climbs southward from 4.6 mi. and reaches Cradle Lake in 6.2 mi. To reach Klonaqua Lakes, take a branch trail (No. 1563) at 5.6 mi. The beautiful lakes are a short, steep ascent westward.

Glacier Basin. This is the approach to the Emmons Glacier and St. Elmo Pass. From the White River Campground at 4400 ft (see White River Road ◆) the trail reaches historic Camp Starbo (5935 ft), with its mining relics, in Glacier Basin at 3.5 mi. and Inter Glacier in less than another mi. The path to St. Elmo Pass (7400 ft +), a route to the Winthrop Glacier and Curtis Ridge, bears W from Glacier Basin. The wind-stunted evergreens at the pass include Engelmann spruce.

The Emmons Glacier moraines provide proof of glacier recession during the past centuries. About 130 years ago the glacier occupied the area where the trail crosses the Inter Fork. The massive terminal moraine from which the glacier started to recede about 1835 can be seen on the main trail about ½ mi. W of the campground. The Emmons began to recede about 1900 from the newly bare ridge SE of the trail bridge. One can reach the most recent lateral moraine easily by a ½-mi. path starting on the wagon road-trail at 0.9 mi., near the Inter Fork bridge.

The valley floor (including moraines) was buried by an avalanche of rock debris from Little Tahoma in 1963. The rockfall deposit buried the floor of White River Valley to depths of as much as 100 ft. The surface of the avalanche deposit is a hummocky accumulation of bare rock debris and is strewn with large boulders.

Glacier Creek Trail No. 1573. Extends 2.3 mi. along Glacier Creek (within about 1 mi. of 6282-ft Lake Charles). The lake is above timberline, nestled in a flat talus basin below snowfields of Snowgrass Peak and Point 7680. Reach the trail via Chiwaukum Creek Trail ◆ ; the Glacier Creek Trail forks from the trail to Chiwaukum Lake.

Goat Peak. The 6473-ft summit is a 4.8-mi. hike from 3100-ft Cougar Flat (see Bumping Lake Road ◆) via trails No. 959 and 958. One can follow the latter SW along American Ridge to Cougar Lakes; the long but scenic hike nearly climbs to 7000 ft on the ridge.

Gold Creek Trail No. 1314. This is a pre-1900 miner's trail, now maintained for about 4 mi., where a branch climbs N to Alaska Lake and meets the Crest Trail ◆ . The relatively deep valley of Gold Creek, with its 2000-ft sloping cliffs on the S flank, shows the effects of recent glaciation. The upper valley

has high avalanche hazard in winter and spring. In 1897 surveyor A. H. Sylvester wrote of the valley head, "Over its walls, the snow water was pouring in a hundred glittering falls and cascades."

Take I-90 ◆ to Exit 54, then follow Road No. 9060 to the Gold Creek entry road (No. 9080); one can drive about 1 mi. to a gate (about 2650 ft altitude). The old trail may be followed beyond Alaska Creek, but probably will be brushy. A branch trail (not maintained) climbs to Joe Lake at about 6 mi.

Granite Mountain Trail No. 1016. See Granite Mountain.

Hatchery Creek Trail No. 1577. This steep trail can be used as a connector to Icicle Ridge (6½ mi.) or as an approach to Big Jim Lakes (6288 ft) in a timberline basin. Begin from spur road No. 7905 (opposite Tumwater Camp on U.S. Hwy No. 2 ◆), which extends to about the 2400-ft level.

Hellroaring Meadows Trail No. 67. Leaves the viewpoint on Bench Lake Road in the Yakima Indian Reservation (see BIA Road ◆). Beyond the floral meadow at Heart Lake (1 mi.) one can easily hike NW to Ridge of Wonders, or follow Hellroaring Creek's basin to the Mazama Glacier. Note: there is a hiking fee within the Reservation.

Highline Trail No. 114. The E flank of Mount Adams can be reached by this trail, which branches from the Crest Trail ◆ at the eastern edge of Killen Creek Meadows. The most direct approach to the Highline Trail is via Killen Creek Trail ◆ , then hiking N on the Crest Trail. The Spring Creek branch of Midway Loop Road ◆ provides the other approach: follow the Crest Trail to Highline Trail. Permits are needed for overnight camping on or near the portion of Highline Trail that is within the Yakima Indian Reservation. The trail has not been maintained beyond about 3 mi., but can be readily followed to Avalanche Valley (about 12 mi. from Spring Creek Road).

The Highline Trail passes "Foggy Flat," a lovely meadow campsite, in 2½ mi.; the trees become juniper and white bark pine in this area. The route crosses one of the largest glacial streams from Mount Adams, then climbs to a plateau (follow cairns) skirting W of a large lava flow and passing 1 mi. W of 7203-ft *Red Butte* — the most perfect cinder cone of the region; one can stroll up the W or S flanks for a fine viewpoint.

Distinctive *Goat Butte* (7484 ft), with its red ash and lava pillars, can be reached by continuing S on the trail (crosses Little Muddy Creek); the trail fades in the direction of the Goat Butte-Mount Adams moraines. Hikers regularly become lost in this area: from the ridgetop S of Red Butte sight the saddle W of Goat Butte, then take a bearing on this destination when the trail fades. A 1-mi. descent leads to Avalanche Valley (camping in this fragile locality has led to serious overuse). Continuing, the Big Muddy can be difficult to cross in warm weather; one can avoid the river and cross the Klickitat Glacier snout.

High Rock Trail No. 266. The 5685-ft summit of Sawtooth Ridge, a craggy subrange S of the Nisqually River, is reached by a 1½ mi. trail from 4301-ft Towhead Gap. High

Rock has an abandoned lookout building perched on the edge of a cliff, and provides a panoramic vista of Mount Rainier, Mount Wow, and the Tatoosh Range. See Berry Creek Road ◆ (17 mi. driving from Ashford).

Sawtooth Ridge. Other hiking trails include Teeley Creek No. 251 to Berta May Lake and branch No. 8410 to Granite Lakes.

Ice Caves Trail (Paradise Glacier). See Skyline Trail ◆.

Icicle Creek Trail No. 1551. Extends from end of Icicle Creek Road ◆ (2900 ft) to connect with the Crest Trail ◆ just W of Lake Josephine in 12 mi. Bark Cabin Camp is at 6.6 mi.

Frosty Creek (Wildhorse) Trail No. 1592 branches off the main trail at 2.7 mi. and in 4.7 mi. reaches Frosty Pass (5680 ft +). Near Lake Margaret one can turn E on Icicle Ridge Trail ◆ and hike to Lake Mary via a fork in ½ mi. The ridge trail meets Upper Florence Lake in 2 mi. and Ladies Pass (6800 ft +) in 3 mi.

Doughgod Creek Trail No. 1569 (poor condition) leaves from Icicle Creek Trail at 4.3 mi. and connects again at 9 mi. as Chain Lakes Trail. This 8.8-mi. highland loop passes Doelle Lakes, climbs over a 6200-ft+ saddle, then passes the Chain Lakes (5690 to 5628 ft).

Icicle Ridge Trail No. 1570. Begins from Icicle Creek Road ◆ at the opposite side of the Wenatchee River bridge (about 1200 ft altitude). It climbs steeply to the ridge crest and reaches the lookout site (7029 ft) in 9.3 mi. It should be noted that there are two shorter methods of reaching the ridge: Fourth of July Trail No. 1579 (5.3 mi. from the road to Icicle Ridge), and Jay Creek Road (No. 7603, then branch No. 140) permits a cross-country ascent of about 1500 ft to a ridge saddle.

The trail continues along the ridge, across the upper watershed of Cabin Creek, passes Lake Augusta (set in a glacial cirque at 6854 ft), Carter Lake, descends to 4800 ft at Index Creek, then climbs to Lake Edna (6735 ft), passes near Cape Horn to Ladies Pass (6800 ft +), and Frosty Pass. The entire route is 24.6 mi. to Frosty Pass; many campsites. Much of the high ridge area is open meadowland with Lyall's larch.

Numerous exotic highland lakes can be easily reached from the trail; high points in Icicle Ridge (such as Point 7763 and Point 7377) can be hiked cross-country. *Cape Horn* (7316 ft) can be hiked by a short path from where the trail passes its N side.

Indian Henrys Hunting Ground. See Tahoma Creek Trail ◆.

Ingalls Creek Trail No. 1215. From the end of the spur road at Ingalls Creek (est. 1950 ft — see Swauk Pass Hwy ◆) the trail begins up this long, straight fault-line valley; there are many camp spots.

The trail reaches Crystal Creek (3800 ft) in 7.7 mi., Porcupine Creek (4100 ft) in 9.6 mi., and Beverly-Turnpike Trail ◆ in 12 mi. Reach the meadows of upper Ingalls Creek (a delightful timberline vale which levels at about 6000 ft) in about 14 mi. Connection here with path to Ingalls Lake and

Ingalls Pass (see Ingalls Lake Trail ◆). Stuart Pass (6400 ft +) is reached in an additional 1½ mi. (see Jack Creek Trail ◆).

Crystal Creek valley offers a good cross-country route to the Enchantment Lakes. Ascend game trails on either side of the creek or the hogback E of the creek; there is a dry tarn at 6000 ft (camping). Rockslides lead to 7020-ft Crystal Lake and 7100-ft Crystal Pass. Allow about 4 hours to reach the pass.

Ingalls Lake Trail No. 1390. From end of Teanaway Road ◆ follow the main trail above the river about ¼ mi., then turn uphill at signpost. The re-routed trail zigzags and contours to Ingalls Pass (6480 ft +) in about 3 mi. from the road. The trail descends N to a fragile meadowed terrace, meanders through lovely subalpine terrain, then climbs through rocks near the second stream; at a small rock draw turn right to the gap above the S end of 6463-ft Ingalls Lake (under 1 mi. from the pass). The gem of water occupies an ice-scoured rock basin, surrounded by reddish peridotite slabs dotted by clumps of whitebark pine; of note are glacial striation grooves and polished roche moutonnées.

In 1872 the U.S. Army sent out a reconnaissance cavalry. Captain Ingalls became separated from his party and near nightfall discovered a greenish alpine lake — the one that now bears his name.

Longs Pass Trail No. 1229 provides a direct route to Mount Stuart and the upper Ingalls Creek valley. Follow the trail to Ingalls Pass about 1½ mi. (5600 ft) then take the right fork about 1 mi. to the 6200-ft + Longs Pass.

A path descends to Ingalls Creek; one can camp at the nearest water, about 500 ft across the pass. In another mi., the path descends to a log across Ingalls Creek (Ingalls Creek Trail ◆ is about 200 ft upslope, and about ¼ mi. to the E, at 4800 ft, is the site of an old outing camp). This area is usually bare by the first of June.

Ipsut Creek Trail. Leaves from the upper end of Ipsut Creek Campground (see Carbon River Road ◆) to climb from 2800 ft to 5120-ft+ Ipsut Pass in 3.9 mi. Tolmie Peak is closely NW. A trail descends from the pass to Mowich Lake in 1.5 mi.

Jack Creek Trail No. 1558. Take Icicle Creek Road ◆ to Chatter Creek Campground. Jack Creek runs through a broad, U-shaped valley; the trail extends to 6400-ft Stuart Pass in 10.2 mi. Begin the trail route via Trout Creek Trail No. 1555 (a private logging road), then at 0.8 mi. bear W on No. 1558.

Meadow Creek Trail No. 1559 is a valley-bottom trail branching SW from Jack Creek at 5 mi. from the road and climbing to Meadow Pass on the French Creek divide (6.5 mi.). The trail continues W to connect with Paddy-Go-Easy Pass (see French Creek Trail ◆).

Cradle Lake Trail No. 1560 climbs NW from 1.4 mi., reaching Cradle Lake (6160 ft) in 2.8 additional mi. The lake, in a high basin, is one of the most beautiful of wilderness lakes. The trail continues to Snowall Creek.

Solomon Creek Trail No. 1593 leaves Jack Creek Trail at 8

mi. from the road and climbs to the Cle Elum River divide at 6160 ft; the trail is seldom used. A connection bears S to the Van Epps Mine.

Fortune Creek-Van Epps Trail No. 1594 leaves Solomon Creek Trail at 0.2 mi. and climbs about 1000 ft to the Van Epps Mine (5300 ft + ; 2.5 mi.), continuing as a jeep road to Van Epps Pass (5840 ft +). See also Fortune Creek Jeep Trail ◆.

Jolly Mountain Trail No. 1307. This trail climbs through open pine forest to the 6443-ft summit. Begin just S of Salmon la Sac (see Cle Elum River Road ◆), taking a short road spur (No. 132) from just S of the guard station. Begin the 6.2-mi. trail at the edge of a corral.

Another route (shorter) is to drive Road No. 4315 at 0.6 mi. S of Salmon la Sac for 4½ mi. to its end (about 4500 ft). Hike upslope to meet the Sasse Ridge Sheep drive; follow N and meet the main trail.

Killen Creek Trail No. 113. This popular trail begins 0.4 mi. SW of Killen Creek Camp on Midway Loop Road ◆ (4584 ft) and reaches the Crest Trail ◆ in 3½ mi. (6084 ft). Killen Creek was once known as "Killing Creek" because of standing ghost forests. From the Crest Trail crossing, an informal route continues SE along the slope of a ridge for another 0.9 mi. to the 6880-ft level at a lava garden. This locality (Mount Adams Camp) faces the Adams Glacier and is the traditional base for ascents. There is insufficient wood for cooking; bring stoves. Be aware of party size limitations.

Klapatche Park. The trail begins at 11.5 mi. on the West Side Road ◆ (4000 ft) and climbs along Klapatche Ridge to the 5500-ft park in 2½ mi. Klapatche Ridge flows, which are sequentially stacked, once filled the canyon of ancestral Puyallup River. By following the Wonderland Trail ◆ southward, 6000-ft St. Andrews Park can be reached in 0.7 mi.

Lake Dorothy Trail No. 1072. Begins at the end of Miller River Road ◆ and reaches the N end of the island-dotted 257-acre lake (3058 ft) in 1½ mi. The trail continues 2 mi. around the lake, then bears W to meet the Taylor River Trail.

From the soggy inlet at the SE end of Lake Dorothy, it is possible to hike cross-country (upvalley); follow the stream and in about 1½ mi. reach a major fork (third fork to right). From here one can (1) ascend S upstream 1 mi. to Fools Gold Lake (4640 ft +) or (2) travel SE up the main stream about 1½ mi. to Gold Lake (4838 ft); keep W of the exit stream on the final rise. This lake hangs at the rim of a timberline basin under the cliffs of Wild Goat Peak (camp at outlet).

Alpine Lakes High Route. Continuing from the NW end of Gold Lake, work N ½ mi. and cross the divide (5240 ft). Drop 100 ft to a pond, then make a traversing descent E on talus to upper Camp Robber Creek; follow the talus (or snow) corridor to Chetwoot Pass (5040 ft +). Skirt the N side of Chetwoot Lake (campsites near outlet), then hike over the sparsely timbered knoll to Azure Lake. Head N several hundred yards to overlook the SW corner of Azurite Lake. Drop and traverse around its S side (a key ledge is at the far E), and on to the exit stream. Make a descending traverse SE

across forest and talus to the inlet stream S of Otter Lake. Pass two small lakes and ascend to Iron Cap Pass (5280 ft +) E of Iron Cap Mountain.

Ascend NE on easy ground to the stream from Tank Lakes. Cross the lovely plateau past the lakes (snow until midsummer), then descend NE to Opal Lake in Necklace Valley (meet East Fork Foss River Trail ◆). A rugged cross-country continuation would be to travel over Mount Hinman, onward to the Lynch Glacier, and then to the trail at Marmot Lake. The entire route can be varied in many ways, with numerous destinations.

Variation. From Chetwoot Lake proceed E up gentle heather and rock shelves, and across talus to a prominent point (5720 ft) with good camping and view. Proceed S over snow and rockslides to Iron Cap Lake with its remnant glacier and opaque water. A natural shelf bears E from the lake outlet — keep between 5200 and 5600 ft and follow to Iron Cap Pass. Note: two steep heather slopes are located about ¼ mi. E of the lake.

Variation. From Iron Cap Pass follow a shelf of flowers, heather, and tarns E to Williams Lake. Nearing the lake the shelf terminates above a cliff (keep altitude until N of the lake at a large rockslide).

Lake Hancock Trail. Turn right at Spur 10 (see Snoqualmie Tree Farm and Tolt River Area ◆) and after about 1½ mi., take Spur 13 road system. Follow signs to the N side of Lake Hancock (2166 ft). Camping and shelter at NW side of lake; trail extends E along shore.

Lake Julius Trail No. 1584. This trail reaches the 5190-ft lake in 6.5 mi. from Coulter Creek Road ◆ (right hand gate). A trail continues 1 mi. to 5508-ft Loch Eileen. A 7000-ft ridge viewpoint to the W can be reached easily. The backcountry of this area offers prime ski-touring opportunities.

Ethel Lake Trail No. 1585 can also be used as an approach to lakes Ethel and Julius; start from Hwy No. 2 ◆ just E of Merritt.

Lake Serene Trail. Drive or hike to the end of Mount Index Road ◆, then hike SE on a cross-slope cat track and trail to the steep, unmaintained miner's trail below and W of Bridal Veil Falls. Follow the classic "tree root" path to an old cabin; here take the tread that begins from the front door and not the one that starts at the waterfall. Continue up the cliffy forest on foot and hand to the 2509-ft lake (total, 1 mi.). This trail is not recommended for inexperienced hikers: the tread usually has wet and slippery areas. Camp spots at the lake are ample, but wood scarce.

Leland Creek Trail No. 1566. Leaves Icicle Creek Trail ◆ at Bark Cabin Camp, extending to Lake Leland (4461 ft) in 5.3 mi. Lake Phoebe (5214 ft), near the valley head, is about 1 mi. farther.

One can hike to the four lovely Swallow lakes from Lake Leland by crossing the ridge through the old Swallow Lake burn.

Square Lake Trail No. 1567 branches from Leland Creek Trail in 1.7 mi. and extends to 4941-ft Square Lake (4 mi.).

CHIMNEY ROCK from Tank Lakes (Alpine Lakes High Route)
JOHN V.A.F. NEAL

NORTH PEAK

CHIMNEY ROCK

Chimney Rock
Col

Finger
of Fate

Overhang

OVERCOAT PEAK

South Arete

East Face

Northeast Snow Finger

OVERCOAT GLACIER

A cross-country hike, following the exit stream of Thunder Mountain Lakes, can be taken to the lovely high lakes, which are set in a small basin just N of Square Lake.

Longs Pass Trail. See Ingalls Lake Trail ◆ .

Manastash Ridge Trail No. 1388. This trail extends along the crest of Manastash Ridge between the Naches-Little Naches and Yakima River drainages. The distance between Bald Mountain to Blowout Mountain on the Crest Trail ◆ is 25.7 mi. The scenic trail provides panoramas of Mount Rainier in one direction and the Stuart Range in the other; the ridge itself is an uplifted block of pre-Tertiary volcanic rock. For road approaches see Bald Mountain ◆ and Quartz Mountain ◆ . There are connecting trails from Little Naches River Road ◆ and various forest roads on the Yakima River flank.

Marmot Lake Trail No. 1066. Extends from Deception Pass to the 4930-ft lake in 3½ mi.; the trail ends on the E shore at a cliffy area (best camp is ¼ mi. to S, where exit flows toward Deception Creek).

There are numerous small craggy unnamed peaks to the S, W, and SE of Marmot Lake (all between 6000 and 6600 ft, and easy hikes).

A continuing cross-country hike from the head of the lake is a gully-scramble to the meadow-divide at No Name Lake (5600 ft) and onward to Jade Lake (5442 ft); skirt this lake on the W. Then travel S up the talus/rubble draw and a small glacier to Dip Top Gap (6640 ft +). One can readily descend to Pea Soup Lake (6200 ft) at the foot of Lynch Glacier (2½ mi. from Marmot Lake). It is feasible from here to traverse back to Deception Pass or make a continuing high-route to La Bohn Gap.

Mazama Glacier Saddle Route. From the road end at Bird Creek Meadows (see BIA Road ◆) start W on a trail, then hike highlands NW to the timberline bench at the height of land between Bird and Hellroaring Creek drainages. Traverse easily for 1 mi. across the upper basin of the latter, then cross moraine slopes (skirt E of the large moraine wave or hike via the obvious dip) to the lower portion of the Mazama Glacier. The prominent 8500-ft saddle is at the W end of Ridge of Wonders, where the glacier divides its flow. A tarn provides water; a rock wall is a windbreak. Time: 3 hours.

An alpine cross-country route is possible to Avalanche Valley, but should be limited to those with glacier travel experience. First descend 1000 ft to the N, cross Klickitat Glacier to Battlement Ridge, descend it E about 1 mi., then cross the ridge and bear N.

A permit is needed for overnight camping on Yakima Indian Reservation lands.

McCue Ridge Trail. This trail and road approach lead to good ski touring terrain. See Coulter Creek Road ◆ . Using the left road fork and gate 1.2 mi. from the highway, one can hike the road 7 mi. to the 5000-ft shelter high on McCue Ridge. A trail extends W, then SW to the ridge crest. A continuation then descends to Chiwaukum Lake to meet Chiwaukum Creek Trail ◆ . Note: one can leave the road on a

southern spur before reaching the shelter and hike more directly to the McCue Ridge crest.

Meeks Table. This is a basalt-capped plateau E of Timberwolf Mountain (4480 ft + altitude) that has been set aside as an ecological study area. Erosion left the unique mesa with its tree cover of ponderosa pine. Take Bethel Ridge Road ◆ and McDaniel Lake branch. At 1.3 mi. SW of McDaniel Lake (about 3 mi. on the branch road) hike a jeep road (No. 130) ½ mi. northward toward the divide about 0.4 mi. W of the Table's high point; easy hiking from here.

Middle Fork Snoqualmie River Trail. See Dutch Miller Trail ◆ and Middle Fork Snoqualmie River Road ◆ .

Mineral Creek Trail No. 1331. This is an old trail route to mining claims near Mineral Creek. In the early 1920s miners had to travel by boat on Kachess Lake to the head of Little Kachess, then continue by a wagon road. The area rock, the Naches Formation, is intruded by Snoqualmie Granodiorite along Mineral Creek, and the contact is the site of copper mineralization.

The new approach is by Cooper Pass Road ◆ . Follow the road beyond the pass to opposite Mineral Creek (11 mi. from Cle Elum River Road at 2400 ft). The trail bears W through a clearcut to cross Kachess River, then enters the valley of Mineral Creek. The trail fords the creek above a miner's cabin and steeply ascends the snowslide sidehill, then traverses to the terminal fork leading to the western Park Lake; the last part climbs steeply to the 4640-ft + lake (6 mi. total). Park Saddle and the Crest Trail ◆ are closely above.

To reach Alta Pass (5440 ft +) ascend the open basin westward from where the trail leaves Mineral Creek (about 4400 ft). One can hike cross-country to Lila and Rachel lakes, or N to the Crest Trail.

Note: fires are prohibited within ½ mi. of Park Lake and Rachel Lake.

Mirror Lake Trail No. 1302. This 1-mi. trail extends from the Yakima Pass Road ◆ at about 3600 ft to Mirror Lake on the Crest Trail ◆ .

Mount Adams Timberline Trail No. 183. See Mount Adams Timberline ◆ (Roads). The Timberline Trail continues upward as a climber's route (see Mount Adams, South Spur).

Mount Defiance Trail No. 1009. Exits at 4 mi. on Pratt Lake Trail ◆ and contours around the N shore of Rainbow Lake (4240 ft +) in 1½ mi. The trail passes above Lake Kulla Kulla in 3 mi. and reaches Thompson Lake (3600 ft +) at about 7½ mi. The trail continues to the 4240-ft saddle just W of the lake; this saddle can also be reached by a jeep-foot trail from Granite Creek.

Pratt Mountain (5099 ft) can be hiked from the trail as it ascends W from the Pratt Lake divide. Hike the SW boulderfield slopes.

Mount St. Helens Trails. See Mount St. Helens, page 47.

Naches Pass. See Little Naches River Road ◆ and Greenwater River Road ◆ .

Nannie Ridge Trail No. 98. This is a possible approach to Goat Rocks. The trail extends from Walupt Lake (see

Johnson Creek Road ◆) and reaches the Crest Trail in 6 mi. Be aware of party size limitations.

Nisqually Moraine Trail. Leaves Skyline Trail ◆ (western branch) at 0.7 mi., and from about 6000 ft makes a ½ mi. descending traverse to the moraine at about 5500 ft.

Noble Knob Trail No. 1184. Begin from Corral Pass at 5600 ft (see Corral Pass Road ◆). Reach the 6014-ft Knob in 3.6 mi. A higher ridge crests at 6205 ft about ½ mi. S.

Norse Peak Trail No. 1191. From Crystal Mountain Road ◆ at 4 mi. (about 3900 ft) this trail begins as a roadway, then climbs steeply to the 6600-ft summit ridge (4 mi.), where there is a grand view of Mount Rainier, the northern portion of the National Park, and the new Clearwater Wilderness.

A right fork along the ridge for ¼ mi. leads atop 6858-ft *Norse Peak;* the left fork descends E for 1 mi. to the Crest Trail ◆ .

North Fork Tieton River Trail No. 1118. This valley trail provides access to both Tieton Pass and the NE flank of Goat Rocks at McCall Basin. Begin at the roadhead of North Fork Tieton River Road ◆ . The trail forks just beyond Tieton Meadows, with the right branch climbing to Tieton Pass and the Crest Trail ◆ (4.6 mi.). The left branch (Army Trail No. 1151) at the fork (2.6 mi.) provides a direct route to McCall Basin and also meets the Crest Trail. An unmaintained trail extends SW into Glacier Basin and McCall Glacier in the Goat Rocks. Be aware of party size limitations.

Northern Loop Trail. This scenic trail, a northern loop to the Wonderland Trail ◆ , branches E from the Carbon River Trail ◆ at 2 mi. and climbs to 5800-ft + Windy Gap in 4 mi. An early lava flow from Mount Rainier spilled through the gap between Crescent and Sluiskin mountains to join an andesite flow at Windy Gap. Here the trail descends to 4370-ft Lake James (at 6 mi.), crosses the W fork of White River and ascends to scenic meadows of Grand Park (5000-5600 ft) at 12 mi. Grand Park is a remnant of an old intercanyon lava flow. The deep canyon of the W fork is entrenched across this flow and divides it. One can continue S on the trail to Berkeley Park and meet the Wonderland Trail ◆ at 15.7 mi.

Owyhigh Lakes Trail. Owyhigh Lakes (5183 ft) are reached in 3.5 mi. from White River Road ◆ at 2 mi. from the Park entrance. These scenic lakes, beneath the cliffs of Governors Ridge, are named for Chief Owyhigh, the Yakima Indian war leader. A 5.2-mi. trail continues from the lakes, crossing a 5400-ft + saddle to Kotsuck Creek. The trail reaches State Hwy No. 123 ◆ at 5 mi. S of Cayuse Pass.

Pacific Crest National Scenic Trail. See Crest Trail ◆ .

Packwood Lake Trail No. 78. Extends to a resort and campground on the lake in 4.3 mi. Reach from Packwood Lake Road ◆ . The Upper Lake Creek Trail No. 81 continues for 7½ mi. to Packwood Saddle (5600 ft +). One can then follow Coyote Trail No. 79 for 1.4 mi. to meet the Crest Trail ◆ at Elk Pass.

Paddy-Go-Easy Pass. This pass (6080 ft +) is reached by a 3-mi. trail (No. 1595) which leaves the Cle Elum River Road ◆ about 11 mi. beyond Salmon la Sac (about 0.8 mi. past Fish Lake Campground, at 3360 ft). Keep left at 2½

mi. From the pass one can descend the trail toward French Creek; one could traverse S to Sprite Lake. See also French Creek Trail ◆ .

To reach Sprite Lake from the pass, contour S along the ridge about ¼ mi. to just above the lake, then descend; camping sites, but no wood.

Palisades Lakes Trail. This route provides good access to an interesting series of lakes, The Palisades, and the Sourdough Mountains. Start at Sunrise Point (about 3 mi. E of Sunrise — at 6125 ft. See White River Road ◆). The trail passes near Sunrise Lake, reaches Clover Lake in 1½ mi., comes near Hidden Lake, then reaches upper Palisades Lake (5800 ft +) in 3½ mi.

Here are The Palisades, one of the Park's outstanding rock formations — a great cliff of columnar jointed black rock, a welded tuff. The rocks on the cliff, up to 800 ft thick, rest upon an underlying plug. It is probable that the Tatoosh magma broke through the surface with explosive violence at The Palisades. See Sourdough Mountains.

Paradise. See Nisqually Entrance Road ◆ and Skyline Trail ◆ (Ice Caves and Paradise Glacier included).

Pete Lake Trail No. 1323. Two parking areas at the road end (Owhi Campground) at Cooper Lake provide access to the Pete Lake Trail (see Cooper Pass Road ◆). From Pete Lake (4½ mi. — 2980 ft), trail No. 1323 continues about 3 mi. to meet the Crest Trail ◆ . An alternative route to reach the Crest Trail (farther N) is Lemah Meadows Trail (see below). In the meadow areas beyond Pete Lake and near Lemah Creek are lush grasses and verdant stands of western white pine and Engelmann spruce.

Spectacle Lake Route. About 1 mi. S of the junction of Pete Lake Trail and the Crest Trail, branch trail No. 1306 makes a short, steep climb to magnificent Spectacle Lake (4239 ft), which lies in a large uneven trough gouged by ice. Note: camp on the lake's NE flank; there is a fire closure within ½ mi. of lake.

The lake's shoreline is irregular and rugged for hiking. Glacier Lake (4720 ft +) lies 1 mi. to the NW; reach the latter by a scramble route upstream from Spectacle Lake's SW bay. The rocks about Glacier Lake were ground smooth by ancient ice; a glacier once flowed E from this basin to the Cooper River valley. The highest lake in the basin is 5785-ft Chikamin Lake, pocketed in a cirque between Lemah Mountain and Chikamin Peak. To reach this lake follow the drainage from Spectacle's NW arm.

Lemah Meadows Trail No. 1323B. From about 1 mi. W of Pete Lake this trail extends 0.8 mi. to join the Crest Trail ◆ at N fork Lemah Creek (Chimney Creek); camping.

Lemah Creek Route. From Lemah Meadows Trail junction with the Crest Trail ◆ , hike S to Lemah Creek. There is a hiker path along the N bank, passing a waterfall. Continue on polished slabs and through some brush to the swampy lakes in the secluded valley under the 200-ft Whinnimic Falls.

Waptus Pass Trail No. 1329. Extends from Pete Lake for 3 mi. to Waptus Pass (4320 ft + — camping). From the pass, trail No. 1329C climbs about 2½ mi. to provide access to the Crest Trail. From Waptus Pass, one can also hike down to Waptus Lake via Quick Creek.

Escondido Lake Trail No. 1320. Leaves the Waptus Pass Trail at about 2 mi. and climbs to the hidden lake in 1.8 mi.

Pratt Lake Trail No. 1007. Take Exit 47 on I-90 ◆ and drive ½ mi. W to the parking area (about 1900 ft altitude). The trail passes above and S of Olallie Lake (3760 ft +) and reaches Lookout Point at 3 mi. At 4 mi. reach Pratt Lake divide (4080 ft +) and a branch trail to Mount Defiance. Reach Pratt Lake (3385 ft) at 6 mi.; the lake is set in a deep virgin forest; camp at N end. Reach Lower Tuscohatchie Lake (3360 ft +), surrounded by dense stands of hemlock and Alaska cedar, at 6½ mi. (shelter). Reach Tuscohatche Lake (4023 ft) by trail from the lake's N end, then hiking ¾ mi. eastward. Kaleetan Lake (3840 ft +) is reached in 3½ mi. via Trail No. 1010 from the W end of Lower Tuscohatchie Lake.

Rachel Lake Trail No. 1313. Approach by Lake Kachess Road ◆. The trail follows Box Canyon and climbs to Rachel Lake (4640 ft +) in 3.5 mi. The lake is in a unique setting near the rim of its rock basin. A northern trail fork climbs 1 mi. to Lila Lake; nearby Three Tarns are located on the SE slope of Alta Mountain.

There is a good cross-country route to Park Lakes. From the Alta slope contour about ¾ mi. on rockslides, then take a path to 6009-ft East Alta. Descend a gully to benches at the head of Mineral Creek below the western Park Lake.

From the N end of Rachel Lake the trail continues SW for 1 mi. to Rampart Lakes (4.8 mi. from the road). The lakes (5040 ft +) are set amid heavenly gardens and rock bowls at the eastern fringe of rocky Rampart Ridge. See also Rampart Ridge Trail ◆. Note: fires are prohibited within ½ mi. of Rachel Lake and Rampart Lakes.

Rampart Ridge Trail No. 1332 (Mount Margaret Trail). Leave I-90 ◆ at Exit 54, turn E and follow Rocky Run Road to its junction with Keechelus Ridge Road No. 4934. Proceed on the latter about ¼ mi. to a parking area about 150 yards from the closed private logging spur that is the trail location for 1 mi. The trail follows the desolate roadway and oversized clearcut for over 2 mi. before entering the timbered slope below the ridgetop.

An eastern trail fork drops to Lake Margaret. The main trail passes the top of Mount Margaret on the W and reaches Lake Lillian in about 6 mi. total (end of trail). To reach Rampart (Archipelago) Lakes, continue cross-country N over a minor divide to Two Tarns, cross a small notch, then descend.

Rat Creek Route. A direct ascent of Rat Creek to the N edge of the Lost World Plateau is brushy and not recommended. A feasible method of reaching upper Rat Creek is to drive the Eightmile Creek Road (see Icicle Creek Road ◆), then drive or hike the logging spur E. Hike up the burn to a level spot, then drop and contour below the Dragon Teeth cliffs to Rat Creek, in the vicinity of The Blockhouse.

One can hike to open slopes and rockslides on the upper E side of the valley, then take a vale to Mesa Lake (6680 ft).

The stream flows in a flat-bottomed, elongated basin which also contains Earle and Shield lakes. Prusik Pass (7480 ft +) is ⅝ mi. SW of Shield Lake and easy to reach; one can continue easily to the Enchantment Lakes.

Musky Pass (7000 ft +) is a saddle E of Lake Earle and provides a route to the Nada Creek drainage.

Just E of Mesa Lake a low saddle (Toketie Pass) leads to the Toketie Lake drainage. Edward Mesa, NE of this saddle, is an extensive upland remnant with a high point of 7276 ft. This isolated tableland is covered with coarse soil and granitic boulders.

Hook Creek provides an alternate route to the mesa. Begin directly from the bridge at 6.1 mi. on Icicle Creek Road (about opposite Hook Creek). Ascend on the creek's left in steep open timber until cliffs force a traverse to center-basin. Then follow a hogback, later keeping to rockslides on the right flank. The route climbs through a gully closely E of The Duolith.

Rattlesnake Peaks Trail (Trails No. 1101, 1114, 1100, 983, 979). This trail connects Bethel Ridge Road ◆ and Deep Creek Road (see Bumping Lake Road ◆) by a scenic high traverse.

Using the eastern approach, begin on Trail No. 1101 at Bethel Ridge Road at 12 mi. from its southern end (5300 ft). Cross the divide to Rattlesnake Creek and reach Trail No. 1114 in 4 mi. at about 3600 ft; climb W on Trail No. 1100 leading to Rattlesnake Peaks. The trail altitude averages about 6400 ft here and climbs slightly higher near Bismarck Peak to the W.

From the W, one can take Trail No. 979 from Deep Creek Road at 15.1 mi. from the American River (at 3700 ft).

Ridge of Wonders. Lava flows from Mount Adams created this scenic 6500- to 7176-ft E-W ridge, which overlooks the magnificent Klickitat Glacier cirque. Little Mount Adams (6821 ft), located on a SE spur of the Ridge of Wonders, is a secondary cinder cone with a perfect crater. Many curious volcanic bombs are scattered over the ridge's surface.

A good route to the ridge and Little Mount Adams is Hellroaring Meadows Trail ◆. From Bench Lake in the Yakima Indian Reservation, Island Spring Trail No. 66 can be taken to the ridge crest. Cross-country travel onward to the E flank of Mount Adams is not recommended except in late summer because of the hazardous Big Muddy River ford. Both this stream and Rusk Creek can be a problem. A route avoiding these crossings is to traverse higher, crossing the glacier snouts and dividing moraines. See Highline Trail ◆.

Riley Camp Trail No. 64. This connection trail extends E from Randle-Trout Lake Road ◆ (at 2 mi. S of junction with Lewis River Road ◆) to the Crest Trail ◆ ½ mi. N of Burnt Rock. This is an excellent approach to climbing routes on the SW flank of Mount Adams. Riley Camp is at about 5400 ft altitude.

Robin Lake Trail No. 1376A. This trail forks E from Deception Pass Trail ◆ at about 4.3 mi. (about ⅓ mi. after the trail zigzags beyond a gully) and climbs steeply to Tuck Lake in 2 mi. The route continues eastward, ascending the ridge dividing the lake from the valley; bear left up a draw and ascend E to the open ridge at 6320 ft just before reaching upper Robin Lake (6178 ft); 3.8 mi.

Tuck and Robin lakes nest in ice-polished granite on the upper western slope of Granite Mountain. No fires at the lakes; camp away from the lakes only at established sites.

Round-the-Mountain Trail No. 9. This scenic trail makes a 10-mi. connection from Bird Creek Meadows (6000 ft) in the Yakima Indian Reservation to Stagman Ridge; see BIA Road ◆. There is a day-use hiking fee in the Reservation.

From the old Timberline Camp intersection (6240 ft +) at 2 mi. and the connecting 1½ mi. trail from Cold Springs, the RTM trail climbs across Crofton Ridge near the Avalanche Glacier at about 6150 ft, then reaches Salt Creek before traversing the subalpine slope above Madcat Meadows and 5580-ft Looking Glass Lake. Reddish rock ridges and a chaos of volcanic mazes are a visual delight between Crofton Ridge and Madcat Meadows. Good camping at Twin Bluffs (W of Salt Creek), Madcat Meadows, and Horseshoe Meadow (just E of the Crest Trail ◆ junction).

Evidence of the vast 1921 Mount Adams avalanche can be seen 100 yards above the trail between Cascade Creek's forks. The SW flank of Mount Adams can readily be visited by leaving the trail at Salt Creek. One can tour cross-country, keeping between the White Salmon Glacier and The Bumper (6470 ft) and The Hump (6584 ft) to join the Crest Trail.

Russell Ridge. This ridge, a raised block of volcanics of the Western Cascade Group (older than the rock at White Pass and Goat Rocks), can be reached by a scenic hike. See Russell Ridge ◆ (Roads). Take Trail No. 1111 at 4920 ft +. Reach Bootjack Rock and Fox Meadow in about 4 mi.; one can hike on to *McNeil Peak* (6788 ft) via Trail No. 1141.

Another approach to Russell Ridge and Fox Meadow is to take Andy Creek Trail No. 1110 to the ridgetop.

Scatter Creek Trail No. 1328. Leaves Cle Elum River Road ◆ at 9.4 mi. beyond Salmon la Sac. A right fork at 2 mi. (County Line Driveway No. 1394) climbs and bears SE to Van Epps Pass. See also Fortune Creek Jeep Trail ◆.

Trail No. 1328 continues up Scatter Creek another 2.8 mi. and ties in with the Solomon Creek trail system.

Silver Creek Trails. From Crystal Mountain Road ◆ several trails connect with the Crest Trail ◆: (1) From the ski area (4600 ft) one can hike to Bear Gap in 1.4 mi.; first hike ¾ of the T-bar hill, then bear right on Silver Creek Trail. (2) Bullion Basin Trail No. 1156 (an old tractor road) begins atop the ski slope E of the day lodge and ends on the Crest Trail at about 6300 ft just N of Blue Bell Pass. See also Norse Peak Trail ◆.

Skyline Trail (Route to Camp Muir). This popular trail (a 4.5-mi. loop) begins at Paradise ◆ (5420 ft). The western loop climbs to Glacier Vista (6336 ft) and Panorama Point (6800 ft), above and E of the Nisqually Glacier. The eastern loop (also called Ice Caves Trail) extends from Paradise to the 1870 climbing memorial, Paradise Glacier, and the Ice Caves area at 6500 ft (2.7 mi.). An alternate approach is the Golden Gate Trail via Edith Creek Basin.

The Skyline Trail begins behind the Paradise Ranger Station: reach Alta Vista in ½ mi., Glacier Vista in 1¼ mi., and Panorama Point in 2½ mi. The hiking route to Camp Muir continues over Pebble Creek (7200 ft), then to Moon Rocks (9200 ft) and the Muir Snowfield (W of 9584-ft Anvil Rock) to Camp Muir (10,080 ft +) — 2.7 mi. from Panorama. Most or all of this route may be snow-covered until midsummer. Note: avoid the rocks of "Little Africa" in order to protect endangered plant species.

Above Pebble Creek the wedgelike slope broadens. Beware of hiking or skiing onto the Nisqually Glacier slope (which is steep) to the W or the Cowlitz Glacier flank during stormy periods and whiteouts. Beware of steep cliffs to the E of McClure Rock and to the E from Anvil Rock to Camp Muir. These cliffs, obscured by snow and cornices in the winter, have been the site of mountaineering tragedies. Panorama Point is a dangerous avalanche area.

The compass bearing from Pebble Creek to Moon Rocks is 350° True N (328° Magnetic N). The reverse reading is 170° T (148° M). The bearing from Moon Rocks to Camp Muir is 344° T (322° M); the reverse reading is 164° T (142° M). Mistakes in routefinding between Paradise and Camp Muir during poor visibility have resulted in lost hikers and climbers. Reference: *A.N.A.M.*, 1984, p. 47.

Snoqualmie Lake Trail No. 1002. Take Middle Fork Snoqualmie River Road ◆ to the Taylor River bridge. Continue ahead, and after about ¼ mi. the road ends at the burnt bridge. The remainder is a hike, following Road No. 5630 for 6 mi. From the end of the old Taylor River Road the trail crosses the 3800-ft divide to the Miller River drainage and Lake Dorothy. The trail passes Snoqualmie Lake, Deer Lake, and Bear Lake; numerous potential cross-country treks and ski tours can be taken in the direction of Big Snow Mountain. See Lake Dorothy Trail ◆.

From the old road end, a 3-mi. trail extends to Nordrum Lake (shelter). One can hike SW to Green Ridge Lake (3838 ft); this is not a practical approach to the Mount Garfield peaks.

Snow Creek Trail No. 1553. This is the normal entry route to the Snow and Enchantment lakes and the high plateau wilderness which is the eastern rampart of the Stuart Range. This splendid highland, the Cashmere Crags, is in danger of being overused: There is a party limit of 12; no campfires; no dogs permitted.

Begin the trail from the parking lot below Icicle Creek Road ◆ at 4.2 mi. (est. 1300 ft), cross Icicle Creek by bridge, then climb to Hart-Nada Lake in 5 mi. (4880 ft); Upper Snow Lake (5420 ft) is an additional 2 mi. (camp between the Snow Lakes or at far end of upper lake). From the dam follow the trail around the S side to the inlet; cross the creek, then ascend NW to Trauma Rib. At about 6600 ft traverse W to the first of the Lower Enchantment Lakes (Lake Viviane — 6785 ft). It is best to hike through a wooded glade, come to the open slabs, then descend them gradually about 150 ft before bearing up to the lake outlet.

To explore the magical lakes and nearby crags, many routes are possible. Keep on used tread or rock slab as much as possible to minimize meadow trampling. The easiest continuing route is to follow Snow Creek, keeping just N of Leprechaun Lake, rounding Rune Lake to the N, and then bearing S of 7190-ft Talisman Lake. Time: 2-3 hours from Snow Lake's outlet. There are countless good camping locations (use existing sites). Leprechaun Lake and both ends of Rune Lake are popular.

To reach the Upper Enchantment Lakes, continue near the creek. The open alpine terrain permits easy travel. The lakes are all small except Brynhild (7700 ft), at the foot of one section of Snow Creek Glaciers. One can hike S up to the high surface of Dragontail Plateau for scenic vistas. Just NW of Brynhild Lake is Aasgard Pass (7800 ft +) and a continuing route to Colchuck Lake (see Colchuck Lake Trail ◆).

Crystal Pass and Crystal Lake can be reached via a short hike from the S side of Rune Lake.

From the N end of Rune Lake, one can hike easily to Prusik Pass at the W end of Mount Temple Ridge; the pass provides an easy high route to upper Rat Creek Lakes and Edward Mesa. The chain of lakes occupies an ice-scoured basin forged during the last Pleistocene glaciation.

Toketie Lake Route. From the main trail at the second switchback beyond a level stretch (at a campsite, about 2900 ft), cross Snow Creek and ascend a rockslide; find a path at its upper left. The route climbs toward a draw between rock crags well S of the Toketie Creek drainage. Cross a ridge to come out about 50 ft above the 6160-ft lake (near the outlet). One can continue on upland to Toketie Pass and Mesa Lake, or from W of Toketie Lake ascend to Edward Mesa.

Nada Creek Route. This is not a hiker-route; there is some rock climbing on the cliffs due W of Nada Lake's midpoint, which are steepest at about 5500 ft. Starting from Nada Lake, ascend the rockslide gully S of Nada Creek, then climb rock on the buttress to the right. Follow a spur of grassy slabs and small evergreens to the flat, forested basin of upper Nada Creek (est. 6100 ft). Follow this basin (Temple Canyon) as it curves rightward, then ascend W to the bench (or follow the creek drainage). Nada Pass (est. 7400 ft) is at the western edge of the bench (also known as Tamarack Meadows) N of Mount Temple. It is an easy traverse to the slopes above Shield Lake and to Prusik Pass.

The parklike benchland of Tamarack Meadows, with its Lyall's larch, heather hollows, and granitic talus is a lovely foreground to the conspicuous trimline higher and the backwall of pinnacled Temple Ridge. The rock surface below the trimline, smooth and polished by recent ice, can be traced from within Temple Canyon to Prusik Pass.

Snow Lake Trail No. 1013. Leaves from Alpental Road (see I-90 ◆) at the NE side of the main parking lot (3200-ft level). Source Lake (1.7 mi.) is located beneath the trail at 3760-ft campsite (1.8 mi.). Reach Snow Lake divide (4320 ft +) at 2.9 mi. and 4016-ft Snow Lake at 3.7 mi. The mi.-long lake rests on an alpine bench below Chair Peak's cliffs; camp near the NE shore (near the outlet).

Gem Lake (4857 ft) decorates the parkland ½ mi. N of Snow Lake's western end. Reach it in 1½ mi. from the outlet

(Wildcat Lake Trail No. 1012). Upper Wildcat Lake (4219 ft) is reached in 1½ mi. from Gem Lake, the trail passing Lower Wildcat Lake.

Source Lake. Can be easily reached from the Snow Lake Trail. A quicker informal route is from the upper Alpental parking lot, then traversing northward on the W side of the river; this route is especially valid when the valley is snow-covered.

Snowgrass Trail No. 96. This route provides a short approach to Goat Rocks and an entry to many scenic panoramas near Snowgrass Flat. See Johnson Creek Road ◆ for approach to Berry Patch. Take the upper (right) fork about ¼ mi. to Hiker's Trail No. 96-A (4500 ft), which intersects Snowgrass Trail in about 200 yards. The distance to Snowgrass Flat is 3½ mi., and the Crest Trail ◆ is 4 mi.

The forest is composed of Douglas fir, hemlock and cedar, with an occasional western white pine at middle altitudes. Salal, blueberry shrubs, and piggyback are common at ground level. The trail crosses several small, picturesque mossy creeks and is of a uniform, easy grade. No camping in Snowgrass Flat. Camp at Bypass (est. 5600 ft) and Alpine (5920 ft +) camps.

South Fork Tieton River Trail No. 1120. Begin hiking at the locked gate at the end of driving on South Fork Tieton River Road ◆ (Conrad Meadows, 3900 ft). Watch for bridge or log jams across the river in 1½ mi. (near where trail crosses a private road). After the crossing the road bears uphill and the trail right. Enter the Goat Rocks Wilderness at 3 mi. and a meadow camp at 4½ mi.

Goat Rocks Trail No. 1132 turns right here: follow this W to Warm Lake (6320 ft +) (1.8 mi.) and Meade Glacier; the trail and route continues NW about 2 more mi. to Conrad Glacier, crossing the Meade-Conrad divide (7160 ft +).

Trail No. 1120 fords the S fork, then climbs to Surprise Lake (5225 ft) at 6 mi. From the lake a seldom-used trail traverses alpine terrain W across Cispus Pass. Be aware of party size limitations. Reference: *100 Hikes in the South Cascades and Olympics.*

South Puyallup River Trail. Leaves West Side Road ◆ at 7.5 mi. (3500 ft) and meets the Wonderland Trail ◆ in 1.5 mi. Hike onto Emerald Ridge at about 5500 ft for views of Mount Rainier or follow the Wonderland Trail toward the Tahoma Glacier. The glacier's NE lobe is the source of the South Puyallup River. The trail southward from the nose of Emerald Ridge follows a prominent lateral moraine toward Tahoma Creek.

Spray Park. The beauty of this park was described as long ago as 1896, when I. C. Russell commented on the "thousands of groves of spire-like evergreens, with flower-enameled glades." The best approach to this lovely parkland is from 4929-ft Mowich Lake (see Mowich Lake Road ◆) in 3-4 mi.

One can make a variety of scenic cross-country hikes: N toward Mother Mountain, or SE to a high viewpoint on Ptarmigan Ridge. The trail crosses a 6400-ft divide to Seattle Park, then descends to the Carbon River.

Stafford Creek Trail No. 1359. Leaves from a northern spur near the end of Stafford Creek Road (see Teanaway Road ◆) at about 3200 ft and climbs to Standup Creek Trail No. 1369 in about 4 mi., then continues to the 6000-ft + divide above Cascade Creek (about 5.5 mi.). Negro Creek Trail No. 1210 extends E to connect with Falls Creek Trail No. 1216 (leading to Ingalls Creek).

Several easy summits can be reached from these trails: *Earl Peak* (7036 ft) from where Stafford and Standup trails meet, and *Bean Peak* (6743 ft) — 1.1 mi. to the NW; *Navajo Peak* (7223 ft) from Negro Creek Trail where it passes high on its S side; *Three Brothers* (7303 ft) is accessible by hiking up the ridge about ½ mi. E from the divide (6040 ft) at Falls Creek Trail. Three Brothers Trail No. 1211 (open to motorbikes) also leads here from Negro Creek Trail (reach via mining road N of the old Blewett townsite on Swauk Pass Hwy ◆).

Miller Peak Trail No. 1379, from the Stafford Creek Road end, leads to the summit of 6402-ft *Miller Peak* (4 mi.) — a scenic viewpoint for the Stuart Range.

Stagman Ridge Trail No. 12. This trail on the SW flank of Mount Adams begins about 14 mi. from Trout Lake. It is accessed by going about 9 mi. N on Randle-Trout Lake Road ◆, then take Road No. 8031 eastward about 0.3 mi., then Road No. 070 for 3.3 mi. N, then Road No. 120 for 1.2 mi. to the E (to about 4400 ft). The first ½ mi. of trail follows a closed spur road. The trail junctions with the Crest Trail ◆ at 3.3 mi. (SW of Horseshoe Meadow). The junction with the Round-the-Mountain Trail ◆ is another ¾ mi.

Stuart Lake Trail No. 1599. Leaves from Eightmile Road (see Icicle Creek Road ◆) at about 3½ mi. (3600 ft), reaching Stuart Lake (5064 ft) in 4.6 mi. The lake is in an ice-scoured basin formed in the last major stage of Pleistocene glaciation. The marshy meadow W of the lake represents a recently filled-in lake. A path continues 2 mi. to Horseshoe Lake (6275 ft).

Mountaineer Creek Cross-Country Route. The S branch of Mountaineer Creek enters opposite the Stuart Lake Trail at about 3 mi. After leaving the trail and fording the stream (windfalls at first), traverse about ¼ mi. and drop alongside creek to find path. Then follow to fork in the open forest — much of it Engelmann spruce.

The western fork of Mountaineer Creek leads to the NE face of Mount Stuart (and other nearby routes); there are camp spots where meadows flatten at about 5400 ft. The continuing main fork and basin (narrowing to a broad couloir at the valley head) leads to Sherpa Pass (6960 ft +); this alpine pass between Sherpa and Argonaut peaks is a feasible route to Ingalls Creek, and is often used as a descent route from Mount Stuart.

Summerland. See Wonderland Trail ◆.

Sunday Creek Trail No. 1000. Drive North Fork Snoqualmie River Road ◆ about 1½ mi. before the forest boundary, to gated spur No. 30; gate may only be open weekends (see Snoqualmie Tree Farm and Tolt River Area ◆). Take Road No. 5720 nearly 2 mi., then the 1.6 mi. trail to Sunday Lake. A faint miner's trail continues about 1 mi.

Sunrise. See White River Road ◆.

Surprise Creek Trail No. 1060. From U.S. Hwy No. 2 ◆ at 10.2 mi. E of Skykomish (before highway bridge) turn S on the Scenic road spur, cross railroad tracks, and bear right on the dirt road to the trail (2240 ft). Climb to 4508-ft Surprise Lake at 4 mi. (camping), then in ½ mi. join the Crest Trail ◆ (leading to Stevens Pass); Glacier Lake's N end is reached at 5 mi.

The trail continues to Surprise Gap (5760 ft +) at 6½ mi., then descends to Deception Lakes (5053 ft) at 8.8 mi. The Crest Trail crosses Pieper Pass to reach Deception Lakes.

Short hikes can be taken to the summits of both *Surprise Mountain* (6330 ft) and *Spark Plug Mountain* (6311 ft). From about ¼ mi. S of Glacier Lake a branch trail climbs W to the shoulder NW of Surprise Mountain; a short hike leads to its summit. From the N flank of Deception Lakes a 1-mi. trail also leads to the summit. The peak offers fine views of Glacier Peak and Mount Daniel.

From the Crest Trail one could travel N along a gentle ridge to the summit of Spark Plug Mountain. Spark Plug Lake (5587 ft) rests atop the divide N of the mountain; while the lake drains NE, its waters nearly reach the level of a divide gap.

Tahoma Creek Trail. Leads to a connection with the Wonderland Trail ◆ and Indian Henrys Hunting Ground, the noted meadowland on Mount Rainier's SW flank. The extensive meadows (5500 ft and above) were named for a Cowlitz Indian with an unpronounceable name who hunted goats there in the 1870s.

The trail leaves the West Side Road ◆ at 4.3 mi. (3160 ft +) to meet the Wonderland Trail in 2.2 mi. Turn S and reach the meadows in 1.4 mi. A spur trail bears E 0.8 mi. to Mirror Lake. A popular viewpoint knoll on the western flank of the meadows is 6010-ft *Mount Ararat.*

Talapus Lake Trail No. 1039. Take Exit 45 on I-90 ◆, then spur No. 9030. Reach Talapus Lake in 2 mi. and Olallie Lake in 2.8 mi.; trail continues to junction with Pratt Lake Trail ◆.

Taylor River Trail. See Snoqualmie Lake Trail ◆.

Turnpike Pass Trail No. 1391. See Beverly-Turnpike Trail ◆.

Twin Sisters Lake Trail No. 980. Reaches the Crest Trail ◆ in 3.4 mi. from Deep Creek Road (see Bumping Lake Road ◆). Leave the road ½ mi. N of Deep Creek Forest Camp.

Van Trump Park. The trail leaves the Nisqually Entrance Road ◆ at 4.3 mi. beyond Longmire, on the W side of Christine Falls bridge (3650 ft). It passes Comet Falls at 2.3 mi. (a slippery danger spot if one gets off trail) on the route to Van Trump Park, then loops SW along Rampart Ridge for a possible direct return to Longmire.

Waptus River Trail No. 1310. This trail takes a gentle valley incline from Salmon la Sac Campground (see Cle Elum River Road ◆) at 2400 ft to Waptus Lake campsite at 9.0 mi. The forested low-level lake (2963 ft) is the second largest

SUMMIT CHIEF MTN.

THREE QUEENS

CHIMNEY ROCK
NORTH PEAK

IRON CAP MTN.

PASS 6140

CHIKAMIN PK.

LEMAH MTN.

MT. THOMPSON

BURNT BOOT PK.

WILD GOAT PEAK

TOURMALINE PK.

AZURE LAKE

CHETWOOT LAKE

ANGELINE LAKE

BIG HEART LAKE

DELTA LAKE

OTTER LAKE

NAZANNE LAKE

in the Alpine Lakes region. Here Spinola Creek Trail No. 1310A ascends 1 mi. to join the Crest Trail ◆.

The main trail rounds the lake and meets Spade Lake Trail (camping) in 0.9 mi. This 3-mi. branch reaches the 5210-ft lake, where ancient ice striations on bare rock are evident. One can hike around the E shore of the lake, then scramble right of a waterfall to reach cliffy, beautiful Venus Lake (¾ mi.).

The main trail merges with the Crest Trail near Spade Creek, then continues as Dutch Miller Trail No. 1362 ◆ from the junction of Waptus River and Chief Creek.

Shovel Lake (4138 ft), set in a confined rocky basin with a narrow exit, can be reached in about 1.5 mi. cross-country by following Shovel Creek. Lake Rebecca (4777 ft) is about 1.5 additional mi. and Rowena Lake (4968 ft), at the southern foot of Mount Hinman, is another ½ mi.

The Dutch Miller Trail reaches 4652-ft Lake Ivanhoe in 2 mi. from Shovel Creek. This lovely lake is sunk in a steep glaciated cirque between ramparts of Bears Breast and Little Big Chief Mountain.

Dutch Miller Gap (4960 ft+) is about ½ mi. past the lake (14.2 mi. from Salmon la Sac). For hiking continuation, see Middle Fork Snoqualmie River Trail ◆. Camp only at established sites on the sloping basin N of the Gap or the existing campsites at Lake Ivanhoe (fire closure). The Gap area is lush with alpine esoterica: floral and heather carpeting, unbelievable pools and drainage systems, all interspersed with boulders and a scattering of dwarf evergreens. The area is very fragile; do not tramp out new meadow trails. Gap area reference: *Mountaineer*, 1945, pp. 24-29.

Summit Chief Pass-Escondido Ridge High Route. One can begin at the last switchback on the trail to Lake Ivanhoe. Ascend along the N valley wall of Chief Creek (light bush). Pass Summit Chief Lake (5347 ft) in a picturesque upland of rolling heather meadows and glaciated knobs. Above the lake and its small glacial cirque the route leads across barrens to the meadowed pass (about 5750 ft).

One can contour on the W slope over heather benches to the two lovely tarns; here are superb views. Or one can travel ½ mi. S to the elbow on the L-shaped ridge that overlooks Escondido Ridge Tarns (Crest Trail ◆ intersects nearby).

Among possible variations: from Summit Chief Lake or on a lower traverse, hike SE to Chief Creek's S fork (meadows), then up ledges and creek bed to Avalanche Tarn. Proceed up a large talus/snow basin to a 5680-ft+ pass in the divide to give access to Escondido Ridge and Vista Lakes; or cross the ridge farther E, taking the 5920-ft+ pass to the Escondido Ridge Tarns (camp away from tarns; no fires).

West Fork Foss River Trail No. 1064. This valley trail provides access to the magnificent group of lakes S of the Skykomish River valley and W of the Cascade divide. Begin the trail from Foss River Road ◆ (1600 ft): reach Trout Lake (2000 ft+) in 1½ mi., pass below Malachite Lake at 3½ mi., pass Copper and Little Heart lakes (camping at NW corners) to reach 4545-ft Big Heart Lake at 6 mi. This is the

end of trail maintenance; camp just SE of the lake's N end. Despite the fact that this is the second largest of the W-side Alpine Lakes, it is so well hidden that it was overlooked on the 1905 Skykomish map quadrangle. Both Big Heart and Angeline lakes drain N from rocky subalpine basins; they are separated by a bedrock hump of Snoqualmie Granodiorite about 750 ft in height.

Chetwoot Lake Route. A fishermen's path follows S along and over this hump to 4905-ft Chetwoot Lake, which lies in a lovely alpine basin (est. 3 additional mi.).

The entire Foss group of high lakes is of special interest to the hiker because of their charm and unique, primitive nature on the periphery of the populous Puget Sound Basin. The largest lakes (Big Heart, Angeline, Otter) nest on the edge of an upland plateau; waterfalls tumble from each lake, ultimately reaching Delta and Trout lakes on the lower W fork of the Foss.

Malachite Lake (4089 ft) is reached from the main trail by taking a short path just S of the outlet creek (which has a 700-ft cascade).

Angeline Lake (4609 ft) nestles in a rock canyon with numerous waterline cliffs and an outlet perched steeply above the lower valley. To reach the lake take the fishermen's trail traversing from the Big Heart outlet (about 0.7 mi. to the Angeline outlet); camp at the lake's NW end.

Bypass Angeline on its E: first climb several hundred ft to get above cliffs, then hike S through open fir clumps and heather sections; it is easier to hold altitude to Azure Lake rather than descend to the southern lake shore. The huckleberry shrub is thick in this entire area, and tends to hold moisture from dew or rain.

Otter Lake Route. A path exists from Trout Lake's S shore, then along the W side of the Foss W fork to Delta Lake. Continue cross-country through heavy forest to 3925-ft Otter Lake (about 1 mi.); the hike along the N side of the stream is preferred except during snow cover. Camp at the lake's NW end.

A continuing route leads to a connection with Alpine Lakes High Route ◆. Hike around the lake's E side, and when S of the lake keep to the valley's W flank; one can continue toward Iron Cap Pass or to Tank Lakes.

Whitepine Creek Trail No. 1582. Beyond the end of Whitepine Creek Road ◆ the trail begins from a rough 2 mi. continuing roadway. The trail meets Icicle Creek Trail ◆ near Lake Josephine (9 mi.).

Wildhorse Creek Trail No. 1592 branches at 2.6 mi., then climbs S for 6.6 mi. to Frosty Pass; this trail continues SW to Icicle Creek Trail.

Wonderland Trail. This 95-mi. trail, which encircles Mount Rainier, connects with the Park's road system at Longmire, North Puyallup River, Mowich Lake, Ipsut Creek (Carbon River), Sunrise, White River, Box Canyon, and Reflection Lakes.

The trail span from Longmire (2761 ft) to the West Side Road ◆ (3500 ft) is 18.6 mi. Campsites include one near Indian Henrys Hunting Ground (6 mi.) and Klapatche Park

(16½ mi.). In its initial portion, the trail crosses over Rampart Ridge, an ancient intracanyon lava flow. While crossing Emerald Ridge, between Tahoma Creek and the South Puyallup River, one can see where the South Tahoma Glacier was joined over 100 years ago by a southern arm of the Tahoma Glacier below Glacier Island.

The trail section from North Puyallup River to Mowich Lake is 15.2 mi.; shelters are at Golden Lakes and Mowich River. The next trail section crosses the divide to Carbon River (see Spray Park ◆ for details), then a section of the trail ascends to Moraine Park and Mystic Lake (see Carbon River Trail ◆ for details). Bearing E, the trail crosses the moraine area the Winthrop Glacier occupied 230-145 years ago. The gravel-covered lower glacier is largely stagnant ice. The trail section from Mystic Lake to Sunrise (Yakima Park), 11.7 mi., is especially scenic and features many interesting surficial deposits. There are numerous branch trails, alternatives, and cross-country hiking opportunities.

The Summerland section of the Wonderland Trail begins from the White River Road ◆ at 3 mi. from the Park entrance (3900 ft). The trail follows Fryingpan Creek to 5400-ft Summerland (4.2 mi.) with its noted floral meadows (shelter here). The trail climbs onward 3 mi. to 6901-ft Panhandle Gap. Recessional moraines are spread over a ½ mi. distance on the valley floor of upper Fryingpan Creek, and are quite visible from the trail. The moraines were formed within the last few hundred years as the Fryingpan Glacier lost volume and shrank back to its present position above a line of cliffs. An interesting cross-country hike can be made from Panhandle Gap, crossing the stagnant Fryingpan Glacier to Whitman Crest — a high ridge between three glaciers. The stagnant ice of Ohanapecosh Glacier lies on a shelf perched above bedrock cliffs.

The 10 mi. Indian Bar trail section extends from Panhandle Gap to Stevens Canyon Road ◆ at Box Canyon (12.7 mi. W of Stevens Canyon entrance). The upper Ohanapecosh is a beautiful isolated valley; above the trail is the bare amphitheatre holding several perennial snowfields and ice of the Ohanapecosh Glacier. There are shelters at Indian Bar (7.6 mi. from the road) and Nickel Creek.

"The scenery around Nisqually is very much enhanced in beauty by the splendid appearance of Mount Rainier, which lies nearly east of it; and from some open prairies there are three of these magnificent snowy peaks in sight. They are all nearly regular cones, with cleft tops, as though they had a terminal crater on their summit."

LT. CHARLES WILKES, 1844

Index

ABOUT THE AUTHOR

Fred Beckey has achieved enduring recognition as the most imaginative, persistent, and thorough explorer and mountain investigator of the Cascade Range wilderness. His intimate knowledge of the topography has been gained through many years of personal experience, including the ascent of hundreds of peaks — many of them first ascents — in all parts of the range, and the study of an untold number of maps and aerial photographs.

This knowledge is reflected in his other guidebooks, and a personal narrative, *Challenge of the North Cascades*.

In addition to becoming a legendary personality, Beckey has also earned a reputation as a student of human history, where he has made his own scholarly contributions. In addition he has carefully perused the body of natural history, ecology, glaciology, and geology, and added his own contributions. Beckey has served as an advisor to Washington State Board on Geographic Names, and has indirectly contributed many feature names in the Cascades, including For-bidden Peak, Crooked Thumb, Phantom Peak, and Cruel Finger.

Through keeping abreast of published literature, seeking out and interviewing other climbers and explorers, and investigating documents in various libraries throughout North America, Beckey has become widely acknowledged as an authority on Cascade history. Many of his findings have been published in the literature of the region.

"The kids up here (Vancouver) talk about you (Fred Beckey) in a legendary way — in the same breath as Buffalo Bill — got to watch out for that! Don't let old age creep up on you."
LES MacDONALD, 1971

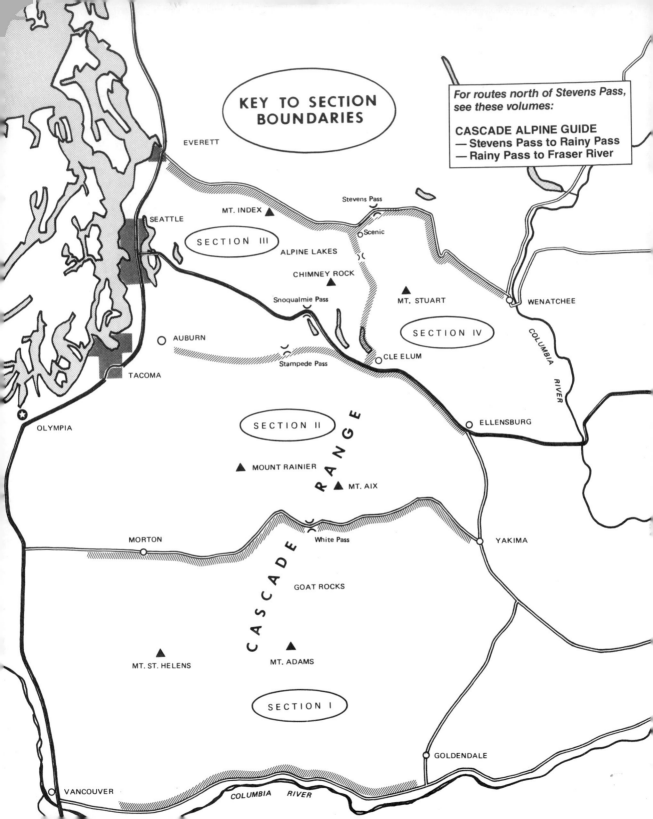

KEY TO SECTION BOUNDARIES

For routes north of Stevens Pass, see these volumes:

CASCADE ALPINE GUIDE
— Stevens Pass to Rainy Pass
— Rainy Pass to Fraser River

EVERETT

MT. INDEX ▲

Stevens Pass

SECTION III

Scenic

ALPINE LAKES

SEATTLE

CHIMNEY ROCK ▲

MT. STUART ▲

Snoqualmie Pass

WENATCHEE

SECTION IV

CLE ELUM

AUBURN

Stampede Pass

COLUMBIA RIVER

TACOMA

SECTION II

OLYMPIA

ELLENSBURG

MOUNT RAINIER ▲

C A S C A D E   R A N G E

▲ MT. AIX

MORTON

White Pass

YAKIMA

GOAT ROCKS

MT. ST. HELENS ▲

▲ MT. ADAMS

SECTION I

GOLDENDALE

VANCOUVER

COLUMBIA   RIVER